The RocketReview Revolution:

THE ULTIMATE GUIDE TO THE NEW SAT®

Adam Robinson

NEW AMERICAN LIBRARY

New American Library
Published by New American Library, a division of
Penguin Group (USA) Inc., 375 Hudson Street,
New York, New York 10014, USA
Penguin Group (Canada), 10 Alcorn Avenue, Toronto,
Ontario M4V 3B2, Canada (a division of Pearson Penguin Canada Inc.)
Penguin Books Ltd., 80 Strand, London WC2R 0RL, England
Penguin Ireland, 25 St. Stephen's Green, Dublin 2,
Ireland (a division of Penguin Books Ltd.)
Penguin Group (Australia), 250 Camberwell Road, Camberwell, Victoria 3124,
Australia (a division of Pearson Australia Group Pty. Ltd.)
Penguin Books India Pvt. Ltd., 11 Community Centre, Panchsheel Park,
New Delhi - 110 017, India
Penguin Group (NZ), Cnr Airborne and Rosedale Roads, Albany,
Auckland 1310, New Zealand (a division of Pearson New Zealand Ltd.)
Penguin Books (South Africa) (Pty.) Ltd., 24 Sturdee Avenue,
Rosebank, Johannesburg 2196, South Africa

Penguin Books Ltd., Registered Offices: 80 Strand, London WC2R 0RL, England

First published by New American Library, a division of Penguin Group (USA) Inc.

First Printing, November 2004
10 9 8 7 6 5 4 3 2 1

SAT is a registered trademark of the College Entrance Examination Board

 REGISTERED TRADEMARK—MARCA REGISTRADA

Printed in the United States of America

To two men I am humbled to know, and whose lives evoke Leigh Hunt's immortal 1834 poem, "Abou ben Adhem."

To Martin Edelston, whose hobby is "saving lives," and who continually reminds me of the importance of contributing to America—and who never fails to inspire by his example.

And to Daniel Rose, Founder of the Harlem Educational Activities Fund, his crowning accomplishment in a lifetime of philanthropy. For more on the astonishing achievements of HEAF, visit www.HEAF.org.

Acknowledgements

This book would not have happened without the support of a large cast of characters. Four parties, however, have to be singled as firsts among equals:

- Luke Janklow, nonpareil literary agent, for making the project a reality. Luke, you're the man. Thanks also to Claire Dippel and Bennet Ashley.

- Kara Walsh and Tracy Bernstein, for their vision in accepting the project, all their help in getting it off the ground, and their unflagging patience in the face of the exasperating delays on my end (so, so sorry, but I trust you'll agree that the finished product was worth the wait)

- Leonid "Lenny" Mirer, indefatigable twenty-two-year-old marketing and multimedia production genius, for giving the book and website so much of its snap-crackle-and-pop, and helping in so many other ways

- Richard Clark, who translated my RocketScore algorithms into computer code

My debt and gratitude extend to many other people as well (in no particular order):

- Tracy's assistant Jessica, Kristin Minnick for promotion, and New American Library's sales force: Go, Team, Go!

- Dan Weiss, for his friendship and support

- Karenj, for her impeccable design taste

- Linda Schmukler, Faye Quam Heimerl, and Brian Aubrey for straightening my grammatical tie

- Lisa Echenthal, for getting behind the book

- Sandi Mendelson, PR guru, for her promotional efforts

- Alexandra Self, independent college consultant extraordinaire

- Nile Lanning, super tutor, for reviewing early drafts

- Victor Niederhoffer, for giving me a chance

- Christopher Ruskis and Wen-Kai Ying, for creating RocketReview's sound brand

- Frank Miller, for his wisdom

- Glen Greenwald, legal paladin

- Michael Pollack and Barbara Marcus, for their friendship

- Kevin Huvane, for so many things

- Samson Day, for keeping me in my place and for all of his advice on the book and the website (it took an impossibly talented twelve-year-old all of five seconds to name OmniProctor)

- Laura Day, my sine qua non, for rescuing me.

CONTENTS

PART I:
Basic Tutorials

CONTENTS

PART II:
Advanced Tutorials

CONTENTS

CONTENTS

PART V:
The SAT Math Test
(REMEMBER: SAT MATH IS DIFFERENT)

CONTENTS

PART VI:
Nuts and Bolts

AVAILABLE ONLINE:
Download from
www.RocketReview.com

Illustrative Problems and Solutions

The Final Word on the 27 Most Frequently Asked Questions about the SAT, PSAT, and SAT II Subject Tests

Welcome to the Revolution

The "New" SAT Is a Big Deal

For many anxious parents and their children, March Madness won't refer this year to the NCAA basketball championships, or to college students' perennial spring break pilgrimage to Florida or southern California. Instead, March Madness will refer to the big changes afoot for you: the college-bound high school student. Unless you've just emerged from a year-long coma, you've probably heard from a million sources—newspapers, magazines, the Net, your friends, your teachers, your panicked parents—that the SAT will undergo radical changes this year.

Believe them, it will. The test publishers have tinkered with the SAT from time to time over the past few decades, but never producing anything like the seismic SAT changes that will show up in the 2004-05 academic year:

- Analogy questions have been dropped to make room for questions about very short reading passages (60-140 words long). These passages, together with the traditional reading passages (450-800 words long) and sentence completion questions, now make up the renamed SAT Reading Test.

- Quantitative comparison questions have been dropped from the SAT Math Test, and the overall difficulty has been ratcheted up a few notches. Previously, the math covered on the SAT was limited to basic topics from seventh-grade through ninth-grade curriculums. (The problems were not always easy, of course, but the underlying concepts were.) Sorry, but now you'll face a few topics drawn from tenth- and eleventh-grade math curriculums, too.

- The really big change is the introduction of the SAT Writing Test. This section will consist of a written essay portion and a multiple-choice portion covering grammatical and other writing problems. (If you're thinking, "Hey, that sounds exactly like the SAT II Writing Test," you're right. Or rather, exactly like the former SAT II Writing Test, which has now been retired.)

And since the new SAT Writing Test will have its own 200 to 800 score, a "perfect" SAT is now 2400 rather than the 1600 your parents and possibly grandparents remember.

Unless You've Taken the Test Before, However, the Newness Is Really *Not* a Big Deal

The vast majority of the 2.3 million students who will take the SAT this year will hardly notice the changes. Why? Because they've never taken the SAT before.

But if you took the PSAT last year as a sophomore, or the year before as a freshman (or even before that, if you were among the many thousands of seventh and eighth graders who took the SAT to gain entry to an academic program for gifted students), you'll probably notice the changes. Like I said, though, this shouldn't be such a big deal for you, personally. After all, why would you care what the SAT used to be like?

The SAT Was Radically Redesigned This Year Because Colleges *Insisted* on It

So you can be sure that college admissions officers, unfamiliar with the nuances of the new test, are going to be scrutinizing applicants' scores—your scores—more closely than ever before. That's why you should care about the changes.

Congratulations!

You now hold the best SAT book available in your hands. Nearly twenty years ago I wrote the only SAT book ever to become a *New York Times* bestseller. This book is completely updated—a new course for a new test—and includes information and test-taking techniques never before revealed to the general public.

I'll show you everything you need to know to do your best on this important exam. I assure you that if you hear something about the SAT—from a friend or a teacher or another book—that's not included in these chapters, it's either information you don't need for the test or it's a useless technique. As I said, I'll cover everything you need to know for this test.

Okay, then, let's get started!

How to Use This Book (Read This Chapter First— I Mean It)

How to Make This Book *Yours*

This is the best SAT book ever written, but it has a defect inherent in all how-to books. Fortunately, it is a defect that you and I can largely correct.

One of the problems in writing an SAT book for everyone is that I have to present a lot of information in the most accessible way to the widest possible audience of likely readers. If I were writing an SAT book *just* for you, I might emphasize certain sections, qualify some of my advice, and maybe even delete whole chapters. And I would certainly present the chapters in a different order.

In short, I would write a different SAT book for *you*. And the book I write I would write for your best friend would be different still. After all, you each have different strengths and weaknesses; your situations could be very different, too.

> The first step in making this book yours is *not* to read it straight through. Just *how* you should read these chapters, and in what order and with what emphasis, will depend on a number of factors. The most important of these factors are whether you are preparing for the PSAT or for the SAT, how much time you have until the test, and your current strengths and weaknesses in the main test areas. We will deal with these factors shortly.

At First, *Dip* into the Book—Don't Plunge

Start with the quiz in Tutorial 3. You'll find it beginning on page 6. This quiz will alert you to any major misconceptions you have about the SAT that we need to correct ASAP. For many students the quiz is a wake-up call.

Then read Tutorial 14, which will take a lot of the pressure off.

Next, get an overview of everything by spending some time scanning the Table of Contents. Check off any chapters that sound interesting, and especially those that sound surprising. **Since you'll be skipping around as you work through the various chapters in the coming weeks and months, use the Table of Contents as a checklist to keep yourself organized.**

Next, read through the tutorials; these important lessons are brief, and set the stage for everything else in the book. **You don't have to read all of these tutorials in one sitting.** I designed the tutorials to be bite-sized so you could digest them at a leisurely pace. **From time to time, return to the tutorials and reread the ones most relevant to you.**

Finally, skim the summary Crash Course beginning on page 650. This summary contains the key ideas of the entire book. **Do not try to remember all these points; they will become second nature soon enough.** Right now you just want to acquaint yourself with the key points so they begin to sink into your brain by osmosis. Remember to read Tutorial 9.

> Resist the temptation—and you will be tempted—to peek at the Diagnostic Test at the back of this book, or you will be wasting a great learning opportunity. You should not see any of the problems on the Diagnostic Test until you are ready to take it *properly*, as if it were your actual SAT. Once you even glance at the practice test, the test loses much of its diagnostic value.

You Can't Cram This Stuff, So Take Tiny Bites

Learning to take the SAT is more a matter of learning test-taking skills than of learning facts. And whereas facts *can*, in a pinch, be crammed, skills—any skills—need to be mastered over time.

If you think about something you excel at, you'll remember that when you first started practicing the skills for that activity, you went through a long period of awkward execution. You knew what you had to do for each particular skill, but you really had to concentrate and the results were less than perfect and far from reliable. But somehow, over time, you gradually improved your skills so that you could perform them without thinking, almost by reflex.

Be consistent! It's far better to spend an average of 15 to 30 minutes a day for two or three months on learning these skills, than to spend an hour or two a day for one month.

But If There's Not Much Time before the Test, Here's Where You'll Make Your Fastest Gains

First, if you're reading this before the PSAT, remember that the real prize is maximizing your SAT score, not your PSAT score. **To maximize your SAT score—and remember, the SAT is still many months away—your primary goal on the PSAT should be to maximize how much you _learn_ from the experience of taking the PSAT, which is _not_ the same thing as trying to maximize your PSAT score itself.**

I know "learning experience" is one of those phrases you hear too annoyingly often from adults, but that's truly the primary value of the PSAT for the 99 percent of high school juniors who don't have their heart set on a National Merit Scholarship. Of course you want to do well on the PSAT, but don't try to master too many techniques or strategies for this test. Better to try to follow a few of the pointers—like _taking pains,_ the subject of the Math Experience Set 3, or using process of elimination on the sentence completions—and see whether you can execute these few skills flawlessly on the PSAT.

Having said that, here are the sections of the book likely to give you the quickest score gains:

- For most students, the fastest gains are likely to be had on the Writing Test. Skim the introduction to this test. Then skim the essay chapters, both basic and advanced principles. In the basic principles chapter on the proofreading questions, read through the illustrative sentences for each type of error and see whether you can correct each sentence on your own. Spend time on the three or four types of errors that give you the most trouble, then skim the advanced principles chapter for these questions.

- On the Math Test—where enormous score gains are also possible in a short period of time, focus on the Techniques chapter and the Experience Sets. Then work through the Top 11 Problems of All Time. If you're really short of time, start with the first problem type and work your way backwards. If you have any time left, skim the refresher chapters.

- On the Reading Test, the fastest gains are likely to be had on the sentence completion questions. Work through the drills in the basic and advanced chapters; you can skim the text. For the reading passages, work through the basic principles chapter. **And however much time you have left, you will *of course* be working on your vocabulary, won't you?** Even memorizing five to ten words a day—which can be done in your spare time—will improve your score significantly.

If you still have some study time left after finishing these sections before your test, use your remaining time to work through any sections you may have skipped.

> **If you're reading this before the PSAT, feel free to ignore the essay chapters—the PSAT does not have a scored essay—and don't worry about any advanced algebra II math (which is tested on the SAT only).**

If You're Not in a Rush, How You Should Read This Book Will Depend on Your Strengths and Weaknesses

If you have two or three months before your SAT, you have plenty of time to work through all the chapters in this book. (If the SAT is only weeks away, see the section above.) Still, as I mentioned earlier, you should tailor the *order* in which you read the chapters to fit your strengths and weaknesses in the various test areas.

- If math isn't your thing, work through the refresher chapters *before* doing any of the Experience Sets. After you've worked through the refresher chapters once—you may need to read certain sections more than once—work through the Experience Sets. Save the Math Hall of Fame chapter for last. By the way, if you're really *strong* at math, pay particular attention to Experience Sets 2 and 3, and review them frequently. **Spend your first two or three weeks of your study time using this book to work through the math refreshers exclusively. This will begin to get you caught up. And then start working on all the areas—math, reading, and writing—together.**

- If you find the reading passages particularly hard—and many students do—you can work through the reading chapters as presented, but you should practice applying the techniques you'll be learning to your everyday reading assignments (at least those outside your English class, which are fiction).

- If grammar is a weak spot, really, *really* take your time on the proofreading questions basic principles chapter. If you take your time, it's not that hard to master the few grammatical concepts tested on the SAT Writing Test.

- If writing is not your strongest area, you can work through the essay chapters as presented, but you should also practice simply *outlining* essays in two or three minutes on random topics. Also, if you don't have two classic literary works and a historical period that you can use for your stock essay examples—the importance of which is discussed in the essay advanced principles chapter—be sure you keep your eye on the lookout in your English and history classes for examples to use.

Otherwise, work through the chapters *in each part* in the order presented.

> In addition, be sure you check the next chapter to see whether you fall into any of the "special cases." If so, you'll find additional information on how to read this book that is directly relevant to *you.*

Work on All Three SAT Areas Simultaneously

It's important that you work on the SAT Math, Reading, and Writing Tests simultaneously. **In this book, that means working on Parts III, IV, and V at the same time.** Do *not* spend a couple of weeks on the SAT Writing Test (Part III), then a few weeks on the SAT Reading Test (Part IV), and then four or five weeks on the SAT Math Test (Part V).

For most students, I would say spend two or three days a week on math, and one or two each on reading and writing. Again, you may have to adjust that depending on your particular strengths and weaknesses.

> Don't simply work on your weak spots. Fast score improvement is also possible in your strong areas, and improving *any* of your SAT scores—math, reading, or writing—contributes to your overall score.

Get a Copy of the Book *The Official SAT Study Guide*

The practice questions in this book (and the additional questions you can download from the RocketReview website) are great, but there's no substitute to working on actual SATs that you'll find in *The Official SAT Study Guide.* You should, however, ignore the official explanations—if the book provides any, as it might in a "Solutions Manual"; the test writers know how to write tests, but their solutions to questions are not especially helpful. (Their "official" solutions are rarely the best ways to answer the questions. Worse, the official solutions always miss the point: they are written from the perspective of students who know all the vocabulary words or who know all of the math or who understood the reading passages. Anyone who could have solved the problems using the "official" explanations wouldn't have gotten the problems wrong in the first place.)

Wait for the edition that contains the new SAT; it should say "March 2005 SAT" on the front cover.) *The Official SAT Study Guide* will have a number of SATs, and it may include a PSAT. **(PSAT students: if *The Official SAT Study Guide* doesn't contain a PSAT—as I write this, *The Official SAT Study Guide* has not yet been released—you'll be able to get a free copy of the new PSAT from your college advisor. You may also be able to download a free copy from the College Board website.)**

I mentioned in Tutorial 6 that only perfect practice makes perfect. Here's what *doesn't* work: flipping through *The Official SAT Study Guide,* doing problems here and there that catch your eye, then checking the answer key to see whether your solutions are correct. If you want to improve your score, you should do at least complete sections at a time, using OmniProctor to simulate test conditions.

> **Use the few tests in *The Official SAT Study Guide* sparingly— they need to last you for the entire time you prepare for the SAT (and possibly for your second SAT). If you're reading this book for the first time before the PSAT, you should save most of the tests in *The Official SAT Study Guide* for your serious preparation *after* the PSAT. Do not use up all these exams before the PSAT. *Not, not, not, not, not.* For more on pacing your preparation, see also questions 12 through 16 and question 20 in the FAQ section that you can find at www.RocketReview.com.**

Important Advice for Girls, PSAT Students, and Other Special Cases

Special Assembly Time

In the last chapter I showed you how you should read this book in the way best suited to you and your strengths and weaknesses. In this chapter I'll have a bit more to say about different types of students and specific *situations*.

As I mention in Tutorial 5 (beginning on page 11), *everything* I say in this book applies to everyone—including you—*unless* I specifically point out an exception. The following categories of students have particular issues surrounding the SAT that merit inviting them to a special assembly. There's a good chance you belong to at least one of these groups, so scan the list closely.

- **Girls**

- **PSAT students**

- **Students retaking the SAT**

- **10th graders**

- **9th graders**

- **Extra-time students**

- **ESL students**

- **Junior high school students**

- **Home schoolers**

You may belong to *more* than of these groups. For example, Mallie, a 10th grader, attends a school that lets 9th and 10th graders take the PSAT. So Mallie should attend three special assemblies: the one for girls, the one for

10th graders, and the one for PSAT students. If you *don't* fall into one of these groups, you're dismissed and can skip to another section of the book.

> When you register at www.RocketReview.com, the computer will ask you a few questions about your status to determine whether you belong to any of these special assembly groups. It's important that you complete these questions accurately because you'll receive additional personalized advice and frequent emailed updates.

Special Assembly for Girls

You may be wondering why I've called this special assembly for girls. Girls do better in high school and college than boys, and yet boys consistently outscore girls on the SAT. **The simple explanation for how and why boys outscore girls on the SAT is the fundamental message of this book: the SAT is way, *way* different from school.**

One of the reasons boys outscore girls on the SAT is that boys treat the test as a game—and so should you. Think of the SAT as a new game that you have to learn. You learned the school game—and I'm sure you excel at it. Now you'll learn to excel at the SAT game.

In addition, the following sections are particularly important for you to read, preferably sooner than later.

- Tutorials 1, 2, 7, 16–21, 27

- Sentence Completions: Advanced Principles

- Introduction to the SAT Math Test

- SAT Math Techniques

- Math Experience Sets 1–6

Asterisk these sections in the Table of Contents so you'll remember to read them. The other chapters in the book are also important, of course, but the ones I just mentioned are *particularly* important for *you*.

Okay, special assembly dismissed.

Special Assembly for PSAT Students

I've addressed students getting ready for the PSAT in different sections throughout the book, but I wanted to make sure I brought these points to your attention as you set out to begin your preparation.

Keep in mind that the ultimate prize is a great SAT score, not a great PSAT score. The preparation you do for the PSAT should set the stage for the SAT. In short, you *should* prepare for the PSAT, but save your big push for the SAT. (Unless you're shooting for a National Merit Scholarship, in which case of course you should prepare actively for the PSAT.)

So don't try to do anything more for the PSAT than get acquainted with the ideas and techniques in this book. **Right now, before you read anything else, read Tutorial 14 (page 26), then come right back.**

I really meant what I said in that tutorial. Do *not* try to remember everything in this book. *Do* skim the Crash Course Summary, and maybe return to it once a week for another *skimming*—nothing more—to give the ideas time to plant themselves in your subconscious. From time to time, skim the tutorial headings also.

Remember also that the PSAT does not have a scored essay, so you can skip the essay chapters until after the PSAT.

In addition, the following sections are particularly important for you to read, preferably sooner than later.

- How to Use This Book

- Tutorial 9

- Math Experience Sets 2, 3, and 6

- A Crash SAT Course with Booster Rockets

- Questions 17–20 in the Final Word on the 27 Most Frequently Asked Questions about the SAT, PSAT, and SAT IIs (online)

Asterisk these sections in the Table of Contents so you'll remember to read them. The other chapters in the book are also important, of course, but the ones I just mentioned are *particularly* important for *you*.

Okay, special assembly dismissed.

Special Assembly for Students Retaking the SAT

This assembly is for all students who have already taken the SAT in 11th grade.

First, if you're in 11th grade now, you should *not* retake the SAT until 12th grade. That means you have at least the remaining time in 11th grade and all of summer vacation to get ready for the SAT, which is plenty of time. In fact, apart from working on your vocabulary, it is probably too early to begin serious preparation for the next time you take the test in the fall. Reread the previous chapter, How to Use This Book, on how to pace your preparation.

If you're now in the 12th grade, there may not be much time remaining before you retake the SAT. Reread the previous chapter, in particular the section on which sections of the book to read to get the maximum score gains in the shortest period of time (page xiii).

In addition, the following sections are particularly important for you to read, preferably sooner than later.

- Taking the SAT

- Questions 8–10 in The Final Word on the 27 Most Frequently Asked Questions about the SAT, PSAT, and SAT IIs (online)

Asterisk these sections in the Table of Contents so you'll remember to read them. The other chapters in the book are also important, of course, but the ones I just mentioned are *particularly* important for *you.*

Okay, special assembly dismissed.

Special Assembly for 10th Graders

First, under no circumstances should you take the SAT. That means as a 10th grader you are either getting ready for a PSAT, or you are getting a *super-*long head start on the SAT.

If you're getting ready for the PSAT, see the previous special assembly. In any event, you have over a year before the SAT. The most important things to be working on now are your vocabulary, and making sure you are thoroughly familiar with the math content on the SAT. (Though a few topics may be new to you, you should recognize most of the math.)

Do *not* take more than one or two practice SATs this year. Not, not, not, not, not. You will have plenty of time for doing practice SATs down the road. The danger in taking practice SATs so far in advance is that you'll get bored, you'll lose your *edge* for the test, and you'll ingrain bad test-taking habits. Having said that, doing one test every four to six *months*—to see where you stand in various test areas—is fine.

In addition, the following sections are particularly important for you to read, preferably before embarking on all the other chapters.

- Tutorials 17–20

- Reading Comprehension: Basic Principles

- Vocabulary for the SAT Reading Test

- Math Experience Set 3 (practice this mind-set in your everyday math class, too)

- Refreshers of SAT Arithmetic, Algebra, Geometry, and Miscellaneous Topics

- The Final Word on the 27 Most Frequently Asked Questions about the SAT, PSAT, and SAT IIs (online)

Asterisk these sections in the Table of Contents so you'll remember to read them. The other chapters in the book are also important, of course, but the ones I just mentioned are *particularly* important for *you.*

Okay, special assembly dismissed.

Special Assembly for 9th Graders

First, under no circumstances should you take the SAT. That means as a 9th grader you are either getting ready for a PSAT, or you are getting a super, *super* long head start on the SAT.

If you're getting ready for the PSAT, see the previous special assembly for PSAT students. In any event, you have over two years before the SAT. As with the 10th graders, the most important things you should be working on now are your vocabulary, and making sure you are thoroughly familiar with the math content on the SAT (as a 9th grader, you probably have not encountered the most advanced topics on the SAT Math Test, but you will be surprised how much you do know).

Do *not* take more than one practice SAT this year. Not, not, not, not, not. You will have plenty of time for doing practice SATs down the road. The danger in taking practice SATs so far in advance is that you'll get bored, you'll lose your *edge* for the test, and you'll ingrain bad test-taking habits. Having said that, taking one test this year—to see where you stand in various test areas—is fine.

In addition, the following sections are particularly important for you to read, preferably before embarking on all the other chapters—which you can put off until next year. There is truly no rush.

- Tutorials 17–20

- Reading Comprehension: Basic Principles

- Vocabulary for the SAT Reading Test

- Math Experience Set 3 (practice this mind-set in your everyday math class, too)

- Refreshers of SAT Arithmetic, Algebra, Geometry, and Miscellaneous Topics

- The Final Word on the 27 Most Frequently Asked Questions about the SAT, PSAT, and SAT IIs (online)

Asterisk these sections in the Table of Contents so you'll remember to read them. The other chapters in the book are also important, of course, but the ones I just mentioned are *particularly* important for *you*.

Okay, special assembly dismissed.

Special Assembly for Extra-Time Students

This special assembly is for students who have a certified condition that qualifies them for taking the SAT (or PSAT) with additional time. **Throughout this book I have stressed the importance of time management, and the likelihood that most students will *not* have time to attempt every question in an SAT section—*without rushing recklessly*.**

This fundamental test-taking principle does not apply to you since you have extra time.

Because you'll have enough time to attempt all the questions in every section, you need to become comfortable with *answering* every question you attempt—even if that means guessing.

In addition, the following sections are particularly important for you to read, preferably sooner than later.

- Tutorials 16–19, 22, and 23

- Tutorials 20 and 27 (but read with the exception in mind that you *should* have enough time to attempt most if not all the questions)

- Reading Comprehension: Basic Principles

- Math Experience Sets 2 and 3 (practice applying these mind-sets in your everyday math class)

- Math Experience Set 6 (but read with the exception in mind that you *should* have enough time to attempt most if not all the questions)

Asterisk these sections in the Table of Contents so you'll remember to read them. The other chapters in the book are also important, of course, but the ones I just mentioned are *particularly* important for *you*.

Okay, special assembly dismissed.

Special Assembly for ESL Students

This assembly is for students whose primary language is not English, or who started studying English only within the last five years. Vocabulary may be an issue on the SAT Reading Test. **When, in the advanced principles chapter on sentence completions, I discuss the "difficulty" of particular words, keep in mind that I am speaking from the point of view of students whose primary language is English.** In general, the longer the word, the more difficult it is; the shorter the word, the easier it is.

When you are answering the reading questions on the SAT Reading Test, do not try to read the passages themselves too closely. The important thing is to get a general idea of each passage's main idea or two, and then spend most of your time on the questions themselves. I explain this point at length in the two reading chapters.

Vocabulary may also be an issue on the SAT Math Test. Make sure you at least skim the math refresher chapters to verify that you know all the words on the SAT Math Test. (All the terms you need to know are in **bold**.)

On the SAT Writing Test, you may find the grammar questions easier than will students who have spoken English their entire lives. The essay, however, may be more difficult if you are not yet comfortable writing in English. The length of your essay is a major factor in your essay's grade, so practice writing quickly without worrying about whether you are using *exactly* the right words.

> **Although I advise students *against* using a personal example in their essays, you *should*, if you can, find a way to reveal that English is not your original language.** Do not—not, not, not, not, *not*—say that English is not your original language *directly*. Instead, reveal *indirectly* that English is a second language for you. ("Another example of our learning more from our mistakes than from our successes is illustrated in Shakespeare's *Hamlet*—which I first read in my original Spanish back in seventh grade.") **Your primary examples should still be literary or historical, as I mention in the essay advanced principles chapter, but letting the SAT graders know that English is not your original language won't hurt your essay's score, and even could help bump your score up a bit.**

In addition, the following sections are particularly important for you to read, preferably sooner than later.

- The Proofreading and Editing Section: Basic Principles

- Sentence Completions: Advanced Principles

- Reading Comprehension: Basic Principles

- Reading Comprehension: Advanced Principles

- Vocabulary for the SAT Reading Test

Asterisk these sections in the Table of Contents so you'll remember to read them. The other chapters in the book are also important, of course, but the ones I just mentioned are *particularly* important for *you*.

Okay, special assembly dismissed.

Special Assembly for Junior High Students

This assembly is for junior high school students taking the SAT for admission to an accelerated academic program. First, remember that the SAT is designed for high school juniors and seniors three or four years older than you.

I promise you that you can get a very respectable score on the SAT simply by answering the easy and medium questions correctly. In fact, a student who answered all the easy and medium questions correctly would achieve a score in the 1800 to 1900 range! **So don't worry about the words you don't know or the math you haven't covered—you can do very well without knowing everything if you just answer correctly the questions you *can* answer.**

Pay particular attention to Tutorial 27. You should spend almost all of your time on the easy to medium questions, and *race* through the difficult questions. Pacing yourself on the SAT is almost the exact opposite of how you're used to pacing yourself on school tests.

Regarding the SAT Reading Test: do not let the words you don't know frighten you—most college students do not know every word on an SAT. I'll show you how to maximize the mileage you get through process of elimination. For the SAT Math Test, skim the math refresher chapters but focus on reviewing the math you already know rather than trying to learn a lot of new math. Instead, focus on the math techniques chapters (the experience sets).

In addition, the following sections are particularly important for you to read, preferably sooner than later.

- Tutorials 13, 17–21, and 26–28

- The Essay: Basic Principles

- The Proofreading and Editing Section: Basic Principles

- Sentence Completions: Basic Principles

- Sentence Completions: Advanced Principles

- Vocabulary for the SAT Reading Test

- Math Experience Sets 1–4

Asterisk these sections in the Table of Contents so you'll remember to read them. The other chapters in the book are also important, of course, but the ones I just mentioned are *particularly* important for *you*.

Okay, special assembly dismissed.

Special Assembly for Home Schoolers

This assembly is for home schooled students. Your SAT scores will be especially important for college admissions officers who will not have high school grades or teacher recommendations to guide them about your application.

The primary theme of this book is that the SAT is very different from school, and it is even more different from home school! What's more, the whole experience of taking standardized tests like the SAT probably feels quite alien to you. (That's not necessarily bad since you probably have fewer *misconceptions* about standardized tests than do most high school students.)

Since you aren't technically in a "grade," do not take the SAT for the first time more than six months before you intend to apply to college. If you are in the equivalent of the 11th grade, see if you can take the PSAT at a local high school.

In addition, the following sections are particularly important for you to read, preferably sooner than later.

- Basic Tutorials

- Advanced Tutorials

- Sentence Completions: Advanced Principles

- Reading Comprehension: Basic Principles

- Math Experience Sets 4 and 6

- Refreshers of SAT Arithmetic, Algebra, Geometry, and Miscellaneous Topics

- Taking the SAT

Asterisk these sections in the Table of Contents so you'll remember to read them. The other chapters in the book are also important, of course, but the ones I just mentioned are *particularly* important for *you.*

Okay, special assembly dismissed.

PART I

BASIC TUTORIALS

The SAT Is Unfair—Get Over It

I know there are dozens of things you'd rather be doing with your time than preparing for the SAT. Hey, I'm on your side. Do I think it's fair that colleges place so much emphasis on a three-and-a-half-hour exam that forces you to wake up early on a Saturday? Nope, but over one million other students have to deal with the same situation.

Look, I'd be lying if I said that preparing for the SAT is all fun and games. But I can say I'll make this process as painless as possible. Given that you want to do your best on the SAT, this RocketReview course is the best way to go. I'll be there with you every step of the way. I won't ever ask you to do something tedious or pointless. I promise everything in this book is designed to raise your score as much as possible, as quickly as possible. In fact, when you see how much and how rapidly you improve your score, you may even enjoy yourself!

But there's no denying it: *the SAT bites*. Now that we've cleared that up, let's move on.

The SAT Is Way Different from Your School Tests

Way, *way* different. That's the main point of this book.

I'm sure you know kids who don't do so well in school, yet somehow manage to ace standardized tests like the SAT. And you probably know other students who do really well in school, yet when it comes to the SAT these same students don't do nearly as well—and sometimes even bomb the test completely.

> **Fact:** Girls get better grades than boys do in high school (in college, too—so come on guys, get your act together). But here's a surprise: boys outscore girls on each section of the SAT (not just the math). Because many scholarships—such as the National Merit Scholarships—are based more on SAT scores than on classroom grades, boys receive far more than their share of such scholarship awards.

Why *do* so many bright students have so much trouble on the SAT? Because taking the SAT is nothing like taking tests in school. I mean *nothing* like it.

- To take one obvious example, school tests rarely last more than an hour.

    Not the SAT. On the SAT you've got to stay mentally focused for over three hours.

- On school tests, your teachers give more weight to the more difficult questions. So it makes sense to spend more time on those questions than on easier ones—they're worth more.

    Not on the SAT. On the SAT, all questions are worth the same, so it doesn't make sense to spend more time on hard questions. But that's exactly what most students do.

- On school tests, your teachers generally give partial credit for partial answers. If your answer to a long, complicated math question was mostly right, except for a "silly mistake," your math teacher would probably give you nearly full credit. If your answer on an English test was not the one the teacher was looking for, but you made a good argument for it, your English teacher would give you at least some credit—possibly full credit for originality!

  Not on the SAT. There's only one right answer for each question, and no partial credit for anything else. On the SAT there's no such thing as "just a careless mistake" since *any* mistake costs you full credit, and then some.

Those are just a few of the many differences between the SAT and the tests you're used to taking. They may seem to be minor differences, but as you'll see in the coming chapters, these differences will have a major impact on how you'll have to change the way you take the SAT if you want to achieve your maximum score.

Trust me: even if you're an excellent student—

- if you solve SAT math questions the way you're used to solving math questions in class

- if you read SAT passages the way you're used to reading novels or even your textbooks

- if you compose an SAT essay the way you're used to writing essays in English class

—then you're in for a *rude* surprise on the SAT.

You'll need to learn a whole new set of skills for the SAT. **Indeed, many of the academic and test-taking skills that lead to success in the classroom will work *against* you on the SAT.** We'll discuss all these points and more in the coming chapters.

> **Throughout this book, I will be alerting you to "classroom-correct, SAT-risky" methods: those methods that work in the classroom, but are risky or downright dangerous on the SAT.**

Forget Everything You Think You Know About the SAT: A Quiz

An amazing number of myths about the SAT have circulated over the years, sometimes spread by well-intentioned teachers. Let me warn you, if you take the test armed with misconceptions, you won't achieve your maximum score.

The following quiz will give you a chance to see whether any test-taking myths are interfering with your success on the SAT. For each of the following questions, choose the option that best indicates what you think about the SAT (or yourself). It's possible that none of the choices precisely reflect your thinking; still, choose only from these options given (no, you can't write in your own answer).

This quiz is for your benefit; nobody's grading it. Choose the answer that is closest to your real opinion, not the one you think you're "supposed" to choose. There are no trick questions in this quiz, so you shouldn't need to spend too much time on any particular question.

How Much Do You Know About Taking the SAT?

1. Since the SAT includes easy, medium, and difficult questions, on which type do you usually spend the *least* amount of time?
   (A) easy questions
   (B) medium questions
   (C) difficult questions

2. On which type of SAT question do you usually spend the *most* amount of time?
   (A) easy questions
   (B) medium questions
   (C) difficult questions

3. Since you lose points on the SAT for errors, if you're unsure after trying to solve a question it's usually better to leave that question blank rather than to answer it and risk losing points.
(A) true (B) false

4. When in doubt on an SAT question, go with your first hunch.
(A) true (B) false

5. Most SAT questions have trick answers.
(A) true (B) false

6. Most students should try to answer every question on the SAT to achieve their highest possible score.
(A) true (B) false

7. It's a good idea to finish each section a few minutes early so you'll have enough time to look over your work.
(A) true (B) false

8. When analyzing a question, you generally try to work out as much as you can in your head rather than waste precious time writing things down—especially on the easy questions.
(A) true (B) false

9. If you're not sure whether you can solve an SAT math problem, you shouldn't necessarily skip the question immediately because maybe you can figure it out with a little time.
(A) true (B) false

10. What is the *last* thing you should do before selecting the answer to an SAT math question?
(A) check your solution
(B) reread the question
(C) rework the problem
(D) check your calculations

11. If you're not sure what an SAT vocabulary word means, you should try to figure it out.
(A) true (B) false

12. How do you pace yourself on an SAT reading passage and the questions that follow it?
    (A) *slowly* on the passage, *quickly* on the questions
    (B) *quickly* on the passage, *slowly* on the questions
    (C) *slowly* on the passage, *slowly* on the questions
    (D) *quickly* on the passage, *quickly* on the questions

13. On the SAT essay, quality is more important than quantity.
    (A) true (B) false

14. On the SAT grammar questions, relying on your "ear" is generally advisable.
    (A) true (B) false

15. Compared with your scores on classroom tests, how do you do on standardized tests like the SAT?
    (A) You do better on the standardized test because you know it counts.
    (B) You do about the same.
    (C) You tend to freak out.

In the following basic and advanced tutorials, I'll tell you what your answers mean in detail. If you're dying to know the answers to specific questions, you'll find a brief discussion of this quiz in Tutorial 14 on page 26.

Don't Take Chances with Your Score!

This book is designed to raise your SAT score as *quickly* as possible, and as *much* as possible, using the least effort possible, and while having some fun along the way. And since we're going to be working together, we've got to establish some important ground rules.

Ground Rule #1: Follow *all* the RocketRules and techniques to get your top score, not just the ones you like or the ones that seem reasonable.

Whenever possible I'll explain *why* each method is best so you can prove it to yourself—and I'll also show you what *doesn't* work and why. But at times, it won't be clear to you why I'm recommending a particular technique or method until you take the actual exam, and that's when you need to trust these methods. I promise you that everything I'm recommending in this book has been field tested by thousands of students over the years.

Ground Rule #2: These techniques will not work unless you practice using them so you'll use them on the actual SAT.

Merely reading about the best SAT techniques in the world won't change the way you take the test, any more than just reading about basketball will improve your free-throw shot. To improve your score, you have to change the way you take the test. I'll show you everything you need to know, but the rest is up to you.

Ground Rule #3: When I give you an exercise or demonstrate a technique, follow my instructions *to the letter,* no more and no less.

For example, if I ask you to get someone to time you on a practice drill, then that's *exactly* what I want you to do. Timing yourself is *not* "the same thing," even though you might not understand why. *Everything* I ask you to do on the SAT matters—whether you see the importance of it or not. I'll try to explain the value of every technique, but sometimes the importance won't be apparent until you take the actual SAT. Until then, I'm asking you to trust me.

> Don't take chances on your actual SAT. Follow all the RocketRules that you'll be learning to the letter, and you'll achieve your maximum possible score.

• • •

Returning to the quiz from the last tutorial, here are the answers and what they mean. If you chose (C) for the first and last questions, and (B) for all the others—congratulations, you are a very sophisticated test-taker! If you chose differently—contratulations, you can improve your score dramatically by learning and using the techniques in this book!

A brief discussion of all the answers can be found at the end of Tutorial 14 on page 26, and in the following chapters I'll explain the principles behind the questions thoroughly. But for now, let's just address question 15, because it goes right to the heart of this tutorial.

Students who select (C)—they *freak out* on tests like the SAT—actually have the *easiest* time adopting the techniques in this book because they're open to new approaches. Students who select (A)—those who think they're *already* good test-takers—tend to resist new approaches. They may indeed *be* good test-takers, but ironically they sometimes have a harder time improving their score until they become more open-minded.

Again, everything in this book will help you achieve your maximum score in the minimum time—so don't take chances with your SAT score. *Use* these techniques; they've worked for thousands of other students, and they'll work for you.

RocketRules Are Absolute—
No Exceptions!

One of the great difficulties in writing a course like this one is that I have to speak to you the same way I speak to everyone else. It's like trying to write a book on baseball for everyone, beginners as well as professionals in the majors. What may be true for everybody else, however, may not apply to Barry Bonds. Once you're that good you can afford to break the rules.

So I'll always begin lessons by laying down absolute test-taking rules—always do this, never do that, and so on. Every RocketRule applies to 98 percent of all students in 98 percent of the situations. Only after you understand the basic principle will I point out any rare exceptions.

If you fall into one or more of the following categories of students, it's more likely that a rare exception will apply to you:

- you've already scored above 720 on a particular section of the test, or you're absolutely certain that you will

- you've already scored below 380 on a particular section of the test, or are fearful that you might

- your first language is not English

- you've got a certified medical condition that entitles you to extra time

- you're in junior high school, taking the SAT for admission to a special program

But even in those situations the exceptions are rare, and I will point them out (some of which I've already done in the opening chapter, "How to Use This Book"). Assume that everything I say in this book applies to you—yes, you—unless I say otherwise.

You'd *Better* Prepare for the SAT—but Practice Alone Is Not Enough

One of the contenders for the title "world's worst SAT advice" is the following sparkler: *Just take the SAT without preparing, to see how you'll do. You can always retake the test later if you're not happy with your score.* This advice is often said especially of the PSAT, because "it's just a practice test, it doesn't count, and colleges won't see your score."

That advice is easy for others to say: they don't have to live with your scores afterwards. Here's the truth: for every hundred students who "just take" the SAT without preparing, 99 will be disappointed with one or more of their reading, writing, or math scores—sometimes crushingly disappointed. (That other student either is incredibly lucky, or doesn't care about the SAT one way or the other.) And once someone is disappointed, that makes the inevitable subsequent preparation all the harder.

Look, there's just no way you're going to do anywhere near your best unless you prepare for the SAT; that just stands to reason. I know you realize how important preparing for the SAT is: that's why you're reading this book. But it's even important to do *some* preparation for the PSAT—the test may not count for others (though it does for many scholarships), but it *does* count for you! You needn't do a lot of preparation for the PSAT, just enough so that you know what to expect and so the test is a positive experience. **The PSAT is especially useful as a trial to see how you handle "curve balls" (the unexpected difficulties that are part of every SAT and PSAT) and how difficult it sometimes is to apply what you know under the pressure of actual exam conditions (see Tutorials 8 and 9).**

Incidentally, a common myth is that students generally improve the second time they take the SAT, even if they don't prepare between tests. Yes, it's true that students at the average score level (500 per section) tend to improve *a bit*. The higher your starting score is, however, the less "practice effect" you get (the improvement resulting simply from retaking the test). In fact, scores greater than 650 on any section tend to *decline* on retesting—*if* a student does not prepare. **Ironically then, the higher your starting scores, the more** important it becomes to prepare between the PSAT and SAT, or between your first SAT and second SAT (if you decide to retake the test).

Another all-too-common fallacy about preparing for the SAT is that all you need to do is "familiarize yourself" with the test by taking some practice exams. Yeah, right, that's like saying the way to become a great basketball player is to familiarize yourself with a basketball court and practice taking a few shots.

Michael Jordan once said that there's a right way and a wrong way to practice basketball. He said that it doesn't matter if you practice eight hours a day—*if you're practicing the wrong way, all you're doing is getting really good at doing the wrong things.*

Merely practicing won't significantly improve anyone's score unless coupled with smarter test-taking strategies. Fortunately, you're holding those strategies in your hands right now.

To Change Your Score, You'll Have to Change the Way You Take the Test

Duh! I know that point seems incredibly obvious but according to many SAT "experts," the best way to improve your math score is to take lots of advanced math classes and the best way to improve your reading score is to read a lot of good books and the best way to improve your writing score is to write a lot. Gee, thanks for the hot tip!

Don't get me wrong. I encourage you to do these things—they'll improve your mind—but they're not going to change your SAT scores very much.

Here's why. First, remember your second tutorial: the SAT requires a very different skill set and mindset than those required to do well in your regular classroom activities.

What's more, apart from some admittedly college-level vocabulary, and reviewing some grammar and math you've already covered in school, there aren't a whole lot of facts or formulas you need to know for the SAT. So the only way to raise your SAT score is to change the way you take the test. And if you want to change your SAT score *a lot,* you have to change the way you take the test—*a lot.*

Fortunately, it doesn't take that long to get the hang of powerful new math, reading, and writing strategies for the SAT. Don't worry, I'll show you how.

Change Is Sometimes Scary

There's nothing natural about taking the SAT. Many of the problem solving techniques you'll be learning here won't feel natural at first, either. Indeed, it's natural to resist change, any kind of change.

So changing the way you take the SAT won't always be easy—especially if you're a good student. After all, you've had a lot of success doing things your way. And then I come along and tell you that if you want to achieve your maximum possible SAT score, you're going to have to change test-taking habits that have served you well in school for years.

Here are some of the major things you're probably going to have to change for the SAT:

- how much time you spend on easy, medium, and difficult questions

- how many questions you leave blank, how quickly you decide which ones to leave blank, and why you leave them blank

- the way you check your work for errors

- the way you read passages, and how much time you spend on the reading questions

- the way you solve math problems

- what you do when you're not sure what a particular word means

- how you guess

- the way you plan and write essays

These aren't difficult things to do, and I'll explain everything step by step. I just wanted to warn you that you may experience some resistance to these changes. Again: if you selected choice (A) on question 15 in the third tutorial— if you already see yourself as a good test-taker—you may resist adopting new techniques more than students who don't think they test well. But it's my job to get you to change the way you take the SAT; you just have to be open to these changes.

There's a Huge Difference Between *Knowing* What to Do on the SAT—and Being Able to *Do* It

The world's worst—and most universal—advice to students about to take the SAT is *relax.* This advice is awful for two major reasons. First, it's flat out wrong: if you want to relax on the SAT, take a pillow into the exam room and put your head down on the desk when the test begins.

There's nothing relaxing about taking the SAT, and most students do better with *some* nervous energy to get their adrenaline pumping and their mind focused on the task at hand.

Admittedly, too *much* adrenaline-induced tension is not a good thing: if the yellow #2 pencil in your hand is vibrating like a tuning fork before the test begins, that's a problem. But a little nervous energy is good. The only students truly relaxed while taking the SAT are asleep, or they don't care what score they receive.

The advice to relax is completely useless, however, for another important reason: it doesn't show you *how* to relax. Even if relaxing were helpful on the SAT, *telling* you to relax isn't going to make you relax. If anything, telling students to relax only makes them more aware of their nervousness. Gee, thanks. Now you've given me something *else* to worry about: I can't relax!

A lot of the SAT advice that people offer students is just like that: they tell you *what* to do, but they don't show you *how* to do it. Here's another piece of well-intentioned but useless advice: *When you get to a difficult question on a test, don't waste time; just skip it and you can always return to it later.*

I'll bet you've heard someone chirp that golden piece of advice to you plenty of times—*as if skipping a difficult question were the easiest thing in the world.* It's not. In fact, being able to recognize a difficult question *at a glance,* and being able to tear yourself away from it *instantly,* is one of the *hardest* things to do on the SAT.

I'll show you how to recognize and skip difficult questions *immediately,* and I'll give you drills that will *force* you to do that. For every technique you need to master for the SAT, I'll show you *what* to do, *how* to do it, and *why* you need to do it. Whenever a technique I'm demonstrating is difficult to use, I'll warn you ahead of time. **Fact: the *right* thing to do on the SAT is often the *hardest* thing to do—that's why so many students haven't learned to test well. It's my job not only to show you how to do something on the SAT, but also to *get* you to do it.** At least, insofar as I can get you to do the right things while speaking to you through a book, an interactive CD-ROM, and some web-based software; unfortunately I'm not in the same room with you so I can't observe and correct you as you rehearse.

Just try to meet me halfway, 'kay?

How Much Can You Raise Your SAT Score?

As we just discussed, how much and how rapidly you can raise your SAT score depends on how willing you are to change the way you take the test. Your potential improvement depends on other factors, of course, so it's impossible to give an average answer. Here are some other general considerations:

- The more time you have to prepare and the more dedicated you are, the more improvement you can expect.

- The higher your starting scores, the less room there is for improvement.

- In general, writing scores improve more rapidly than math scores, and math scores improve more rapidly than do reading scores.

- The more words you memorize, the better you'll do on the sentence completion questions of the reading section (and, as you'll discover, the better you'll do on some of the reading questions and even the essay).

- If we divide all students into tortoises (slow, methodical) or hares (fast, impulsive), tortoises tend to improve more rapidly than hares (it's easier to get tortoises to solve problems more quickly than it is to get hares to solve problems more carefully).

As a rule of thumb, you must pick up four extra questions for every 50 points you want to raise your scores. Keeping in mind that the official statistics by ETS, the test publishers, "show" that the average combined improvement is 60 to 70 points, a 150-point improvement is quite respectable, 200 to 300 points is excellent, and 400 points is phenomenal. Improvements of 500 points are so rare that ETS often examines such answer sheets for evidence of cheating.

Having said all that, nobody can guarantee how well you'll do on the actual exam—nobody. No matter how well prepared you are for the SAT, the actual test is always different. Even Michael Jordan and Tiger Woods had their bad days; it happens. Over half the students who prepare for the SAT will retake it: some because they are disappointed with their scores, but also those who are happy with their scores but know they can do better.

I promise you that this book contains the best SAT information and techniques anywhere. And I promise that if you apply yourself to the lessons and drills and techniques—and use the techniques on the actual exam—you'll do the best you can possibly do on the day of the actual exam. But bad breaks happen to the best of us, so you may need to retake the test.

I just wanted to be totally honest with you. I'll *always* be totally honest with you about the SAT—you can count on it.

Taking the SAT Is a Performance Skill: Improvement Comes in Stages

Like learning anything else, learning how to take the SAT in the optimal way is not something that improves consistently, a little bit each day. At the beginning, you may well experience some quick gains as you master some of the easier techniques. These easy gains, however, are often followed by stretches where your score seems to remain stuck at a certain level.

Or maybe you start off practicing and your scores seem stuck in a rut despite your best efforts. Test after practice test your scores seem to go nowhere.

Hang in there. If you've been practicing diligently—*and applying the techniques I'll show you*—you *are* getting better; the improvement just hasn't been reflected in your score—yet. After a few weeks of seemingly little progress—*pow!*—your score jumps 50, 100 points out of nowhere.

Consider a skill you pride yourself on. Now think back to the time when you first started practicing that skill. Unless you had a natural gift for that skill, you probably struggled quite a bit at the beginning. Perhaps there were times when you considered giving up. And then one day, absolutely unexpectedly, you were surprised, maybe even giddy, that you could suddenly do what had once seemed impossible.

Frustration is a natural part of learning any new skill. Regardless of the activity, the pattern seems to be long periods of boring if not maddening periods of non-improvement—punctuated by brief, joyous periods of rapid and dramatic gains. Don't place too much emphasis on the minor ups and downs of your practice scores from week to week. I say this because all too many students get elated when their score on a practice test goes up—but then they feel crushed when their score dips a bit. Minor fluctuations in your score don't mean anything any more than do fluctuations in a basketball player's score from game to game.

A warning sign are scores that gyrate wildly from week to week: up 70 points; down 60; up 100. Aim for *consistency*. **Consistent scores over a few weeks are a very, very good sign of major score improvements just around the corner.**

How Your Brain's Natural Intelligence Can Get You in Trouble

(Warning: You *Hallucinate* on the SAT More Than You Realize)

Your brain is an amazing organ. It operates all the time, making sense of the world around you. Without your trying, your brain continuously sorts through the stream of impressions it receives from your various senses, and pieces together meaningful information from all this data. Your brain continuously *interprets* what you see and hear—and it does so largely without your awareness. (Bear with me for a few seconds. You'll see how this all creates a hidden danger for you on every section of the SAT shortly.)

So far, so good. In the real world, you *want* your brain to interpret what you see and hear. And by and large, your brain does a pretty good job. In fact, if the brain perceives nonsense, it will interpret *that* for you, too.

Let's say I tell you that the speed limit on Chicago residential streets is 30 miles per hour, and that John is driving at 40 miles an hour. What would you conclude? Probably that John is speeding, right? You might draw other conclusions, such as John's likelihood of getting a speeding ticket if he is caught.

But notice that I did not say *where* John is driving. For all you know, John is driving in the slow lane of a NASCAR race in Daytona Beach, Florida.

Now, in real life it would be ridiculous for someone to say that the speed limit in a city is 30 miles per hour, and that someone is driving 40 miles an hour—but in another city. You know that would be ridiculous, so your brain "figures out" what the other person "really meant."

But on the SAT you don't want to *interpret* ridiculous statements, you want to eliminate them as wrong. Don't interpret on the SAT, or read between the lines, or search for hidden meanings. There are no hidden meanings, and there's nothing between the lines.

Okay, time for an experiment. Let's take an example from an SAT reading passage about warm-blooded and cold-blooded animals and their different physiological responses to climate changes. Then let's say you get to the following question: *"The passage suggests that if the external temperature drops significantly, which of the following would be the effect on the metabolism of a frog compared with the effect on the metabolism of a mouse?"*

Don't worry, SAT reading passages don't test what you know about biology or history or literature; all the information to answer a question like this would have been supplied in the passage. Here's my question for the experiment: *as you think about this question for fifteen seconds or so, what images come to mind?* Close your eyes and imagine the frog and the mouse, create a detailed picture of the situation the question is asking about, and tell me what scene you saw in your mind's eye.

Most people report seeing something like the following: a mouse and a frog, on the ground, in cold weather, probably winter, maybe snow on the ground. Go back to the question and see whether that scenario captures the situation being asked about. Does it?

Unfortunately, that depiction is wildly different from the question being asked. The question did *not* ask what happens to a mouse and a frog when the weather gets cold, it asked what happens when the temperature *drops significantly*. Maybe the temperature dropped from 50 degrees Fahrenheit to 30 degrees; that would be cold. Then again, maybe the temperature dropped from 100 degrees Fahrenheit to 80 degrees; the same significant temperature drop but we're still in warm-to-hot weather. **Notice how easy it is for an SAT question to ask one thing, and for your brain to hear something entirely different.**

Unconsciously interpreting what you read can get you in trouble on every section of the SAT, but especially on the reading questions and on the grammar (proofreading) questions. Misreading questions is another big cause of errors, but at least there you can reread the question and verify that you read it correctly the first time. Once your brain has interpreted some text in a particular way, on the other hand, it's very hard to be objective and seek other interpretations.

Train yourself to take everything you read on the SAT absolutely literally—without interpreting or overanalyzing. I'll give you drills to help you develop this skill on each type of question.

How to Gain (or Lose) 30 IQ Points— Instantly!

(Hint: Your Pencil Is Smarter Than You Are)

Now that you know the tricks your brain can play on you on the SAT, you can better appreciate the importance of being hyper-cautious in every aspect of your work on the test. Remember: *any* mistake on the SAT costs you valuable points; the computer grading your test does not forgive "just silly" mistakes the way your teachers in school often do.

One powerful tool you have right in your hand is your pencil. Einstein himself was fond of saying that his pencil was smarter than he was. If someone *that* smart relied on his pencil, maybe we should, too. You'll understand why using your pencil *all* the time as you take the SAT is so critical once you understand a bit more about another aspect of your brain's operation.

When you think, your brain shuttles information back and forth between your long-term memory (what you know) and your short-term memory (what you're thinking about, for example, when you solve a problem). Unfortunately, the human brain has very limited short-term memory capacity. Psychological experiments have shown that the brain can store about seven items (such as the seven digits of a new phone number) in short-term memory without much difficulty. Beyond seven items, the short-term memory soon becomes overwhelmed (a new area code as well as a phone number is *much* harder to remember than simply a new phone number).

When your short-term memory becomes overwhelmed with too much information, you've got two big problems. First, your thinking ability drops to zero. Literally. Your brain turns to mush.

You can prove this phenomenon to yourself. Ask someone to write down a ten-digit number on a slip of paper and then to read it out loud for you to remember.

You may have to focus a bit but remembering the number's not too hard, right? What's the big deal? Wait a second, we're not finished with the experiment yet.

Now ask this person to give you a simple problem to solve *in your head—as you retain the ten-digit number.* The problem has to be one that requires thinking, not reciting a fact from your long-term memory (a simple math word problem works, or asking for the definition of a difficult word).

Once you've solved the problem, state your solution and then recite the ten-digit number. Have your friend check the number against the slip of paper. (If the number wasn't written down, your friend may have trouble remembering the number accurately, too.)

Did you solve the problem *and* remember all the digits correctly? Almost everyone flubs either the problem or the digit or both. Even if you're a super-genius who solved the problem *and* remembered the number, you'll have to admit that you really had to focus to do so.

So the first problem with taxing your short-term memory is that you have a much harder time even thinking. A couple of items to remember won't have much of an impact, but beyond a few and each new item you try to retain in short-term memory costs you IQ points, literally.

The second problem with taxing your short-term memory is that you are often unaware of when you've reached your limit. The result? Near-total amnesia. I'm not kidding, and if you think about it, you'll realize that this happens all the time. Tell me whether you've ever had the following experience.

You sit down at your desk to read an assignment: an article for a science course, a chapter from a history book, an essay for your English course, whatever. You work your way through the text carefully, maybe underlining key parts and taking notes. *As* you read, you have no trouble whatsoever following along, understanding each and every point the author makes.

Finally, you finish the assignment and close the book. And suddenly you realize a very weird thing: *you can't remember what you just read.* Oh sure, you remember the basic topic, maybe even an idea or two. But otherwise the rest of what you read is a total fog to you.

I know that happens to you because I know it happens to everyone. Here's the explanation. Reading the assigned text closely and carefully, you probably overtaxed your short-term memory somewhere in the first paragraph. So what does your short-term memory do when it "fills up"? It *dumps* the old information to make way for the new. When your short-term memory filled up with information after the first few sentences, it continually dumped the earlier information to make way for the new—*otherwise you wouldn't be able to read.*

Notice that you weren't aware of the problem—that you couldn't remember much of what you'd just read—until you finished the assignment. Now imagine that happens to you on the SAT. Not a good situation in which to find yourself now, is it? The limits of your short-term memory affect you *everywhere* on the SAT: on math problems as well as on the reading passages. **Every time you "do something in your head," you're taxing your short-term memory and leaving that much less brain power for thinking. In other words, the more analysis you do in your head, the dumber you get.**

The solution? Write down as much as possible in your text booklet when you're solving questions. Each time you write something down, however small a step, you free up your short-term memory and thereby give yourself *more* brain power to think with. That's what Einstein was talking about. Write down as much as you can (using abbreviations, of course), no matter how simple or easy or "obvious" it is. Any little math step of a solution? *Write it down.* Using process of elimination on a sentence completion choice? *Write it down.* Locating the main idea of a reading passage? *Write it down.*

If, when you're taking the test, your pencil isn't either writing something down or poised—*I mean this*—at most a few inches off the page, ready to jot down something every five to ten seconds, then you're doing way too much thinking in your head. In short, you're handicapping your thinking ability *big time.* The more you use your pencil, the smarter you become. The SAT is hard enough; don't make it harder than it has to be.

Don't Try to Remember Everything I Say

When was the last time a teacher or coach said that to you?

We're going to be covering a lot of territory in these chapters, but don't let all this new information overwhelm you. And you may think that you have to memorize everything. You don't. Some of the things will stick, you'll learn them almost by osmosis; others won't stick. And that's fine. It takes a lot longer for me to explain techniques than it does for you to use them.

Now, from time to time I will ask you to memorize something, but not often, and not today. Eventually everything will stick. It's my job to make sure it does.

We'll take things slowly, working from basic concepts and principles and building from there, step by step. In each lesson, I'll introduce a few new concepts while reviewing and reinforcing the previous ones. I'll show not only what does work on the test but what doesn't, and why. In very little time, RocketReview's amazing test-taking methods will sink in and—if you apply yourself—become second nature.

Before we move on to consider the SAT itself, here are the answers to the quiz from Tutorial 3, along with references to sections where you'll find more in-depth explanations.

How Much Do You Know About Taking the SAT?

1. Since the SAT includes easy, medium, and difficult questions, on which type do you usually spend the *least* amount of time?
   (A) easy questions
   (B) medium questions
   (C) difficult questions

   Discussion: See Tutorial 27.

2.   On which type of SAT question do you usually spend the *most* amount of time?
     (A) easy questions
     (B) medium questions
     (C) difficult questions

     Discussion: See Tutorial 27.

3.   Since you lose points on the SAT for errors, if you're unsure after trying to solve a question it's usually better to leave that question blank rather than to answer it and risk losing points.
     (A) true **(B) false**

     Discussion: See Tutorials 15, 16, 17, and 24.

4.   When in doubt on an SAT question, go with your first hunch.
     (A) true **(B) false**

     Discussion: See Tutorials 28 and 29.

5.   Most SAT questions have trick answers.
     (A) true **(B) false**

     Discussion: See Tutorials 26 and 28.

6.   Most students should try to answer every question on the SAT to achieve their highest possible score.
     (A) true **(B) false**

     Discussion: See Tutorial 20.

7.   It's a good idea to finish each section a few minutes early so you'll have enough time to look over your work.
     (A) true **(B) false**

     Discussion: See Tutorial 25.

8. When analyzing a question, you generally try to work out as much as you can in your head rather than waste precious time writing things down—especially on easy questions.
    (A) true **(B) false**

    Discussion: See Tutorial 13.

9. If you're not sure whether you can solve an SAT math problem, you shouldn't necessarily skip the question immediately because maybe you can figure it out with a little time.
    (A) true **(B) false**

    Discussion: See Tutorial 23.

10. What is the *last* thing you should do before selecting the answer to an SAT math question?
    (A) check your solution
    (B) reread the question
    (C) rework the problem
    (D) check your calculations

    Discussion: See Tutorial 12, and the Introduction to the Math Test.

11. If you're not sure what an SAT vocabulary word means, you should try to figure it out.
    (A) true **(B) false**

    Discussion: See Tutorial 23, the Introduction to the Reading Test, and Sentence Completions: Advanced Principles.

12. How do you pace yourself on an SAT reading passage and the questions that follow it?
    (A) *slowly* on the passage, *quickly* on the questions
    (B) *quickly* on the passage, *slowly* on the questions
    (C) *slowly* on the passage, *slowly* on the questions
    (D) *quickly* on the passage, *quickly* on the questions

Discussion: See Reading Comprehension: Basic Principles.

13.   On the SAT essay, quality is more important than quantity.
       (A) true **(B) false**

Discussion: See The Essay: Basic Principles.

14.   On the SAT grammar questions, relying on your "ear" is
       generally advisable.
       (A) true **(B) false**

Discussion: See The Essay: Basic Principles.

15.   Compared with your scores on classroom tests, how do you
       do on standardized tests like the SAT?
       (A) You do better on the standardized test because you
            know it counts.
       (B) You do about the same.
       (C) You tend to freak out.

Discussion: See Tutorials 4 and 30.

Remember that this quiz was designed to shake up your thinking. The answer to not one of these questions was obvious, and certainly nothing I would have expected you to know at this point. By the time you finish the tutorials, you'll be saying *duh* to most of these answers.

That was the last of your introductory tutorials. Now we're ready to tackle the SAT itself.

PART II

ADVANCED TUTORIALS

How the SAT Is Scored

(I've Got Good News and Bad News)

The SAT consists of three separate tests—reading, writing, and math—each with its own 200 to 800 score. The lowest possible total score is 600; the highest possible score is 2400.

Now, the moment you enter the exam room and start taking the test, guess how many points you start off with. The answer surprises most people: 2400.

That's right: for signing your name on the answer sheet, you start off the test with 2400 points. I kid you not; when you enter the exam room, your starting score is 2400.

That's the good news.

Here's the catch: you don't necessarily get to keep all those points. In fact, out of every fifteen hundred students taking the SAT, only one will *leave* the exam room with all of his or her original 2400 points.

You see, the bad news is that every time you leave a question blank or get one wrong, they take away points. **Your goal on the SAT is to hang on to as many of your 2400 starting points as possible. How? By leaving the fewest number of questions blank and getting the fewest number of questions wrong.**

Got that? *Hang on to your points!*

Yes, Blanks Do Cost You Points

Most people believe that on the SAT, blanks "don't count." They probably think that blanks don't count because a blank sounds like nothing or a zero, so leaving a question blank must cost zero points.

These people are wrong, and you can prove it to yourself with the answer to a simple question. *What kind of SAT score would you have if you left every question blank?*

Sorry, but blanks *do* count. How much? **Every time you leave a question blank, you lose 10 points from your 2400 starting score.** The cost of each blank varies a bit, but as a rough average, figure 10 points per blank.

If you leave 10 questions blank on the SAT, you lose 100 points; 20 questions, 200 points. **And every time you lose points for a blank, you can never get those points back. Never.**

Guessing Does Not Hurt Your Score

Bad guessing hurts your score; good guessing *helps* your score. I'm serious. Remember our previous tutorial. Only two things hurt your score: blanks and errors.

Here, look at it this way. Every time you get to a question, you have two options: answer the question or don't answer it. **Every time you don't answer a question, you lose 10 points.**

Now, if you answer the question you'll either get it right or get it wrong. If you answer it correctly, you get to keep your points for that question, and you lose nothing. If you answer it *incorrectly,* you lose on average 12 points.

But notice that when you're answering a question, you don't know beforehand whether you'll answer it correctly or incorrectly. A blank is a guaranteed loss of 10 points. By answering a question you're risking about 2 points to save the 10 that you'd otherwise lose for sure.

In short, guessing sometimes helps your score, but *not* guessing *always* hurts your score. In Tutorials 28 and 29 you'll learn more about the art of good guessing (and the logic behind it).

If You've Spent Time on a Question, Answer It—*Always!*

Sometimes, after spending time on a question, you won't be sure how to solve it. Maybe you've been able to eliminate one or more choices but you haven't found the answer. Many students wonder whether they should guess on such a question or leave it blank. You already know the answer: *guess!*

You may be wondering whether you should guess on a question even when you "have no idea." Yes, even then. As you'll see later, if you've spent time on a question, you'll *always* have an idea—even if the idea is simply that the question is a difficult one.

Not knowing an answer and having to guess can be scary. It's not. Many students suffer the mistaken fear that guessing is "taking a chance" while leaving a blank is "playing it safe." Wrong. **Leaving a question blank isn't playing it safe, and it's not taking a chance—it's a guaranteed, irrevocable* loss of 10 points.** If you're not sure of the answer to a question, you can either take a chance or kiss 10 points goodbye. Forever.

Again, notice that you're not taking *much* of a chance by guessing: you're risking 2 or 3 points to save 10. But pay close attention to my words: *if* you spend time on a question, you should always answer it. On some questions, however, it may be better not to spend any time at all.

Wayne Gretzky, unanimously acclaimed as the greatest hockey player of all time (there isn't even a close second), once said, "You miss 100 percent of the shots you don't take." That's true on the SAT as well. If you don't take a shot on a question you've already invested time in, you're definitely going to lose points. **You miss 100 percent of the questions you don't answer.**

* Good SAT word; look it up (GSWLIU).

The *Only* Reason to Leave a Question Blank Is to Save Time

Blanks *do* cost you points, *but they buy you time.* Or rather, blanks had *better* buy you time, or you're sacrificing points for no reason whatsoever.

Unfortunately, all too many students leave a question blank *after* they've spent a lot of time trying to solve it. If you skip a question *immediately,* you save yourself a minute that you can use to solve other questions, and you may need the extra time.

What you don't want to do is spend a minute trying to solve a question, and *then* leave it blank. Now you've lost 10 points *and* 60 seconds. **An important skill you'll be developing is learning to tell—*at a glance*—whether you should leave a question blank or not. If you can't *immediately* decide whether you can do a question, skip it for now—you can return to it later.**

Got all that? *Leaving a question blank means not trying it at all.* Once you spend time on a question, you've got to guess.

Unfortunately, You'll Probably Have to Leave *Some* Questions Blank

(The Speed Versus Accuracy Tradeoff)

Let me put that differently. **Until you're *absolutely* sure that you've got *a shot* at a 750 to 800 on the reading, writing, or math test—only about 1 student in 20 does—you'd *better* leave some questions blank on that part of the SAT.**

Here's the basic problem everyone has to deal with on the SAT: limited time. The SAT has enough questions in a short enough period of time that most students can finish only by rushing. And rushing leads to mistakes.

Yes, blanks cost you points—but so do errors.

Your score on the SAT is determined by how quickly and accurately you can read and solve problems. The dilemma you face is that the higher your speed, the lower your accuracy. The more problems you attempt in the time limit, the more mistakes you're likely to make. If on the other hand you move more slowly to improve your accuracy, you won't be able to answer as many questions. Moving faster means fewer blanks but more errors; moving slower means fewer errors but more blanks. That's the tradeoff everyone faces on the SAT.

The speed versus accuracy tradeoff on the SAT is just like the tradeoff in typing. Up to a certain speed, you can type making few, if any, errors. But then, if you go just a bit faster, you begin to make a few mistakes. And a bit faster than that, you begin to make a lot of mistakes.

So, if you need to leave some blanks, which questions should you sacrifice? Since every question is worth the same amount, the questions to leave blank are the ones that take the most amount of time to answer.

This rule applies to the reading, writing, and math tests. When we get to each test in later chapters, we'll see how to apply this principle on the different question types.

This tutorial may seem to contradict Tutorial 16 but the two rules complement each other. **Until you're scoring consistently above 700, don't attempt every question—but answer every question you attempt.** How many questions you should leave blank will depend on how well you manage the speed versus accuracy tradeoff and what your SAT goal is.

Fortunately, You Can Still Get a Very Good Score Without Finishing

Suppose you received a score of 80 out of 100 on a test at school. Would that be a very good score, a good score, an average score, or a bad score?

Well, on the SAT, 80 percent right is better than a 650 on the reading, writing, or math tests. That's a combined score of 1950, a score level achieved by only one in ten college-bound students. In other words, you could leave one sixth of the questions completely blank, make a few mistakes, and *still* achieve a very good score.

Assuming that you're not rushing, and you're able to maintain a high level of accuracy by allowing *only* a handful of errors, you can leave the following fraction of questions blank and still achieve the corresponding score levels:

- *one-twelfth* of the questions blank and still achieve a 700 (2100 combined)

- *one-fourth* of the questions blank and still achieve a 600 (1800 combined)

- *one-third* of the questions blank and still achieve a 500 (1500 combined)

The mistake most students make is rushing to answer *all* of the questions. In doing so, they make *avoidable* mistakes on easy and medium questions that they *could* have gotten right (had they gone more slowly), in an effort to answer hard questions (on which they make mistakes that are often *unavoidable*).

The possibility that you can do very well on the SAT without attempting a fair number of questions runs counter to your experience in school. On school tests, your teachers almost always expect you to at least attempt every question. On the SAT, unless you are shooting for a score in the top 5 percent or better, you'd be *foolish* to attempt finishing. Allow some time to become comfortable with this notion.

Never Sacrifice Accuracy for Speed

In other words, never rush. **Never, ever, never, ever, never ever.** Repeat after me: *I will not rush on the SAT.*

Rushing is probably the root cause of most *avoidable* errors on the SAT. Students race through each section, doing work in their heads, grabbing at any answer that seems right, all in a mad dash to finish every problem. Paradoxically, rushing itself is caused by one of two opposite states of mind: *over*confidence or *lack* of confidence.

The SAT measures how quickly and accurately you read and analyze questions, but it's much harder to be accurate than it is to be fast. In school classes you may impress your teachers and your classmates with your dazzling speed, but on the SAT you don't get extra points for solving questions quickly.

Look, it isn't hard finishing the SAT. *Anybody* can finish answering every question on the SAT—so long as he or she doesn't mind making mistakes, possibly *many* mistakes. I know that it's not easy being a tortoise; it's much cooler being a hare. Fast and clever are cool; slow and methodical are boring. But as in Aesop's fable, the slow and accurate tortoise will outscore the clever but careless hare any day of the week, I promise you.

How can you tell whether you've rushed on the SAT? Well, one infallible sign is that you finished a section early. Many students express frustration that when they took the SAT, they didn't *try* to rush, they didn't *try* to finish— "it just happened." They say this as if they had no control over their actions, and partly, they're right.

The only way to be sure that you're not rushing is *consciously* to slow yourself down. When I ask these same students whether they wrote everything down (Tutorial 13), they admit, "Well, no, not *everything*. I mean, a lot of the stuff was obvious so I did that in my head."

Busted. What word didn't they understand when I told them to write everything down on the SAT? **The RocketRule is *not* that you write down what you *think* you have to write down, it's that you write down *everything*—**

especially when you think you "don't have to."

A coach will sometimes tell athletes that if they have trouble talking when they're exercising, they're working out too hard. **If you have trouble writing everything down on the SAT, you're moving too quickly—*way* too quickly.**

Your ideal pace lies somewhere between too slow and too fast, and the only way to discover that pace is experimenting. **Your ideal pace is that speed that permits you no more than two or three avoidable mistakes by per section. I say "avoidable" mistakes to distinguish them from unavoidable mistakes— questions you couldn't have gotten right no matter how much time you'd spent on them.**

Your ideal pace will gradually increase as you begin to use the techniques you'll be learning in later chapters. Most students start off their practice in the way-too-fast zone. The thing to do is find your ideal pace—again, the one that balances speed and accuracy—and gradually improve that.

Let me tell you, no matter *what* I say to you here, on the day of the SAT you'll be *so* tempted to rush; so, so tempted. You have to train yourself diligently before the test so you have the self-control when it counts. **Trust me on this point: writing everything down on the SAT makes it impossible for you to rush.**

TUTORIAL 23
Don't Rush on the Test, but Don't Linger Either

What's a few seconds, right? Doesn't sound like very much time, does it? But if you waste even a few seconds on each question of the SAT, you'll have lost 15 minutes by the end of the exam! Gone, vanished. And 15 minutes is enough time to answer fifteen questions. In other words, if you waste just a few seconds per question, you'll be risking as much as 150 points by the end of the exam.

Yes, you want to be accurate on the SAT; on the other hand, you can't afford to waste any time. And the biggest time waster of all on the SAT is trying to "figure out" what to do. Whether it's trying to figure out the definition of a word or figure out what to do on a math problem or figure out what a passage is all about or figure out whether a word is grammatically correct—it's *all* wasted time. **Here are famous last words, and a sure sign that you're about to waste time: "Hmmm, let me think. . . ."**

Look, there's nothing to figure out on the SAT. You either *know* something, or you don't. If you can't decide whether a choice is right or wrong in five seconds—max—squiggle a "maybe" wave in the margin and move on to the next choice. **If you don't know what to do on a question, do *whatever* you can do—it's usually a step in the right direction. If you can't do anything, *move on* to the next choice or the next question.** Move!

Keep your pencil moving. As I mentioned earlier (Tutorial 13), if your pencil lifts off the page for more than a few seconds as you take the SAT— *especially if your elbow goes on the table and you look off into the distance, searching your memory*—you're probably spacing out. Just keep moving, you can always return to the question later.

Train yourself to go through each section in more than one pass. Most students complete a section's questions in numerical order. They answer number one before moving on to number two; number two before moving on to number three; number three before moving on to number four; and so on. And when they get stuck on a question, they come to a complete halt, wasting precious minutes before finally deciding to move on.

43

This is a natural approach to taking the SAT, but a beginner's approach. Smart test-takers are more ninja-like, leaping from question to question according to ease of solution. Smart test-takers also go through each section *at least* twice.

On the first pass you answer every question you can solve quickly. If you misjudge a question, circle the question number and move on—immediately; you can return to it on your next pass. Postponing the question gives your subconscious mind a chance to work on the problem while your conscious mind moves ahead to tackle a new question. This first pass through a section will take half to three-quarters of the available time *because you haven't wasted any wrestling with difficult questions.*

On your second pass through a section, you return to the questions that stumped you on the first pass or that you skipped entirely. Now you step up your pace, spending *less* time per question or per choice. If you're still stumped, no prob—leave the question for a *third* pass. And if you still haven't solved a question as time runs out, guess.

When Time Is Running Out, Always Go for Buzzer Shot Guesses

Yes, you should always be willing to sacrifice some difficult, time-consuming questions to buy yourself time to spend on the other ones. **But never be afraid to guess.** As Wayne Gretzky said, you miss 100 percent of the questions you don't answer.

In Tutorial 22 I said that you should never sacrifice accuracy for speed. Okay, here's the *only* exception to that RocketRule: in the final seconds of any section, take whatever buzzer shot guesses you can.

A buzzer shot in basketball is one taken in absolute desperation, flung in the remaining seconds of a game in the wild hope that it just *might* go in. After all, there's nothing to lose at that point. And amazingly, enough of those wild shots go in to justify taking them.

You'll probably be in the same situation on the SAT at the end of every section. You'll be left with half a minute or less remaining; not enough time to *solve* a problem, but *more* than enough time to make a good guess or two.

Remember: every blank you leave is 10 points deducted from your 2400 starting score, and you're trying to hold on to as many of those points as possible. Some of your buzzer shots may miss, but even when they do they cost you only 2 to 3 points more than the blanks would have cost you anyway. So go for it.

In sum, until the final seconds of any section—say, the last 15 to 30 seconds—you maintain accuracy at all costs. As the final countdown begins, when there's not enough time to solve any more problems, go for broke and take any good guesses you can. When we get to the different question types, I'll show you ways to improve your odds when the time comes.

No Matter What Your Score Level, You'd Better Not Finish Any Section *Early*

If you've finished a section early—it doesn't matter *how* good a test-taker you are—*you've rushed.* Your goal is to pace yourself *throughout* each section so that when the proctor says "Stop, put your pencils down," you've *just* finished answering the last question you were working on or *just* taken your last buzzer shot guesses.

If you finish a section early, you've sacrificed accuracy for speed, and your score is almost certain to suffer a bit as a result. "But I finished early so I'd have time to look over my work," many students say. Too bad. **Nobody in the history of the SAT has ever—and I mean ever—caught a mistake by looking back over his or her work at the end of a section.** Invariably students just flip through the pages of their booklet, glance approvingly at their work—what little they've bothered to write down—and then fold their hands complacently, glancing around the room and waiting patiently for everyone else to finish.

Checking your work at the end of a section is a complete waste of time; unfortunately, it's too late at that point to correct the damage—the avoidable errors—caused by rushing. If you check over any work or review any calculations, you'll just repeat the error you made the first time.

Trust me on this point. You have only one small window to catch an error—either just *before* you make it, *as* you make it, or *just* after you've made it. Later you'll learn how to anticipate mistakes *before* you make them.

SAT Questions Are Arranged in Order of Difficulty

Except for the reading questions, each *type* of question on the SAT is arranged in order of difficulty. The first third of any type of question are easy, the next third are medium, and the last third are difficult. The progression is gradual so that within, say, the hard questions, the difficulty goes from easy-hard to medium-hard to *hard-hard*.

Is this always true? Yes. Sometimes you'll encounter a medium question among the easy ones, or a difficult question among the medium ones, but otherwise the increase in difficulty is something you can count on. **You will never, however, encounter an easy question among the difficult ones.**

An easy SAT question is one that most students get right. A hard question is one that most students get wrong. It's as simple as that.

It's important to realize that a hard question isn't necessarily difficult in the way that, say, calculus or organic chemistry is difficult—but it is *always* dangerous. For *whatever* reason, most students will get a hard question wrong.

How can you tell whether the questions are getting more difficult? The only sure clue is location: easy questions are in the first third; hard questions are in the final third. On the writing questions you'll have no other clues. At least on the sentence completion questions the vocabulary will become noticeably more difficult. Watch your step on the math questions. You'll notice the math problems generally becoming harder, but some of the most difficult questions often look simpler than the easiest questions.

In short, difficult questions do not always *look* difficult. Difficult questions that look easy are *killer rabbits*. We'll examine killer rabbits in depth later, particularly regarding the SAT Math Test.

Each Question Is Worth the Same, So Spend Your Time Where It's Likely to Do the Most Good

In Tutorial 2, we discussed some of the differences between your school tests and the SAT. Your test-taking habits have formed over years of taking school tests, and many of these habits *hurt* your performance on the SAT. One habit in particular gets in the way on the SAT, and that's the habit of spending more time on harder questions and less time on easier ones. That strategy makes sense on school tests since harder questions generally count for a lot more than easier ones. But that strategy is disastrous on the SAT.

Here's what most students do on the SAT. They rush through the easy questions. The questions are easy, after all, and they're trying to finish. They slow down a bit when they get to the medium questions; the questions are getting harder, after all. Then they slow down to a crawl on the most difficult questions. In other words, most students spend the most amount of time on the questions they're least likely to answer correctly!

Since easy, medium, and difficult questions are all worth the same amount, on which type should you spend the most amount of time? Before you answer that question, let's consider an analogy from basketball. Let's say that an easy shot is a couple feet away from the basket, that a medium shot is from the free-throw line area, and a difficult shot is from somewhere in the middle of the court. Now, on which of these three shots would it make the most sense to spend time taking careful aim?

I hope you said the medium shot. It doesn't make sense to spend a lot of time on an easy shot, does it? You don't want to be reckless, of course, but you don't want to be overcautious either. On the other hand, it doesn't make much sense to spend a lot of time on a hard shot, either. Spending time is most likely to make a difference in making the medium shot.

The same principle applies to the SAT. **You want to spend the most amount of time on the medium questions, and the least amount of time on the difficult questions.** To use another analogy, *jog* on the easy questions, *walk—or crawl—*on the medium questions, and *sprint* on the hard questions. **You'll either be able to get a hard SAT question *quickly*, or you'll probably not get it at all.**

Moving slowly during the easy and medium questions on the SAT, and speeding up on the hard questions, runs counter to every test-taking instinct in your body. You'll need to practice this tempo consciously at every opportunity so that it becomes second nature. It helps to remember that easy questions are just as valuable as hard questions. If you want to get a high score, you can't afford to miss any easy questions because you can't be as confident that you'll get all the hard ones.

Easy Questions Have Easy, Obvious, *Popular* Answers— Hard Questions Have Hard, Unexpected, *Unpopular* Answers

It helps to think of SAT questions as popularity contests. The answer to an easy question is the *most* popular choice. The answer to a difficult question is the *least* popular choice. In other words, popular choices on difficult questions are *traps*.

If you think about the SAT for a moment, you'll realize that questions *have* to be designed this way. Since a multiple-choice question provides the answer, the only way they can make a question difficult is to *camouflage* the answer and make the wrong choices more appealing. Another way to look at the choices is whether they are *attractive* or *unattractive*. The answer to an easy question will be an attractive choice; that's why it's an easy question. The answer to a difficult question is an unattractive choice; that's why it's a hard question.

What makes a choice attractive or popular will depend on the type of question. On a math question, any easy numbers that *seem* to solve the problem will be popular choices. On a sentence completion, any easy words that seem reasonable will be popular choices. **Sometimes a question will have more than one attractive choice; sometimes it won't have any.**

If you're stuck on an easy question, remind yourself that the answer should be easy and obvious. If you're stuck on a hard question, remind yourself that the answer should be hard and unexpected. And if you're stuck on a medium question, remind yourself that the answer shouldn't be too easy or too hard.

Knowing the difficulty of the question you're working on is a powerful clue for checking your work. If you've solved a difficult question but your solution is an obvious choice, one that would attract other students—you've probably made a mistake. Knowing the difficulty of the question is also a powerful tool when you're forced to guess.

In later chapters I'll show you how to apply this principle to the different question types.

When You Need to Guess, Beware Your Hunches

You know that whenever you can make a quick guess on a question to avoid leaving it blank, you should take the shot. The key word here is *quick;* you can always afford to guess, but you can never afford to waste time.

So, how *should* you guess? Let's be clear about something: guessing does *not* mean selecting a choice at random. But it also doesn't mean selecting the choice that *seems* to be right. **Guessing means selecting the choice that has the greatest chance of being right, regardless of whether that choice "looks right" or "looks wrong."**

Another adage that needs to be added to our growing list of "world's worst SAT advice" is this: *when in doubt, go with your first hunch.* In real life that advice has some merit. **On the SAT, however, only rarely should you go with your first hunch when you're in doubt.**

Think about it. When are you most likely to be in doubt, on the easy questions, the medium ones, or the hard ones? The hard questions, right? Okay—and make sure you understand this point—the reason a multiple-choice question is hard is that everybody's first hunch on it is wrong. If everybody's first hunch on a hard question were correct, it would be an easy question, not a hard one.

Here's the problem: everybody's first hunch on a question tends to be the same one or two choices. In other words, everybody always goes for the same, popular choices on questions. On easy questions, those choices are correct (Tutorial 28). But on hard questions, those hunches *have* to be wrong—not *might* be wrong, *have* to be wrong.

Now, sometimes you'll find yourself stuck on an easy question. It happens. *Then* you should trust your hunch; after all, it's an easy question. In fact, we could define easy questions as those on which everybody's first hunch—the most popular choice—is usually right.

Medium questions are a bit trickier in this regard. The answer won't be too easy, but it won't be too hard, either. So rely on your hunches on medium questions with caution.

On hard questions, those on which you're most likely to be in doubt, your first hunches are extremely suspect. **The only exception to doubting your first hunch would be if you are consistently scoring in the 700 range or above on the reading, writing, or math tests. Once you're scoring near or above 700, you can** *begin* **to rely on your hunches on difficult questions—so long as those hunches don't point toward a popular answer choice, one that you know would appeal to many students.**

In the coming chapters I'll show you how to apply this principle on the different question types you'll encounter on the SAT. **Incidentally, the best guess on any given question is not always right, but it's always the way to go.** When you're in doubt you have to play the odds. If I asked you which team was more likely to win a game, Team A (first place in the league) or Team B (last place in the league), obviously Team A would be more likely to win. Would Team A *always* beat Team B? Of course not—even though in any given match-up, you'd always expect Team A to beat Team B.

The same is true on the SAT. Easy questions have easy, *popular* answers; hard questions have hard, *unpopular* answers. If you're not sure on a question, that's the way to guess.

RocketReview Techniques Are Designed to Improve Your Speed or Your Accuracy or Both—*Use Them*

To improve your SAT score you've got to learn to improve either your speed or your accuracy or both. In the rest of this book, you'll be introduced to techniques that will help you accomplish this. It's important that you solve the practice problems using the techniques that I show you rather than the methods you've always used.

It's not enough that you answer the practice problems correctly—you also have to solve them in the fastest and most accurate way. And I assure you that if you solve a practice problem in a way other than the method I've recommended, your solution was either slower or riskier or both.

If I were your tennis coach, say, and I were trying to demonstrate proper forehand technique, I would want you to practice using perfect form. I would not be satisfied if you hit the ball over the net using improper form. And in the same way, you should not be satisfied with solving a problem if you haven't used "proper form."

The techniques work, if you use them. If you don't test well, super—RocketReview's techniques will turn you into a test-taking machine. If you're already a great test-taker, these techniques will take your performance up to the next level.

Remember Tutorial 7: if you want to change your score, you have to change the way you take the test.

If you've just finished reading the tutorial series, take a break before moving on to the lessons. You've covered a lot of ground already; you've earned some time off. Taking time off will also give what you've learned time to sink in. From time to time over the coming weeks, return to these tutorials to reinforce the principles we discussed. But for now, take a break!

(Okay, okay, if you're eager to do more work right now, go back to the quiz you took in Tutorial 3 beginning on page 6 and revisit the questions. You'll be surprised at how much your perceptions about the SAT have already changed.)

PART III

The SAT
WRITING
TEST

REMEMBER: SAT Writing Is *Different*

Introduction to the SAT Writing Test:

Raise Your SAT Writing Score by 100 Points (or More) in One Week—(Practically) Guaranteed!

Will This Be on the Test?

Your score on the SAT Writing Test will be determined by how well you do on its two sections.

In the first section, you'll have to write a persuasive essay on an assigned topic in 25 minutes. This will be a general topic that does not require any specific knowledge, and the "prompt" (topic) will be one for which there is no "correct answer." The SAT essay is *not* a test of your knowledge. Right now, as you read this, you know enough information about the world—assuming you haven't slept through the last eleven years of school—to compose an outstanding response to any topic you might be asked to write about on the SAT.

The second section consists of 45 multiple-choice proofreading and editing questions. Your job here is to spot common writing errors in sentences and paragraphs, and sometimes to decide which of five alternatives is the most clear, concise, and correct.

Although this is called the SAT Writing Test, your essay counts for just one-third of your total score; the rest comes from your performance on the 45 proofreading and editing questions.

Important Note for Juniors Taking the PSAT

The 2004 PSAT will *not* include an essay section! Your school may choose to administer an optional essay with the PSAT, but it will not be graded.

This is not an ideal solution. The whole point of the PSAT is to give you a practice SAT. Without an essay grade, however, you will be kept in the dark about your performance on the most significant addition to the SAT.

Fortunately, RocketScore, the online software program you gained access to when you purchased this book, can grade your essay—if your school offers it—in less than a second!

After taking the PSAT (you'll get to keep your essay), simply type your paper into RocketScore's online form and hit "Enter." Your essay grade will be predicted *instantly*, and with decimal-place accuracy. You'll also receive a customized report with specific suggestions to raise your score. (And you'll have the opportunity to use RocketScore on numerous practice essays before you ever take the PSAT or SAT.)

The Most Important Section of the New SAT

If there is anything that all teachers agree on, it's this: *If you can't write well, you can't think well.* If your writing is disorganized and muddy, your reader will most likely assume that your thoughts are, too.

Writing well is an important skill in the "real world" as well as in school. Colleges recognize this fact, which is why they insisted on the new SAT Writing Test.

All three SAT sections—math, reading (formerly "verbal"), and writing—are important, of course, but your performance on this new SAT section in particular will receive close scrutiny from college admissions committees.

Here's a Scary Thought

The SAT essay is far more important than many students (including some of your friends and maybe even you) realize! Sure, you know it's a significant part of your overall Writing Score, but get this: The admissions committees at dozens of selective colleges—Harvard and Yale among them—will now require you to include your actual SAT essay in your applications!

So what? For the first time admissions committees will be able to compare a sample of your actual writing, composed under pressure, with the personal statement and other essays you'll have to write for the application.

It's fairly common for students to receive a lot of editing "help" from their parents, tutors, or college advisors on their application essays (something colleges deplore in the extreme, by the way). These students are now on their own because the SAT essay gives admissions committees a standard by which to judge each applicant's personal statement essay.

And you'd better believe that a big red flag will be raised in the minds of admissions officers (which is a Very Bad Thing) if the quality of a student's SAT essay is markedly different from that of his or her application essays.

> There are important *psychological* reasons for doing well on the SAT essay. The essay section is the first one you'll complete on the test day. By constructing an outstanding essay quickly and efficiently, you'll conserve your energy and put yourself in a positive frame of mind for the rest of the test.

But Here's the Good Part

The ability to write outstanding persuasive essays is not a skill possessed only by geniuses or professional writers, but rather a skill that can be mastered, like playing the guitar or shooting a basketball.

If you learn what *specific* things the SAT essay readers are looking for, and if you then follow a simple formula and some basic rules that you'll discover in the next two chapters, you will be astounded—*astounded*—at how quickly and dramatically your essay score improves.

Here's a Sample of What You'll Be Learning in the Next Few Chapters

Of the three SAT tests—math, reading, and writing—the last is where you'll make the fastest gains, on the multiple-choice questions as well as on the essay. Because grammar is probably not a subject you've studied recently, if ever, you may feel that the proofreading and editing section isn't likely to be one of your stronger areas on the SAT. Fortunately, unlike the math and reading sections for which there's a fair amount of information or vocabulary to master, you don't need to know that much grammar. And what little you *do* need to know, I'll teach you.

In the next four chapters, I'll show you exactly what to expect and how to handle any challenge you might encounter on the Writing Test. For example, you'll learn:

- The twelve simple grammatical and writing concepts that show up in the proofreading questions, and which four will account for half the errors you need to spot. Indeed, you'll learn *precisely* how many errors of each type you can expect to find!

- A simple grammar rule that *doubles* your chances of finding the answer on one-third of the multiple-choice questions.

- The four factors that most influence SAT essay graders—positively or negatively!

- Three simple phrases that *instantaneously* jump-start your pencil if you get writer's block during your 25-minute essay section.

- The specific types of supporting examples that most impress the SAT essay graders—and how to prepare those examples *before* you get to the exam room!

I promise you that no matter what you think of your essay-writing or grammar skills, these two sections will soon be your favorite part of the SAT.

A Few Words on the Essay

It's important to realize that the essay portion of the SAT Writing Test is a particular type of writing: not creative or informative but *persuasive.* You'll be asked to take a position on an issue (usually whether you agree or disagree with a general statement, or "prompt") and to back up that position with reasons and supporting examples drawn from your reading, experience, or observation.

Here are the kinds of essay prompts you can expect for your SAT essay topic:

- *As one door closes, another opens.*

- *Our most challenging battles are not against others, but within ourselves.*

- *The opposite of a profound truth may be another profound truth.*

- *The rights of an individual should never be sacrificed to the interests of the group.*

- *We learn far more from our mistakes and failures than we do from our successes.*

- *To accomplish great things, we must dream as well as act.*

As you can see, there is no single "right answer" for topics like these. First, you must decide whether you agree or disagree with the essay prompt. Then you write a 300- to 500-word essay explaining why or why not. Your grade will be based on two things: what you say and how you say it. In other words, how well do you justify your position? And do you express yourself clearly, coherently, and logically?

A Few Words on the Multiple-Choice Writing Questions

The test writers refer to the three types of multiple-choice questions in the SAT Writing Test as "identifying sentence errors," "improving sentences," and "improving paragraphs." We'll refer to them collectively as "proofreading and editing questions" (or proofreading questions for short) because proofreading is what you're required to do.

Before we consider what grammar and writing topics *are* tested on these questions, here's what's *not* tested:

- Spelling

- Capitalization rules

- Punctuation (though on a question or two you may need to decide which is required in a given sentence, a comma or a semicolon)

So what *is* tested on the proofreading questions? The good news is that five grammatical concepts account for more than half the difficult problems in this section! Here they are:

- Idiom errors

- Pronoun errors

- Singular-plural errors

- Comparison errors

- Lack of parallel structure

All told a mere fourteen simple grammatical concepts are all you need to know to answer every single proofreading and editing question correctly. You're probably familiar with many of them already.

By the way, you'll be relieved to hear that you don't need to know all those formidable grammatical terms that strike terror in the hearts of students everywhere like *gerund* or *subjunctive tense* or *past participle*. We'll need a few simple grammatical terms to discuss the subject matter, of course, but if you have even a passing familiarity with the following words, you'll be fine:

> *noun, verb, pronoun, adverb, adjective, preposition,*
> *phrase, clause, subject, object*

That's not so bad, is it? In the proofreading chapters we'll be covering these terms and everything else you need to answer the multiple-choice questions.

How the Multiple-Choice Section Will Be Scored

The multiple-choice writing questions are scored the same way the multiple-choice math or reading questions are scored. First, a "raw score" is calculated by subtracting those questions left blank (times 1.00) and those answered incorrectly (times 1.25) from the total number of questions in the section (45). For the mathematically inclined, here's the formula used to calculate your raw score on the multiple-choice writing questions:

Multiple-Choice Raw Score = 45 − (1.00 × blanks) − (1.25 × errors)

Notice that blanks *do* hurt your score in this section, just like they do in the multiple-choice math and reading sections. In fact, on the 200-800 writing scale, each blank you leave on a multiple-choice question lowers your eventual score by 10 points—10 points that you can never recover. **So, if you've spent time on a question, be sure to put something down on your answer sheet— even if you have to guess. (This ironclad rule applies throughout the entire test.)**

As I mentioned earlier, this multiple-choice raw score accounts for two-thirds of your overall Writing Score.

Next, I'll discuss how your essay will be scored, and then I'll show you how your two writing section sub-scores are combined into a final 200-to-800 point score.

How Your Essay Will Be Graded

Two graders will independently grade your essay on a scale of 1 to 6, and your score will be the total of their marks. (On the rare occasions when the marks of these two graders disagree by more than one point, an additional grader is called in as a tiebreaker.)

Combining the Two Sections:
How Your Final Writing Test Score Will Be Calculated

Your final score on the SAT Writing Test will be a weighted average of your essay score (on a 2-to-12 scale) and your multiple-choice score (out of 45). The essay counts for about one-third of your overall score. The following table provides a simple way to combine the two writing sub-scores to get your final 200-to-800 Writing Test score.

Essay / Multiple-Choice Scoring Grid

	45	40	36	31	27	22	18	13	9	4
12	800	800	760	720	680	640	600	560	520	480
11	800	780	740	700	660	620	580	540	500	460
10	800	770	730	690	650	610	570	530	490	450
9	800	760	720	680	640	600	560	520	480	440
8	780	740	700	660	620	580	540	500	460	420
7	770	730	690	650	610	570	530	490	450	410
6	750	710	670	630	590	550	510	470	430	390
5	740	700	660	620	580	540	500	460	420	380
4	730	690	650	610	570	530	490	450	410	370
3	710	670	630	590	550	510	470	430	390	350
2	700	660	620	580	540	500	460	420	380	340

To use the table, locate your essay score in the left-most column and your nearest multiple-choice score in the top row. For example, a student who received a 9 on the essay and a raw score of 27 on the multiple-choice section would score a 640 for the combined writing sections.

The scores in bold, running down in a diagonal band across the grid, are rough equivalents of your multiple-choice and essay scores. If the box with your combined score lies *above* the bold band, your essay score was significantly better than your multiple-choice score; you would likely make rapid gains if you reviewed the grammatical concepts tested by those questions. You'll have a chance to do that in the grammar chapters following the essay chapters.

If your combined score lies *below* the bold band, your multiple-choice score was significantly better than your essay score; you would likely make rapid gains if you reviewed the tips on essay writing and practiced applying them. You'll have a chance to do that in the next two chapters.

> In addition to your overall score on the 200-to-800 scale, your score report will include your essay score on the 2-to-12 scale, and your multiple-choice score on a 20-to-80 scale (to distinguish it from your overall score).

That Guarantee, Revisited

The guarantee I made to you at the start of this chapter is not an exaggeration—*if* you apply yourself conscientiously to the upcoming four chapters. The next two chapters will cover the basic and advanced principles of the essay, and in the two chapters after that we'll move on to the proofreading and editing questions.

Okay, let's get started In the next chapter I'll show you *how* to write an essay that will knock the socks off the SAT graders!

The Art of Sprint Writing on the SAT

Strunk and White Would Have *Bombed* on the SAT Essay

The Elements of Style, by William Strunk Jr. and the incomparable essayist E. B. White, is universally acknowledged as one of the best books ever written on crafting nonfiction. And while most of the advice in this slim, 85-page volume is relevant to the SAT essay, it does contain three maxims likely to lead students astray on the test:

- *Write in a way that comes naturally.*

- *Omit needless words.*

- *Avoid fancy words.*

Wrong, wrong, and wrong again! (At least when you're taking the SAT Writing Test.) There's nothing natural about writing an SAT essay, you don't have the time to omit needless words, and the fancier your words the higher your score.

Remember: SAT Writing Is *Different*

As I mentioned in the previous chapter, the kind of writing the graders expect to see is not "personal" or "creative," but rather clear, organized, persuasive, and scholarly. SAT writing is different from the kind of writing you do naturally and informally, like writing letters to friends or journal entries.

Your SAT graders have very definite expectations—and prejudices—about the kind of essay they expect from you. The simple, concise, natural writing advocated by Strunk and White will leave them underwhelmed. (Besides, as even Strunk and White would readily admit: simple, concise writing is anything but natural. Such writing requires painstaking efforts, numerous rewrites, and lots of time to achieve—all luxuries you don't have while writing your SAT essay at breakneck speed.)

Let's get something straight: the SAT essay is *not* designed to test "how well you write." It is designed to test how well—and rapidly—you orient yourself to a new topic, organize your thoughts, and write the *first draft* of a persuasive essay.

How well the SAT essay accomplishes that task, and the relevance of that task for the kinds of writing you are expected to do in college and beyond, are matters you and I will leave to others to debate.

The Only People Faster Than You Writing Your SAT Essay Are the Graders Scoring It

You are most likely used to getting back papers from your English teachers full of carefully written margin notes applauding its graces and subtleties, and gently admonishing its lapses. It's clear that they've spent a lot of time perusing your prose.

Now it's time to wake up to the land of SAT essays! Each grader will probably take less time to grade your entire essay than you did writing the first two sentences.

According to the test publishers, your essay will be graded "holistically," which is a euphemism for very, very quickly. In all likelihood, each grader will spend *at most* 60 seconds speed-reading your essay. Unlike your classroom teachers, your two SAT graders don't have the time to appreciate the brilliant nuances of your thinking or to savor your wonderful prose style. Each SAT grader has dozens, if not hundreds, of essays to mark. As a result, your essay's score will be based entirely on the first impressions formed by two harried graders.

If your essay seems to be organized and well written, if your examples seem to be scholarly, then you'll receive a high mark. Does that sound unfair? Maybe. But since your score depends on the graders' snap judgments of your writing, perhaps you should learn how to turn the graders' haste to your advantage.

You've Got Twelve Seconds to Impress—or Disappoint—the Graders

Okay, I made that number up, but twelve seconds really *is* about the amount of time it will take an SAT grader to read your first paragraph and form his or her initial impression of your essay.

Did I say "initial impression?" That's not quite accurate. By the time a grader finishes reading your first paragraph, that grader will form what is likely to be his or her *only* impression of the grade your entire essay deserves. **And once SAT readers have made up their mind about your essay, they will probably change their opinion little if at all.**

Stop! Please Read This Information before Continuing

The next box contains a sample essay topic that you can do as an online RocketScore practice exercise. If you read the topic now, without composing an essay immediately afterward, you'll deprive yourself of valuable practice.

I strongly recommend that you read the sample instructions below *only* when you have 25 minutes to write a sample essay. Use a legal pad to compose your response. When you're done, transfer your answer into the RocketScore online form to get a score. (You'll find more about the mechanics of using RocketScore in the chapter beginning on page 642.)

If you don't feel like writing a practice essay right now, just skip over the directions box; you can always return to read the instructions later.

The Instructions You'll Probably See

The new SAT Writing Test hasn't settled into a predictable pattern just yet (and the test writers will probably tinker with the precise format over the next few years). Even so, the essay instructions you'll see on the actual test will probably be very close to the following (with a different topic, of course):

> **Directions:** Consider carefully the following statement and the assignment below it. Then plan and write an essay that explains your ideas as persuasively as possible. Keep in mind that the support you provide—both reasons and examples—will help make your view convincing to the reader.
>
> *In his poem, "To a Mouse," the Scottish poet Robert Burns (1759-1796) wrote these immortal lines: "The best laid schemes o' mice an' men / Gang aft a-gley." To paraphrase Burns's archaic dialect in modern English: No matter how carefully we plan our projects, something can still go wrong with them.*
>
> **Assignment:** What is your view of the idea that even our best plans are always at the mercy of unexpected, chance events? In an essay, support your position by discussing an example (or examples) from history, literature, the arts, science and technology, current events, or your own experience or observation.

First things first: *you must respond to the assigned topic!* I'm serious. Two is the lowest total score someone can get on the essay if it bears *some* relevance, however slight, to the topic. But excerpts from the Gettysburg Address, Hamlet's soliloquy, Martin Luther King Jr.'s "I Have a Dream" speech, or any other selection of surpassingly beautiful, but irrelevant-to-the-topic writing would earn the absolute *minimum* possible score on the essay: a zero, zilch, nada. (On the other hand, any one of these works would make an outstanding supporting example, *regardless of the topic*. But more about this point shortly).

As you can see, however, you are given a great deal of latitude regarding *how* you respond to the topic. Take a moment now and review the sample essay prompts I mentioned earlier (page 62) to reassure yourself of just how broad the topics you may face will be.

The SAT Essay Grading Process Is Far Less Subjective Than You Might Imagine

Before they ever score a student's paper, the SAT essay graders are rigorously trained to be consistent. That is, they are trained to agree with each other more or less reliably. It's worth knowing a bit about the training process so you'll understand why the RocketReview formula for high essay marks is so effective.

Initially, all the graders are given the same practice essay to score. Let's pretend that you and I are sitting in on the training process and that we grade the same essay. The average mark, say, was a 4, but you gave the practice essay a 5 (because you were impressed by the subtle metaphors) and I gave it a 2 (because I thought there were too many spelling errors).

All the graders discuss why they scored the essay the way they did. But you and I learn something. You learn that the other graders don't always notice subtle metaphors, and I learn that other graders don't penalize spelling errors as much as I do.

Then we grade a second paper and go through the discussion process again. And again. And again.

Here's the key point: **unlike what you might think, the goal of all the graders is *not* to try to give an essay the score they believe it deserves. Instead, their goal is to give each essay the score they think all the other graders would give it.**

And sooner or later, subconsciously if not consciously, all the graders learn to look for the *same* features and ignore the others. Here are the essay features that most influence the graders:

- **Essay length** (evidence that you have something to say): the longer the better.

- **Number of "SAT words"** (evidence that you're smart and articulate—and yet another benefit of the vocabulary building you were doing for the sentence completion questions): the more the better.

- **Number of paragraphs** (evidence of organization): the more the better.

- **Number of literary, historical, or other scholarly examples** (evidence that you've learned something in high school): at *least* one is good, but two are better, and three are great.

- **Number of "personal words"**: *I, I'd, I'm, I've, I'll, me, myself, mine* (evidence of informality and of failing to provide "hard" evidence): the *fewer* the better.

Again, this grading process is largely subconscious. It's not as if the graders actually count the number of paragraphs you use or tally the number of SAT words they spot.

Five Easy Rules to Ace the Essay

Now that you know what the essay graders are looking for, it's time to apply that knowledge to formulate some guidelines you can actually follow on the test. The rest of this chapter is a piece of cake if you keep in mind the features above. I've boiled down everything you need to know about writing the SAT essay into a handful of simple rules.

You're Following an Essay Formula for a *Reason*

Some of the writing rules I'm about to recommend will have many English teachers gnashing their teeth in exasperation more than any split infinitive or dangling modifier ever did. These teachers hate the whole notion of writing formulas. They believe, with justification, that it's ridiculous if not futile to reduce the complex, intangible skill of writing to a tidy set of simplistic-seeming rules. Indeed, they point to the great writers who became great precisely *because* they flouted the writing rules and conventions of their time.

I agree with these teachers, but let's get something straight here: you are not being judged on whether you can create a literary work of art in 25 minutes. The SAT graders who will be marking your paper have specific expectations about the characteristics of outstanding persuasive essays. If your essay *satisfies* those expectations, it will receive a very high mark. If your essay disappoints those expectations, it will receive a low mark—regardless of the literary or creative merit your paper deserves.

So the upcoming rules are not ideal writing rules, but writing on the SAT is not an ideal situation. **Don't take chances on the actual SAT by getting creative—you have only 25 pressure-cooker minutes to read the question, generate some ideas and examples, organize your thoughts, and compose your essay.** You've only got one shot at the essay, so follow these RocketRules to the letter.

RocketRule #1: Use the First Few Minutes to Plan Your Essay

Even though you have 25 minutes to write your essay, it's crucial that you spend a few minutes planning what you're going to say.

I know it's tempting to dive right in and just start writing the moment the proctor announces, "Open your test booklets and begin." But careful planning is critical to your achieving a high mark.

Use the "scrap paper" space provided in your test booklet to jot down your thoughts and the supporting examples you want to use. If you think of some great words or impressive phrases you'd like to include, jot those down, too. Use abbreviations, of course.

Will you waste what little writing time you have by planning? No, spending a few minutes to organize your thoughts and outline your answer will actually allow you to write much faster. Once you get started, you won't have to stop mid-essay to ponder what to say next because you'll already know. Students who start writing immediately (without planning) quickly find that their writing has run out of steam. By then it's too late for them to get a fresh start on their essay.

Especially Use the Planning Time to Make Sure Your First Paragraph Is a *Zinger*

Your first paragraph will receive the most attention, so make sure you plan one that has snap, crackle, and pop. I'll give you ideas for how to pump up your first paragraph shortly.

As you now know, by the time the SAT graders finish reading your first paragraph they will have largely decided your essay's final grade. They'll merely skim through the rest of your essay. Although the graders will slow down a bit in the final paragraph, they do this merely to confirm their initial impression of your essay.

When students start writing immediately after reading the instructions (without planning their essays), they invariably stumble in their opening paragraph. Even if they catch their stride later in the essay, the SAT graders have already formed their opinions.

RocketRule #2: Write *Fast* and Keep Your Pencil Moving!

If you're a habitual perfectionist in your writing, someone who labors over finding *just* the right word, who agonizes over whether or not to include a comma after a phrase, who mulls over the perfect metaphor to capture the subtle nuances of your thoughts, you'd better get over that habit—and I mean *pronto!*

The SAT essay is a 25-minute all-out sprint, not a marathon. Once you've finished planning your essay, take a deep breath, launch into your paper, and keep that #2 pencil moving. You should be writing at a rate of *one or two sentences per minute* in order to produce 400 words (which is the minimum length graders expect of the highest scoring essays).

Relax: You're Graded on How Well You Write a *First Draft*— *Not* a Polished Final Paper

You bet: *writing fast is scary.* Twenty-five minutes is *not* enough time for you to gather all your thoughts. Or to find the best supporting examples. Or to say exactly what you mean.

Writing fast also means that your handwriting won't be as elegant as it might be otherwise. It means that you'll probably make a spelling mistake or two, not to mention the occasional grammatical error. Writing fast may even mean that you'll change your mind mid-sentence. (If you need to change something, cross it out neatly—erasing takes too much time—and continue writing.

Don't worry about these problems. The graders know that you're writing under enormous pressure, and they make allowances for it.

Obviously, your handwriting or printing should be as legible as possible, and you should avoid flagrant spelling or grammatical gaffes, but most of all you need to focus on getting your thoughts down on paper as quickly as possible.

So be prepared and you'll be better able to handle the pressure.

The Top 33 Misspelled Words in SAT Essays

As I mentioned, spelling is not *that* important to your overall essay score. Still, the fewer spelling errors in your essay, the better.

The following words appear frequently in SAT essays, and are often misspelled: *accept, achieve, apparent, appearance, argument (argues, argued, arguing), beginning, belief, business, describe (description), definite (definitely), different, especially, environment, foreign, government, independent, interest, judgment, knowledge, necessary, occasion (occasionally), occur (occurred, occurring, occurrence), particular, portray, receive, religion, separate (separation), several, similar, tragedy (tragic).*

You don't have to memorize this list, but *do* skim it to see whether any of these words tend to trip you up. Most of us tend to make certain types of spelling errors more frequently than others, so it's helpful to understand the underlying causes of such problems.

Many spelling errors result from your ear for words. Words that sound alike (such as *its* versus *it's,* or *they're* versus *their* versus *there)* cause problems, as do words we pronounce sloppily (*accept, government, particular, different, describe, probably, several),* or words that spell the "uh" sound differently (*definite, separate, independent).* Silent vowels or consonants (*receive, judge, foreign)* or single or double consonants (*occasion, occur)* are also common causes of spelling problems.

RocketRule #3: Write *a Lot*

Your English teacher has undoubtedly stressed that good writing is about "quality, not quantity." And your teacher is right. But this isn't an English paper, and your teacher isn't the one grading it.

On the SAT essay, more is definitely better. The official SAT essay graders believe that good writers have a lot to say, and conversely that poor writers have little to say. (Remember our essay scoring formula?) It's true: on the SAT, 400 well-written words will invariably outscore 200 or even 300 outstandingly well-written words.

The More You Write, the Better—
So Long as What You Write Is *Relevant*

Okay, let's be honest. We've all been in the following situation: we're taking an essay test when we come up against a question that we can't answer adequately. So what do we do?

We *bluff*, of course. We blather on and on, hoping that our teacher won't notice our blindingly obvious ignorance, and that he or she will accept our offering of well-written emptiness as a substitute for a complete lack of facts.

For example, let's say that we get an exam question in our United States history class that asks us to discuss the *technological* causes of the Civil War. Whoops. We know the social causes, sure, and we're fairly knowledgeable about the economic ones, but we don't have a *clue* about the technological causes.

So we ramble on about the social and economic causes of the American Civil War, and we even throw in a bit about how technology affected the course of the conflict. Admittedly this is not *precisely* the question we were asked, but it's pretty close. We cross our fingers, hoping that our teacher won't notice our "near miss" (or that if she does notice that we haven't answered the question, attributes it to a pardonable misreading on our part).

Anyway, you won't ever face that predicament on the SAT Writing Test. The *only* topics you could possibly be assigned will be general ones, like the samples I provided earlier on page 62.

What's more, in the next chapter I'll show you how to pre-write your essay *before* you ever get to the exam room. That's right: that no matter *what* question you're asked, you'll *already* have an essay planned out! Unbelievable? Just wait, you're about to discover how easy it is to pre-plan and even pre-write your future essay.

Provide Specific Details

The best way to write a lot in 25 minutes, apart from knowing what you're going to say before you begin, is to *elaborate.* Give examples. Provide details. Be specific.

You don't have the time to provide too many details in your SAT essay, but even a few can make your points more compelling. Here are some examples of how providing details can transform short, vague statements into lengthier, more interesting sentences.

Vague Sentence #1: *For someone commonly viewed as paralyzed by his own doubts, Hamlet actually did a lot.*

Discussion: Who views Hamlet in this way? What did Hamlet doubt? What exactly did Hamlet do? **Specific details will occur to you naturally if you simply answer the questions your own sentences raise.**

Specifics Provided: *For a character commonly viewed by literary critics as paralyzed by his own doubts about his perceptions, Hamlet feigned madness, dispatched two childhood friends to their likely deaths, staged a play, and killed two men.*

Vague Sentence #2: *Many people were affected by the farming legislation.*

Discussion: How many people? Who? How were they affected? Which farming legislation?

Specifics Provided: *The Eisenhower farming legislation required vast tracts of land to be set aside as fallow. As a result, tens of thousands of migrant farm workers were thrown out of work and forced to leave the countryside to seek their livelihoods in urban centers.*

Notice that there's no rule that requires you to supply all the details you've chosen in a single sentence.

Don't go overboard with details or your essay will lose focus. A sentence or two of details for each example you use is more than enough. In the next chapter, I'll show you how to use impressive examples to back up your points.

State the Obvious, and Then *Restate* It

You're forced to write a lot in a short time, so don't worry about whether something you're saying is "trivial" or "too obvious." Your essay should display some originality, but that doesn't mean that every point you make needs to be important or original.

Once you start writing, don't be afraid to state anything that appears to be relevant to the topic. Will some things you write be less relevant, if not completely off topic? Possibly, but the SAT graders are trained to look at your *overall* essay (one of the *advantages* you get from the hasty reading they'll do of your essay). If your overall essay is otherwise strong, minor flaws are unlikely to have much, if any, effect on your grade.

Remember: you're writing a first draft, not a polished final work; you just don't have the time to weigh every word, phrase, and sentence. After you've planned your essay, write, write, and write!

Three Simple Starter Phrases for Writing Emergencies

You don't have much time to write your essay, so what happens if you get stuck? Writer's block is bad enough when you're trying to compose a paper at home; when you've got 25 minutes to sprint-write an SAT essay, it can be a big problem. Here are three phrases that will help you get unstuck:

- *For example,*
- *In other words,*
- *On the other hand,*

Let's say you're in the exam room, writing your SAT essay. You planned your essay before you started writing so the words have been flowing nicely. Then, all of a sudden, your mind suddenly goes blank. Oh no! You can't think of what to write next, and you can practically hear the exam room clock ticking down.

Here's what you do if you get stuck. *Without thinking*, write down one of these phrases to start off a new sentence and before you know it, you'll find that your pencil begins moving along all by itself. These phrases *force* you to supply more details.

In the next chapter you'll learn a great technique for preparing your examples ahead of time.

Fill Up the Answer Sheet Space Provided for Your Essay

The SAT graders won't tally the exact number of words in your essay, of course. So how do they tell how long your essay is?

They look to see whether or not the 68-line answer form is full! If you've

filled up the form, the graders will be impressed; if you haven't, they won't.

Right now, take a few moments and see what your essay form will look like. You can download one from www.RocketReview.com or you can get a good idea by looking at three blank pages of lined notebook paper. All that white space is scary, isn't it? (Don't worry, I'll show you other ways to expand your essay quickly in a little while.)

If your normal scrawl is tiny, write larger—but not *too* large, because you can't go *beyond* the 68 lines. It's okay to skip a single line between each of your paragraphs but do not skip every other line in the form or you may run out of space. (Skipping every other line will also emphasize to the graders that your essay isn't very long.)

RocketRule #4: Use Smart-Sounding Words

I know that English teachers often tell students not to use big words *just* because they're big, but trust me, on the SAT essay, big words have a better chance of impressing graders than do their smaller synonyms.

I wish I didn't have to write this—and I know that many teachers will object—*but,* smart people *do* use certain words to connect with other smart people. Yes, it's almost a code language.

Don't great writers tend to use simple language? Yes, but so do simpletons, and SAT readers blitzing their way through a mountain of essays can't afford the time to distinguish between the two.

While it's true that the best word is the one that says precisely what you mean, it's also true that big words impress SAT graders. You don't *always* have to use smart-sounding words, but you should sprinkle your essay with at least a few big words so that your opinion *sounds* authoritative.

100 Words That Really Impress SAT Graders— Make Sure Your Essay Includes at Least a Few

Any word from our general list of SAT words (page 80) for the sentence completions and reading questions will impress the SAT graders. It's likely, however, that you'll be able to use certain big words more frequently than others because the same topics and themes show up time and again on SAT essays. The following list emphasizes those SAT words that you can probably work into just about any assigned essay topic (they're also great words to know in any event).

This list is compiled from the words professional writers use most often when writing persuasive essays. It isn't intended to be complete. Examine any op-ed ("opposite-the-editorial") piece in your local newspaper and you'll find *at least* one word, or a variation of it, from this list. I wouldn't be surprised if you found half a dozen or more. Again, this list gives special weight to the rhetorical concepts that occur most frequently in SAT essays.

> *acute adage addressing aesthetic allusion altruism anachronism anecdote antithesis aphorism aspect aspiration assess attribute autonomy coherent compromised concede contend context conventional conviction culminate depict dichotomy discord disparate distinct distinguish doctrine dogmatic echoed egalitarian empirical enduring entail epitome epoch ephemeral ethical evoke exemplify explicit facet feasible ideology immutable implication indifferent indigenous inequitable inevitable inherent intrinsic irony lament legitimacy manifest momentous notably notion nuance objectivity orthodox paradigm paradox pervasive plausible pragmatic predominant premise presumably prodigious profound prominent proponent proposition provocative quintessential realm relentless reminiscent resolve revelation revere rhetorical scrutiny secular subjective subtle sublime thesis tantamount transcend ubiquitous undermine unparalleled unprecedented viable widespread*

Don't get overwhelmed and think you have to use *every* word on this list. Just try to include a few of these words or similar ones in your essay. These words are especially effective in the first and last paragraphs of SAT essays, which the graders read most carefully.

> **It should go without saying that you must use these words correctly or they won't improve your essay's grade. If you're not sure about the word's definition, or if you don't know how to use the word in a sentence, it's probably better not to use it at all in your SAT essay. You'll find definitions of these and other words at the RocketReview.com site that your CD-ROM gives you exclusive access to.**

By the way, *all* these words are "good SAT words" that you should know for the critical reading section; half of these words even make it to our core Power Ranked List of the 323 most valuable words to know for the SAT Reading Test. You'll find this list beginning on page 309.

Practice the List

Try to use these words as often as you can in your everyday school papers. Here's another idea. How about astounding your friends by casually dropping these words into your lunchtime conversation around the cafeteria table?

INSTEAD OF THIS COMMON ESSAY WORD	CONSIDER USING A VARIANT OF ONE OF THESE SAT-WORDS
A lot	*Prodigious*
Argue	*Contend*
Based, basic	*Premise, fundamental*
Cause, because, result	*Evoke, engender, prompt, provoke, elicit, precipitate, animate, inaugurate, attribute*
Common, typical, everyday	*Prevalent, pervasive, conventional, orthodox, status quo, ubiquitous, widespread*
Consequence, result	*Implication, outcome, aftermath, tantamount, ramification*
Difference	*Disparity, dichotomy, discrepancy, diversity, distinction, distinguish*
Hard, difficult, difficulty	*Dilemma, paradox, vexing, quagmire, arduous, intricate, inextricable, problematic*
Easy, practical, quick	*Pragmatic, expedient, viable, tenable*
Example, evidence, instance, illustration	*Paradigm, archetype, empirical, epitome, exemplify*
Experience, story	*Anecdote, chronicle*

INSTEAD OF THIS COMMON ESSAY WORD	CONSIDER USING A VARIANT OF ONE OF THESE SAT-WORDS
False	*Untenable, fallacious*
Free, freedom	*Autonomy, sovereignty*
Help, assist	*Facilitate, bolster, foster, expedite*
Hurt, hinder	*Compromise, undermine*
Illustrate	*Highlight, exemplify, epitomize,*
Important	*Substantiate, embody, underscore Paramount, momentous*
Main character	*Protagonist*
Mother, father, brother, sister	*Maternal, paternal, sibling*
Natural, essential	*Inherent, innate, intrinsic, quintessential, implicit, underlying*
Need, necessary, require	*Unparalleled, unprecedented,*
New, unique, unusual	*Singular, novel*
Opposite	*Antithesis*
Part	*Feature, aspect, attribute, facet*
Period, time, era, centuries, history	*Epoch, millennium (millennia)*
Possible	*Plausible, credible, tenable, viable*
Show, obvious	*Manifest, ostensibly, explicit, depict*
Similar, equivalent	*Parallel, analogous, affinity, reminiscent, echoed, coherent*
Situation	*Context, domain, realm*
Statement, idea, view, opinion, belief, phrase, theme, expression	*Notion, proposition, adage, maxim, doctrine, tenet, credo, thesis, contention, dogma, presupposition*
True, absolute, definite	*Irrefutable, immutable, objective, categorically, inescapable, incontrovertible*
Unfortunately	*Lamentably*
Very, quite, really	*Particularly, notably, exceptionally, singularly*

Refer to the list frequently, especially as you write your school papers. You'll quickly become more comfortable using these words in your everyday conversation and writing. Plus you'll impress your teachers!

Squeeze at *Least* Two SAT Words into Your Very First Paragraph

My research shows that including just two SAT words in the first paragraph or your essay raises your overall essay score a full point on the 2-to-12 scale. That translates to a quick 20 points in your overall 200-800 score on the Writing Test!

The typical SAT essay instructions includes a statement to be commented on—usually you will be asked to agree or disagree—and asks you for examples to support your view. The instructions alone open the door for you to include the words "statement" and "example" in your essay answer. And luckily for you, those words have synonyms on our list of impressive-sounding words. See below:

For instance, instead of ending the first paragraph with this sentence:

> *The idea that our most careful plans sometimes go awry is illustrated by examples in history as well as in literature.*

Clever you could write this:

> *The notion that our most careful plans sometimes go awry is exemplified by a number of prominent instances in history as well as in literature.*

Hey, that's *three* SAT words. A little finesse like that would have boosted your final 200-800 Writing Test score by 20 points or more!

RocketRule #5: Avoid Personal Statements or Qualifiers

Phrases like *I feel, I think, I believe,* and *It seems to me* have no place in your essay. Such phrases are unnecessary (it's a given that you're expressing your opinion) and suck the vitality right out of your writing.

For example, instead of writing,

> *I think that our plans are always at the mercy of events outside our control.*

Write this instead,

> *Our plans are always at the mercy of events outside our control.*

To demonstrate the dramatic difference, here are some famous quotations followed by versions that include personal qualifiers:

FAMOUS QUOTES	SAME QUOTES DILUTED BY PERSONAL QUALIFIERS
Experience is the name we give to our mistakes.	*I feel that experience is the name we give to our mistakes.*
Imagination is more important than knowledge.	*In my opinion, imagination is more important than knowledge.*
Every truly new idea looks crazy at first.	*I believe that every truly new idea looks crazy at first.*
There is more to life than simply increasing its speed.	*I sincerely think that there is more to life than simply increasing its speed.*
The journey is the reward.	*It seems to me, from my point of view, that the journey is the reward.*

See? Omit the humble personal qualifiers and write with confidence; your words will be much more convincing.

This rule is an extension of our general principle to avoid personal words— *I, I'd, I'll, I'm, I've, me, mine, myself*—as much as possible in your SAT essay.

> Note: It is unlikely but still possible that your SAT topic will specifically *require* you to write about a personal experience. Even in this instance, however, you should focus on the other persons involved in the anecdote and put yourself in the background. You'll find a more complete discussion about this rare SAT topic on page 102.

While we're on the topic of phrases to avoid, another common weakness is attempting to make assertions sound more convincing by including any of the following adverbs for emphasis: *a lot, definitely, especially, extremely, greatly, terribly, really, very.* These adverbs are rarely necessary, and using them too often is a hallmark of unsophisticated writing. **One or two of these adverbs in your essay is okay, but avoid using more than two.**

As an exercise, experiment with adding any of these adverbs to the famous quotes above, or indeed any famous quote, and you'll see how these adverbs sap the vigor of writing. Or take a sample of your school writing: if you're using more than one of these adverbs every page, find ways to reduce your dependence on them.

Take a Break Before Moving On

We've already covered most of what you need to know to ace the SAT essay. It's probably a good idea to take some time off—maybe switch to one of the math or reading chapters if you're still feeling energized—before you move on to the advanced essay strategies in the next chapter. Spending some time away from the material will give these rules a chance to sink in.

How to Choose Your Examples and Organize Your Essay—*Before* You Ever Arrive at the Exam Room!

Yes, You *Can* Know What You're Going to Say Before You Say It!

As you know, you don't have much time in the exam room to organize your thoughts and to compose your essay. Wouldn't it be great if you had a game plan *before* the actual test so that you already largely knew how you were going to respond *no matter* what topic you were assigned?

Well, in the next 10 to 15 minutes that's exactly what you're going to learn how to do. Once you complete this chapter you'll know precisely how many paragraphs to write (five), how many supporting examples to include (at least three), and even the sources from which you'll be drawing these examples.

In the last chapter we examined the five basic RocketRules for sprint-writing your SAT essay. Now we'll be moving on to three additional rules that will cover the structure of your essay.

Sorry: SAT Graders Don't Care About Your Opinion

SAT readers are interested in how well you *support* your opinion—and this is what they'll be grading you on—rather than *what* your opinion happens to be.

SAT graders expect you to write an academic persuasive essay. Unlike personal essays, academic ones are characterized by a certain formality and a distinctive structure. Also, academic *persuasive* essays must supply *scholarly* examples to back up the writer's (your) viewpoint.

Once the essay section begins and you've read the question, you won't have the time to debate with yourself whether you agree or disagree with the essay prompt. If you're not sure one way or the other, it's usually easier to agree with SAT essay prompts than to disagree. Sure, if you thought about the topic for an hour or two, you might change your mind. Don't wait to be inspired. Remember: the way you *back up* your opinion is far more important than the opinion itself.

RocketRule #6: Use at Least One "Good" Example to Support Your Thesis—Two Are Better, and Three Are Ideal

SAT graders do not value examples drawn from your personal life as much as they do scholarly examples, such as those drawn from major literary works or from history. **In other words, avoid making a personal experience the focus of your SAT essay; better yet, avoid personal experiences altogether.**

Yes, I realize that the official essay instructions (see our sample on page 70) specifically permit examples "from your own experience or observation." But you need to demonstrate for SAT graders—and later, for the college admissions officers that may be reading your essay, remember—that you've actually *learned something* in school and can apply it in your thinking and writing. Unfortunately, personal observations or anecdotes don't accomplish that goal; they are not considered "good" examples.

When SAT graders see an essay that cites a major literary work, they say to themselves, "Hey, here's a smart kid," and they grade the essay accordingly. An essay that discusses how Hamlet felt about *his* uncle, for example, is invariably more impressive to graders than one that discusses how you feel about *yours*.

What's more, although you might have something truly extraordinary or insightful to share about your uncle or any other person or event in your life, personal examples often turn emotional. That can be dangerous on the SAT. Graders might in turn respond in emotional, and therefore unpredictable, ways—and possibly not in your favor.

Let's examine the various other types of supporting evidence you could use in your paper.

Literary examples are best. Since most SAT readers are English teachers, starting your essay off with a literary example or two is your best bet, by far. Draw your examples from *classics*, not fun reads like romance novels, science fiction epics, or espionage thrillers. Literary classics are works with enduring, universal appeal such as major novels, poems, or plays by William Shakespeare, Mark Twain, Jane Austen, Robert Frost, and the like. Again: your essay should demonstrate to the graders that you've been wide-awake and eagerly absorbing knowledge throughout your high school career.

Three more points worth mentioning about literary examples:

- **Underline the name of the works you cite.** Doing so will help ensure that they will be noticed by the SAT graders blitzing their way through your essay. (Even though by convention the titles of poems and plays should be enclosed by quotation marks, underline them anyway.)

- Certain works—*The Catcher in the Rye, Romeo and Juliet, The Scarlet Letter,* "The Road Not Taken," for example—have presumably been read by each and every high school freshman or sophomore in the United States. While these are excellent literature, they are in danger of becoming SAT clichés. Try using slightly more advanced works, such as those you read this year. Not only are more sophisticated works more likely to impress the graders, but they are also likely to be fresher in your mind, making it easier for you to readily draw concrete examples from them.

- **SAT graders will probably award your essay a higher score if you use three examples from three *different* novels, say, rather than three examples from the *same* novel. Better yet, for variety combine one or two literary examples with one or two historical examples.** That said, if you find three excellent examples from the same literary work to support your thesis, better to use three examples rather than to cite simply one example.

Historical examples are also excellent. It's safer to pick historical examples before 1960. SAT graders are likelier to harbor strong feelings about more recent events, the events that they have lived through and remember vividly, which could hinder their objectivity towards your essay. Even some older historical events, such as the Holocaust, can raise delicate issues with many graders and so are best avoided on the SAT.

Avoid using examples from current events for the same reason; nothing on terrorism or 9/11, for example. Why take the chance of SAT graders imagining that you garnered your examples from skimming newspaper headlines or watching MTV News? An SAT grader likes to see that you've learned your history from textbooks, so stick to examples from them.

> One person's faith may be another person's heresy, so avoid discussing religious works, topics, or doctrines at all costs, even if you feel that you're discussing "history." Also avoid current political topics: your political views could easily conflict with those strongly held by the person grading your essay.

Art, music, and philosophy examples are fine. Here again, make sure you demonstrate what you've learned in school. Discussing examples from classical music or art history is great; discussing graffiti art or pop music, on the other hand, is probably *not* a good idea.

Examples from the "soft sciences" such as psychology, sociology, and economics are good, but beware of intimidating scientific or technical illustrations. Remember that the SAT reader probably studied English and the humanities in college, not quantum theory or esoteric computer-coding algorithms. No offense is intended here, but if you're a science geek lost in an abstract, theoretical world, it's probably best to keep that fact to yourself (at least in your SAT essay).

If you must use an example from the "hard sciences," biology is the most preferable since even the most science-phobic SAT essay grader should be able to relate on some level to plants and animals. Use examples from physics, chemistry, geology—or (horrors) math—only as a last resort.

Here is a summary of subject areas from which to draw your examples (in descending order from best to worst):

- *Literature*
- *History*
- *Art, music, and philosophy*
- *Soft sciences (psychology, sociology, economics)*
- *Hard sciences (biology, physics, chemistry, geology, mathematics)*
- *Current events, modern life, technology*
- *Personal observation*
- *Personal experience*

What's the difference between personal observation and personal experience? Your personal observations are made about other people and the world at large, while your personal experiences are about you. Using personal observations at least demonstrates some awareness of the world around you. **Essays that focus on someone's personal experiences, on the other hand, often come across as emotional or self-absorbed, and these two traits are not likely to win you any points with the SAT graders.**

Use a personal example *if you absolutely must*, but be sure to include at least one scholarly example (ideally two or three) as well. **By the way, one way to give a personal example more academic credibility with SAT graders—who tend to be English teachers, remember—is to describe your experience using literary terms such as *symbolism, plot, narrative, irony, climax, anecdote, metaphor,* and the like.** Other impressive literary terms that can easily be used when recounting a personal experience are *allegory, hyperbole, caricature, genre, epiphany, epilogue, protagonist, euphemism, vignette, subplot, anticlimactic,* and *subtext.*

As I mentioned earlier, SAT graders will award your essay a higher score if you use three examples from *different* novels rather than drawing them all from the *same* novel. Still, other things being equal, *any* literary example is a better choice than an illustration drawn from your personal experience. In other words, if you can think of only one literary work to use on the test, it's probably better to use that work for all your supporting examples than try to add variety to your essay by throwing in a personal experience.

RocketRule #7: Prepare Your Sources *Ahead* of Time!

Yes, that's right: you *can* prepare your examples in advance *even though you don't know what your SAT essay topic is going to be.*

How is that possible? Well, let's consider what I've already told you.

- You now know that literary examples are best. So, what *are* your favorite books, plays or poems? Can you remember *quotations* from them?

- Historical examples are the next best. Which historical period do you know the most about? Have you researched any history topic recently, or better yet, written a paper about such a topic?

Here's the basic idea: no matter what topic you are asked to write a persuasive essay about on the SAT, you should be able to pull at least one supporting example from *any* of your favorite literary works or historical periods—any.

Admittedly, it might take a little creative "forcing" to fit an example from one of your stock works into your essay. Sure, the end result might seem a bit contrived, but the SAT graders don't have enough time to reflect on whether each illustration is "precisely" relevant anyway.

And even if the graders *do* notice that an example is not *exactly* on target, they still realize that you're writing and thinking under pressure and that you have time to pick "the best" examples. Instead of criticizing your choice of examples, they'll be thinking, "Hey, this kid has not only read Jane Austen's *Pride and Prejudice*, but she can also quote entire lines from it. They may not be exactly applicable lines, but I'm impressed that she even tried."

An Illustration Using Prepared Examples on Our Sample Essay Topic

So, in light of the criteria we've just discussed, let's look at an example. A student (we'll call her Sarah) decides that her two favorite literary works (or at least the ones she's most knowledgeable about) are Jane Austen's *Pride and Prejudice* and Shakespeare's *Hamlet*. She'll draw her examples from those two works. And because she recently finished studying World War II in her United States history class, she decides that she'll draw an historical example from that general era.

How might Sarah apply these particular works to our sample topic (found on page 70) addressing the idea that our most careful plans are often thwarted by chance, unanticipated events?

Keep in mind that on this topic alone it's possible to find a dozen or more examples just in *Hamlet*, not to mention Sarah's other two prepared sources (*Pride and Prejudice* and the World War II era).

Sarah agrees with the premise of the sample topic and decides to focus on *Pride and Prejudice* for her first example. Early in the novel, Darcy schemes with the Bingley sisters to break up the blossoming romance between his good friend Charles Bingley and the radiantly beautiful Jane Bennet. He feels that

Jane is "beneath" his friend because she is not a member of the aristocratic social class to which Darcy and Charles belong.

Darcy's plan goes awry when he not only discovers that he is wrong about Jane as a suitable match for his friend, but also that he himself has fallen in love with Jane's sister, the lovely and magnificently talented Elizabeth. Neither he nor Elizabeth had anticipated this ironic development.

Sarah is sure that there are other supporting examples in this novel, but one is more than enough. Besides, she's already thought of several illustrations from *Hamlet:*

- When the ghost of Hamlet's father appears before him (a chance event), the murderous plans of his uncle, the new King Claudius, and his mother, Queen Gertrude, are thwarted.

- When Hamlet intercepts a letter that orders his execution (a chance event), he frustrates his uncle's plan to murder him. In the process, the fates of the helpless Rosencrantz and Guildenstern are sealed (an event *they* did not anticipate).

- Polonius's plans go horribly wrong when Hamlet mistakes him for his evil uncle (another chance event) and stabs him. (Actually, two plans go wrong here.)

- The King's plan to poison Hamlet with tainted wine (should he survive a duel with Laertes, whose sword has also been dipped in poison) goes awry when Gertrude, who has displayed little maternal concern for her bereaved son, grabs the goblet intended for Hamlet and drinks to her son's health (a chance and ironic event).

These examples from *Hamlet* occur to Sarah so quickly that she decides to incorporate them *all*, using a sentence or two for each one, in addition to her example from *Pride and Prejudice* and one from World War II.

> So as not to lose her ideas, Sarah jots them down in an abbreviated form and in a brief outline, rather than writing out full sentences as above. (Although the breathless quality of the sentences above indicates how quickly one must plan the essay.)

From her final source, Sarah remembers that World War II history offers numerous examples of plans gone wrong. She decides she'll use the first example that occurs to her: Hitler's plan to conquer Russia, a country with whom Hitler had previously signed a nonaggression pact. In this example,

Hitler did not count on either the strength and resolve of his adversary or the length and severity of the Russian winter.

Bingo! Sarah's almost done. Sure, she's used a few of her 25 minutes to jot down her thoughts (in abbreviated form, remember), but the time was well spent: now the essay practically writes itself. All Sarah has to do is organize her examples into distinct paragraphs, add a dynamic opening and a compelling conclusion, and she's on her way to nailing a perfect score of 12!

RocketRule #8: Organize Your Essay Around Paragraphs

The quality of your essay's *organization* matters more than the quality of the writing. Why? Because the primary goal of the two SAT graders is consistency: to agree with each other about the scores they award. It is much more difficult (and time-consuming) to judge an essay on the quality of the writing than to evaluate the essay on its organization. Also, the quality of writing is subject to interpretation, meaning that your graders could easily disagree in this area. The question of organization is far less subjective.

Keep this fact in mind: organization is more important than "style," whatever *that* is. SAT graders will be speed-reading your essay in less than a minute, so determining whether your ideas and examples are arranged in distinct paragraphs is one of their quickest and easiest measures for evaluating how well organized it is.

Don't use too few paragraphs, or too many. High scoring SAT essays usually have between four and six paragraphs. Fewer than four paragraphs either means that you're not coming up with enough examples, or you're cramming more than one example into each paragraph. More than seven paragraphs, on the other hand, means that you're probably not developing each example sufficiently.

As a rule of thumb, each of your paragraphs should consist of three to five sentences. Don't bother doing a sentence count of each paragraph on the test, you don't have the time. Simply be on the lookout for super-short or super-long paragraphs, and adjust them as necessary.

Indent Your Paragraphs Clearly

Be sure you indent your paragraphs generously; leaving a line between paragraphs is also acceptable. Either approach will highlight the paragraph structure of your essay for the SAT graders (who are predisposed to think that students who take the time to organize their paragraphs have also organized their thoughts).

The Classic, Foolproof, Five-Paragraph Formula

Some students resent the idea of using a "formula" in their writing. Sure, there is *some* argument to be made against formulas when writing term papers or when taking relatively leisurely essay tests in the classroom (leisurely compared to what you face in this section of the SAT).

But what's great about formulas for writing is this: they save *time* as well as the energy you would otherwise need to think of a format for presenting your ideas during the actual test. And on the SAT, saving time and energy is not an advantage you want to relinquish casually.

You already know that SAT graders expect *academic* persuasive essays. Here's the most basic formula for the traditional academic essay:

- Begin with an opening in which you introduce your topic and present your main idea.

- Follow with a body in which you present your supporting reasons and evidence.

- Wind up with a conclusion in which you restate what you have shown in the rest of the essay, and perhaps briefly address issues that lie outside the scope of your paper.

You don't have enough time on the SAT essay to attempt any of the more complicated variations of academic essays. Beside, this one is perfectly suited to our purposes.

To keep things simple, your ideal SAT essay has five paragraphs: one for your introduction, one for each of your three examples, and one for your conclusion. I realize that this five-paragraph rule is highly restrictive, but sticking to this format will free up your mind to think about your thesis and supporting examples instead of wondering how to organize and present them.

If you're already scoring in the 11-to-12 range on the online practice RocketScore essays using your own formula or judgment for paragraphs, feel free to continue. Your current strategy is clearly working for you. Until you reach that score level *consistently*, however, you should apply the five-paragraph structure religiously.

Don't get creative with your essay in the exam room—doing so takes time and entails enormous risks.

Generalize, Analyze, and Synthesize

The opening of your essay introduces the topic and your general thesis. Your introduction gives the readers a general idea of the point or points you intend to make.

The body of your essay analyzes—breaks down—the topic using different examples. Your analysis is going to be more rushed and superficial than you're used to giving your papers, but everyone's in the same boat.

The conclusion of your essay synthesizes—brings together—your various points into a larger statement about the topic.

About Your Essay's Introduction

Your introductory paragraph, which you will remember is the most important paragraph in your entire essay, and usually the most difficult to write, should accomplish all of the following:

- Introduce the assigned topic in general terms only (in one to three sentences)

- State your thesis simply (in one or two sentences)

- Introduce the *type* of examples you intend to use (in one or two sentences)

As you can see, your opening paragraph should have anywhere from three to seven sentences. Here's how Sarah (our representative student) could incorporate her topic, thesis, and example types into a model introduction:

> *If you want to make the gods laugh, goes the ancient adage, tell them your plans. Though lacking in either the omniscience or wisdom that planning in an uncertain universe would seem to require, human beings persist in drawing up the most detailed goals. No matter how well we plan, however, as the great poet Robert Burns wrote, we often discover that our hopes have been dashed along with our schemes. This universal notion is exemplified throughout literature as well as history.*

Sarah uses the first two sentences to introduce the topic, the third sentence to state her thesis (agreeing with the assigned topic and incorporating the quotation from the question to do so), and her fourth sentence to let the SAT graders know that she will be using literary and historical illustrations, in that order.

Practice using the general structure of this paragraph as a *template* for your introduction. It can be easily adapted to any SAT essay topic you might face.

Sophisticated Introductions: Variations for the Brave Only

If you're feeling ambitious, and the essay topic is broad (as it often is), the following two techniques will immediately impress SAT graders:

Define any key term or terms. Even if the terms of the topic seem "obvious," taking time to define them is done only by experienced writers.

Narrow the scope of the topic to something manageable. Limiting your essay to a single aspect of a broad topic is an entirely legitimate tactic. Be sure you explicitly acknowledge that the topic is broad, and that you are choosing to narrow the topic given the short amount of time you have to write. (SAT essay topics are so broad you could write an entire book in response.)

You can employ either or both of these techniques in the opening paragraph. You might also choose to extend the introduction to a second paragraph and begin your first example in the third paragraph.

About the Body of Your Essay

The middle three paragraphs of your essay—the body—will be devoted to laying out your examples, one example per paragraph. **Be sure that each time you introduce a new supporting example you refer the example back to your thesis.**

Here's how Sarah might compose the paragraph devoted to her first example (see page 91).

One amusing illustration of the futility of human planning occurs early in <u>Pride and Prejudice</u>, Jane Austen's witty and ironic novel about how our pride and our prejudices can get in the way of true love. We are introduced to the imperious aristocrat Darcy, who is scheming with the sisters of his good friend Charles Bingley to scuttle the budding romance between Charles and the sweet and lovely—yet middle class—Jane Bennet. Not only does Darcy's plan fail to deter his understandably love-struck friend, but in the process of carrying out his plan, Darcy himself falls under the spell of Jane's equally lovely sister, Elizabeth.

And here's how she might compose the remaining two supporting paragraphs:

The theme that our plans frequently go awry is also illustrated throughout Shakespeare's signature play, <u>Hamlet</u>. Indeed, there are so many instances of shattered schemes that it is hard to single out just one. Claudius's belief that he can get away with murder goes sour when Hamlet encounters the ghost of his— Hamlet's—murdered father. Claudius's subsequent scheme to have Hamlet executed when the young Prince arrives in England with Rosencrantz and Guildenstern is upended when Hamlet discovers the plot and substitutes the names of his friends for his own—resulting in their demise, not his. And then there's poor Polonius who hatched a plan to discover whether Hamlet was truly mad or merely feigning madness—only to be on the receiving end of Hamlet's sword. (Hamlet, in turn, thought he was skewering Claudius behind the tapestry, not Polonius, so Hamlet's plan failed, too.) Finally, the evil King's plan to poison his nephew backfires when Gertrude, not Hamlet, drinks from the tainted goblet.

Of course, the theme of the frequent (if not virtually inevitable failure) of our best-prepared plans is not limited to literary examples; we see this immutable principle illustrated throughout history, too. Consider the Second World War. The outcome of this conflict was still largely undetermined when Hitler inexplicably decided to attack Russia in violation of the nonaggression pact he had made with the Russians in 1939. This mistake marked one of the decisive turning points in the war.

Note that Sarah used explicit and detailed transition sentences to introduce each paragraph above. Note also that she underlined the literary works she mentioned to follow the accepted format and to make sure the speed-reading SAT graders noticed them.

Now all Sarah has left to do is end her essay with a few strong yet simple concluding sentences.

About Your Conclusion

Your final paragraph wraps up your essay. Sometimes it's hard to think of what to say in your conclusion. After all, you've already said everything you have to say—what more could you add?

Don't worry. Your conclusion doesn't have to be a complicated affair. According to the writer's classic formula for persuasive essays:

- *In the opening, tell the readers what you're going to show them.*

- *In the body, show them.*

- *In the conclusion, recap what you've just shown your readers.*

So all your conclusion has to do is restate your thesis and the areas from which you've drawn your supporting examples. If you're feeling ambitious, however, you could embellish your conclusion using any of the following approaches:

- Qualify your primary thesis by admitting that there are exceptions to your general argument, or by acknowledging that someone could make a case for the opposite point of view. (If you acknowledge opposing views, quickly restate your thesis despite the exceptions you've admitted.)

- Hint at the implications of your thesis. For example, if our plans always go awry (our sample topic), *so what?*

- Raise a rhetorical question about larger but related issues outside the scope of your essay.

- List the *types* of examples that you would have included if you had more time. If you discussed only literary and historical examples, you could mention in the conclusion that there were examples from science or art or other disciplines that also would have supported your argument.

- Refer back to something you mentioned in the introduction.

These are *highly* sophisticated techniques, and you should not feel compelled to attempt any such conclusion unless you are very confident when writing under pressure. Simply restating the topic and your thesis is usually sufficient to guarantee an excellent score (assuming, of course, that your introduction and examples are outstanding).

Here's how Sarah decides to conclude her essay with the little time she has remaining:

> *As we have seen with these literary and historical examples, human beings are apparently doomed to a fate of forever planning and forever having those plans dashed. Indeed, I think ruefully of countless plans of my own in the past, and of the reception they met when I tried to carry out these plans in the real world. Of course, this is not to say that planning is foolish. My father once quoted something General Eisenhower said during World War II: "I have found that plans are generally useless, but the act of planning is indispensable."*

Sarah qualified her thesis, and put a nice spin on it in the closing sentence. She also alluded to examples from her own life, though she felt that her literary and historical examples were more than sufficient.

> Try not to use phrases like "in conclusion" or "to summarize" in your final paragraph. Such phrases sound stilted and should be unnecessary because it should be obvious from the content of your closing paragraph that you're concluding your essay.

Checklist of the Seven Most Common Errors in SAT Essays

When rushed, even excellent writers can fall into traps or forget to do certain things. The following list will help you check your writing. You don't have to memorize this list, but it would be wise to review it carefully. When you complete a practice SAT essay, go through the following questions one by one—especially if your RocketScore essay report mentions that your essay was not as relevant to the topic as it could have been.

1. **Did your essay fail to address the topic directly in one of your first few sentences?** One hallmark of a sophisticated essay is *not* charging right into the essay topic, but approaching the topic *indirectly*. The writer of such an essay deliberately lays a foundation that leads up to the topic and then to the writer's specific thesis. Unfortunately, this indirectness is also a hallmark of an *unsophisticated* essay (and the obvious difference is that unsophisticated writers either never get to the topic, or merely meander into it finally). Knowing this, you may not want to take the risk that speed-reading SAT graders might mistake your sophisticated introduction for an unsophisticated one.

   Remember: SAT writing is different. Don't try to be too clever or too sophisticated regarding your essay's format. In their haste, SAT graders will probably overlook nuances, or worse, *misunderstand* them.

2. **Did you go straight to your first example without even providing an introductory paragraph?** This error is more flagrant than the one we just discussed. Surprisingly, many students (especially those who haven't taken the time to plan their essay) jump into their examples without ever telling the reader what they're writing about.

   Of course the graders "know what the topic is about," but one convention of academic writing is that the writer must proceed as if the reader did not know the topic. **When you write, you must pretend that when SAT graders get to your essay, they are discovering what your topic is for the very first time.**

   So don't be afraid of being "too obvious" in your introductory paragraph; go ahead and tell the readers what the topic is and then what you intend to show them in the body of your essay. (And again, of course, you'll remind them in the final paragraph of what you've just shown in the body of your essay.)

3. **Did your essay drift from the topic by including too many extraneous details?** Yes, your essay's overall length *is* important. Beware, however, of padding your essay with peripheral details. The most common form of this error is providing too much background information for your supporting examples.

   Keep any plot summaries, especially, to a minimum. For instance, if you're using *Romeo and Juliet* as the source of one of your supporting examples, you don't have to go into great detail about its being a tale of star-crossed lovers who belonged to two feuding families, blah, blah, blah. Don't waste time or strain your readers' patience. Get *immediately* to the scene or situation within the play that illustrates your thesis.

In short, assume that your SAT graders will be familiar with any well-known examples you cite. With less familiar illustrations you should provide a sentence or two—*at the absolute max*—of introductory or other background information.

4. **Did your essay explore only one or two examples in great detail rather than three, or even four, examples in less detail?** Once you've made your point by supporting or illustrating your thesis with a particular example, move on: start a new paragraph and begin with a topic sentence that ties your *next* example to your thesis.

5. **Did each example *explicitly* refer back to your thesis?** This error is a variant of the one we discussed in question two. Each time you start a new supporting paragraph, you must introduce the example by announcing its relevance to the topic. Do not open a paragraph within the body of your essay with a sentence like this:

    Another example occurs in Jane Austen's novel, Pride and Prejudice.

    or worse still, with one like this:

    In Pride and Prejudice, *the author Jane Austen describes the courtship of Charles Bingley and Jane Bennet.*

    Instead, open that paragraph with a sentence like this:

    Another illustration that exemplifies the theme that our plans are always at the mercy of chance comes again from literature, this time from Jane Austen's Pride and Prejudice.

6. **Does your essay refer to "the topic" or "the quote" or "the statement," instead of actually repeating (or paraphrasing) your thesis?** It's important that you spell out your thesis and continually and explicitly hammer home the relevance of your points to the specific topic. So instead of concluding your opening paragraph with something like this:

    I will support this statement with examples from literature as well as history.

    Write something like this:

    I will show that our best-laid plans often go awry using examples from literature as well as history.

    The second variation reiterates your thesis; the first variation does not. (The same principle applies to your other paragraphs as well.)

7. **Does your essay end abruptly without a concluding paragraph?** If you notice that you're running short of time—*stop!* Wrap up the example you're working on and write the conclusion, even if all you can manage is a sentence or two. Remember: the SAT graders will spend more time on your final paragraph than the one preceding it. It's more important, then, that you end your essay in grand style, with a proper conclusion, than to leave the grader dangling with a wonderful example that unfortunately ends your essay abruptly.

There's a Teeny-Tiny Chance—Say 1 in 20—That You'll Get a Different Type of Essay Question

ETS, the test publisher, does not like experimenting with something that will be as closely scrutinized as the new SAT. Still, it is remotely possible that you will be confronted with a slightly different question format from the representative one we've been discussing throughout this chapter.

If you keep the basic RocketReview principles in mind, however, you will easily adapt to any question format or topic variation. **The most important principle to remember regarding your choice of examples is that teachers—and virtually all SAT graders are teachers—like to see that you've learned something in school and can apply it in your writing.**

Let's take an extreme case. Let's say, for example, that instead of the formal topic we've discussed, you're faced with a personal topic on the actual exam like: *Who is or was the most influential person in your life?* You've studied and practiced for a formal topic, and then *this* comes up?

Do not panic! With some creativity you can still work a literary allusion or historical reference into your essay, even with such a topic. For example, if Sarah (our representative student) wrote about her mother or father, she could compare either, ironically or not, to the mother or father in *Pride and Prejudice*, or to the King and Queen in *Hamlet*.

Admittedly, finding historical examples from World War II, which Sarah used in our previous example, would be a huge stretch. But it *can* be done, you simply need a little ingenuity. (*My father, ever eager to find grander illustrations for the moral lessons he inculcated tirelessly, often referred to the wartime experiences of his father—my grandfather—in World War II . . .*)

So yes, it's possible that a particular literary, historical, or other scholarly example will seem contrived, but better contrived than not used at all. Remember: your guiding principle when choosing which examples you will use is to show your SAT essay graders that you've learned a lot in high school and that you can apply some of what you've learned to the assigned topic.

That's All There Is to Know about the SAT Essay

Now you know *what* you're going to say on your SAT essay and *how* you're going to say it. Follow these tips and you're sure to ace the essay.

Here is Sarah's completed 526-word essay all in one place. Evaluate it in light of these points, and see whether she committed any of the Seven Most Common Errors in SAT Essays we just discussed.

If you want to make the gods laugh, goes the ancient adage, tell them your plans. Though lacking in either the omniscience or wisdom that planning in an uncertain universe would seem to require, human beings persist in drawing up the most detailed goals. No matter how well we plan, however, as the great poet Robert Burns wrote, we often discover that our hopes have been dashed along with our schemes. This universal notion is exemplified throughout literature as well as history.

One amusing illustration of the futility of human planning occurs early in Pride and Prejudice*, Jane Austen's witty and ironic novel about how our pride and our prejudices can get in the way of true love. We are introduced to the imperious aristocrat Darcy, who is scheming with the sisters of his good friend Charles Bingley to scuttle the budding romance between Charles and the sweet and lovely—yet middle class—Jane Bennet. Not only does Darcy's plan fail to deter his understandably love-struck friend, but in the process of carrying out his plan, Darcy himself falls under the spell of Jane's equally lovely sister, Elizabeth.*

The theme that our plans frequently go awry is also illustrated throughout Shakespeare's signature play, <u>Hamlet</u>. Indeed, there are so many instances of shattered schemes that it is hard to single out just one. Claudius's belief that he can get away with murder goes sour when Hamlet encounters the ghost of his—Hamlet's—murdered father. Claudius's subsequent scheme to have Hamlet executed when the young Prince arrives in England with Rosencrantz and Guildenstern is upended when Hamlet discovers the plot and substitutes the names of his friends for his own—resulting in their demise, not his. And then there's poor Polonius who hatched a plan to discover whether Hamlet was truly mad or merely feigning madness—only to be on the receiving end of Hamlet's sword. (Hamlet, in turn, thought he was skewering Claudius behind the tapestry, not Polonius, so Hamlet's plan failed, too.) Finally, the evil King's plan to poison his nephew backfires when Gertrude, not Hamlet, drinks from the tainted goblet.

Of course, the theme of the frequent (if not virtually inevitable failure) of our best-prepared plans is not limited to literary examples; we see this immutable principle illustrated throughout history, too. Consider the Second World War. The outcome of this conflict was still largely undetermined when Hitler inexplicably decided to attack Russia in violation of the nonaggression pact he had made with the Russians in 1939. This mistake marked one of the decisive turning points in the war.

As we have seen with these literary and historical examples, human beings are apparently doomed to a fate of forever planning and forever having those plans dashed. Indeed, I think ruefully of countless plans of my own in the past, and of the reception they met when I tried to carry out these plans in the real world. Of course, this is not to say that planning is foolish. My father once quoted something General Eisenhower said during World War II: "I have found that plans are generally useless, but the act of planning is indispensable."

Another exercise that you might find interesting would be to submit this essay to RocketScore (the essay is already on the website) in order to see the grade it would have received from actual SAT readers, along with detailed commentary.

What's Coming Up

Now that you're an expert at the SAT essay, it's time to turn our attention to the other part of the SAT Writing Test: the multiple-choice questions. In the next chapter I'll expose the fourteen simple grammatical concepts covered on the proofreading and editing questions.

Feel free to skip to another section of the book if you'd like to take a break from the Writing Test. There's nothing sacred to the order I've selected to present the reading, writing, and math sections. Just follow the sequence of the chapters *within* each section so that you cover the basic principles—yes, even if you're already a high-scoring student—before moving on to the advanced topics.

Finally, get an idea of the amount of space you'll be expected to fill in 25 minutes. **You'll find a printable blank form at the RocketReview website so that you can use it more than once when you practice (although any lined notebook paper will do).** Before you take the SAT, you should practice writing *at least* three essays under simulated (timed) test conditions and submit your papers to RocketScore for a detailed analysis and predicted score.

The Proofreading and Editing Section:
Basic Principles
All the Grammar You Need to Know for the SAT

First Grammar, Then Techniques

In this chapter and the next I'll cover everything you need to know to ace the 35-minute multiple-choice section of the SAT Writing Test. Remember: these proofreading and editing questions are just as important to your final writing score as the essay.

First we'll review the fourteen simple grammatical concepts tested in this section. That may sound like a lot to review, but I'm sure you're familiar with most of these grammatical concepts already. Once we've gotten the basic information out of the way, I'll show you specific techniques for handling the three different question formats.

If you've never taken a grammar course, relax: there's not much you need to know, and we'll be covering everything thoroughly. Still, to move things along we won't linger too long on the fundamentals; students who have trouble telling the difference between a noun and a verb should consider postponing taking the SAT.

> There's a lot of material in this chapter. Even though you are probably familiar with much of it already, I strongly recommend that you skim the chapter first. Spread your in-depth review over several days in small sessions rather than trying to digest everything in one sitting.

SAT-Specific Grammar Only

We'll be reviewing all the grammar you need to know for the SAT, but only that grammar. Moreover, I'll be covering these concepts *as tested on the SAT*. I'll occasionally take liberties with grammatical terms, rules, and even definitions.

For example, if a particular grammatical rule has an exception but that exception never shows up on the SAT, I'll state that rule absolutely. To point out rare exceptions to simple grammatical principles, or to discuss grammatical nuances that vex and confound college English professors, would complicate matters needlessly.

Often a single grammatical misunderstanding will lead to several errors. If so, I will group the analogous grammatical concepts under the same heading even though the concepts may not be related.

In short, I'll take shortcuts to keep things simple (even though some of these shortcuts may horrify traditionalists). My goal here is to raise your SAT Writing score as quickly and efficiently as possible, not to turn you into a grammarian.

Before we get to the details, now's a good time to alert you to a major pitfall awaiting unsuspecting students: using your "ear" to spot writing errors.

First, a Peek Ahead at the Three Question Formats

We'll examine the different formats of the proofreading and editing questions in the next chapter, but we'll have to refer to them occasionally in this chapter so let's take a quick overview.

- The first question format deals primarily with errors with particular words or phrases (usage questions).

- The second question format deals with errors *between* different words and phrases (sentence correction questions).

- The third question format deals primarily with errors between different *sentences* (paragraph correction questions).

If you're not familiar with these question types, take a moment now and skim the introduction, starting on page 62. Again, we'll take a close look at these different formats in the next chapter, along with specific techniques for handling each type.

The Multiple-Choice Questions Can Be Tricky— Beware of Relying Solely on Your "Ear"

Students who aren't sure what they should be looking for on the proofreading questions tend to rely, naturally enough, on their ears: if a sentence "sounds right," they assume it's grammatically correct. (One-sixth of the proofreading questions are error-free.)

Relying on your ear to detect writing problems is natural, even tempting, but it's a big mistake. A big, *big* mistake. Sentences in this section that "sound wrong" are often perfectly okay, while incorrect sentences often "sound okay."

Here's why this natural approach is so faulty. First, our ears are attuned to *informal* speech patterns, but the SAT writing questions reflect *formal* standards of what is correct and acceptable.

In everyday speech, hanging out with our friends or family, we get away with sloppy grammar—and sloppy thinking—all the time. You may have heard your English teacher distinguish between "written English" and "spoken English." ("Hey, it's me" is acceptable in spoken English but unacceptable in written English.) Who can be bothered with the effort required to speak with precision when our friends can figure out what we "really mean" without the effort? What a pain, right?

Isn't it ironic? We've become so attuned to finding informal speech acceptable that sentences that articulate *precisely* what the speaker means with formal correctness sound stilted or somehow alien. Our ears mislead us both ways: bad grammar sounds normal, and good grammar sounds awkward.

The second reason that relying on your ear is dangerous is that a number of the writing problems you're hunting for in the questions are not grammatical errors. Many are actually *logical* errors, and these will sound perfectly okay to the unsuspecting ear.

On the multiple-choice proofreading questions, you must be on the lookout for sentences that *literally* say one thing but were *meant* to say another.

In short, a word or phrase can't simply sound wrong—you have to *know* why it's wrong in order to mark it so.

You Think I'm Kidding About Relying on Your Ear?

To demonstrate the dangers of relying on your ear to judge grammatical correctness, I've prepared the following quiz for you. One or more of the following sentences may contain an error. None of these is a "trick question," but do read each one carefully.

If you spot an error, jot it down on a piece of scrap paper—there are bonus points if you know how to correct it—and then check your responses against the answer key at the end of this chapter.

Good luck. (By the way, the actual format of the SAT proofreading questions differs a bit from these bare sentences, but let's keep things simple for now.)

1) *The two pieces of woodwork by the apprentice carpenters were each so finely sanded that it took the trained eye of their teacher to determine that the oak tabletop was more nearly flat than was the pine tabletop.*

2) *After a thorough examination, the doctor told Melissa that she should exercise more vigorously as well as more regularly.*

3) *The photo-finish of the 100-meter race was so close that each of the first five finishers thought that they had won.*

4) Titus Andronicus, *one of Shakespeare's lesser-known works and the inspiration for the popular movie* Gladiator, *is a play where the noble protagonist suffers a tragic fate.*

5) *The academic habits and expectations of teenage girls are very different from teenage boys.*

6) *The causes of the American Civil War were not just social, but also economical and technological.*

7) *All of the former classmates are planning on attending the formal reunion ceremony, and most have said that they will also attend the reception party afterwards.*

8) *When completely painted with the third and final coat of varnish, Peter set the antique chair outside on the porch to get some sun.*

9) *"By the time you get back," Tim assured his doubtful mother and father as they were preparing to leave for a parent-teacher conference, "I promise I will complete my history term paper."*

10) *Were it not for the downturn of the local economy last year, the then-popular mayor would surely have been reelected.*

Okay, now see how you did by checking the answer key beginning on page 147 at the end of this chapter.

You're Going on a Grammatical Scavenger Hunt

Fortunately, once you know what you're looking for, you won't have to rely on your ear to pick out the writing problems lurking in the multiple-choice questions. It's useful to think of the proofreading and editing questions as a scavenger hunt.

You might be surprised to learn that the test covers quite a narrow range of grammatical and other writing problems. I'm going to arm you with a specific list so that you will know precisely which errors you need to find and how many of each. (Unlike too many hapless students, you will not be wandering through the SAT Writing Test vaguely looking for errors.) After all, it would be hard to go on a scavenger hunt without a list of what you're looking for, right?

A Checklist for Your SAT Scavenger Hunt

Here are the fourteen grammatical concepts you need to know. You *don't* need to memorize these categories (which we'll use for discussion purposes only), and you *won't* need to classify errors on the test, either. The only thing you'll need to do on the SAT is recognize a writing problem when you see it. That said, if you're struggling with a potential error that you can't fit into one of these categories—if the wording merely "sounds wrong"—it probably isn't an error at all.

I've listed the categories in order of their overall importance, combining how frequently the category appears on the SAT with the category's average difficulty. Just skim this chart for now; you can always refer back to it later.

CATEGORY	FREQUENCY	DIFFICULTY
Pronoun Errors	Very High	Medium
Singular-Plural Errors	Very High	Medium
Idiom Errors	High	High
Comparison Errors	Medium	Very High
Parallel Structure Errors	High	Medium
Wordiness and Redundancy**	High	Medium
Modifier Errors*	Medium	High
Ambiguity**	Medium	High
Diction Errors	Low	Very High
Adjective-Adverb Errors	Medium	Medium
Verb Tense Errors	Medium	Low
Sentence Fragments or Run-ons*	Medium	Low
Transition or Punctuation Errors*	Medium	Low
Logic Errors**	Very Low	Very High

The difficulty of each category reflects how easy it is to overlook this type of error on the SAT, not how hard the concept is to learn; the frequency refers to how often the category shows up on an SAT. The two most frequent errors—singular-plural errors and pronoun errors—appear on average three or four times *each*; diction errors, a low frequency category, will appear once, at most twice; logic errors, perhaps not at all.

The asterisked (*) categories appear only on sentence correction questions, all other categories appear on these as well as sentence correction questions. The double-asterisked (**) categories are usually tested indirectly, among the choices rather than in the original sentence. I'll cover those categories in the next chapter, in which I introduce our process of elimination techniques for answering the questions.

For most students, reviewing the top five categories will result in the largest and most rapid score gains:

- Pronoun errors

- Singular-plural errors

- Idiom errors

- Comparison errors

- Parallel structure errors

Again, this order is for the average student, which you are not. No matter how good someone is at grammar, he or she undoubtedly has one or more grammatical blind spots. I have my grammatical blind spots—concepts I overlook more than others—and so do you. As you work through this chapter, become familiar with which grammar categories tend to trip you up and be especially vigilant about them.

Some Basic Grammatical Terms (but No Jargon)

If you ever studied grammar in school, the topic may bring up nightmare memories of terms like "subjunctive tense" and "past participle" and "periodic sentences." Ugh. I promise not to use any complex terms like these.

We will, however, need certain basic terms to discuss grammar on the SAT. I've pared down the list to ten basic words. You probably learned these terms years ago, which is why we'll quickly review them: you may have forgotten their precise meanings. Again, you don't need to memorize any of the following definitions or examples.

> **noun** (*hat, Canada, beaver, equality, apricot*)
> A noun is the name of a person, place, object, or concept. The ten most common nouns in the English language are *time, year, people, way, man, day, thing, child, government,* and *work*.

verb (*run, throw, is, believe, investigated, had forgotten*)
Verbs describe actions or states of being. The ten most common verbs are *be, have, do, will, say, would, can, get, make,* and *go*. Verbs have different *tenses* depending on whether the action is taking place (present tense), has taken place (past tense), or will take place (future tense).

adjective (*bold, fast, solid, thin, funny*)
Adjectives modify or describe nouns or pronouns. The ten most common adjectives are *other, good, new, old, great, high, small, different, social,* and *important*.

adverb (*very, never, really, too, slowly*)
Adverbs primarily modify verbs, but they can also modify adjectives and other adverbs. The ten most common adverbs are *so, up, then, out, then, now, only, just, more,* and *also*.

pronoun (*it, I, you, them, her, something, himself, anyone, none, everybody*)
Pronouns stand in the place of nouns to make our writing smoother and less repetitive. Because pronouns replace other words from which they are usually separated within or between sentences, it's important to verify that the various parts all agree. **Pronoun problems account for more grammatical errors on the SAT than do problems with any other part of speech.**

subject
The subject of a sentence is what the sentence is about. (The rest of the sentence tells you something about the subject.)

object
If a noun or a pronoun receives the action of a verb (if something happens to that noun or pronoun), that word is the object of the verb.

The next three terms are a little trickier, so pay attention.

preposition (*through, between, before, around, against*)
Prepositions usually precede nouns and describe the relationship between things in space or time. The two most common prepositions—*of* and *in*—appear more frequently on SAT grammar questions than all other prepositions combined. The next ten most-common prepositions are *to, for, with, on, by, at, from, as, into,* and *about*.

Notice that a particular word can function as a different part of speech depending on its role within a given sentence. The word *to*, for example, can act as a preposition (*I made a call to my friend*) or be part of a verb (*I need to call my friend*).

phrase (*in the middle, at the corner, of geese*)
A phrase is a group of related words without a subject or verb. Phrases can act as the equivalent of adjectives, adverbs, and other parts of speech. The most important type of phrase for our purposes is the prepositional phrase, which begins, as you might expect, with a preposition and ends with a noun or pronoun. Phrases are best understood in relation to their grammatical cousins: clauses.

clause (*it was early, because the dog barked*)
A clause is a group of words that contains a subject and its verb. A clause can sometimes stand on its own as a complete sentence (as in the first example above) and sometimes not (as in the second example). Don't worry about the distinction between a phrase and a clause, or between different types of clauses. What's important for our purposes is that both phrases and clauses refer to related groups of words.

We'll go into more detail regarding these terms when we discuss the different grammatical concepts you need to know on the SAT, but now we're ready to move ahead. You won't ever be tested on the SAT about your knowledge of these terms, but being familiar with them will help you follow our examination of the most important grammatical errors on the test and will improve your ability to recognize these errors when they appear.

The Simple Principle Behind Many Grammatical Rules

Learning grammar often seems like you have to memorize dozens of bewildering and arbitrary rules. In fact most grammatical rules are based on logical principles, but the principles are rarely explained to students.

Once you understand the principle behind a rule, the rule is easier to remember and to apply. The most fundamental concept underlying grammatical rules is the principle of *agreement*. Different parts of a sentence should not disagree with each other.

Verbs have to agree with the nouns they refer to. For example, in the sentence, *The temperature were cold outside so dress warmly,* the plural verb "were" does not agree with the singular noun "temperature." What's more, the verb "were" is in the past tense, which does not agree with the tense of the verb "dress."

Just as verbs have to agree with their nouns, so do pronouns. Problems between nouns, pronouns, and verbs account for a large number of the errors on the proofreading questions. As a first step on the proofreading questions, make sure that any connected parts are in agreement, *especially* nouns or pronouns, with each other and with their verbs.

> On the proofreading and editing questions, whenever you see a noun or verb or pronoun, whether or not it is underlined—stop! Establish what word or phrase it's related to or referring to, and see whether the two parts are in agreement.

In the rest of the chapter I'll show you every type of error you need to look for. Not all errors in this section are based on noun-verb-pronoun disagreements, but checking for these in a sentence is an excellent first step.

How the SAT Camouflages Simple Grammatical Errors to Make Them Difficult to Spot

If most SAT grammatical errors come down to basic problems in agreement, you may be wondering how the proofreading and editing questions can get so difficult. Here's how.

Even the most grammatically challenged students notice agreement errors—*when the related terms are next to each other.* **The test writers camouflage agreement errors by inserting phrases that *separate* the related terms and distract you from the underlying disagreement.**

Read the next 24-word sentence quickly and see whether the agreement error is obvious (I'm guessing it won't be):

> *The degree of error in calculations done by ancient Mayan astronomers long before the invention of telescopes were, even by modern standards, incredibly small.*

The sentence is a bit cumbersome—though not unusually so by SAT standards. Still, the basic meaning is not too difficult to understand. The agreement error is hard to spot because 15 words separate the subject—*degree*—from its verb—*were.*

Let's work backwards to see how a simple error is made difficult. I'll strip the sentence down to its essential words:

> *The degree were small.*

It's not clear *what* degree the sentence is referring to now, but the disagreement between the subject and the verb pops out. If every proofreading question were four words long like that one, hardly anybody would have trouble spotting most of the errors. The problem is that the average sentence in this section is more than *twenty* words long, so it's easy to get lost and entangled in all the phrases.

Now let's see what happens when the test writers start adding words to the sentence, and watch how the error becomes hidden. They start by adding an adverb:

> *The degree were* incredibly *small.*

The sentence is a bit longer, but the new word did not separate the verb from its subject, so the disagreement between them is still obvious. Okay, the test writers decide to add a prepositional phrase now:

> *The degree* of error *were incredibly small.*

The verb is separated from the subject now, but since the noun "error" now next to the verb is also singular, the verb "were" still seems to disagree with something. Since most students would still immediately spot the problem verb, the test writers get really tricky now by adding a phrase with a *plural* noun next to the verb:

> *The degree of error* in calculations done by ancient Mayan astronomers *were incredibly small.*

All of a sudden the disagreement has become much harder to spot because the plural verb "were" now seems to be referring to the plural noun "astronomers." And just for good measure, to make you work to find the error, the test writers add another bunch of words to throw students completely off track:

> *The degree of error in calculations done by ancient Mayan astronomers* long before the invention of telescopes *were,* even by modern standards, *incredibly small.*

And there you have it: a simple grammatical error camouflaged almost beyond recognition.

> Remember that widely separated parts of a sentence may be grammatically connected, so you can't simply read the questions word by word. You'll sometimes need to read a bit, jump to another part of the sentence, then jump back to continue reading through.

You May Need to Read a Proofreading Question Two or Even Three Times

It's easy to think that because you read and speak English, all you have to do to spot errors on the SAT Writing Test is read the sentences as you read, say, this one.

Wrong.

Just reading through a sentence isn't enough. If you want to spot all the errors—and get a high score—you will have to chop through each sentence suspiciously, word by word and phrase by phrase.

You must read a bit (for example, until you get to a verb), then see what it refers to (which subject and possibly which object), and once you've verified that the two are in agreement, you can move on to the next part of the sentence, and so on. And as you've seen, the two parts that need to be in agreement can be far apart.

The problem, as we've discussed, is the presence of all these usually irrelevant words and phrases that distract and confuse us. **On the first read-through of a sentence—and you may need to read a sentence two or three times before you spot an error—read "around" the phrases and clauses that merely pad the sentence, camouflaging the error.** If you haven't spotted an error yet, then you can go back and examine those phrases one by one to see whether there's anything wrong.

It's easy, focusing on individual phrases in this way as we must, to lose sight of the big picture, so if you *still* haven't spotted an error, read quickly through the sentence a *third* time, as a whole. If you haven't spotted an error at that point—one-sixth of the questions contain no error, remember—move on. Rather than beat your head against the question, mark the sentence as no error and circle the question number. If you have time remaining at the end of the section, return to the questions you weren't sure about and read them with fresh eyes.

The Bracket Technique

A powerful technique that allows us to read around potentially distracting phrases is to enclose them in parentheses. As you read through a sentence for the first time, place parentheses around either of the following:

- any prepositional phrases (by far the most common prepositions are *of* and *in,* followed by *to, for, by,* and *with*)

- any clauses set off by commas

Sometimes you'll find a prepositional phrase within a prepositional phrase, so to keep things simple just open a set of parentheses when you get to the first preposition and close it when you get to the end of the complete phrase. If you get to any other phrases or clauses, open a new set of parentheses. In the sentence we just discussed, we'd have used two sets of parentheses:

> *The degree (of error in calculations done by ancient Mayan astronomers long before the invention of telescopes) were, (even by modern standards), incredibly small.*

Notice that if we read around the parentheses, ignoring the words within them, we're back to our original basic sentence in which the agreement error was obvious. If we didn't find an error outside the parentheses, our next step would be to examine the words within the parentheses.

Using your pencil to break up each sentence into manageable bits also helps you stay focused. Remember Einstein's words of advice that we discussed back in Tutorial 13, "Your pencil is smarter than you are."

As an exercise, why don't you practice applying parentheses to the ten sentences you completed earlier in the drill on page 109.

Learn to Read *Literally*

In school it's important to figure out what your teachers *mean,* rather than listening to what they *literally say.* On the SAT Writing Test, though, the opposite is true: you need to pay attention to what each sentence literally says, rather than to what you think it means or to what the sentence was "trying to say."

Back in Tutorial 12, we discussed the trouble that your brain's natural intelligence can get you into on every section of the SAT. Your brain is programmed to make sense of the information it receives, so it "fills in the blanks" when something doesn't make sense.

Here's the problem: many grammatical errors result in nonsense, literally. When your brain encounters something that doesn't make sense, it instantaneously tries to figure out what's going on. In the real world that's what your brain is supposed to do. On the proofreading and editing questions, however, what your brain "hears" and what a nonsensical sentence actually says can be radically different.

Our introductory quiz on page 109 contained three illustrations of this tendency: questions 2, 5, and 8. If you missed one or more of these questions, you really have to watch out for this problem.

Question 2:   *After a thorough examination, the doctor told*
Melissa that she should exercise more
vigorously as well as more regularly.

What it *seems* to say: Melissa's doctor advised Melissa to get more exercise.

What it *actually* says: We can't tell. The sentence *might* be saying that, but it might be saying that the doctor is admitting to Melissa that she, the doctor, should be getting more exercise.

Question 5:   *The academic habits and expectations of*
teenage girls are very different from teenage
boys.

What it *seems* to say: Girls study differently from the way boys study.

What it *actually* says: The way girls study is different from the way boys *are.* Yes, that's nonsensical, but that's what the sentence says literally.

Question 8:   *When completely painted with the third and*
final coat of varnish, Peter set the antique
chair outside on the porch to get some sun.

What it *seems* to say: That Peter varnished an old chair and then set it outside to dry.

What it *actually* says: That Peter was painted with varnish and then went outside to get some sun, perhaps while sitting in an antique chair. Yes, that's nonsensical—and that's why it's wrong.

Not all grammatical errors result in nonsense, but many do. You're a *proofreader* on these questions, so your job is to be suspicious of *everything* you read.

First, a Look at "Error-Free" Sentences

Before we consider the different types of grammatical errors you need to hunt for on these questions, we need to discuss error-free sentences.

There's a strong temptation to think that all the sentences in this section must have some problem with them. After all, each sentence presents you with four suggested errors. Sometimes, however, you'll read a sentence but you won't find anything wrong with it. The sentence sounded a bit strange, but you couldn't put your finger on anything specific.

You think that maybe you missed something so you reread the sentence, closely examining each choice. But *still* you find no error. In fact, you're absolutely sure that two of the five choices can't be right, but you're not sure about the other choices. You grit your teeth in frustration and decide to read it a third time, and now you *really* focus on each remaining choice. You come up empty-handed again.

I told you back on page 108 that your ear for grammar is not completely reliable. Sometimes grammatically incorrect sentences sound fine to our ears, while grammatically correct sentences sometimes sound strange. Don't drive yourself crazy—and waste time—searching too long for errors where none may exist.

> On average, one-sixth of the 45 proofreading questions are grammatically correct.

Let's take another look at the two error-free examples from our introductory quiz: questions 1 and 10.

Question 1: *The two pieces of woodwork by the apprentice carpenters were each so finely sanded that it took the trained eye of their teacher to determine that the oak tabletop was more nearly flat than was the pine tabletop.*

Discussion: The uncommon phrase "more nearly" sounds alien to most students, who then assume that the phrase *must* be wrong. It's not. **If a word or a phrase in a particular sentence merely "sounds weird" but you can't put your finger on *why* it's wrong, the phrase may be perfectly okay.**

Question 10:   *Were it not for the downturn of the local economy last year, the then-popular mayor would surely have been reelected.*

Discussion: This sentence opens with an uncommon phrase and also ends with a lengthy verb phrase. Could that sentence have been phrased more clearly? Undoubtedly. **But just because you can think of a different or even better way to rewrite a sentence does not mean that the sentence as written is grammatically incorrect.**

Now that you know how awkward or stilted correct sentences can sound, you won't be so tempted to rely on your ear to determine whether some part of a sentence is grammatically incorrect.

> Sometimes a proofreading question will include a difficult or unfamiliar word like one of the following: *inviolable, usurped, inestimable, whereabouts, invasive, attests, belying.* Don't be intimidated and think that the word or the sentence is necessarily incorrect. The proofreading questions do not test vocabulary.

I'll have more to say about the topic of difficult words on these questions when we get to diction errors. Okay, then, let's explore the major grammatical errors on the SAT proofreading questions, arranged roughly in order of importance.

> Each grammatical category begins with sentences that illustrate the different ways that particular error can occur. You will get much more benefit from the remainder of this chapter if you try to identify the errors yourself before reading the explanations that follow. If this is your book, use a pencil to mark up the sentences; use the bracket technique.

Category:
Pronoun Errors

Illustrative Sentences

- *Madeline is a better badminton player than me even though she learned the game only a few months ago.*

- *Between you and I, I'm not sure whether our gym teacher can tie his own shoes much less lead us in calisthenics drills.*

- *The enthusiastic participants in the state fair's pie-eating contest, which ranged in age from seven to nearly seventy, all said that they had eaten nothing that morning.*

- *A paradox is a situation when an apparently reasonable statement leads to contradictory or inexplicable conclusions.*

As I mentioned earlier, pronoun problems are a major source of errors on the SAT Writing Test. To keep this category a reasonable size, I deal with ambiguous pronouns under the ambiguity category and singular-plural pronoun problems in the singular-plural category. (Again, this classification scheme is for our discussion purposes only; I could have classified things differently.) This category consists of using the *wrong* pronoun for the noun it refers to, and here I've included two different types of this error.

The first two illustrations are variations of subject-object pronoun errors. This error occurs when we use a subject pronoun or object pronoun when the other was required.

SUBJECT PRONOUNS	OBJECT PRONOUNS
I	me
you	you
we	us
he	him
she	her
they	them
who	whom

We use subject pronouns when they do things (*I hit the ball*) and object pronouns when they receive the action either of a verb (*I hit the ball*) or a preposition (*the ball is under me*). In certain sentence constructions, these distinctions can be confusing. Once we work through the illustrations you'll understand the principle behind this grammatical rule and it will be much easier to apply on the SAT.

In the first illustration, you wouldn't say *Madeline is better than me is*, would you? Of course not; you'd say, *Madeline is better than I am.* So a longer, correct version of the sentence is *Madeline is a better badminton player than I am,* which we can shorten to *Madeline is a better badminton player than I.* **The same distinction would have been apparent if we had reversed the order of the words without changing the meaning.** *I am a worse badminton player than Madeline* (not *Me is a worse badminton player than Madeline*).

In the second illustration, the word "between" is a preposition. Objects of prepositions require an object pronoun (*me*) not a subject pronoun (*I*). What's confusing the issue here is that the phrase "you and I" is usually heard (correctly) as a subject (*you and I are friends; let's you and I go to the movie*). The word "you" can also be an object (*you hit the ball; the ball hit you*), and in this instance "you" is the object of the preposition, too.

Let's consider a different context in which the distinction will be more obvious. Would you say "Paul stands by I" or "Paul stands by me"? The preposition "by" requires the object pronoun: me. If you're a little shaky on identifying prepositions, a quick review of our discussion on page 113 would be a good idea. The second sentence should begin, *Between you and me, I'm not sure whether . . .*

> Deleting, substituting, and reversing the order of certain words in a sentence are powerful techniques to clear up grammatical confusion when you're uncertain about the correctness of a particular word or phrase in a question.

Before we leave the topic of subject and object pronouns, the ever-popular is-it-who-or-whom question has not yet been tested on the SAT. Explaining when to use "who" and when to use "whom" can cause confusion, so let it suffice to say that the basic rule is that you'd use "who" whenever you'd reply—if it were a question—*he* or *she*, and "whom" whenever you'd reply *him* or *her*.

The third sentence illustrates the use of one pronoun when the noun requires another. The participants are people, so the pronoun "who" is required, not "which."

The fourth illustration is not strictly a pronoun error but it is closely analogous to the pronoun error we just discussed. **Be careful about the incorrect substituting of the words "when" or "where" for the pronouns "who" or "which."** Perhaps this error occurs because all these words are short and begin with "w." In any event, the word "when" refers to a time, but the context of this sentence requires the pronoun "which": *A paradox is a situation in which an apparently reasonable statement leads to contradictory or inexplicable conclusions.*

Related Errors

If this type of error tends to trip you up, you should also review the following categories:

- **ambiguity** (in the next chapter, page 166)
- **singular-plural errors** (page 125)

Category:
Singular-Plural Errors

Illustrative Sentences

- *A picture of the All-Star Team, composed of players from different leagues, were given to each member.*

- *The nature and consequences of the senator's alleged offense is serious, so unless he addresses the charges soon he will face disciplinary action by his fellow senators, and possible expulsion from the senate itself.*

- *For all their size, elephants, a plant-eating animal indigenous to Asia as well as Africa, are remarkably passive.*

- *Lance Armstrong, winner of the Tour de France, recommended that every serious cyclist invest in the best bicycle that they can afford.*

- *Tim and Jack want to get an A in their ethics class, and each student is prepared to do whatever it takes to achieve his goal.*

- *Fire officials attributed the large amount of property damage to the fact that not one of the hotel's more than two thousand rooms were equipped with the latest sprinklers or smoke detectors.*

- *Nobody ever achieved true success—whether in sports, business, or any other field—all by themselves.*

- *Neither George nor Helene were able to decide who should drive to the dance, so they flipped a coin.*

We saw an example of this error in our discussion of the bracket technique on page 118. These errors occur when a singular word or phrase is not in agreement with a plural word or phrase. Singular-plural errors can take a variety of forms, such as a plural pronoun referring to a singular noun or a plural noun taking a singular verb.

The trick to catching these errors is to isolate the true subject of a sentence. **Remember to use the bracket technique to isolate the distracting phrases so that you can focus on the important elements of each sentence.**

In the first example, the subject—*picture*—is singular, but the verb—*were*—is plural.

In the second example, the subject—*nature and consequences*—is plural, but, the verb—*is*—is singular.

In the third example, the subject and verb—*elephants* and *are*—are both plural; the problem is the singular modifying phrase *a plant-eating animal.* An acceptable revision of this sentence would be the following: *For all their size, elephants, plant-eating animals indigenous to Asia as well as Africa, are remarkably passive.* Yes, we could have revised the entire sentence with singular forms: *For all its size, the elephant, a plant-eating animal indigenous to Asia as well as Africa, is remarkably passive.*

The plural pronoun *they* in the fourth example refers to a singular noun, *cyclist.* The correct pronoun for this noun would have been *he* or *she.* An alternative solution would have been to make the phrase *every serious cyclist* plural: *serious cyclists.*

In the fifth example, Tim and Jack want to get As, not a single A.

In the sixth example, the bracket technique would be useful in revealing that the plural verb *were equipped* refers to *one,* a singular noun.

In the seventh example, the plural pronoun *themselves* refers to a singular pronoun, *nobody.*

In the eighth example, the subject of the sentence—*neither George nor Helene*—is singular, but the verb *were* is plural. The expression *neither-nor* is also singular. In fact, all the following pronouns are singular when they appear on the SAT (some rare, minor exceptions confuse most college English professors, so we won't worry about them):

> Singular pronouns: *anybody, anything, anyone, everybody, everything, everyone, somebody, something, someone, nobody, nothing, no one, none, each, either, neither, another*

Notice that some of these singular pronouns *seem* plural. The word *everybody* is really shorthand for "every single body," and so is singular. Everybody *is* present; everybody packed *his or her* lunch for the school field trip. *Everything* and *everyone* are also singular pronouns.

You don't have to memorize this list, but do familiarize yourself with the principle that all these words are singular.

Related Errors

If this type of error tends to trip you up, you should also review the following category:

- **pronoun errors** (page 122)

Category:
Idiom Errors

Illustrative Sentences

- *Many teenagers feel a great deal of pressure to conform with the values, attitudes, and behavior of their peers.*

- *I was prohibited, by my conscience as well as the team dress code, to wear a dress to the football scrimmage.*

- *The labor dispute was caused by both long hours as well as unsafe working conditions.*

This grammatical category is one of the most important in this entire section. The proofreading questions on your SAT will include at least one and as many as three idiom errors.

Preposition idioms make up the majority of these errors. No rule governs which preposition is correct for a given expression; idioms must be learned individually.

I am jealous *of* you; I am worried *about* you; I am grateful *to* you. Sometimes a different preposition can be used with a certain word depending on meaning intended. A scientist can be a credit *to* her university; a scientist can be credited *with* a discovery; a scientist can be given credit *for* her discovery. A common idiom error is the expression "different than"; the correct expression is "different from."

In the first example, the correct expression is "conform to"; the preposition "with" is incorrect. This example was relatively straightforward because the two words in the expression appeared together. When testing a prepositional idiom with both words together, the test writers will underline either both words or just the preposition. If the preposition is wrong, the entire expression is wrong.

Sometimes the same word can take different prepositions depending on the context and the meaning of the expression. When you write a letter to someone, you correspond *with* that person; when two things serve similar functions in different contexts, we say that one thing corresponds *to* the other. On the SAT Writing Test, the context will always be clear in such situations, so you'll always be able to decide which preposition is required.

Idiom errors get tricky when the test writers sandwich a long phrase between the two halves of an idiom to distract you from their connection. When the two halves are separated, the test writers usually just underline the preposition. But because the preposition is now separated from its "other half," it's easy to forget to look back to see whether the preposition is properly used. You have to train yourself to anticipate the second half of these idioms—and look for it—as soon as you encounter the first half.

Once again, the bracket technique comes in handy. In the second example, bracketing the middle phrase isolates the expression "prohibited to." The correct preposition to follow *prohibited* is "from."

Let's say that you weren't sure which preposition goes with *prohibited* and that your ear is no guide in this case. You might ask yourself what preposition goes with a synonym for *prohibited*, like *prevented*. **If you're not sure which preposition goes with a particular word, try substituting a familiar synonym: generally both words will take the same preposition.**

The other type of idiom error you need to look out for involves linking expressions. Certain expressions, a list of which follows, link two sets of words or phrases. These expressions are fixed idioms, and they require both halves to be correct. **Notice that the two parts of each linking expression will be separated: when you see the first half, you must anticipate the second half.** When one of these expressions is being tested on the SAT, often only the second part will be underlined. You'll need to be extremely careful and look back to see whether the underlined second half correctly goes with the first half, which may not be underlined (and which may therefore escape easy notice).

The following common linking expressions, which we will also discuss under parallel errors (page 131), all require both parts to be correct.

both — and

either — or

neither — nor

whether — or

not only — but also

In the third example, the phrase "as well as" incorrectly follows the word "both." Any of the following would have been acceptable versions of this sentence:

- *The labor dispute was caused by both long hours* and *unsafe working conditions.*

- *The labor dispute was caused by long hours* and *unsafe working conditions.*

- *The labor dispute was caused by long hours* as well as *unsafe working conditions.*

You don't have to memorize a long list of idioms. If you're on the lookout—two or three will show up on your test—you should have no difficulty spotting them. The following drill will give you additional practice.

Prepositional Idiom Drill

For each of the following words, supply the correct preposition. You'll find the answers at the end of this chapter on page 148.

1. *able* —
2. *capable* —
3. *comply* —
4. *conscious* —
5. *equivalent* —
6. *identical* —
7. *method* —
8. *opposed* —
9. *preoccupied* —
10. *relevant* —
11. *resemblance* —
12. *respond* —

Related Errors

If this type of error tends to trip you up, you should also review the following categories:

- **diction errors** (page 137)
- **parallel structure errors** (page 131)

Category:
Parallel Structure Errors

Illustrative Sentences

- *A talented athlete just like his older brother, Harold enjoys biking, skiing, and to play golf.*

- *Sharon is a great dancer but, despite years of diligent practice, poor at singing.*

- *The purpose of George Bernard Shaw's plays is more to instruct than providing entertainment.*

- *The short story contains not only comic elements but also it contains tragic elements.*

When a sentence contains related concepts, it should express those concepts in the same (or parallel) grammatical form. In the first example, the sports should be expressed in the same form: *biking, skiing, and golfing.*

In the second example, the related concepts are Sharon's dancing and singing and should take the same grammatical form, so either of the following versions is acceptable:

> *Sharon is a great dancer but, despite years of diligent practice, a poor singer.*

> *Sharon is great at dancing but, despite years of diligent practice, is poor at singing.*

On the SAT, either Sharon's singing or dancing would be underlined for correction. **Notice again that a non-underlined part of a sentence can affect an underlined part and that the two parts can be widely separated.**

In the third example, the sentence lists two purposes of Shaw's plays—instructing and entertaining—but the two ideas are in different grammatical forms. The following would be an acceptable version of this sentence:

> *The purpose of George Bernard Shaw's plays is more to instruct than to entertain.*

Finally, certain expressions connect related ideas, and these ideas must be expressed in the same grammatical form. We discussed these expressions under idiom errors (page 127), but they are important enough to repeat here. Under idiom errors we were concerned that the two parts of an expression both be included. Here we are concerned not with the two halves of the expressions but with the ideas they connect.

> The following expressions all require parallel forms of the phrases (the blanks) that they link:
>
> both — and
>
> either — or
>
> neither — nor
>
> whether — or
>
> not only — but also

In the fourth example, what follows "not only" (*comic elements*) is not in the same form as what follows "but also" (*it contains tragic elements*). The following would be an acceptable version of this sentence:

> *The short story contains not only comic elements but also tragic elements.*

Keep your eye out for these expressions; on average one of them will show up on an SAT.

Related Errors

If this type of error tends to trip you up, you should also review the following categories:

- **idiom errors** (page 127)
- **comparison errors** (page 133)

Category:
Comparison Errors

Illustrative Sentences

- *In some regions of the state, May's average rainfall is greater than April.*

- *The basic policies of the incumbent senator are no different from the candidate challenging her in the upcoming election.*

- *Like many other insects, the camouflage strategy of the viceroy butterfly is imitative: potential predators have a hard time distinguishing the tasty viceroy butterfly from the toxic monarch butterfly.*

Comparison errors are a type of parallel structure error: the two things being compared must have similar forms. These errors are easy to understand once you observe how a comparison error innocently arises. Using the first illustration, let's write out fully the comparison the writer intended:

> *In some regions of the state, May's average rainfall is greater than April's average rainfall.*

Okay, so far so good. The average rainfall in one month is being compared with the average rainfall in another month; no problem, yet. Now let's omit a couple of words that would be implied by the sentence structure:

> *In some regions of the state, May's average rainfall is greater than April's.*

Okay, this sentence is perfectly fine, too. Unfortunately, this version is different from the original sentence: *April* is not the same as *April's*. **It's easy to read right past this type of error because we unconsciously realize what the sentence "really meant." Notice how carefully you must read this sentence: a single letter and an apostrophe—changing a noun into its possessive form—make all the difference between a correct and an incorrect comparison.**

In the second illustration, the basic policies of the senator are being compared with the challenger. A proper comparison could have been the following:

> *The basic policies of the incumbent senator are no different from those of the candidate challenging her in the upcoming election.*

Notice that a mere two words—*those of*—make all the difference.

In the third illustration, a strategy (*the camouflage strategy of the viceroy butterfly*) is being compared with insects (*other insects*). A proper comparison would have been the following:

> *Like that of many other insects, the camouflage strategy of the viceroy butterfly is imitative: potential predators have a hard time distinguishing the tasty viceroy butterfly from the toxic monarch butterfly.*

If you're on your toes about this important error, it should not give you much trouble on the SAT.

Related Errors

If this type of error tends to trip you up, you should also review the following categories:

- **ambiguity** (in the next chapter, page 166)
- **parallel structure errors** (page 131)

Category:
Modifier Errors

Illustrative Sentences

- *While visiting the Statue of Liberty, Mr. Johnson's hat was blown into the harbor waters and quickly sank beneath the turbulent waves.*

- *Unaware the loudspeaker system's microphone was on, the entire school was treated to the principal's musical humming.*

Different variations of this error are referred to as "dangling modifiers" or "misplaced modifiers" or "squinting modifiers," but the underlying principle is simple: modifying phrases should be next to the nouns or pronouns that they're modifying. **Whenever a sentence begins with a modifying phrase followed by a comma, the subject of that modifier follows *immediately* after the comma.**

In the first example, "Mr. Johnson's hat" is the subject being modified by the opening phrase, "while visiting the Statue of Liberty." That's clearly not what the speaker "really meant," but that's literally what the sentence is saying. **Modifier errors are easy to read right past if you're not on the lookout because your brain subconsciously realizes the *intended* meaning—here that Mr. Johnson was visiting the Statue of Liberty—and so ignores the *literal* meaning.**

So you can understand the logic of this important grammatical principle, let's reverse the order of the sentence and put the modifying phrase at the end: *Mr. Johnson's hat was blown into the harbor waters and quickly sank beneath the turbulent waves while visiting the Statue of Liberty.* The sentence's meaning is now unclear: while *who* was visiting the Statue of Liberty? A grammatically correct version of the sentence would be, *While Mr. Johnson was visiting the Statue of Liberty, his hat was blown into the harbor waters and quickly sank beneath the turbulent waves.*

The intended meaning of the second sentence was that the *principal* was unaware the microphone was on, *but that's not what the sentence says.* The sentence says that the entire school was unaware the microphone was on. A grammatically correct version of this sentence would be, *Unaware the loudspeaker system's microphone was on, the principal treated the entire school to his musical humming.*

> Whenever a sentence begins with a phrase followed by a comma, make sure that what immediately follows is the subject of that phrase! These phrases often include a word ending in *ing* (like *visiting*, as in the first example), but not always (as in the second example).

Related Errors

If this type of error tends to trip you up, you should also review the following categories:

- **ambiguity** (in the next chapter, page 166)
- **comparison errors** (page 133)
- **logic errors** (in the next chapter, page 169)

Category:
Diction Errors

Illustrative Sentences

- *The space launch will take place next month, providing that the weather is good.*

- *The range and sheer number of Thomas Edison's inventions are indicative of a uniquely imaginary mind.*

- *Because the elderly dog's physical condition rapidly decreased, the veterinarian decided at long last to undertake the risky operation.*

- *The amount of people who go to the library these days is far less now that so much research is accessible on the Internet.*

- *The latest version of the software has less flaws in it than does the previous version.*

- *The third game of the series was delayed when the two referees disagreed among each other about a critical play.*

- *It was difficult to decide which of the two teachers wore the most outrageous costume to the school Halloween Dance.*

- *The cheering by the home team's fans in the stadium was so deafening as the buzzer went off that the spectators could not hardly hear the announcement that the final play had been disallowed.*

A diction error is using the wrong word for the meaning intended. You have to be very careful to spot this error because the word in the sentence is spelled almost exactly like the word that *should* have been used. The word *providing* in the first example should have been *provided*; the word *imaginary* in the second example should have been *imaginative*. A diction error is *not* a spelling error (which isn't tested on the SAT Writing Test), but rather the *wrong word*.

As I mentioned earlier, don't let a difficult or unfamiliar word intimidate you on the proofreading questions—but *do* be careful that the word is not a diction error. For example, the word "incredulous" (which means disbelieving or highly skeptical) once appeared as a diction error on an SAT when the word "incredible" should have been used.

In the first example, the word should have been *provided* (which means on the condition) rather than *providing* (which means supplying). In the second example, the word should have been *imaginative* (which means creative) rather than *imaginary* (which means unreal).

In the third example, the word "decreased" is incorrectly used. A condition can *deteriorate* but it cannot decrease.

In the fourth example, the word "amount" is incorrectly used. **Amount refers to quantities that cannot be counted; countable quantities (like how many people) require the word *number*.**

The fifth example contains a related diction error. **The words *less* and *more* refer to quantities that cannot be counted; countable quantities (like the number of flaws) require the words *fewer* or *greater*.**

The sixth example uses the word "among" incorrectly. **The word *between* is used when referring to two items; *among* is used when referring to three or more items.**

The seventh example contains a related error. **When comparing two items, use words like *more, happier, better, colder*; when comparing three or more items, use words like *most, happiest, best, coldest*.** The word *most* should have been *more*.

I've included the last example in this category because students who tend to miss diction errors also tend to miss this error. The phrase *could not hardly* should be *could hardly;* the "not" is redundant. **The synonyms *scarcely, barely,* and *hardly* are already negative, and so should not be used with words like *not, no,* or *none* (the correct expressions are *scarcely any, barely any,* or *hardly any*).**

> Don't go crazy second-guessing every word, hunting for suspected diction errors. Your SAT will probably contain just one—*usually among the last few usage questions.* (Breaking news: the last PSAT Writing Test had two *consecutive* diction errors; as predicted, they were among the last few usage questions.)

Related Errors

If this type of error tends to trip you up, you should also review the following categories:

- **adjective-adverb errors** (page 139)
- **idiom errors** (page 127)

Category:
Adjective-Adverb Errors

Illustrative Sentences

- *The exacting editor looked extremely close at the young author's final manuscript, but could find no typographical, grammatical, or other errors.*

- *The team of surgeons worked slowly and steady during the most delicate phase of the operation on the newborn infant's heart.*

I'm sure you know the difference between an adjective and an adverb (and if you're a little shaky on these terms you should take a moment to review the definitions on page 113). Adjectives modify only nouns or pronouns; adverbs modify primarily verbs, but also adjectives and other adverbs. What's the big deal? **What makes these errors so pesky is that the adjective and adverb forms of many words look almost identical, with two or three letters making all the difference.**

In the first example, the word "close" is supposed to modify the verb "looked" so it should take the adverb form, "closely." It's easy to misread this sentence because of the expression "taking a close look," in which the word "close" now modifies the noun, "a look," and so is in the correct adjective form.

In the second example, the adjective "steady" should be the adverb "steadily" because it modifies the verb "worked." Here again, if you weren't on the lookout for this type of error, you can see how it would be possible to miss it entirely (just like diction errors).

Related Errors

If this type of error tends to trip you up, you should also review the following category:

- **diction errors** (page 137)

Category:

Verb Tense Errors

Illustrative Sentences

- *After months of campaigning the councilmember finally had enough support for her proposal, so she calls for an immediate vote.*

- *The marathoner paused briefly in the race to drink a few sips of water after he had ran the first half at a record-setting pace.*

- *If both parties would have known how long and difficult the conflict was likely to be, the earlier settlement talks might have been more fruitful.*

We tend to think of tenses in terms of past, present, and future, but in fact variations of these tenses arise depending on when the action takes place relative to other events. Consider the following examples and you'll see that different situations would require different tenses.

Present Tenses

- *I clean up my room.*

- *I am cleaning up my room.*

- *I have cleaned up my room.*

- *I have been cleaning up my room.*

Past Tenses

- *I cleaned up my room.*

- *I was cleaning up my room.*

- *I had cleaned up my room.*

- *I had been cleaning up my room.*

Future Tenses

- *I will clean up my room.*

- *I will be cleaning up my room.*

- *I will have cleaned up my room.*

- *I will have been cleaning up my room.*

A sentence can contain more than one tense. (Because I *was* sick yesterday I *am* studying for a make-up test that I *will* take tomorrow.) If so, however, these tenses must be consistent with each other. In the first example, the past tense switches inconsistently with the present.

In the second example, the correct form of the past tense would be "had run." Occasionally the SAT will include a tense of an "irregular" verb like "to run." There are too many irregular verbs to list here, but usually your ear will be reliable detecting any such tense errors (a notable exception to our general caution about relying on your ear on the proofreading questions).

The verb phrase "would have" in the third example is used to construct conditional forms, as in the sentence, *I would have called you if I hadn't lost your phone number.* In this sentence, however, a past tense is required. The correct version of this sentence would have been, *If both parties had known . . .*

You don't have to memorize dozens of verb tenses. Just read carefully and realize that this error *does* show up once or twice on a test.

Related Errors

If this type of error tends to trip you up, you should also review the following category:

- **sentence fragments or run-ons** (page 142)

Sentence Fragments or Run-ons

Illustrative Sentences

- *The supportive words of the teacher offering little consolation to the despondent athlete who had been disqualified on a technicality.*

- *Although the two poets wrote about similar themes and used similar techniques.*

- *Since the migration patterns of many bird and other species were altered dramatically by greatly increased sunspot activity.*

- *The gymnastics coach told the audience of aspiring gymnasts that it takes ten years for athletes to develop their full potential, they should start serious training as early as possible.*

In informal writing a sentence fragment is sometimes used for emphasis, but on the SAT Writing Test sentence fragments are always incorrect. The basic grammatical principle is that every sentence requires a subject and a verb, and that sentence fragments lack one or both.

The tricky thing about sentence fragments is that if you read one too quickly, you may not notice that it is indeed a fragment. **In the first example, simply changing a single word—"offering" to "offered"—would have transformed the fragment into a complete sentence.**

The second and third examples are clauses that cannot stand on their own; they just hang there, incomplete. Although the poets had some things in common—what? Since the migration patterns were altered—what? Notice that deleting the first word of the second or third example would have transformed either into a complete sentence.

A sentence fragment, then, is incomplete; it cannot stand on its own. A run-on sentence has the opposite problem: it consists of two or more parts, either one of which could stand on its own.

The fourth example is a run-on sentence. **If we replaced the comma with a period, the two clauses could stand as complete sentences.** We'll discuss how to repair run-on sentences in the next section.

Sentence fragments and run-ons should not be difficult to spot now that you know to be on the lookout for them.

You know you shouldn't read proofreading and editing questions casually and that you need to break them down word by word and phrase by phrase. Analyzing sentences in this way presents its *own* danger, however: getting so caught up in the parts of the sentence that you lose sight of its meaning as a whole.

We'll go into more detail about this point in the next chapter but it bears repeating: you will usually need to read sentences in this section *at least* twice. The first time you chop the sentence down, making your way through it word by word and phrase by phrase. The second time, after you've analyzed all its parts, make sure you put them back together again and read through the entire sentence normally.

Related Errors

If this type of error tends to trip you up, you should also review the following categories:

- **transition or punctuation errors** (page 144)
- **verb tense errors** (page 140)
- **diction errors** (page 137)

Category:
Transition or Punctuation Errors

Illustrative Sentences

- *Many students are intimidated by math, they do not realize that solving problems is a lot like following simple recipes.*

- *Discount coupons are accepted at the store's Manhattan location, and they are not accepted at the store's New Jersey locations.*

- *The summer program offered intensive immersion sessions in the following languages, French, German, Spanish, Italian, Russian, Korean, Chinese, Japanese, and even Latin and ancient Greek.*

- *The principle is this, all contestants should be given an equal opportunity to prepare for the science fair.*

Sentence fragments and run-on sentences can be fixed with proper punctuation and by transitional words or phrases. I've included punctuation and transitional words together because they both serve the same function: indicating the transition between ideas and sentences.

You may have recognized after our previous discussion that the first example is a run-on sentence. When two halves of a sentence can both stand on their own, a comma is not the correct punctuation. The comma here should be replaced by either a period or a semicolon. Since most of the proofreading questions involve single sentences, providing a semicolon is the typical solution to this error. **On the SAT Writing Test, the semicolon is used primarily to link two independent thoughts.**

The second example illustrates a transition error. The word *and* should be *but* because the second clause introduces an idea contrary to that in the first clause. We can revise this sentence in two primary ways, so please examine the following sentences closely:

> *Discount coupons are accepted at the store's Manhattan location, but they are not accepted at the store's New Jersey locations.*

> *Discount coupons are accepted at the store's Manhattan location; they are not, however, accepted at the store's New Jersey locations.*

Notice that the subtle but important change from *but* to *however* requires

144

that we switch from a comma to a semicolon. The rationale for this grammatical point is too complicated for our purposes, so just notice the difference. You will not be asked to choose between these two solutions; all you need to do is recognize that both solutions are acceptable.

The third and fourth examples illustrate situations in which a colon is required. A colon is used to introduce specific information discussed earlier in a sentence, or to clarify the first half of the sentence. The correct versions of these sentences would be the following:

> *The summer program offered intensive immersion sessions in the following languages: French, German, Spanish, Italian, Russian, Korean, Chinese, Japanese, and even Latin and ancient Greek.*

> *The principle is this: all contestants should be given an equal opportunity to prepare for the science fair.*

Errors requiring the use of a colon do not appear often on the proofreading questions, but it's an easy concept, so it was worth covering quickly.

Related Errors

If this type of error tends to trip you up, you should also review the following category:

- **sentence fragments or run-ons** (page 142)

Moving On to Our Techniques

We've covered most of the grammatical errors you need to be on the lookout for on the proofreading and editing questions. I've saved a few categories for the next chapter because these categories are usually tested indirectly, in the answer choices, rather than directly in the original sentence.

Let's move on to our advanced lesson on general strategy and specific test-taking techniques for each proofreading question format. Remember to determine your grammatical blind spots. From time to time, return to this chapter to refresh yourself on the general categories. With practice, you should be able to spot any grammatical error they throw your way.

Answers to the Grammar Quiz on Page 109
(Please Don't Read These Explanations Until You've Taken the Quiz)

Only the first and last sentences were grammatically correct. The other eight sentences contained precisely the kinds of errors you're likely to see on your test. Give yourself credit only if you spotted the specific error. Remember: it's not enough merely to say something within a sentence "sounded wrong."

1) *The two pieces of woodwork by the apprentice carpenters were each so finely sanded that it took the trained eye of their teacher to determine that the oak tabletop was more nearly flat than was the pine tabletop.* (**Error-free sentence:** although this sentence may seem awkward, the idea it expresses has to be phrased this particular way. It's impossible for one thing to be flatter than another—something is either flat or it's not—but one thing can be more *nearly* flat.)

2) *After a thorough examination, the doctor told Melissa that she should exercise more vigorously as well as more regularly.* (**Ambiguity error:** we aren't sure whether the doctor was advising Melissa that she should exercise more regularly, or admitting that she herself should exercise more regularly.)

3) *The photo-finish of the 100-meter race was so close that each of the first five finishers thought that they had won.* (**Singular-plural error:** the pronoun *each* is singular, so instead of the word *they*, which is plural, the sentence should use the singular *he* or *she.*)

4) Titus Andronicus, *one of Shakespeare's lesser-known works and the inspiration for the popular movie* Gladiator, *is a play where the noble protagonist suffers a tragic fate.* (**Pronoun error:** the sentence should read, *a play in which . . .*)

5) *The academic habits and expectations of teenage girls are very different from teenage boys.* (**Comparison error:** this sentence compares girls' academic habits with boys, but the writer meant to compare girls' habits with those of boys.)

6) *The causes of the American Civil War were not just social, but also economical and technological.* (**Diction error:** *economical* means thrifty. Whoops. The word should have been *economic.*)

7) *All of the former classmates are planning on attending the formal reunion ceremony, and most have said that they will also attend the reception party afterwards.* (**Idiom error.** You don't plan *on* doing something, you plan *to* do it.)

8) *When completely painted with the third and final coat of varnish, Peter set the antique chair outside on the porch to get some sun.* (**Modifier error:** presumably the chair was painted, not Peter! The sentence should read, *When Peter had completely painted the antique chair, he set it outside on the porch.*)

9) *"By the time you get back,"* Tim assured his doubtful mother and father as they were preparing to leave for a parent-teacher conference, *"I promise I will complete my history term paper."* (**Verb tense error:** Tim is promising that by the time his parents return, he *will* have completed his paper.)

10) *Were it not for the downturn of the local economy last year, the then-popular mayor would surely have been reelected.* (**Error-free sentence:** the sentence could have been phrased differently and certainly more clearly, but it contains no grammatical errors.)

If you got them all right, you did *amazingly* well. Good for you. But if you had trouble with a few or even more than a few of these questions, you can dramatically improve your score on the proofreading questions. How? With two or three hours of easy review in this chapter and the next. That's a promise.

Back to the discussion on page 110. (Don't peek at the answers to the next drill!)

Answers to the Prepositional Idiom Drill on Page 130

1. *able to*
2. *capable of*
3. *comply with*
4. *conscious of*
5. *equivalent to*
6. *identical to*
7. *method of*
8. *opposed to*

9. *preoccupied with*

10. *relevant to*

11. *resemblance to*

12. *respond to*

If you missed more than a few of these, try to be more alert to idioms in your regular classroom reading assignments. Now that you know to be on the lookout for prepositional idioms, you'll quickly become familiar with the more common ones.

RocketRules for Attacking the Different Question Formats

A Quick Recap of the Previous Chapter

In the previous chapter we covered the major grammatical concepts you'll be tested on in the proofreading and editing section. We actually have a few remaining grammatical concepts to discuss, but we'll introduce those topics when we examine the three different question types individually. So now you're ready to learn RocketReview's techniques for answering the major question types.

You'll Have 35 Minutes to Answer 45 Questions—
So You'll Have to *Fly!*

A simple calculation of 45 questions in 35 minutes reveals an average of just under 50 seconds per question for you to read each sentence, identify its error (if any), locate and darken the appropriate oval on your answer sheet, and then find the next question in your test booklet. When you consider how much time the mechanics of filling in your answer sheet takes up, you're left with five to ten seconds to read and evaluate each choice.

That's not very much time. Once you know how to analyze these questions, however, you'll slice through this section with remarkable efficiency.

An Overview of the Section

The 45 questions in this section include the following:

- 22 *usage questions*

- 16 *sentence correction questions*

- 7 *paragraph correction questions*

The usage questions ask you to identify isolated errors in otherwise correct sentences. Here's a simple example:

Example: No matter how hard an artist <u>tries</u>, no
                                                            A
                 individual <u>is</u> truly free <u>from</u> the influences
                             B   C
                 of <u>their</u> predecessors. <u>No error</u>
                    D   E

The sentence correction questions ask you to revise poorly written sentences or parts of sentences. Here's a simple example:

Example: Most people seem to prefer realistic art <u>than abstract art</u>.

    (A) than abstract art
    (B) than they prefer art that is abstract
    (C) to abstract art
    (D) instead of abstract art
    (E) rather than abstract art

> **Both the usage questions and the sentence correction questions are arranged roughly in order of difficulty, progressing from easy to medium to difficult. Be especially careful on the last four or five questions of both of these types.**

The paragraph correction questions ask you to revise poorly written portions of a student's rough essay. Rather than reprint an entire essay here, I'll direct you to examples of these questions on page 175.

Okay, now that you have the big picture, let's examine each of these question types thoroughly.

The First Question Type:
Usage Questions

The first 22 of the 45 questions in this section are usage questions. The typical sentence of this format is 23 words long. Four segments, of one to three words long each, will be underlined, followed by a fifth underlined option ("No Error").

Here are the directions. These directions will not change on the actual test, so do not waste time reading them in the exam room.

Strategies for Answering the Usage Questions

The usage questions can seem tricky but are straightforward, so I'll quickly summarize our strategies for answering them.

As always, you don't have to memorize the following strategies. With just minimal practice (which you're getting here), you'll find that techniques will soon become second nature to you.

- **These questions come first, but tackle them second. Because this question format is the trickiest of the proofreading and editing questions, begin instead with the sentence correction questions (questions 23 through 38).** Using diligent process of elimination on the sentence correction questions provides an excellent warm-up for the trickier usage questions.

- **The 22 usage questions are arranged roughly in order of difficulty.** The first seven or so are relatively easy, the next seven or so are medium, and the last seven are difficult. Don't second-guess your analysis on the earlier easy questions, and be especially careful on the harder ones near the end.

- First, **as with every other question type on this entire test—math, verbal, and other grammar—**you must, must, *must* mark up your test booklet as you analyze each usage question. There are simply too many things to keep track of to attempt your analysis "in your head." **As Albert Einstein said, your pencil is smarter than you are—so use it!**

- An excellent use of your pencil, as I recommended in the previous chapter, is to insert parentheses around clauses and prepositional phrases. These phrases usually add distracting detail to the basic *idea* of the sentence and often distract you from the grammatical error by separating parts of the sentence in disagreement.

- An underlined word or phrase must be *grammatically incorrect* to qualify as an error. It's not enough to say of a particular underlined segment that you "could have said it differently." In other words, you're looking for grammatical errors on these questions, not stylistic differences.

- Remember that the non-underlined portions of a sentence can cause one of the underlined words or phrases to be wrong, so don't just examine the underlined segments. Indeed, an underlined segment can be wrong because it does not agree with a word or phrase earlier in the sentence.

- Don't fall for the trap of grabbing the first choice that sounds like it might be correct. Make sure you use process of elimination. If you're not sure whether an underlined word or phrase is correct—let's say choice A—circle that choice and continue looking for errors in choices B, C, and D. Don't waste time thinking about something that confuses you when there may be a more obvious error later in the sentence.

  (So from the example in the directions, if you couldn't decide whether choice A was correct, you should use your pencil to put a squiggly mark next to the letter and then immediately move on to the other choices. By the time you get to choice D you might be absolutely certain that it is wrong, saving you the time and energy of wrestling with choice A.)

- Choice E—No Error—is correct on approximately three or four of the 22 usage questions, but the choice tends *not* to be correct on the difficult questions (the last five or six of this type). So if you're stuck on a difficult question between, say, choice D and choice E, the odds favor choice D slightly over choice E. See the next point, however.

- If you're really stuck on a question and can't decide whether a particular choice—say, choice B—is incorrect, or whether the answer is choice E, No Error, jot down "B/E" in the margin, circle the question number, and move on. When you've finished attempting all the 22 usage questions, count up how many choice Es you're already sure are answers.

  Let's say that you have only one choice E so far and three questions you're still unsure about. Since you're expecting three to four Es here, and you have only one so far, the odds favor at least two Es out of the three remaining questions. **These are just odds to help tilt you one way or another when you're really stuck.**

Okay, let's move on to the next question type.

The Second Question Type:
Sentence Correction Questions

The next 16 of the 45 questions in this section are sentence corrections. The typical sentence of this format is 21 words long. Some or even all of each sentence—on average a bit less than half—will be underlined, usually with one or more errors (unlike the usage questions, which have at *most* one error). Your job is to consider which, if any, of the offered alternatives is better than the original version.

Here are the directions to the sentence correction questions; these directions will not change on the actual test, so do not waste time reading them in the exam room.

Strategies for Answering the Sentence Correction Questions

Like the usage questions, approximately one-sixth of the 16 sentence correction questions will be error-free, though here choice A is the error-free selection. **Since the section contains 16 questions of this type, we're expecting 2 or 3 As here.** If haven't found a single "no error" sentence or even just one "no error" sentence, you've very likely been too critical and one of the "corrections" you found wasn't a correction at all.

On the other hand, getting four "no errors" (choice A) out of the 16 sentence correction questions is already getting a bit high, and five is definitely too many: you've overlooked an error in one or two of those five sentences.

Unlike the usage questions, sentence correction questions *can*, and often do, contain more than one error, so it's important that you use your pencil all the time as you mark the sentences using process of elimination.

155

Although sentence correction questions come second, I strongly recommend that you attack them *first, before* the usage questions. The big danger on the usage questions is reading "right past" the error. The nice thing about the sentence corrections is that the process of elimination you use to answer the questions will remind you of the different types of errors you need to be on the lookout for, giving you an excellent warm-up for the trickier usage questions. Students who answer the sentence correction questions first gain an average of a question or two over those students who answer the questions in their normal order.

As you read these questions, remember that a non-underlined part of a sentence can make an underlined part wrong, so be sure to read the entire sentence—not just the underlined portion. Then follow our three simple steps to find the answer.

Step 1:   Identify any errors in the original sentence.

Step 2:   Eliminate all options that contain any of the original errors.

Step 3:   Apply process of elimination to the remaining choices to isolate the error.

Let's take a quick look at the first two steps; the third will require a more detailed discussion.

Step 1 on the Sentence Corrections

Your first goal is simply to identify any error or errors in the original sentence—assuming it has any. As you know, not every sentence correction question *has* an error, but you should *try* to identify any error or errors in the original sentence.

If you can't identify any errors in the original sentence—don't worry, it happens—go immediately to the third step below: process of elimination.

Step 2 on the Sentence Corrections

Assuming you've identified an error in the original sentence, your next step is to eliminate choice A, the original sentence, and any other sentence that contains that error.

Usually one or two of the other five choices will contain the same error as the original sentence, so you can eliminate those choices, too.

Step 3 on the Sentence Corrections

Once you've narrowed the field to the remaining choices, apply process of elimination to find the answer. This third step includes four powerful elimination techniques to isolate the answer.

Process of Elimination Techniques on the Sentence Corrections

We have four simple process of elimination techniques that almost always lead directly to the answer:

Sentence Corrections Elimination Technique #1: Avoid long choices.

Sentence Corrections Elimination Technique #2: Avoid ambiguous choices.

Sentence Corrections Elimination Technique #3: Avoid choices that mangle the original meaning.

Sentence Corrections Elimination Technique #4: Avoid choices that introduce *new* errors.

I'll show you how to apply these powerful techniques to a sample question on page 172, but before we do so, let's spend a little time examining each one.

Process of Elimination Technique #1: Avoid Long Choices

Nobody likes wading through wordy text to extract information that could have been expressed more simply and directly. Conciseness, then, is a characteristic of all good writing (though it often takes several editing drafts to remove all unnecessary words from a single sentence, much less a paragraph or more). Fortunately, on the SAT you won't be required to edit wordy sentences. Instead, all you'll have to do is select the most concise choice from the options offered—assuming, of course, that the choice is also grammatically correct.

> On the sentence correction questions, the shortest choice is correct almost half the time; two-thirds of the time the answer is the shortest or second shortest choice! (You don't have to count up the number of words; just eyeball the choices.) On the flip side, only one-sixth of the time is the answer to a sentence correction question either the longest or second longest choice. In other words, the answer is *four times* more likely to be one of the two shortest choices than it is one of the two longest choices. If you're stuck between two choices and you just can't decide, select the shorter choice.

Wordiness can arise from many sources, such as awkwardly lengthy phrases when shorter alternatives exist, repeating words or ideas that can be implied in the structure of the sentence, and even logical redundancies. As usual, reviewing a few examples is more enlightening than academic explanations.

Illustrations of Wordy Phrases

To give you an idea of the range and types of wordiness on the test, I've prepared the following chart of examples. If you want to get some practice reducing redundancies without hints, cover up the second two columns with a piece of paper.

INSTEAD OF THIS WORDY PHRASE	WHY NOT SIMPLY SAY	DISCUSSION
ask a question whether	*ask whether*	What else could you ask?
because of the fact that	*because*	The other words are unnecessary.
end result	*result*	Results are almost always at the end, and intermediate results can be specified as such.
small number of	*few*	The definition of "few" is "small number of," so why not use the word rather than its definition?
financial cost	*cost*	Costs are almost always financial; other costs (such as human costs) can be specified as such.
reach a conclusion	*conclude*	Conclusions are always reached, just as something asked is always a question.
large in size	*large*	Large already refers to size, so the other words are unnecessary.
the month of September	*September*	What else is September?
is a cause of	*causes*	"Is" is a form of the verb "to be," and generally speaking, such "passive verbs" are wordier than their "active" equivalents.

Scavenger Hunting for Wordy Phrases

As I mentioned in the previous chapter, the proofreading and editing questions are just one big grammatical scavenger hunt: half the battle is simply knowing what you should be looking for.

Now we'll be looking for examples of wordy phrases and ways these phrases can be revised or simply eliminated. After you've had a little practice here you'll be a pro at catching them on the actual exam.

I'll walk you through the following examples of eliminating needless words from sentences. If you want to try your hand at the examples before you read my revisions, use a sheet of paper to cover the lines below each original version.

Original Version: *Paul is a talkative person.*

Revised Version: *Paul is talkative.*

> **Discussion:** What else would Paul be but a person? (Okay, perhaps Paul is a talkative parrot, but let's stay on planet Earth.)

Original Version: *The ball was hit by the bat.*

Revised Version: *The bat hit the ball.*

> **Discussion:** Replacing passive verbs—usually those with a variation of "to be"—with active verbs almost always results in shorter sentences.

> On the sentence corrections, choices containing variations of the verb "to be"—*is, am, are, be, been, being, was, were*—are overwhelmingly frequently wrong, especially those containing the word "being." When you're trying to decide between equally long choices, avoid those options that contain such words.
>
> Using forms of "to be" is not intrinsically wrong; indeed, many ideas cannot be expressed without that verb. The point is to avoid *wordy phrases*, which often include forms of "to be."

Original Version: *The board of directors debated whether the mandatory* *retirement age should be lowered to sixty years old.*

Revised Version: *The board of directors debated whether the mandatory retirement age should be lowered to sixty.*

Discussion: When speaking about human beings beyond their infancy—and not about fruit flies or infants—age can always be assumed to be years and not days or months.

Original Version: *The reason the meeting was cancelled is because not enough people responded to the invitation.*

Revised Version: *The meeting was cancelled because not enough people responded to the invitation.*

Discussion: "The reason is because" is a common redundant expression. The word "because" means to give reasons, so we need either one word or the other but not both. An equally acceptable version of this sentence would be the following: *The reason the meeting was cancelled is that not enough people responded to the invitation.*

Original Version: *The reason Paula moved to Paris is because she wished to exchange her dull lifestyle for something more exciting.*

Revised Version: *The reason Paula moved to Paris is that she wished to exchange her dull lifestyle for something more exciting.*

Discussion: The revision isn't shorter than the original sentence, but "reason" and "because" are redundant: use one word or the other but not both.

Original Version: *When students are late to school, they must check in at the principal's office before going to class.*

Revised Version: *When late to school, students must check in at the principal's office before going to class.*

Discussion: "Students" is implied in the opening phrase, so it's unnecessary to repeat it.

Original Version: *Steven is the team captain, and he is over six feet tall in* *height.*

Revised Version: *Steven, the team captain, is over six feet tall.*

Discussion: Strictly speaking, we probably need to retain "tall" but "tall in height" is definitely redundant.

Original Version: *The widespread computer failures were because of the electrical storm that occurred last night.*

Revised Version: *Last night's electrical storm caused the widespread computer failures.*

Discussion: Changing the sentence from the passive form to the active saved us three words; introducing the possessive form for "last night" saved us another two words. **Notice that on this type of question, a sentence or choice can be wordy in more than one place.**

Original Version: *This is the long-lost abstract painting by Picasso which was recently purchased in a garage sale.*

Revised Version: *This long-lost abstract painting by Picasso was recently purchased in a garage sale.*

Discussion: Notice the subtle but important difference between the phrase we used—*painting by Picasso*—and a shorter phrase that seems the same but is not: *Picasso's painting.* This alternative changes the meaning by introducing an ambiguity: is Picasso's painting one that he owns, or one that he painted? **Be careful that a shorter version does not change the meaning of the original sentence.**

Original Version: *Stanley loves comedies, and Carrie loves dramas.*

Revised Version: *Stanley loves comedies; Carrie, dramas.*

Discussion: The revised version is an extreme form of word reduction, and may even sound odd, but it is a grammatically correct variation of the original sentence. **Notice that concise versions sometimes sound a bit strange when compared to longer versions.** It takes even experienced authors a great deal of editing and revising to find the most concise and powerful way to express a particular thought. In everyday speech, which is what our ears are attuned to, we rarely bother to search for the most concise versions of our thoughts.

Original Version: *Meredith, who is an excellent swimmer, is also an excellent runner.*

Revised Version: *Meredith, a fine swimmer, is also an excellent runner.*

Discussion: Here's another variation: *A fine swimmer, Meredith is also an excellent runner.*

Original Version: *It is possible that the spring outdoor dance may be rained out, in which case the dance will take place in the school gymnasium.*

Revised Version: *The spring outdoor dance may be rained out, in which case the dance will take place in the school gymnasium.*

Discussion: Notice that "it is possible" and "may" are redundant.

Original Version: *Some members on a soccer team play offense. All the others play defense.*

Revised Version: *Members of a soccer team play either offense or defense.*

Discussion: Combining two sentences often allows you to eliminate repetitive elements, although you're more likely to encounter combining sentences in the last question type—paragraph correction questions—than on the sentence correction questions.

Original Version: *After conducting an investigation of possible interactions, the pharmaceutical company combined together three different kinds of existing treatments with the result being the creation of a new wonder drug.*

Revised Version: *After investigating possible interactions, the pharmaceutical company combined three kinds of existing treatments to create a new wonder drug.*

Discussion: *Conducting an investigation* is the same as *investigating; combined together* is redundant; *three* *different kinds* is redundant; and *with the result being* is embarrassingly wordy. Remember: a sentence can be wordy in more than one place.

On the sentence correction questions, choices containing forms of verbs ending in "ing"—like *being, going, having, looking, making, using, taking, getting*—are overwhelmingly frequently wrong. (Though on this particular sentence, we were able to eliminate only one of the two gerunds: *being* but not *conducting.*) Interestingly, the word "being" is doubly dangerous: it's a verb ending in "ing" *and* it's a form of the word "to be."

Okay, now it's your turn. The following exercise will help sharpen your eye for the various ways prose can tightened—and thereby made more powerful—by deleting extraneous words. Again, on the actual exam you won't have to come up with the most concise way of expressing an idea, but rather choose the most concise and effective version from among the choices offered.

Conciseness Drill

Directions: Edit each of the following sentences to make it more concise. As a hint, the revised versions—and there may be several ways to make any particular sentence more concise—saved an average of two and a half words over the original versions. **Be careful not to eliminate so many words that you introduce an ambiguity into the sentence, or otherwise change its meaning.** You'll find the answers on page 183 at the end of this chapter.

1. *Clancy's latest novel is an exciting one.*

2. *Grace is taller than her brother is.*

3. *Mia was granted a two-week extension by our teacher for the term paper.*

4. *It was a blow to the varsity volleyball team to lose to the junior varsity squad.*

5. *Mr. Phillips, the man who was last year's winner, came in second place in this year's pie-eating contest.*

6. *Scholars often work hard and they often work in isolation.*

7. *There were two cats trapped in the tall oak tree.*

8. *Any individual person who submits an application after the cutoff date will be ineligible for the competition.*

9. *The delay caused our principal to be angry.*

10. *The dog that Molly has is so lazy that he practically expects to be carried on his walks.*

11. *Theo provided a summary of the novel for his World Literature class.*

12. *The board of directors did not succeed in reaching a consensus on who should be elected treasurer.*

Remember that conciseness is almost always tested in the sentence corrections section; only very rarely is redundancy tested in the usage questions. Almost all of the time regarding this type of error, your job is to pick the shortest version presented (assuming that choice is otherwise grammatically unobjectionable). On the usage questions, don't fret too much over whether a particular underlined word or phrase is redundant or wordy—if it is it will be *screamingly* obvious.

Process of Elimination Technique #2: Avoid Ambiguous Choices

As I mentioned earlier, eliminating words in a sentence has two potential dangers: creating ambiguities or changing the sentence's original meaning. We'll consider them separately in our second and third elimination techniques.

Ambiguities often, but not always, arise from pronouns that can refer to more than one noun in a sentence. In the previous chapter we discussed pronoun errors (see page 122). A pronoun error consists of using the wrong pronoun for a given noun. *Ambiguous* pronouns arise when a pronoun can refer to more than one noun in a sentence.

Ambiguities, like modifier errors and comparison errors, can be difficult to spot because we subconsciously figure out what the speaker *meant* to say, even though the sentence is literally saying something different or can be interpreted in more than one way. Since your brain instantly and subconsciously figures out what the sentence is *trying* to say—even though the sentence doesn't—it's easy to miss the error completely because your brain ignores the error it has already corrected.

Ambiguities are usually tested *indirectly*, among the suggested alternatives in the sentence correction questions rather than as the original version.

I'll walk you through the following examples of eliminating needless words from sentences. If you want to try your hand at the examples before you read my revisions, use a sheet of paper to cover the lines below each original version.

Illustrations of Ambiguity

Original Version: *If your arm hurts after lifting a weight during exercise, you should apply ice to it immediately rather than wait until the next day.*

Possible Revision: *If your arm hurts after lifting a weight during exercise, you should apply ice to your arm immediately rather than wait until the next day.*

Discussion: Ambiguities are often funny. The pronoun "it" is ambiguous—not wrong—because it can refer either to "arm" or "weight." **It is not sufficient to point out the absurdity of applying ice to a weight, or think "of course" the sentence "meant" to say that the ice should be applied to your arm; the sentence is still ambiguous.**

Original Version: *Because weather conditions vary greatly between seasons, farmers must learn to adjust their methods when changing.*

Possible Revision: *Because weather conditions vary greatly between seasons, farmers must learn to adjust their methods when the seasons change.*

Discussion: Here we have an instance of an ambiguous phrase—*when changing*—rather than an ambiguous pronoun. Did the sentence mean when the *seasons* change or when the *weather conditions* change? (We could even argue that possibly the *farmers* were changing!) Of course, perhaps the sentence should have read, *when the weather conditions change.* **On the SAT you won't have to resolve the ambiguities you find, but rather just avoid choices containing ambiguities.**

Original Version: *Culver City nearly gained 3,000 inhabitants since the last census was taken a decade ago.*

Possible Revision: *Culver City gained nearly 3,000 inhabitants since the last census was taken a decade ago.*

Discussion: Although the sentence *probably* means that Culver City gained approximately 3,000 inhabitants, the original version *could* be interpreted literally to mean that it was about to gain 3,000 new inhabitants, but didn't.

Okay, now you're on your own.

Spotting Ambiguities Drill

Directions: Each of the following sentences contains one or more ambiguities. When you've identified an ambiguity, revise the sentence to remove the error. Again, you'll be able to devise at least two ways of resolving any ambiguity: one for each way of interpreting it. You'll find the answers on page 185 at the end of this chapter.

1.   *Randolph's sister gave him a present on his twenty-first birthday, which was nice.*

2.   *Kara was less satisfied with her painting than her art teacher.*

3.   *Millicent's music teacher demonstrated proper keyboard technique with a smile.*

4.   *In some European capitals such as Madrid, they eat dinner very late in the evening and go out afterwards for even more entertainment.*

5.   *Sophomores outnumbered juniors and seniors at the school dance, so the principal decided that she should open an additional room for them.*

Process of Elimination Technique #3:
Avoid Choices That Mangle the Original Meaning

The second danger in creating more concise versions of a sentence is altering its meaning. Choices that change the meaning of the original sentence can be eliminated.

If you read the choices carefully, you'll have no difficulty spotting the more obvious changes in meaning. Sometimes, however, the changes are more subtle (such as the distinction between "Picasso's painting" and "painting by Picasso" we discussed in the Scavenger Hunting for Wordy Phrases exercise on page 160).

The problem once again is the tendency of our brains subconsciously to correct minor changes in a sentence's meaning. Instead of taking what a subtly incorrect option says *literally,* our brains figure out what the sentence was *trying* to say—so our conscious minds all too easily "read past" the error unwittingly.

A related error occurs when an option has a subtle flaw in logic that did not appear in the original sentence. The following examples illustrate the kinds of errors in logic that might occur on your SAT. If you want practice spotting this kind of error, see whether you can spot the flaw by covering up the discussion that follows each example.

Illustration: *The principal announced that to his great surprise, the combined contributions to the school fund-raising drive by juniors and the seniors was less adequate than those by sophomores and freshmen.*

Discussion: "Adequate" is one of those words—like flat, circular, or perfect—that are absolute. Something cannot be more adequate than something else: it's either adequate or not adequate.

Illustration: *The population gains it made since 1980 more than made up for the losses in the decade prior to 1980, so New York City remains larger than any metropolitan area in the United States.*

Discussion: Since New York City *is* a metropolitan area in the United States, the sentence—*when taken literally*—is a logical impossibility. The sentence *meant* to say that New York City is larger than any *other* city in the United States.

Illustration: *Despite the incumbent governor's optimistic public statements regarding his chances for reelection, privately he was unsure whether he would win or lose the election.*

Discussion: If we take this sentence literally—which we always should on the SAT—it's nonsensical. The governor *can't* be unsure whether he will win or lose the election; if he's running for reelection he will *definitely* either win or lose. The governor could be unsure whether he will *win* the election; the governor could be unsure whether he will *lose* the election; but he cannot be unsure of both!

> Don't go crazy. Logic errors are far less common than the other errors we've discussed, and are almost always tested in the sentence corrections section. Only exceedingly rarely is this error tested in the usage questions.

Process of Elimination Technique #4:
Avoid Choices That Introduce *New* Errors

Although by this point you've identified any error or errors in the *original* sentence, you still have to be on guard against choices that clear up the original error, but introduce a new one!

For example, the original sentence might contain a faulty comparison error. So you eliminate choice A, the original sentence, and choices B and D, say, that also contain that error. So now you have to decide between choices C and E. You're about to choose choice E because it's more concise than choice C when all of a sudden you notice—whoops, choice E introduces a pronoun error that wasn't present in the original sentence. So process of elimination compels you to select choice C even though it's a bit longer than choice E.

> An excellent way to narrow your search during process of elimination is to focus only on the *differences* between two choices. If two remaining choices are identical except that one ends in a comma, say, and the other ends in a semicolon, you know that you should focus your attention on the punctuation. If two remaining choices are identical except that one contains the word "is" and the other contains the word "are," you should focus on whether the subject of the verb is singular or plural.

Putting It All Together:
A Powerful Strategy for the Sentence Correction Questions

We've covered a lot of ground on this question type, so a quick recap is in order.

- First, if possible, identify any errors in the original sentence. (On average, three of the sixteen sentence correction questions will be error-free.)

- Next, eliminate any choices that repeat those errors.

- Finally, use process of elimination to isolate the answer. **Once you've eliminated any options that contain the original error, the answer is the shortest remaining option nearly 90 percent of the time!** Beware of options that clear up the original error but introduce a new one.

Work through all the choices methodically, especially on the harder sentence correction questions. Since these questions are arranged in order of difficulty, the harder questions will be the last four or five of the sixteen questions. **If you're really stuck, the answer to hard sentence correction questions—the last few—also tends *not* to be choices A or B.**

The process of elimination techniques are simple, but there's no way you can keep everything straight if you attempt to do it all "in your head." **As always, use your pencil to mark up the choices. If you get stuck on a question, write down your remaining options in the margin ("A/D" for example) and move on to the next question.** Later questions often remind you of error categories you may have forgotten about.

Applying Our Techniques to a Sentence Correction Question

Again, you don't have to memorize these strategies. In the next example you'll see how simple it is to apply all of our sentence correction techniques.

Example: After playing the decisive role in winning World War II, more economic aid was delivered by the United States to its former enemies than to its allies.

   (A)   After playing the decisive role in winning World War II, more economic aid was delivered by the United States to its former enemies than to its allies.

   (B)   After playing the decisive role in winning World War II, the United States delivered more economic aid to their former enemies than their allies.

   (C)   After playing the decisive role in winning World War II, the economic aid delivered by the United States to its former enemies was more than its allies.

   (D)   More economic aid was delivered from the United States to its former enemies than to its allies after it played a decisive role in winning World War II.

   (E)   After playing the decisive role in winning World War II, the United States delivered more economic aid to its former enemies than to its allies.

Discussion: First we see whether we can identify any error or errors in the original sentence. Choice A is a modifier error, since the United States played the decisive role, not economic aid. So we eliminate A, but also C, which contains the same modifier error. Two down, two to go.

Choice B corrects the modifier error, but introduces a singular-plural error because United States is a singular noun (it's a country) but "their" is a plural pronoun. **Once you spot one error in a choice, eliminate that choice and move on!** You don't have to search for additional errors in that choice—unless, of course, you were unsure whether the "error" you caught was indeed an error.

(Did you notice that B contains an ambiguity error? The sentence could mean that the United States delivered more aid to its former enemies than its former allies delivered to these enemies. The more likely meaning intended, of course, was that the United States gave more aid to its former enemies than the United States gave to its allies.) Three down, one to go.

Choice D not only is longer than E, but also contains an ambiguous pronoun ("it" could refer to the United States or to the economic aid). So D is out and E is the answer.

The No-Error Sentences Are Sometimes Clunkers

Sometimes you'll encounter an absolute clunker of a sentence in the sentence correction questions and you're convinced that it *has* to be wrong. You can't put your finger on the exact error, but you decide that there's just no way the original version—choice A—could be correct.

So you apply process of elimination to B, but that's got a definite wordiness error. So you cross it off and then move on to C—but that choice is even worse. And so on to D and E, in which you find yet additional concrete errors.

After which you're surprised to discover yourself back at choice A, the original version, as the only option left standing since each of the suggested alternatives was even worse.

I just wanted to warn you that many of the no-error sentences are *not* good examples of English prose. In short, the *best* option is not necessarily a good option.

The Third Question Type: Paragraph Correction Questions

The last seven questions in the proofreading and editing section are paragraph correction questions. You'll find a brief 200- to 250-word student's essay, or rather the *first draft* of an essay. The essay will typically consist of four paragraphs comprising 14 sentences, with each sentence numbered for your reference.

Here are the directions to the paragraph correction questions; these directions will not change on the actual test, so do not waste time reading them in the exam room.

The good news is that these questions tend to be much, much easier than the other two types of proofreading questions. You'll be able to apply everything you've already learned about proofreading and editing to these questions, too.

The Rough Draft Essay That You're Asked to Correct Is *Very* Rough

Because the paragraph correction questions follow an essay that looks a lot like a typical reading passage, you may be tempted to read the essay carefully before answering the questions.

Don't.

The student draft is so badly written, with so many errors, that if you read it closely you may get very confused and waste valuable time trying to make sense of everything. All you need to answer the questions is a rough idea of what the essay is about, which you can get from a quick skimming of the passage—15 to 30 seconds; at most a minute.

The New Paragraph Correction Question Types

The five paragraph correction questions on the rough draft essay are in sequential order rather than in order of difficulty. These questions are an amalgam of the other two types you've already seen (which deal with errors *within* sentences) and questions that cover errors *between* sentences or even paragraphs. You may even encounter a reading-comprehension-type question, although, again, the question will be much easier than the questions you face in the regular reading passages.

Of the seven types of paragraph correction questions, only three are new; the other four are variations of questions you've already seen. Here are examples of the three new question variations:

First Example: Which of the following is the best way to combine sentences 1 and 2 (reproduced below)?

John Smith was introduced to the Indian princess Pocahontas. He was an explorer from England.

(A) John Smith was introduced to the Indian princess Pocahontas and was an explorer from England.

(B) John Smith was introduced to the Indian princess Pocahontas and he was an explorer from England.

(C) John Smith, an explorer from England, was introduced to the Indian princess Pocahontas.

(D) John Smith, who is an explorer from England, was introduced to the Indian princess Pocahontas.

(E) Being an explorer from England, John Smith was introduced to the Indian princess Pocahontas.

Discussion: Applying what you've already learned about process of elimination on the sentence correction questions, choice C is clearly the most concise and effective option.

Second Example: (1) *The Montgolfier Brothers—Joseph and Jacques—were actually the first human beings to take to the skies in 1783. (2) More than a century earlier, however, that technological feat had been accomplished in France. (3) Orville and Wilbur Wright are widely credited with achieving, at the start of the twentieth century, the first manned flight in the skies over Kitty Hawk, North Carolina. . . .*

Which of the following is the best way to order sentences 1, 2, and 3?

(A) Sentence 1, sentence 3, sentence 2
(B) Sentence 2, sentence 1, sentence 3
(C) Sentence 2, sentence 3, sentence 1
(D) Sentence 3, sentence 1, sentence 2
(E) Sentence 3, sentence 2, sentence 1

Discussion: Remember that the student essay is a *first draft,* so don't be surprised if you have to unscramble a few sentences. **You might need to read a sentence or two before and after the specified sentences to get a sense of the context.**

Sentence 2 might seem to follow from sentence 1, but then sentence 3 makes no sense because it references a time *after* 1783 rather than "a century earlier." Sentence 2 refers to something earlier, so that sentence cannot begin the essay. That leaves sentence 3 as the best opening of the three possibilities.

Once you have sentence 3 in place, sentence 2 must be next, and then sentence 1. Choice E is the answer.

Third Example:

(1) *One of the greatest challenges facing scholars who study ancient history is the lack of written or other "solid" evidence.* (2) *Ancient myths were commonly passed down from generation to generation orally, and then set down in writing by the great poets and philosophers.* (3) *It is often difficult for us today, then, to distinguish ancient fact from ancient fiction.*

(4) *Plato, however, was as gifted an author as he was a philosopher.* (5) *Plato often employed powerful and elaborate metaphors to convey his ideas.* (6) *On what basis are we to decide, then, whether Plato's mentioning Atlantis should be taken literally or figuratively?* (7) *Perhaps one way to investigate this question is indirectly.* (8) *We could examine all of Plato's writings, and see whether any of the geographical areas he mentioned were actual places or fictitious creations.*

Which of the following sentences would be most logical to insert at the start of the second paragraph, between sentences 3 and 4?

(A)   An example of this was the story of Atlantis.

(B)   Plato himself provides no additional clues, nor do any of his contemporaries from this time.

(C)   The oldest written record of Atlantis occurs in two of Plato's famous "dialogues," Timaeus and Critias.

(D)   Those who study ancient history have long lamented the burning of the Library of Alexandria, which archived hundreds of thousands of documents from Assyria, Greece, Persia, Egypt, and even India.

(E)   Is the legend of Atlantis perhaps more than just a legend?

Discussion: This type of question is the paragraph equivalent of a sentence completion. Instead of needing a word or phrase to complete a sentence, we need a sentence to complete a paragraph.

This example is a bit harder than our previous ones, because we have to determine the context and *direction* of the passage. Notice that the student's essay leaps from a general discussion in sentences 1, 2, and 3 to a specific discussion—of Plato and Atlantis—in sentences 4 and 5. What we need, then, is a sentence that bridges sentences 3 and 4 and introduces Plato and possibly Atlantis so that sentences 4 and 5 don't seem to come out of the blue.

Choice A contains an ambiguous pronoun ("this"), a tense error ("was" should be "is"), and no mention of Plato. Choice B mentions Plato, but it clearly refers to a prior mention of Plato (choice B would follow logically *after* sentence 5); choice B also contains a redundancy. Choice C, the answer, mentions both Plato and Atlantis in a way logically consistent with the current essay. Choice D follows logically from the first three sentences but does not lead naturally into sentence 4 because it fails to mention Plato. Choice E mentions Atlantis but not Plato.

> On the paragraph correction questions, you can apply all the grammatical concepts and elimination techniques that we explored for the usage and sentence correction questions.

Strategies for Answering the Paragraph Correction Questions

As I mentioned earlier, the paragraph correction questions are much easier than the usage questions (which can be very tricky indeed) and the sentence correction questions (which can often require simple yet laborious process of elimination). Difficult paragraph correction questions are extremely rare. Still, since you'd like to ace this section, the following points are worth stressing:

- All the error types you're already familiar with—pronoun errors, modifier errors, parallel structure errors, wordiness, ambiguity—apply here, too, and may be tested indirectly, in the choices rather than the passage itself. You can safely eliminate any choice that contains a grammatical error.

- In the previous chapter (page 114), we discussed the grammatical principle of agreement. On the usage and sentence correction questions, you have to make sure that any related parts of a sentence are in agreement. **On the paragraph correction questions, you have to make sure that related parts of *different sentences* are in agreement.** If a pronoun refers to a plural noun in the previous sentence, for example, that pronoun must also be plural. It's exactly the same principle; you just need to expand the scope of your search from a single sentence to two or more.

- Don't waste your time trying to understand each sentence—*the essay is not a reading comprehension passage.* Just skim through the essay as quickly as possible to get an overall sense of the topic and the main points.

- The sample essay is a rough—very rough—draft or "work in progress." This student paper will often lurch from one idea to the next without appropriate transitions. Keep the big picture of the essay in mind as you answer the detail questions. Be especially aware of awkward transitions between sentences and the need to maintain continuity and a coherent organization.

Applying Our Techniques to a Sample Essay and Paragraph Corrections

The following passage and questions are representative of the types of paragraph correction questions and their difficulty. You'll find the answer to these questions on page 187.

Sample Draft:

(1) *The average child watches three to four hours of television a day.* (2) *By the time a child graduates from high school, they have seen 15,000 hours of television spending only 11,000 hours in school.* (3) *Children have many more opportunities to absorb messages from television shows than they do from classes in their schools.* (4) *Unfortunately, many of these glorify violence.*

(5) *Surprisingly, programming specifically aimed at kids is frequently the most violent kind.* (6) *Children's shows like Power Rangers not only feature many fight scenes, but also don't make any kind of statement about violence being wrong.* (7) *It has been found in studies that in three quarters of Power Ranger fight scenes, violent characters go unpunished.* (8) *Young children watching programs like this see the violence and see that there is nothing wrong with being violent in their actions.* (9) *Public television often works to create nonviolent children's programming, but more should be done to address this problem.* (10) *In particular, younger children are not able to tell the difference between what is real and what is not.* (11) *They can only learn to act more aggressively from watching programs like this.*

(12) *Both parents and the programmers need to work together.* (13) *Instead of blaming each other they could try to find what is best for children to watch.* (14) *What is most profitable to broadcast could be found too.* (15) *They have blamed each other for the problems that exist for so long they have forgotten that they cannot exist without each other.* (16) *Only by their cooperating will there be an end to the threat to children being known today.*

1. In context, which of the following is the best way to revise the underlined portion of sentence 4 (reproduced below)?

   Unfortunately, many <u>of these</u> glorify violence.

   (A) of these are ones that
   (B) of these classes in their schools
   (C) of these lessons
   (D) of these opportunities
   (E) of these children

2. The main rhetorical purpose of the first paragraph is to

   (A) question the available statistics
   (B) summarize the argument the passage will make
   (C) present an opposing viewpoint
   (D) cite an interesting anecdote
   (E) explain why the subject is important

3. Sentence 9 would make the most sense if placed immediately after

   (A) Sentence 6
   (B) Sentence 7
   (C) Sentence 10
   (D) Sentence 11
   (E) Sentence 15

4. Which of the following is the best way to combine sentences 10 and 11 (reproduced below)?

In particular, younger children are not able to tell the difference between what is real and what is not. They can only learn to act more aggressively from programs like this.

(A) In particular, younger children unable to tell the difference between what is real and what is not can only learn to act more aggressively from such programs.

(B) Particular younger children are not able to tell the difference between what is real and what is not and can therefore only learn to act more aggressively from programs like this.

(C) Only learning to act more aggressively from programs like this, younger children in particular are not able in the telling of the difference of what is real and what is not.

(D) In particular, younger children, only learning to be acting more aggressively from programs like this, are not able to tell the difference between what is real and what is not.

(E) Unable to tell the difference between what is real and what is not, particular younger children can only learn their acting more aggressively from programs like this.

5. Which of the following is the best version of sentence 16 (reproduced below)?

Only by their cooperating together will there be an end to this threat to children being known today.

(A) Only by their cooperation together can this threat to today's children be ending.

(B) Only their cooperation can end this threat to today's children.

(C) Only if they cooperate together will they be able to end this threat to children they know.

(D) This threat being known to children today can only be ended by their cooperation.

(E) Known only to children today, this threat can only be ended by their cooperation together.

Congratulations: You're Done!

By completing the last two chapters, you now know everything there is to know about the multiple-choice questions on the SAT Writing Test. And since we've already covered the essay section, you've completed everything you need to know about the entire SAT Writing Test.

Take a break; you've earned it. But before you do, take five or ten minutes now—right now, while everything is still fresh—and skim all the chapters of Part III, beginning on page 57. You'll be amazed how much you've learned. A ten-minute review is more than enough for today, though you should refer to these chapters from time to time so the material stays fresh.

Answers to Exercises

Conciseness Drill (Page 165)

The following revisions are the ones I came up with; perhaps you devised even shorter versions. **Notice that eyeballing the revised versions reveals them to be significantly shorter than the original sentences.** On the actual exam you don't want to be bothered with counting up the words in each choice on the sentence correction questions, so simply scanning the choices is a useful skill to zero in on the most likely answers.

1. **Original:**   *Clancy's latest novel is an exciting one.*

   Revised: *Clancy's latest novel is exciting.*

   (Net savings: 2 words)

2. **Original:**   *Grace is taller than her brother is.*

   Revised: *Grace is taller than her brother.*

   (Net savings: 1 word)

3. **Original:**   *Mia was granted a two-week extension by our teacher for the term paper.*

   Revised: *Our teacher granted Mia a two-week extension for the term paper.*

   (Net savings: 2 words)

4. **Original:**   *It was a blow to the varsity volleyball team to lose to the junior varsity squad.*

   Revised: *Losing to the junior varsity squad was a blow to the varsity volleyball team.*

   (Net savings: 2 words)

5. **Original:**   *Mr. Phillips, the man who was last year's winner, came in second place in this year's pie-eating contest.*

   Revised: *Mr. Phillips, last year's winner, came in second in this year's pie-eating contest.*

   (Net savings: 4 words)

6. **Original:** *Scholars often work hard and they often work in isolation.*

   Revised: *Scholars often work hard and in isolation.*

   (Net savings: 3 words)

7. **Original:** *There were two cats trapped in the tall oak tree.*

   Revised: *Two cats were trapped in the tall oak tree.*

   (Net savings: 1 word)

8. **Original:** *Any individual person who submits an application after the cutoff date will be ineligible for the competition.*

   Revised: *Individuals who submit applications after the cutoff date will be ineligible for the competition.*

   (Net savings: 3 words)

9. **Original:** *The delay caused our principal to be angry.*

   Revised: *The delay angered our principal.*

   (Net savings: 3 words)

10. **Original:** *The dog that Molly has is so lazy that he practically expects to be carried on his walks.*

    Revised: *Molly's dog is so lazy that he practically expects to be carried on his walks.*

   (Net savings: 3 words)

11. **Original:** *Theo provided a summary of the novel for his World Literature class.*

    Revised: *Theo summarized the novel for his World Literature class.*

    (Net savings: 3 words)

12. **Original:** *The board of directors did not succeed in reaching a consensus on who should be elected treasurer.*

    Revised: *The board of directors failed to reach a consensus on who should be elected treasurer.*

    (Net savings: 2 words)

> Remember: on the actual test you won't be asked to come up with a shorter version, merely recognize which of the choices—assuming they are grammatically okay—is the most concise.

Spotting Ambiguities Drill (Page 168)

The revision alternatives below are the ones I came up with; other versions are possible.

1. **Original:** *Randolph's sister gave him a present on his twenty-first birthday, which was nice.*

   Revisions: *Randolph's sister gave him a present on his twenty-first birthday, which was a nice gesture.* OR

   Randolph's sister gave him a nice present on his twenty-first birthday. OR

   Randolph's sister gave him a present on his twenty-first birthday, which was a nice occasion.

Discussion: As you can see, the phrase *which was nice* could apply to Randolph's birthday, his sister's present, or to her giving him the present.

2. **Original:** *Kara was less satisfied with her painting than her art teacher.*

   Revisions: *Kara was less satisfied with her painting than her art teacher was.* OR

   Kara was less satisfied with her painting than she was with her art teacher.

Discussion: Although the second alternative was less likely the speaker's intention than was the first, both alternatives were possible interpretations of the original sentence.

3. **Original:** *Millicent's music teacher demonstrated proper technique with a smile.*

185

Revisions: *Smiling, Millicent's music teacher demonstrated proper technique.* OR

Millicent's music teacher demonstrated the proper smiling technique.

Discussion: Yes, the first version is *probably* what the speaker intended, but we can't be sure.

4. **Original:**   *In some European capitals such as Madrid, they eat dinner very late in the evening and go out afterward for even more entertainment.*

   Revisions: *In some European capitals such as Madrid, travelers eat dinner very late in the evening and go out afterward for even more entertainment.* OR

In some European capitals such as Madrid, local residents eat dinner very late in the evening and go out afterward for even more entertainment.

Discussion: The "they" in the original sentence is not so much ambiguous as it is completely unclear: just *who* are they?

5. **Original:**   *Sophomores outnumbered juniors and seniors at the school dance, so the principal decided that she should open an additional room for them.*

   Revisions: *Sophomores outnumbered juniors and seniors at the school dance, so the principal decided that she should open an additional room for the sophomores.* OR

Sophomores outnumbered juniors and seniors at the school dance, so the principal decided that she should open an additional room for the juniors and seniors. OR

Sophomores outnumbered juniors and seniors at the school dance, so the principal decided that she should open an additional room for all the students.

Discussion: We can't be sure whether the pronoun "them" refers to the sophomores, the juniors and seniors, or *all* of the students.

Remember: on the actual test you won't be asked to resolve an ambiguous phrase, merely to recognize one and eliminate any choice containing it. This concept is not nearly as important as is conciseness on these questions, so don't go crazy with hunting for ambiguities that aren't there (especially on the usage questions, since ambiguities invariably show up on the sentence correction questions).

Answers to the Sample Paragraph Correction Questions (Page 179)

1. In context, which of the following is the best way to revise the underlined portion of sentence 4 (reproduced below)?

   Unfortunately, many _of these_ glorify violence.

   (A) of these are ones that
   (B) of these classes in their schools
   (C) of these lessons
   (D) of these opportunities
   (E) of these children

Discussion: The pronoun "these" is *ambiguous*; it could refer to several plural nouns in the previous sentence. Choice A retains the ambiguity and adds wordiness. It's clear from the context that the messages from the television shows are what the writer intended. **The answer paraphrases more concisely the noun from the previous sentence.** Instead of saying "many of these messages from children's television shows," it says more simply, "many of these lessons." The answer is C.

2. The main rhetorical purpose of the first paragraph is to

(A) question the available statistics
(B) summarize the argument the passage will make
(C) present an opposing viewpoint
(D) cite an interesting anecdote
(E) explain why the subject is important

Discussion: The first paragraph introduces the topic of children's exposure to violence by providing statistics that show the extent of that exposure. The answer is E.

3. Sentence 9 would make the most sense if placed immediately after

(A) Sentence 6
(B) Sentence 7
(C) Sentence 10
(D) Sentence 11
(E) Sentence 15

Discussion: Sentence 9 qualifies the main point (that children are exposed to too much violence on television) by admitting that some programming is a step in the right direction but adds that more needs to be done to solve the problem. Since the third paragraph suggests a solution (parents and programmers need to work together), sentence 9 leads naturally into sentence 10, the first sentence of the final paragraph. The answer is D.

4. Which of the following is the best way to combine sentences 10 and 11 (reproduced below)?

In particular, younger children are not able to tell the difference between what is real and what is not. They can only learn to act more aggressively from programs like this.

(A) In particular, younger children unable to tell the difference between what is real and what is not can only learn to act more aggressively from such programs.

(B) Particular younger children are not able to tell the difference between what is real and what is not and can therefore only learn to act more aggressively from programs like this.

(C) Only learning to act more aggressively from programs like this, younger children in particular are not able in the telling of the difference of what is real and what is not.

(D) In particular, younger children, only learning to be acting more aggressively from programs like this, are not able to tell the difference between what is real and what is not.

(E) Unable to tell the difference between what is real and what is not, particular younger children can only learn their acting more aggressively from programs like this.

Discussion: This type of question is a variation of the sentence correction questions we're already familiar with. We're looking for the choice that retains the meaning of the original sentences in the most concise and unambiguous way and that does not introduce any grammatical errors. The answer is A.

5. Which of the following is the best version of sentence 16 (reproduced below)?

Only by their cooperating together will there be an end to this threat to children being known today.

(A) Only by their cooperation together can this threat to today's children be ending.

(B) Only their cooperation can end this threat to today's children.

(C) Only if they cooperate together will they be able to end this threat to children they know.

(D) This threat being known to children today can only be ended by their cooperation.

(E) Known only to children today, this threat can only be ended by their cooperation together.

Discussion: This question is also a sentence correction variation. The original sentence is redundant (all cooperating is done together) and awkwardly wordy. The answer is B, the most concise choice.

PART IV

THE SAT
READING
TEST

REMEMBER: SAT Reading Is *Different*

Introduction to the SAT Reading Test
They Should Call This the SAT Reading and Vocabulary Test

What Does the SAT Reading Test Measure?

The SAT Reading Test consists of three sections—two 25-minute sections and one 20-minute section—containing 18 sentence completion questions and 44 reading comprehension questions for a total of 62 questions.   In no particular order, you'll encounter the following:

- 25-minute section: 9 sentence completions and 13 reading questions

- 25-minute section: 9 sentence completions and 13 reading questions

- 20-minute section: 18 reading questions

There may be some slight variation from test to test, but you can expect this general layout.

Although this is officially called the SAT Critical Reading Test, over one-third of the questions measure your vocabulary.   Other than vocabulary, no other specific knowledge is required.   Everything you need to answer the reading questions is contained in the passages.

The SAT Reading Test is difficult for two reasons: time pressure and vocabulary.   Let's consider time pressure first.   You have an average of one minute per question.   That's more than enough time for the sentence completions but you'll find yourself pressed for time on the reading passages. We'll talk about how to manage your time later, but for now I'll just leave you with the thought that you'll probably need to leave some reading questions blank.

Sacrifice reading questions, not sentence completions.   Sentence completions can be solved more quickly than reading questions, so you buy yourself more time leaving a reading question blank than a sentence completion blank.   What's more, as you'll learn, on sentence completions you can always make a good guess if you find yourself in trouble (because these questions are in order of difficulty and the answers are short). It's more difficult to make a good guess on the reading questions (because they're *not* in order of difficulty, and the answers are relatively long).

In short, the SAT Reading Test measures your vocabulary, and how well you read *under pressure*.

The More Words You Know, the Better

I'm giving you fair warning: it's highly unlikely to near impossible that you're going to know every vocabulary word that appears on the SAT Reading Test. In fact, many college graduates would have trouble defining every word on a typical SAT. If you know a lot of words, you'll do very well. If you don't know a lot of words, you're facing a struggle.

The sentence completions directly test your vocabulary, and at least three of the reading questions will also ask you to determine the meaning of a word in context. But that's not to mention the difficult words that can appear in other reading questions. Here are some tough words I selected from reading questions and their choices: *allude, benevolence, configuration, dissipation, exalted, incongruous, juxtapose, laudatory, premonition, rapacious, refute, scorn, subordinate, urbanity.*

The more words you know, the higher your SAT reading score. **If you're serious about doing well on the SAT Reading Test, you'll make a point of learning as many words as you reasonably can.** I'll show you how to memorize words, and which words are the most important to learn, in the chapter beginning on page 303.

Help Is on the Way

Fortunately, you don't have to know the definition of every word in a question to answer the question correctly. As you'll learn shortly, using process of elimination means that you'll have to know at most four of the five choices on any question in order to determine the answer. If the answer isn't one of the four choices you know, it's in the fifth choice that you don't know. And sometimes you can answer a question knowing even fewer than four of the five choices.

I don't mean to suggest that you'll need an incredible vocabulary to answer the sentence completions and many of the reading questions, but that the more words you learn, the easier the entire SAT Reading Test will be. In addition to the tangible benefit of knowing words, there's also the psychological edge—the kick of seeing a word that you know, especially one that you recently learned.

Here are some of the ways you'll be learning to improve your reading score:

- how to use your time more efficiently by learning which questions you should spend the most amount of time on, which you should spend the least amount of time on, and which you should consider skipping entirely

- how to avoid the *dangers* of process of elimination, and how to use it properly to answer questions even when you don't understand the answer

- how to improve your comprehension of the passages by reading *less*

- how to use order of difficulty on the sentence completions to catch potential errors and to improve your odds when you're forced to guess

These techniques are designed to help you get the most mileage from the words you already know, but at the same time you should be working assiduously* on your vocabulary. To get you started, you'll find the most important SAT words and effective ways to memorize them on page 303.

Before we get to specific techniques for answering sentence completions and reading questions, the rest of this chapter will introduce you to some general skills that you'll be applying later.

*GSWLIU

Process of Elimination on Sentence Completions and Reading Questions

The great thing about a multiple-choice test is that the answers are always right in front of you. You don't have to come up with the answer to a question out of the blue, you just have to recognize the answer among the choices. It's better than that: you don't even have to recognize the answer if you are able determine that all the other choices are wrong.

Everyone has heard of process of elimination but most students do not apply it correctly. For example, many students decide on the answer to a question first, and then eliminate all the other choices. The key to process of elimination is *not* looking for the answer, but remaining open-minded until you *discover* the answer by eliminating all the other choices.

There's a more serious mistake that even you are likely to make from time to time, so pay close attention. There's an *enormous* but subtle difference between the following two situations:

- eliminating a choice that you *know* is wrong,

    versus

- eliminating a choice that merely *seems* wrong.

Consider an easy question. The question and answer choices look something like this:

Easy Question: blah, blah, blah, blah, blah, blah, blah, blah
(A) *Wrong.*
(B) *Bingo, the answer!*
(C) *Wrong.*
(D) *Wrong.*
(E) *Wrong.*

No prob, right? It's an easy question and the answer practically pops out at you.

Now consider a hard question. The answer doesn't pop out at all. Now the question and choices look something like this:

Hard Question: blah, blah, blah, blah, blah, blah, blah, blah
(A) *Wrong.*
(B) *Could be right, I suppose; I'm not sure.*
(C) *Hunh? Nah, I don't think this is right.*
(D) *What? Hunh? No, this doesn't seem right either.*
(E) *No way, wrong.*

The *hunh?* choices are the ones you have to be careful about. Most students are too quick to eliminate "odd" choices that "seem wrong." I'm *not* saying that seemingly strange choices are always right. Don't be too quick, however, to eliminate a choice you're not sure about, whether it's a tough vocabulary word on a sentence completion or a choice on a reading question that you don't quite understand.

If You Can't Define a Word, You Can't Eliminate It

It's very tempting to eliminate difficult words that you don't know. They aren't nice, they're scary. You don't like really hard words. That's natural.

An easy sentence completion will have an easy answer, so on those questions you don't have to worry about words you can't define. **But on a medium or difficult sentence completion, never eliminate a word you can't define—at least not initially.** Sometimes you'll have to choose between two or more words you can't define. In that situation of course you'll have to eliminate a word you can't define, but initially any difficult word should be treated as a "maybe."

An exception to this rule is that you can eliminate a word you can't define *if* you know that it's a *positive* word, say, but the question calls for a *negative* answer. We'll consider this exception shortly but our general principle stands: on medium and difficult questions, don't eliminate a word you can't define.

> In your head, the *rhythm* of process of elimination should sound something like the following: *Could be (A). Definitely not (B). I don't think it's (C), but maybe. Not (D). Not (E). It's either (A) or (C), I'll focus on (A). Oh, it can't be (A) either. I guess the answer is (C) after all.*
>
> That's the rhythm you want to establish on all the sentence completion and reading questions, even the easy ones: *not-this-not-this-maybe-that-not-that-not-that-I-guess-the-answer-is-that.*

Overconfidence Causes Many Mistakes on the SAT Reading Test

Most students get scared on the SAT, but ironically they don't get scared enough about the right thing. Students should be scared about being overconfident. **Overconfidence is thinking you know what a word means when you *don't*.** Overconfidence may even happen to you from time to time.

Being overconfident won't happen to you on an easy word like *apparent* or *controversy*. You know what these words mean, no problem.

And you won't get overconfident on difficult words, either. On hard words like *anarchy, reticent,* and *parsimony,* at least you know where you stand. Either you looked up a hard word in a dictionary—in which case you know what it means—or you haven't looked it up—in which case you at least realize that you don't know what it means.

If it's not easy words that you have to be on guard against, and it's not hard words, then which type of word *should* you be most careful about?

Medium Words Are the Trickiest

You're most likely to be overconfident about words of medium difficulty. Medium words are sneaky because nobody ever looks them up. We hear them and read them all the time. Sometimes we even use medium words correctly, even though we don't know precisely what they mean. And because most students do not know what medium words mean, they often either choose them incorrectly or eliminate them incorrectly.

The following drill will give you some experience trying to define some medium difficult words.

Defining Medium Words Drill

In the following table, use the space provided to write a brief definition of the words below. Write a definition rather than supplying synonyms or words associated with the medium word. No credit for merely using the word in a sentence.

1. plastic	
2. discriminating	
3. parochial	
4. formidable	

Compare your definitions with the ones I provide on page 207.

Either You *Know* What a Word Means—or You *Don't*

The most common and dangerous mistake on the SAT Reading Test is not being aware of the difference between *knowing* what a word means, and *thinking* you know what a word means.

Knowing a word means that you can *define* it. There's no in-between, like *sort of* knowing what the word means, or *kind of* knowing what it means, or being *able to use it in a sentence.*

If you can't define a word in a few seconds—if you aren't "dictionary-sure"—you don't know what it means!

Trying to Figure Out What a Word Means Is Usually a *Huge* Waste of Time

Many students try to figure out the meaning of words they don't know or can't remember on the SAT. They may have been told, for example, to use Latin or Greek "roots" to "decipher" a strange word.

This sometimes works on easier questions, but more often it's a big waste of time. Some students will puzzle over a particular word for as much as 15 seconds or more. What's worse, after spending time wrestling with a difficult word, you can't be sure whether you've correctly deciphered what the word means.

If you can't define a word in a few seconds—leave the choice as a "maybe" and move on! On sentence completions you can *sometimes* deduce what a word within the sentence means. And, as you'll learn shortly, once you know the meaning of a word you're looking for, you can work backward from the choices to the definition.

Otherwise, don't labor over difficult words. You'll need the time for the words you *do* know, and for the reading passages.

Beware of Easy Words with Hard Second Definitions

Sometimes, usually on the hard sentence completions, you'll see a simple word that seems out of place. Be very, very careful: it's possible that the word is being used in a different sense from the one you usually associate it with.

For example, the word *distant* means far away. If we say a person is distant, however, we don't mean that he or she is literally far away; we mean he is reserved, or lost in thought. The word *qualify* means to meet some standard, but it can also mean to make an exception to a general statement. Or take the word *guarded*. It can mean closely watched, but it can also mean cautious.

Sometimes parts of speech will be a clue. **All the choices on a question—whether sentence completions, or vocabulary-based reading questions—will be the same part of speech.**

For example, consider the word *pedestrian*. You know what it means as a noun, but do you know what it means when used as an adjective? (It means ordinary, common, uninspired.) Or take the word *champion*. Again, as a noun the meaning is easy, but do you know what it means when used as a verb? (It means to stand up for something, as in fighting for a noble cause.)

The following drill will hone your skill at spotting easy words with hard second definitions.

> **Don't start second-guessing whether every easy word on the SAT Reading Test has a hard second definition. On the sentence completions, easy words with hard second definitions will show up—if they show up at all—once, at most twice, on the hard questions. These words can show up several times, however, on the vocabulary-in-context reading questions.**

Second Definition Drill

The following words have all appeared on SATs in the context of their second definitions rather than their more common first definitions. See if you can match the easy word with its hard second definition. **Use process of elimination; some of these are *very* hard words.** You'll find the answers on page 208.

	EASY WORD		HARD SECOND DEFINITION (SCRAMBLED)
1.	conviction	(A)	calm
2.	buoyant	(B)	endanger
3.	slight	(C)	seriousness
4.	complex	(D)	certainty
5.	composed	(E)	insult
6.	eclipse	(F)	equivalent
7.	parallel	(G)	seize
8.	diversion	(H)	cheerful
9.	detached	(I)	entertainment
10.	gravity	(J)	network
11.	appropriate	(K)	uninvolved
12.	compromise	(L)	surpass

Beware of Easy *Looking* Words That You Don't Know

Sometimes you'll encounter a word on a difficult sentence completion that *looks* a lot like an easy word you know, but whose meaning is completely unrelated to the word it reminds you of. **Again: be very careful about trying to figure out what a new word means on the SAT.**

For example, the word *impassive* does *not* mean "not passive" (it means dispassionate, without feeling, coldly objective). The word *fatalism* has nothing to do with death or dying (it means being resigned to defeat). Or take the word *decorum,* which has nothing to do with decoration (it means socially accepted behavior). *Disinterested* does not mean not interested (it means neutral or impartial).

The stronger your vocabulary, the more you can rely on your ability to deduce a word's meaning. Still, trying to figure out the precise definition of a new word is dangerous. It's much safer to determine whether the unknown word is a "good" word or a "bad" word.

If You Can't Define a Word, *Immediately* Establish Whether It's Positive or Negative

You either know what a word means or you don't. But even when you can't define a word you will usually have enough of a sense of the word to decide whether it's positive or negative. You may have heard your English teacher referring to this concept as the *connotations* of a word.

Why is knowing a word's connotations so important? **Often all you need to know about a word to eliminate it is whether it's positive or negative.** If you know the connotations of a word, you'll often be able to eliminate it regardless of whether you can define the word or not.

When we speak of positive words on the SAT, we mean it in the most general sense. *Warmth,* for example, is a positive word; *argument* is a negative word.

Some words, like *table* or *water,* are neither positive nor negative. On the SAT, however, most words will at least lean one way or the other. **Whenever possible, even with neutral words, try to decide whether a word is positive or negative.**

Don't flip a coin to decide whether a word is positive or negative. It's worth spending a few seconds to try to get a "sense" of the word. Compare the *spelling* of the word with words you already know. You're trying to "get a feel" for the word by comparing it with words you know with similar spellings. If you know a foreign language like French or Spanish or Italian, you can use your knowledge of these words, too.

Beware of relying solely on the prefix of a word. Many students, for example, assume that any word beginning with "dis" is negative, until I point out words like *discover* or *display*. Negative prefixes—like *un, dis, a,* and sometimes *in*—reverse the root following it, and so "flip" an otherwise positive or negative word. Take the word *discover*. *Cover* is a negative word, so the negative prefix *dis* flips the entire word to positive.

When comparing the unknown word to words you know, try to find overlaps that are at least three or four letters; the more the better. If the comparison words are positive, then the odds are overwhelming that the mystery word is positive, too.

You won't always be able to tell whether a word is positive or negative, but most of the time you will. The following drill will give you practice.

Positive or Negative Drill

The following words are very difficult; if you know more than a few I'm super impressed. Spend a moment or two—no more than five seconds each—and decide whether a word is positive or negative. Indicate your choice with a plus (+) or a minus (−). You'll find the answers on page 208.

1. *amity* ( )	2. *vogue* ( )	3. *foible* ( )
4. *placate* ( )	5. *virulent* ( )	6. *revere* ( )
7. *plaintive* ( )	8. *equanimity* ( )	9. *disparage* ( )
10. *virtuoso* ( )	11. *acerbic* ( )	12. *salutary* ( )

Keep the Difficulty of a Word in Mind

Knowing the difficulty of a word is important on the sentence completion questions because these questions—unlike the reading questions—are arranged in order of difficulty. As you'll learn in "Sentence Completions: Advanced Principles," the answer to an easy sentence completion will be an easy word; the answer to a hard sentence completion is almost always a hard word. Being able to judge a word's difficulty quickly is an enormously powerful tool when it comes to selecting the answer to sentence completions when you're undecided or even completely stuck.

We determine the difficulty of a word *not* **by whether we know it, but by estimating how many people in general know it.** An easy word is one everyone knows; a hard word is one very few people know. Medium words fall somewhere in between.

It's important to remember that the difficulty of a word is not your *opinion* of the difficulty, but rather an objective standard. You and I should be in close agreement on the difficulty of any given word. Just because you happen to know the definition of a difficult word does not make the word easy. Easy words are easy for everyone; difficult words are difficult for everyone.

So you and I both mean the same thing when we refer to easy, medium, or difficult words, I've prepared the following quick drill. With practice you should be able to recognize the difficulty of a word at a glance.

> If you have trouble judging the difficulty of a word, rely on the general rule that longer words tend to be harder than shorter words. If English is not your first language, judging the difficulty of words may not be easy. If your first language is a Romance language such as French, Spanish, Italian, or Portuguese, you may have an easier time recognizing longer, harder words (which are more likely to be related to your original language) than you will recognizing shorter, easier words (which are more likely to be related to Old English or Germanic roots).

Judging Word Difficulty Drill

The following table of words are representative of the full range of difficulty you will encounter on the choices to sentence completion questions. They are in random order. Your job is to assess the difficulty of each word.

Start by deciding first whether a word is easy, medium, or hard. Once you've got a general bearing, refine your estimate up or down to easy-medium or medium-hard if necessary.

Before you rate any words, read through the whole list first so you have a sense of the words as a whole. Use a scale of 1 (easy) to 5 (hard), with 3 as average (medium). Here's a rough translation of the various difficulty levels to help guide you:

1	*easy*	(most students probably knew this word in sixth grade)
2	*easy-to-medium*	(most students could give an accurate definition of this word)
3	*medium*	(most students could offer at least a rough definition of this word)
4	*medium-to-hard*	(some students would recognize this word, but many would not be able to define it)
5	*hard*	(most students would not have a sense of this word, and many might not even recognize it)

Remember to read through the entire list once before rating any words. Work carefully but quickly; try to spend no more than a second or two on each word. Once you've finished rating all the words, feel free to go back and reassess any words you were unsure about. As a first step, consider finding the two or three very easiest words and the two or three hardest words and rating those with 1s and 5s respectively. See page 209 for the answers.

1. *voluntary* ( )	2. *expenditures* ( )	3. *munificent* ( )
4. *confide* ( )	5. *adequate* ( )	6. *innate* ( )
7. *repel* ( )	8. *somber* ( )	9. *proclivity* ( )
10. *subtle* ( )	11. *fertile* ( )	12. *formal* ( )
13. *validity* ( )	14. *serene* ( )	15. *capricious* ( )
16. *articulate* ( )	17. *viable* ( )	18. *apathy* ( )

Okay, You're Ready to Tackle the Sentence Completion Questions

You've absorbed a lot in this chapter, so here is a good spot to stop for the day. Throughout the next four chapters we'll be returning to the concepts we've just covered, so don't worry about having fully digested everything at this point.

Answers to the Defining Medium Words Drill (page 198)

I chose the medium words of this drill as examples of ones that students typically get overconfident about being able to define. Don't get discouraged if you tripped up on some of these, the point of the drill was to make you more cautious.

1. plastic	Capable of being shaped or formed; easily molded or influenced; malleable
2. discriminating	Showing careful judgment; perceptive; astute
3. parochial	Having a limited outlook; narrow-minded; provincial
4. formidable	Arousing fear, dread, awe, or wonder; threatening; intimidating

Answers to the Second Definition Drill (page 201)

EASY WORD		HARD SECOND DEFINITION	
1.	conviction	(D)	certainty
2.	buoyant	(H)	cheerful
3.	slight	(E)	insult
4.	complex	(J)	network
5.	composed	(A)	calm
6.	eclipse	(L)	surpass
7.	parallel	(G)	seize
8.	diversion	(I)	entertainment
9.	detached	(K)	uninvolved
10.	gravity	(C)	seriousness
11.	appropriate	(F)	equivalent
12.	compromise	(B)	endanger

Answers to the Positive or Negative Drill (page 203)

As I mentioned, the words in this drill are all very difficult. Even without knowing the precise definition of these words, however, you probably got most of these right.

1. *amity* (+)	2. *vogue* (+)	3. *foible* (−)
4. *placate* (+)	5. *virulent* (−)	6. *revere* (+)
7. *plaintive* (−)	8. *equanimity* (+)	9. *disparage* (−)
10. *virtuoso* (+)	11. *acerbic* (−)	12. *salutary* (+)

If you missed more than two or three of these, you should work on developing your sense of words more *before* you look them up. Whenever you encounter a new word, try to decide whether it's positive or negative *without* relying on the context; you won't have context to help you on the answer choices.

Answers to the Judging Difficulty Drill (page 206)

The following assessment of difficulty is based on the percentage of high school students who know the words in the list, ranked from 1 (easy) to 3 (medium) to 5 (difficult).

Sometimes it's a judgment call whether a word is an easy or an easy-medium, say, or a medium versus a medium-hard. So long as you're within plus or minus 1 of the rankings below, you're fine. If you're off consistently, determine whether you tended to overestimate or underestimate the rankings. If your vocabulary is strong, for example, you may tend to underestimate the difficulty of words; if your vocabulary is on the weak side, you may tend to overestimate the difficulty of words.

1. *voluntary* (2)	2. *expenditures* (3)	3. *munificent* (5)
4. *confide* (3)	5. *adequate* (1)	6. *innate* (4)
7. *repel* (2)	8. *somber* (3)	9. *proclivity* (5)
10. *subtle* (4)	11. *fertile* (2)	12. *formal* (1)
13. *validity* (2)	14. *serene* (3)	15. *capricious* (5)
16. *articulate* (3)	17. *viable* (5)	18. *apathy* (3)

Sentence Completions:

Basic Principles

Whole Sentences Can Be Confusing, So Read Them in Chunks

I'll Say It Again: Start Memorizing Words *Today*

Two of the three SAT Reading Test sections will contain a group of sentence completion questions. Each group contains nine questions, making a total of 18 sentence completions on the test.

Both groups of sentence completions are arranged from easy to medium to difficult: the first few questions are easy (safe), the middle few are medium, and the last few are hard (dangerous). Although sentence completions require some comprehension, they are primarily a test of your vocabulary. You won't have much trouble with the easy ones, but the last few sentence completions contain very hard words. Indeed, on the last couple of completions you may not even recognize some of the words in the sentences themselves as well as the choices. I'll show you how to memorize words, and which words are the most important to learn, in the chapter beginning on page 303.

In this chapter I'll show you a simple three-step method for analyzing sentence completions. In the next chapter I'll show you ways to attack questions when you can't define one or more of the words either in the sentence itself or among the choices. If that happens, a fourth step—guessing—may be necessary. As you'll learn, you can often solve the hardest sentence completions even without knowing what the answer means.

What Is a Sentence Completion?

Each question consists of a sentence from which a word has been omitted and replaced by a blank (indicated by a dashed line). Half the questions replace two words with blanks. Your job is to find the word or set of words that completes the main idea of each sentence—what the sentence is "getting at."

Each sentence below has one or two blanks. Each blank indicates that something has been omitted from the sentence. Choose the word or set of words that best completes the meaning of the sentence as a whole.

Example:

> Trends are difficult to spot until they are well established because they usually begin as minor, seemingly ------ events.
>
> (A) momentous   (B) popular   (C) insignificant
>   (D) current   (E) recent

(A) (B) **(C)** (D) (E)

Here are the directions. These directions will not change on the actual test, so do not waste time reading them in the exam room.

Solving Sentence Completions in Three (or Four) Simple Steps

Although there are innumerable types of sentences in the English language, sentence completions can be solved applying a simple, three-step method:

Step 1: Find the main idea of the sentence.

Step 2: Anticipate what word or type of word will fit in the blank or blanks.

Step 3: Apply process of elimination to the choices until you find the answer.

This approach works for any sentence completion, though if you don't know one or more words in the sentence or the choices, you may not be able to eliminate enough choices to find the answer in the third step. If that happens, a fourth step is necessary:

Step 4: If you haven't found the answer by Step 3, guess.

Again, in this chapter we'll focus largely on the first three steps. In the next chapter I'll show you additional methods to apply when you aren't sure of all the words in Step 3, and how to guess in Step 4.

Let's begin with the first step.

Step 1: Look for Clues to Find the "Main Idea" of the Sentence

Consider the following "incomplete" sentence completion:

Peter is -------.

(A) popular   (B) hyperactive   (C) tall
(D) gullible   (E) paranoid

This example is incomplete because it has no main idea; any adjective could fit here. Peter is popular. Peter is hyperactive. Peter is paranoid. **(Incidentally, notice that all the choices are grammatically consistent.** Here the choices are all adjectives; on another question they might be all verbs.)

You will never see such a question on the SAT because it is too simple. You are not given enough information to choose a "best" answer. Peter could be popular, hyperactive, tall, gullible, and paranoid!

On the SAT, each sentence will give you clues pointing to its main idea. Consider now the following variations of our original sentence:

Variation 1:   Peter is -------, so he plays center for his high school basketball team.

(A) popular   (B) hyperactive   (C) tall
(D) gullible   (E) paranoid

Discussion: The clue here is the phrase following the blank. The only choice that fits now is C.

Variation 2:   Peter is -------, so he continually looks over his shoulder for hidden dangers.

(A) popular   (B) hyperactive   (C) tall
(D) gullible   (E) paranoid

Discussion: The only choice that fits now is E. **Even if you weren't familiar with the answer, you could use process of elimination to rule out the other choices.**

Variation 3: Peter is -------, so on weekends he has more party invitations than he can handle.

(A) popular   (B) hyperactive   (C) tall
(D) gullible   (E) paranoid

Discussion: The only choice that fits now is A.

Variation 4: Peter is -------, so his friends are always playing practical jokes on him.

(A) popular   (B) hyperactive   (C) tall
(D) gullible   (E) paranoid

Discussion: The only choice that fits now is D. Again, if you weren't familiar with the answer, process of elimination would have allowed you to deduce the answer by eliminating the other choices. In the next chapter we'll discuss what to do when you can't define all the words.

Variation 5: Peter is -------, so he finds it nearly impossible to sit still through long, tedious lectures.

(A) popular   (B) hyperactive   (C) tall
(D) gullible   (E) paranoid

Discussion: The only choice that fits now is B.

Of course, SAT sentence completions will get a lot harder than that, but the basic principle is the same. Don't forget that half the questions include two blanks, but our overall method does not change significantly, so for now let's just nail down our basic approach.

Chunking the Sentence into Phrases

The sentences you'll have to answer on the test are more difficult than the ones above because they're longer. The average sentence on the SAT contains more than 20 words. With sentences that long, you'll have to dig to uncover the clues.

The way not to answer long questions is to plug in each choice and read the sentence as a whole over and over until you find the answer. This process is too confusing and time-consuming. Indeed, reading a lengthy sentence under time pressure just once is difficult enough to take in. As we discussed in Tutorial 12, your brain can handle only so much information in short-term memory before it crashes, just like a computer. Reading a lengthy sentence for clues can overload your short-term memory, making it very difficult to think clearly, if at all.

The solution is to work with chunks of a sentence at a time, eliminating as many choices as you can, and then working with another chunk of the sentence. By working in this way you'll find that you can often determine which word or type of word fits without reading the entire sentence.

Focus on the Neighboring Words near the Blank

As a first step—before you read the sentence as a whole—see how far you can get by using the words immediately before and after the blank, especially any phrases that include the blank.

Let's consider the following sentence to see how this chunk-eliminate-chunk-eliminate process works.

> Though he invariably took his time to consider carefully any new potential venture, once he made up his mind to invest the successful businessman moved quickly and ------- to exploit the opportunity.
>
> (A) patiently   (B) recklessly   (C) occasionally
> (D) decisively   (E) publicly

The sentence is over 30 words long, quite a mouthful. So let's take the sentence in small bites at a time. We skip all the words at the beginning of the sentence and jump right to the phrase that includes the blank: "quickly and -------." The answer must be a word that is consistent with the idea of moving quickly.

Just that little bit of information allows us to eliminate choices A, C, and E. Now all we have to do is search for another clue to decide between the remaining choices B and D. The first few words of the sentence tell us that the businessman took his time and was careful, so we eliminate B and select the answer, choice D.

With shorter, easier sentences, you may not need to chop the sentence down like that. Read the longer sentences whole, however, only as a last resort.

The Two Types of Sentence Completion Clues:
Direction Clues and Concept Clues

To find the main idea of a sentence, the two types of clues you can use are direction clues and concept clues. Direction clues are grammatical and relatively easy to spot and apply. If a sentence offers a direction clue—not all sentences do—this clue is often sufficient to select the answer.

A concept clue, as the name suggests, involves two or more related or contrasting concepts within a sentence. Concept clues are harder to spot than direction clues, but often come in handy on the more difficult questions.

A sentence will offer either a direction clue or a concept clue or both, so use whichever one presents itself. Let's take a closer look at each type.

Looking for Direction Clues

If we view the main idea of a sentence as having a flow or a direction, that direction can do one of three things:

- *continue*

- *reverse*

- *go to extremes*

By far the most common instances on the SAT are sentences whose direction continues. **Unless you have grammatical or other clues indicating otherwise, you should assume that the direction continues.**

On the medium to difficult questions, direction reversals become more common. On the most difficult questions, you'll occasionally encounter a sentence whose direction goes to extremes, but the last variation is far less common than the other variations.

Here's an example of each possible direction a sentence can take. We'll look at the same basic sentence with different direction clues.

The direction continues: Faced with a seasoned champion as an opponent, the inexperienced fencer was frightened as well as ------- before his upcoming match.

Discussion: The direction clue here is the phrase "as well as." A word like "pessimistic" would fit here since "frightened" and "pessimistic" indicate negative and related states of mind. A silly response would be a word like "rich." The inexperienced fencer could be both frightened and rich, but it makes no sense to speak of these concepts together in the same sentence (especially in light of the opening phrase here). **Note that when the direction of a sentence continues, the missing word should complement the clue or clues, though it may not be an exact synonym.** We would not say, for example, that the inexperienced fencer was "frightened as well as scared."

The direction reverses: Faced with a seasoned champion as an opponent, the inexperienced fencer was frightened yet ------- before his upcoming match.

Discussion: The direction clue here is the word "yet." A word like "determined" would fit here since it qualifies the word "frightened" without absolutely contradicting it. **Note that when the direction of a sentence reverses, the missing word should complement the clue or clues—without necessarily being an exact antonym.** We would not say that the inexperienced fencer was "frightened yet brave." When the direction of a sentence reverses, a contrasting or qualifying idea is introduced, but it need not be an exact opposite.

The direction goes to extremes: Faced with a seasoned champion as an opponent, the inexperienced fencer was frightened if not ------- before his upcoming match.

Discussion: The direction clue here is the phrase "if not." A word like "panicked" or "terrified" would fit here. This last variation of sentence direction is rare, and is found only in the final two or three (most difficult) sentence completions.

Before giving you a list of the different types of expressions that offer direction clues, the following brief drill will give you practice.

Direction Clues Drill

For each of the following sentences, decide first which type of direction is indicated by the italicized phrases and then choose a word that would fit the blank. On the actual test the clues will not be italicized for your convenience, of course, but this drill is designed to sharpen your awareness of the different types of direction clue expressions.

It's possible that many words can fit in the blank, so you have some flexibility. If you'd like, you can select more than one word for an answer.

SENTENCE COMPLETION	DIRECTION	POSSIBLE ANSWER
1. The coach praised *and* ------- her athletes.		
2. The proposed solution was expensive *rather than* -------.		
3. The prototype exhibited excellent design *as well as* -------.		
4. *Neither* agreeing *nor* disagreeing with either side, the mediator remained ------- during the opening presentations.		
5. The audience was quiet *if not* ------- throughout the opera.		
6. The author's anecdote is *as* enjoyable *as it is* -------.		

You'll find the answers to this drill on page 227. **Please try your hand at these sentences before reading on.**

Examples of Direction Clues

The following table provides you with a comprehensive list of the variety of direction clues you can expect. The ellipses (. . .) indicate the words before and after each expression. We have already reviewed many of these expressions in the previous drill.

I've arranged these expressions in terms of your likely familiarity with them. **Some of the phrases toward the end of each list may be unfamiliar to you. If so, you should practice using any such expression by writing a practice sentence.**

As always, you don't have to memorize anything here. Just review the table so that you are familiar with the different types of direction clues.

DIRECTION CONTINUES (most common)	DIRECTION REVERSES	DIRECTION GOES TO EXTREMES (least common)
. . . and . . .	. . . but . . .	. . . became . . .
. . . also . . .	. . . not . . .	. . . and eventually . . .
. . . as well as . . .	. . . instead of . . .	. . . and even . . .
as . . . as it is . . .	. . . unlike . . .	. . . almost . . .
not only . . . but also . . .	. . . although . . .	. . . if not . . .
	. . . except for . . .	
	. . . however . . .	
	. . . rather than . . .	
	this . . . is no . . .	
	. . . on the contrary . . .	
	. . . nonetheless . . .	
	. . . surprisingly . . .	
	. . . was previously . . .	
	. . . paradoxically . . .	
	this hitherto . . . is now . . .	
	. . . save for . . .	
	. . . notwithstanding . . .	
	for all its . . . it was still . . .	

The Role of the Colon and Semicolon

Some sentence completions will contain a colon (:) or semicolon (;). **In almost every instance, the sentence direction continues after the colon or semicolon.** In fact, the second half of the sentence following the colon or semicolon usually does nothing more than paraphrase the first half.

Here's an example:

> Elliot's analysis of the manuscript is disappointingly ------; Elliot seems content to remain on the surface of the intricate text.
>
> (A) superficial   (B) overdue   (C) derivative
>   (D) critical   (E) scholarly

The semicolon tells us that the second half of the sentence merely echoes the first half. Since the second half tells us that Elliot remained on the surface of the text, the first half of the sentence must be saying the same thing. The only choice that fits here is A. Choices B and C are negative, as required by the word disappointingly, but are not consistent with the second half of the sentence.

Be Alert for Concept Clues

Grammatical clues (such as the words and phrases we just discussed) and punctuation clues are often enough to solve the sentence completion, but sometimes you will need to use concept clues. **A concept clue is an idea that is repeated or contrasted within a sentence.**

We find a simple example of this technique in the instructions. Here is the illustrative sentence:

> Trends are difficult to spot until they are well established because they usually begin as minor, seemingly ------ events.
>
> (A) momentous   (B) popular   (C) insignificant
>   (D) current   (E) recent

Notice the repetition of the ideas "difficult to spot" and "minor." This concept clue points us to the answer, "insignificant."

Sometimes an idea will be contrasted with another, and such contrasts are also important concept clues. On the two-blank sentence completions, you will often find two concept clues, but the principle we have discussed is the same.

Use Common Sense

Simply using what you know about people and the world often helps you solve sentence completions. Consider the following example:

> The young poet, apparently eager to ------ academic commentators who criticized his earlier work for pandering to plebian sensibilities, began to include more erudite references and classical allusions in his poems.
>
> (A) appease   (B) embody   (C) describe
>   (D) antagonize   (E) confirm

This sentence is packed with several difficult to very difficult words, so let's start by chunking the sentence and applying some common sense.

What would a young poet be eager to do regarding academic commentators of his work? Unless he were self-destructive, a young poet would be eager to please or impress commentators of his work, especially those who had criticized his work earlier. The answer to this question is choice A. **Even if you weren't familiar with this word, you could have eliminated the other choices using process of elimination. Once again, notice how we can sometimes—though not always—get away with ignoring difficult words in a sentence completion.**

You've learned an astonishing amount about the world and the people in it—use it. As you'll see when we get to the reading passages, common sense often rescues us on those questions, too.

Don't Be Too Clever on the Sentence Completions

Sentence completions are straightforward, as are the reading questions. Unlike the kind of reading you are required to do in your school literature classes, the sentences contain no subtleties or surprises.

I say this because if I were giving a lecture right now on sentence completions to you and a dozen classmates, it's about this point that some braniac would raise his hand and challenge me with a comment like, "Well, maybe a young poet would be angry at the critics of his previous work, and so maybe he'd actually be trying to antagonize them."

Yeah, right. Heck, why stop there? Maybe the poet hates poetry and is trying to sabotage his own career. No way. **Whenever a sentence includes something contrary to common sense, the sentence will highlight this fact by including a word like "surprisingly" or in some other way letting us know that something unusual is going on.**

Keep things simple. If you start to overanalyze a sentence or choice, you can quickly find yourself in deep water. Being clever may win points with your English teacher, but this isn't school. On the SAT, being too clever is likely to cost you time as well as points. Let's move on to step two.

Step 2: Fill in the Blank (or Blanks) Before Looking at the Choices

Once you've determined the direction of a sentence, you should be able to make a good guess about a word that would complete the main idea. Some students actually quickly write a word in the blank, though this is not necessary.

The point of coming up with the word on your own, before you glance at the choices, is not to let the choices confuse your analysis. Now when you look at the choices you're like a heat-seeking missile: you have a definite target in mind.

If You Can't Come Up with a Specific Word for the Blank, Use the Positive-Negative Method

Sometimes the clues don't immediately suggest a specific word. Since you don't have a lot of time during the test to ponder over the sentence, your quick fallback position is to use the positive-negative method. Even when you can't determine a precise word that would fill the blank, you can usually figure out whether the missing word is positive or negative.

Consider the following example and decide whether a positive or negative word would fit. Be careful!

> The point of most advertising of new products,
> after all, is to make us on some level feel ------- our
> current lives so that we feel compelled to purchase
> the products being peddled.
>
> (A) aware of (B) discontent with
>   (C) consumed with (D) hopeful about
>   (E) harmonious with

While advertising is supposed to make us want to buy a particular product or service, it accomplishes this by making us feel discontented with our current situation. (The concept clue in the repeated theme of "new" and "current" helped here.)

Be careful using the positive-negative method. **Whether the missing word is positive or negative often depends on the particular context.** Consider the following example:

Unfortunately, in preliminary trials the experimental vaccination actually ------ the spread of the harmful bacteria.

(A) curbed   (B) altered   (C) defined
(D) cured   (E) promoted

Clearly the main idea of the sentence is negative, but since we're talking about harmful bacteria, the blank would actually be a positive word like "accelerated." The answer is choice E, "promoted," a positive word.

If You Can't Even Decide Whether the Missing Word Should Be Positive or Negative

If you're really stymied, glance at the choices for inspiration. Sometimes a choice triggers an association that will reveal the main idea you're looking for.

Here's another point worth making. **Whenever a sentence discusses a woman or a member of a minority group—and especially his or her achievements—the main idea is invariably positive.** The test writers go out of their way not to offend anyone, so the tone of sentence completions or reading passages that discuss members of a minority is always upbeat and laudatory.

(This political correctness extends—I kid you not—to the SAT's math problems. If there's an SAT word problem involving boys and girls, I promise you that a girl or girls will win the race or have the highest grade point average or whatever. It never fails.)

Step 3: Attack the Choices Using Process of Elimination

You've already done the hard work, now all you have to do is go through the choices, matching them against the word you anticipated or against the positive-negative connotation you determined.

Don't, however, expect an exact match for the word you anticipated in the previous step, although this often happens. Instead you now have a "key" that allows you to assess each choice quickly using process of elimination. If a particular choice is not consistent with the word you devised, that choice can safely be eliminated—so long as you're sure of the choice's definition, or at least sure whether the choice is positive or negative.

Let's say on a question that the word you came up with is "regular," or something close in meaning. At the very least you've determined that the word should be positive. Consider the following five choices:

(A) imprecise
(B) fortunate
(C) likely
(D) unbalanced
(E) expected

Let's work with the connotation first—always safer than going out on a limb looking for a precise word. We're looking for a positive word, so we can eliminate any negative choices. Choices A and D are out. Now we match each of the remaining choices against our target word—"regular"—and eliminate any that are inconsistent. The only choice consistent with regular is choice E, "expected." **Of course, if none of the choices comes close to the word you were expecting, you should reevaluate the sentence.**

Again, Don't Be Too Clever

Let's say that you're looking for a negative word on a sentence and you have the following choices to work with:

(A) honest
(B) sufficient
(C) complex
(D) impressive
(E) necessary

Clearly the only negative choice here is C; the other choices are positive-to-neutral. But there's always some smarty pants at this point who says, "Whoa, wait a second. How do we know that the word 'honest' is always positive? I can think of situations in which a person can be too honest. And for that matter, 'necessary' could be negative, too."

Give me a break. **If you get caught in the trap of finding justifications for various choices, you'll never be able to reach a decision. Your goal is to eliminate choices, not justify them.**

Two-Blank Completions Give You More to Work With

So far we've discussed only one-blank sentence completions, but everything I've said so far applies equally to the two-blank versions. Two-blank sentence completions take a bit more time to analyze than one-blank questions, so it may appear that they're more difficult. Remember, however, that we have twice as much information per choice during the process of elimination stage. If you can eliminate either word of a pair, the entire choice is out.

Work with one blank at a time. Focus on one of the two blanks—whichever you have more information about—and eliminate as many choices as you can. Then, apply process of elimination to the other blank of the remaining choices.

You might determine, say, that the first blank of a sentence is positive and the second blank negative. Glance at the choices and select the blank that has easier words to work with—which may be the second. Eliminate every choice that does not have a negative second word. If you're lucky you may already have found the answer! If not, simply review the remaining choices and eliminate every one that does not have a positive word in the first position.

On Two-Blank Questions, You Can Also Focus on the Relationship *Between* the Blanks

Although two-blank questions seem more difficult than those with one blank, remember that we now have twice as much information to work with in selecting or eliminating each choice. On a two-blank question if you can't even decide whether the blanks are positive or negative, you can often focus on the relationship between them.

Consider the following sentence:

> Like most -------, Tom was primarily interested
> in ------- people.
>
> (A) leaders . . enslaving
> (B) frauds . . swindling
> (C) scientists . . describing
> (D) teachers . . intimidating
> (E) criminals . . evading

It's impossible to tell whether the blanks are positive or negative, but it is absolutely clear that the two blanks are both positive or both negative. Choice D we can quickly eliminate since only one of the words is negative. The two blanks in choices A, C, and E are somewhat consistent, but only by stretching things. The only choice that works is B.

On more difficult questions, the relationship is sometimes more difficult to establish. Consider the following sentence:

> The table was ------- as well as large, so moving it
> up the narrow staircase required strength as well
> as -------.

The two "as well as" phrases establish what English teachers call *parallelism* (a topic we covered in the grammar review). We can make this structure more evident by setting up the phrases as follows:

-------	as well as	large
strength	as well as	-------

Here the first blank refers to the word "strength," while the second refers to the word "large." A possible answer would be "heavy" for the first blank and "agility" for the second.

But What Happens If You Don't Know All the Words?

So far you've learned a basic procedure for analyzing any sentence completion. Things get tougher when you don't know one or more of the words, but in the next chapter you'll learn additional techniques for handling these situations. As I've said before and I'll remind you again, the more words you know, the easier you'll find the SAT Reading Test.

Answers to the Direction Clues Drill (page 217)

Keep in mind that many possible words might satisfy a particular blank. So long as you've found an appropriate type of word for these sentence completions, you're fine. **Remember that on the SAT you're not looking among the choices for an exact match with the word you've anticipated.** The important thing in this drill is whether you recognized the correct direction indicated by the clue phrase.

1. The coach praised and ------- her athletes.

Discussion: The direction of this sentence continues, so a word like "encouraged" or "supported" or "congratulated" would work here. The answer would have to be a positive word consistent with the word "praised."

2. The proposed solution was expensive rather than -------.

Discussion: The direction of this sentence reverses, so a word like "practical" or "affordable" would work here. The answer would have to be a positive word contrasting with the word "expensive."

3. The prototype exhibited excellent design as well as -------.

Discussion: The direction of this sentence continues, so a word like "construction" would work here.

4. Neither agreeing nor disagreeing with either side, the mediator remained ------- during the opening presentations.

Discussion: The direction of this sentence reverses, so a word like "neutral" or "objective" would work here.

5. The audience was quiet if not ------- throughout the opera.

Discussion: The direction of this sentence goes to extremes, so a word like "silent" would work here. The expression "if not" is a difficult direction clue, so you may not have been familiar with it.

6.   The author's anecdote is as enjoyable as it
         is -------.

Discussion: The direction of this sentence continues, so a word like "instructive" would work here. The answer would have to be a positive word consistent with the word "enjoyable."

Sentence Completions: Advanced Principles
What to Do When You Don't Know All the Words

It's Scary Seeing a Word on the SAT That You Don't Know

When you get to a tough sentence completion on which you don't know all the words, it's easy to think, "Oh no, what's that word? And that one? What am I supposed to do?"

That's scary, absolutely. And no matter how good your vocabulary is, no matter how many words you memorize between now and your SAT, you'll encounter sentence completions with a word or two or more that you won't know. Guaranteed.

But just because you don't know all the words on a sentence completion doesn't mean you can't figure out the answer. And that's what you'll be learning in this chapter: how to attack a question when you don't know all the words.

This situation can come up in one of two ways. Either you won't know all the words within the sentence itself, or you won't know all the choices—or both. We'll consider each situation separately.

If You Don't Know a Particular Word in the Sentence

You will often, especially on the more difficult questions, encounter a word within a sentence that you don't know—and may not even recognize! Don't give up, you're just getting started. In most cases you can figure out what the word means from the context by using common sense or direction clues; if not you can often figure out whether the word is positive or negative. Even when you can't figure out what the mystery word means, you may not even need to know what it means to answer the question.

Here's an example:

> After decades of internecine warfare, both sides in
> the civil conflict were at long last ready for -------.
>
> (A) adversity   (B) escalation   (C) publicity
>   (D) separation   (E) peace

If you didn't trip over the word "internecine," you have the vocabulary of a college professor.

Not to worry. It's clear from the context that internecine, describing warfare, is a negative word. Actually, you can ignore the word completely and not miss any of the sentence's meaning. You were probably able to conclude that the answer has to be something like "peace," coincidentally choice E. By the way, internecine means mutually destructive, usually in a bloody sense. It is not a common SAT word.

Let's consider another example:

> Though the university awards ceremony was
> austere and -------, the celebration afterwards was a
> raucous, almost bacchanal affair.
>
> (A) studious   (B) official   (C) dignified
>   (D) glamorous   (E) festive

Yikes, three difficult words in the sentence: austere, raucous, and bacchanal. Well, let's see how far we can get using direction clues and common sense. The word "though" tells us that the direction of the sentence reverses from the awards ceremony to the celebration afterward.

Now let's use some common sense. What do you imagine university awards ceremonies versus celebrations to be like? Let's see, we eliminate choice A but an awards ceremony could be official, dignified, glamorous, or festive. The direction clue tells us that the ceremony was somehow different from the celebration, so which of these choices fits best now? The answer is choice C.

Okay, now I'm going to give you an important clue for the next example. **This is a medium question.**

Many celebrity assistants have thankless jobs,
trying to keep up with the mercurial and
unpredictable moods of their capricious and
demanding -------.

(A) producers   (B) taskmasters   (C) fans
     (D) sycophants   (E) entrepreneurs

Another question with difficult words: mercurial and capricious. The
direction clue (the word "and") connecting mercurial to unpredictable, and
capricious to demanding, gives us a lot of information about what these words
might mean. The meaning of mercurial must be consistent with the word
unpredictable, and the meaning of capricious must be consistent with the
word "demanding." Let's examine the sentence without the tough words.

Many celebrity assistants have thankless jobs,
trying to keep up with the unpredictable moods of
their demanding -------.

(A) producers   (B) taskmasters   (C) fans
     (D) sycophants   (E) entrepreneurs

Without the scary hard words, the sentence is less intimidating. We're
looking for a word that means "bosses." We can quickly eliminate choices A
and C, leaving us with choices B, D, and E. At this point, you may be unsure
of the meanings of one or more of the remaining choices. Remind yourself
that this is a medium question, so the answer should be a medium word.
Choice D would be a bad choice, since this is a very difficult word. The
answer is B, though E is a good shot (*always* take the shot).

Now we've got to consider the second case, when you don't know all the
words in the answer choices.

I don't want to mislead you here. You won't always be able to
figure out the answer to sentence completions when you don't
know all the words. The key is to analyze the question quickly yet
carefully. Then, if you haven't figured out the answer, guess. I'll
show you how to put the odds even more in your favor shortly.

If You Don't Know a Word among the Answer Choices

On your SAT, you will undoubtedly face several sentence completions that contain one or more choices you can't define. Difficult words among the choices occurs most frequently on the harder questions, but you'll sometimes come across a difficult choice even on an easy, early question.

Let's deal with the easy, early questions first. **The answer to an easy question is never a difficult word.** If you see a difficult choice on an easy question, you don't have to worry about it since it won't be the answer.

As the questions become increasingly difficult, it becomes increasingly likely that the answer will be a difficult word.

Avoid Easy or "Obvious" (Popular) Choices on Difficult Questions

Students are always attracted to easy words that seem to fit the context of the sentence. If the sentence is about art, for example, many students will be attracted to easy, art-type words like "creative" or "imaginative." If the sentence is about science, many students will be attracted to words like "experimental" or "hypothesis." **Since difficult sentence completions have difficult answers, on these questions you should avoid easy words that would remind people of the sentence subject matter.**

Try your hand at the following difficult question. Remember to anticipate the word that would fill in the blank, and then to apply process of elimination as far as it will take you. If you haven't determined the answer, guess. (Difficult questions have what kind of answers?)

> Kuhn, a scholar of the history of science, asserted
> that a scientific revolution occurs in a field when a
> new paradigm ------- an older, less successful model.
>
> (A) supplants   (B) invents   (C) corroborates
>   (D) verifies   (E) explores

The word paradigm is difficult so you might not be able to define it. Perhaps you noticed the concept clue: the contrasting ideas of "new" and "older." If you did, you might have inferred that a paradigm is a model. If you didn't, no biggie, let's try to apply some common sense. What would you do to an older, less successful model? You'd want to replace it with something better.

232

You were probably able to eliminate choices B, D, and E. These are easy words associated with the subject of science. Then you have to choose between the two remaining difficult choices, A and C. If you know what either word means, you don't have to guess; you can simply select the answer. But assuming you don't know what both words mean, you'll now have to guess between them. The answer is choice A.

If you selected choice C you made a great guess even though it wasn't successful. **Keep guessing. Not every guess you make will be correct, but if you've spent time on the question, it's always the correct thing to do.** It's tough to choose between those two words unless you have a "sense" about one or the other.

Before You Guess, Try to "Get a Sense" of Each Remaining Choice

If you can't eliminate a choice because you don't know the definition, spend a few seconds to get a feel for what the word could possibly mean. For this your knowledge of word roots or a foreign language may come in very handy.

For example, let's say you're on the last sentence completion looking for a word that means "stubborn" and—this is the hardest sentence completion in the section—these are your choices:

(A) duplicitous
(B) quiescent
(C) pragmatic
(D) munificent
(E) obdurate

Ugh. Sit with these words for a few moments and if you still can't eliminate any, circle the question and move on. As you're working on other sentence completions—or beyond that on the reading questions—your subconscious can search your memory for related words. Often, out of the blue, you'll work out what a word means.

If you don't get a sense of any of the words, make your best guess—difficult questions have difficult answers—and move on to the next question. (The answer here was obdurate. If you didn't select that choice don't fret, it was a very tough question. Your guesses on hard questions won't always be right, but you should always take the shot.)

As I mentioned earlier, don't attempt to figure what a word means unless your vocabulary is good to very good. If your vocabulary is not as strong as it could be, you're better off not trying to get a sense of the word. Simply guess and move on. **The important thing is not to spend more than a few seconds of conscious thought on each choice because you'll quickly run out of time wrestling with the words you don't know.**

> Notice precisely what you're doing when you're trying to get a sense of words. Instead of trying to figure out what each word means, you're asking whether a choice could have the specific meaning you're looking for.

Adjust Your Guesses to the Question's Difficulty

If you're stuck on an easy question, the answer will be easy, so guess accordingly. If you're stuck on a medium question, remind yourself that the answer can't be too easy, but it shouldn't be too hard, either. A word like "supercilious" is not going to be the answer to an easy or medium sentence completion—though it's the kind of word that would very likely be the answer to a difficult question.

On the two-blankers, be sure you weigh the difficulty of both words. A choice like *evanescent . . corporeal* contains two difficult words and so would be more difficult than a choice like *transitory . . solid*, which contains only one difficult word. To be consistent, rank both words in the choice. So one choice might be easy-medium, one might be medium-hard, and another might be hard-hard; then compare the difficulty with each other.

The following table will help you develop your intuitive sense about the difficulty you should expect on each third of the sentences: easy, medium, and difficult. The list shows a random sampling of representative answers from actual SATs.

On the first (easy) third, expect answers like the following	On the middle (medium) third, expect answers like the following	On the final (difficult) third, expect answers like the following
gradual	contentment . . enjoy	acrimonious
omits . . essential	vulnerable . . damages	cryptic . . lucid
enriched	predecessors	monolithic . . mosaic
modified	widespread	flouted
erode	value . . extraneous	mundane

As we discussed on page 202, remember that sometimes simple looking words can be much more difficult than they appear at first glance. **Rarely—at most once on your SAT—the answer to a difficult sentence completion will be an easy looking word with a difficult second definition.**

Sentence Completion Self-Assessment Exercise

So far we've discussed the likelihood of the answer to sentence completions being an easy, medium, or difficult word. This exercise will help you internalize the likelihood from *your* point of view.

In the table on the previous page, circle every word that you can define. Be honest; this exercise is for your benefit.

Notice the difficulty as you move across the columns from easy to medium to difficult. There's no "right answer" to this exercise, but take your time.

Then complete the three questions below from your point of view. Again, be honest.

1. On easy sentence completions I personally:

 (A) can define the answer to the question all the time
 (B) can define the answer to the question most of the time
 (C) can define the answer to the question some of the time
 (D) can rarely define the answer to the question, but I usually at least recognize the answer
 (E) have a hard time even recognizing the answer most of the time

2. On medium sentence completions I personally:

 (A) can define the answer to the question all the time
 (B) can define the answer to the question most of the time
 (C) can define the answer to the question some of the time
 (D) can rarely define the answer to the question, but I usually at least recognize the answer
 (E) have a hard time even recognizing the answer most of the time

3. On hard sentence completions I personally:

 (A) can define the answer to the question all the time
 (B) can define the answer to the question most of the time
 (C) can define the answer to the question some of the time
 (D) can rarely define the answer to the question, but I usually at least recognize the answer
 (E) have a hard time even recognizing the answer most of the time

Once you've completed these questions, reflect on your answers. What do they tell you about what to expect on the actual SAT? What do your answers tell you about how you should guess on easy, medium, and difficult questions?

Now answer the following questions:

4. If I am stuck on an easy sentence completion, the best guess for me would be a word that I:

   (A) can define easily
   (B) can usually define
   (C) can sometimes define, but I usually at least recognize the answer
   (D) can rarely define, but I sometimes recognize the answer
   (E) hardly even recognize, if at all

5. If I am stuck on a medium sentence completion, the best guess for me would be a word that I:

   (A) can define easily
   (B) can usually define
   (C) can sometimes define, but I usually at least recognize the answer
   (D) can rarely define, but I sometimes recognize the answer
   (E) hardly even recognize, if at all

6. If I am stuck on a hard sentence completion, the best guess for me would be a word that I:

   (A) can define easily
   (B) can usually define
   (C) can sometimes define, but I usually at least recognize the answer
   (D) can rarely define, but I sometimes recognize the answer
   (E) hardly even recognize, if at all

Again, reflect on your answers. They will help give you the courage to make the best guess on the actual SAT when you might be scared to do the right thing.

Never Leave a Sentence Completion Blank—Never!

On the hardest sentence completions, you'll almost certainly be forced to guess. Yes, I realize that you may not feel comfortable guessing, but you know that every question you leave blank costs points that you can't get back.

You may be wondering, "But what if I have no idea on a question, should I guess even then?" Yes, even then. You see, you'll always have some idea about a question. Even in those rare cases when you haven't been able to eliminate any choices, you'll know whether the sentence completion is easy, medium, or difficult.

- On an easy question, the answer will be an easy choice (eliminate the choices that don't work and guess among the remaining easy ones)

- On a medium question, the answer will be a medium choice (eliminate the choices that don't work and select a remaining choice that's neither too easy nor too difficult)

- On a hard question, the answer will be a hard choice (eliminate the choices that don't work and guess among the remaining hard ones)

So if you're completely stuck on a difficult question, select the most difficult, unattractive choice. And if you're stuck on a medium question—it happens—remember that the answer can't be too easy or too difficult.

The best guess on any given question will not always be correct, but making the best guess is always the correct thing to do.

Pace Yourself Properly!

Since the sentence completions are arranged in order of difficulty, you'll need to pace yourself accordingly. Move through the easy early questions quickly but carefully. Slow down a lot on the medium questions—the ones where the extra time will make a difference in your getting the question right or wrong. Then, on the hardest questions—sprint.

Unless you have an outstanding vocabulary, one or more of the words on the hardest questions will stump you. And as we've already discussed, spending more than a second or two trying to determine the meaning of the word is a waste of time—time that you'll need to use on the passages and reading questions still remaining in the section.

In short, work as fast as you can on the hardest questions to eliminate any choices that you know are wrong, and then guess. Just guess quickly, because you'll need the time for the reading questions that follow the sentence completions. As you'll learn shortly, if you have to leave any questions blank in the reading sections, they'll be reading questions rather than sentence completions.

Moving On to the Reading Passages

Congratulations, you now know everything there is to know about sentence completions. You can practice these techniques in your daily reading when you come across difficult words. See how far you can get figuring out what a difficult word means from any concept clues or direction clues in the sentence.

Why Your Comprehension Improves the *Less* You Read of a Passage

The Other Half of the SAT Reading Test

Two of the three sections of the SAT Reading Test begin with sentence completion questions before the reading passages; one section consists of reading questions. To give you a better idea of the layout of the passages within the SAT Reading Test, let's take another look at its three sections:

- 25-minute section: 9 sentence completions and 13 reading questions (3 medium passages)

- 25-minute section: 9 sentence completions and 13 reading questions (1 long passage)

- 20-minute section: 18 reading questions (1 long passage, 6 short-to-medium-length passages)

Again, there might be some variation from test to test, but you can expect this basic layout.

These passages are primarily nonfiction, and cover a broad range of topics. SATs have included passages as diverse as the hunting of whales, women in the workplace, religious freedom, and even professional wrestling. Apart from vocabulary, the reading questions do not require any specific knowledge. **All the information you need to answer the questions is provided in the passages.**

The passages usually express someone's point of view in a discussion or explanation of something. Unlike the kind of fiction reading you do in English class, the passages require little or no "interpretation." Instead, your main job is simply to follow the author's argument or explanation or whatever, and answer questions on the content or implications of the passage.

Here are the instructions to the reading passages:

As you can see, these directions are straightforward. They will not change, so do not waste time reading these directions again during the test.

Like I Said, SAT Reading Is Different

Reading seems like a skill you learned a long time ago, but SAT reading is different from the kind of required reading you do all the time in school or from the kind of reading you do outside of school for pleasure. If you read an SAT passage the way you read a textbook or a novel for homework, you're going to be in big, big trouble on the test!

Let's consider the how and what you typically read. One important aspect of your reading is that you always have background information about the subject or at least a context in which to place it. When you read it's either a subject you're studying or an area or genre of personal interest. If it's for class, the book or article is in a subject you're familiar with, and your teacher has probably discussed the main points. If you're reading for your personal enjoyment, you're probably quite comfortable with even difficult material.

Don't underestimate how much all this background information paves the way for what you read. And if you get stuck on something, no prob—you can take your time to reread it as many times as necessary. You're not in any rush, so you can ponder what you've read for additional insights. If you're still confused, you can seek out additional references or perspectives in other resources or on the Internet. In short, for your normal reading you have it pretty easy.

Now let's consider how and what you'll be reading on the SAT. On an SAT passage, you're reading an excerpt in an unfamiliar area, totally divorced from context that would help you understand it. If you're confused, tough luck: there are no class notes to refer to for an explanation, there's no glossary or index, nor any other source material for an explanation. If you don't understand a word—whoops—there's no dictionary or online encyclopedia in which to look it up. Then of course there's the time pressure factor. You have barely enough time to read a passage once and still answer the questions, much less read it a second or even third time as you might at home.

And that's just what you have to cope with for a passage. Reading the *choices* correctly presents its own set of even more difficult challenges.

How *Not* to Read an SAT Passage

Okay, tell me whether any of the following sounds familiar from your experience reading an SAT passage.

You read the first paragraph carefully, but by the end of the first paragraph you realize you're a bit confused. Undaunted, you push on (Mistake #1). You plod through the text conscientiously, sentence by sentence, trying to take in as many facts as you can. Perhaps you underline key words or phrases that seem important. You move through the passage doggedly, determined to get as detailed an understanding as possible (Mistake #2).

You've spent quite a bit of time on the passage (Mistake #3), so you're surprised that when you arrive at the end of the passage, you don't understand very much of the text and can remember even less. Yikes, but now you're short of time—can't reread the whole passage—so you rush through the questions (Mistake #4).

Here's the deal. You simply don't have enough time to understand and remember all the information in even a brief SAT passage. As we discussed in Tutorial 13, your short-term memory has a very limited capacity. Once it "fills up" with half-a-dozen facts or ideas—likely to happen some time in the first paragraph—your short-term memory hits overload and your thinking capacity drops to near zero. Not only is getting a detailed understanding of a passage impossible on a timed test like the SAT, but trying to do so is only going to get you confused. Moreover, you'll need that time to spend on the questions.

Since you're operating under extremely rushed conditions, all you can hope for is a very general understanding of the passage. Fortunately, since a multiple-choice test provides you with all the answers, a cursory understanding of the passage is all you need to answer the questions. After all, you don't have to come up with the answer to a question; you just have to recognize the answer among the choices.

> You may have heard or read the suggestion that you not try to read the passage at all, but instead go directly to the questions. This approach is extremely ill-advised—unless you're running out of time during the last few minutes of a reading section. We'll discuss how you should handle this situation in the next chapter.

The Real Challenge of the Reading Section Is the Questions and Choices—*Not* the Passages

You'd think that the difficulty on the reading section comes from not understanding what the passages are about. In fact, most avoidable mistakes arise from not understanding precisely what a question is asking or what a choice is.

That may seem remarkable. After all, how hard can it be to understand a simple question or the short choices compared to understanding a difficult and sometimes lengthy passage? Think of it this way: if you misread or misinterpret an entire *sentence* in a 900-word passage, your overall understanding of the entire passage probably won't be seriously affected. If you misread even a key *word* of a brief question or answer choice, however, you'll very likely get the question wrong.

As we discussed briefly in Tutorial 12 and as you're about to discover firsthand in the following drill, you need to learn to read what a choice is *actually* saying, instead of what it *seems* to be saying!

> The *shorter* the passage—and some SAT passages may be fewer than 100 words long—the *more* carefully you have to read it.

Read Carefully Drill

Part A: To demonstrate just how carefully you have to read individual choices, I've prepared the following single-sentence passage for you. Don't guess here; really try to work out the answer—you'll never see a passage this short again! Take your time, but don't take any chances: use process of elimination to be sure you've found the answer. **If more than one choice seems correct, keep working until you find a reason to eliminate every choice but the answer.**

> The last supernova in our galaxy visible from Earth was observed only five years before the telescope was first used for celestial observation in 1609.

1. Which of the following can be inferred from the passage above?

    (A) Telescopes were first used for celestial observation.
    (B) Since astronomers began using telescopes, they have observed no supernovas in our galaxy.
    (C) The last supernova in our galaxy occurred in 1604.
    (D) Supernovas can be seen from Earth by the unaided eye.
    (E) The telescope was invented five years before the last visible supernova occurred.

You'll find a discussion of this drill on page 264. **Check your answer before attempting the next passage.**

Part B: To hammer home just how important spending the time to read the choices correctly is, take a shot at the question below. This passage is the length of one of the shorter passages on an actual SAT.

The nation's health system requires a continual supply of new blood from donors to replenish its stockpiles. Freezing blood for long-term storage is a delicate, expensive, and time-consuming process; moreover, many doctors believe that the resulting product is unreliable. When stored in a solution of plasma and nutritive dextrose (a sugar), fresh red blood cells can survive and remain viable for transfusion for only six weeks.

2. The passage above suggests which of the following?

    (A) Additional facilities must be created to prepare and store blood for future transfusions.

    (B) Without special storage procedures, red blood cells cannot exist for long outside the human body.

    (C) The public should be reminded frequently of the need to donate blood, not merely appealed to in times of crisis.

    (D) The nation's stockpile of blood is dangerously low and needs an immediate infusion of donations.

    (E) The nation's stockpile of blood supplies is exhausted on average once every six weeks.

Check your answer on page 265—and be sure to read the analysis of the wrong choices, too.

Don't be discouraged if you found this drill difficult. I designed it to underscore how easy it is to be fooled by the apparent simplicity of even a few words, and to demonstrate why you have to slow down on the questions rather than the passage.

Improve Your Score by Unlearning Old Habits and Acquiring New Ones

You know that to change your score you have to change the way you take the test. Changing the way you approach the reading passages will likely be harder than changing the way you approach sentence completions. Your reading habits have formed over the past ten years or more, and have probably served you well in school. These same habits, however, are ill-suited to the demands of the SAT Reading Test. Still, by practicing the use of the new techniques in this chapter and the next, you can develop new reading habits for the SAT.

If you're already scoring high on the reading questions—say, one or two reading mistakes in the entire test, *under timed conditions*—don't change your overall approach; it's clearly working for you. Still, the techniques in this and the next chapters can be added to your repertoire. So *until* you're consistently achieving a perfect or near perfect score on the reading questions, you should adopt these new techniques.

Repeat after Me:

Quickly through the Passage,
Slowly through the Questions

Most students spend far more time on the passages than they should, not leaving enough time for the questions. The key is to get through your *initial* read of a passage as quickly as possible so that you have enough time to work through the questions carefully. As you answer the questions you will need to reread a passage every so often to verify a detail or to clarify a point, but your initial reading of the passage should be quick.

Your goal is to read a passage quickly for the one or two key ideas, then read the questions and the choices very, very slowly! If you have eight minutes left for a medium-length (500-word) passage followed by six questions, you should try to get through the passage in two minutes or less so you'll have six minutes for the questions. **As a rule of thumb, pace yourself so that you have *at least* a minute on average for each question.** If you generally need more time than that to read a passage or to analyze and answer the questions, you'll need to leave some blanks.

We'll talk about leaving blanks later. The key point here is to recognize the importance of speeding up on the passage and slowing down on the questions.

> As I said earlier, the shorter the passage the more carefully you must read. Indeed, you may paradoxically need to spend *more* time reading a 150-word, one-paragraph passage than you will to read a 450-word, three-paragraph passage.

Our Approach to the Passages in a Nutshell

Since your ultimate aim is to answer the questions, you'll want to spend as little time on the passage as possible and as much as possible on the actual questions. Here in a nutshell is our general approach to reading a passage and answering its questions:

Step 1: Read the passage *slowly* until you get to its main idea, then race through the rest of the passage as quickly as you can.

Step 2: As much as possible, force yourself to skim over specific facts and details.

Step 3: The passage may have a secondary idea but your primary goal now is to get an overview of the passage's organization (the basic way each paragraph *develops* the main idea).

Step 4: Get to the questions as quickly as you can and chop your way through the choices using aggressive process of elimination. Refer back to the passage frequently to verify details.

That's all there is to it. We'll have to modify this approach slightly for certain types of passages, but those four steps form the basis of a powerful method for answering reading questions as quickly and accurately as possible. We'll spend the next two chapters elaborating on each of these steps in great detail.

Before I throw you into the deep end by giving you a full-length SAT passage and its questions, I'd like to discuss the first two steps above.

Step 1: Read Slowly *Until* You've Identified the Author's Main Idea

No doubt about it, you don't have enough time on the SAT to read the passages at a leisurely pace. You'll have to *push* yourself to read the passages faster than you might like.

Now, when I say you'll have to read quickly, I don't mean that you should try to skim through an entire passage at the same rapid pace.

Surprisingly, skilled readers actually read more *slowly* than unskilled readers over the few important ideas, and skilled readers make up for the lost time by reading *much* faster over the larger mass of less important details. It's a bit like driving a race car: knowing when you have to slow down on the dangerous curves, and then letting the car rip on the straightaways.

Focus Especially on the Four Key Sentences of Every Passage

Regardless of the subject matter, the main idea of SAT reading passages is almost always located in one of four key places. You are probably familiar with the notion of "topic sentences," and this concept is helpful to us, also. **The first and last sentences of each paragraph tend to summarize the paragraph's content.** For the passage as a whole, though, where are we likely to find the main idea?

> **The main idea of a passage will probably be located in the first or last sentence of the *first* paragraph, or in the first sentence of the *second paragraph*. The main idea of the passage is often echoed in the final sentence of the passage.**

In other words, by the time you get through the first sentence of the second paragraph, you should already know the main idea of the passage, and be prepared to accelerate the pace of your reading dramatically.

Be Absolutely Sure You Distinguish the Author's Opinion from What "Other People" Think—the Conventional Wisdom

One of the dangers in finding the author's main idea is that, on the SAT, the passages often begin not with the author's belief, but rather with what other people think, also known as the conventional wisdom. Many of the passages on your SAT will not be strictly factual passages, but rather "opinion" passages. The author usually presents his opinion on a topic, and then supports it. **Before the author presents his or her view, however, he usually presents the conventional wisdom, or the "other side" of the issue.**

Think about it: if the author agreed with what other people thought, what would be the point of writing the passage? On the SAT you'll never find a passage that begins with a sentence like the following: "Most historians of technology believe that the mechanism of differential gears is relatively modern—and hey, I think they're right." **The author will not necessarily disagree with the conventional wisdom completely, but his viewpoint *will* be different.**

You have to read carefully—especially the first paragraph—because it is easy to mistake the conventional wisdom for the author's perspective, especially when the author goes back and forth between the two as the passage progresses.

The author will usually introduce the "other side" with a sweeping statement attributed to a large group (*scientists, historians, critics, artists, educators, philosophers, rock musicians*). Here are illustrative phrases that tip off that the author is merely articulating the common viewpoint he or she will go on to oppose in some way: *widely thought, commonly believed, often asserted, previously speculated, one approach, some feel.*

Again, don't feel that you have to memorize this list. With a little practice you'll be able to instantly recognize whether the author is speaking for himself or the "other side."

The tricky thing is that the author may be articulating the conventional wisdom without clearly indicating he or she is doing so. Read the following passage carefully and see whether you can determine in which sentences the author discusses his or her view and in which sentences the other side's:

> It is commonly assumed that the government's insurance of bank deposits makes them safer. If the bank somehow fails by investing customer deposits in risky loans that are not repaid, the government will make good the lost funds. Thus reassured, the public will not find itself in the grips of financial panic and create "runs" on the bank to demand back their money such as occurred during the Great Depression in the 1930s.
> Ironically, however, the perception of this "safeguard" induces banks to extend far riskier loans than they would otherwise, thereby increasing the likelihood of catastrophic bank failures. In the final analysis, bank deposit insurance may undermine rather than bolster public confidence in our financial institutions.

1. Which of the following is the main idea of this passage?

    (A)   The government's insuring of bank deposits may have unintended consequences.

    (B)   Financial panics and bank runs are not likely to occur in the future since bank deposits are insured.

    (C)   If the government had taken the proper steps, the Great Depression could have been prevented.

    (D)   The government should take greater steps to insure customer deposits.

    (E)   Banks should not put customer deposits at risk by making loans that might not be repaid.

Discussion: The phrase *it is commonly assumed* in the first sentence tips us off that the author is discussing the conventional wisdom. The second and third sentences are elaborations of a commonly held view, *not* statements of the author's position. What the author is actually saying in the first three sentences is this:

> It is commonly assumed that the government's insurance of bank deposits makes them safer. *It is assumed that* if the bank somehow fails by investing customer deposits in risky loans that are not repaid, the government will make good the lost funds. *It is assumed that* thus reassured, the public will not find itself in the grips of financial panic and create "runs" on the bank to demand back their money as occurred during the Great Depression.

I've inserted phrases (italicized) to clarify that the author is articulating what *other* people think. It is not until the fourth sentence—the clue is the word *however*—that the author tells us what he or she thinks. The answer is choice A. You'll find a more complete examination of this question in the next chapter on page 287.

So again: read slowly and carefully until you've nailed down the author's point of view. If you aren't clear about which side—the author's or the other's—you're dealing with as you read a paragraph, you'll lose the train of the author's argument.

> If the passage begins with the conventional wisdom, the author's main idea will most likely be located either in the *last* sentence of the first paragraph or the *first* sentence of the second paragraph. The sentence will usually contain a direction reversal word like *but, although,* or *however.*

The First Paragraph Will Open in One of Three Ways

You'd think SAT passages could have hundreds of possible openings. Amazingly, however, you can count on one of three variations for the first sentence of *any* SAT passage. In order of likelihood, here are the three possibilities for the first sentence of every SAT passage:

Opening Variation #1: The first sentence will set out the conventional wisdom. You already know that if this is the case, the main idea will almost certainly appear in the last sentence of the first paragraph or the first sentence of the second paragraph.

Opening Variation #2: The first sentence will be an introductory statement providing background for the topic. The main idea will occur anywhere in the first paragraph, probably in the last sentence. **If a question is asked in the first paragraph, the main idea will be the answer to that question.**

Opening Variation #3: The first sentence will articulate the author's main idea. The rest of the first paragraph will go on to elaborate on that idea. Sometimes the author then contrasts his main idea with the conventional wisdom before returning to develop his idea with details and examples.

Once you've "gotten a fix" on the opening paragraph and the author's main idea, you'll have a much easier time following the rest of the passage as it unfolds.

If You're Confused by the End of the First Paragraph—Stop!

Sometimes you'll come across a passage so difficult—or poorly written—that you're confused way before you even reach the second paragraph. You may think that if you continue reading, sooner or later the passage will begin to make sense. Unfortunately, what usually happens is that you become even *more* confused.

It's absolutely crucial that you come to grips with the main idea of the passage. Until you do, the details won't make much, if any, sense. Since the author frequently sums up his or her point in the last sentence or two of the passage, go directly to the last paragraph. By reading the last few lines carefully, you should get a much better grasp of the author's main idea.

> If you don't understand the first paragraph, immediately skip down to the final paragraph and read the last sentence carefully. Once you've gotten a handle on the main idea, return to the first paragraph and proceed with the rest of the passage. Now the text should make a lot more sense.

Step 2: Once You've Identified the Main Idea, Speed Up and Force Yourself to Ignore the Details

No question about it, skimming a passage under time pressure is uncomfortable and sometimes quite scary. (Like many other things about taking the SAT, the best way is often the scariest—if it weren't scary, many more students would be achieving outstanding scores, as we discussed in Tutorial 9).

So you have to train yourself *not* to pay attention to the details, because your natural inclination will be to try to absorb as much as possible, and probably underline the material you can't absorb.

Big mistake. As we've discussed at length, your short-term memory can handle only so much before it gets overwhelmed and short-circuits your ability to think. What's more, a typical passage on the SAT contains dozens if not *hundreds* of facts—and yet the number of factual questions on a passage will be at most *eight*. **In other words, most of the facts in an SAT passage are completely unrelated to any questions you have to answer.** Remember, too, that when you get to the questions, you can always look back to the passage to find any fact or detail you need to verify.

A helpful mindset to adopt is to think of reading an SAT passage in the same way you would listen to a long-winded friend who blathers on and on until you want to scream out in exasperation*, "Could you *please* get to the point?!"

* GSWLIU

251

> Important facts and secondary ideas are often found in sentences that contain direction reversal words. By far the most common such word on the SAT is *but*. Other words include *although, despite, except, however, though,* and *yet.* Whenever you see one of these words in a passage, circle the word—the sentence may come in handy when you reach the questions.

Underline as You Read Sparingly Only, If at All

You know you're getting lost in the details if you find yourself underlining every other phrase or sentence. These are precisely the things that clog up your short-term memory and clog your brain. If underlining helps you focus while you read, fine—but try to keep it to a minimum. And whatever you do, don't waste time *wondering* whether you should underline something or not. The clock's ticking. Underline it or not, but keep moving.

Take a Long Breath Now—I'm Throwing You into the Deep End

We'll examine our basic approach in more detail shortly. Before we do, I want you to complete the next drill. The following passage is typical of the subject matter and of the kinds of questions you can expect on the SAT. You'll have 12 minutes to read the passage and answer the questions. The passage is long, and of medium-to-hard difficulty. **Longer passages on the SAT contain more details than do the shorter passages, but they rarely contain more *ideas*.**

> The longer SAT passages may be preceded by a brief italicized introduction. This two- or three-sentence preface contains background information about the author or the passage to place the excerpt in a context for you.
>
> You may be tempted to skip a passage's introduction "to save time." Don't. No questions will be asked about the introduction, but you can scan it in a few seconds and the background it provides may offer you a useful insight.

Sample Passage Drill: 12 Minutes

To get the most out of this and the next chapter, it's important that you appreciate the difficulties of reading on the SAT. To experience these difficulties, you'll have to set aside some time and complete the following drill at a desk as you would on the actual exam. And no, it's not the same thing to do this drill reading comfortably on your bed while listening to some MP3 tunes you've downloaded.

This passage is slightly more difficult than average, though some of the questions are quite difficult. Do the best you can; you're just getting warmed up to the reading techniques.

Time yourself using OmniProctor.

The following excerpt is from a book by Umberto Eco, an internationally renowned scholar and prolific Italian author (nonfiction as well as bestselling fiction).

I frequently feel irritated when I read essays on the theory of translation that, even though brilliant and perceptive, do not provide enough examples. I think translation scholars should have had at least
(5) one of the following experiences during their life: translating, checking and editing translations, or being translated and working in close cooperation with their translators. As an editor, I worked for twenty years in a publishing house. As a translator,
(10) I made only two translations of others' works, which took me many years of reflection and hard work. As an author, I have almost always collaborated with my translators, an experience that started with my early essays and became more
(15) and more intense with my four novels. Irrespective of the fact that some philosophers or linguists claim there are no rules for deciding whether one translation is better than another, everyday activity in a publishing house tells us that it is easy to
(20) establish that a translation is wrong and deserves severe editing; maybe it is only a question of common sense, but common sense must be respected.

Let us suppose that in a novel a character says,
(25) "You're just pulling my leg." To render such an
idiom in Italian by *stai solo tirandomi la gamba* or
tu stai menandomi per la gamba would be literally
correct, but misleading. In Italian, one should say
mi stai prendendo per il naso, thus substituting an
(30) English leg with an Italian nose. If literally
translated, the English expression, absolutely
unusual in Italian, would make the reader suppose
that the character (as well as the author) was
inventing a provocative rhetorical figure; which is
(35) completely misleading, as in English the expression
is simply an idiom. By choosing "nose" instead of
"leg," a translator puts the Italian reader in the
same situation as the original English one. Thus,
only by being literally unfaithful can a translator
(40) succeed in being truly faithful to the source text.
Which is like echoing Saint Jerome,* patron saint
of translators, that in translating one should not
translate *verbum e verbo sed sensum exprimere de
sensu* (sense for sense, and not word for word),
(45) even though the notion of the right sense of a text
can imply some ambiguities.

   In the course of my experiences as a translated
author, I have always been torn between the need
to have a translation that respected my intentions
(50) and the exciting discovery that my text could elicit
unexpected interpretations and be in some way
improved when it was re-embodied in another
language. What I want to emphasize is that many
concepts circulating in translation studies (such as
(55) adequacy, equivalence, faithfulness) can also be
considered from the point of view of negotiation.
Negotiation is a process by virtue of which, in
order to get something, each party renounces
something else, and at the end everybody feels
(60) satisfied since one cannot have everything.
Between the purely theoretical argument that,
since languages are differently structured,
translation is impossible, and the commonsensical
acknowledgement that people, after all, do translate
(65) and understand each other, it seems to me that the
idea of translation as a process of negotiation
between author and text, between author and
readers, as well as between the structure of two

languages and the encyclopedias of two cultures is
(70) the only one that matches our experience.

1. In lines 3–8 ("I think translation . . .
    translators."), the author expresses the
    opinion that translation scholars

    (A) should have practical experience in
         their field
    (B) should have open minds about the
         opinions of others
    (C) are brilliant and perceptive, if
         somewhat academic
    (D) should be less concerned with
         theories of translation
    (E) should have more than one degree,
         and ideally in different fields

2. In lines 8–15 ("As an editor . . . novels."), the
    author

    (A) displays the scope of his erudition on
         multiple topics
    (B) reveals conflicting attitudes about the
         work of translators
    (C) elaborates on the source of his
         irritation with theories of translation
    (D) summarizes the breadth of his
         background and perspectives on the
         subject
    (E) confesses that he lacks the academic
         qualifications of typical translation
         scholars

3.   In lines 25–28 ("To render such . . .
      misleading."), the author says that it would
      be misleading to so translate the English
      statement because

      (A) in Italian there are two equally valid
           ways of translating the words
      (B) the word-for-word translation would
           not have the same sense
      (C) an English character would not speak
           in Italian
      (D) in Italian there is no equivalent idiom
      (E) the Italian translations use far more
           words than does the original version

4.   In line 34, "figure" most nearly means

      (A) body
      (B) thought
      (C) picture
      (D) character
      (E) expression

5.   In lines 38–40 ("Thus, only by . . . text."), the
      author

      (A) raises a question
      (B) employs an idiom
      (C) poses a paradox
      (D) proves a theory
      (E) introduces a metaphor

6. In referring to the "ambiguities" (line 46), the author

    (A) admits that two translators might very well differ regarding their determination of the sense of a text

    (B) points out that words can often have more than one meaning

    (C) criticizes translators who offer only one version of a work

    (D) rejects the commonsensical notion that literal translations are ineffective

    (E) anticipates the possible objection that translations cannot be as clear as the original work

7. What is the author's view of the concepts mentioned in lines 53–56?

    (A) These concepts are not useful in understanding the translation process

    (B) These concepts are theoretical, and refer to things that do not actually exist

    (C) These concepts do not adequately reflect the tradeoffs translators must weigh in practice

    (D) These concepts are outdated, and should be replaced by new ones

    (E) These concepts unnecessarily distort the meaning of translations

8.   It can be inferred that the author mentions "encyclopedias" (line 69) rather than dictionaries because unlike dictionaries, encyclopedias

(A)   are revised frequently, making them more up-to-date
(B)   are compilations of contributions from individual experts in many fields
(C)   do not contain literal definitions of words, making them more reliable
(D)   contain cross-referenced indexes, affording translators easy comparisons
(E)   contain the cultural contexts and connotations of the original and the new language

9.   Based on the passage as a whole, the author's approach towards translation, as contrasted with that of theoretical translation scholars, can best be characterized as

(A)   mercenary
(B)   untenable
(C)   literal
(D)   pragmatic
(E)   rhetorical

You'll find the answers to these questions on page 267. We'll return to these questions from time to time, but for now let's return to our exploration of the RocketReview steps to reading the passages and answering the questions.

Step 3: Once You've Identified the Main Idea, Focus on How Each Subsequent Paragraph *Develops* That Main Idea

In the first step you identified the main idea of the passage. This should have occurred by the end of the first paragraph, or by first sentence of the second paragraph at the absolute latest.

In the second step you then picked up the pace, forcing yourself to ignore the details as much as possible. The passage might have a second major idea, but on the SAT such passages are rare. You're underlining very little if at all, but you're circling words like *but*, *although*, and *however* if you encounter them; sentences that contain those words often come in handy later.

Now, in the third step, your goal is to see what the main idea of each paragraph is; its function in the overall passage. Each paragraph will develop the author's main idea in some way, and the only thing you care about now—before you get to the questions—is how each paragraph as a whole fits in to the passage as a whole.

An SAT Passage Can Unfold in Only So Many Ways

Under the previous step we discussed the role of the opening paragraph of an SAT passage as either presenting the main idea itself or setting up the main idea, in which case the main idea would occur in the first sentence of the second paragraph.

After the passage states the main idea, the main idea will be elaborated or supported. The author can elaborate or support the main idea in various ways, including the following:

- defining a key term

- providing details

- offering examples

- comparing a related idea

- quoting an expert

As you're reading the passage, you shouldn't care about the specifics of an

example, but rather simply that an example is being offered. As soon as you recognize that an example is being offered, you should race ahead in the passage—slowing down only when you get to the next example or the next definition or whatever other way the author is using to develop the main idea.

After the author supports the main idea, be alert for any opposing ideas or—especially—qualifications. An idea is *qualified* when its scope is limited, such as when exceptions to the idea are pointed out. Qualifications to the main idea will almost always be introduced with the direction reversal words we discussed earlier, "but" being the most common, followed by words like *although, despite, except, however, though,* and *yet.* Qualifications are also sometimes introduced with words and expressions like *of course, admittedly, not the only,* and so forth.

The passage will not always qualify the main idea of the passage, but it often does. So, after the passage states the main idea and supports it, and then possibly qualifies it, how else can the main idea be developed; where else can it go?

The final way the main idea may be developed is by extending or *applying* the idea into another area, to show the idea's significance or wider relevance. The main idea is applied when the author answers the further question, *So what?*

> The basic format of all SAT passages, then, is simple: *introduce* the main idea (possibly with the conventional wisdom); *elaborate* and *support* the main idea with details and examples; and then possibly *qualify* the main idea or *apply* it.

Following the Development of a Passage: An Illustration

The next passage illustrates a wide range of development techniques. Before reading the discussion below the passage, try to determine how each sentence moves the passage forward.

In the past, how has one civilization conquered [Q] another? Many historians have concentrated on [Conventional wisdom] the technological superiority of one side over the other's. Undoubtedly, technological advances such [example] as the development of metal weapons or gunpowder or even the stirrup for horses enabled one civilization to defeat another.

260

But the conquering side often had invisible allies, too. Europeans took over the North American continent from the native population as much by introducing—not always unwittingly—microbes and viruses into a populace that had no immunity to them, as by their muskets and other technologically advanced weapons. A growing acknowledgement among historians of the role of this phenomenon will undoubtedly lead to a radical reinterpretation of many historical events.

Discussion: The first sentence is a *rhetorical question* that is answered in the second sentence by the *introductory statement*. The third sentence *supports* the introductory statement with two examples (metal weapons and gunpowder). The fourth sentence *contradicts* the introductory statement with opposing idea (invisible allies). The fifth sentence *qualifies* the opposing idea by saying that both factors (technological superiority and invisible microbes) can answer the initial rhetorical question, and that many historians were not completely mistaken. The sixth and final sentence *applies* the main idea to the larger scope of history in general.

If You Can, Anticipate the Passage's Likely Development

One way to stay actively engaged in the passage is to anticipate how it is likely to develop. For example, if a question is asked in the passage, we would expect an answer to follow. A problem stated in one paragraph should be followed by a solution in the next paragraph. A general statement should be followed by an example.

You won't always anticipate the development correctly, but that doesn't matter. What's important is that you *think* as you read. Apart from thinking being a good idea on its own, thinking as you read *prevents* you from overloading your short-term memory with details because your brain is already occupied.

Writing IM (Instant Message) Summaries to Yourself Can Be Helpful

You know you shouldn't underline details on the SAT as you read, but if you're used to writing margin notes in the books you read for school—an outstanding practice that I highly recommend—this next technique may appeal to you.

When you read the newspaper, most articles start off with a main headline that summarizes the entire article. Every few paragraphs you will often see a sub headline that summarizes the next few paragraphs. If you were to read *only* those headlines, you'd understand the gist of the entire article without getting swamped by all the details.

Unfortunately, SAT passages don't come with helpful titles or subtitles, but you *can* write them yourself. I call these IM Summaries to emphasize that you should keep them super-short, as if you were writing a text message to a friend.

Keep it brief. Your IM summaries don't need to be grammatically correct, and of course you should abbreviate as much as possible. Your IM summaries are for your benefit; it's not like anyone else will read them.

Creating these IM summaries is an active process that forces you to come to grips with the main idea of each paragraph. Many students find that this process helps them focus and helps them ignore the details (which won't help you write a summary).

> If you have trouble summarizing a paragraph, you're reading the text too closely and getting lost in the details. In other words, read only enough of a paragraph to summarize its contents. As soon as you've read enough of a paragraph to write an IM summary, jump to the next paragraph and continue the process. Get to the questions; get to the questions.

IM Summary Drill

In the sample passage you just read, create IM summaries for each of the three paragraphs. Try to create your summaries without rereading the entire passage, which would defeat the point. You'll find my summaries on page 272.

The Fourth and Final Step: Answering the Questions

The first three steps of our approach to the reading passages and questions are designed to let you extract the gist of the passage as quickly as possible so that you'll be prepared to spend most of your time on the questions. We'll consider the fourth step in the next chapter.

After we finish discussing our process of elimination techniques, we'll discuss the minor modifications we need to make to our general method for special situations. Finally, we'll consider how to manage your time to maximize the number of questions you're able to answer correctly.

Take a Break from the Reading Section for Now

We've covered a lot of ground in this chapter so you've earned a breather. If you'd like to do more work today, I'd recommend switching to a different SAT subject—math, vocabulary, whatever—but give the basic reading concepts you've just learned a day or so to gel before you move on to the advanced reading concepts.

> The reading method you've learned in this chapter can be applied to your everyday school reading as well. Try using this approach when you have lengthy nonfiction reading assignments—*not* fiction—and you'll be amazed at how much time you'll save. The more you use these techniques, the more comfortable you'll be using them under pressure on the actual SAT.

Answers to the Read Carefully Drill (page 242)

Read the discussion of the first passage only, and then return to page 243 to complete the second passage.

> The last supernova in our galaxy visible from Earth was observed only five years before the telescope was first used for celestial observation in 1609.

1.   Which of the following can be inferred from the passage above?

     (A) Telescopes were first used for celestial observation.
     (B) Since astronomers began using telescopes, they have observed no supernovas in our galaxy.
     (C) The last supernova in our galaxy occurred in 1604.
     (D) Supernovas can be seen from Earth by the unaided eye.
     (E) The telescope was invented five years before the last visible supernova occurred.

Discussion: If you selected choice A—careful—you misread the passage *and* didn't consider all the choices. It says that telescopes were first used for celestial observation in 1609; it doesn't say that this was the first use of telescopes.

If you selected choice B—careful—you misread the passage *and* didn't consider all the choices. The choice says that no supernovas were visible from Earth, but astronomers could have observed supernovas from satellite-based telescopes. If you hadn't considered that possibility, you still should have worked your way through the other choices, because choice D is unquestionably the answer without any need to read between the lines.

If you selected choice C—careful—you misread the passage *and* didn't consider all the choices; you may also have misread the choice. The choice refers to when supernovas *occurred*, whereas the passage refers to when they were *observed*. Moreover, it would be impossible for us to know enough about our galaxy to say when the last supernova occurred.

If you selected choice D, you used process of elimination correctly and found the answer. Congratulations, this was a deceptively difficult question. If the last supernova was observed five years before telescopes were used to explore the night sky, then clearly supernovas were visible to the unaided eye.

If you selected choice E—careful—you misread the passage *and* the choice. The passage did not say when the telescope was invented, just when it was first used for astronomical purposes. See also the discussion to choice C, a similar error. Notice also that the choice refers to the last supernova visible—but the passage refers to supernovas *in our galaxy,* a very big difference.

Stop. Return to page 243. Do not read the following discussion until you have completed the question on the second passage.

The nation's health system requires a continual supply of new blood from donors to replenish its stockpiles. Freezing blood for long-term storage is a delicate, expensive, and time-consuming process; moreover, many doctors believe that the resulting product is unreliable. When stored in a solution of plasma and nutritive dextrose (a sugar), fresh red blood cells can survive and remain viable for transfusion for only six weeks.

2. The passage above suggests which of the following?

   (A)   Additional facilities must be created to prepare and store blood for future transfusions.

   (B)   Without special storage procedures, red blood cells cannot exist for long outside the human body.

   (C)   The public should be reminded frequently of the need to donate blood, not merely appealed to in times of crisis.

   (D)   The nation's stockpile of blood is dangerously low and needs an immediate infusion of donations.

   (E)   The nation's stockpile of blood supplies is exhausted on average once every six weeks.

If you selected choice A—careful—you misread the passage *and* didn't consider all the choices. Nothing was said about the need for additional storage facilities. New facilities would be of little use if the blood supply were not replenished continually.

If you selected choice B—careful—you misread the choice *and* didn't consider all the choices. The passage says that blood cannot *survive* for long; the passage does *not* say that blood ceases to *exist*. Indeed, common sense tells us that blood exists for a long time (think of a blood stain), although the blood would not long remain viable for transfusions.

If you selected choice C, you used process of elimination correctly and found the answer. Congratulations, this was a deceptively difficult question, too. If blood remains viable for transfusion for a limited time, then the public must replenish blood stockpiles continually.

If you selected choice D—careful—you misread the passage. The first sentence says that the nation requires a continual supply of new blood; the passage does not say that the current supply is inadequate.

If you selected choice E—careful—you misread the passage. The passage said that blood in solution remains viable for only six weeks. The stockpile of blood would be exhausted six weeks from today only if no new blood were donated.

Answers to the Sample Passage Drill (page 253)

1. In lines 3–8 ("I think translation . . . translators.") the author expresses the opinion that translation scholars

   (A) should have practical experience in their field
   (B) should have open minds about the opinions of others
   (C) are brilliant and perceptive, if somewhat academic
   (D) should be less concerned with theories of translation
   (E) should have more than one degree, and ideally in different fields

Discussion: This was an easy question. Some students select choice B. Of course *everyone* should have an open mind about the opinion of others; unfortunately, this is beside the point the author is making in these lines.

2. In lines 8–15 ("As an editor . . . novels."), the author

   (A) displays the scope of his erudition on multiple topics
   (B) reveals conflicting attitudes about the work of translators
   (C) elaborates on the source of his irritation with theories of translation
   (D) summarizes the breadth of his background and perspectives on the subject
   (E) confesses that he lacks the academic qualifications of typical translation scholars

Discussion: This was a relatively easy question. Some students select choice B, but the author does not say and does not imply that he has conflicting attitudes about translation. Consider *why* the author is mentioning his background. He begins the passage by teasing translation scholars for not having any practical experience in translating (the subject of question 1). He cites his own background, then, to demonstrate that he has plenty of experience translating.

3. In lines 25–28 ("To render such . . . misleading.") the author says that it would be misleading to so translate the English statement because

(A) in Italian there are two equally valid ways of translating the words

(B) the word-for-word translation would not have the same sense

(C) an English character would not speak in Italian

(D) in Italian there is no equivalent idiom

(E) the Italian translations use far more words than does the original version

Discussion: This was a relatively easy question. Some students select choice A which is a true statement, but which does not answer the question!

4. In line 34, "figure" most nearly means

(A) body
(B) thought
(C) picture
(D) character
(E) expression

Discussion: This was a medium question, although many students get snookered by choice C. **If we convert the question into a sentence completion, with the word "figure" as the blank, the answer becomes fairly obvious.** If we refer back to the passage—which you should do as often as necessary, *especially on this type of question*—we see that the author mentions "inventing . . . a figure." There's only one choice that can be invented: an expression.

5. In lines 38–40 ("Thus, only by . . . text."), the author

(A) raises a question
(B) employs an idiom
(C) poses a paradox
(D) proves a theory
(E) introduces a metaphor

Discussion: This was an extremely difficult question. Some students select choice A, but the author does not raise any questions with this statement (though of course anything anyone says can raise a question in somebody's mind). Many students select choice D, but this choice is *far* too extreme. **The author of any passage can make a *case* for his or her point of view, but he or she can't *prove* it.** Even though the answer contains a moderately difficult word—paradox—students who use process of elimination rigorously are able to identify the answer even without knowing the meaning of the answer. (A paradox is a seemingly contradictory statement that may in fact be true; a self-contradictory yet possibly true statement.)

6. In referring to the "ambiguities" (line 46), the author

    (A) admits that two translators might very well differ regarding their determination of the sense of a text
    (B) points out that words can often have more than one meaning
    (C) criticizes translators who offer only one version of a work
    (D) rejects the commonsensical notion that literal translations are ineffective
    (E) anticipates the possible objection that translations cannot be as clear as the original work

Discussion: This was a difficult question. Some students select choice E but the author is not discussing whether or not translations can be as clear as the original works on which they are based. Many students select choice B, which does *seem* to answer the question. While ambiguous words do have more than one meaning, that is *not* why the author refers to ambiguities. If we refer back to the passage—which again we should do frequently—we see that the author first claims that translators should focus on the sense of the work's words rather than their literal meaning. The author then says that these *senses* might involve some ambiguities, not the words' meanings.

7. What is the author's view of the concepts mentioned in lines 53–56?

  (A) These concepts are not useful in understanding the translation process

  (B) These concepts are theoretical, and refer to things that do not actually exist

  (C) These concepts do not adequately reflect the tradeoffs translators must weigh in practice

  (D) These concepts are outdated, and should be replaced by new ones

  (E) These concepts unnecessarily distort the meaning of translations

Discussion: This was a very difficult question. Many students were attracted to choices A and B. Choice A is too extreme. The author does not say that these choices are not useful; if he did, he would say that they should be scrapped altogether. Choice B is incorrect because although the concepts themselves are theoretical, they refer to aspects of the translation process that do exist.

8. It can be inferred that the author mentions "encyclopedias" (line 69) rather than dictionaries because unlike dictionaries, encyclopedias

  (A) are revised frequently, making them more up-to-date

  (B) are compilations of contributions from individual experts in many fields

  (C) do not contain literal definitions of words, making them more reliable

  (D) contain cross-referenced indexes, affording translators easy comparisons

  (E) contain the cultural contexts and connotations of the original and the new language

Discussion: This was a fairly difficult question. Some students select choice B, but while this choice is true, it does not answer the question! Many students choose choice C—perhaps because they are attracted to the word "literal" in this choice—but C is wrong on at least two counts. First, encyclopedias *do* contain literal definitions of words. Second, this choice misses the point of the passage, which is that translators need to consider numerous aspects of the original and new languages. Encyclopedias are more likely to contain different perspectives than are dictionaries, which are primarily confined to definitions.

9. Based on the passage as a whole, the author's approach towards translation, as contrasted with that of theoretical translation scholars, can best be characterized as

    (A) mercenary
    (B) untenable
    (C) literal
    (D) pragmatic
    (E) rhetorical

Discussion: The difficult vocabulary words in the choices made this a fairly difficult question. Choice C was probably the easiest of the choices to eliminate because the author was arguing *against* literal translations. If you weren't sure of the definitions of the other choices, you should still have guessed among them. Remember that every blank you leave lowers your potential maximum score by 10 points. The answer, pragmatic, is an important SAT word, and means practical. Mercenary means motivated by money (which, if you knew what it meant, you should have eliminated). Untenable means unjustified or hard to maintain (which, if you knew what it meant, you should have eliminated). Rhetorical means relating to the use of language, especially persuasive language (which, if you knew what it meant, you should have eliminated).

Summary: As I mentioned, this passage was slightly harder than average but some of the questions were extremely difficult. As a rough performance measure—for this passage only—use the following formula:

$$\text{Reading Score} = 800 - 60 \text{ (blanks)} - 70 \text{ (errors)}$$

So someone who left two questions blank and got two wrong would lose 120 points for the blanks and 140 points for the errors, for a rough—very rough—score of 540.

Answers to the IM Summary Drill (page 262)

Here are my IM summaries for the three paragraphs from the sample passage. Keep in mind that yours may be quite different from mine; the important thing is to get the gist right.

Paragraph #1:   translators need common sense

Paragraph #2:   Italian example, sense more important than words

Paragraph #3:   translation equals negotiation

On the actual exam I would have used abbreviations, so actually my test booklet would have had margin notes more like the following:

Paragraph #1:   trans. need com. s.

Paragraph #2:   Ital. ex, sense > words

Paragraph #3:   trans. = neg.

The Real Challenge Is Comprehending Not the Passage—but the Answer Choices

Our Final Step: Attacking the Questions

In the last chapter we covered everything you need to know to grasp the key ideas of a passage as quickly as possible. Now you're ready to attack the questions. I say "attack" the questions because that is what you'll have to do during process of elimination. On the easiest questions the answer will be relatively apparent, but on the medium and difficult reading questions, you'll have to work hard to *earn* the answer.

The Two Primary Question Categories: Explicit Versus Inferential

An explicit question asks about some word or fact or detail *stated* in the passage: *according to the passage* . . . . Explicit questions are relatively straightforward. Inferential questions, on the other hand, ask you to draw conclusions beyond what is stated: inferential questions ask you to determine what a word or sentence or idea in the passage *implies.*

Inferential questions are either general or specific. A general question asks about the passage as a whole, such as the author's overall theme or tone or purpose. A specific question asks about words, phrases, facts, ideas, or other details used by the author.

Explicit questions tend to be relatively easier than inferential questions. Most of the questions, however, are inferential.

Recognizing and Handling Inferential Questions

General inferential questions, such as the author's primary purpose or the main idea of the passage or the function of the third paragraph, are easy to spot. Specific inferential questions can be worded in various ways, such as the following:

- *The passage suggests . . .*

- *The author probably . . .*

- *It can be inferred that . . .*

- *The use of the quotation implies . . .*

- *The most likely reason . . .*

Even though you won't find the answer to an inferential question directly stated in the passage, you'll probably still have to refer back to the passage to verify details.

Let's say a passage includes the statement "Peru exports copper." You can *infer*—although the three-word sentence did not explicitly state—that Peru has more copper than it needs. The two examples from the Read Carefully Drill in the previous chapter (page 242) are excellent illustrations of the kind of thinking you have to do to answer inferential questions.

The answer to a specific inferential question is often the "flip side" of the author's statement. The flip side of Peru's having *more* copper than it needs is that at least one other country has *less* copper than it needs. The following drill will give you practice anticipating flip side inferences.

Drawing Inferences Drill

For the following three statements from passages, see what "flip side" inferences you can draw. You'll find my responses on page 301.

- In the presidential election of 1936, the Democratic Party won widespread national support of black Americans for the first time.

  In past years, blacks voted Republican

- Astronomers identified the pulsar as relatively old because of its slow rate of rotation. *when the pulsar was young, it rotated fast*

- Scientists believe that a human body's bone mass decreases under prolonged exposure to weightlessness because the lack of stress from bearing weight slows the formation of calcium-building cells. *people who tend to form calust*

Warning, Warning, Warning! Do *Not* "Read into" Things!

One of the most dangerous traps smart students fall into on the SAT reading passages is reading into things. As I discussed at length in Tutorial 12—which you should reread now in the context of what you've learned about the reading passage—you do *not* want to interpret what a passage says, or make any subtle assumptions. Restraining yourself from making unwarranted "leaps" on the passages may be something you must consciously remind yourself to do.

There's a huge difference between drawing a valid inference, and making an unwarranted assumption. Watch your step! For example, if a passage says that a university social committee invited a famous writer to speak at a conference, you *can* conclude that the committee felt that the writer was an appropriate choice for the conference—but you *cannot* conclude, say, that the committee admired the author's works.

The Five Most Common SAT Reading Questions— and a Conjecture about a Sixth

Certain SAT reading questions tend to go in and out of style every few years. "Best title" questions used to be very popular on the SAT, but are extremely rare now. General "author's attitude" used to be popular, too, but now attitude questions are much more specific.

Since the SAT is changing this year, all we have to go on are recent SATs. The following five types, in order of importance, have been the most popular questions over the past five years:

- *literary technique (mini-purpose)*

- *vocabulary-in-context*

- *main idea (primary purpose)*

- *tone (attitude)*

- *reference*

These questions appear frequently enough that I'd like to say a few words about each so you'll know how to handle them. If anything dramatic changes regarding the types of questions you'll have to handle on the test, I'll keep you posted on the website.

> I have a strong suspicion that the new SAT will introduce argument structure questions, especially on the smaller, paragraph-length passages.

Since these questions can be difficult if you don't understand the fundamental structure of an argument, we'll discuss arguments later in the chapter.

Literary Technique Questions: Literary technique questions ask you to determine why the author uses a particular literary device—a quote, an analogy, a particular phrase, even a quotation mark—so in a sense these are mini-purpose questions. Here are some variations and their respective answers:

- *The first sentence of the passage functions primarily as (the foundation of a particular argument)*

- *The quotation in the first line serves primarily to (express a widely held point of view)*

- *The second paragraph primarily serves to (anticipate a potential objection)*

Keep in mind that whatever the author does in a passage is ultimately to support the main idea or drive the argument forward. You might want to review our earlier discussion beginning on page 246 of the different ways an author can develop the main idea.

These are straightforward questions, so don't overcomplicate things. Focus first on the initial verb of each choice. The answer tends to include words like *illustrate, suggest, link, indicate, emphasize*—and tends *not* to be words like *show, prove, demonstrate.*

Vocabulary-in-Context Questions: Vocabulary-in-context questions ask you to determine the meaning or sense of a particular word or phrase—*as used in the passage*. These questions test you on simple *looking* words (*cold, fixed, light, set, touch, device, fabric, passion, signal, subscribe, designated*), but you must refer back to the passage for the context! **Several choices will offer plausible definitions, and the answer will *not be* the most common definition of the word.**

Refer back to our earlier discussion of second definitions under sentence completions (beginning on page 199). **In fact, if you aren't sure of the definition of a particular word, it's a good idea to convert the question into a sentence completion by pretending that the word in the passage is a blank and substituting each choice until you find the answer.**

> Since the new SAT has eliminated the analogy questions that used to test your knowledge of difficult words, the test writers may be forced to include more difficult words on the vocabulary-in-context questions.

Main Idea Questions: Main idea or primary purpose questions are medium to medium-difficult, but they can usually be answered quickly. These questions will appear either first or last in a question set, so if you're running short of time glance ahead to see if one is coming up.

Be careful to distinguish the author's main idea or main purpose from his secondary ones. The answer will be general rather than detailed, so look for answers that include broad words like *explore, examine,* and *assert*.

Tone Questions: Tone questions include the author's general tone as well as the author's attitude about specific things. These are among the easier reading questions to answer. Just as you can tell a friend's mood almost instantly when they start speaking to you, you can readily glean the author's tone or attitude. **Read the question carefully, however: the author may display different attitudes toward different things within the same passage.**

Start your analysis by getting a general bearing: is the author's tone positive, negative, or neutral? Eliminate some choices based on your general take of the answer, and then narrow your focus with the remaining choices.

Don't get subtle on the tone or attitude questions. The answer tends to include simple and unambiguous words like *appreciation, disapproval, respect, disrespect, sarcasm, reflective,* or *ambivalent* (having mixed feelings)—the answer is virtually never *indifferent* (not caring one way or the other).

Reference Questions: Reference questions ask you to determine what a particular word or phrase refers to. Read very carefully, the reference may not be obvious. You may need to read a sentence or two before the particular line number to discover the reference.

Chop through the Choices Using Aggressive Process of Elimination, Referring Back to the Passage Frequently to Verify Details

I'll bet the following situation sounds all too familiar. You're answering a reading question. You quickly eliminate three of the five options and get the choice down to the two remaining options. Let's say you had reached the following situation on a question.

1.   Which of the following best describes Arthur's response as he was about to enter the forest (lines 1-4)?

    (A)   fear of attack by hidden enemies
    (B)   (eliminated)
    (C)   (eliminated)
    (D)   awe at unknown mysteries
    (E)   (eliminated)

Then you think to yourself, "Wait a second—*both* these choices seem right!" *Now* what do you do? Selecting the answer to a reading question often seems like a matter of opinion: could be choice A, could be choice D. The words seem to mean pretty much the same thing. *How do you choose?*

It's important to realize that after you've eliminated the easy choices is when the hard thinking *begins*. Unfortunately, this is where most students get frustrated and wind up picking whichever choice "seems right." Sometimes this works; sometimes it doesn't. Fortunately, you're about to learn a series of techniques that will help you decide conclusively which is right and which is wrong.

There is one and only one answer to each reading question, and the other choices can always be *proven* wrong.

When You Can't Decide Between Two Choices—
Attack the *Simpler* One

It's easy to get stuck vacillating* between two choices like A and D above. The reason you get stuck is that you're still looking *for* the answer and both choices *seem right*.

> The art of process of elimination is *not* looking for the answer—it's looking for reasons to get *rid* of choices. If you're uncertain about a question, you can't choose an answer until you have found reasons to eliminate *all* the other choices.
>
> Repeat after me: "If I'm unsure on a question, I will not select the answer until I've found reasons to physically cross off—with my pencil—*all* the other choices. I will not select the answer until I've crossed off all the other choices. I will not select the answer until I've crossed off all the other choices."

When you get stuck between two choices, focus on each choice one by one. Start with the choice *least* open to interpretation—*not* the choice you think is more likely the answer—and attack that choice, looking for any little reason to get rid of it.

You attack a choice by taking apart a choice term by term and phrase by phrase, taking every single word literally. If you find *any* reason—however tiny—to eliminate that target choice, it's out and the other one is the answer. Obviously, if you *can't* eliminate the target choice you've attacked, it's the answer. (Unless you're dealing with more than two choices, in which case repeat the process with the remaining choices.)

So, between the choices A and D, of which are you more certain? The first choice seems straightforward, breaking it down into easy bits: fear, fear of attack, fear of attack by hidden enemies. Not much to interpret there. Let's look at the other choice.

The other choice is a bit more uncertain: awe, awe at unknown mysteries.

So our *target choice* is A. We're looking for any reason we can find to eliminate it. Notice that a "feeling" or a "hunch" is not enough to eliminate the choice—we need a specific *reason*.

At this point, if we hadn't earlier in the question, we'll have to look back to the passage to have some basis for our attack.

* GSWLIU

Refer Back to the Passage *Frequently* to Verify Details

Okay, here are the lines in the passage the question refers to:

> Arthur paused at the edge of the dark, dense
> forest, a towering sylvan palisade that extended to
> the left and the right as far as he could see. He
> had no choice; to complete his journey he would
> have to enter the forest, at once forbidding and
> majestic. He trembled at the prospect. . . .

Now let's turn our attention back to our target choice, probing word by word, phrase by phrase, until we find a reason to eliminate the choice—if we can.

Is Arthur *afraid?* Does the passage give us any *tangible evidence?* He's trembling, which could be a sign of fear. On the other hand, trembling could also be a sign of excitement, or awe. The forest is described as forbidding, so perhaps Arthur is fearful.

We're stuck, so let's expand our search to encompass more of the choice. Is there any evidence that Arthur is afraid of attack? Again, no. And certainly there's no evidence that he's afraid of attack by hidden enemies. **Again, don't "read into" things.**

Bingo, we've eliminated choice A. **Choice D is the answer by default, even if we aren't sure *why* it's the answer.** That's the way process of elimination works.

Here are some general points to keep in mind when referring back to the passage:

- Some questions refer you to specific line numbers. You may have to read a few lines before and after the specific line mentioned to grasp the context fully.

- Reading questions are in sequential or chronological order, so you should have a pretty good idea where to look generally. If a question doesn't refer to line numbers, check the line numbers of the questions before and after it to sandwich the location between those line numbers.

- Theme or general questions will not have specific locations since they usually pertain to the passage as a whole. (Theme or general questions about the passage as a whole will appear at the beginning or the end of the question set.)

- Inferential questions may not have specific information that you can refer to in the passage, but even on these questions you should see what clues the passage lines may offer.

> **Don't get overwhelmed by all these process of elimination steps.** It takes much longer to describe process of elimination—like every SAT method—than for you to execute the technique. If I tried to describe every step needed to tie your shoes, the instructions might run half a page or more, even though you could tie your shoes in several seconds. Remember, too, that you need to employ several steps only on the most difficult reading questions; most choices "crack" quickly after a probe or two.

The Answer Is Almost Always the Most *Defendable* Statement

The test writers have a difficult job writing reading questions. The writers must come up with a single choice that they can defend as the answer, and four more or less plausible choices that *cannot* be defended. That is why I speak of *attacking* the choices. Wrong choices are *easy* to attack. The answer, on the other hand, is usually the choice that offers you the *least* to attack.

What makes a statement or a choice defendable? The following joke will illustrate what I mean.

A Logic Joke

A mathematician, a biologist, an astronomer, and an engineer were traveling together from the United States on a train to a science convention in Canada. This was their first trip to the far north, and as they crossed the border from the United States into Canada, they all looked out the window to admire the beautiful scenery. There, in the distance, they saw a solitary black sheep grazing in a field.

The astronomer exclaimed, "Look, all sheep on

earth are black."

"No," the biologist quickly corrected, "in *Canada* the sheep are black."

"You're both wrong," the engineer interceded, "in Canada *some* of the sheep are black." The mathematician, who had patiently listened to his fellow travelers, rolled his eyes and said, "You're *all* wrong. In Canada, there exists at least one field, in which there is at least one sheep, which is black—on at least one side."

The process the scientists engaged in is called *qualifying* a statement. The astronomer started with an unqualified statement, a universal claim. A universal claim is hard to defend, so the biologist *restricted the scope* of the original statement. The biologist tried to make the statement still more defensible, followed by the engineer, and then the mathematician.

An *extreme* statement is very difficult to defend—or, what is the same thing, very easy to attack. Let's start with an extreme statement and see how we could make it progressively more defendable:

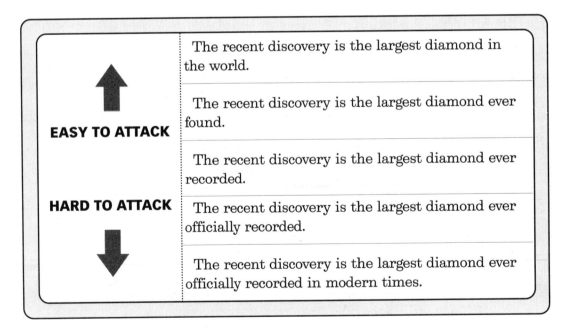

EASY TO ATTACK	The recent discovery is the largest diamond in the world.
	The recent discovery is the largest diamond ever found.
	The recent discovery is the largest diamond ever recorded.
HARD TO ATTACK	The recent discovery is the largest diamond ever officially recorded.
	The recent discovery is the largest diamond ever officially recorded in modern times.

The first and final statements both seem to be saying "about the same thing." While the first statement can be easily challenged (and would therefore not be the answer to an SAT question), however, the final statement is much easier to defend.

The answer to a reading question is not necessarily the longest or most qualified choice. Indeed, the answer is often so simple and so general that you can't argue with it. Each incorrect choice can be attacked on one or more grounds—often because they are too specific. If you're stumped on a reading question, the answer tends to be the least complicated choice.

This time let's start with a general statement and see how we could make it progressively less defendable:

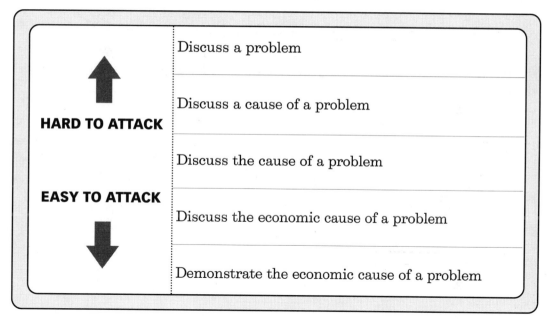

HARD TO ATTACK ↑	Discuss a problem
	Discuss a cause of a problem
	Discuss the cause of a problem
EASY TO ATTACK ↓	Discuss the economic cause of a problem
	Demonstrate the economic cause of a problem

Each time specifics were added to the original phrase, we gained more "points of attack" during process of elimination. The more detailed a choice, the more likely it is that one of those details is incorrect.

Just because a choice is defendable does not make it the answer. The important point is that on each question, every single word of every single choice was specifically chosen by the test writers to make one choice right, and the other four choices wrong. The easier it is to quibble with a choice, the easier it is to eliminate that choice.

Remember to Take Every Word of a Choice *Literally*

Many students have trouble with the reading questions because they're too smart for their own good on the SAT. Instead of taking every word of the questions and choices literally, they try to read between the lines to interpret what the choices "really mean," much as I'm sure they do in English class when they're hunting for symbolism in a novel.

On the SAT, however, there is no symbolism to be uncovered. As we discussed in Tutorial 12, because nobody ever says *precisely* what he or she means in everyday speech, we get accustomed to "figuring out" what someone "meant to say." This tendency *not* to take things literally can get anyone—including you—in big trouble on the reading questions. (We also saw the dangers of this phenomenon on the proofreading questions back on page 117.)

Because we do this interpreting unconsciously and instantaneously, you have to train yourself to be absolutely, *ruthlessly*, literal. To show you how difficult this can be, consider the two seemingly innocuous* statements below, one an opinion, the other a fact:

- *Every child should read as much as possible.*

- *The population of Dallas, Texas, is one million.*

I'm already giving you a big hint by warning you ahead of time not to interpret them, but I think you'll admit that both statements appear reasonable enough; certainly neither choice would be likely to set off alarm bells in your head if you were to see them as choices on an SAT reading question. But let's take a closer look at each statement.

The first statement is the kind of thing we would expect a well-intentioned schoolteacher to say. Unfortunately, if we put the statement under our SAT microscope's literal lens, it falls apart completely. So, every child should read as much as possible. *Every* child? Even three-year olds? And as much as possible? Outside of sleep, then, every child should be reading *continuously,* even during meals?

Now, you may be thinking that I'm being ridiculous, that *of course* "the person didn't mean that." But that's what the statement says. If "the person" *meant* to say that children who can read should do so as much as they reasonably can, why didn't he or she say so? **By the way, that was an actual SAT choice; I didn't make it up.**

* GSWLIU

Okay, let's consider the second statement. I'll bet even now, after everything we've discussed, it's hard not to read that sentence as saying that the population of Dallas is *about* one million. But it doesn't say that: it says the population of Dallas *is* one million, *exactly* one million. Well, if that figure were true when the sentence was written, it wouldn't be true a few minutes later, when someone in Dallas was born, or died, or moved away, or moved in.

Keep in mind that those were relatively *simple* examples; SAT choices can get much more complex. **It's not that the test writers try to "trick" you—it's your own brain that's hallucinating.**

Bottom line: read every choice literally. Pay close attention to all adjectives and adverbs: they can often make or break an answer choice. Remember that every single word of a choice was *carefully* selected by the test writers—either to make a choice right, or to make it wrong.

What Makes a Choice Easy to Attack?

The answer to any SAT reading passage question will be an easily defended statement. Factual statements are more easily defended than are judgments or opinions, which must be worded especially carefully to be correct.

The more extreme or committal a choice, the easier it is to attack. Consider the simple yet significant difference between the verbs *prove* and *assert.* Proving something to be true is far more committal (and easier to attack) than merely asserting it to be true. Or consider the difference between the meanings of *to explain* and *to suggest an explanation.* Explaining something is far more committal (and easier to attack) than merely suggesting an explanation.

Certain extreme words and phrases are very easy to attack, such as the following:

- *all, most, none, the only, same, equal, entirely, solely, first, last, always, never, "est" words (like best, tallest, greatest), "less" words (like useless, meaningless, endless)*

Choices that contain any of these or similar words give you an easy point of attack and are often wrong. Watch out especially for any choice containing the phrase *the only;* it's probably wrong. **Extreme choices are not always wrong, but they are always easy to attack—and so are *often* wrong.**

Other words are vague and slippery and noncommittal, which makes them difficult to attack:

- *some, possible, about, approximately, seems, apparently, primarily, generally, sometimes*

You don't have to memorize these words and phrases once you understand the basic principle of defendable statements.

I can't give you any hard and fast rules about extreme words, however, because you must always consider the context. The phrase "the only" is almost always wrong, but the phrase "*not* the only" is often correct. Consider the examples below:

EASILY *ATTACKED* WORDS	EASILY *DEFENDED* VERSIONS
all	not all
always	not always
the only	seemed the only
oldest	oldest known
the first	among the first
same	about the same

As you can see, it is simplistic to think that any words by themselves are always right or always wrong.

Finally, definite statements about the future—*predictions*—are always easy to attack (so they tend to be wrong). Be wary of choices that include words like the following:

- *cause, must, will, would, likely*

On the other hand, *qualified* statements about the future—*possibilities*—are hard to attack (so they tend to be right). Look for choices that contain words like the following:

- *may, might, can, could*

Again, you don't have to memorize any of these words; the important point is to be aware of the different ways choices can be easy to attack or hard to attack.

Let's apply what you've learned by revisiting a question from a passage in the previous chapter. The passage was on page 249 but don't refer back to it just yet. Instead, I'd like you to focus *solely* on the wording of the choices to see which ones are easy to attack and which ones are hard to attack. As you'll see, this basic principle is a powerful tool in your process of elimination arsenal.

1. Which of the following is the main idea of this passage?

   (A) The government's insuring of bank deposits may have unintended consequences.

   (B) Financial panics and bank runs are not likely to occur in the future since bank deposits are insured.

   (C) If the government had taken the proper steps, the Great Depression could have been prevented.

   (D) The government should take greater steps to insure customer deposits.

   (E) Banks should not put customer deposits at risk by making loans that might not be repaid.

Discussion: Choice A, the answer, is absolutely indisputable and impossible to attack: *any* action can have unintended consequences. Choice B is a prediction, so it is very hard to defend (especially since it is the opposite of the point the author was making in the passage). Choice C is a hypothetical situation that is impossible to defend: how would we ever know? Choice D is an opinion that is less defendable than is choice A; this choice is also at odds with the main point of the passage. Choice E is another opinion, again less defendable than choice A.

Other Points of Attack

Your goal during process of elimination is to find reasons to eliminate the four wrong choices, leaving you with the one right answer. In addition to attacking choices in terms of their general wording, as we've already discussed, there are a number of specific ways you can attack tough choices.

I'm going to give you a laundry list of reasons to avoid or prefer choices on a reading question. As always, you do *not* have to memorize this list, which takes much longer to describe than to use. **And don't get overwhelmed by all these methods; you'll remember what you remember.** I just wanted you to be aware of different perspectives to use to analyze choices when you're stuck. Add these tools to your process of elimination arsenal; they may come in handy.

- **Prefer paraphrased choices.** If the test writers have gone to the trouble of paraphrasing the wording of the passage to create a choice, that choice is very likely the answer. A choice that borrows a lot of the same words from the passage, on the other hand, is usually a trap. Such choices *seem* right because they appear to be saying *exactly* what the passage said. The only trouble is that those verbatim words usually don't answer the question. If the passage says that someone was "polite," the answer might paraphrase that word to say that the person was "courteous." If the passage says that a certain ritual takes place "after the summer," the answer might paraphrase that wording to say that the ritual takes place "in the fall." Naturally, the correct answer may have to use *some* words from the passage. But if a choice seems to say exactly what the passage said in exactly the same way, that choice is probably a trap. If you have to choose between a choice containing a verbatim phrase from the passage and a choice that paraphrases the text, go with the paraphrase.

- **Prefer choices that echo the passage's overall theme.** On the longer passages, the questions and answers often overlap each other to a great degree. Look for "themes" among the answers to the questions you've already completed—they will often provide clues about the ones you're having trouble with. In our sample passage on translation back on page 253, a number of the answers (1, 2, 7, and 9) echoed the theme of practical experience versus theoretical approaches.

- **Avoid choices that refer to the wrong passage location.** Since the questions are in chronological order, you can eliminate any choice that refers to a fact or idea that did not appear until later in the passage.

- **Avoid politically incorrect choices.** Invariably when an SAT passage describes the life and achievements of a specific person, the overall tone will be positive. The person may have his or her faults—who doesn't?—but on the whole, the author's attitude towards this person will be positive. If a question asks about a woman or a member of any minority group the answer will *always* be positive. Eliminate any choice that sounds even slightly critical of women or members of any minority group.

- **Avoid choices that violate common sense.** The test publishers warn students not to answer questions based on what they know, but rather limit themselves to the passage only. Nonsense. Although the passages do not require "outside knowledge" of the topic, that doesn't mean you can't use what you know—which includes common sense. It's easy to get so lost in the details of the passage that you forget to eliminate choices that are downright ridiculous. Indeed, there is always a choice or two you can eliminate on this basis even if you aren't clear about the passage.

> Don't start off being too critical in attacking the choices or you may eliminate the answer itself. It helps to go through the choices of a question *twice*, or even three times. Your first time through the choices should be *casual*; if a choice might possibly be right, don't eliminate it—yet. If you haven't found the answer on your first pass, begin to attack the choices a bit more critically on your second pass. And if you haven't found the answer on your second pass, attack the choices even more aggressively on your third pass. Questions of medium difficulty will probably require two passes to find the answer; really difficult questions may require three passes.

Postpone Making a Final Decision on Super Tough Questions

If, after attacking a question with everything you've got, you're still left with two or more choices, don't keep hitting your head against the problem. Circle the question number—*immediately*—and move on to the next question in the set. You'll find that as you work your way through a passage's questions, your understanding of the content improves considerably. And later questions may give you insight to answer earlier ones.

When All Else Fails, the *Simplest* Remaining Choice Is the Best Guess

Sometimes, no matter how many different angles you've used to try to eliminate one or the other of two remaining choices, you still find yourself stuck. You postponed making a final decision and moved on to other questions, but now you've returned to the question and you *still* can't decide. What should you do?

When you're stymied on sentence completions, you have the difficulty of the question to guide you: easy questions will have easy answers; hard questions will have hard answers. **Unlike sentence completions, unfortunately, questions on the reading passages are not in order of difficulty.** (As we discussed earlier, the questions for each passage are arranged "sequentially" or "chronologically" or "geographically": the first question will refer to lines early in the passage, the second question will refer to something a bit later, and so on.) That means you have no way of knowing whether the question is actually easy or hard. If you're really stuck the question is probably hard but not necessarily; you could, after all, just be missing something on a medium or even easy question.

Anyway, the guessing rule on reading comprehension is almost the opposite of what you'd expect.

> When you're *completely* stymied no matter how many different ways you attack the remaining choices, choose the *least* complicated answer. Avoid choices with strange looking words. Other things equal, the shorter and easier a remaining choice, the better. Why? Because long, complicated, difficult choices are easier to attack.

Two Question Formats You Should Know How to Handle

Two different question formats appear infrequently on SATs but are worth mentioning so you know how to approach them should you encounter either. These formats are EXCEPT questions and three-part questions.

EXCEPT Questions: These reading questions are among the trickiest because you're looking for something that did *not* appear in the passage rather than something that did. On these questions you're looking for something that is *not* true, and switching gears to a "reverse" process of elimination is difficult under the pressure of exam conditions. **Be very, very careful on EXCEPT (and LEAST and NOT) questions. Avoid them entirely if you're running short of time.**

Three-Part Questions: These questions—also known as Roman Numeral (I, II, III) Questions—aren't tricky, but they *are* more time-consuming since you're answering three questions but you're getting credit for only one.

Start with the easiest option first, which may not be the first numeral. Decide whether it is true or false, and eliminate as many choices as you can with that information. You'll usually be able to eliminate at least two choices right off the bat.

Then look at the remaining *choices* to see which numeral you should check next. **If you approach a three-part question methodically, you may not need to consider all three options. Take your time on these questions; if you make a mistake on any one of the three options, you lose full credit.**

Be Willing to Sacrifice Some Questions Entirely

Reading questions are the most time-consuming on the entire SAT, even without taking into account the time required to read the passage itself. Until you're consistently scoring above, say, 650 on the SAT Reading Test, you almost surely will need to skip some reading questions.

As we discussed in Tutorials 19 and 20, needing to sacrifice some questions is not easy to accept. Indeed, it's always at this point in my lecture on the reading passages that some student raises his or her hand and challenges, "But I scored a 550, and I still had time to answer all the reading questions!" "Sure," I respond, "but how many of the questions did you get right?"

I wasn't trying to be rude, but rather bringing the person back to planet Earth. Anybody can answer all the reading questions if he or she rushes fast enough. **The trick is *not* to maximize the number of questions you answer, but to maximize the number you get *right*.** Out of the 13 reading questions in a section, it's better to attempt 10 questions, say, and get 8 or 9 right, than to attempt all 13 questions, but get only 7 right.

> If you're making more than 3 reading mistakes in a section or more than 7 reading mistakes on the overall test, you're moving *way* too fast. Slow down to spend more time on fewer questions, and get more right!

How Many Reading Questions Should You Sacrifice?

Each reading section contains from 13 to 18 reading questions. The number of reading questions you should sacrifice will depend on how quickly and accurately you read the passages and answer the questions. **Instead of wondering how many reading questions you should sacrifice, it's better to think of maintaining your optimal pace—and the blanks will take care of themselves.**

Remember that your ability to work through the passages and questions will improve as you master the techniques you've learned in the last two chapters. What's more, as you get more efficient answering the sentence completions, you'll buy yourself more time for the reading passages.

You'll need to experiment to find your optimal pace. Again, if you're making more than 3 reading mistakes in a section, slow down. By the way, if you're making *fewer* than 3 reading mistakes in a section and you're leaving blanks, try picking up the pace a bit; you may be working too cautiously.

Which Questions Should You Sacrifice?

Since the only reason to sacrifice questions by leaving blanks is to save time, it makes sense that you should sacrifice the most difficult, time-consuming questions. **On the actual SAT, you'll need to be able to tell *at a glance* whether you should skip a particular reading question or not.** Unfortunately, as we've discussed, the reading questions are *not* in order of difficulty, so you'll have to make a judgment on the actual test of which questions would make the most sense to sacrifice.

When you have five to ten minutes left in a reading section, take a few seconds to glance ahead at the remaining passages and reading questions to budget your remaining time. You're looking for the length and subject matter of each remaining passage as well as the number and type of questions following each.

You may want to review our earlier discussions of different question types back on page 275, and of different question formats on page 290. Here are some rules of thumb to guide your decisions about which questions you should sacrifice:

- *It takes less time to answer a longer passage with four questions than two shorter passages with two questions each.*

- *In general, the longer the answer choices, the more difficult and time-consuming the question.*

- *EXCEPT and Roman numeral questions are time-consuming and are often confusing; avoid these when short of time.*

- *Vocabulary-in-context questions are sometimes difficult, but they can usually be solved quickly.*

- *Author's tone or attitude questions can usually be answered quickly.*

- *Main idea or primary purpose questions can usually be answered quickly.*

- *Literary technique questions are straightforward and can usually be answered quickly.*

- *Inferential questions are generally more time-consuming than explicit questions.*

Weighing all these considerations may seem like a lot to handle, but with practice you'll be able to make those assessments in a couple of seconds.

> **When you're down to the last few minutes of a reading section— even if you're not counting on having to sacrifice questions—do the remaining problems *not* in sequential order, but in order of their perceived difficulty and time-consumption.**

The Main Types of Passages

So far we've adopted a basic method for reading the passages and answering the questions. We're finally ready to begin modifying that method to handle specific types of passages. First, let's consider the different types of passages.

The test writers go to a great deal of trouble to find passages on topics they don't expect you to have encountered in your school curriculum. Once in a great while you'll happen to know about the subject matter of a passage, but don't count on it. As I mentioned earlier, however, all the information you need to answer the questions is contained in the passage.

Here are the most important types of passages, roughly in order of their importance (as always, you don't have to memorize this list):

Science Passages: Science passages run the gamut from astronomy to zoology. This category also includes philosophy. Science passages sometimes deal with unexplained phenomena. Don't be intimidated by any terminology. Despite the apparent difficulty of the subject matter, science passages are straightforward.

Social Science Passages: Social science passages include topics from history, economics, politics, sociology, or cultural studies. These passages often express strong opinions, and can sometimes be quite difficult.

Humanities Passages: Humanities passages include topics from literature, literary criticism, linguistics, art, and music. These passages are often about the life and achievements of a great author or other artist. Like the social science passages, humanities passages often express strong opinions.

Personal Narrative Passages: Personal narrative passages are someone's reminiscences or memoirs or even journal entries. Although they are nonfiction, the tone of these passages is so personal that they almost seem like fiction. In recent years, these passages have very often been written by women, often professional writers, and usually tell the story of the individual's arrival in America as an immigrant and his or her problems adjusting to the new culture.

Fiction Passages: Fiction passages are excerpts from novels. The novels will probably be ones most students will not immediately recognize (recognizing the source of an excerpt would not help answer the questions, anyway). Fiction passages present unusual challenges so I will deal with these passages in more detail below.

Modifying Our Basic Approach
to Handle Fiction Passages

Unlike all the different types of nonfiction passages, fiction passages don't have a main idea. **Instead, your primary goal in reading a fiction passage is to establish the relationships of the characters depicted.** What complicates the process is that you're *thrown* in to the middle of a scene or conversation already in progress and it's sometimes hard to get your bearings.

SAT fiction passages will be big on irony, so don't expect straightforward questions. Pay *especially* close attention to the difference between what *seems* to taking place on the surface, and what's *really* going on beneath the surface. (Fiction passages, in this regard, sometimes require you to interpret the text in a way you *never* should on all the nonfiction passages. As we discussed in Tutorial 12 and throughout the reading chapters, you must take what SAT passages say at face value *only*, without reading into things. Even with the interpretation you'll need to do on the fiction passages, however, try to limit yourself to the minimum needed to answer the questions.)

> **Everything I've said about fiction passages on the SAT applies equally well to the passages on the SAT II Literature and AP Literature tests.**

Modifying Our Basic Approach
to Handle the Mini-Passages

As you know, some of the passages on the SAT may be only a paragraph or two in length and contain even fewer than 100 words. You've already seen examples of these short passages in the previous chapter.

Remember that the shorter the passage, the more carefully you have to read it. Otherwise our basic approach to passages works equally well regardless of the length. Pay closer attention to sentences containing direction reversing words like *but, although,* and *however.* **If the passage contains only one or two questions—max—read the questions *before* you read the passage.** (If a passage contains three or more questions, *never* read the questions first or you'll overload your short-term memory.)

Modifying Our Basic Approach to Handle
the Paired Comparison Passages

SATs have featured a pair of related passages for nearly a decade, so there's good reason to expect the new SAT to feature them, too. The two passages will be followed by a set of questions: one-third of these questions will be on the first passage, one-third will be on the second passage, and one-third will compare the two passages. The joint questions ask how the passages are either similar (joint-agreement) or different (joint-contrast).

Our basic approach works well on the paired passages, but keep the following additional points in mind:

- **Although the two passages will not express the same opinion, they will not necessarily be opposing points of view.** Think of the paired passages as two different perspectives on the same topic. Typically the two passages will agree on some points and disagree on others. For example, the two passages may both agree that a certain problem exists, but differ on how to solve it.

- **Read the first passage and go immediately to the questions that refer to it.** Then go to the joint questions and answer any that refer to agreement between the two passages. Based on what you know from the first passage, you should be able to eliminate a number of the choices on each of these questions. Then go to the second passage and repeat the process: answering the second-passage-only questions before returning to the comparison questions you've partially answered. **Save questions that ask you to *contrast* the two passages for last; these questions tend to be difficult.**

- The questions on either passage are equally difficult, but students tend to have more trouble with questions on the second passage (perhaps because students are running out of steam, running short of time, or confusing the two passages).

- **If you're running short of time, you may have to limit yourself to the questions on one passage and the joint-agreement questions.** If you still have a couple of minutes left to tackle the second passage, consider tackling either the vocabulary-in-context questions (especially if you have a strong vocabulary), which can generally be answered quickly, or read the first and last few lines and tackle any remaining joint questions.

A Quick Course in Argument Passages

The word "argument" may conjure up a picture of a shouting match, but an argument is also a formal discussion in which reasons are given to support a certain conclusion. Consider the following mini-argument a father gives to his teenaged daughter as she is preparing to leave the house:

> *You should take an umbrella to the homecoming football game because the barometric pressure is falling.*

The father is trying to convince his daughter to bring an umbrella with her. That's his main idea, or the conclusion he's trying to support. His *stated* reason is that the barometric pressure is falling. His *unstated* reasons are that falling barometric pressure means that rain is likely, and that she doesn't want to get wet. If we add those unstated reasons to the original argument, the father would have said something like this:

> *The barometric pressure is falling, which means it's likely to rain, and since you don't want to get wet you should take an umbrella to the homecoming football game.*

If we wanted to *strengthen* this argument, we would need to provide additional reasons to support the conclusion; *in other words, we would need to provide additional reasons to convince the daughter that she should take an umbrella.* (Since you're wearing your favorite dress to the dance afterward, you especially don't want to get wet.)

If we wanted to *weaken* the argument, on the other hand, we would want to provide reasons to convince the daughter that she should *not* bring an umbrella. (It's not cool to carry an umbrella. The game is being played in an indoor stadium.)

With that argument as background, let's summarize what we know about the main parts of an argument:

conclusion: The conclusion of an argument is the main idea; what the author is trying to convince the reader of; what the author is *claiming*; the *point* of the argument. Even though the conclusion suggests the end of the argument, the conclusion can appear anywhere in the argument. Sometimes the conclusion is not stated but implied.

stated reasons: The stated reasons are also known as the *premises* of the argument. **It's important to recognize that on the SAT, the reasons won't** *prove* **the conclusion, but rather just** *support* **it.**

unstated reasons: The unstated reasons are also known as *assumptions.* Since arguments would be much longer if every single reason needed to be stated, we *assume* certain reasons that seem sensible and logical—such as you don't want to get wet, in our example.

SAT arguments—if there are any—are most likely to be the short, paragraph-length passages. There are different types of arguments, but they all follow the same basic structure. **Keep in mind that an argument may or may not be valid.**

The Four (Actually Two) Types of Argument Questions

Four types of questions can be asked about SAT argument passages:

- *Which of the following is the main point of the passage? What is the conclusion of the passage? The passage above provides the most support for which of the following conclusions?*

- *Which of the following, if true, would most strengthen the author's conclusion? Which of the following, if true, would strengthen the author's argument?*

- *Which of the following, if true, would most weaken the author's argument?*

- *Which of the following is an assumption the author makes?*

Notice that the third question is just the reverse of the second question. And since assumptions are unstated reasons to believe the conclusion, the fourth question is actually a variation of the second question.

Your primary goal in reading an argument is to isolate the conclusion. Once you've identified the conclusion—which may be unstated—you can answer any other question that can be asked about the argument.

If the question asks you which of the choices is an assumption, or which of the choices most strengthens the argument, you're looking for a choice that will make you more likely to believe the conclusion. If the question asks you which of the choices most weakens the argument, you're looking for a choice that will make you *less* likely to believe the conclusion—or even which choice will make you believe the *opposite* of the conclusion.

Sample Argument Drill

The following passage and its questions are representative of what you can expect on the new SAT if argument passages begin to appear, as I believe they might. You'll find the answers at the end of the chapter on page 309.

The popular conception of extraterrestrial visitors to Earth, as depicted in dozens of Hollywood films and science fiction shows, generally conjures pictures of tall, gaunt, pallid creatures with long thin fingers and enormous dark eyes. But if we reflected on our own initial forays into the depths of space, such as the Voyager mission—which has yet to leave the solar system after having been launched nearly 30 years ago—we would realize that our first treks into space were done by robots and not human beings. Human beings did not travel into space until many years after we had launched unmanned spacecraft. If we are ever visited in the future by crafts from distant interstellar worlds, we are more likely to be greeted by the mechanical R2-D2 from *Star Wars* than by the cute E.T.

1. Which of the following is the main point of the passage?

(A) Unmanned spacecraft were launched into space well before human beings.

(B) We will be visited in the future by interstellar spacecrafts.

(C) Extraterrestrials probably do not appear as they have been depicted in popular films and other media.

(D) Any future visits by alien beings would probably be preceded by automated exploratory spacecraft.

(E) We are not the only beings exploring space.

2. Which of the following, if true, would most weaken the author's argument?

   (A) We are the most advanced form of life in the universe.
   (B) Earth has already been visited by alien spacecraft many times in the past.
   (C) We will reach life on other worlds before life on other worlds reaches us.
   (D) Any other forms of life in the universe could not survive the rigors of interstellar travel.
   (E) We would probably not understand the greeting of an artificial alien creation.

Congratulations!

You've just completed the last lesson on the SAT Reading Test. As always, I strongly recommend that you take a break now—as if you needed any prodding!

Answers to the Drawing Inferences Drill (page 274)

You may very well have drawn other inferences from the statements in the drill; the ones I've provided here are flip side inferences.

- In the presidential election of 1936, the Democratic Party won widespread national support of black Americans for the first time.

Discussion: You could infer that *before* 1936, black Americans primarily supported the *Republican* Party in national elections.

- Astronomers identified the pulsar as relatively old because its rate of rotation was comparatively slow.

Discussion: You could infer that *young* pulsars have a comparatively *fast* rate of rotation.

- Scientists believe that a human body's bone mass decreases under prolonged exposure to weightlessness because the lack of stress from bearing weight slows the formation of calcium-building cells.

Discussion: You could infer that bone mass *increases* when a body is exposed to increased weight-bearing stress.

Answers to the Sample Argument Drill (page 299)

1. Which of the following is the main point of the passage?

    (A) Unmanned spacecraft were launched into space well before human beings.
    (B) We will be visited in the future by interstellar spacecrafts.
    (C) Extraterrestrials probably do not appear as they have been depicted in popular films and other media.
    (D) Any future visits by alien beings would probably be preceded by automated exploratory spacecraft.
    (E) We are not the only beings exploring space.

Discussion: The main point of any argument is what the author is trying to persuade us of. **An argument will *say* many things, but it is trying to convince us of one thing in particular.** Here the passage wants to persuade us that UFOs will not be "manned" by alien beings, but are more likely to be "unmanned," like the Voyager spacecraft. The answer is choice D.

2.   Which of the following, if true, would most weaken the author's argument?

(A)   We are the most advanced form of life in the universe.

(B)   Earth has already been visited by alien spacecraft many times in the past.

(C)   We will reach life on other worlds before life on other worlds reaches us.

(D)   Any other forms of life in the universe could not survive the rigors of interstellar travel.

(E)   We would probably not understand the greeting of an artificial alien creation.

Discussion: To weaken any argument, we're looking for a choice that will make us believe something *other* than the author's main idea—ideally, a choice that will make us believe the opposite of the author's claim. Here, then, we're looking for a choice that will make us believe that any future UFOs *will* contain actual alien beings. Choices A, C, and especially D *support* the argument; choice E is just off base. The answer is choice B: if we've already been visited many times in the past, it's far more likely that future spacecraft will not be unmanned exploratory alien spacecraft.

RocketReview's Unique Power Rankings of the 323 Most Important SAT Words

Hey, I Forget: Did I Mention How Important Vocabulary Still Is on the SAT?

As you know, vocabulary is tested not just on the sentence completions, but also on the reading questions. In this chapter you'll get a list of the most important words to know for the SAT. I'll also show you how to memorize these words as easily as possible—and how *not* to memorize them.

> Even small improvements in your vocabulary can lead to *explosive* gains in your SAT reading score—and I can prove it.
>
> Let's say a student knows three out of the five (60 percent) of the choices on a difficult sentence completion. Assuming the answer is not one of the three words she already knows, this student has a 50 percent chance of answering the question correctly (since the answer is one of the two remaining choices).
>
> But a student who knows four out of the five (80 percent) of the choices has a 100 percent chance of answering the question correctly—since only one choice remains!
>
> Notice how dramatically process of elimination translates vocabulary improvements into score gains. Remember: you don't have to know *all* of the words on any SAT sentence completion or reading question to answer it correctly—you just have to know *most* of the words.

How the Power Rankings Were Compiled

The more frequently a word appears on past SATs, the more likely it is to appear on *your* SAT. But the value of any particular word *to your SAT score* is not just how often the word has appeared in the past on SATs, but whether your knowing that word will make a difference to your answering the question correctly or not.

To take an absurdly simple example, "the" is the word that has appeared most frequently on past SAT Reading Tests, but obviously knowing that word will not make a difference to your answering a sentence completion or reading question correctly. The more difficult a word, the more valuable your knowing it is to your SAT score.

RocketReview's Power Rankings combine all these factors—the frequency of a word on SATs, its value to you, and the likelihood of your knowing it—into a single number. Every word that has appeared on an SAT in the past twenty-five years has been ranked and the results provided here, in descending order of importance.

A Line Had to Be Drawn Somewhere

The #1 word on the list is *conventional.* As the second-most top ranked SAT word, *undermine* has a power ranking of 100. That doesn't mean it has a 100 percent chance of showing up on an SAT; it's just a round number that permits us to compare the relative SAT value of knowing that word compared to another. The 323rd word on the list—*circumspect*—has a power ranking of 20; significant, but only 20 percent as valuable to your SAT score as the word *conventional.*

By the time we drop to *cunning,* the 813th word on the list, the power ranking is down to 10. At a certain point, learning additional words—always a good thing—offers diminishing SAT returns. The SAT point value of the top 323 words equals the point value of the 904 words below them in the rankings, and the next couple of *thousand* words below those.

Don't get me wrong—there are *lots* of words worth knowing for school, for expressing your ideas, or for understanding others. Whenever you get a chance to memorize the definition of any new word you come across, *do so!* But for your immediate purposes, I wanted to keep this list to manageable proportions. Your time is valuable, and I know how crazy busy you probably are, so it makes sense to focus first on the words *most* likely to improve your SAT score.

Just how good is this list? Of the 54 sentence completions and reading questions in the SAT Reading Test, you can expect the *answers* to 10 to 16 of those questions to include variations of the words from this core list. In addition, between 30 and 60 of the wrong choices will contain words from this list. That's not to mention the times these words will appear elsewhere in the SAT Reading Test.

These estimates assume that the test writers will not depart radically from the way they have constructed previous SATs. SAT test writers are creatures of habit, so this is a fairly safe assumption. Still, check out the RocketReview website for any breaking news.

This Core List Is Just a Start

Obviously this list of 323 words is just a starting point. You'll find additional power ranked SAT words at the RocketReview site that the CD-ROM gives you access to. These words can be easily printed out for further study. You'll also find an extended discussion of each word, including notes on pronunciation and etymology.

As I mentioned, you should make a point of memorizing new words that you encounter in your daily reading—not just in English class. Whether you're studying history, reading a cheesy novel, or skimming a newspaper, you encounter many words each day that you could add to your vocabulary if you made learning words a priority, and you should. No matter *what* you want to do in college and beyond, the better able you are to express your ideas, the better you will do. End of sermon.

Oh, by the way, get a good paperback dictionary that you can consult when you come across a new word—and keep that dictionary in your knapsack at all times so that you'll *use* it. The best paperback dictionaries are the *Merriam-Webster Dictionary,* the *Oxford Dictionary and Thesaurus, Webster's New World Dictionary and Thesaurus,* and the *American Heritage Dictionary.* Check them out and buy one that feels comfortable in your hands.

You're Probably Familiar with a Lot of the SAT Power Words Already—but Read the Definitions Anyway (Just in Case)

Unfortunately, merely being familiar with a word, or being "able to use it in a sentence," is not enough on the SAT. Don't assume you know the "easy"

words on this list! Most words have more than one meaning—sometimes very different meanings—so the definitions provided here are the meanings of words as tested on the SAT. **If you can't provide a dictionary definition of *all* the meanings of a power ranked word, memorize the definition or definitions provided.**

A good example of a word's various meanings can be found in *compromised,* #115 in the power rankings. I know you know the simple definition of *to compromise* as to give up something during a dispute or to settle differences. But *to compromise* also means to expose something to danger or loss, as in the sentence, "Some students complained that the fairness of the pop quiz had been compromised because the teacher had given some a few people advance warning." It's this second definition of *compromise* that is usually tested on the SAT, not the first.

Other power words whose SAT definitions are *not* the meanings that spring first to mind include the following: *animated, champion, detached, discriminating, engaging, exacting, parallel, parochial, reserved, resigned, restrained,* and *temper.*

Don't Take All the Definitions Literally

What's more, even if you *are* familiar with the literal meaning of a word, you may not be familiar with all the contexts in which the word can be used. **Be alert to the *metaphorical* uses of a word.**

The word *embellish,* for example, means to make something more beautiful by adding decorations or ornaments. But embellish *also* means to fib, as in making a story more interesting by adding *fictitious* details, as in the sentence, "Steve embellished his college application by saying that he had been a member of his school's varsity football team since freshman year—without mentioning that he was the team's water boy."

Chip Away at the List in Your Spare Time

First, do *not* try to set aside special time to memorize definitions every day; we both know you're not likely to stick to any formal schedule like that. Instead, you'll find it much easier, and more effective, to *chip away* at the list during spare moments that otherwise go wasted.

Think about all the times throughout the day when you're between activities with nothing to do—especially times when you're bored or annoyed, *waiting* for something: waiting for a bus, waiting to use a school computer, waiting for a class to start, waiting in a movie line. It doesn't seem like much time, but a minute here, a couple of minutes there . . . by the end of the day all those spare moments add up to as much as a half an hour a day—*wasted*.

Those occasions are usually too short or too inconvenient to get any homework done, or even to take out your MP3 player. But they are ideal times to memorize a vocabulary word or two. From the RocketReview site, you'll be able to check off as many words as you want for that day and print out a sheet to carry around with you in your knapsack or hip pocket during the day.

Get in the habit of pulling out the day's vocabulary sheet the moment you realize you're bored or annoyed because you're not doing anything. Not only will you be improving your vocabulary and SAT score, you'll also be making productive use of your time.

See Whether You Can Define Each Word before Peeking at Its Definition

You'll memorize the words more easily if you make a sincere try at defining each word before reading the definition provided. **If you can't define a word before peeking at the definition, try to decide whether the word is positive or negative. If you can't define a word but you know you've seen it before, try to determine in what class you might have encountered the word.** Sometimes just recognizing that you heard a particular word in English class or history or biology or art or whatever is enough on the SAT to decide whether the word is the answer you're looking for on a question or not.

Each word is followed by a quick definition, and then an extended discussion that often includes related words. **Be sure you familiarize yourself with any spelling variations of the different parts of speech since the word may appear in a different form on the SAT.**

How to Memorize These Words—and How Not To

First, do *not* make flash cards. Apart from the time wasted in creating them, flash cards are one of the *least* effective ways of memorizing anything. Repeating the definition of a word over and over is not only ineffective and time-consuming, it's *boring*.

Your brain is good at remembering four things: *pictures, patterns, stories,* and *rhymes*. All mnemonics, or memory tricks, are based on one or more of these four methods. If you want to remember something permanently, find a way to create a *picture, pattern, story,* or *rhyme* out of it. Here are some examples:

- Let's say you noticed that the etymology of a word you didn't know—like *immutable*—is related to the etymology of a word you do know, like mutation. Here the common pattern of letters of "mut," meaning to change, helps you remember the meaning of the new word and enhances your understanding of both words.

- Let's say you wanted to memorize that *undermine* means to weaken the support of something from underneath or within. You could use a picture and story by visualizing a person digging a mine underground that collapses a building above it.

- Let's say you wanted to memorize that *mitigate* means to lessen the severity of something. You could break the word down into words you could visualize, like *mitt* and *gate*. Then you could create a story with those pictures by visualizing a gate slamming on your hand but a mitt softening the blow. **The sillier the image, the more memorable.**

- Let's say you wanted to memorize that *daunting* means discouraging or intimidating someone. *Daunting* rhymes with *haunting*, which means being visited by a ghost or some other supernatural being. The two words do not have exactly the same meaning, but the meanings are close enough that knowing *haunting* helps you remember *daunting*.

I'm sure you've already used these techniques to memorize foreign language vocabulary for a test. These methods work equally well for memorizing English vocabulary.

The Power Ranked Core Words

The following list provides the 323 top power ranked SAT words, beginning with the most valuable word—*undermine*—and working its way down. Each entry includes the core word, followed by its power ranking (just to give you an idea of each word's relative SAT worth).

- **If the core word can appear in variations that differ significantly from the core word's spelling or meaning, these forms are included in a parenthesis following the definition.**

- **I have sometimes taken liberties with precise definitions in the interests of simplicity, or to connect one core word to another closely related core word. Italicized words in a definition are themselves power ranked core words.**

PART V

THE SAT
MATH TEST

REMEMBER: SAT Math Is *Different*

Introduction to the SAT Math Test

How SAT Math Is Different from Classroom Math

The Good News: Even Though SAT Math This Year *Is* a Bit Tougher, It's Still Pretty Basic Stuff

Most students are surprised to find out just how basic SAT math is: arithmetic, geometry, algebra, and a smattering of elementary logic and probability. Yes, the SAT Math Test for the first time now includes a *bit* of algebra II—*not much*—but most of the concepts tested were familiar to you by ninth grade, if not earlier. You won't need the quadratic formula, or any trigonometry; and you won't need to prove any geometry theorem. Indeed, one of the problems many students face on the SAT Math Test is *remembering* their basic math from junior high school.

> As I'll remind you frequently in the math chapters, you *already* know all of the math covered on the SAT. The trick is learning how to *reason* in new ways with fairly basic math concepts.

The SAT Math Test will probably consist of 52 questions in three sections. Forty of the questions are regular, multiple-choice questions. Twelve of the questions are more like the math problems you solve in school. These questions do not provide choices; you must work out the answer to these "student response" questions and "grid-in" your result into special boxes on your answer sheet. **Unlike your math tests in school, however, you will *not* receive any "partial credit" for your work.**

More Good News: They Provide Most of the Formulas You Need

Here are the instructions you'll find on each section of the SAT Math Test:

Directions: You may use any available space in your booklet for scratch work, but only your answer sheet will be graded. When you have determined the answer to a question, fill in the corresponding oval on your answer sheet.

Notes:

1. You may use a calculator. All numbers used are real numbers. All figures lie in a plane unless otherwise indicated.

2. Figures that accompany problems are intended to provide information useful in solving the problems. They are drawn as accurately as possible EXCEPT when a specific problem states that the figure is not drawn to scale.

Reference Information

$A = \pi r^2$
$C = 2\pi r$ 　　 $A = lw$ 　　 $A = \frac{1}{2}bh$ 　　 $V = lwh$ 　　 $V = \pi r^2 h$ 　　 $c^2 = a^2 + b^2$ 　　 Special Right Triangles

The number of degrees of arc in a circle is 360.
The measure in degrees of a straight angle is 180.
The sum of the measures in degrees of the angles of a triangle is 180.

You probably know most or all of these formulas already, but spend a minute to review this information so you do not waste precious seconds on the actual exam doing so.

Because the new SAT math instructions may provide a bit more information to cover the slightly more advanced concepts now in the test, glance—just glance—at any *new* formulas; one may come in handy. The *only* important facts in the instructions are the formulas; the "notes" will not change significantly.

The Bad News: The SAT Math Test Camouflages Simple Concepts

If the math on the SAT is so basic—and it is—you may be wondering how anyone can find it difficult. One of the big reasons that students have trouble on the SAT Math Test is that the test writers do an excellent job of transforming very simple math concepts so that these concepts are barely recognizable. But the real reason students have trouble is that the SAT tests their knowledge very differently from the way you're used to being tested in school.

> Never let an unfamiliar term on an SAT math problem bamboozle you. The test writers often stumble in their efforts to remove ambiguities from problems that only a mathematics professor would quibble with—creating needless confusion for hundreds of thousands of SAT students. One of my favorite terms in this regard is "non-overlapping," which just means touching in one point at most.

SAT Math Is *Way* Different from School Math

The SAT Math Test is remarkably different from the kind of math tests you're used to taking in school. **As I said in Tutorial 2: if you take the SAT Math Test the way you're used to taking math tests in school, you're in for a rude surprise.** Consider the following differences:

- **The SAT Math Test is a multiple-choice test; you receive no partial credit for your work if the solution isn't correct.** In school if your math solution is "mostly correct," you will probably receive close to full credit even if your exact answer is off the mark. *Not on the SAT.* On the SAT, if you're even a bit off the answer—for whatever reason—you'll lose *full* credit for that question. This difference is *huge,* and will completely reverse your priorities from being quick and clever (but sometimes sloppy) on school tests, to being ruthlessly, *obsessively* accurate on the SAT.

- **SAT math questions are all worth the same amount.** Again, this will completely upend your usual priority on school math tests to spend the most amount of time on the most difficult questions. On a school test you can't afford to miss a difficult question (because it's usually worth a lot of points). On the SAT Math Test, you can't afford to miss an easy question.

- **SAT math questions are in order of difficulty.** On school math tests this is often the case, but remember that the later questions on those tests are worth more. You have been trained, in other words, to sprint in the early part of a test so that you can spend enough time on the questions that count more near the end. On the SAT, you should do exactly the *reverse:* go slowly on the easy and medium questions in the early part, and then sprint on the hardest questions at the end.

- **The SAT Math Test covers a hodgepodge of material.** Yet again, this aspect will require a much, much larger adjustment of their problem-solving methods than most students realize. When you're studying a math topic in school—say, solving simultaneous equations—you can expect that your quiz or test on that material will involve *just* simultaneous equations. Granted, sometimes your math teacher may make a test cumulative, but even then the test will cover relatively recent material. On the SAT, one question can be on percentages that you studied back in junior high, followed by an algebra II question on material you may have studied last year, bouncing back to geometry you covered a year or two ago, and continuing all over the place. **The SAT Math Test requires that you orient yourself *instantaneously* to each new question, and then leap nimbly to the next question, reorienting yourself all over again.**

> One of the biggest differences of all is that the SAT Math Test is what the test writers call a "reasoning test." Unlike an achievement test—like the SAT II Math Ic and IIc Tests—the SAT Math Test rewards students who see *past* what the problems *seem* to be asking to what the problems are *actually* testing. On the SAT Math Test, for example, a problem may *seem* to require that you solve for x, when in fact you don't need to solve for x at all. In fact, trying to solve for x on some problems will send you on a wild goose chase *away* from the solution.

As you'll see in the coming chapters, not all of these differences make the SAT more difficult; indeed, some of these differences will give you powerful leverage. **But these differences will require a complete overhaul in the way you approach solving math questions.**

SAT Math Questions Are Arranged in Order of Difficulty

Each math section is arranged in order of difficulty. Here's the question layout of the entire SAT Math Test:

20 Multiple Choice 25 minutes	20 Multiple Choice 25 minutes	12 Grid-In 20 minutes

You won't see warning signs in your booklet like this: *Warning! You are about to leave the medium questions—hard questions coming up!* The only clue you'll have regarding the difficulty of a question is where in its section it appears, so you'll have to keep an eye open for the question number at all times.

The only exception to this rule about order of difficulty (danger) occurs on compound questions. Your SAT Math Test may have two or three consecutive questions based on the same information. **If so, the second and third ones will be medium to hard—regardless of where these questions appear in the section.**

Normally, for example, questions 10 and 11—smack in the middle of a 20-question section—would be medium questions. If this were a pair of questions on the same information, however, the first question would be medium and the second question would be *difficult*. If it were a trio of questions on the same information—say, 10, 11, and 12—the first question would be easy, the second question would be medium, and the last question would be difficult. Not a big deal since these compound questions appear maybe once every SAT, but worth watching out for.

This section arrangement is the best I have been able to piece together from what little information has been released so far about the new test. It is possible, though unlikely, that the grid-in questions will be distributed into more than one section. If so, each *type* of question within each section will be arranged in order of difficulty. The multiple-choice questions will progress from easy to medium to hard, and if these are then followed by grid-in questions, these too will progress from easy to medium to hard. **Visit the RocketReview website for any breaking updates about the test; I'll keep you posted about any significant changes.**

Here's How You'll Improve Your Math Score

I'll show you everything you need to know to achieve your maximum SAT math score in the minimum time.

Of course I'll show you all of the math you need to know for the test (it's surprisingly little). But I'll also show you the most common tough SAT problems of the past twenty-five years—these problems show up over and over—and how to solve each one in a snap.

I'll show you the true secret behind solving SAT math problems, and four specific master math moves that can solve just about any SAT math problem they may throw at you—sometimes in mere *seconds*. Every SAT has its little surprises, so I'll show you the best way to *rescue* problems that you can't solve, and the best way to bail out of difficult situations.

I'll show you how to make the best use of your limited time—and what to do if you run out of it. Finally, I'll show you how to catch errors that you make (it's not the way you think), and how to avoid most errors in the first place.

Have a Calculator Handy for Emergencies, but Try *Not* to Use It

The instructions say that you can use a calculator on the SAT Math Test, but relying on a calculator on the actual exam is *not* recommended for the following reasons.

- Using your calculator wastes time. Unless you're ambidextrous, stopping to use a calculator means juggling with your pencil, punching numbers into the calculator, and then readjusting your pencil to resume writing—and that's just for a single step of a problem.

- It's easy to get confused with order of operations on a calculator, or with multi-step calculations; heck, even punching in the numbers incorrectly is a source of error. If you make a mistake, it won't be clear where you went wrong and you won't have any written record you can review.

- Most risky of all, when you use a calculator you take your eyes off the problem and you stop *thinking*. It's easy to get caught up in the calculation and forget what you were solving for.

Besides, you shouldn't need your calculator: if you think you need it for a tough or lengthy calculation, you've probably missed the point of the question.

Still, you *should* have a calculator with you in case your brain freezes in

338

the exam room on the Big Day and you can't remember what 9 times 8 equals—it happens! Calculators are not supplied so bring one you're familiar with, not a calculator you borrowed from someone at the last minute. The last thing you need when you're taking the SAT is to be fumbling around with your best friend's super-calculator.

Most four-function, scientific, or graphing calculators are fine. The calculator needs to solve only simple calculations, so avoid anything too complicated; the simpler the model, the better. **Hand-held minicomputers, laptop computers, and pocket organizers (such as those with typewriter-style keypads) are *not* allowed.**

A Few *Important* Words about the Open-Ended Questions

Twelve of the 52 questions on the SAT Math Test will consist of what the test writers call "student-produced response" questions. The open-ended questions do not have choices, so you will have to "grid-in" your exact answer.

These questions will require us to modify some of the techniques you'll be learning shortly—our four "math moves"—but the important thing is to become comfortable with bubbling-in your answer in the special grids.

I'll give you some practice bubbling-in on your answer sheet shortly, but first here are the main points to keep in mind regarding these questions:

- Before filling in the ovals on a question, it's a good idea to write your solution to each problem in the space provided on the answer sheet above the bubbles. Doing so takes only a couple of seconds and reduces the chances of filling-in the wrong bubbles.

- Some questions have more than one correct answer. If so, you can bubble in anyone of the possible answers; the choice is up to you.

- All answers are non-negative. If you get a negative answer to an open-ended question, you've made a mistake. (The answer to any open-ended question must also be no greater than 9999, which is the maximum number that the answer sheet will allow for these questions.) **In other words, the answer to an open-ended question on the SAT Math Test must range from 0 to 9999 inclusive.**

- The answer sheet gives you the option of filling in the answer to a question as a fraction or as a decimal. Choose whichever way seems most natural to the problem you've just solved.

- Mixed numbers (like 1½) are not allowed, so either convert any mixed number to a fraction (3/2) or convert it to a decimal (1.5) before filling in the bubbles.

- The answer sheet has room for four-digit answers. If your answer has fewer than four digits, you can start bubbling your answer into any column that space allows. For example, the two-digit number 28 could be bubbled into the first and second, second and third, or third and fourth columns.

- Ignore the decimal point for integer answers.

- If you're entering a decimal answer with a repeating digit (such as 2/3, which equals 0.6666. . .), you should enter the decimal point (ignoring the zero to the left of the decimal point) and the first three digits to the right. You can round the answer or not (.666 or .667 are equally acceptable versions of 2/3; .66 or .67 are not); it's up to you. Of course, simply entering in the fraction version of such answers may be easier than wondering which digits to include or how you should round them.

> Be especially careful—but then you're *always* careful, aren't you—on the open-ended questions. If you're off on a question by even a one-thousandth, you will receive no credit for your answer.

Answer Sheet Practice for the Open-Ended Questions

In the space provided below, fill in the ovals for the following sample answers to the open-ended questions.

1. 962

2. 2.4

3. 1/7

4. 2 ¼

5. 0.01

You'll find the correct version or versions of each answer at the end of this chapter on page 343.

My Job—Your Job

My job is to provide you with all the skills and knowledge you need to achieve your maximum possible SAT math score, but you have to master these things. Hey, I'm just your coach, remember—you've got to do most of the work. Fortunately, the work won't seem that hard when you see how quickly your SAT math score starts improving.

It doesn't matter whether you're a whiz at math or whether math's your worst subject: I'll show you how to improve your score. The key point to keep in mind now is that you'll be learning a whole new way to take the SAT Math Test. Your most important job is *changing* the way you approach and solve math problems. I'll show you how, but you've got to do the changing.

As we discussed way back in Tutorials 6, 7, 8, and 9, changing old habits isn't easy—*especially* if you're already good or even great at math. (If math's not your thing than you'll be eager to change.) Remember Michael Jordan's advice: if you practice eight hours a day incorrectly, you get very good at doing the wrong thing. When you solve practice SAT math problems here or on your own, the crucial thing is *not—repeat: not*—merely getting the answer. I can't stress that point enough. The *entire* point of practicing for the SAT Math Test is *rehearsing* the techniques you're about to learn. These problem-solving and test-taking techniques are the key to your improvement.

Remember: to change your math score, you've got to change the way you take the test. If you want to change your math score dramatically, you've got to change what you're doing—dramatically.

I'll Cover Techniques before Content—but You May Need to Reverse the Order

The content of the SAT Math Test is relatively simple, and won't require much time to review. Changing your problem-solving and test-taking habits, on the other hand, will require stronger measures, so we'll start there.

- If you're a strong math student, immediately begin with the techniques (the experience sets) that follow this chapter. Then review the most common SAT math problems (page 584) before returning to review any math concepts you may need brushing up on.

- If you're good at math but it's not your strongest subject, simply follow the chapters as they are organized (techniques, math review, most common SAT math problems).

- If you don't feel comfortable with math, skip the technique chapters and begin instead with the math review (page 445) and most common SAT math problems before returning to the techniques.

Solutions for the Answer Sheet Practice Drill (from page 341)

Here are the acceptable ways of bubbling-in the sample answers. When more than one version was possible, I have provided each one.

1.

2.

3.

4.

2	.	2	5

(Grid-in answer: 2.25)

9	/	4	

(Grid-in answer: 9/4)

	9	/	4

(Grid-in answer: 9/4)

5.

.	0	1	

(Grid-in answer: .01)

	.	0	1

(Grid-in answer: .01)

SAT Math Techniques

Learning to Test Well—
or Even Better

It's Not Enough to Be a Good Math Student—
You Also Have to Test Well

Let's face it: your SAT math score will reflect how well you take standardized tests as much as it reflects how much math you know. Indeed, when you see in the content chapters that follow how little algebra, geometry, arithmetic, and other concepts the SAT Math Test actually includes, you'll realize that the difference between a good score and a great score—or between a great score and an amazing score—comes down to your test-taking skills.

Fortunately, you can become a great test taker in relatively little time—*provided* that you're willing to change your problem-solving and test-taking habits. Even if you *hate* math in school, I promise you that you'll soon learn to *love* math on the SAT.

Revealing RocketReview's Unique Approach to Math Instruction:
The Experience Sets

Changing your problem-solving and test-taking techniques will mean that you'll have to unlearn habits that may have served you well in your math classes and learn a whole new set of habits.

Changing anyone's habits about anything is always a challenge, all the more so here because you and I are not together. I can't observe what you're doing when you solve problems, for example, or whether you're following the explanations.

Merely reading about new techniques is usually not enough to compel most students to change the way they take the SAT Math Test. **So I've arranged a series of math test-taking *experiences* that will *force* you to change your problem-solving habits.**

Each experience set is carefully designed to target a major SAT test-taking skill. I'll introduce each experience with a *prelude* to set the stage. The experience itself will consist of one or more problems that you should complete exactly as the instructions direct you. After each experience, I'll *debrief* you and we'll discuss the lessons you just learned from the experience. Some debriefings will include supplementary exercises.

The six experience sets have been arranged in a specific order. Work through the six experience sets in the order presented; do not skip around.

Brace Yourself: Frustration Ahead

Improving any skill—learning a dance routine, shooting a free throw, playing a musical instrument, mastering a new language—is enormously rewarding. In the beginning, however, it is also enormously frustrating.

Improving your SAT math skills is no different. I can promise you a lot of frustration in the coming chapters. In fact, making sure the drills are *just* frustrating enough is my job. Frustration is a sign that you haven't yet mastered a new skill, that you still have things to learn—that there's still *lots* of improvement ahead.

You won't improve your SAT math score by doing a lot of easy problems that you can solve quickly, any more than lifting a light weight all day is going to make you much stronger. The fastest way to improve your math score is to find out immediately what gives you a hard time on the SAT—whether it's catching mistakes or solving algebra problems or whatever—and then to work through the frustration of mastering new skills.

I say all this so you won't get discouraged, or think that you're "just no good at math." Frustration is part of the improvement process. Hang in there—I promise that your gains will be worth the frustration.

Math Experience Set 1

Avoid Math on the SAT Whenever Possible— and Try *Thinking* Instead

PRELUDE

The SAT Is a Reasoning Test, *Not* an Achievement Test

An enormous difference that we haven't yet explored between the SAT Math Test and the math tests you're used to taking is that the SAT Math Test is *not* designed to measure how much math you know, but how well you *reason* with relatively basic math concepts. In school your math teacher might want to see how well you've learned, say, how to solve simultaneous equations. The SAT Math Test, on the other hand, would measure how well you handle a problem that *seems* to require that you solve simultaneous equations—but in fact does not.

And so, without further ado, try your hand at the following questions.

EXPERIENCE SET 1

These questions are fairly difficult, so just do the best you can to solve them. If you can't remember any formulas that seem relevant, try *thinking* about the problems. If you want to practice handling time pressure, give yourself 5 minutes for the entire set of problems, but for this drill you can also do the problems without timing yourself.

1. Calvin traveled from his home to another city at an average speed of 32 miles per hour, and then returned home along the same route at an average speed of 40 miles per hour. If his total traveling time for the trip was 3 hours, how many <u>minutes</u> did it take Calvin to drive from his home to the other city?

   (A)   100
   (B)   90
   (C)   80
   (D)   72
   (E)   60

2. The line that passes through (–4, 2) and (0, 3) also passes through which of the following points?

   (A)   (1, 7)
   (B)   (4, 4)
   (C)   (4, 8)
   (D)   (7, 1)
   (E)   (8, 4)

3. M can complete a certain job on her own in 9 hours, but while working with N the two can complete the same job in 6 hours. How many hours would it take for N to complete the job on his own?

   (A)   3
   (B)   4.5
   (C)   6
   (D)   9
   (E)   18

Stop! Please do not continue reading this section until you have completed the problems above. The solutions will be revealed shortly.

1. Calvin traveled from his home to another city at an average speed of 32 miles per hour, and then returned home along the same route at an average speed of 40 miles per hour. If his total traveling time for the trip was 3 hours, how many <u>minutes</u> did it take Calvin to drive from his home to the other city?

(A) 100
(B) 90
(C) 80
(D) 72
(E) 60

SOLUTION IF YOU NOTICED

Calvin travels the first half of the trip slower than the second half of the trip, so his time going to the other city must be more than half of three hours, or 90 minutes. Only one choice is greater than 90: choice (A).

CLASSROOM SOLUTION IF YOU DIDN'T

Begin by assigning variables. Let T_g be the time going and T_r be the time returning; R_g and R_r would be the two rates (32 and 40 miles per hour respectively). The distance is the same both ways so let that be D. Since distance equals rate times time, time equals distance divided by rate. Knowing this relationship gives us the equation for both times: $T_g + T_r = 3$ hours $= \frac{D}{32} + \frac{D}{40}$. Solving this equation—ugh—gives us $D = 53\frac{1}{3}$ miles. Still with me? I ask because we're not finished yet. *Assuming* you haven't made a mistake so far with these equations, you now have to plug D back into the equation $T_g = \frac{D}{32}$ to get $T_g = 1\frac{2}{3}$ hours. Whoops, still not finished: we have to convert that figure to minutes. Multiplying $1\frac{2}{3}$ by 60, we get 100 minutes. **Anybody who could wade through all that without making a mistake would have avoided the solution altogether.**

(Note: there's a faster mathematical solution, but it depends on your noticing that the times vary inversely with the speeds—and anyone who noticed *that* would have adopted the SAT-correct solution in the upper box.)

2. The line that passes through (–4, 2) and (0, 3) also passes through which of the following points?

(A) (1, 7)
(B) (4, 4)
(C) (4, 8)
(D) (7, 1)
(E) (8, 4)

SOLUTION IF YOU NOTICED

In moving from (–4, 2) to (0, 3), we moved four to the right and up one. If we again move from four to the right and up one, this time from (0, 3), we get to (4, 4), or choice (B).

CLASSROOM SOLUTION IF YOU DIDN'T

(Note: As a RocketReview apprentice, you would have drawn a diagram of this problem to help your thinking.)

First we'll need to determine the equation of the line by plugging in the points (–4, 2) and (0, 3) into the basic formula $y = mx + b$. This gives us the equations $2 = –4m + b$ and $3 = 0m + b$. Fortunately the second equation tells us immediately that $b = 3$. Substituting that value into the first equation, we can solve for m. *Assuming* we do all this correctly, we get $y = \frac{1}{4}x + 3$. Hold on, because we're not finished yet. *Now* we have to substitute the x value of *each* choice into *that* equation—and we need to do that substituting correctly, too. Plugging in the 1 from the first choice, the equation does not yield 7 as the y value. Plugging in the 4 from the second choice yields 4 as the y value. That's a match, so we finally have the answer.

3. *M* can complete a certain job working on her own in 9 hours, but while working with *N* the two can complete the same job in 6 hours. How many hours would it take for *N* to complete the job on his own?

(A) 3
(B) 4.5
(C) 6
(D) 9
(E) 18

SOLUTION IF YOU NOTICED

N must work more slowly than *M* because if they worked at the same rate of 9 hours each, the combined time would have been half of *M*'s time working solo. Only one choice is greater than 9: choice (E).

CLASSROOM SOLUTION IF YOU DIDN'T

If you've memorized the formula for work problems—and it's not easy to remember if you don't understand it—you know that if T_1 and T_2 are the two individual times, and TT is the total time, $\frac{1}{T_1} + \frac{1}{T_2} = \frac{1}{TT}$. Substituting the two values, we get $\frac{1}{9} + \frac{1}{T_2} = \frac{1}{6}$. Subtracting $\frac{1}{9}$ from both sides, we get $T_2 = \frac{1}{6} - \frac{1}{9}$, or $\frac{1}{18}$, so $T_2 = 18$. We still have to check our answer; and it works.

(Note: it would have been easy to misapply this formula and get
$\frac{1}{6} + \frac{1}{9} = \frac{1}{T_2}$ **, which would have yielded $T_2 = 4.5$—whoops.)**

The Problem with Formulas

The trouble with formulas is that virtually all students—and quite possibly *you*—go into panic mode trying to remember some formula or other for a problem. When these same students find a formula, they go on automatic pilot solving it. **In short, searching for and solving formulas often short-circuits *thinking* about the problem in front of you—especially when the problem may not require any formula to solve it in the first place.**

To be sure, many SAT questions will *require* you to use a formula. But before you rush off in a mad dash to find and apply some formula to a problem, see how far you can get applying a few moments of thinking about the question. At the very least, thinking about a question will clarify the issues you need to consider to avoid potential blunders.

The SAT Math Test Rewards Students Who *Notice* Things— and Punishes Students Who Don't

I said that the SAT Math Test is what the test writers call a "reasoning test," but they could also call it a "noticing test." The SAT Math Test is all about *noticing* things, which is no surprise since most thinking and reasoning begins with noticing something unusual about a situation—in our case, about a problem.

How does the SAT Math Test reward students who pause for a moment to notice things about each problem before solving it? By allowing such students to solve even complicated-looking questions quickly, sometimes in mere *seconds*. Students who rush into every problem with their blinders on, however, quickly find themselves mired* in lengthy solutions that practically invite errors.

*GSWLIU

Unlearning "Classroom-Correct, SAT-Risky" Problem-Solving Approaches

We've already discussed the critical differences between the SAT Math Test and the math tests you're used to taking in school. These differences mean that you'll need to adopt an entirely new strategy of problem-solving and test-taking techniques if you want to achieve your maximum SAT math score.

The techniques you're about to learn for the SAT Math Test work so amazingly well that it's easy to dismiss them as "tricks" or "gimmicks." **These new techniques are not tricks or gimmicks, but are ways of *reasoning* under pressure.**

Welcome to SAT Math Land
(Hint: You're Not in Kansas Anymore)

Some students—often girls, who, let's face it, tend to be a whole lot more conscientious about school than boys are—are uncomfortable with new approaches that seem like shortcuts to avoid solving math problems the way they're used to solving problems. "But what's the *right* way to solve the problem?" such students invariably ask when shown a clever solution that does away with the need for a formula or some other laborious method.

What they really mean is, "But what's the way we're used to solving this kind of question in school?" Well, school math is school math, and SAT math is SAT math.

In the coming experience sets you'll learn the enormous differences between the two. Okay, let's compare the solutions of a student who spent a few seconds to notice things about the questions with the solutions of someone who blindly attempted classroom methods.

Don't Worry If You Didn't Completely Follow All the Solutions

As I mentioned at the outset, those were fairly difficult problems. **The important point is just to realize that anyone who *could* have solved the problem—correctly—with the classroom solutions would have avoided them entirely.**

Not every SAT math question rewards students who notice things as generously as these illustrations did, but many SAT problems do. In the upcoming experience sets—especially Experience Set 4—you'll learn how to solve problems like these in a snap.

If Thinking about a Problem Provides No *Quick* Insights— Try *Fiddling* with the Problem

I said earlier that you should think for a few moments about each problem before attempting a "mathematical" solution. I want to emphasize the phrase *a few moments.* If you haven't noticed anything about the question to suggest a rapid solution, by all means don't get lost in thought. You don't want to waste precious time looking for a quick solution.

Keeping your pencil moving continually is a good safeguard on the SAT Math Test. **If your pencil isn't moving on the page every few seconds—you're in danger of** *spacing out!*

***Fiddling* with a problem often reveals the solution.** Fiddling with a problem means quickly—*without thinking*—trying *random* possibilities in the hope that one of your attempts will either solve the question, or provide you with an insight that will lead to the solution. Do *not* spend a lot of time fiddling with the question; it will either work quickly or it won't. **The key point is that simply *staring* at a question, trying to "figure it out," is always a huge waste of time.**

Sometimes neither thinking nor fiddling works quickly on a question, and you can't think of the mathematical solution either. In Experience Set 5, I'll show you what to do when you get *totally* stuck on a problem.

Killer Rabbits and the Secret to Catching Math Errors on the SAT

PRELUDE

SAT Math Questions Are Arranged in Order of Difficulty— Even If They Don't Seem to Be

As we've already discussed, the questions in each section of the SAT Math Test are arranged in order of difficulty. Not all difficult problems, however, *seem* difficult.

And so, without further ado, try your hand at the following difficult problems.

EXPERIENCE SET 2

Do these difficult questions *timed*. If you're a strong math student, give yourself 3 minutes; otherwise take 5 minutes.

1. The probability of choosing a red marble at random from a certain jar containing only red and blue marbles is $\frac{1}{3}$. If there are 18 red marbles in the jar, how many blue marbles are in the jar?

   (A) 6
   (B) 9
   (C) 12
   (D) 36
   (E) 54

2. What was the initial membership of a club that now has P members after the club gained Q members and then lost 10 members?

(A) $P + Q - 10$
(B) $Q - P + 10$
(C) $P + Q + 10$
(D) $Q - P - 10$
(E) $P - Q + 10$

3. A certain rectangle has twice the width and 5 times the length of another rectangle. If the smaller rectangle has an area of R, then the area of the larger rectangle is greater than the area of the smaller rectangle by what amount?

(A) $7R$
(B) $8R$
(C) $9R$
(D) $10R$
(E) $14R$

Stop! The following debriefing is based on this problem set. Please do not read any further if you haven't yet completed these questions. Also, please do *not* peek ahead at the solutions.

DEBRIEFING

Did You Catch Yourself Making Any Errors?

I know you're eager to see how you did on these questions, but before I give you the answers spend a few moments to see whether you made any mistakes. Once you've reviewed your solutions and are satisfied, we'll be ready to continue.

Oh, by the way, did you catch any mistakes? I realize that I haven't given you the answers yet; I'm just curious to see whether you caught any errors on your own.

Again: please do not peek ahead at the solutions; the experience set is not quite over yet.

SAT Math Lessons from the Movies

If you haven't seen the movie *Monty Python and the Holy Grail,* rent this 1975 cult classic. This spoof on the King Arthur legend could very well be the funniest movie ever made, and it's certainly the looniest. (If you're in a giggly mood, you won't stop laughing convulsively, so do *not* eat while watching this movie if you don't want food bits coming out of your nose.) But make no mistake: One outrageously funny scene in this movie offers you an invaluable lesson about taking the SAT Math Test.

If you and I were in an SAT class together I'd tell everyone that this is the film portion of class and roll out the television and VCR for a five-minute film clip, but you'll just have to rely on your imagination as I re-create the scene.

Anyway, King Arthur and his small band of stalwart knights—Gawain, Robin, Galahad, Lancelot, Belvedere—are in search of the Holy Grail. They encounter a flame-throwing wizard named Tim the Enchanter who not only knows their names, but also knows of their quest for the Holy Grail.

Arthur and Galahad and the other knights ask Tim if he could help them find the Holy Grail. Yes, he says in a great booming voice. "Follow. But! Follow only if ye be men of valor, for the entrance of this cave is guarded by a creature so foul, so cruel, that no man yet has fought with it and lived! Bones of full fifty men lie strewn about its lair. So brave knights, if you do doubt your courage or your strength, come no further, for death awaits you all with nasty, big, pointy teeth."

The knights follow Tim through some stark, bleak lands. The "horses" grow jittery as they approach the cave. "Behold the cave of Caerbannog!" announces Tim.

Arthur and his knights are cowering some distance from the cave, but close enough to see the bones and armor of all the knights who had been vanquished by the terrifying creature. They're wondering how best to enter the cave when, all of a sudden, Tim the Enchanter shouts, "Too late! There he is!"

"Where?" asks a puzzled Arthur, who is obviously expecting some enormous beast. "There!" Tim says, pointing at a furry little rabbit that has just bounded out of the cave. "What, behind the rabbit?" asks Arthur. "It *is* the rabbit," says Tim in hushed tones.

Arthur and his knights roll their eyes and stand up, greatly relieved. "You silly sod," says Arthur, "you got us all worked up."

"That's no ordinary rabbit," warns Tim. "It's got a vicious streak a mile wide! It's a killer. I'm warning you."

The knights think Tim the Enchanter is off his rocker. "What's he do, nibble your bum?" asks Robin.

"He's got huge, sharp . . . he can leap about . . . look at the bones!" Tim reminds them.

One of the knights pulls his long sword out of its scabbard and announces that he'll make a quick rabbit stew out of the little creature. But just as he approaches the cute bunny, its little pink nose twitching, the rabbit leaps six feet in the air at his neck and rips the knight's head clear off!

That scene sounds gruesome, I know, but the image of this cute little bunny chomping off the head of a knight in full armor is ferociously funny. "I warned you," says Tim, with an I-told-you-so smirk, "but did you listen to me? Oh no, you knew it all, didn't you? Oh, it's just a harmless little bunny, isn't it? Well, it's always the same, I always tell them."

Now, you'd think that Arthur and his men, having seen with their own eyes the horrible truth of Tim's warning, would have beat a quick retreat to regroup and reconsider their plan of attack. But no. "Charge!" the knights announce in unison, storming all at once towards the not-so-defenseless rabbit.

Duh, smart move, guys. The rabbit leaps from knight to knight, blood spurting everywhere, until the brave Arthur shouts, "Run away! Run away!" "We'd better not risk another frontal assault," decides a breathless Arthur. "That rabbit's dynamite!"

Back to the SAT Math Test

Okay, you may be thinking, that's funny, but what's it got to do with the SAT Math Test? Here's what. I told you that the problems in each section get progressively more difficult. In other words, the problems get progressively more *dangerous*. The problems in the final third of each math section are *super* dangerous.

The tricky thing is that dangerous math questions on the SAT don't always *look* dangerous—sometimes they look simple and innocent. Easy-looking questions in the final third of any math section are anything but easy—they're super-dangerous killer rabbits.

358

You've been warned.

A Riddle with a Moral

Two students answered exactly the same questions on the SAT Math Test and made exactly the same errors—yet one received a score 150 points higher than the other. How is that possible?

Here's how: the high-scoring student *caught* many of her mistakes; the low-scoring student did not.

Learning to Catch Errors Is One of the Fastest Ways to Improve Your SAT Math Score

No matter how "good" you are at math, if you don't know how to catch your math errors—and believe me, you'll make them on the SAT—you won't achieve your top score. On the flip side, once you *do* know how to catch your errors, your score will leap virtually overnight.

The real problem many students have on the SAT Math Test is that they make errors—sometimes *many* errors—completely unaware that they are doing so. No matter how carefully you solve SAT math problems, and we'll get to *that* shortly, you'll make errors. Indeed, students who finish an SAT math section without catching any errors probably made lots of them. Great test takers make many of the same mistakes as other students—but they've learned to catch them. So will you.

Remember that when you make an error on a problem, it's not like a loud buzzer goes off and a flashing red light starts spinning. You just make the mistake and move on. Now, I know what you're going to say. "But I check my work at the end of the section." Like you just did on the quiz, right? Did you catch any errors? I'm guessing that you didn't.

Checking Your Work at the *End* of a Section Is a Complete—*Complete*—Waste of Time!

Most students work through a problem, find their answer among the choices, select the appropriate letter on their answer sheet, and then tackle the next question. These students continue working through questions in this way until they finish the section or run out of time, whichever comes first.

Many students do finish early and use their remaining time to "go back and check" their work. They flip through their test booklets, casually glancing over their work. They look around the room, mighty pleased with themselves that they finished "with time to spare," while everyone else is feverishly working to complete as many problems as possible.

Boy, are these students in for a shock. Unless you're scoring at or near 800 on the SAT Math Test, if you have time left over at the end of any math section it means two things. First, that you made at least a few, and possibly many, avoidable errors. But it also means that you are *not* going to catch any of those errors.

How do I know this? I know this because no student in the *history* of the SAT has ever found an error by checking his or her work at the end of a section. At least nobody I've ever known, and I've dealt with thousands of students.

"Looking over work" for errors at the end of the section is a waste of time for three reasons. First, if you're like most students you probably did a lot of your work "in your head." So there's not a whole lot written down to check, right? Second, if you made a mistake the first time you solved the problem, then when you look over your work later, you'll probably just repeat your mistake.

But third, and most important, you probably don't know what you did wrong in the first place, or where you're likely to find any of your errors. When checking over your work, what exactly should you be looking for, anyway? If there's something wrong with a car engine, the mechanic knows the likely places to check for trouble. Do you know where you should look for trouble in your solution to an SAT math problem?

I'll tell you shortly, but the bottom line is that once you leave a question and move on to the next problem, it's almost certainly too late to catch any errors in the problem you just finished.

The Only Time to Catch an SAT Math Error
Is *Either* Just After You've Made the Mistake—or *Just* Before

Looking over your work at the *end* of a section is a waste of time, but you *should* look over each step as you complete it.

> Always verify each step of your solution *as* you work through the question. Step, verify, next step, verify, next step, verify. *Always* verify—right to the very end of the solution.

The Most Common Cause of SAT Math Errors Is *Not* a Math Error

The biggest cause of avoidable math errors on the SAT is not miscalculations, but rather misreading the question! The primary way you'll catch errors just after you've made them is by rereading the question! You heard it here first. The last, *last* step in solving any SAT math problem—the step *right* before you fill in your answer—is to say, *Wait, let me reread the question!*

You don't have to reread the entire question, just the final line that tells you what you're looking for.

> Reread the question! Reread the question! Reread the question! *Reread the question!* Repeat after me: *I always reread the question before selecting the answer. I always reread the question. Always.*

Revisiting the Experience Set

When I asked you to review your work on the quiz for errors, did you reread any of the questions? Please reread each of the questions now (page 355) before continuing, and *before* you see the solutions later in this chapter.

Developing Your SAT Spider Sense to Catch Errors *Before* They Happen!

As you probably know, Spider-Man (aka Peter Parker) has a special sense that tingles to warn him when danger is near. Your inner voice often alerts you to errors as you make them—listen to it! Trust me: you've either just made a mistake or you're *about* to make one when any of the following thoughts flash through your head:

- *That seemed pretty easy . . .*

- *Isn't there a rule that says. . . ?*

- *I just figured . . .*

- *This choice is too obvious for a difficult question but I don't see how any of the other choices could work . . .*

- *Of course . . .*

- *I can do this problem in my head . . .*

- *Obviously . . .*

- *The answer has to be . . .*

- *No way is the answer . . .*

- *What a stupid question!*

If you hear yourself thinking any of these phrases, it's a virtual certainty that you've either just made a mistake or you're just about to make one.

> Never *anticipate* the answer to an SAT math problem; let the answer come as a *surprise*. It's always a *good* sign if the answer to a medium to hard question seems a little *strange*. If your solution seemed a little too easy, a little too obvious—*red alert!*

Finding Your Solution among the Choices Is No Guarantee— Especially If You Got a "Popular" Answer Choice

Many students are tricked into thinking they solved an SAT math problem correctly simply because they see their solution among the choices. Sorry, but things aren't quite so simple. The test writers work through each question a number of *incorrect* ways to see what sorts of answers students are likely to get. They then include those *incorrect* solutions among the choices.

Another thing to beware of on any medium to difficult question are those answer choices likely to be popular with students. You know that medium to difficult questions have medium to difficult—*unpopular*—answers.

Popular choices are traps on hard questions. After you've *glanced* at a hard question, *immediately* cross off any popular-looking choices (traps) *before* you begin solving the question.

Learning to Spot the Popular Choices— and the Unpopular Ones

A popular choice is one that will probably attract a lot of students. A popular choice will "just seem right." Most (but not all) difficult questions will have at least one popular-looking choice, and many have two or more popular choices.

Here are some guidelines to help you spot popular choices on SAT math questions:

- Any choice containing a solution that can be derived from the numbers in the problem will be popular.

- Any choice with a "nice" number will be popular. The fraction $\frac{1}{4}$ is nice; the fraction $\frac{2}{7}$ is not. What makes a number nice will depend on the context. If the problem involves angles, for example, the numbers 30, 45, 60, 90, 180, and 360 are nice; the number 18 is not nice in this context.

Sometimes it isn't clear which, if any, choices on a hard question will be popular with many students. If so, don't sweat it. With practice, however, you should be able to spot any popular choices *at a glance.*

The Answer to a Hard Question Will Be an Unpopular-Looking Choice

You know now that you should avoid popular choices on hard questions. But popular choices can point us in the direction of the answer. **The most obvious choice on a hard question is obviously wrong—but it's not far off.**

If, on the other hand, you get stuck on an easy or medium SAT math question—it happens—remind yourself that the answer should be a relatively popular choice.

Revisiting the Experience Set Problems One Last Time

Please return to the problem set you just completed on page 355—I warned you ahead of time that all the questions in it were difficult—and identify any popular answer choices. I'll show you the popular choices when I discuss the solutions on page 365—don't peek!—but try to figure them out on your own.

Would a lot of students choose any of your answers? What does that tell you?

If You Suspect You Made a Mistake but Aren't Sure, What Should You Do?

In fact, the only time you can be absolutely sure you've made an error is when you don't find your answer listed among the choices. **By the way, if you *don't* find your solution among the choices, it often means you're *way* off base, so don't select "the closest choice."** For example, if you work out a question and get 48 but it's not among the choices, do *not* think the answer is 50, which just happens to be among the choices.

If you get stuck on a question—for whatever reason—*immediately* circle the question number in your test booklet and move on to the next question. Solving other questions often gives you new insights into or a fresh perspective on a problem that had previously stumped you.

Postponing a question on the actual SAT is very, very difficult to do if you haven't *trained* yourself to do so *as a reflex.* Practice postponing questions even on your school math tests and homework, or you'll have to use extreme willpower doing so on the SAT.

When you *return* to the question, start over. Do *not* check your work or you're likely to repeat the same mistake. **The first thing to do is to reread the question carefully.** Next, check to see whether you made any faulty assumptions. Work out the question *completely.*

If you *still* haven't found the answer, and time is running out, do *not* leave the question blank or you'll sacrifice 10 points as well as all the time you've spent. Guess! If you're stuck on a medium question, remember that the answer won't *look* easy; but it won't look too hard, either. **And if you're stuck on a difficult question, select a hard, unpopular-looking choice.**

I'll show how to rescue tough questions in Experience Set 6.

Finally, the Answers to Those Killer Rabbit Questions

1. The probability of choosing a red marble at random from a certain jar containing only red and blue marbles is $\frac{1}{3}$. If there are 18 red marbles in the jar, how many blue marbles are in the jar?

   (A)   6
   (B)   9
   (C) 12
   (D) 36
   (E) 54

SOLUTION

If you drew a picture of the jar (*did you draw a picture?*) and labeled it correctly, you would see that if the 18 red marbles are one-third of the total number of marbles, the blue marbles must make up the other two-thirds. In other words, there are twice as many blue marbles as red marbles, so the answer is choice (D). If you got choices (A) or (E)—whoops, popular choices on a hard problem—you misread the question. *If you missed this question, did you check your solution? Did you reread the question?*

2. What was the initial membership of a club that now has P members after the club gained Q members and then lost 10 members?

(A) $P + Q - 10$
(B) $Q - P + 10$
(C) $P + Q + 10$
(D) $Q - P - 10$
(E) $P - Q + 10$

SOLUTION

If you swapped numbers for the variables (*did you swap numbers?*), you'd quickly see that the answer is choice (E). If you got choice (A)—whoops, a popular choice on a hard problem—you misread the question. *If you missed this question, did you check your solution? Did you reread the question?*

3. A certain rectangle has twice the width and 5 times the length of another rectangle. If the smaller rectangle has an area of R, then the area of the larger rectangle is greater than the area of the smaller rectangle by what amount?

(A) $7R$
(B) $8R$
(C) $9R$
(D) $10R$
(E) $14R$

SOLUTION

If you drew a picture of two rectangles (*did you draw a picture?*) and substituted numbers for the length and width of the two rectangles (*did you swap numbers?*), you would see that the area of the larger rectangle exceeds the area of the smaller rectangle by $9R$, or choice (C). If you got $10R$—whoops, a popular choice on a hard problem—you misread the question. **Notice that the answer—$9R$—is not far off from the popular answer.** *If you missed this question, did you check your solution? Did you reread the question?*

How Did You Do?

Remember: All three problems were difficult. If you got even one of the three questions right, you did pretty well. If you got two right, you did very well indeed. And if you got all three right, you did extraordinarily well.

If you got any or even all of the problems wrong, not to worry: You have plenty of room to improve your SAT math score. Here's a final question to ponder before leaving this experience set: If you missed any questions, *why—exactly*—did you miss them?

You'll learn the answer in the next experience set.

> Never, ever, never, ever, never dismiss any mistake on the SAT Math Test as "stupid" or "just careless." You'll rarely if ever hear a professional athlete saying that he or she lost a big game because of a "stupid" mistake. *Any* mistake on the SAT costs you points—the grading computer doesn't care—and "stupid" mistakes are the *hardest* to get rid of. I'll have a whole lot more to say on this topic in the next experience set.

How Do You *Know* Whether a Question Is Difficult?

A difficult question is one that most students get wrong—*for whatever reason.* As you learned in this experience set, how difficult a question *seems* may have little to do with how hard the question actually *is.* The difficulty of an SAT math question is determined solely by its placement within a section. Questions in the first third of each section are easy; most students get these right. **Questions in the final third of each section, however, are** *difficult*—**even if they don't** *seem* **difficult.**

> A killer rabbit question is any easy-looking problem in the final third of any SAT math section. You've been warned!

No Pain, No Gain—
Avoiding Errors in the First Place

PRELUDE

What's Your Pain Threshold?

In the last experience set we discussed how to catch errors on the SAT Math Test. Catching errors is a crucial math skill you need to develop for the SAT, but of course it's better to try avoiding errors *in the first place!*

> The key to avoiding and catching errors on the SAT Math Test is—listen to the words I'm about to use—*being willing to take pains.* The tricky thing is that the only way to be sure that you've been careful *enough* on an SAT math problem is to be *more* careful than you think you have to be. *Always.* In other words, if you want to achieve your maximum possible SAT math score, you need to be paranoid about making errors, even on the easiest-looking math questions on the SAT—*especially* on the easiest-looking questions.

I mean that literally. If you solved any medium or difficult SAT math problem without experiencing any *pain,* you've *greatly* increased the odds that you've made an error. If you take *pains* to avoid and catch errors—I'm about to show you how—I promise you that your SAT math score will *skyrocket.*

Achieving rapid score improvement on the SAT Math Test is as easy—and as hard—as that. Many students *aren't* willing to take the pains to be *obsessively* careful on the SAT. Some of these students may even be math whizzes, but not one of them will achieve his or her maximum possible score on the SAT.

And so, without further ado, try your hand at the following difficult problems.

Do these difficult questions *timed*. If you're a strong math student, give yourself 4 minutes; otherwise take 6 minutes.

1. If the third Tuesday of a certain month falls on the 21st day of that month, on what date does the second Friday fall?

   (A) 10th
   (B) 11th
   (C) 17th
   (D) 18th
   (E) 24th

2. In a certain sequence of numbers, each term after the first differs from the preceding term by the same amount. If the 20th term of the sequence is 60 and the 10th term is -40, what is the 1st term of the sequence?

   (A) -140
   (B) -130
   (C) 10
   (D) 150
   (E) 160

3. One number is 4 times another number. If their sum is -1, what is the smaller of the two numbers?

   (A) -0.20
   (B) -0.25
   (C) -0.75
   (D) -0.80
   (E) -4.00

Stop! The following debriefing is based on this problem set. Please do not read any further if you haven't yet completed these questions. Also, please do *not* peek ahead at the solutions.

DEBRIEFING

Pain Is Your Error Barometer

I used the phrase "willing to take pains" for a reason. It's hard to tell whether a question was "easy" or "difficult" to solve. On the other hand, pain—a sign that you're exerting *effort*—is a tangible feeling. If you felt no pain when you solved a medium or difficult question, there's a good chance you made an error.

As I said in the last experience set, it's *absolutely critical* that you not dismiss *any* of your SAT math mistakes as "stupid" or "silly" or "just careless." What still absolutely amazes me after all these years of working with thousands upon thousands of students is that as soon as I've said that, a student will raise his or her hand and say, "But *my* mistakes really *were* careless."

Please return to the questions you just completed on page 369 and see whether any problems seemed particularly easy to solve. Were any solutions relatively *painless?* What does that tell you?

There Are No "Just Careless" Mistakes on the SAT Math Test— Just *Reckless* Mistakes or Unavoidable Ones

When they get back their math exams in school (or they review their practice SAT math problems), most students look over their errors and say of many of them, "Oh yeah, that was just a careless mistake" or "Dang, I knew that answer. I could have gotten that question right." They think that "just careless" errors are trivial, and easy to eliminate.

Wrong. Students make these comments as if eliminating errors were the easiest thing in the world. Wrong! **Solving problems is a piece of cake compared to avoiding errors, and "just careless" errors are the *hardest* ones to eliminate.** Students who dismiss a mistake as "just careless" couldn't *ever* have caught it because they probably weren't willing to take pains to *make sure* they got the question right. Reckless is a much better word to describe what's really going on than careless. So from now on, we'll use the phrase "reckless mistakes" for any mistakes you could and *should* have avoided.

Can most students avoid reckless mistakes? Absolutely—*if* they're willing to take pains. The next time you hear the words "it was just a careless mistake" forming in your head when you review an error, change the sentence

370

to this: "It was just a reckless mistake that I couldn't be bothered to avoid."

Some mistakes on the SAT Math Test are unavoidable, like on a math section when you have 30 seconds left and 3 problems to solve. Or you're up against an impossibly difficult question. Or a brain cell misfires and you think 3 times 4 is 7 (it happens).

Most of your SAT math mistakes, however, are probably *completely* avoidable: You had enough time to solve the question correctly, and knew enough to solve the question correctly—but you didn't. Why? I'll tell you why you make avoidable math mistakes. (This will sound harsh but remember, I'm your coach.) **You make avoidable mistakes because in *school* you get away with it.** You won't, however, on the SAT.

The SAT Grading Computer Is Like the Terminator, Not Your Teacher

It amazes me how absolutely casual most students are about making mistakes on the SAT Math Test. A casual mistake here, a casual mistake there—pretty soon we're talking about some really major damage to your math score. If you make just one slip every ten minutes during the SAT Math Test—bang!—your score drops 100 points! And you can't get those points back.

Most students are casual about "just careless" math mistakes—*reckless mistakes*—because in school their teachers *let* them be casual. Perhaps you tend to dismiss such mistakes, too, abetted by an accommodating math teacher who overlooks such "trivial" errors because "of course" you understood the "main concepts" on the test.

Let's say your math teacher is grading a really tough test that consisted of a single, super-complicated problem. He notices that although your answer was slightly off, all the steps in your solution were completely accurate—except one. At one point in your analysis you misread a simple condition in the problem (say, that x was *nonnegative,* which you took to mean *positive;* nonnegative includes zero, but positive does not). Not a super-big deal, and all the rest of your work was flawless, so your teacher gives you nearly full credit.

And when your math teacher *doesn't* give you full credit, when your work was "mostly right," you probably plead or cajole* after class that it wasn't fair, that you've "been working hard and of course you understood the material and could have gotten the question right," and that it was just a "stupid mistake." Under that kind of unrelenting* pressure, most math teachers will finally give in and award you partial or even full credit for the question.

*GSWLIU (Yes, you should be looking up words *all* the time.)

But the SAT grading computer doesn't care one bit *why* you got a question wrong (on the plus side, it doesn't care how you got a question *right*, either). To borrow the classic line from the original *Terminator* movie, the SAT grading computer "can't be bargained with. It can't be reasoned with. It doesn't feel pity. And it absolutely will not stop . . ." until it has penalized you for every error you make (or blank you leave) on the SAT.

All it takes on an SAT math problem is one little slip, and you lose *full* credit for that question: 10 to 20 points—whoosh, *gone,* in the blink of an eye. And you won't be able to convince the SAT grading computer that you *should* have gotten the question right.

On the SAT Math Test, there are no do-overs.

Value Accuracy over Speed on the SAT Math Test: The Tortoise Beats the Hare Every Time

Most students need to develop a whole new set of priorities for the SAT Math Test. In school it's okay to be quick and clever because your teacher can bail you out by not punishing reckless mistakes. On the SAT Math Test, the methodical, painstaking tortoise will beat the clever but reckless hare every single time.

I'll show you how to solve SAT math problems quickly but it won't do much good if you aren't willing to take pains to avoid and catch errors. If you're serious about improving your math score, you'll focus more attention on avoiding errors than you will on solving problems.

Golf, Grounders, and Getting It Right

I realize that it's not cool to be meticulous and methodical in school; that it seems boring. Worse, it's so *hard.* If you want to see people who are extraordinarily, painstakingly careful, watch professional athletes—the winning ones, anyway.

Here's an assignment for you: Watch a professional golf tournament the next time one is televised. Excruciatingly boring, isn't it? Most people find golf boring *precisely* because golfers go to such extreme lengths to avoid errors. Watch Tiger Woods lining up a simple putting shot. He may take a full minute or more to be sure a simple ten-foot putt will go in when he takes the shot. Only when he's *absolutely* sure nothing will go wrong: tap, and the crowd goes wild.

But it's not just golf. You will never, *ever* hear any professional athlete casually saying he or she lost a game because of a "careless mistake" or a "careless shot." In professional sports, a single error can cost an entire game; in 1986, it cost the Boston Red Sox the World Series. Even if you're not a baseball fan (I'm not), the next scenario has been voted by sports writers as one of the most exciting sports moments in the last century.

Okay, picture this. It's October 25, 1986. We're in the sixth game of the World Series between the Boston Red Sox and the New York Mets. The Red Sox are leading the series, three games to two; if they win this game, they'll be the world champions.

And in the bottom of the tenth inning, the Red Sox look absolutely set to win. They are ahead by one run and, with the Mets up at bat, the Red Sox are one out away from clinching the game and the series.

Suddenly, a wild pitch allows the Mets to tie the score. Up at bat is Mookie Wilson. Wilson has pop-fouled several times, so he's just one strike away from an out. Finally Wilson connects, just barely, with the ball, this time in bounds. Unfortunately, the ball is an easy grounder headed for the one person you don't want to hit an easy grounder to: the first baseman, Bill Buckner.

Buckner leans over to scoop up a slow ground ball that any Little League fielder could have gotten. *All* he had to do is scoop up the ball, take a couple of steps, and touch first base before Wilson, racing hopelessly towards the base for what is surely an "easy out," and the Red Sox would be up at bat again in the eleventh inning.

Oh no! Buckner, in the perfect position to get the ball and tag first base, lets the grounder roll right between his legs! Wilson gets on base, another run scores, and the Red Sox lose the game.

In a flash the Mets turned certain defeat into an incredible victory. The Red Sox were so demoralized that the Mets had little trouble defeating them in the next and final game of the series.

A simple, "just careless" error once cost the Boston Red Sox the World Series. Many SAT math problems are easy grounders: if you take pains to get them right, you will. **Take pains.**

Pay *Close* Attention: The Three Most Common Causes of Avoidable SAT Math Errors

What we've been talking about here are *general* math errors; the kind you can make on any type of problem. Later we'll address specific kinds of errors like sign errors or decimal-place errors or whatever. And we're not talking now about manipulation errors like failing to distribute a term when multiplying. And we're most certainly not talking about calculation errors, which are surprisingly rare.

You already know what the cause of avoidable errors on the SAT Math Test is: *not taking pains.* **Interestingly, the fundamental cause of not taking pains to get things right on SAT problems is one of two mental states at opposite ends of the extreme: panic and overconfidence.** Of the two, overconfidence is the harder to overcome; students who panic are generally more willing to take pains. (Now is a good time to revisit a discussion of question 15 from the Tutorial 3 quiz you took back on page 6; you'll find a discussion of that question on page 26.)

Panic and overconfidence both lead to rushing, to cutting corners, to "doing things in your head," to grabbing at a solution—any solution—so you can just move on to the next question and *finish the section in time.* In order of importance, here are the three consequences of not taking pains:

- Misreading the question.

- Taking faulty shortcuts or not working out the problem *fully.*

- Forgetting what the question was asking for.

These errors can occur anywhere in a math section, although they tend to occur more often on medium to difficult questions.

Let's consider each one in turn.

Cause #1: **Misreading the question.** As you learned in the last experience set, the most common math error on the SAT has nothing to do with math. Students often think they've read a question when all they've done is pass their eyes over the words in the problem without all of those words actually registering. So these students rush into their computations, solving for something that wasn't asked for, using information that wasn't given. **Solution: Read the problem with extra-special care the first time, before you solve it—and then reread the question one last time** *after* **you've solved the problem.**

The following exercise will help you.

Exercise: Spot the Difference

If you misread an entire sentence of a reading passage, it will probably have little if any impact on your overall understanding. But if you misread even a single *word* of a math problem, your answer could be completely off base.

To highlight the importance of reading carefully word by word on the SAT Math Test, I've prepared the following exercise for you. The table below consists of pairs of problems that are *nearly* identical—only a phrase or even a single word distinguishes the left-side problem from the right.

For each pair, underline the minor difference between the two wordings and notice how dramatically this difference changes the respective answers. If you're feeling ambitious you can work out the problems on your own, but the point of this exercise is simply to have you notice the major impact that minor changes in wording can have.

	VERSION A	VERSION B
1.	Points *A, B,* and *C* lie on a line. If *AB* is 2 and *BC* is 4, what is *AC*? (Answer: It cannot be determined)	Points *A, B,* and *C* lie on a line in that order. If *AB* is 2 and *BC* is 4, what is *AC*? (Answer: 6)
2.	$\frac{2}{3}$ is $\frac{1}{2}$ of what number? (Answer: $\frac{4}{3}$)	What is $\frac{2}{3}$ of $\frac{1}{2}$? (Answer: $\frac{1}{3}$)
3.	Set $R = \{1, 2, 3\}$ and set $S = \{2, 3, 4\}$. If *r* is a number in set *R* and *s* is a number in set *S*, then how many different combinations of the product *rs* are possible? (Answer: 9)	Set $R = \{1, 2, 3\}$; set $S = \{2, 3, 4\}$. If *r* is a number in set *R* and *s* is a number in set *S*, then how many different values of the product *rs* are possible? (Answer: 7)

VERSION A	VERSION B

4. Paula completed $\frac{1}{4}$ of her homework assignment in school and $\frac{1}{2}$ of the assignment on the bus ride home. What fraction of her homework assignment remains to be done?

(Answer: $\frac{1}{4}$)

Paula completed $\frac{1}{4}$ of her homework assignment in school and $\frac{1}{2}$ of the balance on the bus ride home. What fraction of her homework assignment remains to be done?

(Answer: $\frac{3}{8}$)

5. If the sum of three consecutive positive integers is 42, what is the least number?

(Answer: 13)

If the sum of three consecutive even integers is 42, what is the least number?

(Answer: 12)

6. If the average of three numbers is 10 and the average of two of them is 8, what is the third number?

(Answer: 14)

If the average of three numbers is 10 and the sum of two of them is 8, what is the third number?

(Answer: 22)

7. 4 is what percent of 5?

(Answer: 80%)

What percent of 4 is 5?

(Answer: 125%)

8. The numbers 6 and 8 have a total of how many positive factors greater than 1?

(Answer: 6)

The numbers 6 and 8 have a total of how many distinct factors greater than 1?

(Answer: 5)

Cause #2:* Taking faulty shortcuts or not working out the problem *fully. This error tends to occur on simple *looking* questions (like the ones in the problem set you just completed). Cutting corners comes from underestimating a problem or not realizing what a problem is *really* asking—especially when the solution seems "pretty obvious." But the biggest cause of this error is relying on "common sense" or some *supposed* "rule." Here are some supposed "rules" that students misapply:

- *When multiplying two numbers raised to powers, add the exponents.* (Whoops, only if it's the same number.)

- *If one rectangle has a larger perimeter than another, it has a larger area.* (Whoops, only if the two rectangles are squares; otherwise it's not necessarily true.)

- *A fraction of a number is less than the number itself.* (Whoops, only if the number is positive; if the number is negative, a fraction of it will be *greater* than the number itself; if the number is zero, a fraction of it will remain zero.)

- *To find the distance between points A and C, add the distance between A and B to the distance between B and C.* (Whoops, only if the points are in a line—and only if the points are in that order.)

- *If the ratio of x to y is 3 to 2, then x equals 3 and y equals 2.* (Whoops, x equals 3 only if y equals 2.)

Never assume anything on the SAT Math Test. Remember that the solution to a medium to difficult question is rarely obvious. If common sense or some quick solution worked on a difficult question, it would be an easy question. Write out every single step of your solution to the very end. Don't "grab" at an answer; let it come to you as a surprise. **Solution: Never cut corners: *assume nothing; verify everything; check it out!***

***Cause #3:* Forgetting what the question was asking for.** After you've started solving a problem, it's very easy to get lost in the calculations or in setting up the formulas—and forgetting what you were looking for in the first place. Forgetting what you're looking for happens a lot in your daily life. You're in your room, get up, walk into the living room, and then realize, "Hey, what did I come in here for?" The same thing happens on the SAT Math Test. This error is similar to misreading the question, and it has the same solution. **Solution: reread the question one last time *after* you've solved the problem.**

Force—and I Mean *Force*—Yourself to Write Every Step Down

Rereading the question *after* you've solved a problem is easy enough to do, though you may have to remind yourself consciously until this step becomes a habit. Writing everything down, however, requires a major act of willpower.

Students—especially math jocks—are often reluctant to write down "simple" or "obvious" steps because they save time by completing calculations or manipulations mentally. **Yes, I realize that you can often "do things in your head"—unfortunately, that's where mistakes occur, too.** As we discussed in Tutorial 13, the more steps or information you "do in you head," the more you tax your short-term memory—and the dumber you get.

So yes, writing everything down takes a little more time, but just a bit more, and the payoff is well worth the second or two you invest. Here are some general thoughts:

- Don't do any work in your head—ever!—even on the simplest questions. Write everything down, *not* just the stuff that you think you should.

- Write down numbers and computations in an *organized* way, rather than haphazardly, all over the page.

- Use parentheses whenever possible.

- Whenever possible on a problem, draw a figure or diagram. Draw your diagrams to scale to assist your thinking.

- If a figure or diagram is provided, mark it up.

- Do *not* erase your work. Erasing takes up valuable time, and you may need to retrace your steps.

> Whenever you review one of my solutions to a math problem in this book, the way the question is marked up is the way *your* problem should be marked up; it is *not* the way I'm explaining the solution.

As Much as Possible, Represent SAT Math Problems Graphically

Your brain was designed to process visual information, not algebraic equations, not even numbers. Almost any math problem can be solved more simply, and certainly more accurately, if you begin by representing the information in pictures. You probably do this already with geometry problems, but you can represent just about any type of math problem with pictures or diagrams.

Always try to draw the information to scale. Remember that the pictures you draw will influence how your brain processes the problem, so if you misrepresent the information with a casual or even sloppy drawing, your thinking could very well be sloppy, too.

Use variables that suggest the quantity being indicated—*b* for base; *s* for side; *r* for red—rather than the standard variables *x* and *y*. The trouble with *x* and *y* as variables is that they don't stand for anything, which makes thinking about them difficult and increases the chances that you'll forget what the variables represent.

Exercise: Representing Information Graphically

For each of the following statements, represent as much of the information provided as you can with pictures or diagrams. There are no problems to solve here, just information to represent. Remember to draw the diagrams to scale. You'll find my diagrams and an explanation of each one on page 387.

INFORMATION	YOUR DIAGRAM OR PICTURE
1. Sarah spends half of her salary on rent and a quarter on food. She spends half the remainder on clothing and entertainment.	
2. Alex drives from home to work at 40 miles per hour, and without stopping returns home at 60 miles per hour.	

INFORMATION	YOUR DIAGRAM OR PICTURE
3. The ratio of boys to girls at Lincoln High School is 3 to 2.	
4. On Bill's first four biology quizzes he scored an average of 85, while on his fifth quiz he scored a perfect 100.	
5. A square and a circle have equal areas.	
6. The height of a triangle is one-half its base.	
7. A certain sequence of 100 terms begins with 1. Each successive term after the first is determined by adding 3 to the preceding term.	

INFORMATION	YOUR DIAGRAM OR PICTURE
8. Five badminton teams play each other in a round-robin, with each team playing every other team exactly once.	

Other Ways to Avoid Math Errors

In addition to rereading a question *after* you've solved the problem, and writing every step down without taking shortcuts, here are some additional methods you should incorporate whenever possible.

- **Underline or circle the unknown before you do any calculations.** (Like rereading the question, this step reduces the chances of forgetting what you're looking for.)

- **On medium to difficult questions, eliminate any popular choices before you begin working on the question.** (We discussed how to spot popular and unpopular choices in the previous experience set.)

- **Whenever possible, solve a problem using one or more of our four master math moves.** (You'll be learning these moves in the next experience set.)

- **Set up the problem *completely* before you begin doing any intermediate steps or calculations.** (Many students jump from one part of a problem to another while working on a solution. Be organized.)

- **Avoid using your calculator unless *absolutely* necessary.** (Your calculator is largely a distraction and using it takes your focus away from the problem. Another big drawback to using your calculator is that you have no record of anything but your final calculation; if you need to retrace your steps to locate the source of an error, you're in trouble.)

You don't have to memorize these steps, most of which follow naturally from our habit of writing everything down and rereading the question often.

Question: What Is the Point of Fastening Your Seatbelt?

I'm guessing that you're taking driver's ed now or you've just taken it or you're about to take it, but you've certainly ridden in cars before. Okay, before I answer the question above, notice that you wear your seatbelt *always*—not just when you think you need to. **In the same way, you should *always* take pains to avoid errors on the SAT Math Test**—writing everything down, rereading the question, you know the drill—not just on the harder questions, which you may already do, but even on the very easiest questions. *Always.*

Okay, now let's get back to that driving question. The point of fastening your seatbelt is *not* just to keep you inside the car should the car's forward momentum abruptly decelerate and Newton's first law of motion threaten to propel you into the dashboard or windshield or worse. *Of course* that's one point to wearing a seatbelt, but it's not the only point. A major reason experienced drivers fasten their seatbelts is this: *the very act of fastening the seatbelt puts them into a drive-with-extreme-caution frame of mind.* Fastening a seatbelt doesn't *just* reduce the chances of serious physical harm in case of an accident—it reduces the chances of an accident's occurring *in the first place.*

That's why you *always* go through our error checklist. Not just to *catch* errors, but to prevent them from occurring in the first place.

Become Aware of Your Unique Error Patterns— before the SAT Math Test Does It for You

In addition to these general causes of errors that everyone has to guard against, each person has his or her personal weak spots. I do, and so do you. My big problem is misreading things. I'm so aware of my Achilles' heel that I sometimes put my pencil or even my index finger on key words of math problems to make sure I've read everything correctly.

Your weakness might be making decimal errors, or misreading diagrams, or screwing up exponents, or forgetting to distribute all the terms when multiplying, or botching operations with negative numbers, or whatever. **Such errors are often a sign that you aren't taking pains to avoid errors—like rereading the question, or writing all your steps down, or working the problem through to completion—but sometimes your personal error pattern is just idiosyncratic.**

Anyway, as you work through this course and you review *actual* SAT questions, and even as you do math problems in school, keep track of the *specific* kinds of errors you make. When you know your personal weak spots, you'll be better able to watch out for them.

> Repeat after me: read, solve, check, *reread!* Read, solve, check, *reread!* Read, solve, check, *reread!* Read, solve, check, *reread!* Read, solve, check, *reread!* Read, solve, check, *reread!*

Can You Get Away without Completing All These Precautions?

Will following these precautionary steps take you a little longer? Sure, maybe five or ten seconds a question. But doing so will almost guarantee you'll get the question right. I don't care how great a math student you are—if you're not using these methods consistently, you're taking reckless chances with your score.

Let's settle on a compromise: you can begin to experiment with not taking all these steps once your SAT math score is *consistently* 800. I'm not being sarcastic. But once you reach that score level, why would you want to stop taking the precautions that got you there?

If you want to see whether or not you can get away without taking all those precautions, let's see how you did on the problems of the experience set.

Finally, the Answers to Experience Set 3 (page 369)

Remember, I warned you that these were difficult questions. If they seemed easy, then I guess they were killer rabbits.

1. If the third Tuesday of a certain month falls on the 21st day of that month, on what date does the second Friday fall?

(A) 10th
(B) 11th
(C) 17th
(D) 18th
(E) 24th

SOLUTION

If you took the pains to write out a calendar (*did you draw a picture?*) and filled in the dates correctly, you would see that the second Friday of this month occurs nearly two weeks before the third Tuesday—on the 10th. Most students count the dates out on their fingers and get (C), the easiest and most popular answer—and wrong. *If you missed this question, did you do the problem in your head or did you actually verify your analysis? Did you reread the question? Did you take the pains needed to get the question right?*

2. In a certain sequence of numbers, each term after the first differs from the preceding term by the same amount. If the 20th term of the sequence is 60 and the 10th term is -40, what is the 1st term of the sequence?

(A) -140
(B) -130
(C) 10
(D) 150
(E) 160

SOLUTION

If you took the pains to write out the basic terms of the sequence (*did you draw a picture?*) and actually verified your analysis, you would see that there are 10 "jumps" between the 10th term and the 20th—but only 9 jumps between the 10th term and the 1st. **Notice that the answer—choice (B)—is not far off the easiest and most popular choice, (A).** *If you missed this question, did you do the problem in your head or did you actually verify your analysis? Did you reread the question?*

3. One number is 4 times another number. If their sum is –1, what is the smaller of the two numbers?

   (A) –0.20
   (B) –0.25
   (C) –0.75
   (D) –0.80
   (E) –4.00

SOLUTION

If you're like most students, you probably solved this difficult question in a snap: $x + 4x = -1$, so $x = -0.2$, right? *Wrong!* **That solution is far too easy and pain-free, so there must be something wrong with that analysis.** Whoops, –0.2 is the *larger* number; the answer is –0.8, the smaller number. *If you missed this question, did you do the problem in your head or did you actually verify your analysis? Did you reread the question? Did you take the pains needed to get the question right?*

How Did You Do?

Again: all three problems were difficult. If you got even one of the three questions right, you're did pretty well. If you got two right, you did very well indeed. And if you got all three right, you did extraordinarily well.

I think you'll agree that what made these questions difficult were simply the pains required to get them right. Probably any high school ninth grader could get all three questions right—if he or she were willing to take pains.

Answers to the Representing Information Graphically Exercise
(page 379)

Your diagrams may differ from mine in minor ways, but please read the discussion so that you understand *why* I represented the information as I did—and not in some other way.

INFORMATION	MY PICTURE OR DIAGRAM
1. Sarah spends half of her salary on rent and a quarter on food. She spends half the remainder on clothing and entertainment.	$\frac{1}{2}$ $\frac{1}{4}$ $\frac{1}{8}$ (rectangle divided: r, f, c & e)

DISCUSSION

You're probably used to drawing figures for geometry questions, but figures also help your thinking on word problems. I used a rectangle to represent Sarah's total salary, and divided the rectangle to represent how the salary was spent. **Use rectangles to represent information rather than circles; it's difficult to divide up a circle to scale.**

INFORMATION	MY PICTURE OR DIAGRAM
2. Alex drives from home to work at 40 miles per hour, and without stopping returns home at 60 miles per hour.	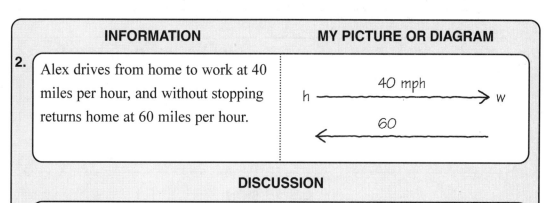

DISCUSSION

This diagram is pretty straightforward. If the problem provided us with distance, I would have inserted that below the two lines I drew.

INFORMATION	MY PICTURE OR DIAGRAM

3. The ratio of boys to girls at Lincoln High School is 3 to 2.

$$\begin{array}{cc} 3 & 2 \\ \boxed{\quad b \quad} & \boxed{\quad g \quad} \end{array}$$

DISCUSSION

Again, rectangles are convenient figures with which to represent information. Notice that I drew the figure to scale.

INFORMATION	MY PICTURE OR DIAGRAM

4. On Bill's first four biology quizzes he scored an average of 85, while on his fifth quiz he scored a perfect 100.

$$\underset{85}{\underline{\quad}} \; \underset{85}{\underline{\quad}} \; \underset{85}{\underline{\quad}} \; \underset{85}{\underline{\quad}} \; \overset{100}{\underline{\quad}}$$

DISCUSSION

Whenever a problem includes a list or a sequence or a series, I provide draw "slots" for each item. If I know an exact number, I place it on top of the slot; any other information I place it below the slot.

INFORMATION	MY PICTURE OR DIAGRAM

5. A square and a circle have equal areas.

DISCUSSION

Again, notice that I drew the figure to scale.

388

INFORMATION	MY PICTURE OR DIAGRAM

6. The height of a triangle is one-half its base.

$\frac{1}{2} b$

b

DISCUSSION

Another figure drawn to scale.

INFORMATION	MY PICTURE OR DIAGRAM

7. A certain sequence of 100 terms begins with 1. Each successive term after the first is determined by adding 3 to the preceding term.

$$\frac{1}{1st} \quad \frac{4}{2nd} \quad \frac{7}{3rd} \quad \cdots \quad \frac{x}{100}$$

DISCUSSION

See my earlier discussion of question 4.

INFORMATION	MY PICTURE OR DIAGRAM

8. Five badminton teams play each other in a round-robin, with each team playing every other team exactly once.

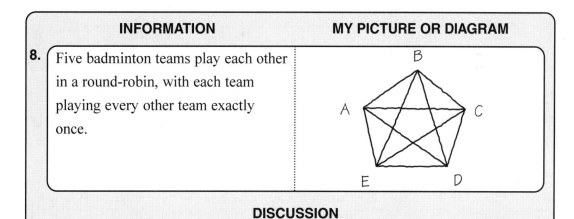

DISCUSSION

When you have people or things interacting with one another, it's often helpful to draw them as if forming a circle—rather all on a straight line—so that you can draw the various interactions. Here, each line represents a game between the two respective teams.

The Karate Kid Introduces Our Four SAT Math Moves

PRELUDE

Today We Have *Fun*

Today you and I are going to have a lot of fun, I promise you, even if you *hate* math. You'll see how another movie—this time *The Karate Kid*—changes the way you look at SAT math problems forever.

But make no mistake: this is important material, so pay close attention to *everything* I say. **The simple "math moves" I'll demonstrate in this chapter can raise your SAT math score 50 to 150 points or more—provided that you use these techniques without fail.**

You'll Never Be Bullied by an SAT Math Problem Again

Did you ever see the movie *The Karate Kid*? The two sequels were lame but the original is a teen classic. Here's the plot.

Daniel LaRusso, a loser from the moment you set eyes on him, has just moved from some nowhere town in New Jersey to this hip California high school. It isn't clear why the audience should care about Daniel, but whatever. Daniel is socially clueless, so of course he doesn't fit in at his new school. For some unknown reason, the cutest girl in school—Ali—is impressed with some lame soccer dribbling skills Daniel demonstrates, or something. This state of affairs does not bode well for Daniel because Ali's possessive boyfriend is not only a bully, he's also the southern California karate champion.

Daniel's a glutton for punishment, so after getting his nose rubbed in the sand and generally humiliated in front of all the cool kids, he continues to pursue Ali the prom queen. Daniel really doesn't get it; I told you he was a chump. As you might expect, Daniel's infatuation doesn't sit well with the bully or his posse, so Daniel becomes a marked man.

Enter the diminutive sage Mr. Miyagi. Mr. Miyagi tends bonsai plants, restores vintage cars, and practices catching flies with chopsticks when he isn't repairing screen doors or fixing plumbing leaks around Daniel's apartment building. Instead of trying to talk some sense into Daniel—*Hey stupid, back off the bully's girlfriend*—Mr. Miyagi violates California child labor laws by putting Daniel to work from dawn to dusk sanding his floor, painting his fence, and waxing his cars.

All day long: sand the floor, paint the fence—*both sides*—wax-on-wax-off. By twilight, Daniel's had enough of his servitude. He's plenty steamed, no question. And who can blame Daniel? He signed on to learn some karate, not to sweat doing chores for Mr. Miyagi, who enjoyed a relaxed day of fishing. Naturally, even someone as obtuse* as Daniel begins to resent being taken advantage of sooner or later. What's more, his shoulder's all sore from all the manual labor, so he tells Mr. Miyagi that's it, I quit.

"Ha, Daniel-san!" the mild-mannered Mr. Miyagi shouts abruptly. And if that shout didn't get Daniel's attention, Mr. Miyagi's neat rubbing-his-hands-together healing trick sure did. All of a sudden, Mr. Miyagi fake attacks Daniel.

Only *then,* when he fends off Mr. Miyagi's attack, does Daniel realize that he hasn't been wasting his time sanding the floor, painting the fence, and waxing on and waxing off. No way. You see, Daniel's *actually* been mastering three ancient karate moves. Cool! And before long, with those three simple moves, and a devastating crane kick—"If done right, no defense," says Mr. Miyagi, gravely—Daniel proves that he can take anything the bully and his fellow karate thugs can dish out.

Anyway, rent the movie.

I like to joke about *The Karate Kid,* but the movie does demonstrate an important truth about strategy. **Daniel learned only four simple *moves,* that's it.** Count them: sand the floor; paint-the-fence; wax-on-wax-off; and the crane kick. Four moves—four *great* moves, mind you, but just four. And with those moves, even a complete wimp was able to defeat bigger, stronger, and more experienced opponents who were using a whole variety of karate styles.

Today you'll be learning the math equivalent of martial arts moves. I'm going to show you a few simple math moves that can solve just about *any* SAT math problem, no matter *how* difficult. I'm not kidding.

*GSWLIU

Warning: I'm about to Throw You in the Deep End Again

The best way to appreciate the power of RocketReview's math moves is first to have you wrestle with some questions. Then I'll toss you a lifeline and show you how quickly you can solve these problems using the math moves.

The following questions are equivalent to the hardest ones you'll find on any SAT Math Test. Do not get discouraged. Do the best you can with the problems, and then I'll show you the best way to solve them using four simple math moves.

And so, without further ado, try your hand at the following questions.

EXPERIENCE SET 4

Take as long as you want on this drill, but time yourself so you know how much time you spent on average for these difficult questions.

Struggle with these problems as best you can. **If you get even one of these questions right, you're doing quite well.** Give each problem at least two or three minutes, and take longer if you're ambitious. I promise you that in a short while you'll solve any question below faster than a four year-old child can recite the alphabet.

Good luck, my young RocketReview apprentice. **If you can't solve a problem, take your best guess (remember to avoid popular-looking choices). These are all difficult questions, so each answer should come as a *surprise*.**

PS: Remember: *take pains.*

1. When each side of a square is decreased by 2 meters, the area of the square is decreased by 36 square meters. What is the length of a side of the original square, in meters?

   (A) 12
   (B) 10
   (C) 9
   (D) 8
   (E) 6

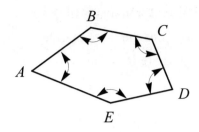

2. In figure *ABCDE* above, what is the average (arithmetic mean) degree measure of the 5 marked angles?

   (A)   72
   (B)   90
   (C) 108
   (D) 120
   (E) 180

3. In a certain class, $\frac{2}{5}$ of the students are ninth graders and $\frac{1}{4}$ of the ninth graders are boys. What fraction of the class are ninth-grade girls?

   (A) $\frac{1}{10}$

   (B) $\frac{3}{20}$

   (C) $\frac{3}{10}$

   (D) $\frac{9}{20}$

   (E) $\frac{3}{5}$

$$K = 23 \times 29 \times 31 \times 37 \times 41$$

4. A decrease of 1 in which of the factors above would result in the greatest decrease in K ?

   (A)   23
   (B)   29
   (C)   31
   (D)   37
   (E)   41

5. There are fewer than 40 marbles in a jar. If $\frac{3}{4}$ of the marbles are large and $\frac{7}{9}$ of the large marbles are blue, how many marbles are in the jar?

(A) 21
(B) 27
(C) 28
(D) 36
(E) It cannot be determined from the information given.

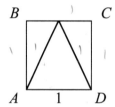

Note: Figure not drawn to scale.

6. In the figure above, an equilateral triangle of side 1 is inscribed in rectangle ABCD. What is the area of the rectangle?

(A) 4

(B) $2\sqrt{3}$ (approximately 3.46)

(C) $\sqrt{3}$ (approximately 1.73)

(D) 1

(E) $\frac{\sqrt{3}}{2}$ (approximately 0.87)

7.	A watch loses x seconds every y hours. At this rate, how many <u>minutes</u> will the watch lose in 1 day?

(A) $24xy$

(B) $\dfrac{1440x}{y}$

(C) $\dfrac{x}{24y}$

(D) $\dfrac{2x}{5y}$

(E) $\dfrac{5x}{2y}$

8.	$\dfrac{(x^8 + x^7 + x^6 + x^5 + x^4 + x^3 + x^2)}{(x^7 + x^6 + x^5 + x^4 + x^3 + x^2 + x)} =$

(A)   1
(B) x
(C) $7x$
(D) x^7
(E) x^8

Stop! The following debriefing is based on this problem set. Please read no further if you haven't yet completed these questions. The solutions will be discussed throughout the debriefing. If you're really curious to find out how you did, you'll find the answers on page 415.

Our Four Math Moves Versus Classroom-Correct, SAT-Risky Solutions

If you attempted to solve the questions above using the traditional mathematical approaches you learned in the classroom, you probably experienced an enormous amount of difficulty. Classroom-correct, SAT-risky solutions work on problems when you are relaxed, are able to think clearly, and have plenty of time to review your work for errors. In the pressure-cooker situation of taking the SAT Math Test, however, you *won't* be relaxed, you *won't* always be able to think clearly, and you *won't* have a lot of time to review your work for errors.

What's worse, the SAT Math Test includes *seemingly* typical questions that are not typical at all—problems *designed* to frustrate typical classroom approaches. **Remember that the SAT Math Test is a *reasoning* test that rewards students who *notice* things—like when a complicated solution to a question is unnecessary.**

The four math moves that you're about to learn—especially the master math move of them all—WIBNI—are designed to help you notice things about even the most difficult problems on the SAT. **These moves are not "tricks" at all, but rather ways of math thinking under pressure.**

> You will find detailed, step-by-step animations of each math move in this section online at RocketReview.com. If you haven't yet used your CD-ROM to register and gain access to all the special features that accompany this book, please do so.

Math Move #1: Checking the Choices

We use this math move on any SAT word problem. The standard (classroom-correct, SAT-risky) method of solving word problems has four steps:

1. Assign variables for the unknowns.

2. Set up equations.

3. Solve equations.

4. Check your answer.

On the SAT you know that one of the five choices is the answer—so you can skip the first three steps and jump right to checking the choices. **Since the choices for word problems are almost always arranged in order of size you start in the middle with choice (C). You "pretend" this number is the answer and you see if your "answer" was correct by plugging it right back into the problem.**

About one-fourth of the time choice (C) is the answer, and you can stop right there. If not, you'll usually know whether the answer should be larger or smaller than the number you just tried. If choice (C) was too small, you only have to try one of the two larger choices—check whichever choice is simpler: if it's not right, the other larger choice is the answer. If choice (C) was too large, you only have to try one of the two smaller choices—check whichever choice is simpler: if it's not right, the other smaller choice is the answer.

On some problems you'll try choice (C) and discover that it doesn't work, but you aren't sure whether you should try one of the larger choices or one of the smaller choices. On the rare occasions when that happens, just pick one direction or the other—larger or smaller—whichever direction seems simpler.

"But won't this method take too long?" students often ask. No way! You'll have to check your answer *anyway,* so you may as well start off by checking the potential answers. You'll almost always get the answer on the first or second try. Best of all, you'll be *alert* throughout the entire process of checking the choices, rather than going brain-dead on automatic pilot, solving equations without thinking about what you're doing.

We can use this move on two problems from the experience set: questions 1 and 5.

1. When each side of a square is decreased by 2 meters, the area of the square is decreased by 36 square meters. What is the length of a side of the original square, in meters?

    (A) 12
    (B) 10
    (C) 9
    (D) 8
    (E) 6

SOLUTION

Let's start with choice (C). If the side of the original square was 9, the side of the new square is 7. The area of the square decreased from 81 to 49, or 32: too small. Cross off choices (C), (D), and (E).

Let's check choice (B). If the side of the original square was 10, the side of the new square is 8. The area decreased from 100 to 64, or 36. Bingo: That's our answer.

The classroom-correct, SAT-risky solution would have required your *correctly* setting up the equation $x^2 - (x - 2)^2 = 36$, *correctly* solving the equation, and then you'd *still* have to check your answer. I think you'll agree that checking the choices immediately is safer, faster, and more efficient.

5. There are fewer than 40 marbles in a jar. If $\frac{3}{4}$ of the marbles are large and $\frac{7}{9}$ of the large marbles are blue, how many marbles are in the jar?

(A) 21
(B) 27
(C) 28
(D) 36
(E) It cannot be determined from the information given.

SOLUTION

If you tried to set up an equation on this question, you probably got confused because the problem didn't give you much information to work with. So let's check the choices.

There is no middle choice, so let's just start with choice (C), 28. Let's see, $\frac{3}{4}$ of 28 is 21, but hey—wait a second! We can't take $\frac{7}{9}$ of 21. Whoops. Cross off choice (C). Since we're not sure whether we should try a larger choice or a smaller, let's just try choice (B). Hey—wait a second! We can't take $\frac{7}{9}$ of choice (B) *or* choice (A). So let's try choice (D). Let's see, $\frac{7}{9}$ of 36 is 28, and $\frac{3}{4}$ of 28 is 21. Bingo, choice (D) works.

At this point we should realize that the answer has to be divisible by both 4 and 9, and only one positive integer less than 40 has both those factors: 36. The answer is choice (D).

Keep the following points in mind about checking the choices:

• Check the choices on any word problems rather than setting up and solving elaborate equations!

• The move often works on equations and inequalities as well as on word problems. Alas, this move does not work on the open-ended questions since these problems give use no choices to work with.

• Start with the middle choice. If it's too large, try one of the two smaller choices; if it's too small, try one of the two larger choices. You'll usually find the answer on your first or second try.

Math Move #2: Using the Figure

The instructions to each section of the SAT Math Test tell us that any figures "are intended to provide information *useful* in solving the problems" (italics supplied). Figures "are drawn as accurately as possible" unless a problem specifically states that the figure "is not drawn to scale." (Most figures on the SAT are drawn to scale.)

Great! If the figures provide useful information, we'd be fools not to use the figures, right? In fact, most of the time you'll be able to eliminate two or three choices simply by estimating the answer from the figure provided. Sometimes you'll even be able to eliminate four choices and find the answer— especially if the answer choices are far apart in size.

Even when estimating from a figure does not provide the answer, it is *always* worth *trying* to estimate the answer. Doing so makes you *mindful* of the process—unlike the brain-dead application of formulas and equations—and provides a safety check from which to judge the reasonableness of your solution.

We can use this move on two problems from the experience set: questions 2 and 6.

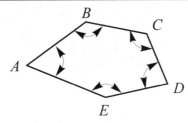

2. In figure *ABCDE* above, what is the average (arithmetic mean) degree measure of the 5 marked angles?

(A)   72
(B)   90
(C) 108
(D) 120
(E) 180

SOLUTION

Let's see how far estimating from the figure gets us since the answer choices are fairly far apart. **First we need a benchmark.** Since we're estimating angles, 90° is a good starting point. So, estimating from the figure above, would you say that the angles are mostly smaller than 90°, about 90°, or larger than 90°?

I think you'll agree that the angles are mostly larger than 90°, so we can eliminate choices (A) and (B). (Whoops, did you divide 360° by 5 and get 72 as an answer? That's much too easy-and-painless—a solution for such a difficult problem).

Now let's take another benchmark, this time larger: 180°. Clearly every angle above is less than 180°, so we can eliminate choice (E).

Alas, choices (C) and (D) are too close together to safely distinguish their size, especially since we're talking about five different angles. At this point you'd either have to work out the exact answer, or make a guess. Since this is a difficult question, which choice, (C) or (D), do you think will be more popular—we're selecting the *other* choice. The answer is 108, but (D) would have been a decent guess—as opposed to choice (A), which couldn't even have been in the running.

By the way, the exact solution for this average (arithmetic mean) involves finding the total degree measure of the marked angles, and then dividing by 5. If you draw line segments AC and AD, you'll see that we can divide this pentagon into 3 triangles. The total degree measure of their angles is 3 times 180, or 540. Dividing 540 by 5, we get 108.

I told you it was a difficult question. But notice how quickly using the figure allowed us to narrow down the choices dramatically.

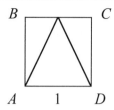

B   C

A   1   D

Note: Figure not drawn to scale.

6. In the figure above, an equilateral triangle of side 1 is inscribed in rectangle ABCD. What is the area of the rectangle?

(A) 4

(B) $2\sqrt{3}$ (approximately 3.46)

(C) $\sqrt{3}$ (approximately 1.73)

(D) 1

(E) $\frac{\sqrt{3}}{2}$ (approximately 0.87)

SOLUTION

Okay, now we're estimating an area. The area of a rectangle is base times height. We need a benchmark: a known length from which we can estimate. From the figure we know that the base of the rectangle equals the base of the triangle, which is 1.

Super. Now all we have to do is estimate the height. Drop a line down from the top of the triangle to the base. We know that the sides of the equilateral triangle all equal 1. Is the height you've just drawn greater than 1, equal to 1, or less than 1? If the sloping sides are 1, the height must be less than 1, right?

Okay, that means the base (equal to 1) times the height (less than 1) must equal less than 1. Bingo! Only one choice is less than 1: choice (E).

If you chose (D)—a super-popular-looking choice—you were reckless. You should have been suspicious of such a painless answer on a difficult question.

To figure out the solution *exactly* (had this been an open-ended question without choices), you can use the Pythagorean relationship to determine the height of the triangle: the height splits the original triangle into two smaller triangles, each with a base of $\frac{1}{2}$ and a hypotenuse of 1. Using the formula $\left(\frac{1}{2}\right)^2 + h^2 = 1^2$, you could have determined the height to be $\frac{\sqrt{3}}{2}$.

Keep the following points in mind about our using the figure move:

- The farther apart the choices, the easier it is to use the figure.

- Even on open-ended questions, you should still use the figure to estimate the answer and provide a rough check on your solution.

- You can use a figure to estimate any geometric quantity: lengths, angles, areas, whatever.

- Start the estimation process by finding an easy benchmark you can use as a "ruler." Find benchmarks above and below the quantity you're trying to determine (as we did with 90° below and 180° above in the previous problem), and then make your estimate successively closer to the answer.

- If there's a figure on a question and it's drawn to scale, you should *always* use the figure.

- Even figures "not drawn to scale" are still *pretty close* to scale, so you can still use them to some degree.

- If the figure is not drawn to scale, by the way, you can always *redraw* it more closely to scale.

- On questions involving inequalities with figures, it sometimes helps to redraw the figure even *less* to scale so that minor differences in the original drawing are exaggerated to the point where you notice the inequality.

- Of course, if a figure is *not* provided at all on a geometry question, draw one yourself—and draw it as closely to scale as you can.

Math Move #3: Swapping Numbers for Variables

"What is algebra, exactly? Is it those three-cornered things?" wondered James Matthew Barrie, author of *Peter Pan*. The trouble with algebraic variables and expressions is that these abstract quantities don't mean anything to your brain. What's more, it's easy to mangle algebraic manipulations. And when you get an algebraic—as opposed to a numeric—answer, it's difficult if not impossible to tell whether you've solved an equation correctly.

Wouldn't it be great if you could convert messy algebra problems into simple arithmetic problems? Well, you can!

On questions with algebraic answer choices, our math move is to exchange a simple number for every variable in the problem and choices, calculate the answer with numbers, and then find the algebraic choice that leads to the same numeric result.

That sounds complicated but you won't believe how easy this method actually is in practice. We can use this move on three problems from the experience set: questions 3, 7, and 8 (although for question 8 we'll also need WIBNI, our *master* math move).

3. In a certain class, $\frac{2}{5}$ of the students are ninth graders and $\frac{1}{4}$ of the ninth graders are boys. What fraction of the class are ninth-grade girls?

(A) $\frac{1}{10}$

(B) $\frac{3}{20}$

(C) $\frac{3}{10}$

(D) $\frac{9}{20}$

(E) $\frac{3}{5}$

SOLUTION

I don't know about you, but I *hate* fractions. Since the problem doesn't tell us how many students are in the class, we can treat the class size as a variable that we'll swap a number for. Since the largest denominator among the choices is 20—also a multiple of the two denominators in the problem—let's use 20 as the class size. Here's what we just transformed the question into:

3. In a certain class, $\frac{2}{5}$ of 20 students are ninth graders and $\frac{1}{4}$ of the ninth graders are boys. What fraction of the 20 students are ninth grade girls?

That problem is a whole lot easier to think about, isn't it?

If $\frac{2}{5}$ of the students are ninth graders, that means we have $\frac{2}{5}$ of 20 (or 8) ninth graders. If $\frac{1}{4}$ of the 8 ninth graders are boys, that means we have 2 ninth-grade boys and 6 ninth-grade girls. So 6 of the 20 students in the class are ninth grade girls, or $\frac{3}{10}$: choice (C).

If you chose (A), you forgot to reread the question: $\frac{1}{10}$ is the fraction of the class that are ninth-grade boys. If you chose any other answer, you probably got lost in manipulating fractions.

405

7. A watch loses x seconds every y hours. At this rate, how many <u>minutes</u> will the watch lose in 1 day?

(A) $24xy$

(B) $\dfrac{1440x}{y}$

(C) $\dfrac{x}{24y}$

(D) $\dfrac{2x}{5y}$

(E) $\dfrac{5x}{2y}$

SOLUTION

This question is super-difficult for anyone who attempted to solve the problem algebraically. Watch how easy the problem is when we convert it into an arithmetic question by swapping numbers for the variables.

We want to use "good" numbers for x and y—numbers that help us solve the problem. **It helps to read the problem quickly all the way through so you can decide what kinds of numbers would be helpful to exchange for the variables.** Since we have to find out how many minutes are lost in a day, let's use 60 for x seconds and use 12 for y hours. **Remember that the x and y in each choice are also now 60 and 12.**

Here's the embarrassingly easy arithmetic question we just transformed that impossible algebra question into:

7. A watch loses 60 seconds every 12 hours. At this rate, how many <u>minutes</u> will the watch lose in 1 day?

(A) 17,280

(B) 7,200

(C) $\dfrac{5}{24}$

(D) 2

(E) $\dfrac{25}{2}$

Duh: It loses 1 minute every 12 hours, so it loses 2 minutes every 24 hours: the answer is choice (D). If this problem doesn't sell you on the beauty of our swapping numbers move, nothing will.

Keep the following points in mind about swapping numbers:

- You should *always* swap numbers on any question—arithmetic, algebraic, geometric—with algebraic answer choices.

- You can also swap numbers on questions where some of the number for some key variable is not supplied.

- To keep track of what you're doing, *always* write the number just over the variable you're swapping for. *Whenever* you see that variable in the question or the answer choice, swap the same number.

- Once you substitute a number for a variable, that number *sticks* wherever that variable appears in the problem and the choices.

- Once you select one number for a variable, you may not have complete freedom to determine the numbers for any other variables.

- Use "nice"—small, simple—numbers that will help you solve the problem. Consider any *units* in the question when choosing helpful numbers to swap (60 for minutes; 10 or 100 for percent).

- You may need to read the problem through once to determine what sort of number would be appropriate.

- Avoid using 0 or 1 (except on coordinate geometry questions, where 0 is especially useful).

- Avoid using any numbers already present in the problem.

- Avoid using the same number for different variables in the problem.

- If more than one answer choice works—and that should not happen if you've selected good numbers—simply substitute another set of numbers into the remaining answer choices.

Math Move #4: WIBNI

I saved our coolest, most powerful SAT math move for last. WIBNI is an acronym that stands for "wouldn't it be nice if." **The basis of WIBNI is to solve an *easier* version of a hard question to discover a general rule that allows us to solve the original, harder version. WIBNI is actually a *mindset*, a habit of thinking when you are confronted by a difficult, complicated, *ugly* math problem.**

You can apply this mindset in countless ways. The principle behind WIBNI actually underlies our other three math moves. Wouldn't it be nice if we could:

- Avoid setting up and solving equations on word problems and just check the choices?
- Estimate the answer to geometry questions simply using the figure?
- Solve a complicated algebra question using simple arithmetic?

WIBNI, then, is our *master* math move. We can use WIBNI on two problems from the experience set: questions 4 and 8. We'll start with question 8 because this problem demonstrates the *combined* use of WIBNI and our swapping numbers move.

8. $\dfrac{(x^8 + x^7 + x^6 + x^5 + x^4 + x^3 + x^2)}{(x^7 + x^6 + x^5 + x^4 + x^3 + x^2 + x)} =$

(A) 1
(B) x
(C) $7x$
(D) x^7
(E) x^8

SOLUTION

If you thought of swapping numbers on this question, bravo! We could translate all the algebra into simple arithmetic by swapping, say, 2 for x. (**On problems with algebraic answer choices, remember, we avoid swapping using 1 or 0 because these numbers "dissolve" away.**)

Unfortunately, there are so many exponents here that substituting 2 still involves a healthy amount of arithmetic, even for a calculator. "There must be an easier way" is the signal to start WIBNI thinking. Wouldn't it be nice if we do away with all the big exponents?

The simpler version we'll create must retain the essence of the original problem. So we notice that the essence of this question is the sum of consecutive powers of x divided by a sum of consecutive powers of x, all 1 less than those in the numerator.

Okay, here's our WIBNI version of the question:

8. $\dfrac{(x^4 + x^3 + x^2)}{(x^3 + x^2 + x)} =$

Now let's swap 2 for x, and we get

8. $\dfrac{(x^4 + x^3 + x^2)}{(x^3 + x^2 + x)} = \dfrac{(2^4 + 2^3 + 2^2)}{(2^3 + 2^2 + 2)} = \dfrac{(16 + 8 + 4)}{(8 + 4 + 2)} = 2$

Okay, if we let x equal 2, we get 2—that is, x—as the answer; that's our solution rule. So applying that rule to the original problem, we get choice (B) as the answer.

Now, if you are one of those rare students who *happened* to notice that an x can be factored out of the numerator to equal the denominator—bravo. But very, very few students notice that because of the unusual nature of the fraction. *Everyone* acquainted with WIBNI and swapping numbers, however, sees through this question almost immediately.

$$K = 23 \times 29 \times 31 \times 37 \times 41$$

4. A decrease of 1 in which of the factors above
    would result in the greatest decrease in K ?

    (A) 23
    (B) 29
    (C) 31
    (D) 37
    (E) 41

SOLUTION

If you were tempted to use your calculator on this question—despite my earlier warning about the dangers of calculators—you determined that K equals 31,367,009. Ugh. If you tried to push ahead with this approach, you'd have to subtract 1 from each of the factors above, and find the new product each time. Then you'd have to subtract each of those products from the original value of K to see which factor's decrease by 1 resulted in the greatest overall decrease.

So, as I recommended in the first experience set: Whenever possible on the SAT math test, avoid math and try thinking instead. Almost everyone realizes that the answer must be either choice (A) or choice (E); a few students suspect choice (C) might somehow be the answer as the median.

So, what exactly don't we like about the problem that we could use WIBNI to change? The huge product, of course. Okay, here's my WIBNI version of the question:

$$K = 2 \times 3 \times 4$$

4. A decrease of 1 in which of the factors above
    would result in the greatest decrease in K ?

    (A) 2
    (B) 3
    (C) 4

Okay, *this* problem is a piece of cake. The original value of K is 24. If we decrease the 2 by 1, we get a new product of 12 (a difference of 12). If we decrease the 3 by 1, we get a new product of 16 (a difference of 8). If we decrease the 4 by 1, we get a new product of 18 (a decrease of 7).

CONTINUED ON NEXT PAGE ▷

From the WIBNI version, we learned that the solution rule is to select the smallest value among the choices. Applying this rule to the original version, we get the answer as 23, or choice (A).

With a little practice our WIBNI master math move will become second nature to you. The following drill will help you develop your awareness of the endless variety of SAT math situations in which WIBNI can come to your aid.

WIBNI Drill

Each example below is the whole or partial situation of an SAT math problem. Use WIBNI to create an *easier* version of the situation to work with—do not work with the original situations. Some of these are quite difficult, so do the best you can; you'll soon get the hang of this math move. You'll find my versions on page 415. **If you find these questions too difficult, review my version after each question before trying the next.**

THE ORIGINAL SITUATION	YOUR WIBNI VERSION
1. The three sides of a triangle are 7, 7, and 6.	
2. A certain sequence of numbers begins with –5, and every succeeding term after the first is 3 greater than the preceding term.	
3. Three brothers share the cost of a present in the ratio of 3:4:5.	

$$\boxed{\text{CONTINUED ON NEXT PAGE} \triangleright}$$

411

THE ORIGINAL SITUATION	YOUR WIBNI VERSION
4. The coordinates of point A are (4, 1) and those of point B are (6, 1). A line is drawn from the origin that passes between points A and B.	
5. How many numbers from 1 to 1000 are divisible by 2 or 5?	
6. $3^{60} + 3^{60} + 3^{60} = 3^x$	
7. In x years, Kyle will be $(y + 1)$ times his current age. In terms of x and y, what is Kyle's current age?	
8. Steven can do a certain job in 3 hours and Gary can do the same job in 2 hours. How many hours will it take Steven and Gary to do the job working together?	

> **Keep the following points in mind about our WIBNI move:**
>
> - You can use WIBNI on any every type of question on the SAT, including the open-ended questions.
>
> - Whenever you aren't sure what to do on a problem, create a *simpler* version of the question that retains the *essence* of the original problem. Solve the easier problem to discover the solution rule, and then apply this principle to the original version of the question.
>
> - The WIBNI process begins by noticing what you don't *like* about a problem.

Use These Four Math Moves Whenever You Can—Always

The math moves you've just learned are always the most efficient way to solve any question. By most efficient, I mean the fastest *safe* way to solve a question.

When students first encounter these moves, they often remark, "But I *never* would have thought of solving questions that way." I didn't *expect* you to know these methods; after all, that's why you're reading this book.

Remember that you can combine these methods on individual problems, as we did on question 8 from the experience set.

> Our math moves work on the SAT Math Ic and SAT Math IIc tests as well as on the SAT Math Test—they even work on the Advanced Placement AB and BC calculus exams!

Your Goal When Practicing for the SAT Math Test Is *Not* to Solve Problems— But Rather to Practice Using Our Math Moves

Although the SAT grading computer doesn't care how you answer questions, I *do*. As your SAT coach, my job is to make sure that you learn the math moves—and to make sure that you actually *use* them.

If you continue to solve questions using classroom-correct, SAT-risky methods when you practice, you're not changing the way you take the SAT math test. And as you know from Tutorial 7, if you want to change your math score, you *must* change the way you solve math problems.

Using our math moves is guaranteed to change the way you take the test. So if your solution to a problem is different from the solution I offer, you should at least master the method that my solution illustrates.

Practice Solving Problems in More than One Way

In math class at school, you're used to solving one problem and then moving on to the next. That's fine for math class. But if you're serious about improving your math score—and I trust you are—you'll practice different approaches to each question. **When practicing it's much more effective to solve one question in three different ways than to solve three different questions.**

For example, you can:

- Solve a question slowly, the way your math teacher might show you.
- Solve it quickly using one or more math moves.
- Rescue it, by pretending you have only ten seconds to go.

Use your OmniProctor to practice answering questions under different time scenarios. We'll revisit this topic in Experience Set 6.

Answers to Experience Set 4 (page 392)

You'll find detailed solutions to each problem in the debriefing.

1. B
2. C
3. C
4. A
5. D
6. E
7. D
8. B

Discussion of WIBNI Drill (page 411)

Your WIBNI versions of these questions may be different from mine and yet just as good; the important thing is that your version be *essentially* the same as the original situation—yet simpler.

1.

THE ORIGINAL SITUATION	MY WIBNI VERSION
The three sides of a triangle are 7, 7, and 6.	The three sides of a triangle are 7, 7, and 7.

DISCUSSION

I didn't like the unequal sides, which were mostly equal. So I created an equilateral triangle because I know all of its angles are equal. Now it would be a simple matter to work out the question using the equilateral triangle. **I'll have to remember to adjust my answer at the end to return to the original triangle.**

2.

THE ORIGINAL SITUATION	MY WIBNI VERSION
A certain sequence of numbers begins with –5, and every succeeding term after the first is 3 greater than the preceding term.	A certain sequence of numbers begins with 3, and every succeeding term after the first is 3 greater than the preceding term.

DISCUSSION

I didn't like starting with –5 because the resulting series is not easy to count: –5, –2, 1, 4, 7, yuck. So I created a series beginning with 3 (by adding 8 to the first term) so that I could count the terms as consecutive multiples: 3, 6, 9, 12, and so on. At the end of the problem I'll have to remember to subtract back the 8 to return to the original series.

3.

THE ORIGINAL SITUATION	MY WIBNI VERSION
Three brothers share the cost of a present in the ratio of 3:4:5.	Three brothers share the cost of a present in the ratio of 4:4:4.

DISCUSSION

I didn't like the unequal shares, which were mostly equal. So I made them equal. At the end of the problem I'll have to remember that the smallest share is a bit less than the equal shares, and the largest share is a bit more.

4.

THE ORIGINAL SITUATION	MY WIBNI VERSION
The coordinates of point *A* are (4, 1) and those of point *B* are (6, 1). A line is drawn from the origin that passes between points *A* and *B*.	The coordinates of point *A* are (4, 1) and those of point *B* are (6, 1). A line is drawn from the origin that passes through point A at (4, 1).

DISCUSSION

I didn't like not knowing exactly where the line was drawn. So I simply chose to have the line drawn through point *A*. I could have drawn it through point *B*, or even through (5, 1) midway between points *A* and *B*. At the end of the problem I'll have to remember to adjust my answer to return to the original situation.

5.

THE ORIGINAL SITUATION	MY WIBNI VERSION
How many numbers from 1 to 1000 are divisible by 2 or 5?	How many numbers from 1 to 10 are divisible by 2 or 5?

DISCUSSION

I didn't like the huge number, and having to count so high. So I dropped the two zeroes and made the counting a whole lot more manageable. At the end of the problem I'll have to remember to adjust my answer by adding the zeros back.

6.

THE ORIGINAL SITUATION	MY WIBNI VERSION
$3^{60} + 3^{60} + 3^{60} = 3^x$	$3^2 + 3^2 + 3^2 = 3^x$

DISCUSSION

I didn't like the huge exponents, which makes the numbers hard to think about (even for my calculator). So I adjusted the exponents way, way down. Now the problem is easy to solve, and I learn x is 3, or 1 more than the exponent I used. That's my solution rule for this question. At the end of the problem I'll have to remember to adjust my answer by applying the rule I learned to the original situation.

7.

THE ORIGINAL SITUATION	MY WIBNI VERSION
In x years, Kyle will be $(y + 1)$ times his current age. In terms of x and y, what is Kyle's current age?	Kyle is 10. In 30 years, Kyle will be 40, or 4 times his current age of 10.

DISCUSSION

What I didn't like about this problem was that swapping numbers for the variables x and y for once produced a *complicated* arithmetic question. So I started with an answer and chose simple numbers that satisfied the question. At the end of the problem I'll have to remember to adjust all the values of x and y in the choices to reflect the numbers I've chosen.

8.

THE ORIGINAL SITUATION	**MY WIBNI VERSION**
Steven can do a certain job in 3 hours and Gary can do the same job in 2 hours. How many hours will it take Steven and Gary to do the job working together?	Steven can do a certain job in 3 hours and Gary can do the same job in 2 hours. How many jobs can they complete in 6 hours working together?

DISCUSSION

What I didn't like about this problem was being forced to deal with fractions. So I chose a simple number of hours that 2 and 3 both divide evenly into—6— that they work together. Now it's easy to figure out how many jobs Steven can do and Gary can do in this time. At the end of the problem I'll have to adjust my answer to reflect that I want to know how long it takes them to do a single job.

Knowing What to Do
When You Don't Know What to Do

PRELUDE

Solving SAT Math Problems Often Seems Like
Driving in the Fog—at Night

E. L. Doctorow, the author of *Ragtime,* once said, "Writing is like driving at night in the fog. You can see only as far as your headlights, but you can make the whole trip that way."

Solving an SAT math problem often seems exactly like you're driving in a fog: you read the question but you don't have a clue how to go about solving it. You think and think but you come up blank; you have no idea of even where to begin. So, what *do* you do when you don't know what to do? The answer is surprisingly simple. But first, another brief experience set.

EXPERIENCE SET 5

Time yourself on these questions, but take as much time as you need. (I just want you to develop your awareness of how much time you spend on questions.) These are super-tough problems, so it may take a while to solve them; most students cannot solve them at all. You may experience a lot of frustration with this problem set, but struggle with the questions as long as you can; the frustration is part of this experience set.

1. Set N consists of the digits from 1 through 7, inclusive. If one of the digits from set N is removed, the units' digit of the sum of the remaining digits is 2. What number was removed from the set?

    (A) 1
    (B) 4
    (C) 6
    (D) 7
    (E) It cannot be determined from the information given.

2. If $\dfrac{x}{y} + \dfrac{y}{x} = 6$, then $(x + y)\left(\dfrac{1}{x} + \dfrac{1}{y}\right) =$

    (A) 4
    (B) 8
    (C) 12
    (D) 24
    (E) 36

> Stop! The following debriefing is based on this problem set. Please do not read any further if you haven't yet completed these questions—or at least given them your *best* shot. Also, do *not* peek ahead at the solutions.

DEBRIEFING

The Amazingly Simple Secret to Getting Unstuck on Tough SAT Math Problems

What I'm about to reveal will seem so blindingly obvious that you'll think I'm just joking around, but I couldn't be more serious. The clue is in the E. L. Doctorow quote: you only have to see a bit ahead to make progress. **If you don't know what to do on a problem, do *whatever* you can do—it's almost always a step in the right direction. You don't *have* to see how to solve the problem in order to solve it; you just have to see what to do *next*.**

Think about what I've just said for a moment. The trap that students fall into on the SAT Math Test is that when they don't see the *complete* solution to a problem, they stop dead in their tracks. Wrong! You don't have the luxury to contemplate the problem; and you can't afford to stand still.

Staring at a Tough Question Won't Help— *Do* Something on the Problem—*Anything*

The great poet Robert Frost once commented, "The brain is a wonderful organ; it starts working the moment you get up in the morning and does not stop until you get into the office."

Trying to "figure out" what to do on a tough question won't help. Keep your pencil moving and do whatever you *can* do on the problem.

For example,

- *If an algebraic expression can be factored—factor it!*

- *If you can draw a diagram of the problem—draw one!*

- *If an equation can be simplified—simplify it!*

- *If like terms can be combined—combine them!*

- *If two fractions can be added—add them!*

- *If you can write down a geometry formula—write it down!*

Any—and I mean *any*—step you can take when you're stuck will move you forward. Even a simple step may open a door that reveals the way to the eventual solution.

The process is not unlike solving one of those video game mysteries: To find the treasure you have to find a key. Once you find the key you have to find the box it opens. When you open the right box, a map is inside, but it's missing the half that contains vital information.

Step by step, without knowing where you'll eventually wind up, you make your way toward solving the mystery. But you have to *do* something on a difficult problem—*anything*—if you expect to make progress towards a solution.

The Best Place to Start Solving a Tough SAT Math Problem Is Often at the *End*

Each SAT problem begins by providing some information—*If blah, blah, blah*—and then asking you to solve for something—*then what does blah-blah equal?* It's natural to assume that you should work through the problem in the order in which the information is presented.

Not always. In fact, on the medium to difficult questions you'll often find that the path toward the solution presents itself immediately if you start instead at the end and work backward.

Consider the following question:

1. If *blah blah blah blah blah blah blah blah blah blah blah blah blah blah blah blah blah blah blah blah blah*, then what does $3x + 3$ equal?

So, what can you do on this question? Well, the first thing to do is to do *whatever* you can do, which here is factor the expression $3x + 3$ to get $3(x + 1)$. Then you'd look back to the rest of the problem and see how to get $(x + 1)$—not x alone—from the information provided.

The following drill will give you some practice to help develop the habit of *immediately* doing *whatever* you can do on a problem—*as a reflex.*

The Blah-Blah Drill

In the following drill, do whatever you can do on each problem. You will not be given enough information to solve any of the questions, but do whatever you can do.

1.	If *blah blah blah blah blah blah blah blah blah blah blah blah blah blah blah blah blah blah blah blah blah*, then what is the area of triangle *ABC*?
2.	If $\frac{1}{2} < \frac{x}{18} < \frac{5}{6}$, and *blah blah blah blah blah blah blah blah blah blah blah blah blah blah blah blah blah blah blah blah blah blah blah*, then which of the following must be true?

3. If *blah blah blah blah blah blah blah blah blah blah blah blah blah blah blah blah blah blah blah*, then the average of the remaining three scores =

4. If $(x + y)^2 < (x - y)^2$, and *blah blah blah blah blah blah blah blah blah blah blah blah blah blah blah blah blah blah blah*, then which of the following must be true?

5. If a certain trip was made by foot, by car, and by bus, and *blah blah blah blah blah blah blah blah blah blah blah blah blah blah blah*, then what fraction of the distance traveled was made by car?

6. If $2 - \dfrac{m}{n} = \dfrac{m}{n} - 4$, and n ≠ 0 *blah blah blah blah blah blah blah blah blah blah blah blah blah blah blah blah blah blah*, then which of the following must be true?

You'll find a discussion of the questions at the end of this experience set on page 427.

Finally, the Answers to Those Super-Difficult Questions

1. Set N consists of the digits from 1 through 7, inclusive. If one of the digits from set N is removed, the units' digit of the sum of the remaining digits is 2. What number was removed from the set?

   (A) 1
   (B) 4
   (C) 6
   (D) 7
   (E) It cannot be determined from the information given.

DISCUSSION

Let's start with our basic rule: *Do whatever you can do.* Well, the problem involves the sum of the remaining numbers, so let's use WIBNI (one of our math moves from the last experience set) and find the sum of *all* the numbers: 28. The units' digit of that sum is 8. Okay, well, we can cross off choice (D) since we haven't removed any digits yet. If you *check the choices* (another math move), you'll see the answer must be 6, choice (C). **On hard questions, the choice (E) (It cannot be determined from the information given) tends to be a popular—and therefore wrong.** But if you quickly checked *all* the digits from 1 to 7, you'd quickly see that 6 is the only possible solution.

2. If $\dfrac{x}{y} + \dfrac{y}{x} = 6$, then $(x + y)\left(\dfrac{1}{x} + \dfrac{1}{y}\right) =$

(A)   4
(B)   8
(C)   12
(D)   24
(E)   36

DISCUSSION

Again, let's start with our basic rule: *Do whatever you can do.* Well, if we start with the expression we're asked to find, we could multiply the two parentheses, so let's do that. If we multiply the two parentheses (FOIL: first, outer, inner, last), we discover that we're looking for $1 + \dfrac{x}{y} + \dfrac{y}{x} + 1$, or $2 + \dfrac{x}{y} + \dfrac{y}{x}$. Hey, how convenient! The problem tells us that $\dfrac{x}{y} + \dfrac{y}{x}$ equals 6, so adding 2 we get choice (B).

Very Important Postscript: If you tried to solve for x or y, you probably quickly got lost in a maze of algebraic expressions. **As you'll learn when we get to SAT algebra, never try to solve for x if the problem doesn't ask for x.** Many RocketReview students attempt to swap numbers on this problem, but then they get stuck when they realize that they they'd have to answer the question to swap the right numbers. For example, many students try to let $x = 1$ and $y = 6$, but then the give up when they get $\dfrac{x}{y} + \dfrac{y}{x} = 6\dfrac{1}{6}$ instead of 6. **But what do we do when we get stuck? We do whatever we can do.** Let's use our WIBNI move: wouldn't it be nice if the problem said that the $\dfrac{x}{y} + \dfrac{y}{x}$ equaled $6\dfrac{1}{6}$ instead of 6. After all: $6\dfrac{1}{6}$ is pretty close to 6. So let's push ahead and swap 1 and 6 for x and y into the parenthetical expressions. Now we get a WIBNI answer of $8\dfrac{1}{6}$. Hey, there's only one choice close to $8\dfrac{1}{6}$ choice (B), 8, the answer.

And If You're *Still* Stuck . . .

If you've done everything you *can* do on a problem and you're *still* stalled, circle the question number and move on! *Now!* Return to it later when your subconscious mind has had some time to mull the problem over, or when another question in the section triggers an association that offers a fresh perspective. And if you're running out of time on the section, take a buzzer shot guess.

Discussion of the Blah Blah Drill (page 423)

Remember that the purpose of this drill was *not* to have you solve questions (since not enough information was provided), but simply to get you in the *habit* of doing whatever you can do without wondering whether the step leads to the soultion—it usually does.

1. If *blah blah blah blah blah blah blah blah blah blah blah blah blah blah blah blah blah blah blah,* then what is the area of triangle *ABC*?

    DISCUSSION

    You could write down the formula for the area of a triangle: $\frac{1}{2}bh$. You should also draw a picture of a triangle and label the base and height.

2. If $\frac{1}{2} < \frac{x}{18} < \frac{5}{6}$, and *blah blah blah blah blah blah blah blah blah blah blah blah blah blah blah blah blah blah blah blah blah,* then which of the following must be true?

    DISCUSSION

    You could use 18 as a common denominator, and get $\frac{9}{18} < \frac{x}{18} < \frac{15}{18}$. At that point, you could multiply each term through by 18 and get $9 < x < 15$. **Notice how much simpler the problem has become simply by doing whatever you can do.**

3. If *blah blah blah blah blah blah blah blah blah blah blah blah blah blah blah blah blah,* then the average of the remaining three scores =

    DISCUSSION

    You could write down the formula for the average of three items: $\frac{x+y+z}{3}$.

4. If $(x + y)^2 < (x - y)^2$, and *blah blah blah blah blah blah blah blah blah blah blah blah blah blah blah blah blah blah blah blah blah,* then which of the following must be true?

DISCUSSION

You could FOIL both sides of the inequality to get $x^2 + 2xy + y^2 < x^2 - 2xy + y^2$. That's a good start, but then you could subtract $x^2 + y^2$ from both sides of the inequality to get $2xy < -2xy$. Now you could add $2xy$ to both sides of the inequality to get $4xy < 0$. Almost done: Now you can divide both sides by 4 to get $xy < 0$. **Notice how much simpler the problem has become simply by doing whatever you can do.**

5. If a certain trip was made by foot, by car, and by bus, and *blah blah blah blah blah blah blah blah blah blah blah blah blah blah blah blah blah blah blah,* then what fraction of the total distance traveled was made by car?

DISCUSSION

You could write down the formula for this fraction: $\frac{c}{t}$ where c is the distance traveled by car and t is the total distance. **Notice that I used the initial letters of the variables rather than x or y.** At this point you could express t in terms of the other variables and get $\dfrac{c}{f + c + b}$.

6. If $2 - \dfrac{m}{n} = \dfrac{m}{n} - 4$, and n ≠ 0 *blah blah blah blah blah blah blah blah blah blah blah blah blah blah blah blah blah blah blah blah,* then which of the following must be true?

DISCUSSION

You could add 4 to both sides of the equation to get $6 - \dfrac{m}{n} = \dfrac{m}{n}$. Now you could add $\dfrac{m}{n}$ to both sides of the equation to get $6 = 2\left(\dfrac{m}{n}\right)$. Then you could divide both sides of the equation by 2 to get $3 = \dfrac{m}{n}$. If you don't like fractions (and I certainly don't), you could multiply both sides of the equation by n to get $3n = m$. **Notice how much simpler the problem has become simply by doing whatever you can do.**

Learning to Handle Time Pressure, Rescue Questions, and Take Buzzer Shots

PRELUDE

Face It: You Probably Won't—and Shouldn't— Have Time to Finish Each Math Section

The vast majority of students who take the SAT Math Test fall into one of two categories: those who work too slowly, and those who work too quickly. Those who work too slowly are easier to help; after learning the math moves and the most common types of SAT problems, their problem-solving speed improves dramatically.

Those who move too quickly, however, present a greater challenge. Look, anybody can finish an SAT math section with plenty of time to spare—if he or she is willing to throw accuracy *out the window*. I know that it seems like you shouldn't have much difficulty finishing an SAT math section. After all, the questions don't seem *that* difficult; you *ought* to be able to finish them all, right? Don't be deceived.

Take one of the regular multiple-choice sections. You have 25 minutes in which to answer 20 questions. That works out to an average of 75 seconds for each question. Sounds like more than enough time to solve each problem, doesn't it?

Hold on. Consider all the steps you have to complete for each question in that 75 seconds. First you have to read the question—*carefully*—at least once and maybe twice, just to be sure. Then you have to figure out what the question is asking, and decide on the best approach to solving it. You then have to compute the answer *and* check your solution. Then—*always*—you have to reread the question one last time. Then you have to find the answer among the choices and verify that your solution is there. Then you have to find the correct spot on your answer sheet and fill in the corresponding bubble. And finally, you have to return to your test booklet and find the next problem.

On second thought, maybe 75 seconds doesn't sound like so much time after all. Just filling in the answer sheet can eat up five to ten seconds per question. That adds up to two or three minutes—*per section*—consumed simply by filling in answers. That's two or three minutes less per section that you have for solving questions.

Introducing Sprint Drills

Please review Tutorials 25, 26, and 27 on the importance of focusing on your accuracy rather than your speed. **Until you are *consistently* scoring in the mid-700 plus range on the SAT Math Test, you absolutely must be willing to sacrifice some questions.** The need to sacrifice some math questions may be difficult to accept, *especially* if you're a strong math student. The following multipart experience set will *force* you to focus on accuracy rather than speed.

EXPERIENCE SET 6

For this experience set you'll need access to your OmniProctor on your RocketReview CD-ROM or at our website, RocketReview.com. (If you aren't familiar with OmniProctor, you'll find a description beginning on page 647, as well as on the CD-ROM and on the RocketReview website.) If you don't have access to OmniProctor, you can use a timer that you can set accurately to the minute.

This experience set consists of three pairs of medium to difficult questions that you will complete one pair at a time. **Do not even glance at the questions until you are ready to complete the questions; this is a strictly timed drill.**

For the first pair of questions, set OmniProctor (or your timer) for *exactly* two minutes. Warning: Unless you are an extraordinarily strong test-taker, if you attempt to answer both questions in two minutes, you run the risk of getting both questions wrong. Your goal is to choose *one* of the two questions and get it right, spending however much of the two minutes you need. Then, if you have any time left, either try to solve the other question or take a buzzer shot guess on it. **Remember to avoid any popular-looking choices if you're taking a guess—these are difficult questions.**

This is a very, very, *very* tough drill, but it will make a dramatic difference in your test-taking ability.

First Sprint Drill: Two Minutes

1. What is the least integer greater than -1.8?

   (A)   0.0
   (B) -1.0
   (C) -1.7
   (D) -1.9
   (E) -2.0

2. How many positive, 2-digit integers are there such that if the digits of the number are reversed, the resulting number is 9 more than the original?

   (A) 9
   (B) 8
   (C) 4
   (D) 2
   (E) 1

STOP! Please turn to page 441 to see how you did before proceeding to the next sprint drill.

Second Sprint Drill: Two Minutes

1. If the present time is 6 PM, then what time was it 46 hours ago?

    (A) 12 PM
    (B)   8 PM
    (C)   4 PM
    (D)   8 AM
    (E)   4 AM

2. If the radius of a circle is decreased by 20 percent, by what percent is the area reduced?

    (A)   4%
    (B) 20%
    (C) 36%
    (D) 40%
    (E) 64%

STOP! Please turn to page 442 to see how you did before proceeding to the next sprint drill.

> Remember to take pains. Don't rush. Remember to take pains. Don't rush. Remember to take pains. Don't rush. Remember to take pains.

Third Sprint Drill: Two Minutes

1. A certain gymnastic club has 8 more girls than boys. If there is a total of 60 boys and girls in the club, how many members are boys?

    (A) 38
    (B) 34
    (C) 28
    (D) 26
    (E) 22

2. If a line contains the points (−2, 2) and (1, 11), then its *x*-intercept is

    (A) 8

    (B) 3

    (C) $\frac{3}{11}$

    (D) $-\frac{3}{4}$

    (E) $-\frac{8}{3}$

Please turn to page 443 to see how you did before moving on to the debriefing.

Stop! The following debriefing is based on this problem set. Please do not read any further if you haven't yet completed these questions.

Work through Each SAT Math Section in at *Least* Two Passes— Three Is Even Better

Most students march through an SAT math section as if they were tin soldiers. They complete the first question, and then move on dutifully to complete the second question, then on to the third, and the fourth, and so on, until time runs out.

Listen, no rule requires you to answer questions on the SAT in numerical order. You should complete SAT math in the order most convenient to *you*.

Now, you may be thinking, "Hey, I thought the questions on the SAT Math Test were in order of difficulty. Shouldn't I do the easy questions before the hard ones?"

Well, yes, and no. In general, the more difficult the question, the more time-consuming it will be—but not necessarily. More important, what may be hard for most test-takers may not be hard for you, now that you're armed with all the knowledge you've been gaining here.

An enormous danger on the test—I know this has happened to you because it happens to *everyone*—is getting stuck on a question early on in a section; sometimes on an easy question. And before you know it, several *minutes* have gone by and you're still stuck!

The problem with frustration on the SAT Math Test is that once you become frustrated with—or worse, panicked about—a question, that frustration or panic doesn't disappear once you've (we hope) solved the question. **Once frustration or panic sets in on the SAT, it's very hard to shake for the rest of the test!**

Because of this danger, you need to *train* yourself to be a lazy procrastinator! Keep postponing the most difficult and time-consuming questions whenever you encounter them. Jump through a section the way a monkey jumps from tree to tree, from quick question to the next quick question.

The best way to accomplish this goal is to work through each SAT math section in waves or passes.

- On the first pass through a math section, answer only those questions you *know* you can solve *quickly*. If you know a question will take you some time, *skip it for now*. And if you aren't *immediately* sure whether you can solve a question, don't risk getting stuck—*skip that question.* **By the way, any time you skip a problem, circle the question number in your test booklet so you can remember to return to the problem on your second or third pass.**

- On the second pass, tackle the questions you know you can do, or can probably do, but will take some time. You might glance at some of the problems skipped on the first pass and decide to postpone them again for your final pass.

- And on the final pass, tackle those questions you're not sure of. If you can't solve a question completely and less than a minute remains, take a buzzer shot guess.

Remember: if you can't tell whether you can solve a problem quickly, that question will almost certainly give you some trouble—skip it on your first pass through the section.

The following table is an example of how a smart test-taker—let's call her Mallie—might make three passes through one of the 25-minute math sections:

 First Pass: Jog (10 minutes)	Second Pass: Walk (12 minutes)	Third Pass: Sprint (3 minutes)
1 DONE ✓		
2 DONE ✓		
3 DONE ✓		
4 (skipped) ⇨	DONE ✓	
5 DONE ✓		
6 DONE ✓		
7 DONE ✓		
8 (skipped) ⇨	DONE ✓	
9 DONE ✓		
10 DONE ✓		
11 (skipped) ⇨	DONE ✓	
12 (attempted) ?	(skipped) ⇨	DONE ✓
13 DONE ✓		
14 (skipped) ⇨	(skipped) ⇨	DONE ✓
15 (skipped) ⇨	(skipped) ⇨	(blank) ✗
16 DONE ✓		
17 (skipped) ⇨	(attempted) ⇨	(buzzer shot guess) 🏀
18 (attempted) ?	DONE ✓	
19 DONE ✓		
20 (skipped) ⇨	(skipped) ⇨	(buzzer shot guess) 🏀

Notice the following points about Mallie's progress through the section:

- Mallie answered a couple of hard questions on the first pass; Mallie recognized them and knew they could be solved quickly.

- Notice also that Mallie skipped an easy question on the first pass because it looked a little long and she didn't want to get bogged down.

- Even on the second pass Mallie sidestepped a number of questions that she didn't immediately know how to solve; she figured that with a bit more time solutions might occur to her, possibly triggered by another question. **As she passed by these questions on the second pass, she made mental notes of good buzzer shot guesses for her final pass if she couldn't figure out solutions to the last few remaining questions.** We'll talk a lot more about buzzer shots shortly.

- On the third pass, Mallie finally figured out how to solve two of the remaining questions and took buzzer shot guesses on two. On one of the questions, number 15, she didn't spot any good guesses so she let that one go by unanswered.

It may take you some time to become comfortable with this three-pass approach but with sufficient *rehearsing*, working in passes will become second nature. Indeed, highly experienced test-takers might even take a fourth or fifth pass through a section. **Apply this approach to completing your regular classroom homework assignments and tests; you'll see that it works well in school, too.**

> **Always be sure you write your answers in your test booklet as well as on your answer sheet. If you get out of sequence on your answer sheet—it happens—you'll be able to reconstruct the correct answers.**

No, Working in Passes Does *Not* Take More Time

A common question at this point is, "But don't all these passes take more time?" Not one bit, because you haven't ever allowed yourself to get stuck. **Another benefit of postponing questions is that your subconscious mind has a chance to work on them while your conscious mind is busy solving the question at hand.**

Which Questions Should You Postpone—or Sacrifice Entirely?

How do you decide which questions you should postpone attempting on your first pass, if not sacrifice entirely? As I just mentioned, sometimes a medium question will take much longer to solve than a difficult one.

Since each question is worth the same amount, regardless of how long it takes to solve, you must learn to recognize *at a glance* whether a question is worth attempting. Which questions you decide to do on your first pass through a math section is partly a matter of personal preference. For example, you may prefer algebra questions while another student prefers geometry questions.

Having said that, the following factors will help you decide whether a question is worth attempting on your first pass, or whether you should postpone it for a second or third pass:

- Shorter questions usually take much less time to solve than longer questions. Any question longer than three lines is going to take some time to solve.

- Questions with *simple* diagrams usually take less time to solve than questions without diagrams.

- Keep your eyes out for *familiar* question types; these questions can often be solved in mere seconds.

You just learned four amazingly powerful *math moves* that can solve many medium-to-difficult questions in a flash. And later, when we cover the top 11 SAT math problems of all time (well, of the last quarter-century anyway), you can expect at least several of these problem types to show up on *your* SAT Math Test.

By the end of this book, then, you'll be familiar with many types of problems. A problem that might have stumped you today will soon seem like a snap.

You Should Be Able to Tell How Time-Consuming a Question Will Be—*at a Glance!*

Just as a good batter knows in a flash whether to swing at a pitch or let it go by, you should know in a flash whether to tackle a question or let it go by— at least on your first pass. You shouldn't need to read the question!

You may be wondering, "How can I tell if a question will take a lot of time to solve unless I read it?" **If you have to read a question all the way through to decide whether you can solve the problem, that question is likely to give you some trouble.** Circle the question number and skip the problem on your first pass, you can return to it later.

Keep in mind that your ability to assess accurately how long a question will take you to solve will improve as you become familiar with the problem-solving math moves you're learning in this book.

If You Misjudge a Question, Cut Your Losses and Move On

It may happen on your first pass that you attempt a question you *thought* you could solve, only to realize as you get into details that you find yourself stumped. I'll show you later what to do when you get stuck on a problem, but until then, as soon as you realize that you may be spinning your wheels on a problem, circle the question number and move on.

On the other hand, you don't want to give up too early, either. Sometimes just a little more pushing unlocks a problem. **As a rule of thumb, if you aren't making forward progress on a question for ten to twenty seconds, consider yourself stalled if not stumped.** *Tear* yourself away from the problem and return to it later.

Remember to Take Buzzer Shot Guesses If You Can't Solve a Question Completely

Okay, you've skipped a few questions that stumped you on your first or second passes through a math section, but now time is about to run out. What should you do?

Rescue the question as best you can by eliminating as many choices as you can, and guessing among the remaining choices. Remember that easy questions have easy, obvious, *popular-looking* answers; hard questions have hard, strange, *unpopular-looking* answers.

> If you're taking a buzzer shot guess on a difficult question, your best guess is the hardest-looking choice *nearest* in size to the most obvious choice. The obvious choice on a difficult question is obviously *wrong*, but it's usually not far off.

By the way, it's much harder to take a buzzer shot guess on an open-ended question because you have no choices to work with. Still, if you have a rough idea of an answer, by all means go for it and guess.

Moving on to SAT Math Content

This was our final experience set on SAT math techniques. While you may not be comfortable yet with all of our test-taking techniques, I promise you that you are now familiar with the most powerful test-taking skills and drills available anywhere. You will find additional drills at RocketReview.com, our website.

Take a break before moving on to the section on SAT math content—you've just completed a grueling experience set.

Answers to the Experience Set Sprint Drills (page 432)

Please review the answers to the sprint drills you completed; don't peek ahead.

First Sprint Drill

1. What is the least integer greater than –1.8?

   (A) 0.0
   (B) –1.0
   (C) –1.7
   (D) –1.9
   (E) –2.0

   DISCUSSION

   If you took the pains to draw a number line and mark off some integers to either side of –1.8, you saw that the next greater integer is –1.0, or choice (B). Choice (E) is the greatest integer *less* than –1.8. If you missed this question, you were reckless. Slow down and take pains to get things right.

2. How many positive, 2-digit integers are there such that if the digits of the number are reversed, the resulting number is 9 more than the original?

   (A) 9
   (B) 8
   (C) 4
   (D) 2
   (E) 1

   DISCUSSION

   If you took the pains to write out 2-digit integers at random, you'd soon discover that 12, 23, 34, and 45 work, as do 56, 67, 78, and 89. The answer is choice (B). These numbers all come in pairs (as shown in the table to the right).

   If you missed this question but got the first question, you did well. If you got them both right, you did very well. If you got them both wrong, you're too reckless. Slow down and take pains on the second sprint drill.

valid	-	invalid
12	-	21
23	-	32
34	-	43
45	-	54
56	-	65
67	-	76
78	-	87
89	-	98

STOP! Please return to the second sprint drill on page 433. Do not peek ahead at the answers below.

Second Sprint Drill

1. If the present time is 6 PM, then what time was
    it 46 hours ago?

    (A) 12 PM
    (B)   8 PM
    (C)   4 PM
    (D)   8 AM
    (E)   4 AM

DISCUSSION

If you took the pains to write out the hours, you absolutely should have gotten this question right. Using our WIBNI math move, we could use 48 hours as a benchmark. Two days ago would bring us back to 6 PM, but we went too far back so we have to come forward two hours, to 8 PM, or choice (B). If you chose (C), you either didn't take sufficient pains to write everything out, or you misread the question. Again, if you missed this question, you were reckless. Slow down and take pains to get things right.

2. If the radius of a circle is decreased by 20
    percent, by what percent is the area reduced?

    (A)   4%
    (B) 20%
    (C) 36%
    (D) 40%
    (E) 64%

DISCUSSION

If you took the pains to draw two circles, and then used our swapping numbers math move, this question was not *that* tough. Let the radius of the circle be 10; its area is 100. If the radius decreases by 20 percent, it's now 8, and the area of the circle has decreased to 64. That's a 36 percent reduction, or choice (C). If you chose (D)—the most popular-looking choice—you forgot that this was a difficult question. If you chose choice (E), you misread the question.

If you missed this question but got the first question, you did well. If you got them both right, you did very well. If you got this question but missed the first one, take more pains on the medium questions. If you got them both wrong, you're too reckless. Slow down and take pains on the final sprint drill.

STOP! Please return to the third sprint drill on page 434. Do not peek ahead at the answers below.

Third Sprint Drill

1. A certain high school gymnastic club has 8 more girls than boys. If there are a total of 60 boys and girls in the club, how many members are boys?

   (A) 38
   (B) 34
   (C) 28
   (D) 26
   (E) 22

DISCUSSION

If you took the pains to use our checking the choices math move, you discovered that choice (D) works: 26 boys and 34 girls equals 60 members. If you started off the question by estimating that there were fewer than half boys, and crossed off choices (A) and (B)—bravo! If you got this question wrong, you didn't check your answer and you are still being too reckless. Slow down and take pains to get questions right.

2. If a line contains the points $(-2, 2)$ and $(1, 11)$, then its x-intercept is

(A)   8

(B)   3

(C) $\dfrac{3}{11}$

(D) $-\dfrac{3}{4}$

(E) $-\dfrac{8}{3}$

DISCUSSION

If you took the pains to draw the two points on a coordinate graph, you could have used our estimating math move to answer this question in seconds. If you draw the line connecting these points, you'll see that the x-intercept falls to the left of the first point, so the x-intercept must be less than -2. Only one choice is less than -2: choice (E).

Notice that the classroom-correct, SAT-risky solution of finding the equation of the line running through these two points would take way too long for this sprint drill. (For a similarly lengthy computation, see our discussion question 2 on page 350 of the first experience set.)

If you missed this question but got the first question, you did well. If you got them both right, you did very well. If you got this question but missed the first one, take more pains on the medium questions. If you got them both wrong, you're still way too reckless. Slow down and develop the habit of taking pains.

That's it for the sprint drills. Please return to begin the debriefing on page 435.

SAT Math Content

Reviewing What You Already Know—with Fresh Eyes

One of the Problems with SAT Math Is That You May Have *Forgotten* Some of It

The SAT covers arithmetic, algebra, geometry, and some miscellaneous topics like sets and probability. Yes, the test writers added some algebra II to the SAT Math Test this year, but on the whole, the math concepts covered on the SAT are surprisingly basic—so basic, in fact, that you may have forgotten some of the material. It's probably been some time since you had to solve a math problem involving a remainder, for example, or had to express consecutive integers algebraically. And when was the last time you had to solve a percentage problem?

Learning to Think about Really Simple Math Concepts

In most math classes, you've got to cover so much material that you rarely have time to pause and *reflect* about what you're learning. Sure, you can solve complex trigonometry problems by rote, but do you know how many heights a triangle has? (Three: one for each base.) Sure, you've mastered advanced algebra, but do you know what the remainder is when 5 is divided by 6? (Five: 6 goes into 5 zero times, with 5 left over.)

As we've already discussed, the test writers call the SAT Math Test a *reasoning* test because it measures your ability to think about basic math concepts in novel situations. **The test writers camouflage basic concepts in novel situations to see how well you *think*.** If the math concepts were placed in typical situations, you could solve the problems using rote memory.

In the technique chapters I gave you the tools you need to look at math problems through fresh eyes, but you'll still need to review the basic concepts covered on the test. That's what you'll be doing in the following section.

Reducing the Subject to Bite-Sized Bits:
Introducing Concept Boxes

To make it easier for you to digest all the math you need to know, I've chopped everything up into bits that you can review in brief sessions—even during spare moments. You learned all these concepts ages ago, so we'll move through the topics quickly. Any terms you need to know appear in bold; terms used for discussion purposes and that do not appear in SAT problems themselves will appear in italics.

On your first pass through any of the refresher sections, don't linger too long on any topic. Use the check boxes to indicate those areas you're familiar with and those that deserve a longer review on a second or even third pass through the section. When there's something especially important that I want you to notice or that deserves closer study, I'll highlight the information.

So skim each refresher section first, and then return for a closer review. Don't worry if every concept doesn't sink in on your first or second reading. Trust me: All this material will come back to you soon enough. Keep in mind that every concept will be reinforced in the illustrative questions that you will find online.

Refresher of SAT Arithmetic

Back to Grade School Basics

A big believer in returning to basics, legendary professional football coach Vince Lombardi used to begin each season's training camp by holding up a ball in his hand and announcing, "Gentlemen, this is a football." (One of his players once quipped, "Uh coach, could you take it a little slower?")

You may be studying algebra II or trigonometry or even calculus in school, but don't skip this arithmetic chapter. Pure arithmetic questions will probably make up one-fifth of the new SAT Math Test, not to mention the algebra and geometry questions that involve arithmetic concepts or manipulation. And remember: You haven't covered arithmetic since sixth or seventh grade.

By the way, just because you're allowed to use a calculator doesn't mean arithmetic concepts—like how to divide fractions, or what a remainder is, or how to set up a ratio—are less important; you may have to contend with their algebraic equivalents, which of course your calculator is not equipped to handle. (Although admittedly, as you know, using our math move of swapping numbers for variables is usually able to convert an unwieldy algebra question into a simple arithmetic one.)

So please be patient as we work through this chapter. All the subsequent sections—on algebra, geometry, and miscellaneous math topics—will build on this foundation.

> Perhaps the biggest cause of arithmetic (and algebraic) mistakes on the SAT is forgetting that numbers include fractions. Repeat after me: *Numbers include fractions. Numbers include fractions. Numbers include fractions.* What do numbers include?

> *Manipulation* errors are the second biggest cause of arithmetic (and algebraic) mistakes on the SAT Math Test. Use parentheses whenever possible in setting up and in solving equations. Repeat after me: *The parenthesis is my friend. The parenthesis is my friend. The parenthesis is my friend.* Who's your friend?

Ready? Our Refresher of SAT Arithmetic Is about to Begin

I've divided SAT arithmetic into the following topics:

- Different types of numbers
- Number lines
- Absolute value
- Arithmetical operations
- Parentheses and order of operations
- Factors and divisibility
- Multiples
- Remainders and fractions
- Decimals
- Digits and place value
- Exponents and scientific notation
- Radicals (roots)
- Ratios
- Percentages
- Averages: mean, median, and mode

> Read through all the concepts boxes quickly first, checking the boxes that need further review. Keep in mind that all the concepts will be reinforced in the explanations to the illustrative problems that you'll find on the RocketReview website.

DIFFERENT TYPES OF NUMBERS

N1

Numbers come in many varieties.	$1, 2, 300, -3, \frac{1}{4}, 0, 0.6, \sqrt{2}, \pi$

☐ I KNOW THIS   ☐ I NEED TO REVIEW THIS

N2

Positive numbers are *greater* than zero. No, zero is not positive. **Do not confuse *positive* with *even*.**	

☐ I KNOW THIS   ☐ I NEED TO REVIEW THIS

N3

Negative numbers are *less* than zero. Negative numbers are indicated by a minus sign (−). Positive numbers are usually written without the positive, or plus, sign (+).

☐ **I KNOW THIS**   ☐ **I NEED TO REVIEW THIS**

N4

Zero is neither positive nor negative.

☐ **I KNOW THIS**   ☐ **I NEED TO REVIEW THIS**

N5

Non-negative numbers are positive numbers or zero.

☐ **I KNOW THIS**   ☐ **I NEED TO REVIEW THIS**

N6

Integers are also known as **whole** numbers.

☐ **I KNOW THIS**   ☐ **I NEED TO REVIEW THIS**

N7

Integers can be positive, negative, or zero. Yes, zero is an integer.

☐ **I KNOW THIS**   ☐ **I NEED TO REVIEW THIS**

N8

Even numbers are integers **divisible** by 2, such as 4, 8, −12, or 0. Notice that even numbers can be zero or negative. Yes, zero is even.

☐ I KNOW THIS   ☐ I NEED TO REVIEW THIS

N9

Odd numbers are not divisible by 2.

☐ I KNOW THIS   ☐ I NEED TO REVIEW THIS

N10

Notice the following important behavioral facts about products:

- An even plus an odd is an odd; an even plus an even, or an odd plus an odd, is an even.
- An odd times an odd is an odd; an even times an even, or an even times an odd, is an even.

☐ I KNOW THIS   ☐ I NEED TO REVIEW THIS

N11

Prime numbers are positive integers divisible only by 1 *and* themselves. 1 is *not* a prime number. The numbers 2, 3, 23, and 37 are all prime. **Notice that 2 is the only even prime number.**

☐ I KNOW THIS   ☑ I NEED TO REVIEW THIS

N12

Consecutive numbers are any series of integers increasing by 1, unless otherwise stated. Consecutive numbers can begin as negative, such as the series −2, −1, 0, 1. The series 2, 4, 6, 8 consists of consecutive even numbers. The series 2, 3, 5, 7, 11 consists of consecutive prime numbers.

◻ **I KNOW THIS**   ◻ **I NEED TO REVIEW THIS**

NUMBER LINES

NL1

All numbers can be represented on a number line. The equally spaced divisions are for reference only. The point 2.5, for example, is located midway between the points 2 and 3.

2.5
↓

1   2   3   4

◻ **I KNOW THIS**   ◻ **I NEED TO REVIEW THIS**

NL2

Although most SAT problems involving number lines are marked by consecutive integers, other divisions are possible; we can even use variables.

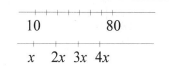

10   80

x $2x$ $3x$ $4x$

◻ **I KNOW THIS**   ◻ **I NEED TO REVIEW THIS**

NL3

On a number line, numbers to the right are greater than those to the left. Numbers increase as we move to the right, and decrease as we move to the left.

decrease ← → increase
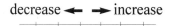

◻ **I KNOW THIS**   ◻ **I NEED TO REVIEW THIS**

NL4

The value of zero is sometimes called the **origin**. Numbers to the right of the origin are positive; numbers to the left of the origin are negative.

negative ← → positive

0

☐ I KNOW THIS   ☐ I NEED TO REVIEW THIS

NL5

Be very, very careful when asked to compare the relative size of numbers; sketching a quick number line could save you from making an embarrassingly reckless mistake.

What is the smallest integer greater than −2.1?

What is the largest integer less than −3.6?

☐ I KNOW THIS   ☑ I NEED TO REVIEW THIS

ABSOLUTE VALUE

AV1

The **absolute value** of a number is its distance from the origin. The symbol for absolute value is | | . Since 3 and −3 are both 3 units from the origin, | 3 | = | −3 | = 3.

☐ I KNOW THIS   ☐ I NEED TO REVIEW THIS

Be careful when dealing with absolute values of negative numbers, especially when subtracting. Absolute values can be applied more than once in the same equation.

$$| 3 - | 3 - 8 | | =$$
$$| 3 - | -5 | | =$$
$$| 3 - 5 | =$$
$$| -2 | =$$
$$2$$

☐ **I KNOW THIS** ☐ **I NEED TO REVIEW THIS**

ARITHMETICAL OPERATIONS

It's not a big deal, but you need to know the following terms:

- **Sum** or **total:** the result of adding numbers
- **Product:** the result of multiplying numbers
- **Quotient:** the result of dividing numbers (the first number divided by the second number)
- **Difference:** the result of subtracting numbers (the first number minus the second number)

☐ **I KNOW THIS** ☐ **I NEED TO REVIEW THIS**

$$10 \times 10 = 10^2 = 100.$$
$$10 \times 10 \times 10 = 10^3 = 1000.$$

Another way of stating these facts is 10 **squared** is 100 (or 100 is the **square** of 10), and 10 **cubed** is 1000 (or 1000 is the **cube** of 10). The numbers 2 and 3 here are **exponents** or powers. Raising a number to a **power** is essentially repeated multiplication.

☐ **I KNOW THIS** ☐ **I NEED TO REVIEW THIS**

454

PARENTHESES AND ORDER OF OPERATIONS

PO1

When different operations are involved in the same expression or equation, they must be carried out in the following order:

- Parentheses (any operations within parentheses, or within an absolute value sign)
- Exponents (or roots)
- Multiplying
- Dividing
- Adding
- Subtracting

The grade school mnemonic for remembering this sequence is "Please Excuse My Dear Aunt Sally," for the first initials of these operations. Also remember that any absolute value sign is a sort of parenthesis.

$49 - (3 + 2)^2 =$
$49 - 5^2 =$
$49 - 25 =$
24

$49 - 3 + 2^2 =$
$49 - 3 + 4 =$
50

If you use parentheses whenever you can, order of operations should present little problem.

☐ **I KNOW THIS**   ☐ **I NEED TO REVIEW THIS**

PO2

Whenever you see an expression with any terms that can be distributed, distribute them by multiplying! Whenever you see a distributed expression that can be factored, factor it!

$2(a + b) = 2a + 2b$

$5x + 5y = 5(x + y)$

☐ **I KNOW THIS**   ☐ **I NEED TO REVIEW THIS**

FACTORS AND DIVISIBILITY

FD1

As you know, prime numbers such as 3, 5, and 17 are **divisible** only by 1 and themselves. The number 14 is divisible by 2 because 2 goes into 14 evenly (7 times); similarly, 14 is divisible by 7 because 7 goes into 14 evenly (2 times). The numbers 2 and 7 are **factors** or **divisors** of 14, along with 1 and 14. The factors of an integer are all the positive integers that divide into that integer evenly. **When factoring a number, don't forget the number itself and 1. To find all the factors of a number *systematically*, begin with 1 and the number, then try 2 and its "partner," then 3 and its partner, and so on, as if you were working your way up a ladder.**

Work systematically to find factors of, say, 60:

1 and 60
2 and 30
3 and 20
4 and 15
5 and 12
6 and 10

☐ **I KNOW THIS** ☐ **I NEED TO REVIEW THIS**

FD2

A problem might restrict your search for factors to the even factors, say, or the **prime factors. I recommend listing *all* the factors of a number, and then circling the particular factors that a problem may call for. Notice that the *prime* factors of any integer x are the same as the prime factors of x^2.**

The prime factors of 60 are 2, 3, and 5. The prime factorization of 60 is $2 \times 2 \times 3 \times 5 = 2^2 \times 3 \times 5$.

The prime factors of 3600 are 2, 3, and 5. The prime factorization of 3600 is $2^4 \times 3^2 \times 5^2$.

☐ **I KNOW THIS** ☐ **I NEED TO REVIEW THIS**

FD3

To determine the **greatest common factor** (GCF) between two numbers, break down each number into its prime factorization and "pull out" the largest factor common to both. As is often the case, simply checking the choices may be the fastest and safest way to solve a problem like this.

To find the greatest common factor of 24 and 300:

$$24 = 2 \times 2 \times 2 \times 3$$
$$300 = 2 \times 2 \times 3 \times 5 \times 5$$

$$\text{GCF} = 2 \times 2 \times 3$$

☐ I KNOW THIS ☑ I NEED TO REVIEW THIS

FD4

The word "distinct" means different or unique.
The numbers 24 and 300 have three *distinct* prime factors: 2, 3, and 5.

Prime factors of 24: 2, 3

Prime factors of 300: 2, 3, 5

☐ I KNOW THIS ☑ I NEED TO REVIEW THIS

FD5

A number divisible by x and y is also divisible by xy.

A number divisible by 2 and 3 is also divisible by 6.

☐ I KNOW THIS ☑ I NEED TO REVIEW THIS

FD6

You may be asked to count how many numbers between 1 and n are divisible by d. This is another way of asking how many positive multiples of d are less than n. Listing a lot of numbers is risky and time-consuming (though doing so may be the most efficient solution if you can't think of a shortcut).

How many numbers from 1 to 250 are divisible by 6?

($250 \div 6 = 41$ with a bit left over, so the answer is 41.)

☐ I KNOW THIS ☐ I NEED TO REVIEW THIS

FD7

In the old, pre-calculator days of the SAT, you needed to know the various divisibility tests for numbers like 2, 3, and 5. With a calculator, such problems no longer pose any difficulty. You are more likely today to be hit with a question that would be too cumbersome to solve with a calculator. If $J = 2^2 \times 3^8 \times 5^6 \times 7^8$, is 49 a factor of J? Is 8 a factor of J?

J is a 16-digit number that will overload your calculator display, assuming you were able to enter the factors correctly. So *think*. J is divisible by 49 because 7×7 requires two 7s as factors, and J has eight 7s. J is not, however, divisible by 8 since $2 \times 2 \times 2$ requires three 2s, and J has only two.

☐ I KNOW THIS ☐ I NEED TO REVIEW THIS

MULTIPLES

MU1

Multiples are the inverse of factors: A multiple of a number is any integer—positive, negative, or zero—times that number. **Notice that multiples, unlike factors, can be negative.**

Some random multiples of 8:
$$-16 = (-2 \times 8)$$
$$0 = (0 \times 8)$$
$$24 = (3 \times 8)$$
$$400 = (50 \times 8)$$

☐ I KNOW THIS ☐ I NEED TO REVIEW THIS

MU2

A series of consecutive integers times a number creates **consecutive multiples** of that number.

The integers 2, 3, 4, and 5 are consecutive, so the numbers 16, 24, 32, and 40 are consecutive multiples of 8.

☐ I KNOW THIS ☐ I NEED TO REVIEW THIS

To find the **least common multiple** (LCM) of two numbers, take the larger number and create consecutive multiples of that number until you find a number that is also a multiple of the smaller number. Again, checking the choices would be effective on this type of question.

The least common multiple of 75 and 500: The first few consecutive multiples of 500 are 500, 1000, 1500, and 2000; since 75 is a factor of 1500, 1500 is the LCM of 75 and 500.

☐ **I KNOW THIS** ☐ **I NEED TO REVIEW THIS**

REMAINDERS AND FRACTIONS

RF1

When an integer is not evenly divisible by another integer, the amount left over is the **remainder**. **Remainders are always integers.**

The remainder when 14 is divided by 5 is 4. The remainder when 122 is divided by 6 is 2.

☐ **I KNOW THIS** ☐ **I NEED TO REVIEW THIS**

RF2

The top part of a fraction is the **numerator** and the bottom part is the **denominator**. The **reciprocal** of a fraction is the denominator over the numerator.

In $\frac{3}{4}$, the numerator is 3 and the denominator is 4. The reciprocal of $\frac{3}{4}$ is $\frac{4}{3}$. Since 2 equals $\frac{2}{1}$, the reciprocal of 2 is $\frac{1}{2}$.

☐ **I KNOW THIS** ☐ **I NEED TO REVIEW THIS**

RF3

To prevent manipulation errors, if a problem contains any fraction, *immediately* convert any integers or variables in the problem to fractions by placing them over 1.

If a problem contains $\frac{1}{2}$, 3, and x, make them *all* fractions: $\frac{1}{2}$, $\frac{3}{1}$, and $\frac{x}{1}$.

◯ I KNOW THIS　◯ I NEED TO REVIEW THIS

RF4

In the old, pre-calculator days, you had to know how to compare the size of different fractions. With calculators these problems have disappeared. More likely you are asked to compare two fractions that force you to *think*.

Which is greater, $-\frac{1}{8}$ or $-\frac{1}{9}$?

(Careful: $\frac{1}{8}$ is larger than $\frac{1}{9}$, of course, but that means $-\frac{1}{8}$ is more *negative* than $-\frac{1}{9}$, so $-\frac{1}{9}$ is greater.)

◯ I KNOW THIS　◯ I NEED TO REVIEW THIS

RF5

To convert a *mixed number* to a fraction, multiply the denominator by the integer, add the numerator, and then place the result over the original denominator. As always, be careful when negative numbers are involved.

$$1\frac{7}{8} = \frac{(1 \times 8) + 7}{8} = \frac{15}{8}$$

$$-2\frac{1}{3} = -\frac{[(2 \times 3) + 1]}{3} = -\frac{7}{3}$$

◯ I KNOW THIS　◯ I NEED TO REVIEW THIS

To convert a fraction into a mixed number, simply perform the division indicated. Do not confuse this process with calculating a remainder.

$$\frac{14}{6} = 2\frac{2}{6}$$

Calculating the remainder is not the same: 6 goes into 14 twice, with a remainder of 2.

☐ **I KNOW THIS** ☐ **I NEED TO REVIEW THIS**

To *reduce* a fraction, divide out any factors' common factors.

$$\frac{24}{300} = \frac{12}{150} = \frac{6}{75} = \frac{2}{5}$$

☐ **I KNOW THIS** ☐ **I NEED TO REVIEW THIS**

To add (or subtract) two fractions, find a common denominator, add the numerators, and then reduce.

$$\frac{1}{2} + \frac{3}{8} = \frac{4}{8} + \frac{3}{8} = \frac{7}{8}$$

$$\frac{3}{4} - \frac{2}{5} = \frac{15}{20} - \frac{8}{20} = \frac{7}{20}$$

☐ **I KNOW THIS** ☐ **I NEED TO REVIEW THIS**

Yes, adding fractions is grade school stuff, but on the SAT, you may have to add *algebraic* fractions.
When possible, convert algebraic manipulations into arithmetic manipulations by using our math move of swapping numbers for variables.

$$\frac{1}{x} + \frac{1}{y} = \frac{y}{xy} + \frac{x}{xy} = \frac{(y+x)}{xy}$$

$$1 + \frac{1}{y} = \frac{y}{y} + \frac{1}{y} = \frac{(y+1)}{y}$$

☐ **I KNOW THIS** ☐ **I NEED TO REVIEW THIS**

RF10

To multiply two fractions, divide the product of the numerators by the product of the denominators. **When possible, reduce the fractions before multiplying.**

$$\frac{5}{24} \times \frac{16}{25} =$$

$$\frac{(5 \times 16)}{(25 \times 24)} = \frac{(1 \times 2)}{(5 \times 3)} = \frac{2}{15}$$

☐ I KNOW THIS   ☐ I NEED TO REVIEW THIS

RF11

Dividing a number by a fraction is equivalent to multiplying the number by the fraction's reciprocal. When dividing an integer by a fraction, convert the integer to a fraction by placing the integer over 1.

$$\frac{1}{2} \div \frac{3}{8} = \frac{1}{2} \times \frac{8}{3} = \frac{4}{3}$$

$$1 \div \frac{2}{5} = \frac{1}{1} \times \frac{5}{2} = \frac{5}{2}$$

☐ I KNOW THIS   ☐ I NEED TO REVIEW THIS

RF12

Raising a fraction to a power should present no problem if you're careful to write everything out. We'll take a closer look at raising numbers to fractional and negative exponents shortly.

$$\left(\frac{2}{5}\right)^3 = \left(\frac{2}{5}\right)\left(\frac{2}{5}\right)\left(\frac{2}{5}\right) = \frac{8}{125}$$

☐ I KNOW THIS   ☐ I NEED TO REVIEW THIS

To take the square root of a fraction, divide the square root of the numerator by the square root of the denominator. To take the cube root of a fraction, divide the cube root of the numerator by the cube root of the denominator. **Notice that the root of a positive fraction less than 1 is greater than the fraction itself.**

$$\sqrt{\frac{16}{25}} = \frac{\sqrt{16}}{\sqrt{25}} = \frac{4}{5}$$

$$\sqrt[3]{\frac{8}{27}} = \frac{\sqrt[3]{8}}{\sqrt[3]{27}} = \frac{2}{3}$$

☐ **I KNOW THIS**   ☐ **I NEED TO REVIEW THIS**

The numerator of a fraction can be 0, but the denominator cannot (dividing by 0 results in an *undefined* fraction).

$$\frac{0}{x} = 0$$

☐ **I KNOW THIS**   ☐ **I NEED TO REVIEW THIS**

DECIMALS

Decimals should pose no particular difficulty for you on the SAT Math Test. If you're uncomfortable manipulating decimals, by all means use your calculator. The most common error in working with decimals is, of course, misplacing the decimal point.

☐ **I KNOW THIS**   ☐ **I NEED TO REVIEW THIS**

In general, working with fractions is easier and safer than working with decimals. It's a good idea to convert any decimals in a problem into equivalent fractions and solve the problems with fractions. (I'll cover converting decimals to fractions when we get to place value shortly.) If you have any trouble adding, subtracting, multiplying, or dividing decimals, use your calculator.

☐ **I KNOW THIS** ☐ **I NEED TO REVIEW THIS**

To convert a fraction to a decimal, simply divide the numerator by the denominator. A *repeating decimal* is one whose digits form a series that repeats forever. The repeating is indicated with an ellipsis (three periods), sometimes with a bar over the sequence of digits that repeats. **Watch out when rounding repeating digits on the open-ended questions. The answer sheet provides room for only three decimal places, so rounding 0.1666 . . . becomes 0.167.**

$$\frac{1}{6} = 0.1\overline{6666}\ldots$$

$$\frac{1}{7} = 0.\overline{142857}\ldots$$

☐ **I KNOW THIS** ☐ **I NEED TO REVIEW THIS**

DIGITS AND PLACE VALUE

DP1

Be careful not to confuse the **digits** used to write a number with the number itself. Think of digits as the "alphabet" used to write numbers. There are ten digits: 0, 1, 2, 3, 4, 5, 6, 7, 8, and 9. **Notice that 0 is a digit.**

27 is a two-digit number
456 is a three-digit number
1089 is a four-digit number

☐ **I KNOW THIS** ☐ **I NEED TO REVIEW THIS**

DP2

The value of a digit varies depending on its place within a number. In the number 42, the value of the digit 4 is 40 since the 4 represents four 10s. In the number 6432, the value of the digit 4 is 400 since the 4 represents four 100s.

☐ **I KNOW THIS** ☐ **I NEED TO REVIEW THIS**

DP3

Moving to the left of a decimal place, the **place value** of the first digit is 1. This digit is called the **ones digit** or the **units digit.** Moving to the left, the next digit is the **tens digit**, and then the **hundreds digit**, and so on. Moving to the right of the decimal place, the first digit is the **tenths digit.** The next digit to the right is the **hundredths digit**, and then the **thousandths digit**, and so on.

☐ **I KNOW THIS** ☐ **I NEED TO REVIEW THIS**

The value of a number is the sum of the products of each digit and its respective place value. That's a mouthful but the concept itself is easy to illustrate.

The number 3478 is the sum of three 1000s, four 100s, seven 10s, and eight 1s:

$$8 \times 1 = 8$$
$$7 \times 10 = 70$$
$$4 \times 100 = 400$$
$$+ 3 \times 1000 = 3000$$
$$\overline{3478}$$

☐ **I KNOW THIS**   ☐ **I NEED TO REVIEW THIS**

Careful: on the SAT Math Test, lowercase letters such as *x* or *y* are usually used to indicate numbers, while specific digits are usually represented by upper case letters like *A* or *B*. This convention can cause a lot of confusion. Variables like x and y can, unless otherwise stated, be equal—letters, however, cannot represent the same digit. If we use *A* to represent the digit 2, we can *write* the number 22 as *AA*. *AA* here does *not* represent $A \times A$. **If a problem states that *A* represents a digit and *B* represents a digit, then *A* and *B* are *different* digits.**

Number	Value
ABC	$100A + 10B + C$
328	$100(3) + 10(2) + 8$
705	$100(7) + 10(0) + 5$

☐ **I KNOW THIS**   ☐ **I NEED TO REVIEW THIS**

One of the most common SAT math problems asks you to determine what digits different letters represent in a simple calculation. **Focus on determining one digit—often a digit that is carried—and use trial and error to determine the other digits. Be careful about carrying from one column into another. Do *not* attempt questions like these algebraically unless you are absolutely stuck.** When you're pressured it's hard to think clearly, so trial and error is often the fastest solution.

$$
\begin{array}{r}
AA \\
+ \quad AB \\
\hline
CCC
\end{array}
$$

What digit does B represent?

(The largest sum of two two-digit numbers is 198, so C must represent 1. Trial and error quickly reveals that A is 5 and B is 6.)

☐ **I KNOW THIS** ☐ **I NEED TO REVIEW THIS**

EXPONENTS AND SCIENTIFIC NOTATION

The best way to illustrate everything you need to know about non-negative integer exponent rules for the SAT is to illustrate these rules with examples. **Don't rely on "rules"! The safest procedure when dealing with exponents is to write out all the terms (assuming you're not dealing with huge exponents) so that you don't overlook something. Remember to use parentheses!** If you write all the terms out, you'll *understand* the rules rather than attempt to apply them blindly.

$2^3 = 2 \times 2 \times 2 = 8$

$(2^2)(2^3) = (2 \times 2)(2 \times 2 \times 2) = 2^5$

$(2^2)^3 = (2 \times 2)(2 \times 2)(2 \times 2) = 2^6$

$\dfrac{2^4}{2^3} = \dfrac{(2 \times 2 \times 2 \times 2)}{(2 \times 2 \times 2)} = 2$

$(1^4) = (1 \times 1 \times 1 \times 1) = 1$

$(0^4) = (0 \times 0 \times 0 \times 0) = 0$

$16^1 = 16$

$16^0 = 1$

$(2x)^3 = (2x)(2x)(2x) = 8x^3$

$\left(\dfrac{2}{5}\right)^2 = \left(\dfrac{2}{5}\right)\left(\dfrac{2}{5}\right) = \dfrac{2^2}{5^2} = \dfrac{4}{25}$

$(-2)^5 = (-2)(-2)(-2)(-2)(-2) = -32$

$(2^3)(5^3) = (2 \times 2 \times 2)(5 \times 5 \times 5) = 10^3$

☐ **I KNOW THIS** ☐ **I NEED TO REVIEW THIS**

Negative exponents may not seem as familiar as positive exponents, but the same principles apply. **Don't rely on "rules"! Write all the terms out and use parentheses.**

$$2^{-3} = \frac{1}{2^3} = \frac{1}{8}$$

$$\frac{1}{2^{-3}} = \frac{1}{\frac{1}{8}} = 8$$

$$(2^{-4})(16^2) = \frac{16^2}{2^4} = 16$$

☐ **I KNOW THIS**   ☐ **I NEED TO REVIEW THIS**

Fractional exponents obey the same basic rules as integer exponents, so don't be frightened. If you don't understand the principle, just follow the basic pattern illustrated. **Write all the terms out, as we did with integer powers, and you should be okay.**

$$64^{\frac{1}{2}} = \sqrt[2]{64^1} = \sqrt[2]{64} = 8$$

$$64^{\frac{1}{3}} = \sqrt[3]{64^1} = \sqrt[3]{64} = 4$$

$$64^{\frac{2}{3}} = \sqrt[3]{64^2} = \sqrt[3]{64}\,\sqrt[3]{64} = 16$$

$$64^{\frac{3}{2}} = \sqrt[2]{64^3} = \sqrt[2]{64}\,\sqrt[2]{64}\,\sqrt[2]{64} = 512$$

☐ **I KNOW THIS**   ☐ **I NEED TO REVIEW THIS**

If you get stuck with fractional exponents, remember that you can estimate the answer—one of our math moves. Estimating won't give you the exact answer, but it may get you close enough to one of the choices to determine the answer.

Let's say you were trying to estimate $8^{\frac{2}{3}}$. Since $0 < \frac{2}{3} < 1$, then $8^0 < 8^{\frac{2}{3}} < 8^1$, so $1 < 8^{\frac{2}{3}} < 8$. So $8^{\frac{2}{3}}$ lies somewhere between 1 and 8. The exact calculation is $8 = \sqrt[3]{8^2} = \sqrt[3]{8}\,\sqrt[3]{8} = 4$.

☐ **I KNOW THIS**   ☐ **I NEED TO REVIEW THIS**

ES5

Be very, very, *very* careful on SAT exponent problems. The test writers often set up difficult exponent questions in a deceptive way to lure students into thinking a certain exponent "rule" applies—when the rule actually does *not* apply. If you're in the habit of writing out all the terms, you will not be trapped.

$9^3 \times 3^4 =$
$(9 \times 9 \times 9) \times (3 \times 3 \times 3 \times 3) =$
$(3 \times 3) (3 \times 3) (3 \times 3) \times$
$(3 \times 3 \times 3 \times 3) =$
3^{10}

☐ **I KNOW THIS**   ☐ **I NEED TO REVIEW THIS**

ES6

Exponents are written smaller and slightly above "regular" numbers and variables, so be careful *reading* exponents correctly—especially if a variable appears in the exponent.

In the number 3^{x+2}, the 2 is in superscript along with the x. The exponent of 3 is $(x + 2)$, not x. In the number 3^{x^2}, the exponent of 3 is (x^2).

☐ **I KNOW THIS**   ☐ **I NEED TO REVIEW THIS**

ES7

You may encounter a problem on the SAT Math Test involving **scientific notation**. A number expressed in scientific notation is the product of some integer power of 10 and k, where $1 \le k < 10$. When determining the scientific notation, make sure you correctly count the number of places you are moving to the right or the left of the decimal.

Number	Scientific Notation
1024	1.024×10^3
102.4	1.024×10^2
0.01024	1.024×10^{-2}

☐ **I KNOW THIS**   ☐ **I NEED TO REVIEW THIS**

RADICALS (ROOTS)

R1

We've already touched on radicals (roots), but here are examples of the range of operations regarding radicals that you'll need to know how to do on the SAT Math Test.

$$10 \times \sqrt{2} = 10\sqrt{2}$$

$$\sqrt{3}\sqrt{3} = \sqrt{9} = 3$$

$$\sqrt{8} = \sqrt{4}\sqrt{2} = 2\sqrt{2}$$

$$\sqrt{2}\sqrt{32} = \sqrt{64} = 8$$

$$\sqrt{\frac{4}{25}} = \frac{\sqrt{4}}{\sqrt{25}} = \frac{2}{5}$$

$$\sqrt{2} = 1\sqrt{2}$$

$$\sqrt{2} + 3\sqrt{2} = 1\sqrt{2} + 3\sqrt{2} = 4\sqrt{2}$$

☐ **I KNOW THIS** ☐ **I NEED TO REVIEW THIS**

R2

You will *not* encounter problems on the SAT Math Test involving the square root of a negative number (such roots are called *imaginary numbers*). However, you *might* encounter a problem involving the *cube* root of a negative number.

$\sqrt[2]{-8}$ is an imaginary number (it will not appear on the SAT).

$$\sqrt[3]{-8} = -2$$

(might appear on the SAT)

☐ **I KNOW THIS** ☐ **I NEED TO REVIEW THIS**

470

RATIOS

RA1

A **ratio** of j to k is simply the fraction of j divided by k, reduced to lowest terms. A ratio can be expressed in several different ways.

the ratio of j to k

$$\frac{j}{k}$$

$$j:k$$

☐ **I KNOW THIS**   ☐ **I NEED TO REVIEW THIS**

RA2

Let's say that a certain class consists of 8 girls and 12 boys. The ratio of 8 girls to 12 boys is 2 to 3. **Notice that this ratio does *not* express the actual number of girls and boys. The ratio of 2 girls to 3 boys means that for every 2 girls, there are 3 boys.**

A class contains 8 girls and 12 boys, so the ratio of

- Girls to boys is 2:3
- Girls to students is 2:5
- Boys to students is 3:5

☐ **I KNOW THIS**   ☐ **I NEED TO REVIEW THIS**

RA3

It helps to think of ratios in terms of "parts." If the ratio of girls to boys is 2 to 3, then there are 5 parts: the girls have 2 of the 5 parts, and the boys have 3 of the 5 parts.

If the ratio of red to white to blue marbles is 1:2:3, then there are 6 parts, so $\frac{1}{6}$ of the marbles are red, $\frac{2}{6}$ or $\frac{1}{3}$ of the marbles are white, and $\frac{3}{6}$ or $\frac{1}{2}$ of the marbles are blue.

☐ **I KNOW THIS**   ☐ **I NEED TO REVIEW THIS**

Watch out: ratio problems are *very* easy to misread. It's also very easy on ratio questions to mistake any fraction in the problem for the ratio in question.

In a certain class of juniors and seniors, if $\frac{3}{8}$ of the students are juniors, what is the ratio of seniors to juniors?

(Let's say the class consists of 8 students: 3 would be juniors and 5 would be seniors, so the ratio of seniors to juniors is 5:3.)

☐ **I KNOW THIS**   ☐ **I NEED TO REVIEW THIS**

Sometimes a ratio problem will not use the word "ratio." A common variation of word problems uses a phrase like "at this rate," which is a proportion. When two ratios are equal, a proportion is established. To solve problems like these, orient yourself by finding a unit rate, like how many feet traveled in *one* second, or how many pages read in *one* hour, and then "step up or down" to the answer as the problem requires. **Pay close attention to units, which often switch within a problem.**

A certain machine stamps a letter every 5 seconds. At this rate, how many letters will the machine stamp in an hour?

1 letter every 5 seconds =
12 letters every 1 minute =
720 letters every 60 minutes

☐ **I KNOW THIS**   ☐ **I NEED TO REVIEW THIS**

PERCENTAGES

P1

Percentage problems often confuse students who haven't encountered them since junior high school, but these problems really are no big deal if you remember that percent literally means "per 100" or divided by 100. Of course, each of the fractions could then be converted into equivalent decimals.

Percent	Fraction	Reduce
25%	$\dfrac{25}{100}$	$\dfrac{1}{4}$
1%	$\dfrac{1}{100}$	$\dfrac{1}{100}$
100%	$\dfrac{100}{100}$	1
200%	$\dfrac{200}{100}$	2
$x\%$	$\dfrac{x}{100}$	$\dfrac{x}{100}$

☐ I KNOW THIS ☐ I NEED TO REVIEW THIS

P2

Just as percentages can be converted into fractions, fractions can be converted into equivalent percentages by creating a proportion. To convert a percentage into a fraction, you know to divide by 100 (and drop the percentage sign). To convert a fraction into a percentage, simply *multiply* by 100 (don't forget the percentage sign).

$$\frac{3}{4} = \frac{75}{100} = 75\%$$

$$\frac{1}{2} = \frac{50}{100} = 50\%$$

$$\frac{3}{2} = \frac{150}{100} = 150\%$$

$$\frac{1}{8} = \frac{12}{100} = 12\frac{1}{2}\%$$

$$\frac{1}{3} = \frac{33\frac{1}{3}}{100} = 33\frac{1}{3}\%$$

☐ I KNOW THIS ☐ I NEED TO REVIEW THIS

The key to answering any percentage problem is to convert it *immediately* into a fraction problem.

Terms	Equivalent
percent, %	÷ 100
of	×
is, equals	=
what	w, x, y

As with any fraction question, convert all integers into decimals by placing them over 1; as always, the parenthesis is your friend.

What is 25 percent of 8?

$$w = \left(\frac{25}{100}\right) \times \left(\frac{8}{1}\right)$$

25% of 48 equals 50 percent of what number?

$$\left(\frac{25}{100}\right) \times \left(\frac{48}{1}\right) = \left(\frac{50}{100}\right) \times \left(\frac{w}{1}\right)$$

A certain cheerleading squad consists of 5 juniors and 25 seniors. What percent of the club are seniors?

$$\left(\frac{w}{100}\right) \times \text{club} = \text{seniors, or}$$

$$\left(\frac{w}{100}\right) \times 30 = 25$$

What is 20 percent of 30 percent of 50?

$$w = \left(\frac{20}{100}\right) \times \left(\frac{30}{100}\right) \times \left(\frac{50}{1}\right)$$

☐ **I KNOW THIS** ☐ **I NEED TO REVIEW THIS**

To calculate the **percentage increase** (or decrease, sometimes called **percentage discount**), simply divide the change by the "starting value" and convert the fraction into a percentage. **Don't confuse equivalent absolute changes with equivalent percentage changes. Be *absolutely* sure you read these percentage questions correctly.**

The increase from 8 to 10 is 2, so the fractional increase is $\frac{2}{8}$ or $\frac{1}{4}$, so the percentage increase is 25 percent. The decrease from 10 to 8 is 2, so the fractional decrease is $\frac{2}{10}$ or $\frac{1}{5}$, so the percentage decrease is 20 percent. **Notice the different percentages.**

☐ **I KNOW THIS** ☐ **I NEED TO REVIEW THIS**

P5

When a problem states that a number increased or decreased by some percent, the phrase "of itself" is implied.

So saying, "*x* increased by 20 percent"

is equivalent to saying,

"*x* increased by 20 percent *of itself*."

☐ **I KNOW THIS** ☐ **I NEED TO REVIEW THIS**

P6

Some students get bamboozled by percentage increases greater than 100 percent. **The same basic principle applies: find the absolute increase, convert this change to a fraction of the original number, and then convert the fraction to a percentage. Notice that doubling a number results in a percentage increase of 100%; tripling a number results in a percentage increase of 200%.**

An increase from 4 to 6 is an absolute increase of 2, a fractional increase of 2 out of 4 (or $\frac{1}{2}$), and a percentage increase of 50%. An increase from 4 to 8 is an absolute increase of 4, a fractional increase of 4 out of 4 (or 1), and a percentage increase of 100%. An increase from 4 to 12 is an absolute increase of 8, a fractional increase of 8 out of 4 (or 2), and a percentage increase of 200%.

☐ **I KNOW THIS** ☐ **I NEED TO REVIEW THIS**

AVERAGES: MEAN, MEDIAN, AND MODE

The **average** or **mean** of a set of items is the total of those items divided by the number of items. On the SAT Math Test, the average is often referred to as the **arithmetic mean**.

Items	Total	Number	Average
1, 2, 9	12	3	4
1, 2, 9, 0	12	4	3
−4, 14	10	2	5
$k, k + 2$	$2k + 2$	2	$k + 1$

Average (arithmetic mean) =

$$\frac{\text{Total of items}}{\text{Number of items}}$$

☐ I KNOW THIS ☐ I NEED TO REVIEW THIS

The key to solving any problem involving averages is to find the *total* of the items as your first step. Once you find the total, you can calculate anything else the problem asks you.

Total =

Average × Number of items

☐ I KNOW THIS ☐ I NEED TO REVIEW THIS

The average of a set of items lies somewhere in the middle of the items, though not necessarily *exactly* in the middle. Notice that for an odd number of consecutive integers, the middle number *is* the average.

Set A =

{10, 11, 12, 13, 14, 15, 16}

Average (arithmetic mean) = 13

☐ I KNOW THIS ☐ I NEED TO REVIEW THIS

Careful: The average of two averages is not necessarily midway between the two averages. If one average has more items than does the other average, the combined *weighted* average will lie closer to it than to the average with fewer items.

If the average of x, y, and z is 20 and the average of p and q is 30, what is the average of x, y, z, p, and q ?

The total of x, y, and z is 60, and the total of p and q is 60. The total of the five items is 120, so the overall average is 24.

☐ I KNOW THIS ☐ I NEED TO REVIEW THIS

A common type of weighted average problem involves average speed on a trip when the average speed changes during the trip. **Again, be careful: The overall average speed is not necessarily midway between the two average speeds.**
A car that travels 200 miles at 40 miles per hour and then 200 miles at 50 miles per hour has traveled a total of 400 miles in a total of 9 hours (5 hours for the first leg of the trip; 4 hours for the second leg), for an average speed of $44\frac{4}{9}$ miles per hour.

Average speed =

$$\frac{\text{Total distance}}{\text{Total time}}$$

☐ I KNOW THIS ☐ I NEED TO REVIEW THIS

AVG6

In addition to the "regular" average (arithmetic mean), two other kinds of averages appear on the SAT Math Test: **median** and **mode**. The median of a set of items is the "middle" item (when ranked by size); the mode is the item—if any—that appears the most frequently in the set.

☐ I KNOW THIS ☐ I NEED TO REVIEW THIS

AV7

These mean, median, and mode averages *can* all be the same, but on the SAT they will usually be different. One of the Most Common SAT Math Problems of All Time is a question that asks about the relationship of these different averages for a given set of numbers. **One difference, for example, is that the median and the mode of a set of items must actually be an item in that set, while the mean need not be.**

Set $A = \{1, 2, 2, 4, 9, 11, 20\}$
- Mean of Set $A = 7$
- Median of Set $A = 4$
- Mode of Set $A = 2$

Notice that the average (arithmetic mean) is not a member of the Set A, while the median and the mode are.

☐ I KNOW THIS ☐ I NEED TO REVIEW THIS

AV8

The median is the middle element when the items are ranked by size. **Be careful: A problem may not present the items in terms of size. If a set has an even number of elements, the median is the arithmetic mean of the middle two elements.**

If Set $B = \{2, 10, 4, 1, 3\}$, what is its median?

(Rearranging the items by size—1, 2, 3, 4, 10—we find that the middle element is 3.)

☐ I KNOW THIS ☐ I NEED TO REVIEW THIS

478

Now that you've read through the concepts quickly, return to those concepts that you checked for further review. Remember that all these concepts will be reinforced in the explanations of the illustrative problems.

Apply What You've Learned to Our Practice Arithmetic Problems

That completes our survey of *all* the arithmetic you need for the SAT Math Test. Trust me: you will not encounter an arithmetic problem on the SAT that requires a concept or combination of concepts other than those we have covered here. **Don't be bullied: If you** *think* **an arithmetic problem on the SAT calls for more advanced concepts or formulas than those we've just discussed—you've missed the point of the question.**

You'll find our latest examples of SAT arithmetic problems at www.RocketReview.com. These printable problems will give you all the arithmetic practice you need.

Refresher of SAT Algebra

SAT Algebra Covers Only Basic Concepts—with a Twist

As with the arithmetic concepts, the algebra concepts tested on the SAT are pretty basic. You don't have to worry about the intricacies of synthetic division or the quadratic formula, for example.

The twist, however, is that the algebra concepts on the SAT are often disguised. As I mentioned earlier, in school you're used to solving for x, say. On the SAT, an algebra problem will *seem* to require that you solve for x—when in fact you may not need to solve for x at all. **Indeed, if you blindly apply the algebra methods you've learned in your classroom to an SAT math problem, you will often be missing the point of the question altogether.**

Drill: Think I'm Kidding about Not Always Solving for *x*?

Each of the following *difficult* SAT algebra questions can be solved in less than ten seconds, some in less than five—if you know what you're doing. I've already given you a huge clue (don't try to solve for an individual variable). Even with that warning, however, you'll see how difficult it is to get out of the habit you've acquired in your math classroom of automatically—that is, *unthinkingly*—solving for individual variables.

Hey, want to have a bit of fun? Ask your *math teacher* to solve these SAT questions—in an average of two steps each. Unless he or she has already seen this book, get ready for some squirming. **I'm not putting math teachers down—I'm stressing how *different* SAT math is from regular classroom math.**

Hint: *Look* at what the question is asking you to solve for.

1. If $x^2 + y^2 = 80$ and $(x + y)^2 = 144$, then $xy =$

2. If $x + 2y = 10$ and $2x + 3y = 17$, then $x + y =$

3. If x, y, and z are all positive and $xy = 1$, $yz = 32$, and $xz = 2$, then $xyz =$

4. When three numbers are added in pairs, their respective sums are 11, 13, and 16. What is the sum of the three numbers?

Remember: each problem can be solved in an average of two steps. If your solution to any problem here requires four or five or even more steps, you've missed the point of the question.

You'll find the solutions at the end of this section on page 513. **Do not peek at the solutions until you've struggled with the questions for a bit or you will be missing out on an important math lesson for the SAT.** The more you struggle with a math problem before seeing the solution, the more permanently the *method* of the solution will be etched in your brain.

I'd *Never* Have Thought of Those Solutions

Well, maybe you would have thought of those solutions (in which case, on the SAT Math Test at least, you probably don't need much help at all).

But if you didn't—good!—you'll learn a lot in the coming pages. I promise you that in a very short time, you'll learn how to *reason* through SAT math questions just like those above.

Although We're Covering Algebra, Try to Avoid Algebraic Solutions Whenever Possible

The two big math moves for algebra questions are swapping numbers for variables (when the choices contain variables) and checking the choices (on word problems); WIBNI (wouldn't it be nice if) also comes in handy. In this refresher of SAT algebra, I'll point out when one of these methods applies. For a review of these methods, see Experience Set 4.

These two methods allow you to you avoid all the hassles and dangers of algebraic solutions on a major chunk of the SAT Math Test. Anyway, in this section I'll be refreshing you on all the algebra because some of it is unavoidable—but whenever possible use one of our math moves to avoid algebra.

The problem with using algebra in pressure situations like the SAT Math Test is that algebra is even more abstract than numbers—neither of which your brain was designed to handle (as opposed to pictures). But at least when you manipulate numbers you have some common sense notions of numerical relationships and magnitudes to guide your thinking; if you screw up an algebraic manipulation, on the other hand, and get, say, $x - y$ instead of $y - x$, you'll have nothing to warn you that anything is amiss.

> Watch out! Algebraic manipulation errors (especially failing to distribute all terms when multiplying, and most especially failing to distribute negative signs properly) are major pitfalls on SAT algebra questions.

Some Really Basic Algebra Definitions and Conventions You Should Know for the SAT Math Test

Although you will probably not encounter the following words on your SAT Math Test, we'll need them to discuss algebra so let's just run through some quick definitions.

- A *variable* is a letter that stands for any number, possibly subject to restrictions (such as standing for any positive number). SAT algebra questions often restrict a variable from being zero ($x \neq 0$), or a group of variables from being zero ($xyz \neq 0$).

> There is nothing magical or sacred about the typical use of the letters x and y as variables. Indeed, if the problem does not assign letters to variables, you should use a letter that suggests the quantity being discussed (d for distance, h for height, p for price) so that you keep the variable or variables straight in your head.
>
> Another point: Two different variables in a question—say x and y—*can* equal the same number unless the problem states otherwise. If the test writers want the variable to represent a specific number (and no other), they often use capital letters such as C.

- A *constant* is a quantity that does not change, such as the number 14, for example. A constant can also be identified with a letter (often uncommon ones like k so that the constant is not confused with a letter that represents a variable, like x, or with capital letters as discussed above).

- An *unknown*, as the name suggests, is a quantity that we do not know in a problem (but that can possibly be solved from other information the problem provides). Unknowns, like variables, are often represented with lower case letters.

- A *term* is a quantity, either expressed as a number or a variable: 3, x^2, and $4y$ are terms.

- Two terms are *like terms* if they consist of the same variable raised to the same power: $2x$ and $3x$ are like terms, but $4x$ and $4x^2$ are not.

- An *expression* is a group of two or more (quantities) such as $(x + 2)$ or $(y^2 - 1)$.

> I'll say it again: You'll avoid a *lot* of grief on the SAT Math Test if you get in the habit of *immediately* bracketing any expression in parentheses. Trust me on this point.

There are different types of expression, like *binomial, trinomial, polynomial, or quadratic,* but rather than make your eyes glaze over I'll just reassure you that the meaning of these words will always be clear from the context.

Again, the definitions above are important for our discussion purposes only; you almost certainly will not encounter them on the actual SAT. **Any terms you need to know for an SAT math problem will be as basic as the ones we just discussed, so don't let unfamiliar words bully you.**

I've divided SAT algebra into the following topics:
- Expressions
- Equations
- Absolute value equations
- Direct and inverse variation
- Inequalities
- Simultaneous equations
- Quadratics
- Algebraic thinking
- Functions
- Symbol operations
- Word problems

So let's begin.

> Read through all the concepts boxes quickly. Check the boxes that need further review. Keep in mind that all the concepts will be reinforced in the illustrative problems that you'll find at the RocketReview website.

EXPRESSIONS

EX1

On the SAT Math Test you'll often need to translate simple English statements into their mathematical equivalents. We're talking really simple translations here, like translating "x is 2 more than y" into $x = 2 + y$. Even simple statements can make students stumble, however, like "x is 2 less than y," which becomes $x = y - 2$, not $x = 2 - y$. The key, as I'll repeat over and over until you repeat the warning in your sleep, is to read math problems with extraordinary care. If you misread a single word of a math problem, you can botch translating the information and wind up solving the wrong equation.

☐ **I KNOW THIS**   ☐ **I NEED TO REVIEW THIS**

EX2

You may need to keep simple arithmetic definitions in mind when translating statements into their mathematical equivalents. The words "product of two numbers" translates into xy, which requires that you know what a product is. Consider the simple statement "x is positive." Since "is positive" means the same thing as "is greater than 0," we can translate that statement into $x > 0$. Similarly, "the difference between x and y is negative" becomes the inequality $x - y < 0$.

☐ **I KNOW THIS**   ☐ **I NEED TO REVIEW THIS**

EX3

For some reason many students have trouble translating the word "of"; it means "times." Translating "one-half of a number" becomes $\frac{1}{2}$ times x, or $\frac{x}{2}$. The word "per," by the way, means "divided by."

☐ **I KNOW THIS** ☐ **I NEED TO REVIEW THIS**

EX4

If you ever get stuck translating words into their mathematical equivalents—it can happen to the strongest math students on the simplest problems—check your translation out on some simple numbers, just to be sure.

☐ **I KNOW THIS** ☐ **I NEED TO REVIEW THIS**

EX5

When an algebraic expression is a quotient, as in $\frac{(x + 1)}{(x - 1)}$, the denominator cannot equal zero, because the resulting fraction would then be *undefined*. In such cases, a problem may specify that a variable cannot equal some number (in this case x cannot equal 1) to avoid such an outcome. It is highly unlikely that the new SAT will expect students to be familiar with the notion of undefined expressions (though there's a teeny, tiny chance the concept may come up indirectly on a question about *domain* and *range*, which we will cover shortly. This topic isn't a big deal, but worth mentioning in passing.

☐ **I KNOW THIS** ☐ **I NEED TO REVIEW THIS**

Whenever you see in an SAT math problem an expression that can be simplified—*simplify it before doing anything else, even if you don't see where the simplification gets you.* Nine times out of ten, the simplification is the first step on a direct road to the solution. For example, if you see an expression that can be *factored,* factor it. **This rule is an application of our fundamental RocketRule for problem-solving on the SAT Math Test: whenever you see something that you can do in a problem—** *do it.*

In the expression $\dfrac{(4x + 2y)}{20z}$, we can pull out a 4 from all the terms—so we should.

$$\frac{(4x + 12y)}{20z}$$

$$= \frac{4(x + 3y)}{4(5z)}$$

$$= \frac{(x + 3y)}{5z}$$

In general, gather all like terms and factor whenever you can.

☐ **I KNOW THIS** ☐ **I NEED TO REVIEW THIS**

There is no such mathematical operation as "crossing out" or "canceling." In the expression $\dfrac{(x^2 + x)}{x}$, many students fall into the trap of "crossing out" the x in the denominator with the x in the numerator, getting x^2 as a result. Whoops.

$$\frac{(x^2 + x)}{x}$$

$$= \frac{x(x + 1)}{x}$$

$$= x + 1$$

☐ **I KNOW THIS** ☐ **I NEED TO REVIEW THIS**

You may encounter a problem that asks you to evaluate a simple expression for a certain value—usually *not x*. For example, if $4x = 10$, then what does the expression $\frac{(4x - 2)}{2}$ equal? **The key on this type of question is to look for the most efficient way to get from the information provided to the unknown—most of the time the most efficient solution will *not* involve solving for *x*.** I can't tell you how many times in the problem above students solve for *x* by reflex in the original equation (dividing both sides of the equation by 4), and then turn around and multiply *x* by 4 to evaluate the expression. **Always look at how the information is being presented—the SAT Math Test rewards *insight*.** Here we can just substitute 10 directly into the expression for $4x$.

If $4x = 10$, then what does

$\frac{(4x - 2)}{2}$ equal?

$4x = 10$, so

$$\frac{(4x - 2)}{2} = \frac{(10 - 2)}{2} = 4$$

☐ **I KNOW THIS**   ☐ **I NEED TO REVIEW THIS**

EQUATIONS

EQ1

On the SAT Math Test you'll need to be able to solve very—*very*—simple equations. Don't be deceived, however: Simple equations are remarkably easy to botch if you let your guard down. **A great habit to adopt is circling the unknown as soon as you read the question, to reinforce what you're solving for—it may not be *x*.** You'll find representative equations among the illustrative SAT algebra problems on the RocketReview website, but a few words are in order here.

☐ **I KNOW THIS**   ☐ **I NEED TO REVIEW THIS**

EQ2

The complete set of values (say, of x) that can satisfy an equation is called the **solution set**, for which the test writers sometimes use the set notation symbol $\{x\}$. **Equations may have more than one solution, so when *any* choice contains one of your solutions, check the *other* solutions that choice contains, too.** Notice how dangerous attempting to solve an equation can be when simply checking the choices is a safer and often quicker solution.

If $x^3 = 25x$, what is the solution set of x ?

(A) $x = \{5\}$
(B) $x = \{5, -5\}$
(C) $x = \{0\}$
(D) $x = \{5, 0\}$
(E) $x = \{5, 0, -5\}$

The best way to solve questions like this is to check the solutions offered in the choices: 5, 0, and -5. All these choices satisfy the equation, so the answer is choice E.

The classroom-correct solution is SAT-risky:

$$x^3 = 25x$$
$$x^3 - 25x = 0$$
$$x\,(x^2 - 25) = 0$$
$$x\,(x + 5)\,(x - 5) = 0$$
$$x = 0, -5, 5$$

(Dividing by x as a first step is wrong because we eliminate one of the solutions: 0.)

☐ **I KNOW THIS** ☐ **I NEED TO REVIEW THIS**

EQ3

Just as it's possible to *overlook* a solution, it's possible to introduce a false solution if you're not careful. As with the previous concept box, raising a variable to a power sometimes *adds* a solution, just as taking the root of a variable sometimes loses a solution. **This danger—illustrated here—is avoided if you are in the habit of checking choices whenever possible. Besides, you'll have to check your solutions at the end *anyway*, so you may as well *start* by checking the solutions offered in the choices.**

If $\sqrt{x-1} = x - 3$, what is x?

(A) 5 only
(B) 2 only
(C) –1 only
(D) 5 or 2 only
(E) 5 or –1 only

(Here's the classroom-correct, SAT-risky solution:

$$\sqrt{x-1} = x - 3$$
$$(\sqrt{x-1})(\sqrt{x-1}) = (x-3)(x-3)$$
$$x - 1 = x^2 - 6x + 9$$
$$0 = x^2 - 7x + 10$$
$$(x-5)(x-2) = 0$$
$$x = 5 \text{ or } 2$$

You're not finished: Remember to check both solutions! When you do you'll see that 5 works, but 2 does not: the answer is choice A.)

☐ **I KNOW THIS** ☐ **I NEED TO REVIEW THIS**

EQ4

You'll get plenty of practice solving the different types of SAT equations in the illustrative algebra questions (at the RocketReview website), but two equations are worth examining here because you probably don't see them often in your math class: absolute value equations and variation equations.

☐ **I KNOW THIS** ☐ **I NEED TO REVIEW THIS**

ABSOLUTE VALUE EQUATIONS

ABE1

An equation or two on the SAT Math Test may include absolute value. **It's very easy to screw up equations involving absolute value. Rather than risk incorrectly breaking up the absolute value, not to mention all the risks of incorrectly subtracting negatives, I urge you instead simply to check each solution using process of elimination.**

If $|x - 3| = 6$, then what is x ?

Classroom-correct, SAT-risky solution:

$$(x - 3) = 6 \text{ or } (x - 3) = -6$$
$$\text{So } x = 9 \text{ or } x = -3$$

(Instead, just check any choices.)

☐ **I KNOW THIS**   ☐ **I NEED TO REVIEW THIS**

DIRECT AND INVERSE VARIATION

DIV1

Two particular kinds of equations that the test writers say will now appear on the new SAT are **direct variation** and **inverse variation**. To say that y **varies directly** (or is **directly proportional**) with x means that y increases as x increases (or the reverse). To say that y **varies inversely** (or is **inversly proportional**) with x means that y increases as x *decreases* (or the reverse).

To take a real-world example, the distance a car travels in a certain time varies directly with the car's speed: The greater a car's speed, the greater the distance traveled by the car. Similarly, the *time* it takes a car to travel a certain distance varies inversely with the car's speed: The greater a car's speed, the *less* time it takes for the car to travel a given distance.

☐ **I KNOW THIS**   ☐ **I NEED TO REVIEW THIS**

These equations aren't particularly difficult to set up, but you have to be familiar with how these problems are worded. If we let k equal some number (a constant), then here are different examples of direct and inverse variation, from simple to a bit more complicated. To take an example from geometry, the area of a circle varies directly with the *square* of its radius (π is the constant), or $A = \pi r^2$

- "*y* varies directly with *x*" ($y = kx$) or ($\frac{y}{x} = k$)

- "*y* varies directly with the square of *x*" ($y = kx^2$)

- "*y* varies inversely with *x*"   ($k = xy$)

- "*y* varies inversely with the square root of *x*" ($k = y\sqrt{x}$)

- "*z* varies directly with the square of *x* and inversely with the cube of *y*" ($zy^3 = kx^2$)

☐ **I KNOW THIS**   ☐ **I NEED TO REVIEW THIS**

Problems involving direct or inverse variation will probably state so explicitly, but you may instead have to infer the type of variation either from a table or a graph. In such cases you might be required to calculate the constant (k) from the information provided.

x	y
2	24
3	36
4	48

(So y varies *directly* with x, and k equals 12.)

x	y
1	36
2	9
3	4

(So y varies *inversely* with x^2, and k equals 36.)

☐ I KNOW THIS   ☐ I NEED TO REVIEW THIS

INEQUALITIES

You'll get at least a question or two on the SAT Math Test involving inequalities. **(The new SAT may have *more* inequalities now that the math test has done away with quantitative comparison questions, which used to test inequalities).** Here's a simple example: What are all values of x such that $10 < x + 2 < 20$? **When an expression is sandwiched between two inequalities, *both* inequalities must be satisfied.**

$$10 < x + 2 < 20 =$$

$$10 < x + 2 \text{ and } x + 2 < 20 =$$
$$8 < x \text{ and } x < 18 =$$
$$8 < x < 18$$

☐ I KNOW THIS   ☐ I NEED TO REVIEW THIS

IN2

Inequalities can be solved the same way as equations. **Remember that multiplying both sides by a negative number reverses the direction of the inequality.**

$$-x < 4 =$$
$$-1(-x) > -1(4)$$
$$x > -4$$

☐ **I KNOW THIS**   ☐ **I NEED TO REVIEW THIS**

IN3

Careful: The direction of the inequality can be reversed in some other situations. You'll avoid potential pitfalls, as I mentioned, by simply trying the solutions among the choices.

$$2 < \frac{1}{x} < 4 =$$
$$\frac{1}{2} > x > \frac{1}{4}$$

☐ **I KNOW THIS**   ☐ **I NEED TO REVIEW THIS**

As with absolute value equations or absolute value inequalities, your best bet on inequalities is to check every choice rather than trying to "solve" the equation. To check each choice, throw *any* number into the inequality—0 is always easy to check—and if that number works, eliminate every choice that *excludes* the number; if the number doesn't work, eliminate every choice that *includes* the number. Repeat with a different number until you've eliminated all choices but the answer. That process may *seem* to take longer, but I promise you that in the pressure cooker situation of the actual SAT, trying the choices is both faster and safer than the traditional classroom methods of solving inequalities.

If $5 < x < 9$ and $5 < y < 8$, then which of the following best describes $x - y$?

(A) $-3 < x - y < 4$

(B) $1 < x - y < 5$

(C) $4 < x - y < 5$

(D) $4 < x - y < 8$

(E) $5 < x - y < 8$

Throw in a couple of simple permissible values for x and y. If x is 8 and y is 6, then the difference $(x - y)$ equals 2. Choices (C), (D), and (E) are out because none include 2 as a possible result. Next we try a different pair of values, say 6 for x and y. Now, the difference equals 0. Since choice (B) does not include 0, choice (A) is the answer.

I KNOW THIS ☐   I NEED TO REVIEW THIS ☐

494

Watch your step if the inequality contains an absolute value! Your best bet, as illustrated in the previous concept box, is to throw in different values of x and use process of elimination until you find the answer. **Although I do *not* recommend classroom-correct, SAT-risky solutions, *do* notice that I've replaced the absolute value sign with parentheses.**

If $|x + 5| > 3$, then $x =$

Here's the classroom-correct, SAT-risky solution:

$$(x + 5) > 3 \text{ or } (x + 5) < -3$$
$$x > -2 \text{ or } x < -8$$

Notice that this solution *cannot* be expressed in the sandwiched form $m < x < n$.

☐ **I KNOW THIS**   ☐ **I NEED TO REVIEW THIS**

Remember with inequalities that numbers include decimals as well as integers (unless a problem states otherwise). If $x < 10$, everyone's first instinct is that the maximum value of x is 9, but x could equal 9.999999, or practically 10. When dealing with inequalities, you'll usually find it easier to pretend that the maximum or minimum values can equal the inequality limit, and then take care of the inequality sign as the last step of the problem.

☐ **I KNOW THIS**   ☐ **I NEED TO REVIEW THIS**

IN7

Read inequality problems carefully: It's easy to reverse which side of the symbol is greater (it's the "open side" of the < or > sign). By the way, the symbol ≥ means greater than or equal to, though most SAT inequalities are pure inequalities.

☐ **I KNOW THIS**   ☐ **I NEED TO REVIEW THIS**

SIMULTANEOUS EQUATIONS

SE1

You will almost certainly encounter at least one simultaneous equations question on your SAT. With simultaneous equations you're given two or more equations involving two or more variables and asked for a solution that satisfies the equations given (usually just two equations). Avoid solving simultaneous or other equations on the SAT by the "substitution method" (using one equation to solve for one variable in terms of the other, and then substituting that solution into the other equation). **This method is time-consuming and creates an enormous risk of manipulation errors.** Instead, determine which variable you want to get rid of—the one you're *not* solving for.

If $x + 2y = 10$ and $3x + y = 20$, then $x = ?$

Since you're solving for x, you want to get rid of y. So we multiply the second equation by 2 to get $6x + 2y = 40$. Then subtract the first equation from this equation and simplfy:

$$\begin{array}{r} 6x + 2y = 40 \\ -\ (x + 2y = 10) \\ \hline 5x \quad\ = 30 \\ x\ = 6 \end{array}$$

☐ **I KNOW THIS**   ☐ **I NEED TO REVIEW THIS**

In math class you're used to solving simultaneous equations by multiplying one of the two equations by one number, the other equation by another number, and then subtracting the two equations to solve for one of the variables. Then, by plugging the value of that variable back into either equation, the other variable can be determined. **That's the way you solve simultaneous equations in the classroom because that's the way you determine both variables.** But on the SAT Math Test, it's virtually certain that you won't need to solve for both variables of a simultaneous equations question, so you'll almost certainly never need to carry out such a laborious solution process.

On SAT simultaneous equations, simply lining up and then adding the two equations is often all you need to do (sometimes you'll need to simplify the solution). If adding the two equations doesn't lead to the solution, subtracting the two equations usually does the trick. (In rare cases, you'll first need to multiply one of the two equations through by a **number—and then add or subtract the two equations.)** It's usually a simple matter of mentally *jiggling* the various coefficients in the given equations to arrive at a desired unknown expression.

If $x + 2y = 3$ and $2x + y = 18$, then $x + y = ?$

Method A: add the two equations and reduce (Ans.:7)

If $3x + 2y = 13$ and $x - y = 1$, then $2x + 3y = ?$

Method B: subtract the second equation from the first equation (Ans.: 12)

If $4x + 3y = 3$ and $2x + 4y = 18$, then $5x + 5y = ?$

Method C: double the first equation and add the result to the second equation, then simplify (Ans.: 12)

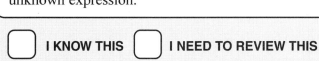

☐ **I KNOW THIS** ☐ **I NEED TO REVIEW THIS**

QUADRATICS

QD1

To multiply two binomial expressions, use the FOIL method (first, outer, inner, last). **Whenever a problem provides you with a binomial that you can FOIL, *do so*—it's almost always the first step on a direct road to the final solution.** This rule is another application of our general approach to solving SAT math questions: Whatever we *can* do on a problem, we *should* do, even if it's not clear how the step leads to the final solution—it will!

$$(x + 2)(x - 3) =$$

$$x^2 - 3x + 2x - 6 =$$
$$x^2 - x - 6$$

☐ I KNOW THIS   ☐ I NEED TO REVIEW THIS

QD2

Conversely, whenever you see a quadratic expression that you can factor—*factor it!* Just fiddle around with the factors of the last term until you find a pair that adds up to the coefficient of the middle term. The quadratics on the SAT Math Test are always simple to factor.

$$x^2 + 8x - 20 =$$

$$(x + 10)(x - 2)$$

☐ I KNOW THIS   ☐ I NEED TO REVIEW THIS

QD3

You may be asked for the **roots** (or the solution) of a quadratic equation (roots in this sense are not the same as square roots or cube roots). **Careful: the roots themselves add up to the *negative* of the middle term's coefficient.**

$$x^2 + 8x - 20 = 0$$

$$(x + 10)(x - 2) = 0$$
$$(x + 10) = 0 \text{ or } (x - 2) = 0$$
$$x = -10 \text{ or } x = 2$$

☐ I KNOW THIS   ☐ I NEED TO REVIEW THIS

QD4

An SAT problem might combine a quadratic with an inequality. **As I mentioned earlier, the most efficient way to solve inequalities on the multiple-choice questions is to check different values of x and use process of elimination on the answer choices so you can *avoid* the numerous pitfalls of the traditional classroom solution as shown here.**

$$x^2 + 8x - 20 > 0$$
$$(x + 10)(x - 2) > 0$$
either
$$(x + 10) > 0 \text{ and } (x - 2) > 0 \text{ or}$$
$$(x + 10) < 0 \text{ and } (x - 2) < 0$$
so either
$$x > -10 \text{ and } x > 2 \text{ or}$$
$$x < -10 \text{ and } x < 2$$
so $x > 2$ or $x < -10$

(*Avoid* this classroom-correct, SAT-risky process!)

☐ **I KNOW THIS**   ☐ **I NEED TO REVIEW THIS**

QD5

Two super, *super*-important quadratics on the SAT are $x^2 + 2xy + y^2$ (or $x^2 - 2xy + y^2$) and "the difference of two squares," $x^2 - y^2$. Be absolutely sure you are comfortable with both expressions. (By the way, whenever you see an "xy" in a an SAT Math Test problem, there's a good chance that the solution will somehow involve the expression $x^2 + 2xy + y^2$, even if this is not immediately apparent in the problem.)

$$(x + y)(x + y) = x^2 + 2xy + y^2$$
(Notice the middle term, $2xy$!)
$$(x - y)(x - y) = x^2 - 2xy + y^2$$
$$(x + y)(x - y) = x^2 - y^2$$

☐ **I KNOW THIS**   ☐ **I NEED TO REVIEW THIS**

QD6

Don't be bamboozled on the SAT by polynomials with exponents greater than 2 or 3—they can be factored using methods we've already discussed.

$$x^4 - y^4 =$$

$$(x^2 + y^2)(x^2 - y^2) =$$
$$(x^2 + y^2)(x + y)(x - y)$$

(Notice that the expression $x^2 + y^2$ cannot be factored.)

☐ **I KNOW THIS** ☐ **I NEED TO REVIEW THIS**

ALGEBRAIC THINKING

AT1

Algebraic thinking problems involve the properties or *behavior* of numbers that are expressed algebraically. In other words, algebraic thinking is really about arithmetic! **Beware: algebraic thinking questions are among the most difficult and dangerous on the SAT Math Test, often appearing as killer rabbits.** As I mentioned earlier, your thinking (and unconscious assumptions) about all numbers is based on the behavior of a limited type of number: positive integers greater than 1—so you must be hyper-careful about drawing conclusions about numbers in general. **Remember: The behavior of numbers like 1, 0, fractions, and negative numbers differs *greatly* from the behavior of "regular numbers" like 2 or 24 or 500.**

If $(x + y)$ is an integer and $(x - y)$ is an integer, which of the following must be integers: $x, y, 2x$?

(Both x and y could be integers, but they could also be fractions. If we add the two expressions, each of which is an integer, the result of $2x$ must be an integer.)

☐ **I KNOW THIS** ☐ **I NEED TO REVIEW THIS**

Let's take an operation as easy as doubling a number. Doubling a number makes it bigger, right? Not necessarily. If the number is zero, doubling it has no effect; if the number is negative, doubling it makes it smaller. Squaring a number makes it larger, unless the number is 0 or 1—or a fraction between them. **Very, very important: If you swap numbers for variables on algebraic thinking questions, as you should, be absolutely sure that you try different *types* of numbers.** (Algebraic thinking questions, which ask about the properties or behavior of numbers, are different from "regular" questions with algebraic answer *choices,* which we can usually get by swapping one set of numbers. Refer to our discussion beginning on page 404 of the swapping numbers math move.)

- Which is greater, x or $x + 1$?

No matter what x is, $x + 1$ is 1 more than x, so $x + 1$ is greater.

- Which is greater, x or $2x$?

You can't tell; the answer depends on what x is.

- Which is greater, x or x^2?

You can't tell.

[ ] **I KNOW THIS** [ ] **I NEED TO REVIEW THIS**

As we discussed in the arithmetic refresher, number lines are helpful when comparing the relative sizes of numbers. When numbers are expressed as variables, sketching a quick number line is even more helpful—especially when dealing with negative numbers or with powers of fractions. For example, normally we might think that, of course, $x < x^2 < x^3$, but see the examples here.

When x is -2, then x^2 is positive but x^3 is -8, so now $x^3 < x < x^2$.

When x is $\frac{1}{2}$, then x^2 is $\frac{1}{4}$ and x^3 is $\frac{1}{8}$, so now $x^3 < x^2 < x$.

When x is $-\frac{1}{2}$, then x^2 is $\frac{1}{4}$ and x^3 is $-\frac{1}{8}$, so now $x < x^3 < x^2$.

[ ] **I KNOW THIS** [ ] **I NEED TO REVIEW THIS**

Notice—rather than memorize—the following *very* important behavioral facts about the product of numbers such as *xyz* or *pqrs.*

- The product of integers must be even if one or more of the integers is even.

- In other words, the product of integers can be odd only if *all* the numbers being multiplied are odd.

- The product of some numbers must be zero if one or more of the numbers is zero.

- The product of some numbers is negative only if none of the numbers is zero *and* the number of negative numbers is odd.

- A positive number raised to any power is positive; a negative number raised to an even power is positive, otherwise it is negative.

Play around with different combinations of positive and negative numbers until you become comfortable with questions like these.

If *p, q, r, s,* and *t* are all integers, and their product *pqrst* is even, at most how many of these integers can be odd?

Four, since at least one of the numbers must be even.

If $xyz \neq 0$ and $xy^2z^3 > 0$, what can we conclude about *xz* ?

Since y^2 must be positive, we know that xz^3 must also be positive. So if *x* is positive, *z* must also be positive so *xz* is positive; if *x* is negative, *z* must also be negative, and once again *xz* is positive.

☐ **I KNOW THIS**   ☐ **I NEED TO REVIEW THIS**

Notice—rather than memorize—the following *very* **important behavioral facts about divisibility. Let** k **be any integer.**

- An even number can be expressed as $2k$, whether k is even or odd, because $2k$ is divisible by 2. For that matter, $6k$ is even because $6k = 2 \times 3k$, so it's divisible by 2 (of course, it's also divisible by 3 and 6).

- An odd number can be expressed as $2k + 1$, because it leaves a remainder of 1 when divided by 2.

- Consecutive numbers can be expressed in the form k, $k + 1$, $k + 2$, $k + 3$, and so on.

- Consecutive even numbers differ by 2, and so can be expressed in the form $2k$, $2k + 2$, $2k + 4$, $2k + 6$, and so on. Consecutive odd numbers also differ by 2, and so can be expressed in the form $2k + 1$, $2k + 3$, $2k + 5$, $2k + 7$, and so on.

Play around **with different combinations of factors and multiples until you become comfortable with questions like these.**

If $J = (2 \times 3 \times 5 \times 7 \times 11 \times 13) + 1$ then J is a prime number because it leaves a remainder of 1 when divided by all the prime factors a non-prime number would have had.

That's a tough prime number concept, but notice that you can convince yourself that J is prime by using the WIBNI math move and considering smaller, easily verifiable "versions" of J such as the following:

$(2) + 1 = 3$ (prime)
$(2 \times 3) + 1 = 7$ (prime)
$(2 \times 3 \times 5) + 1 = 31$ (prime)

For more on WIBNI, see the discussion beginning on page 408.

☐ **I KNOW THIS**   ☐ **I NEED TO REVIEW THIS**

A common algebraic thinking question asks you to determine the maximum (or minimum) value of an expression. **As always, read the problem carefully, because it may ask you for what value of x the expression becomes a maximum (or minimum).**

If $y = (1 + x)^2$, what is the minimum possible value of y?

The minimum possible value of anything squared is 0. Notice, however, that the minimum value for y occurs when x itself is -1.

☐ **I KNOW THIS**   ☐ **I NEED TO REVIEW THIS**

Be very careful when you are required to maximize or minimize an expression or related variables: Maximizing the value of one thing may require something else to be *minimized*.

If x, y, and z are different positive integers whose sum is 10, what is the maximum possible value of z?

To maximize z we must *minimize* x and y. The minimum possible values here are 1 and 2, so the maximum value of z is 7.

☐ **I KNOW THIS**   ☐ **I NEED TO REVIEW THIS**

FUNCTIONS

FN1

Function questions, formerly limited to the math SAT II subject tests, will now appear frequently on the SAT Math Test. A function is an instruction to perform an operation or a series of operations on a variable that produces a certain result. A function, then, is a rule or a set of rules.

☐ **I KNOW THIS** ☐ **I NEED TO REVIEW THIS**

FN2

Imagine a special box into which we provide an input and the box produces a certain output. This particular box "adds 1" to the input. If the input were 5, the box would produce an output of 6.

$x \rightarrow \square \rightarrow x + 1$

$5 \rightarrow \square \rightarrow 6$

☐ **I KNOW THIS** ☐ **I NEED TO REVIEW THIS**

FN3

No matter what we put inside this particular box, the box will perform the same operation ("add 1"). If the input is 10, the output will be 11. If the input is 2.2, the output will be 3.2. If the input is $x + 2$, the output will be $x + 3$. If the input is x^2, the output will be $x^2 + 1$.

$10 \rightarrow \square \rightarrow 11$

$2.2 \rightarrow \square \rightarrow 3.2$

$x + 2 \rightarrow \square \rightarrow x + 3$

$x^2 \rightarrow \square \rightarrow x^2 + 1$

☐ **I KNOW THIS** ☐ **I NEED TO REVIEW THIS**

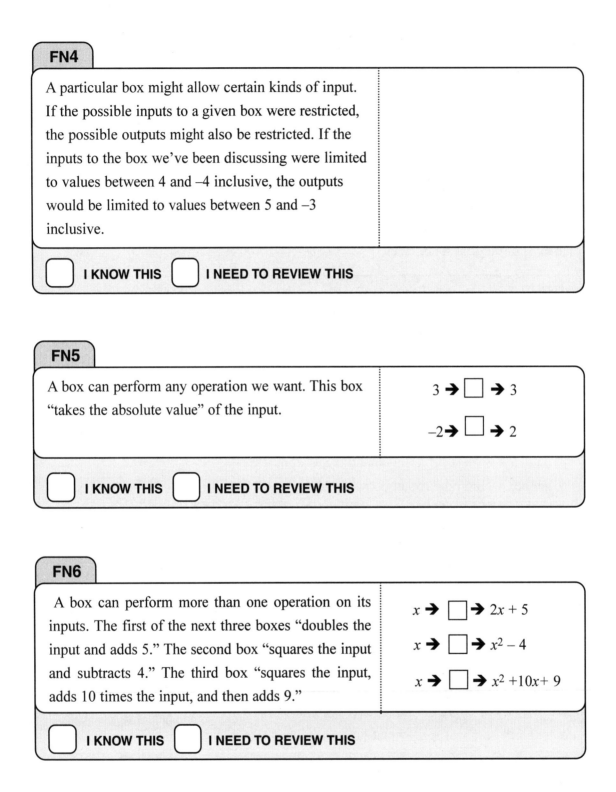

FN4

A particular box might allow certain kinds of input. If the possible inputs to a given box were restricted, the possible outputs might also be restricted. If the inputs to the box we've been discussing were limited to values between 4 and –4 inclusive, the outputs would be limited to values between 5 and –3 inclusive.

☐ I KNOW THIS ☐ I NEED TO REVIEW THIS

FN5

A box can perform any operation we want. This box "takes the absolute value" of the input.

$3 \rightarrow \square \rightarrow 3$

$-2 \rightarrow \square \rightarrow 2$

☐ I KNOW THIS ☐ I NEED TO REVIEW THIS

FN6

A box can perform more than one operation on its inputs. The first of the next three boxes "doubles the input and adds 5." The second box "squares the input and subtracts 4." The third box "squares the input, adds 10 times the input, and then adds 9."

$x \rightarrow \square \rightarrow 2x + 5$

$x \rightarrow \square \rightarrow x^2 - 4$

$x \rightarrow \square \rightarrow x^2 + 10x + 9$

☐ I KNOW THIS ☐ I NEED TO REVIEW THIS

Mathematicians call boxes like these **functions** and use the notation $f(\ \ )$ instead of a box. Think of the parenthesis as the box itself, and the "f" as the name of the box. (Different functions can be denoted with different letters.) Let's call the input x. Each of the boxes we have discussed so far could have been written in functional notation.

$$f(x) = x + 1$$

$$g(x) = |x|$$

$$h(x) = 2x + 5$$

$$j(x) = x^2 - 4$$

$$k(x) = x^2 + 10x + 9$$

| I KNOW THIS | I NEED TO REVIEW THIS |

If any of these equations reminds you of coordinate geometry, it should. Another way to write $f(x)$ is simply y. In other words, $f(x) = y$. All of the functions above could have been written in (x, y) notation, and mapped on a coordinate graph. (Please take a moment to review the discussion of functions under the coordinate geometry heading beginning on page 553 in the SAT geometry refresher.)

$$y = x + 1$$

$$y = |x|$$

$$y = 2x + 5$$

$$y = x^2 - 4$$

$$y = x^2 + 10x + 9$$

| I KNOW THIS | I NEED TO REVIEW THIS |

When a function raises x to the first power, we call that equation a **linear function**. The equation, $y = x + 1$ is a linear function. A linear function is just a fancy way of saying a line. When a function raises x to the second power, we call that equation a **quadratic function**. The equation, $y = x^2 - 4$, is a quadratic function.

| I KNOW THIS | I NEED TO REVIEW THIS |

FN10

We discussed earlier that a particular box (function) might restrict the allowable inputs (x), which might in turn restrict the possible outputs (y). The complete set of inputs a particular function allows is the **domain** of that function. The complete set of possible outputs that a particular function can provide is the **range** of that function.

☐ I KNOW THIS   ☐ I NEED TO REVIEW THIS

FN11

Function questions on the SAT will be fairly simple, so don't let the notation bully you.

If $f(x) = x^2$, what is $f(5)$?

(This function squares the input, so when we square 5 we get 25.)

☐ I KNOW THIS   ☐ I NEED TO REVIEW THIS

Again, function questions on the SAT will be fairly simple, so don't let the notation bully you. Just follow the instructions the function gives you.

If $f(x) = x^2$, what is $f(x + 1)$?

(Squaring the input $x + 1$, we get the output $x^2 + 2x + 1$.)

If $f(x) = x^2$, what does $f(x + k) - f(x)$ equal?

(Just take the question one step at a time: $f(x + k) = x^2 + 2kx + k^2$ and $f(x) = x^2$, so the difference is $2kx + k^2$.)

☐ **I KNOW THIS**   ☐ **I NEED TO REVIEW THIS**

SYMBOL OPERATIONS

To disguise function questions, the old SAT used random symbols that the test writers made up instead of the $f(x)$ notation. The new SAT Math Test will retain this type of question, perhaps for nostalgic reasons.

If $x* = x^2$, then $6* = ?$

(Substituting the 6 for x, we get 36.)

☐ **I KNOW THIS**   ☐ **I NEED TO REVIEW THIS**

The use of a random symbol also allows the test writers to create certain types of problems that would be cumbersome with function notation.

If $x* = x^2$, then

$3* + 4* =$

(A) $5*$

(B) $6*$

(C) $7*$

(D) $12*$

(E) $25*$

(Squaring each of the inputs, we get 9 plus 16, or 25. But notice that 25 is not in the answer choices (Choice E is $25*$, or 625), so we must convert each of the answer choices into their numerical equivalents. Choice (A) is the answer; choices (C) and (E) are traps.)

☐ **I KNOW THIS**   ☐ **I NEED TO REVIEW THIS**

WORD PROBLEMS

WP1

In order of importance, almost all SAT word problems fall into one of the following six types:

- Average problems
- Distance-rate-time problems
- Percentage discount problems
- Fraction-whole problems
- Branching category problems
- Ratio problems

We've already discussed average problems, percentage discount problems, and ratio problems in the SAT arithmetic refresher section. Since you'll find representative examples of each type of word problem in the arithmetic illustrative problems, I'll just say a few words here about word problems in general.

☐ **I KNOW THIS**   ☐ **I NEED TO REVIEW THIS**

WP2

On the multiple-choice questions, word problems should be solved using our checking the choices math move (see the discussion beginning on page 397 if you are not already familiar with this method).

☐ **I KNOW THIS**   ☐ **I NEED TO REVIEW THIS**

Now that you've read through the concepts quickly, return to those concepts that you checked for further review. Remember that all these concepts will be reinforced in the explanations of the illustrative problems.

Apply What You've Learned to Our Practice Algebra Problems

That completes our survey of *all* the algebra you need for the SAT Math Test. Trust me: you will not encounter an algebra problem on the SAT that requires a concept or combination of concepts other than those we have covered here.

Don't be bamboozled. The SAT Math Test measures how well you *reason* with basic concepts, not advanced ones. **Don't let a scary looking algebra question intimidate you: if you *think* an algebra problem on the SAT calls for more advanced concepts or formulas than covered in this chapter—you've missed the point of the question.**

You'll find our latest examples of SAT algebra problems at RocketReview.com. These printable problems will give you all the algebra practice you need.

Solutions to the "Think I'm Kidding about Not Always Solving for *x*" Drill (page 480)

We'll examine these questions in detail, as well as the underlying SAT logic involved, in our refresher of SAT algebra.

1. If $x^2 + y^2 = 80$ and $(x + y)^2 = 144$, then $xy =$

Solution: If we multiply the second equation out, we get $x^2 + 2xy + y^2 = 144$. Subtracting the first equation, we get $2xy = 64$, so $xy = 32$. Three steps.

2. If $x + 2y = 10$ and $2x + 3y = 17$, then $x + y =$

Solution: Subtracting the first equation from the second equation, we get $x + y = 7$. One step.

3. If x, y, and z are all positive and $xy = 1$, $yz = 32$, and $xz = 2$, then $xyz =$

Solution: Multiplying the three equations, we get $x^2y^2z^2 = 64$. Taking the square root of both sides, we get $xyz = 8$. Two steps.

4. When three numbers are added in pairs, the respective sums are 11, 13, and 16. What is the sum of the three numbers?

Solution: Each number is paired with two of the other numbers, so that means each number appears twice. Adding the three sums, we get 40. Since each number appears twice, we must take half of that sum: 20. Two steps.

(If you need to set the problem up algebraically to see the solution, let the three numbers equal x, y, and z. The resulting equations are $x + y = 11$, $x + z = 13$, and $y + z = 16$. Adding the three equations, we get $2x + 2y + 2z = 40$, so $x + y + z = 20$.)

Pretty cool, eh?

> Not one of the solutions is a "trick," but rather based on the basic SAT principle *not* to solve for *x* (or any other individual variable) unless the question *asks* you for *x*. Notice the unknown in all these cases—*xy*, *x* + *y*, *xyz*, and *x* + *y* + *z*—was an *expression*—not a single variable.

Return to the discussion on page 481.

Refresher of SAT Geometry

SAT Geometry Covers Only Basic Concepts

The geometry concepts tested on the SAT are pretty basic. As I mentioned earlier, the SAT Math Test instructions provide you with most of the geometry formulas you need (though you probably memorized these formulas back in ninth or tenth grade). And you won't have to prove any theorems.

A Generous Invitation in the Instructions

It's worth quoting the following directly from the official math instructions:

"Figures that accompany problems are intended to provide information useful in solving the problems. They are drawn as accurately as possible EXCEPT when it is stated in a particular problem that the figure is not drawn to scale."

In other words, the test writers are not even hinting—they're out-and-out *telling* you to *estimate* as much as you can directly from any figures provided, even answers! That's awfully generous of the test writers, since estimating answers is one of our master math moves—and especially since almost every geometry problem on the SAT provides a figure.

The only limit to this generosity, as pointed out in capital letters, are those problems that specifically state that the accompanying figure is *not* drawn to scale. About one-fourth of the geometry figures on the SAT Math Test provide a warning underneath: "<u>Note</u>: Figure not drawn to scale."

> Good news: even the few figures *not* drawn exactly to scale on the SAT are drawn *pretty close* to scale, so you can still make rough estimates. Important: Take a few *seconds* to verify just how close the drawing is to scale by comparing your visual estimates with the numerical information provided. If the figure is too far away from scale to be helpful in estimating, quickly *redraw* the figure to scale.

You'll find a more in-depth look at using estimation beginning on page 400 in our SAT math moves chapter.

Estimate as Much as You Can on Geometry Questions— *Before* Doing Any Calculations

Yes, estimating on a question before doing any calculations sometimes *does* take a *little* more time. But it's just a bit more time, and sometimes it's a *lot* less time. If the answer choices on a problem are far enough apart, sometimes a quick estimation reveals the answer *in seconds.*

Even when estimation only narrows the range of possible answers to a question, however, the few seconds you've spent estimating are *always* well spent. Estimating orients you to the problem and helps point the way toward the solution. Estimation is also a precautionary step that gives you a check on possible errors in your analysis should your "exact" solution deviate too far from your estimation. And finally, if you get stuck on the question later, your prior estimation will give you a good guess.

As I mentioned earlier, fastening a seatbelt and checking the rearview mirror *before* you start to drive takes a little time, too, but you can't afford not to take those precautions. Estimating on geometry problems is like fastening your seatbelt.

Ready? Our Refresher of SAT Geometry Is about to Begin

I've divided SAT geometry into the following topics:

- Lines and angles
- Triangles
- Squares and rectangles
- Parallelograms
- Other polygons
- Circles
- Solid geometry
- Coordinate geometry

> Read through all the concept boxes quickly. Check the boxes that need further review. Keep in mind that all the concepts will be reinforced in the illustrative problems that you'll find on the RocketReview website.

LINES AND ANGLES

LA1

Unless a problem states otherwise, the word **line** means *straight* line. Lines are identified either by the script letter ℓ or by two points the line passes through, as in $\overleftrightarrow{MN}$. A **ray** is identified by its **endpoint** S and a point T it passes through, as in $\overrightarrow{ST}$. Line drawings may or may not include the arrows sometimes used to distinguish them from **line segments**.

$$\overleftrightarrow{MN} = \ell_1$$

$\overrightarrow{MN}$ is a segment of ℓ_1

$\overline{ST}$ lies on ℓ_2

☐ **I KNOW THIS** ☐ **I NEED TO REVIEW THIS**

LA2

The length of a line segment can be indicated by a number or variable next to the segment. The test writers have introduced a needless ambiguity by sometimes referring to the length of a line segment by its endpoints, as in $CD = 6$. ***Watch out:* It's easy to become confused on SAT geometry questions and think that *CD* means *C* times *D* as if *C* and *D* somehow referred to values on a number line; they don't.**

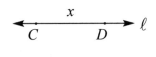

$$\overline{CD} = 6$$

$$x = 6$$

☐ **I KNOW THIS** ☐ **I NEED TO REVIEW THIS**

LA3

By definition, a line contains 180° on a side. A complete move around both sides of the line—a circle—contains 360°.

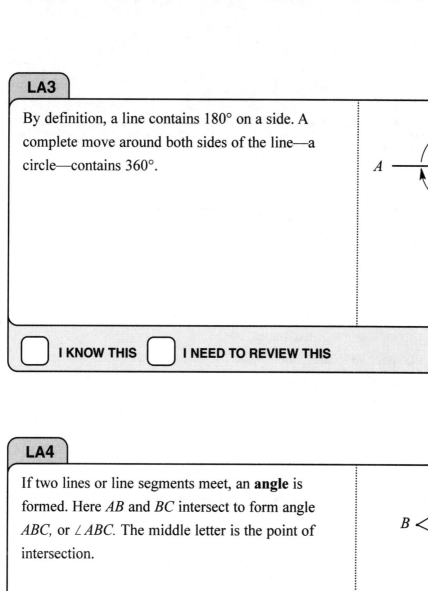

☐ **I KNOW THIS**   ☐ **I NEED TO REVIEW THIS**

LA4

If two lines or line segments meet, an **angle** is formed. Here *AB* and *BC* intersect to form angle *ABC,* or ∠ *ABC.* The middle letter is the point of intersection.

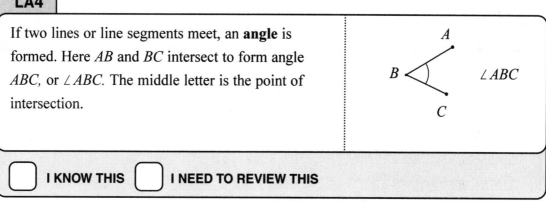

☐ **I KNOW THIS**   ☐ **I NEED TO REVIEW THIS**

LA5

A line **bisects** an angle if the two resulting angles are equal. *BD* bisects ∠ *ABC.*

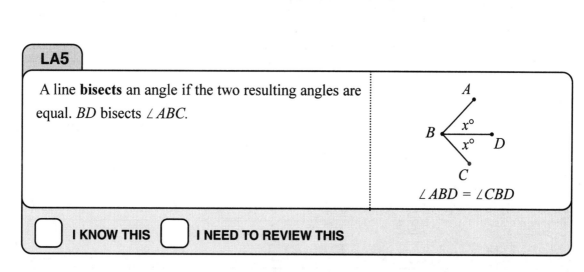

☐ **I KNOW THIS**   ☐ **I NEED TO REVIEW THIS**

LA6

If two lines intersect to create four angles, the opposite—or *vertical*—angles are equal.

☐ **I KNOW THIS** ☐ **I NEED TO REVIEW THIS**

LA7

If two lines intersect to create four equal angles, the two lines are said to be **perpendicular**; the symbol for perpendicular is ⊥. Each resulting angle is 90°, also known as a **right** angle. **Acute** angles are less than 90°; **obtuse** angles are greater than 90°.

$$\overline{AB} \perp \overline{CD}$$

☐ **I KNOW THIS** ☐ **I NEED TO REVIEW THIS**

LA8

Two lines in the same plane are **parallel** if they do not intersect. (As the instructions to each math section reassure us, all figures lie in a plane unless otherwise indicated.) The symbol for parallel is ∥.

$$\ell_1 \parallel \ell_2$$

☐ **I KNOW THIS** ☐ **I NEED TO REVIEW THIS**

LA9

If a third line intersects two parallel lines, two angle measures result.

$$\ell_1 \parallel \ell_2$$

☐ **I KNOW THIS** ☐ **I NEED TO REVIEW THIS**

LA10

When a third line intersects two parallel lines, it helps to think of the eight resulting angles as "small" or "big." All the small angles are equal, and all the big angles are equal. The sum of any small angle and any big angle is 180°.

$\ell_1 \parallel \ell_2$ $x° + y° = 180°$

☐ **I KNOW THIS**   ☐ **I NEED TO REVIEW THIS**

LA11

Learn to visualize these angles even if the parallel lines are truncated, as in this example.

$\ell_1 \parallel \ell_2$ $x + y = 180$

☐ **I KNOW THIS**   ☐ **I NEED TO REVIEW THIS**

LA12

Don't assume that two parallel-looking lines are parallel unless you are told that they are parallel (especially when the problem states that the figure is not drawn to scale). Sometimes you are not told directly that two lines are parallel, but you can deduce the fact from the information provided.

☐ **I KNOW THIS**   ☐ **I NEED TO REVIEW THIS**

LA13

Notice that lines that look parallel may not be parallel unless we are told so directly, or are given enough information to conclude that the lines are parallel. In the top figure, ℓ_1 and ℓ_2 are parallel if and only if $x + y = 180$. If instead $x + y > 180$ (middle figure), ℓ_1 and ℓ_2 would intersect when extended to the left of ℓ_3. If $x + y < 180$ (bottom figure), ℓ_1 and ℓ_2 would intersect when extended to the right of ℓ_3.

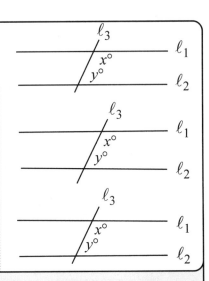

☐ **I KNOW THIS** ☐ **I NEED TO REVIEW THIS**

TRIANGLES

T1

A **triangle** is identified by its three corners, or **vertices** (the singular is **vertex**). The symbol for triangle is $\triangle$. The sum of the three angles of a triangle is 180°.

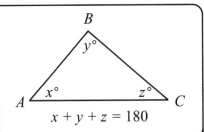

$$x + y + z = 180$$

☐ **I KNOW THIS** ☐ **I NEED TO REVIEW THIS**

T2

Knowing two angles of a triangle allows us to determine the third angle.

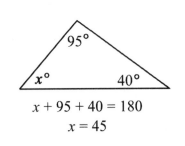

$$x + 95 + 40 = 180$$
$$x = 45$$

☐ **I KNOW THIS** ☐ **I NEED TO REVIEW THIS**

T3

Knowing an angle of a triangle allows us to determine an exterior angle.

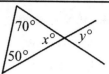

$$50 + 70 + x = 180$$
$$x = 60$$
$$y = 60$$

☐ **I KNOW THIS**   ☐ **I NEED TO REVIEW THIS**

T4

Knowing an angle outside a triangle can help us determine its interior angles.

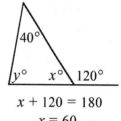

$$x + 120 = 180$$
$$x = 60$$
$$y + 40 + 60 = 180$$
$$y = 80$$

☐ **I KNOW THIS**   ☐ **I NEED TO REVIEW THIS**

T5

A triangle with three equal sides is **equilateral**. (Another way of saying that the sides are equal is that the three vertices are **equidistant**.) The angles of an equilateral triangle are also equal.

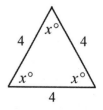

$$3x = 180$$
$$x = 60$$

☐ **I KNOW THIS**   ☐ **I NEED TO REVIEW THIS**

T6

A triangle with two equal sides is **isosceles**. The two angles opposite the equal sides are also equal.

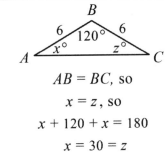

$AB = BC$, so

$x = z$, so

$x + 120 + x = 180$

$x = 30 = z$

☐ I KNOW THIS ☐ I NEED TO REVIEW THIS

T7

Sometimes a problem does not state that a triangle is isosceles, but this fact can be determined (because it has either two equal sides or two equal angles). It is always helpful to indicate equal angles or equal sides by marking the diagram.

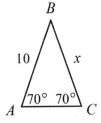

Since $\angle A = \angle C$,

$x = 10$

☐ I KNOW THIS ☐ I NEED TO REVIEW THIS

T8

Sometimes it takes a step or two to determine that a triangle is isosceles.

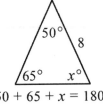

$50 + 65 + x = 180$

$x = 65$

☐ I KNOW THIS ☐ I NEED TO REVIEW THIS

T9

The larger the angle of a triangle, the larger its opposite side. The smaller the side of a triangle, the smaller the opposite angle.

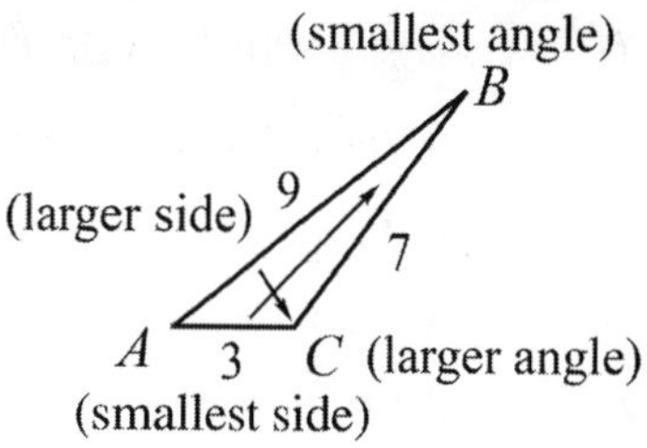

(smallest angle)

(larger side) 9

7

A 3 C (larger angle)
(smallest side)

☐ **I KNOW THIS** ☐ **I NEED TO REVIEW THIS**

T10

The **perimeter** of a triangle is the sum of its sides.

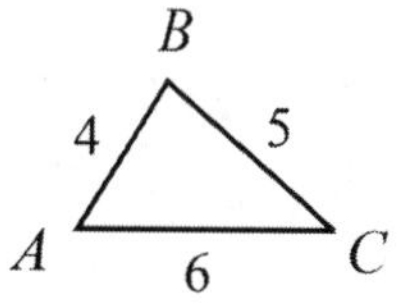

B

4   5

A 6 C

perimeter = $4 + 5 + 6 = 15$

☐ **I KNOW THIS** ☐ **I NEED TO REVIEW THIS**

T11

The sum of any two sides of a triangle is greater than the remaining side. This relationship arises because the shortest distance between any two points is a straight line. Consider $\overline{AB}$. This segment is the shortest distance between the points A and B. It follows that any other "route" from A to B—through point C, for example—is longer. So going from A to C ($\overline{AC}$) and then from C to B ($\overline{CB}$) is longer than $\overline{AB}$.

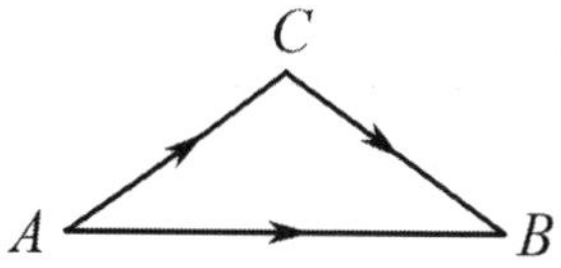

C

A B

☐ **I KNOW THIS** ☐ **I NEED TO REVIEW THIS**

To give you better feel for this relationship between the sides of a triangle, imagine that two sides of ∠ABC—say, $\overline{AB}$ and $\overline{AC}$—are made of wood, connected by a hinge at vertex A. The third side—$\overline{BC}$—is a rubber band. If we open the hinge as far as possible so that $\overline{AB}$ is almost on the same line as $\overline{AC}$, you can see that the maximum the third side, BC, can reach is smidgen less than AB + AC. If we close the hinge to make the third side as small as possible, you can see that the minimum BC can reach is a smidgen more than AC – AB.

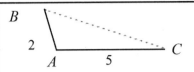

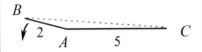

BC must be less than 7

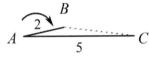

BC must be greater than 3

A **right triangle** includes a right angle. The side opposite the right angle is the **hypotenuse**.

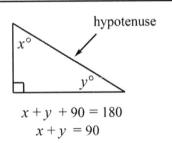

hypotenuse

$$x + y + 90 = 180$$
$$x + y = 90$$

T14

The sides of a right triangle obey the *Pythagorean* theorem, illustrated here.

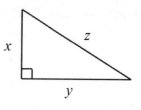

$$z^2 = x^2 + y^2$$
$$z = \sqrt{x^2 + y^2}$$

☐ **I KNOW THIS** ☐ **I NEED TO REVIEW THIS**

T15

Most of the time, determining the hypotenuse involves a radical in the result. **If you see radicals in the answer choices, there's a good chance a right triangle is involved in the solution—even if a right triangle is not immediately apparent in the problem or its diagram.** Determining the length of the diagonal of a box or cube, for example, is a notable example as we'll see shortly.

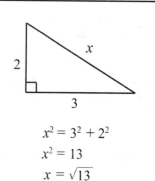

$$x^2 = 3^2 + 2^2$$
$$x^2 = 13$$
$$x = \sqrt{13}$$

☐ **I KNOW THIS** ☐ **I NEED TO REVIEW THIS**

T16

Integer solutions of the Pythagorean theorem often appear on the SAT, especially the 3:4:5 "triple" and its multiples (6:8:10, 15:20:25). If you see any two of the three numbers (3:4, 3:5, 4:5) involved in a triangle question, there's a good chance a 3:4:5 triangle is involved in the solution—even if it's not immediately apparent in the problem.

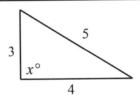

Since $3^2 + 4^2 = 5^2$,
$$x = 90$$

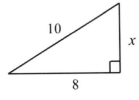

$$x^2 + 8^2 = 10^2$$
$$x^2 = 36$$
$$x = 6$$

☐ **I KNOW THIS** ☐ **I NEED TO REVIEW THIS**

T17

Two other integer solutions of the Pythagorean relationship are 5:12:13 and 7:24:25 (rare, but it's a new SAT Math Test, so you never know). If you see two of the three numbers of either triple (5:12, 5:13, 12:13, 7:24, 7:25, 24:25), there's a good chance the missing side is involved in the solution of the problem—even if a right triangle is not immediately apparent.

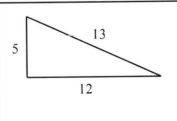

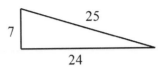

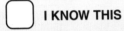
☐ **I KNOW THIS** ☐ **I NEED TO REVIEW THIS**

Notice that the Pythagorean theorem ($c^2 = a^2 + b^2$) holds if the largest angle of a triangle *equals* 90°. If the largest angle is *greater* than 90°, then $c^2 > a^2 + b^2$. If the largest angle is *less* than 90°, then $c^2 < a^2 + b^2$. Take some time to satisfy yourself how this relationship occurs.

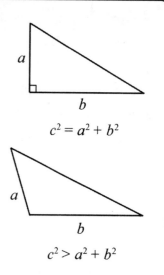

$$c^2 = a^2 + b^2$$

$$c^2 > a^2 + b^2$$

$$c^2 < a^2 + b^2$$

☐ **I KNOW THIS**   ☐ **I NEED TO REVIEW THIS**

If two right triangles share the same hypotenuse, we can equate the sum of the squares of the respective sides.

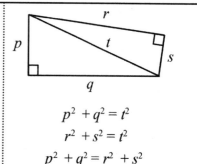

$$p^2 + q^2 = t^2$$
$$r^2 + s^2 = t^2$$
$$p^2 + q^2 = r^2 + s^2$$

☐ **I KNOW THIS**   ☐ **I NEED TO REVIEW THIS**

T20

A problem may require that you apply the Pythagorean relationship more than once. In the figure shown, we use the Pythagorean relationship first to determine x (actually x^2), then we plug that value into the larger triangle's Pythagorean relationship to determine y.

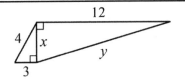

$$3^2 + 4^2 = x^2$$
$$25 = x^2$$

$$x^2 + 12^2 = y^2$$
$$25 + 144 = y^2$$
$$169 = y^2$$
$$13 = y$$

☐ **I KNOW THIS**   ☐ **I NEED TO REVIEW THIS**

T21

An **isosceles right triangle** is a right triangle with two equal sides. You may have heard your math teacher refer to it as a 45:45:90 triangle. **This triangle will be extremely important on the new SAT, so spend some time to familiarize yourself with its side relationships.** Notice that the hypotenuse of this triangle can also be the diagonal of a square.

$$x + x + 90 = 180$$
$$x = 45$$

$$a^2 + a^2 = c^2$$
$$2a^2 = c^2$$
$$a\sqrt{2} = c$$

☐ **I KNOW THIS**   ☐ **I NEED TO REVIEW THIS**

Another hugely important right triangle on the new SAT is the 30:60:90 triangle. It helps to understand how we can derive the 30:60:90 triangle by chopping an equilateral triangle in half. Notice that the 60° angle that we bisected becomes the 30° angle of the 30:60:90 triangle. Notice especially that the side opposite the new 30° angle gets chopped in half, too. As a result, the side opposite the 30° angle is half the hypotenuse. This 2:1 ratio on a triangle question is a tip-off that a 30:60:90 triangle is probably involved in the solution of the problem—even if a 30:60:90 triangle is not immediately apparent.

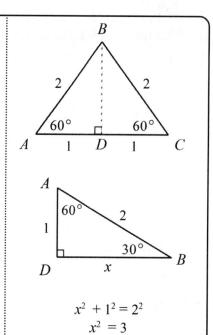

$$x^2 + 1^2 = 2^2$$
$$x^2 = 3$$

Another tip-off that a 45:45:90 triangle or a 30:60:90 triangle is involved in the solution of a problem is seeing one or more choices containing $\sqrt{2}$ in the answer (in the case of the 45:45:90), or one or more choices containing $\sqrt{3}$ in the answer (in the case of the 30:60:90). To keep these two very important triangles straight, think "two equal sides, radical two; three different sides, radical three."

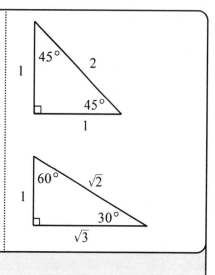

With both a 45:45:90 and a 30:60:90 triangle, if you know any single side or other single feature you can determine every other feature of the triangle. If you know just one side, for example, you can determine the other two sides, the perimeter, and the area.

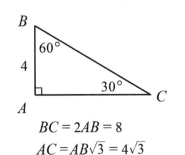

$BC = 2AB = 8$

$AC = AB\sqrt{3} = 4\sqrt{3}$

☐ I KNOW THIS   ☐ I NEED TO REVIEW THIS

The **area** of a triangle equals one-half the product of a **base** and the corresponding **height**.

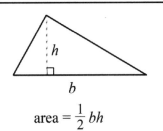

$$\text{area} = \frac{1}{2}bh$$

☐ I KNOW THIS   ☐ I NEED TO REVIEW THIS

The height corresponding to a base is the perpendicular distance from the opposite vertex. **Notice that if the opposite vertex is not "above" the base, the perpendicular distance is measured to the line containing the base.** This concept is more easily illustrated than described.

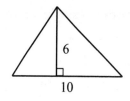

$$\text{area} = \frac{1}{2} \cdot 10 \cdot 6 = 30$$

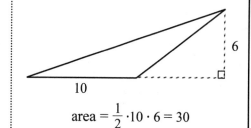

$$\text{area} = \frac{1}{2} \cdot 10 \cdot 6 = 30$$

☐ **I KNOW THIS**   ☐ **I NEED TO REVIEW THIS**

Any one of a triangle's three sides can be the triangle's base. A triangle with sides of three different lengths has three potential bases, each one of which has a corresponding height. The triangle shown has been rotated to different sides to demonstrate the different heights. We are used to thinking of a triangle's base as its "bottom" side, but sometimes a problem makes it more convenient to use a different side as the base.

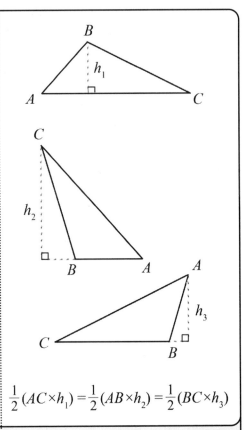

$$\tfrac{1}{2}(AC \times h_1) = \tfrac{1}{2}(AB \times h_2) = \tfrac{1}{2}(BC \times h_3)$$

☐ **I KNOW THIS** ☐ **I NEED TO REVIEW THIS**

If two or more triangles have the same base and the same height, they have the same area. In the figure shown, $\ell_1 \parallel \ell_2$. The distance between the two lines at points C, D, and E is therefore equal. Since all three triangles have the same height and share the same base ($\overline{AB}$), they all have the same area.

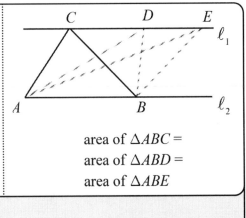

area of $\triangle ABC =$
area of $\triangle ABD =$
area of $\triangle ABE$

☐ **I KNOW THIS** ☐ **I NEED TO REVIEW THIS**

Two triangles are **similar** if their corresponding angles are all equal. The symbol for similar is ≃. Similar is just a fancy way of saying exactly the same shape. Two similar triangles are **congruent** if they are also exactly the same size. The symbol for congruent is ≅.

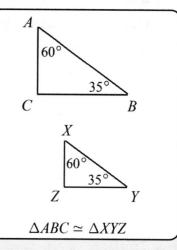

$\triangle ABC \simeq \triangle XYZ$

☐ **I KNOW THIS** ☐ **I NEED TO REVIEW THIS**

The ratio of any two corresponding sides of similar triangles is equal. To keep the corresponding sides of similar triangles straight, it's helpful to dub the three sides as "small side," "middle side," and "long side." For example, the small side of ∠ABC over the small side of ∠DEF equals the middle side of ∠ABC over the middle side of ∠DEF. Or the long side of ∠ABC over the small side of ∠ABC equals long side of ∠DEF over the small side of ∠DEF.

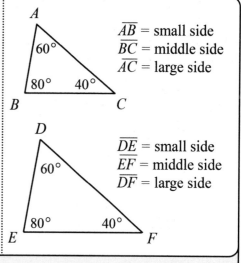

$\overline{AB}$ = small side
$\overline{BC}$ = middle side
$\overline{AC}$ = large side

$\overline{DE}$ = small side
$\overline{EF}$ = middle side
$\overline{DF}$ = large side

☐ **I KNOW THIS** ☐ **I NEED TO REVIEW THIS**

T31

A problem may require you to determine that two triangles are similar. In the figure shown, the sides of $\triangle DEF$ are all twice the corresponding sides of $\triangle ABC$ so the two triangles are similar.

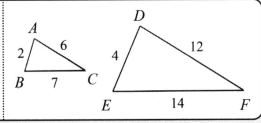

☐ **I KNOW THIS** ☐ **I NEED TO REVIEW THIS**

T32

A common way the test writers disguise similar triangles is to put one on top of the other. (This method of camouflaging similar triangles is sometimes done with cones, which we'll discuss shortly under solid geometry.)

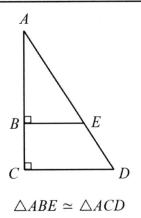

$\triangle ABE \simeq \triangle ACD$

☐ **I KNOW THIS** ☐ **I NEED TO REVIEW THIS**

Notice the indirect way that the test writers sometimes tell us that two triangles are similar—here by requiring us to apply what we know about the angle relationships formed when two parallel lines are cut by a third line. In the figure shown, $\overleftrightarrow{AB}$ is parallel to $\overleftrightarrow{DE}$.

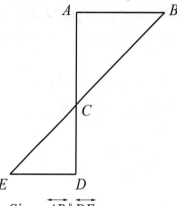

Since $\overleftrightarrow{AB} \parallel \overleftrightarrow{DE}$, $\angle EDC = \angle CAB$ and $\angle CED = \angle ABC$. Substitute numbers for these angles and convince yourself that $\triangle ABC \simeq \triangle DEC$.

This variation of disguised similar triangles is the most rare, but one I suspect will be more common on the new SAT. Notice that three similar triangles are produced by taking a right triangle and drawing a perpendicular from the hypotenuse to the opposite vertex. The original triangle is similar to the two resulting interior triangles.

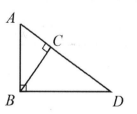

$\triangle ABD \simeq \triangle ACB \simeq \triangle BCD$

Be careful: The ratio of the sides of similar triangles is not the same as the ratio of their areas. Expressed in the language of direct variation that we encountered in the SAT algebra refresher section (beginning on page 480), the ratio of the areas of two similar triangles varies directly with the square of the ratio of their sides. Again, this relationship is more easily illustrated than described.

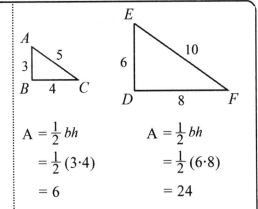

$$A = \tfrac{1}{2}\,bh \qquad\qquad A = \tfrac{1}{2}\,bh$$
$$= \tfrac{1}{2}\,(3 \cdot 4) \qquad\quad = \tfrac{1}{2}\,(6 \cdot 8)$$
$$= 6 \qquad\qquad\qquad = 24$$

Note that $AB:DE = 2:1$, but the area of $\triangle ABC$: area of $\triangle EDF = 4:1$.

☐ **I KNOW THIS** ☐ **I NEED TO REVIEW THIS**

SQUARES AND RECTANGLES

SR1

A **rectangle** is a four-sided figure with four right angles.

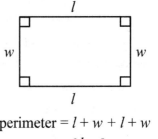

$$\text{perimeter} = l + w + l + w$$
$$= 2l + 2w$$
$$\text{area} = lw$$

☐ I KNOW THIS ☐ I NEED TO REVIEW THIS

SR2

A **square** is a rectangle with four equal sides. Notice that a square is a particular kind of rectangle.

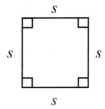

$$\text{perimeter} = s + s + s + s$$
$$= 4s$$
$$\text{area} = s^2$$

☐ I KNOW THIS ☐ I NEED TO REVIEW THIS

SR3

A **diagonal** of a rectangle is a line drawn between opposite corners. Notice that the diagonal of a rectangle creates two congruent triangles. We can determine the length of the diagonal using the Pythagorean theorem.

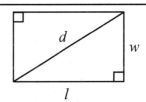

$$d^2 = l^2 + w^2$$
$$d = \sqrt{l^2 + w^2}$$

☐ I KNOW THIS ☐ I NEED TO REVIEW THIS

PARALLELOGRAMS

A four-sided figure (quadrilateral) whose opposite sides are parallel is a **parallelogram**. Notice that rectangles are just a particular kind of parallelogram. Notice that opposite sides of a parallelogram are equal, but that all four sides are not necessarily equal.

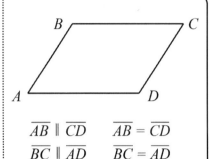

$$\overline{AB} \parallel \overline{CD} \qquad \overline{AB} = \overline{CD}$$
$$\overline{BC} \parallel \overline{AD} \qquad \overline{BC} = \overline{AD}$$

☐ **I KNOW THIS** ☐ **I NEED TO REVIEW THIS**

Notice that the opposite angles of a parallelogram are equal, and that the sum of *adjacent* angles is 180° (see concept boxes LA10 and LA11 on page 519). A problem may require you to *determine* that a particular quadrilateral is a parallelogram rather than stating that the quadrilateral is a parallelogram.

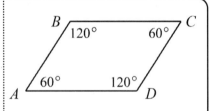

☐ **I KNOW THIS** ☐ **I NEED TO REVIEW THIS**

Just as with triangles, the height of a parallelogram is the perpendicular distance from the base to the opposite vertex. Notice that the height of a parallelogram is *not* the length of the "slanting" side.

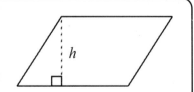

☐ **I KNOW THIS** ☐ **I NEED TO REVIEW THIS**

PL4

Notice that we can take apart a rectangle and reassemble it into a parallelogram with the same base and the same height. The area of a parallelogram is given by the formula A = *bh*.

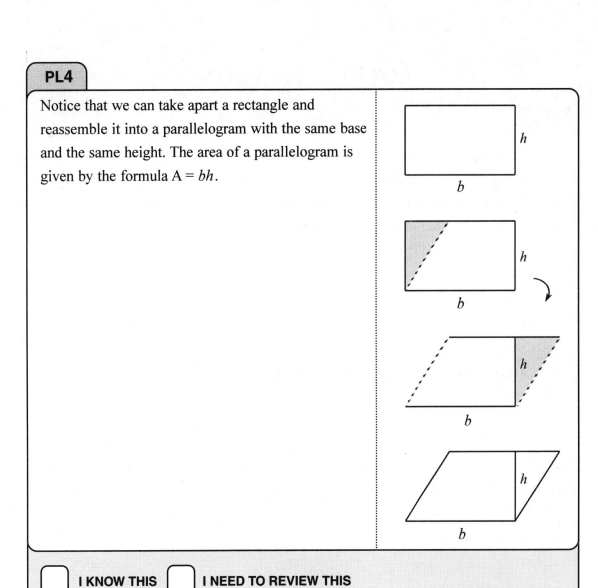

☐ **I KNOW THIS**   ☐ **I NEED TO REVIEW THIS**

PL5

Note that parallelograms with the same base and height have the same area. In the figure to the right, the two parallelograms have the same base and the same height, so they both have an area of 80.

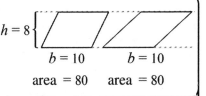

☐ **I KNOW THIS**   ☐ **I NEED TO REVIEW THIS**

OTHER POLYGONS

OP1

A **polygon** is any figure formed by three or more sides. *Triangles* are three-sided polygons; *quadrilaterals* are four-sided polygons; *pentagons* are five-sided polygons; *hexagons* are six-sided polygons; *octagons* are eight-sided polygons. As with triangles, two polygons are similar if they have the exact same shape, and congruent if they have the exact same shape *and* size.

triangle   quadrilateral

pentagon   hexagon

☐ **I KNOW THIS** ☐ **I NEED TO REVIEW THIS**

OP2

A **regular** or equilateral polygon has equal sides. Do not assume that a polygon is equilateral unless you are told so.

☐ **I KNOW THIS** ☐ **I NEED TO REVIEW THIS**

OP3

The perimeter of a polygon is simply the sum of its sides.

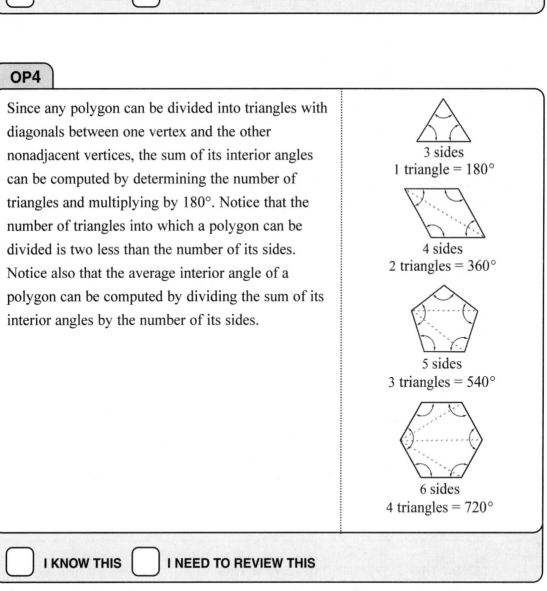

perimeter $= 5 + 6 + 6 + 9 + 7$
$= 33$

☐ **I KNOW THIS** ☐ **I NEED TO REVIEW THIS**

OP4

Since any polygon can be divided into triangles with diagonals between one vertex and the other nonadjacent vertices, the sum of its interior angles can be computed by determining the number of triangles and multiplying by 180°. Notice that the number of triangles into which a polygon can be divided is two less than the number of its sides. Notice also that the average interior angle of a polygon can be computed by dividing the sum of its interior angles by the number of its sides.

3 sides
1 triangle = 180°

4 sides
2 triangles = 360°

5 sides
3 triangles = 540°

6 sides
4 triangles = 720°

☐ **I KNOW THIS** ☐ **I NEED TO REVIEW THIS**

OP5

Notice that a regular hexagon can be divided into six equilateral triangles. Different features of the hexagon (such as its area) can be computed by calculating the corresponding feature of one of the interior equilateral triangles and multiplying the result by six.

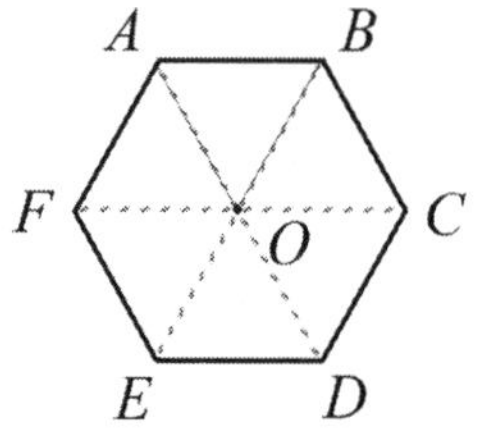

area of $ABCDEF =$
$6 \times$ area of $\triangle ABO$

☐ **I KNOW THIS**   ☐ **I NEED TO REVIEW THIS**

CIRCLES

CL1

A **circle** is often identified by its **center**. The perimeter of a circle is known as its **circumference**.

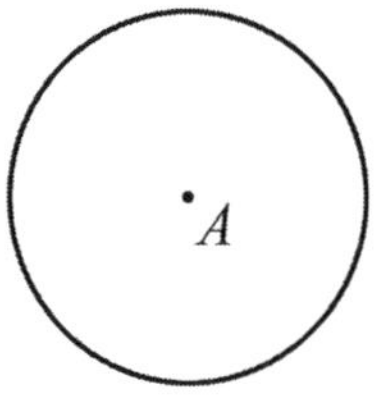

circle A

☐ **I KNOW THIS**   ☐ **I NEED TO REVIEW THIS**

CL2

The distance from the center of a circle to its circumference is the circle's **radius** (plural: *radii*). Twice the radius equals the **diameter**.

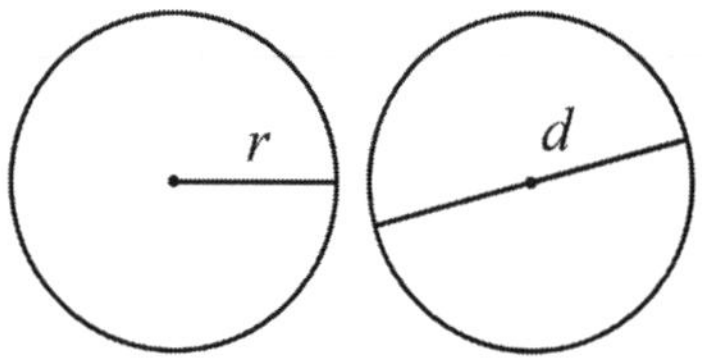

$d = 2r$

☐ **I KNOW THIS**   ☐ **I NEED TO REVIEW THIS**

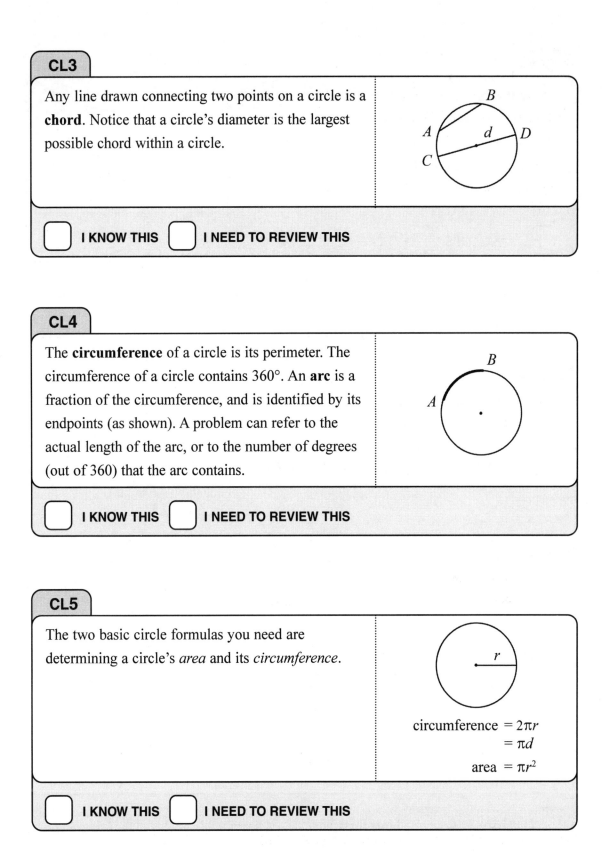

CL3

Any line drawn connecting two points on a circle is a **chord**. Notice that a circle's diameter is the largest possible chord within a circle.

☐ I KNOW THIS   ☐ I NEED TO REVIEW THIS

CL4

The **circumference** of a circle is its perimeter. The circumference of a circle contains 360°. An **arc** is a fraction of the circumference, and is identified by its endpoints (as shown). A problem can refer to the actual length of the arc, or to the number of degrees (out of 360) that the arc contains.

☐ I KNOW THIS   ☐ I NEED TO REVIEW THIS

CL5

The two basic circle formulas you need are determining a circle's *area* and its *circumference*.

$$\text{circumference} = 2\pi r$$
$$= \pi d$$
$$\text{area} = \pi r^2$$

☐ I KNOW THIS   ☐ I NEED TO REVIEW THIS

Notice that one complete move around a circle's circumference is a **revolution** (or **rotation**). We can calculate the distance a circle rolls by multiplying the number of revolutions the circle makes by its circumference.

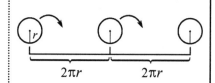

A **semicircle** is half a circle, so it contains 180°. A semicircle has half the whole circle's area and half the circle's circumference.

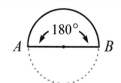

Notice that in addition to one half, we can calculate other fractions of a circle's area or circumference if we know what fraction of the circle's full 360° is involved.

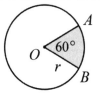

$$\text{arc } AB = \tfrac{1}{6} \times \text{circumference}$$
$$= \tfrac{1}{6} \times 2\pi r = \tfrac{\pi r}{3}$$
$$\text{shaded area} = \tfrac{1}{6} \times \text{area}$$
$$= \tfrac{1}{6} \times \pi r^2 = \tfrac{\pi r^2}{6}$$

CL9

Be careful: The ratio of the radii of two circles is not the same as the ratio of their areas. The ratio of the areas of two circles varies directly with the square of the ratio of their radii. Once again, this relationship is more easily illustrated than described. In the circles to the right, doubling the radius doubled the circumference but quadrupled the area.

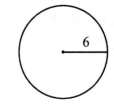

$C = 2\pi r = 6\pi$ $\quad C = 2\pi r = 12\pi$

$A = \pi r^2 = 9\pi$ $\quad A = \pi r^2 = 36\pi$

◻ **I KNOW THIS** ◻ **I NEED TO REVIEW THIS**

CL10

A polygon whose vertices all lie on a circle is said to be **inscribed**. (Conversely, the circle is said to **circumscribe** the polygon.)

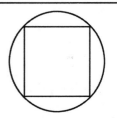

◻ **I KNOW THIS** ◻ **I NEED TO REVIEW THIS**

CL11

Notice that we can calculate the degree measure of the arcs determined by an inscribed regular polygon by dividing the number of sides into 360.

$x = \dfrac{360}{5} = 72$

◻ **I KNOW THIS** ◻ **I NEED TO REVIEW THIS**

CL12

If a square is inscribed in a circle, we can calculate any feature of either figure (such as area) by knowing any feature of the other. (Having said that, such problems on the multiple-choice questions are usually better solved by using a math move—such as estimating the answer or swapping numbers—rather than by laboriously calculating the respective formulas algebraically.)

$$r = x\sqrt{2}$$

circle	square
$A = \pi r^2$	$A = (2x)^2$
$C = 2\pi r$	$P = 8x$

☐ **I KNOW THIS** ☐ **I NEED TO REVIEW THIS**

CL13

If one vertex of a triangle is the center of a circle and the other two vertices lie on the circle, the triangle is isosceles (because two of its sides are radii, which are equal by definition).

 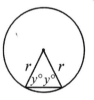

☐ **I KNOW THIS** ☐ **I NEED TO REVIEW THIS**

CL14

A line that touches a circle at one point only is called a **tangent line**. A radius drawn to the point of *tangency* is perpendicular to the tangent line.

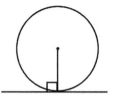

☐ **I KNOW THIS** ☐ **I NEED TO REVIEW THIS**

SOLID GEOMETRY

SG1

A **box**, or **rectangular solid**, has three dimensions: a length, a height, and a width. The **volume** of a box is the product of its length, width, and height.

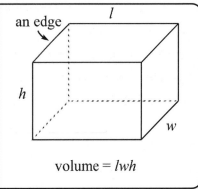

volume = lwh

☐ I KNOW THIS   ☐ I NEED TO REVIEW THIS

SG2

A box has six **faces**: top, bottom, front, back, left, right. Notice that the top and bottom faces are equal, as are the front and back faces, and the left and right faces. A box's **surface area** is the sum of the areas of its six faces.

The surface area of
the box above =
$lw + lw + lh + lh + hw + hw$

☐ I KNOW THIS   ☐ I NEED TO REVIEW THIS

SG3

A **cube** is a box all of whose **edges** are equal. Since every edge is equal, the area of each of a cube's six faces is equal.

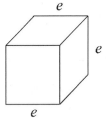

Volume = e^3
Surface area = $6e^2$

☐ I KNOW THIS   ☐ I NEED TO REVIEW THIS

SG4

Notice that if we were to divide each edge of a cube in half, we create eight smaller cubes. If we divide each edge in thirds, we create twenty-seven smaller cubes. Notice that the sum of the volumes of the smaller cubes equals the volume of the original cube—but the sum of the surface areas of the smaller cubes is much *larger* than the surface are of the

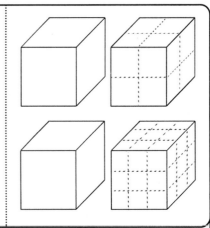

◯ **I KNOW THIS** ◯ **I NEED TO REVIEW THIS**

SG5

From the previous figure (SG4), notice that a cube's surface area and its volume do not vary linearly with its edge. Let's say that the edge of one cube is twice the edge of another cube. The larger cube has four times the surface area of the smaller cube's, and eight times the volume. If the edge of one cube is three times the edge of another cube, it has nine times the surface area and twenty-seven times the volume. Spend some time trying drawing different pairs of cubes with different ratios of their edges, and calculating the resulting ratios of their surface areas and their volumes.

e = edge
f = face = e^2
sa = surface area = $6e^2$
v = volume = e^3

e	f	sa	v
1	1	6	1
2	4	24	8
3	9	54	27
4	16	96	64
5	25	150	125
6	36	196	196

◯ **I KNOW THIS** ◯ **I NEED TO REVIEW THIS**

SG6

The volume of a **cylinder** is the product of its height and the area of its base (a circle). The height is the perpendicular distance from one base of the cylinder to the other. This formula is provided in the instructions to each SAT math section.

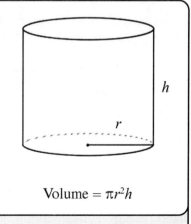

$$\text{Volume} = \pi r^2 h$$

☐ **I KNOW THIS**   ☐ **I NEED TO REVIEW THIS**

SG7

Imagine taking a cylinder (say, a soda can) and wrapping it—except for the top and bottom—with a sheet of paper that exactly covers its lateral surface area. Now let's unwrap the paper and lay it out flat. Notice that the width of the paper equals the height of the cylinder, and that the circumference of the cylinder equals the length of the paper.

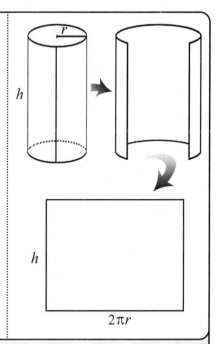

☐ **I KNOW THIS**   ☐ **I NEED TO REVIEW THIS**

In general, if we take a polygon or any other figure and extend up perpendicular line segments, the volume of the resulting solid is the area of the base times the height.

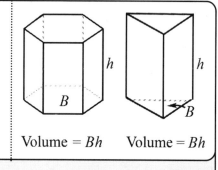

Volume = Bh Volume = Bh

Imagine a circle, and a point above that circle. If we draw every a line segment from every point on the circle to the point above the circle, we create a **cone**. When a cone appears on the SAT, it tends to be a **right cone**, with its vertex directly above the center of the circle. If a problem calls for the volume of a cone, the instructions to the new SAT will provide the formula. (For what it's worth, the volume of a cone is one-third the volume of a cylinder with the same base and height.)

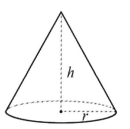

SG10

As I mentioned earlier, right cones are sometimes used to disguise similar triangle questions. If you look at a cone from the side—a two-dimensional view—a cone appears as a triangle. If we were to "slice" the cone with a plane parallel to the base, we would create a smaller cone (a triangle, when viewed from the side) similar to the original cone.

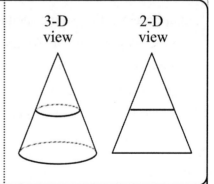

3-D view   2-D view

☐ **I KNOW THIS**   ☐ **I NEED TO REVIEW THIS**

SG11

Imagine a polygon, and a point above that polygon. If we draw a line segment from every point on the polygon to the point above the polygon, we create a **pyramid**. When a pyramid appears on the SAT, it tends to be a **right pyramid**, usually with a square base. If a problem calls for the volume of a pyramid, the instructions to the new SAT will provide the formula. (For what it's worth, the volume of a pyramid with a square base is one-third the volume of a box with the same square base and height.)

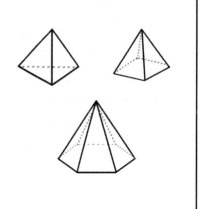

☐ **I KNOW THIS**   ☐ **I NEED TO REVIEW THIS**

A **sphere** is a three-dimensional circle (in other words, a ball). You may be asked to visualize various features of a sphere (such as the circle that results when a plane intersects a sphere), but if a problem calls for the volume or surface area of a sphere, the instructions to the new SAT will provide the formula.

☐ **I KNOW THIS**   ☐ **I NEED TO REVIEW THIS**

The Pythagorean theorem that we use in two dimensions to calculate the hypotenuse of a right triangle or the diagonal of a rectangle can be extended to three dimensions to calculate the diagonal of a box. **It may be hard to visualize, but the three-dimensional application results from applying the Pythagorean theorem twice.**

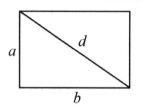

$$d = \sqrt{a^2 + b^2}$$

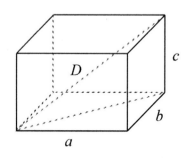

☐ **I KNOW THIS**   ☐ **I NEED TO REVIEW THIS**

SG14

You may encounter a problem on the SAT Math Test that requires you to visualize something going on in three-dimensional space without a diagram to help you. Here are examples: a cube inscribed in a sphere; three perpendicular lines intersecting at a point, not all three lines lie on the same plane; a right triangle is rotated about its height to create a solid figure. Drawing your own two-dimensional figure is simple, but drawing an accurate three-dimensional figure—even something as simple as a cube—can be difficult. If you get stuck, look around your room (or the test room, if it's on the actual test day) for things that can help you imagine the information. A stack of bookshelves could represent parallel planes; the proctor's desk, a box; a wall clock, a sphere.

☐ **I KNOW THIS** ☐ **I NEED TO REVIEW THIS**

COORDINATE GEOMETRY

CG1

The coordinate graph is formed by two intersecting number lines. The horizontal (side-to-side) axis is called the **x-axis**; the vertical (up-down) axis is called the **y-axis**. The x-axis and y-axis intersect at the **origin**, which is usually designated 0. Each axis has a positive and a negative direction. Moving up or to the right is positive; moving down or two the left is negative.

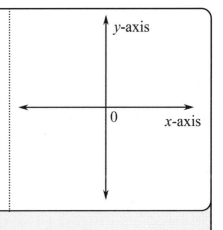

☐ **I KNOW THIS** ☐ **I NEED TO REVIEW THIS**

Points in the coordinate plane can be located by an **ordered pair** of numbers (x, y). Be very careful: switching the two values is an all-too-common error. The first number is the *x*-**coordinate**; the second number is the *y*-**coordinate**. Keep them straight. **(Note: Misreading math questions, always a big danger, is especially dangerous on coordinate geometry questions, owing to the heavy use of notation.)**

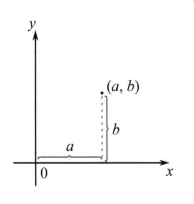

On the SAT Math Test, the coordinate plane is usually used to graph functions. The y value is the same thing as $f(x)$. Review our earlier discussion of functions in the SAT algebra refresher section beginning on page 505. In function notation, $f(6) = 4$ is the point $(6,4)$.

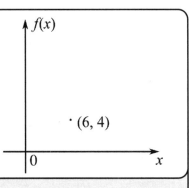

On the SAT, the coordinate plane is sometimes used to graph geometric figures. You will not be expected to know the formula for the equation of a circle, for example, but you will be expected to deduce information provided about a circle from its coordinates. Instead of being told that the radius of a circle is 5, say, you might be given the coordinate values that enable you to calculate the radius.

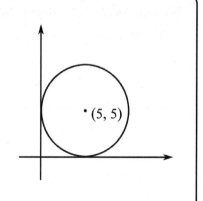

☐ **I KNOW THIS**   ☐ **I NEED TO REVIEW THIS**

To calculate the distance between two points with the same x or y value, simply subtract the difference between the two coordinate values—x or y—that differ. As always, be careful when subtracting negatives. Remember also that the distance between two points must be positive.

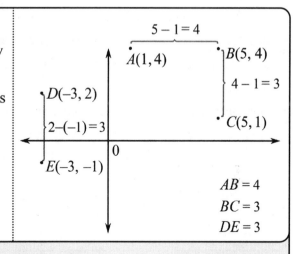

☐ **I KNOW THIS**   ☐ **I NEED TO REVIEW THIS**

To calculate the distance between two points with different x and y values requires just a bit more effort. The *distance formula* is nothing more than the Pythagorean theorem, with the distance between two points being the hypotenuse of a triangle.

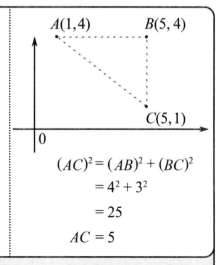

$A(1,4)$ $B(5,4)$

$C(5,1)$

$$(AC)^2 = (AB)^2 + (BC)^2$$
$$= 4^2 + 3^2$$
$$= 25$$
$$AC = 5$$

☐ **I KNOW THIS**   ☐ **I NEED TO REVIEW THIS**

If a question seems to require that you calculate the distance between more than two points, look before you blindly apply the Pythagorean theorem to the problem. To solve a question it may be sufficient either to estimate the distances required, or to compare horizontal and vertical "movements" (to get from point A to point B, for example, move up 3 and over 2; from C to D, move over 2 and down 2).

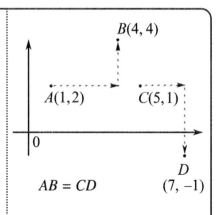

$B(4,4)$

$A(1,2)$ $C(5,1)$

D
$(7,-1)$

$AB = CD$

☐ **I KNOW THIS**   ☐ **I NEED TO REVIEW THIS**

CG8

To calculate the **midpoint** of a line segment (the point that **bisects** the line segment), take the average of the coordinates of the line segment's **endpoints**. Notice that the midpoint lies halfway between the two endpoints horizontally and halfway between the endpoints vertically. Careful: You may be given the midpoint and one of the endpoints and then asked to calculate the other endpoint.

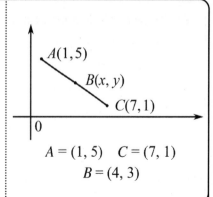

$A = (1, 5) \quad C = (7, 1)$

$B = (4, 3)$

⬜ **I KNOW THIS** ⬜ **I NEED TO REVIEW THIS**

CG9

The equation of a line is $y = mx + b$, where m is the **slope** and b is the **y-intercept**. This equation is equivalent to $f(x) = mx + b$.

⬜ **I KNOW THIS** ⬜ **I NEED TO REVIEW THIS**

CG10

The slope of a line is determined by dividing the up-down change between any two points on the line (the difference in their y coordinates) by the side-to-side change (the difference in their x coordinates).

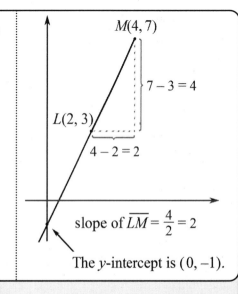

$7 - 3 = 4$

$L(2, 3)$

$4 - 2 = 2$

slope of $\overline{LM} = \dfrac{4}{2} = 2$

The y-intercept is $(0, -1)$.

⬜ **I KNOW THIS** ⬜ **I NEED TO REVIEW THIS**

To determine the equation of a line given two points, you need to solve for m (the slope) and b (the y-intercept). Begin by calculating the slope (the difference in y-coordinates divided by the difference in x-coordinates). Once you have the slope, substitute it for m in the formula $y = mx + b$. Then take either point—it doesn't matter which—and substitute the point's x and y values into the revised equation to solve for b. (Note: On a multiple-choice question, this laborious process can be circumvented* simply by plugging the points into the answer choices and seeing which equation satisfies both points.)

*GSWLIU

(From the previous concept box)

$L = (2, 3)$ $M = (4, 7)$

$$\text{slope} = \frac{y_2 - y_1}{x_2 - x_1} = \frac{7 - 3}{4 - 2} = 2$$

$$y = mx + b$$
$$7 = 2(4) + b$$
$$-1 = b$$

so the final equation is:

$$y = 2x - 1$$

Check your equations:
$$7 = 2(4) - 1 \quad \text{(okay)}$$
$$3 = 2(2) - 1 \quad \text{(okay)}$$

☐ **I KNOW THIS** ☐ **I NEED TO REVIEW THIS**

Notice that the slope of a line measures how y changes as x changes.

- Positive slope: y increases as x increases.
- Negative slope: y decreases as x increases.
- Zero slope: y remains constant as x increases.
- A line that slopes upward as you move to the right has a positive slope; a line that slopes downward as you move to the right has a negative slope. A horizontal (flat) line has a slope of 0.

☐ **I KNOW THIS** ☐ **I NEED TO REVIEW THIS**

The simplest line is $y = x$. For every point on this line, the y-coordinate equals the x-coordinate. Notice that for every point above the line, $y > x$; for every point below the line, $y < x$.

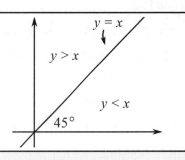

☐ **I KNOW THIS** ☐ **I NEED TO REVIEW THIS**

A horizontal line takes the form $y = k$, where k is some number. Notice that the equation of the x-axis is $y = 0$. A vertical line takes the form $x = k$, where k is some number. Notice that the equation of the y-axis is $x = 0$.

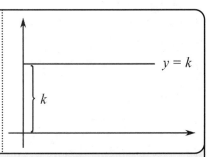

☐ **I KNOW THIS** ☐ **I NEED TO REVIEW THIS**

The **x-intercept** of a line is where the line intersects the x-axis. In other words, at the x-intercept of a line, y equals 0. The y-intercept of a line is where the line intersects the y-axis. At the y-intercept of a line, x equals 0.

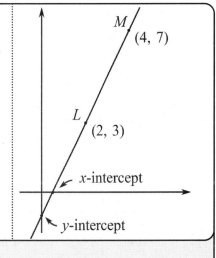

☐ **I KNOW THIS** ☐ **I NEED TO REVIEW THIS**

CG16

The easiest way to determine the *x*-intercept of a line is to substitute 0 for *y* and solve for *x*. To determine the *y*-intercept, substitute 0 for *x* and solve for *y*. In CG11, we calculated the equation of the line containing the points (2,3) and (4,7) as $y = 2x - 1$.

$y = 2x - 1$

$y = 2(0) - 1 = -1$

so the *y*-intercept is $(0, -1)$

$0 = 2x - 1; x = \dfrac{1}{2}$

so the *x*-intercept is $(\dfrac{1}{2}, 0)$.

☐ **I KNOW THIS** ☐ **I NEED TO REVIEW THIS**

CG17

Two lines are parallel if their slopes are equal. To determine whether two lines are parallel, you need only compare their slopes; their *y*-intercepts do not matter.

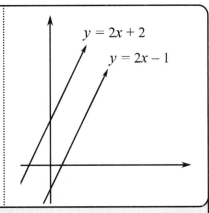

$y = 2x + 2$

$y = 2x - 1$

☐ **I KNOW THIS** ☐ **I NEED TO REVIEW THIS**

CG18

Two lines are perpendicular if their slopes are negative reciprocals. Notice that the product of the slopes of two perpendicular lines is always –1. To determine whether two lines are perpendicular, you need only compare their slopes; their *y*-intercepts do not matter.

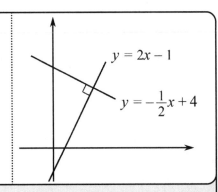

$y = 2x - 1$

$y = -\dfrac{1}{2}x + 4$

☐ **I KNOW THIS** ☐ **I NEED TO REVIEW THIS**

CG19

Linear equations (lines) are characterized by x raised to the first power (or to the **first degree**). You may be required to identify features of graphs of equations involving x raised to the power of 2 (quadratics) or greater. For example, the **roots** (sometimes referred to as the **zeroes**) of an equation are where that graph intersects the x-axis (in other words, where the y-value equals zero; in other words, where the function equals zero). Or you might be asked to identify for what values of x a particular function takes on the value of, say, 2 (in other words, where the y-values of the equation equal 2). Don't let these problems intimidate you. Just remember that $f(x)$ is the same thing as y, and that you need to read the problem carefully.

☐ **I KNOW THIS**   ☐ **I NEED TO REVIEW THIS**

CG20

If you're asked to identify an equation of degree greater than 2, just substitute some simple values for x and y—the numbers 0 and 1 are always excellent places to start—and then sketch a quick graph connecting the resulting points.

☐ **I KNOW THIS**   ☐ **I NEED TO REVIEW THIS**

Another question you might be asked about graphs is the **domain** (all possible x values) and **range** (all possible y values). For the equation $y = 2x^2$, the domain is all values of x. The range, however is limited to non-negative values only (since x^2 can not be negative).

☐ **I KNOW THIS** ☐ **I NEED TO REVIEW THIS**

A problem may involve the **transformation** of a figure or of the graph of a function. Three types of transformations appear on the SAT Math Test: **rotations**, **reflections**, and **translations**. These transformations do not change the shape of the original figure or graph, they merely shift it.

☐ **I KNOW THIS** ☐ **I NEED TO REVIEW THIS**

Rotations on the SAT Math Test apply to figures only. The easiest way to view the rotation of a figure is to imagine that one point in the figure is "pinned" to the coordinate graph and then the figure is rotated a certain amount, usually 90° (a quarter circle), or 180° (half a circle). Make sure you keep straight the difference between rotating *clockwise* or *counterclockwise*. In the figure shown, $\triangle ABC$ is rotated 90° clockwise about point C.

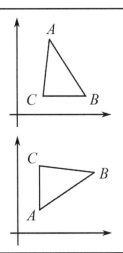

☐ **I KNOW THIS** ☐ **I NEED TO REVIEW THIS**

Reflections on the SAT Math Test apply to figures only. A figure is reflected *across* a line, such as the *x*-axis, or the *y*-axis, or the line $y = x$, or the line $x = 2$. Think of the reflection line (sometimes called the *axis of symmetry*) as a mirror (hence the term, reflection). When reflected, every point in the original figure remains the same perpendicular distance from the reflection line after the figure gets reflected. Reflections can be difficult to visualize, so pick two reference points on the original figure—the point closest to the reflection line and the point farthest away—and *map* those points to the opposite side of the reflection line, maintaining the same perpendicular distance. As usual, it's easier to illustrate this concept than to define and describe it.

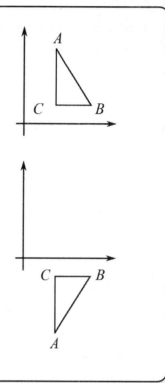

☐ **I KNOW THIS**   ☐ **I NEED TO REVIEW THIS**

Translations on the SAT apply to graphs of functions only. Translations shift a graph up or down, or left or right. Translations can get tricky, and at most you will find a single example on the SAT, so the following brief explanation will have to suffice. Once again, it is far easier to illustrate than to describe. With that in mind, the graph of $y = f(x)$ will shift up k units when translated $y = f(x) + k$. Vertical translation behaves as you might expect, since we're adding k to y. Horizontal translation defies our initial expectations, however: the graph of $y = f(x)$ will shift to the left k units when translated $y = f(x + k)$. I don't want to make a big deal of this topic. If you get stuck on this type of question, choose a couple of reference points (as always on coordinate graphs, letting x and y equal 0 and 1 is a good starting point) and plot the new, translated function to see how the original graph shifts.

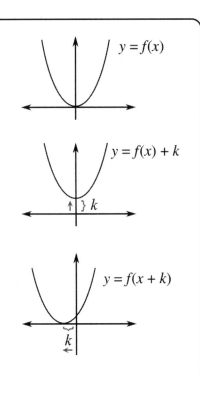

☐ **I KNOW THIS**   ☐ **I NEED TO REVIEW THIS**

Now that you've read through the concepts quickly, return to those concepts that you checked for further review. Remember that all these concepts will be reinforced in the explanations of the illustrative problems.

Apply What You've Learned to Our Practice Geometry Problems

That completes our survey of *all* the geometry you need for the SAT Math Test. Trust me: you will not encounter a geometry problem on the SAT that requires a concept or combination of concepts other than those we have covered here.

Don't be intimidated. The SAT Math Test measures how well you reason with basic concepts, not advanced ones. **Don't let a complicated-looking problem fake you out: if you** *think* **a geometry problem on the SAT calls for more advanced concepts or formulas than those we covered in this chapter—you've missed the point of the question.**

> **Generally speaking, the square, rectangle, and triangle are the only figures you need to be familiar with on the SAT Math Test. Any "weird" or complicated figures can be broken down into the sums or differences of those three basic figures.**

You'll find our latest examples of SAT geometry problems at RocketReview.com. These printable questions will give you all the geometry practice you need.

Refresher of Miscellaneous SAT Math Topics

A Grab Bag of Topics

Most of the math questions on the SAT fall into one of the three categories that we've already discussed: arithmetic, geometry, or algebra. Your SAT Math Test will also include some problems that cannot be neatly classified under a single heading. Here are the major topics:

- Sets
- Tables and graphs
- Counting
- Combinations
- Probability
- Patterns (series and sequences)
- Visualizing objects
- Logic

These disparate* topics may seem completely unrelated, but there are common denominators. Counting, for example, forms the basis of combinations, probability, and patterns. Although some problems in these areas can be quite difficult on the SAT, I assure you that all of these topics are so elementary that you probably encountered them in junior high school.

*GSWLIU

Ready? Our Refresher of Miscellaneous SAT Math Topics Is about to Begin

Any problems with these topics can be solved without formulas. Casual sloppiness is the real danger here. **But if you are *organized* and painstaking about searching for and listing things (numbers, pairings, patterns) and visualizing and inspecting things (tables, graphs, objects, diagrams), you will have no major trouble with these questions.**

SETS

S1

A **set** is just a group of **elements.** A set is usually identified by a capital letter. The elements of a set are called its **members**. A set's members can be listed individually, or by a rule or group of rules that qualifies the elements. Sets B and C are **subsets** of Set E; Set E is a subset of Set F. All the members of a subset are members of the larger set.

Set $A = \{-2, -1, 0, 1, 2\}$
Set $B = \{\text{odd integers}\}$
Set $C = \{\text{even integers}\}$
Set $D = \{\text{prime numbers} < 10\}$
Set $E = \{\text{integers}\}$
Set $F = \{\text{numbers}\}$

☐ I KNOW THIS ☐ I NEED TO REVIEW THIS

S2

The SAT Math Test may use the formal notation for describing a set. Don't let this notation throw you.

(Referring to the sets above)
Set $B = \{x: x \text{ is an odd integer}\}$
(means the same thing as)
Set $B = \{\text{odd integers}\}$

☐ I KNOW THIS ☐ I NEED TO REVIEW THIS

S3

The **union** of two sets is another set containing all the members—and only the members—of the given sets. The symbol for union is ∪, just like the letter "u" for union. The **intersection** of two sets is another set containing only those members the given sets have in common. The symbol for intersection is ∩, an upside-down version of the union sign.

(Referring to the sets in S1)

$A \cup B = \{-1, 1\}$
$B \cup C = \{\text{all integers}\}$
$B \cap D = \{3, 5, 7\}$
$C \cap D = \{2\}$

☐ I KNOW THIS ☐ I NEED TO REVIEW THIS

S4

If two sets have no members in common, the intersection of those sets is called the **null (empty) set**. The symbol for null set is $\varnothing$. **The null set does *not* equal zero, though its symbol resembles one.**

(Referring to the sets in S1)

$$B \cap C = \{\varnothing\}$$

☐ I KNOW THIS ☐ I NEED TO REVIEW THIS

S5

Think of union and intersection as operations, so if a sequence of union or intersection operations is applied, perform the operations within any parentheses first.

(Referring to the sets in S1)

$$A \cap (C \cap D) = \{2\}$$

☐ I KNOW THIS ☐ I NEED TO REVIEW THIS

S6

A set is said to be **closed under an operation** if the result of any two elements under that operation is also a member of that set. The set of even integers is closed under multiplication, for example, because the product of any two even integers is another even integer. The set of even integers is also closed under subtraction and addition. The set of even integers is *not* closed, however, under division, since the quotient of two even integers could be a fraction or an odd integer.

☐ I KNOW THIS ☐ I NEED TO REVIEW THIS

568

One way of analyzing sets is to use a **Venn diagram**. Venn diagrams use circles to indicate different sets. The overlap, if any, between circles indicates those members that belong to both sets. Two circles that do not touch have no members in common. A circle within another circle indicates a subset of the larger circle. By the way, there is nothing sacred about circles with Venn diagrams, they're simply easy to draw.

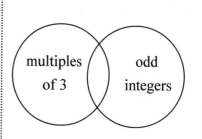

I KNOW THIS   I NEED TO REVIEW THIS

Let's say Circle *J* indicates students at Jackson High School. Circle *F* indicates Jackson students who take French, Circle *S* indicates Jackson students who study Spanish. The overlap indicates Jackson students who take both French and Spanish. Jackson students who take neither French nor Spanish are outside Circles *F* and *S* but within Circle *J.* Anyone who does not attend Jackson is outside Circle *J.* We could add other circles to the diagram, such as Circle *L* for those Jackson students, if any, who take Latin.

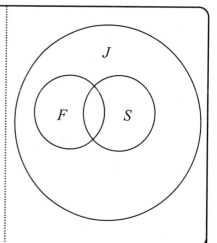

I KNOW THIS   I NEED TO REVIEW THIS

The big error on Venn diagram problems is either overlooking the presence, or assuming the absence, of the word "only." If a problem states that 80 language students at Jackson study Spanish, for example, you cannot assume these 80 students study *only* Spanish. Indeed, every language student who studies Spanish at Jackson might also study French and Latin. Similarly, if a problem states that 20 language students at Jackson study Latin only, there might be 40 *other* language students at Jackson who study Latin and French or Latin and Spanish. If a problem states that 100 language students at Jackson study Spanish, 100 study French, and 100 study Latin—it's possible that there are a total of 100 language students at Jackson, and each one studies French, Spanish, and Latin.

Notice the differences in the following pairs of statements about Jackson High School:

- 80 language students study only Spanish
    (versus)
- 80 language students study Spanish

or

- 40 language students study both French and Spanish
    (versus)
- 40 language students study French or Spanish

☐ **I KNOW THIS**   ☐ **I NEED TO REVIEW THIS**

TABLES AND GRAPHS

TG1

You may encounter a problem on the SAT Math Test involving a table or a graph. There are too many possible variations of these questions to list them all, but these questions are rarely difficult. **The big error on these questions is failing to read the captions (explanatory information) of the table or graph closely enough, or failing to notice the relationship between diagrams when more than one is provided. Be _especially_ careful about units.** You'll find sample table and graph questions among the illustrative miscellaneous SAT math problems at the RocketReview website.

☐ **I KNOW THIS**   ☐ **I NEED TO REVIEW THIS**

COUNTING

C1

Questions involving counting objects or events are among the 11 Most Common SAT Problems of All Time. You've known how to count since you were three, so counting problems are easy to take for granted. **Watch your step: Counting problems are among the _most_ dangerous killer rabbit questions on the SAT Math Test. Any easy, obvious, popular-looking choice is almost certainly wrong, even on a medium counting problem—and _absolutely_ wrong on a difficult counting problem.**

☐ **I KNOW THIS**   ☐ **I NEED TO REVIEW THIS**

Yes, it's easy to count—and it's easy to *miscount,* too. The two ways of miscounting are caused by overlooking a possible event (undercounting), or by counting the same event more than once (overcounting). Never, *ever* do a counting question in your head using some not-so-clever shortcut. **Always write the entire list of things out, or at least enough of the list to be absolutely sure you understand how you *might* have miscounted on the question. Be especially careful with any counting problem on the open-ended (grid-in) section because you won't have any choices to alert you if you're off base.**

A car odometer indicates that the car has been driven 955 miles. What is the least number of additional miles that the car must travel before two of the odometer digits are again the same?

(If you got 11 as the answer, you were reckless and failed to take pains. The answer is 4.)

☐ **I KNOW THIS** ☐ **I NEED TO REVIEW THIS**

Two important words on counting problems are **distinct** and **inclusive**. Distinct means different or unique. The word "banana" has six letters, but only three *distinct* letters (*a, b,* and *n*). Inclusive means including. There is one integer between the numbers 1 and 3, but there are three integers between 1 and 3 *inclusive.*

The number 15 has four positive factors: 1, 3, 5, and 15.

The number 6 has four positive factors: 1, 2, 3, and 6.

The numbers 6 and 15 have six *distinct* positive factors: 1, 2, 3, 5, 6, and 15.

☐ **I KNOW THIS** ☐ **I NEED TO REVIEW THIS**

COMBINATIONS

CO1

Combination problems are similar to counting problems. Here you determine—count—how many different ways two or more things can happen together.

☐ I KNOW THIS   ☐ I NEED TO REVIEW THIS

CO2

If you've studied elementary probability in school, you probably came across the distinction between *combination* and *permutation*. These words are not used on the SAT, but it's important that you understand the distinction: With combinations, the order of the items does not matter, with permutations it does. **By the way, if you've learned factorial formulas for calculating combinations and permutations, I strongly advise you to *avoid* using these factorial formulas.** Instead, either list the possible combinations, or apply the logic behind the factorial formulas. I'll show you how to do that shortly.

Let's say we wanted to find out how many different ways two co-captains could be selected from among team members Paula, Robert, Sara, Tom, and Ula. Here Paula-Robert is the same as Robert-Paula; order does not matter. If we were selecting a captain and a manager, however, then Paula-Robert is not the same as Robert-Paula—now order matters.

☐ I KNOW THIS   ☐ I NEED TO REVIEW THIS

The logic behind the factorial formulas for combinations and permutations is easy to understand. The basic rule—we'll modify it shortly—is simply to multiply the number of elements of each type of item to be combined. For the sample question to the right, if you listed each of the meals (you could call them *A*, *B*, and *C*) and each of the appetizers (you could call them 1, 2, 3, and 4), you would find a total of 12 different combinations: A1, A2, A3, A4; B1, B2, B3, B4; C1, C2, C3, C4.

Let's say that a certain restaurant offered 3 main courses and 4 appetizers. How many different meals of one appetizer and one main course can the restaurant serve?

(For each main course, there are 4 appetizers, making a total of 3 times 4, or 12 different meals.)

☐ **I KNOW THIS** ☐ **I NEED TO REVIEW THIS**

Okay, now we're going to modify the basic multiplication rule for determining combinations so we avoid double-counting. Instead of calculating combinations by picking one item from one group and one item from another group, say, let's see what happens to the combination count when we want to select two items from the same group. **Again, if the logic here of multiplying elements is confusing, you can always list the possible combinations individually—for a small number of elements, listing will not take much time. If you list the combinations, do so in an orderly fashion so you don't overlook some possibilities.** Choose one element and list every combination with that element. Then repeat the process with the next element, and so on.

Let's say a clothing store offers 5 different shirts on sale and customers can pick any two different shirts for the price of one. To calculate the number of possible combinations, notice that customers can choose one of 5 possible shirts for their first selection, but then only one of 4 remaining shirts for their second selection. So here the number of combinations is 5 times 4, or 20.

☐ **I KNOW THIS** ☐ **I NEED TO REVIEW THIS**

If you're dealing with a combination problem on which order matters (a permutation), you will have to multiply the combination count by the number of ways any combination can be reordered. That procedure sounds complicated, but the example at right should make it clear. Notice the difference in the two variations. **Again, if you get stuck on problems like these, listing all the possible combinations will solve the problem.** The two drawbacks to listing combinations is that doing so can take a bit of time, and there is always the danger that you will miscount the possibilities by overlooking some or double-counting others.

How many different ways can we select 2 people from among 5 possible candidates?

(We have 5 possibilities for the first selection, and then 4 remaining for the second, so there are 5 times 4, or 20 combinations.)

How many different ways can 2 persons finish first and second in a 5-person race?

(This problem is exactly the same as the previous problem, only now order matters. So for each of the 20 combinations we found above, each "pair" has two different arrangements. We have twice as many permutations, then, or 40.)

☐ **I KNOW THIS** ☐ **I NEED TO REVIEW THIS**

PROBABILITY

PR1

The probability of an event's occurring is measured on a scale of 0 (definitely *won't* happen) to 1 (definitely *will* happen). **Notice that the probability of any event's occurring cannot be more than 1. Notice also that probability has much in common with combinations and counting: all three concepts involve counting things or events or possibilities. Just about every probability problem can be solved by listing possibilities, so do not be intimidated by formulas.**

Probability of $x = P(x) =$

$$\frac{\text{Number of desired events}}{\text{Number of possible events}}$$

If a jar contains 2 blue marbles and 4 red marbles, the probability of choosing a blue marble is 2 (the number of desired events) out of 6 (the number of possible events), or $\frac{1}{3}$.

☐ **I KNOW THIS** ☐ **I NEED TO REVIEW THIS**

PR2

The probability of an event's *not* occurring is 1 minus the probability of the event's occurring. If the probability of choosing a blue marble from a jar is $\frac{1}{3}$, then the probability of not choosing a blue marble is $\frac{2}{3}$.

$P(\text{not } x) = 1 - P(x)$

☐ **I KNOW THIS** ☐ **I NEED TO REVIEW THIS**

Probability can be expressed geometrically. If we were throwing a dart at the dartboard shown here, we could calculate the probability that a dart that hit the dartboard landed in the shaded inner region by comparing the relative areas of the shaded region to the total area of the dartboard. The probability that a hit was a bull's-eye is the area of the bull's-eye over the total area of the dartboard.

The radius of the bull's-eye is 1 and the radius of the dartboard is 4. So the probability that a hit will be a bull's-eye is $\frac{\pi r^2}{\pi R^2}$ or $\frac{1}{16}$.

☐ **I KNOW THIS**   ☐ **I NEED TO REVIEW THIS**

Probability questions on the SAT usually involve multiple events. **The basic rule is that the probability of Event *A and* Event *B* is the *product of their individual probabilities.*** This rule assumes that the two events are unconnected, which is almost always the case on the SAT.

The probability of getting a heads on a fair toss of a coin is $\frac{1}{2}$. The probability of getting heads on the first toss *and* heads on the second toss is $\frac{1}{2}$ times $\frac{1}{2}$ or $\frac{1}{4}$. You can arrive at this probability as easily by listing the possible events: HH, HT, TH, TT.

☐ **I KNOW THIS**   ☐ **I NEED TO REVIEW THIS**

Be careful if one event changes the probability of the next event. Notice in this example that the number of red marbles changed on the second draw—*and* the total number of marbles changed. The probability of drawing a red marble on the first try and a red marble on the second try is $\frac{2}{5}$ times $\frac{1}{3}$, or $\frac{2}{15}$. Notice that the probability of drawing a red marble on the first try and a blue marble on the second try is $\frac{2}{5}$ times $\frac{2}{3}$, or $\frac{4}{15}$.

Assume an urn has 4 red marbles and 6 blue marbles. The probability of drawing a red marble is $\frac{4}{10}$ or $\frac{2}{5}$ on the first draw. But if we've drawn a red marble on the first draw, the probability of pulling a red marble on the second draw drops to $\frac{3}{9}$ or $\frac{1}{3}$.

☐ **I KNOW THIS** ☐ **I NEED TO REVIEW THIS**

The probability that Event *A or* Event *B* will occur is determined by adding the number of Event *A*s and event *B*s, and dividing by the total number of possible events. Watch out: This calculation is *not* necessarily equivalent to adding their respective probabilities. Notice that if we incorrectly added the two respective probabilities of drawing a red marble, we'd get $\frac{2}{5}$ plus $\frac{4}{5}$, or $\frac{6}{5}$ but the probability can never be greater than one. **Sometimes the easiest way to compute "*or*" probabilities is to calculate the probability of both events *not* happening—an "*and*" probability—and then subtract the result from one.**

This probability concept is as difficult as any you will ever encounter on the SAT Math Test; most probability problems are more straightforward.

Urn *A* has 2 red marbles and 3 blue marbles; Urn *B* has 4 red marbles and 1 blue marble. The probability of drawing a red marble from *A and* a red marble from *B* is $\frac{2}{5}$ times $\frac{4}{5}$ or $\frac{8}{25}$. The easiest way to calculate the probability of drawing a red marble from *A or B* is to consider the probability of *not* drawing a red marble from *A and* not drawing a red marble from *B* (which is $\frac{3}{5}$ times $\frac{1}{5}$, or $\frac{3}{25}$). The probability of drawing a red marble from *A or* from *B* is 1 minus $\frac{3}{25}$, or $\frac{22}{25}$.

☐ **I KNOW THIS** ☐ **I NEED TO REVIEW THIS**

PATTERNS (SERIES AND SEQUENCES)

PA1

A group of numbers that come one after the other according to some rule is a **series**. The numbers 4, 5, 6, 7, and 8 form a series of five consecutive integers. The two primary types of series that appear on the SAT Math Test are **arithmetic** and **geometric**. An arithmetic series is one that increases (or decreases) by a set amount each time. In other words, the *difference* between any two consecutive numbers in an arithmetic series is constant. A geometric series is one that increases (or decreases) by a constant multiple. In other words, the *ratio* between any two consecutive numbers in a geometric series is constant. (Geometric series are sometimes referred to as *exponential* series.)

Arithmetic Series

2, 4, 6, 8, 10: Notice that
$(4 - 2) = (6 - 4) = (8 - 6) = (10 - 8)$

20, 14, 8, 2: Notice that
$(20 - 14) = (14 - 8) = (8 - 2)$

Geometric Series

2, 4, 8, 16, 32: Notice that
$(4 \div 2) = (8 \div 4) = (16 \div 8) = (32 \div 16)$

9, 3, 1, $\frac{1}{3}$: Notice that
$(9 \div 3) = (3 \div 1) = (1 \div \frac{1}{3})$

☐ **I KNOW THIS** ☐ **I NEED TO REVIEW THIS**

The two main types of series questions ask either for the sum of an arithmetic series, or for the nth term of an arithmetic or geometric series. Unlike our simple examples above, a series on the SAT Math Test may have 100 terms or more, but the basic principle is the same. (For an example of how tricky a series question can be, see the second question from Experience Set 2 on page 356.)

Although you may have learned formulas in your algebra II class for determining these series calculations, these formulas are unnecessary on the SAT. I strongly recommend that you work out such problems without blindly relying on a formula. **The trick for both these question types—finding the sum of a series or computing a particular term— is to write out as much of the series as necessary so that you can "predict" what will happen with the rest of the series. The big danger here is miscounting.** The illustrative question to the right is as hard a series question as you're likely to encounter on the SAT, but if you sketch things out, it isn't too bad.

If the sum of twenty consecutive integers is 550, what is the sum of the next twenty consecutive integers?

(The 21st term—the first term in the second group—is 20 more than the 1st term. The 22nd term is 20 more than the 2nd term, and so on. Each term of the second group is 20 more than its "twin" in the first group. So the sum of the second group is 20 times 20, or 400, more than sum of the first group, or 950.)

☐ **I KNOW THIS** ☐ **I NEED TO REVIEW THIS**

A **sequence** is a small group of things—digits, letters, colors—that repeats itself. Once you identify the rule that creates the pattern, you can predict what the pattern will be in the future.

1, 4, 9, 6, 5, 1, 4, 9, 6, 5 . . .
r, y, b, g, r, y, b, g . . .

☐ **I KNOW THIS** ☐ **I NEED TO REVIEW THIS**

A hard sequence question will not give you the sequence explicitly, as in the previous examples. Instead, you will have to calculate the sequence. **As I said before regarding series, beware of using your calculator for lengthy sequence questions.** Using your calculator for the first few terms is okay, but if you think you need your calculator beyond that on a sequence question, you're missing the point of the problem.

What is the sequence of units' digits of 3^n?

$3^0 = (1)$, $3^1 = (3)$, $3^2 = (9)$, $3^3 = 2(7)$, $3^4 = 8(1)$, $3^5 = 24(3)$ . . . , which is far enough for us to see that the sequence of units' digits 1, 3, 9, 7 repeats.

A popular SAT math problem is a sequence question that asks for the nth term. **The trick is to divide n by the number of terms in a group that repeat—4, 5, whatever—and calculate the remainder. Then** *count* **the remainder into a new group and you've found the nth term.** If you get confused, remember that the term of the last item in the group will always be a multiple of the number of items in the group.

If the five digits 4, 1, 3, 2, 6 repeat indefinitely, notice that since the last term is a 6; the 5th term is a 6, so:

- the 10th term will be a 6
- the 15th term will be a 6
- the 50th term will be a 6
- the 500th term will be a 6
- the $1,045^{th}$ term will be a 6

VISUALIZING OBJECTS

V1

You may encounter a problem on the SAT Math Test that asks you to describe what will happen when an object (possibly not depicted) is changed in some way. For example, a problem might ask what number is on the top of a circular clock if the clock is rotated one-quarter turn clockwise and then flipped over. These problems are rarely difficult. **If you get stuck on one of these problems that does not provide a diagram, either draw a diagram or look around the room for an object—a desk, a bookcase, whatever—that will help you visualize what is being described in the question.**

☐ **I KNOW THIS**   ☐ **I NEED TO REVIEW THIS**

LOGIC

L1

You may encounter a problem on the SAT Math Test that requires simple logical reasoning. These problems are rarely difficult, and do not involve any formal terms used in traditional logic courses.

You'll find logic problems among the illustrative miscellaneous SAT math problems at the RocketReview website.

☐ **I KNOW THIS**   ☐ **I NEED TO REVIEW THIS**

> Now that you've read through the concepts quickly, return to those concepts that you checked for further review. Remember that all these concepts will be reinforced in the online illustrative problems.

Apply What You've Learned to Our Practice Miscellaneous Problems

That completes our survey of the major miscellaneous topics you need for the SAT Math Test. If you've completed the other refresher chapters and the math techniques chapters, you're now ready to move on to the Top 11 SAT Problems of All Time.

> The four refresher chapters on arithmetic, algebra, geometry, and miscellaneous math topics cover every major concept ever to appear on an SAT Math Test, but with the new SAT, you should be ready for a surprise or two—and I mean *at most* two surprises out of the 52 total questions. If you apply what you've learned here, especially our math moves, you should be able to handle any question the test writers throw your way.

You'll find our latest examples of miscellaneous SAT math problems at RocketReview.com. These printable problems will give you all the practice you need on miscellaneous math topics.

The Top 11 Problems of All Time
(Six or More Will Show Up on *Your* SAT)

You Can't Teach an Old Test New Tricks

The SAT Math Test has been revised a lot this year, but certain things won't change. The test writers like to maintain consistency from year to year so that a 600 on the SAT Math Test in 2005 "means the same" as a 600 on the SAT Math Test from 2004.

But this very consistency contributes to a self-referential weakness: the test writers consider a "good" SAT question to be one that predicts how well you'll do on *other* SAT questions. The "best" SAT math questions (from the test writers' point of view) are the most predictive.

As it turns out, certain specific types of math questions do a much better job of predicting than do others—and that's great news for us. In other words, the most *predictive* SAT math questions (good for the test writers) also happen to be the most *predictable* ones (great for you).

Creating RocketReview's Math Hall of Fame

In a way similar to the method I used to compile our Power Rankings for vocabulary words (page 303), I compiled those math problems that occurred the most frequently *and* that tripped students up most frequently. The more frequently a problem type occurred on past SATs, and the more trouble that problem type gave students, the higher the problem rose in the Hall of Fame rankings.

I had to leave emotion out of the selection process to keep the list at just eleven problems. I have to admit that I'm fond of certain types of SAT math problems, but if they didn't make the cut, they weren't inducted into the Math Hall of Fame.

All the online illustrative problems—algebra, geometry, arithmetic, and miscellaneous—were in the running for the Hall of Fame. When you add the illustrative problems to the eleven here, you will be familiar with the top fifty-odd problems ever to appear on the SAT Math Test. **As always, you do *not* need to memorize these problems.** Once you've worked through them and understand the *logic* behind the solutions, you'll remember how to solve the problems naturally.

Seek Out Hall of Fame Problems—
Especially When Time Runs Short

All of the Hall of Fame problems are medium to difficult, meaning that they will appear in the second half of a math section, if not among the very last few questions. **Once you learn how to solve these problems, most can be solved very, very quickly indeed. The counting and combination questions are notable exceptions, so keep an eye out for them.** As we discussed in Experience Set 6 (page 430), you should solve familiar math questions before unfamiliar ones, especially as time begins to run short.

As an example, the #1 and #3 ranked math problems can usually be solved in less than fifteen seconds—once you know how to solve them. These two problems, however, often show up among the very last questions in a section. You don't want to get bogged down in a bunch of time-consuming questions towards the end of a section and overlook some questions that could be solved in a snap.

So at the start of each section, quickly glance at the last six or seven questions to see how many problem types you recognize—you'll want to be sure you answer these, even if that means sacrificing other, more time-consuming, questions. Just scan through the difficult questions and make a mental note to leave enough time to answer any Hall of Fame problems before you get too bogged down in the section.

Be Sure You Read the Solution Notes—
Even on the Problems You Solved Here Correctly

I strongly recommend—if you were in front of me, as your SAT coach I'd insist—that you work through each type of problem one at time, reviewing the solution notes carefully. **It's not enough that you answer these questions correctly—you've also got to solve them the best way.**

I'll outline the ideal solutions for each of the eleven problem types, and point out any potential pitfalls. Read the solution notes carefully, but don't try to memorize them. Then, when you're finally familiar with all the intricacies* and nuances* of one problem type, you can move on to the next problem type. If you have a fair amount of time before the SAT—say, more than two months—I'd tackle one problem type each week before moving on to the next. Distributing your learning in this way will allow you more time to master each problem type in an unhurried way, and to allow the solution methods to sink in fully.

*GSWLIU

> Before attempting any problems in this section, I strongly recommend that you briefly review Experience Set 3 (beginning on page 368) and Experience Set 4 (page 390). Whenever possible, use our math moves to answer questions.

Will These Rankings Change?

Probably not much, if at all. I analyzed every SAT Math Test released over the past twenty years, not to mention dozens of PSATs—over 100 SATs in all. For the new material on the SATs, I extrapolated* from what I know about the math Ic and IIc subject SATs. From year to year certain question types go in and out of favor, and certain trends become apparent. For example, as students have increasingly prepared for the SAT over the past two decades, it's clear that some math problems that used to appear frequently no longer do so.

The most important trend that concerns you is the growing importance of problem types that require taking pains to get right. Two of the top eleven math problems involve counting or combinations (as you know, a variation of counting)—yet these problems were rare even ten years ago. Compared with other SAT math questions, counting and combination problems require enormous pains to get right, which explains why they have become increasingly important on SATs. **The ability to take pains while solving math problems is one of the last remaining traits that distinguish the highest scoring SAT math students from everyone else.** Ten years ago it was enough to be a strong test taker to achieve a super-high SAT math score—now you have to be a strong test taker *and* be willing to take pains. That's why we devoted two entire experience sets (2 and 3) to error-catching and error-avoidance.

*GSWLIU

It's possible that the test writers will release new information after this book goes to press that will require updating these rankings, but the rankings won't change significantly. The problems here will remain highly ranked, but another problem type or two may join them in the Hall of Fame. **As with any breaking news about the SAT, stay tuned at RocketReview.com.**

Uh, No, You Won't Find *Exactly* These Problems on Your SAT— but You *Will* Find Close Variations of Them

The following eleven problems are paradigms* that exemplify* the important themes you'll need to recognize when you encounter an example of the problem on your SAT. When a problem here can appear in different guises, I've also included archetypes* of each variation.

*GSWLIU

Before You Begin

Keep the following points in mind as you work through the problems illustrated:

- All of the questions in this section are medium to very difficult. Take pains to get them right.

- Avoid popular-looking choices.

- I strongly recommend that you solve a problem and read its solution *before* moving on to the next problem, so you can apply what you've just learned. Of course, try not to peek ahead at the solution to the next problem.

SAT Math Hall of Fame Problem #11:
Percentage Change Questions

Introduction: Percentage change problems often trap unwary students, so watch out—these questions are often killer rabbits.

> Swapping numbers is the math move of choice on percentage change questions—10 and 100 are great numbers here. Avoid popular-looking choices on hard percentage change questions—but remember that the answer will not be too far off from the most popular choice.

Archetypes: The following difficult problems illustrate the major themes and variations you need to be familiar with on percentage change problems. Before attempting these questions, you may want to review our earlier discussion of percents in the arithmetic refresher beginning on page 473.

1. The radius of a circle is increased by 10 percent. By what percent is the area increased?

   (A)   1%
   (B)   10%
   (C)   20%
   (D)   21%
   (E)   100%

2. If p is 50 percent greater than m and q is 60 percent greater than n, then pq is what percent greater than mn ?

   (A)   55%
   (B)   110%
   (C)   140%
   (D)   210%
   (E)   240%

3. The price of a book is p dollars after a 20 percent discount. What was the initial price of the book?

    (A) 5.00p
    (B) 1.25p
    (C) 1.20p
    (D) 0.80p
    (E) 0.75p

SAT Math Hall of Fame Problem #10:
Pythagorean Theorem (Special Cases) Questions

Introduction: Some applications of the Pythagorean relationship appear so frequently on SATs that you should be familiar with their peculiarities. These problems include the 30:60:90 and 45:45:90 triangles, shared hypotenuses, and the Pythagorean relationship in three dimensions.

> As I mentioned earlier regarding SAT geometry questions, always try estimating the answer *before* attempting a laborious mathematical solution. If a problem does not provide a figure, draw a diagram.

Archetypes: The following questions, arranged from medium-difficult to very difficult, illustrate the major themes and variations you need to be familiar with on Pythagorean relationship problems. Before attempting these questions, you may want to review our earlier discussion of the Pythagorean relationship in the geometry refresher beginning on page 525.

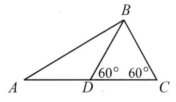

1. In the figure above, $AD = BD = 4$. What is the value of AB ?

    (A) $2\sqrt{3}$ (approximately 3.46)
    (B) 4
    (C) $4\sqrt{2}$ (approximately 5.66)
    (D) $4\sqrt{3}$ (approximately 6.93)
    (E) 8

Note: Figure not drawn to scale.

2. What is the radius of the circle above?

    (A) $\sqrt{2}$ (approximately 1.41)
    (B) 2
    (C) $2\sqrt{2}$ (approximately 2.82)
    (D) 4
    (E) It cannot be determined from the information given.

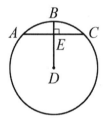

3. In the figure above, the circle with center D has a radius 5. If $BE = 1$, then $AC =$

    (A) $2\sqrt{26}$ (approximately 10.20)
    (B) 9
    (C) 8
    (D) 6
    (E) $\sqrt{26}$ (approximately 5.10)

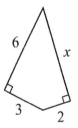

4. In the figure above, $x =$

    (A) $\sqrt{33}$ (approximately 5.74)
    (B) $\sqrt{35}$ (approximately 5.92)
    (C) $\sqrt{41}$ (approximately 6.40)
    (D) 7
    (E) 8

5.   The pyramid above has a square base and four
      identical triangular faces. The edge of each base
      is 2 and the height of the pyramid is 3. What is
      the length of PQ ?

      (A) $\sqrt{11}$ (approximately 3.32)
      (B) $\sqrt{13}$ (approximately 3.61)
      (C) $\sqrt{15}$ (approximately 3.87)
      (D) $\sqrt{17}$ (approximately 4.11)
      (E) 5

SAT Math Hall of Fame Problem #9:
Coordinate Geometry (Slope) Questions

Introduction: Slope problems on the SAT often require you to go beyond the
mere mechanical application of slope formulas.

Don't let these problems bully you. Before immediately wondering
what formulas you might need on a question, try *thinking*
through the problem. If a problem does not provide a figure, draw
one—to scale—to help your thinking and possibly estimate the
solution.

As I've mentioned elsewhere, you should *always* try to estimate
the solution to geometry questions on the SAT—even on those
questions without choices—before working out any formulas.
Estimating the solution helps you *think* about the question, and
gives you a benchmark to judge whether or not your final solution
is *reasonable*.

To help you estimate the answer to slope questions, you should be
able to tell *at a glance* the difference between a positive and
negative slope. You should also be able to distinguish between a
slope greater than 1, a slope of 1 (as a benchmark), and fractional
slopes.

Archetypes: The following questions, arranged from difficult to very difficult, illustrate the major themes and variations you need to be familiar with on slope problems. Before attempting these questions, you may want to review our earlier discussion of coordinate geometry and slope in the geometry refresher beginning on page 553.

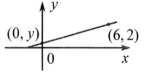

1. In the figure above, the slope of the line is $\frac{1}{4}$. What is the value of y?

    (A) 2

    (B) $\frac{3}{2}$

    (C) 1

    (D) $\frac{1}{2}$

    (E) $\frac{1}{4}$

2. Line ℓ has a slope of 4. If line ℓ contains the point (0, 1), then which of the following points could line ℓ also contain?

    (A) (0, 4)
    (B) (1, 5)
    (C) (2, 4)
    (D) (4, 1)
    (E) (4, 4)

3. Point A has coordinates (0, 0) and point B has coordinates (n, n) where $n > 1$. If point B is moved from its current location, which of the following coordinates would result in the <u>least</u> slope of $\overline{AB}$?

    (A) B $(n + 1, n)$
    (B) B $(n - 1, n)$
    (C) B $(n, n + 1)$
    (D) B $(n, n - 1)$
    (E) B $(n - 1, n - 1)$

$$\ell_1: \ y = ax + b$$
$$\ell_2: \ y = cx + d$$

4. Which of the following conditions ensure that lines ℓ_1 and ℓ_2 above have no points in common? (Assume that the two lines lie in the same plane.)

    (A) $a \neq c$ and $b \neq d$
    (B) $a \neq c$ and $b = d$
    (C) $a = c$ and $b \neq d$
    (D) $a > c$ and $b > d$
    (E) $a < c$ and $b < d$

SAT Math Hall of Fame Problem #8: Weighted Average Questions

Introduction: Once you know the basic approach to solving weighted average problems, you'll smile when you see them on the SAT.

> The key to solving weighted average problems is to find the *total* of the elements and then work from there. Remember that the weighted average of a set is *not* midway between the smallest and largest elements in the set—the weighted average *tilts* towards the "heavier" side, the one with more elements.

Archetypes: The following questions, arranged from medium-difficult to very difficult, illustrate the major themes and variations you need to be familiar with on weighted average problems. Before attempting these questions, you may want to review our earlier discussion of averages in the arithmetic refresher beginning on page 476.

1. The average (arithmetic mean) of p and q is 6 and the average of p, q, and r is 8. What is the value of r ?

    (A) 18
    (B) 14
    (C) 12
    (D) 10
    (E) 2

2.   On a history quiz, the average (arithmetic mean) score for 12 students was 40. If 2 students had an average score of 45, what was the average score for the remainder of the class?

(A) 35
(B) 36
(C) 37
(D) 38
(E) 39

3.   The average of a set of 4 numbers is 8. When one of the four numbers was removed from the set, the average increased by 1. What number was removed?

(A) 5
(B) 7
(C) 9
(D) 11
(E) 13

4.   A bicyclist rode from her home to her training center at an average speed of 20 kilometers per hour. She returned home along the same route at an average speed of 30 kilometers per hour. If her total travel time to and from the training center was one hour, what was the total distance of her commute in kilometers?

(A) 22
(B) 24
(C) 25
(D) 26
(E) 28

SAT Math Hall of Fame Problem #7:
Combination Questions

Introduction: We discussed combination questions in our refresher of miscellaneous math topics, so you know that these problems have a lot in common with counting questions, Hall of Fame Problem #4.

As I mentioned then, I urge you *not* to use any combination or permutation formulas you may have learned in math class. These formulas aren't necessary and are easy to *misapply*—what's worse, blindly relying on these formulas prevents you from *thinking* clearly about the question in front of you.

Just be methodical and painstaking—as always—about listing all the possibilities, and you'll be fine. Our WIBNI math move comes in handy here to simplify especially complicated problems: If too many combinations are possible to make a complete listing practical, list enough of the combinations so that you understand the basic logic behind the solution process and *then* use a formula.

Also, it's often possible to *estimate* the answer to a combination if you get stuck. The answer tends to be in the middle towards the higher range of choices.

Finally, be especially cautious about combination problems on the open-ended (grid-in) questions since you won't have choices to let you know whether you're on track or not.

Archetypes: The following two moderately difficult questions illustrate the major themes and variations you need to be familiar with on combination problems. Before attempting these questions, you may want to review our earlier discussion of combination problems under the miscellaneous math topics beginning on page 573.

1.   How many different committees of 3 people can be selected from a group of 5 people?

   (A)   10
   (B)   15
   (C)   25
   (D)   60
   (E) 120

2.   Five runners—*A, B, C, D,* and *E*—enter a race. In
how many different ways can the runners finish
the race if we know that either *A* or *B* finished
first? (Assume there are no ties.)

(A) 12
(B) 15
(C) 30
(D) 48
(E) 120

SAT Math Hall of Fame Problem #6:
Coordinate Geometry (Locating Points) Questions

Introduction: Locating coordinate point problems involve using what you
know about geometry to draw conclusions about points in the *xy*-coordinate
plane.

> Draw a diagram if one isn't provided, and try estimating the
> answer *before* attempting a laborious mathematical solution.

Archetypes: The following questions, arranged from medium-difficult to
difficult, illustrate the major themes and variations you need to be familiar
with on locating coordinate point problems. Before attempting these
questions, you may want to review our earlier discussion of coordinate
geometry in the geometry refresher beginning on page 553.

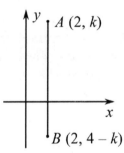

1. In the figure above, if $AB = 10$ then $k =$

   (A) 12
   (B) 10
   (C) 8
   (D) 7
   (E) 6

2. Which of the following points could be the center of a circle tangent to the x-axis and y-axis?

   (A) $P(-4, -2)$
   (B) $P(-4, 4)$
   (C) $P(0, -4)$
   (D) $P(2, -4)$
   (E) $P(2, 4)$

3. Isosceles triangle JKL is drawn on the coordinate plane so that K is on the x-axis, base JL is parallel to the y-axis, and $JK = KL$. If the coordinates of point J are $(-4, -3)$, what are the coordinates of point L?

   (A) $(-3, -4)$
   (B) $(-4, 3)$
   (C) $(-3, -4)$
   (D) $(4, -3)$
   (E) $(4, 3)$

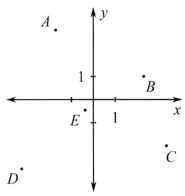

4. In the figure above, for which point is the product of its *x*- and *y*-coordinates greatest?

    (A) A
    (B) B
    (C) C
    (D) D
    (E) E

5. What is the area of the triangle created by the *x*-axis, the *y*-axis, and the line $y = 2x - 4$?

    (A) 1
    (B) 2
    (C) 4
    (D) 8
    (E) 16

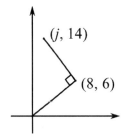

Note: Figure not drawn to scale.

6. In the figure above, what is the value of *j* ?

    (A) 0
    (B) 2
    (C) 4
    (D) 6
    (E) It cannot be determined from the information given.

SAT Math Hall of Fame Problem #5:
Triangles (Angle Relationship) Questions

Introduction: You know that a triangle contains 180 degrees, and other simple facts regarding angle relationships. Still, it's amazing how clever the test writers are at disguising simple concepts to trip up unwary students.

> **Beware: Do not rely on "rules" (which may or may not apply) to answer angle relationship questions. Work with all the information provided and *check things out*. Whenever possible, estimate the answer *before* relying on a mathematical solution. Swapping numbers, one of our math moves, often comes in handy, too.**

Archetypes: The following questions, arranged from medium to difficult, illustrate the major themes and variations you need to be familiar with on angle relationship problems. Before attempting these questions, you may want to review our earlier discussion of triangles and angle relationships in the geometry refresher beginning on page 520.

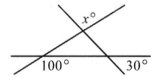

1.   In the figure above, what is the value of *x* ?

    (A) 130
    (B) 90
    (C) 70
    (D) 60
    (E) 50

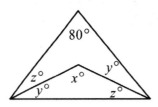

2.   In the figure above, what is the value of x ?

   (A) 140
   (B) 130
   (C) 120
   (D) 110
   (E) 100

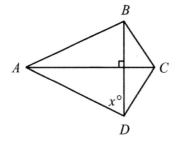

Note: Figure not drawn to scale.

3.   In the quadrilateral above, $AB = AC = AD$. If $\angle BCA = 65$, then $x =$

   (A) 25
   (B) 35
   (C) 40
   (D) 45
   (E) 50

SAT Math Hall of Fame Problem #4:
Counting Questions

Introduction: We discussed counting questions in our refresher of miscellaneous math topics, so you know that these problems have a lot in common with combination questions, Hall of Fame Problem #7.

> **As I've mentioned, do not take counting problems for granted—these questions are often *killer rabbits*.** Just be methodical and painstaking about writing everything out—don't do steps "in your head"—and you'll be fine. Our WIBNI math move comes in handy to simplify especially complicated counting problems. So if you have to count to a high number, determine the *logic* behind a simpler version of the problem and then apply that principle to the problem in front of you.
>
> Also, it's often possible to *estimate* the answer if you get stuck. The answer tends to be in the middle towards the higher range of choices.
>
> **Finally, be especially cautious about counting problems on the open-ended (grid-in) questions since you won't have choices to let you know whether you're on track or not.**

Archetypes: Although many different types of counting questions can appear on the SAT Math Test, the following difficult questions illustrate the major themes and variations you need to be familiar with on counting problems. Before attempting these questions, you may want to review our earlier discussion of counting problems under the miscellaneous math topics refresher beginning on page 571.

1. How many numbers from 60 to 180 inclusive are divisible by 3?

   (A) 20
   (B) 39
   (C) 40
   (D) 41
   (E) 60

2. The first two numbers of a sequence are 1 and 1. Every number after the second is the sum of the two numbers immediately preceding it, so the third number is 2, the fourth number is 3, the fifth number is 5, and so on. How many of the first 200 numbers in this sequence are odd?

(A) 66
(B) 67
(C) 100
(D) 133
(E) 134

3. How many positive integers less than 101 are divisible by either 2 or 5 or both?

(A) 10
(B) 50
(C) 60
(D) 70
(E) 80

4. Four lines can divide a rectangle into a maximum of how many nonoverlapping regions?

(A) Eight
(B) Nine
(C) Ten
(D) Eleven
(E) Sixteen

SAT Math Hall of Fame Problem #3:
Algebraic Expression Questions

Introduction: These questions can be recognized instantly by the presence of one or more algebraic—as opposed to numeric—answer choices.

> Algebraic expression questions can be answered in a snap, so seek them out when time is running short. Never, ever, solve these questions by algebraic manipulation—*always* swap numbers for the variables.

Archetypes: The following questions, arranged from medium-difficult to difficult, illustrate the major themes and variations you need to be familiar with on algebraic expression problems. Before attempting these questions, you may want to review the earlier discussion of our swapping numbers math move beginning on page 404.

1. Let k be the least of 4 consecutive positive integers whose sum is s. What is the sum of 8 consecutive integers, the least of which is k?

   (A) $s + 16$
   (B) $s + 22$
   (C) $2s$
   (D) $2s + 16$
   (E) $2s + 22$

2. If x equally priced items cost a total of c cents, what is the cost, in <u>dollars</u>, of y of the items?

   (A) $\dfrac{xc}{y}$

   (B) $\dfrac{yc}{x}$

   (C) $\dfrac{yc}{100x}$

   (D) $\dfrac{100yc}{x}$

   (E) $\dfrac{100xc}{y}$

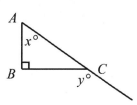

3. If side $\overline{AC}$ of right triangle ABC is extended as shown above, what does x equal in terms of y?

(A) y
(B) $y - 180$
(C) $y - 90$
(D) $90 - y$
(E) $180 - y$

4. If $\dfrac{(mx)}{(n + x)} = 1$ and $n \neq -x$, then $x =$

(A) $\dfrac{m}{(n - 1)}$

(B) $\dfrac{n}{(m - 1)}$

(C) $\dfrac{(n - 1)}{m}$

(D) $\dfrac{(n + 1)}{m}$

(E) $\dfrac{(n - 1)}{(m - 1)}$

5. If x and y are positive integers, then which of the following expressions is equivalent to $\dfrac{(2^x)^y}{2^x}$?

(A) 2^y
(B) 2^{xy-1}
(C) 2^{xy-x}
(D) 2^{xy-y}
(E) $2^{xy} - 2^x$

604

SAT Math Hall of Fame Problem #2:
Algebraic Thinking Questions

Introduction: We've already discussed algebraic thinking questions in the algebra refresher. Algebraic thinking questions are often disguised *arithmetic* thinking questions about basic concepts like odd or even integers, or positive or negative numbers. You can convert algebraic thinking questions back to arithmetic thinking questions by swapping numbers for variables. But watch out!

> Sometimes the fastest—and safest—way to solve these questions is *not* to think but to *fiddle* with a problem by tossing in numbers and seeing what happens to the choices, using aggressive process of elimination. These problems are *trickier* than algebraic expression questions— the Hall of Fame problem #3—which should *always* be solved by swapping numbers. Algebraic thinking questions often ask what *could* be true rather than what *must* be true—so you may have to try swapping different *types* of numbers for the variables.

Archetypes: The following questions, arranged from medium to very difficult, illustrate the major themes and variations you need to be familiar with on algebraic thinking problems. Before attempting these questions, you may want to review our earlier discussion of algebraic thinking in the algebra refresher beginning on page 500.

1. The sum of four different positive integers is 24.
   The greatest that any of the integers could be is

   (A) 21
   (B) 20
   (C) 28
   (D) 14
   (E) 6

2. If $\frac{p}{3} = q = 2r = 7s = 5t$ and $p, q, r, s,$ and t
   are all positive numbers, which of the following
   must be true?

   (A) $p < q < r < s < t$
   (B) $p < q < r < t < s$
   (C) $s < t < r < q < p$
   (D) $p < s < t < r < q$
   (E) $t < s < r < q < p$

3. If x and y are positive odd integers, which of the following must be an even integer?

I. $\dfrac{(x+y)}{2}$

II. $xy + 1$

III. $\dfrac{(xy+1)}{2}$

(A) None
(B) I only
(C) II only
(D) I and II only
(E) I, II, and III

4. If $x < 2$ and $y < -1$, then the sum of x and y could equal which of the following values?

(A) 0
(B) 1
(C) 2
(D) 3
(E) 4

$$xy < 0$$
$$xz > 0$$

5. Given the information above, which of the following must be true?

(A) $x > 0$
(B) $yz > 0$
(C) $yz < 0$
(D) $xyz > 0$
(E) $xyz < 0$

SAT Math Hall of Fame Problem #1:
Symbol (Function) Operation Questions

Introduction: Symbol operation questions are disguised function operation questions you probably encountered in your algebra class. Don't let a strange symbol confuse you; it is *not* something you missed in school. The test writers just make up a symbol to stand for an operation or series of operations to perform on numbers. Think of the operation as an instruction to do something.

    If you are painstaking and methodical, these questions are practically giveaway points—never, ever leave one of these problems blank. You simply follow the instructions defined by the symbol and crank out the answer.

> **Since the new SAT Math Test is placing an increased emphasis on algebra II, the symbol notation of these problems may be replaced to some extent with the conventional function—$f(x)$—notation you are used to seeing in your math class, but the principles discussed here apply to all variations.**

Archetypes: The following questions, arranged from medium to very difficult, illustrate the major themes and variations you need to be familiar with on symbol operation problems. Before attempting these questions, you may want to review our earlier discussion of symbol operation questions in the algebra refresher beginning on page 509.

1.   For all j and k, let $j \boxtimes k$ be defined by $j \boxtimes k = jk - 1$. What is the value of $3 \boxtimes (2 \boxtimes 1)$?

(A) 6
(B) 5
(C) 4
(D) 3
(E) 2

2. For all positive integers x, $\trianglerighteq x$ is defined as the least integer greater than x, and $\trianglelefteq x$ is defined as the greatest integer less than x. What is the value of $\trianglerighteq 3.1 - \trianglelefteq 1.9$

(A) 3
(B) 2
(C) 1
(D) 0
(E) −1

3. For all numbers j and k, let the operation $j \oplus k = \dfrac{(j - k)}{(j + k)}$. If $2 \oplus 1 = 1 \oplus x$, what is the value of x ?

(A) 2

(B) 1

(C) $\dfrac{1}{2}$

(D) $-\dfrac{1}{2}$

(E) −1

4. $\boxplus x \boxplus$ is defined by $\boxplus x \boxplus = (x + 1)^2$. Which of the following is equal to $\boxplus 4 \boxplus + \boxplus 11 \boxplus$?

(A) $\boxplus \sqrt{15} \boxplus$
(B) $\boxplus 4 \boxplus$
(C) $\boxplus 12 \boxplus$
(D) $\boxplus 13 \boxplus$
(E) $\boxplus 15 \boxplus$

5. If $f(x) = x^2 + 1$, then $f(f(x)) = $

(A) $x^4 + 1$
(B) $x^4 + 2$
(C) $x^4 + x^2 + 1$
(D) $x^4 + 2x^2 + 1$
(E) $x^4 + 2x^2 + 2$

Solutions for Hall of Fame Problem #11

1. **Swap a number for the radius—10 is great—and then calculate the new radius.** A 10 percent increase from 10 would make the new radius 11. *Now* we use the formula for the area of a circle: πr^2. The original area was 100π, and the new area is 121π: a 21 percent increase, or choice (D). Choice (C) is a popular-looking trap. **Notice that the most popular-looking choice was not correct—but it wasn't far off.**

    (PS: Swapping a different number for the original radius would have worked, too, but 10 provides us with a nice "base" to calculate percentage change from.)

2. **Swap a number for m and n: Once again, 10 is an outstanding choice.** A 50 percent increase from 10 would make p 15, and a 60 percent increase from 10 would make q 16. The product pq (240) is 140 greater than mn (100), or choice (C). Choice (B) is a popular-looking trap. **Notice that the most popular-looking choice was not correct—but it wasn't far off.** If you selected choice (E), you misread the question.

    (PS: When we swap numbers for variables in algebraic expression questions—as on Hall of Fame Problem #2—we avoid using the same number twice (say, for x and y) because then we wouldn't be able to tell the difference between the variables. Since this question had only numeric choices, we didn't have to worry about that confusion.)

3. **First, estimate the answer to avoid potential errors.** If the price of the book is p dollars *after* a discount, the original price had to be *more* than p, right? Eliminate choices (D) and (E), which are both less than p. **Now let's toss in a number *not* for p, but for the original price.** Let's use 10 again. If the original price is 10 dollars, a 20 percent discount would bring the new price—p—down to 8 dollars. Now the question is a snap: If p is 8, the answer to the question is 10. Swapping 8 for p in the choices, we find that the answer is choice (B). Choice (C) is a popular-looking trap. **Notice that the most popular-looking choice was not correct—but it wasn't far off.**

    (PS: If you had used 10 for p, you would have arrived at the same answer, but the calculations would have been a bit messier—but only a bit.)

Solutions for Hall of Fame Problem #10

1. **First, estimate the answer to avoid potential errors—and who knows, maybe even answer the question.** By examining the diagram, it's clear that *AB* is greater than *AD*, but not twice as great. So *AB* is greater than 4 but less than 8: eliminate choices (A), (B), and (E). **If you're good at estimating, you should be able to distinguish between the two remaining choices—5.66 and 6.93—to determine the answer without any more work.** But if you're just getting used to estimating, we'll have to find the solution the long way. Okay, angle *ADB* equals 120° (since angle *BDC* equals 60°). Since *AD* and *BD* are equal, angles *DAB* and *DBA* are equal—so they're both 30°. Now let's switch perspective and look at triangle *ABC*. Triangle *ABC* is a 30:60:90 triangle, with *AC* as the hypotenuse. Now we apply the Pythagorean relationship: $(AC)^2 = (BC)^2 + (AB)^2$. We know that *AC* is 8 and *BC* is 4 (since we've determined that triangle *BCD* is equilateral). Plugging these values into the equation, we determine—at long last—that *AB* is $4\sqrt{3}$, or choice (D).

    (PS: If you weren't able to work out a complete solution—either because you didn't have enough time or because you just didn't see it—you could still have gotten very close to the solution by estimating and you should have guessed between choices (C) and (D). As I mentioned, meticulous estimating could have distinguished the answer between these two choices.)

2. The figure is not drawn to scale, so we can estimate with extreme caution only. The triangle is an isosceles triangle (since two of its sides are radii of the circle), so two angles equal 45°. The remaining central angle, then, is 90°. **(At this point you might see that the radius must be less than 2, since 2 is opposite the largest angle in the triangle. Only choice (A) is less than 2, so we could eliminate choices (B), (C), and (D) at this point.)** Since the triangle is a right (45:45:90) triangle, we can use the Pythagorean relationship: $r^2 + r^2 = 2^2$. Solving this equation, we can determine that r = $\sqrt{2}$, or choice (A).

    (PS: Because the figure is not drawn to scale, we could have redrawn the figure to scale to help us estimate the answer.)

3. **First, estimate the answer to avoid potential errors.** Since BD is 5, it's clear from the diagram that AC is greater than 5—but not much greater. Choices (A), (B), and (C) are much too big. **If you're good at estimating, you should be able to distinguish between the two remaining choices—6 and 5.10—to determine the answer without any more work.** But if you're just getting used to estimating, we have some more work ahead of us. Since AD is a radius, it equals 5. Since BE equals 1, ED equals 4. Now we can use the Pythagorean relationship: $(AD)^2 = (AE)^2 + (ED)^2$. Since AD equals 5 and ED equals 4, we can determine that AE equals 3, so AE equals 6, or choice (D).

4. **First, estimate the answer to avoid potential errors.** It's clear from the diagram that x is greater than 6, but not *much* greater. Choices (A) and (B) are definitely out, and choice (E) is probably too large. Choices (C) and (D) may be too close together to permit a conclusive estimation, so let's see if we can work out the solution. If we split the quadrilateral lengthwise, we create two right triangles that share a hypotenuse. Applying the Pythagorean relationship, we get $6^2 + 3^2 = x^2 + 2^2$. Solving this equation, we get $x^2 = 41$, or $x = \sqrt{41}$. The answer is choice (C).

5. **First, estimate the answer to avoid potential errors.** Estimating solid geometry figures is a bit tougher than estimating two-dimensional figures in a plane, but not much tougher. Anyway, from the figure it's clear that PQ is greater than 3, but probably not a whole lot greater. Choice (E) is way too big, but the other choices may be too close together to permit a conclusive estimation. If we construct a triangle using P, Q, and the center of the base, we have a right triangle with a height of 3, and a diagonal that runs from the center of the base to P. The diagonal along the base has two sides of 1 and 1, so it's a 45:45:90 triangle with a hypotenuse of $\sqrt{2}$. Now we can apply the Pythagorean relationship again: $(PQ)^2 = (\sqrt{2})^2 + 3^2 = 11$, so $PQ = \sqrt{11}$.

(PS: If you remembered that the Pythagorean relationship in three dimensions is the same as the Pythagorean relationship in two dimensions, you could determine PQ directly: $(PQ)^2 = 1^2 + 1^2 + 3^2 = 11$, so $PQ = \sqrt{41}$.)

Solutions for Hall of Fame Problem #9

1. **First, estimate the answer to avoid potential errors.** It's clear from the diagram that y is less than half of 2—using the point (6, 2) as a guide—so we can eliminate choices (A), (B), and (C) right off the bat. Choices (D) and (E) are too close together to permit a conclusive estimation, so let's see if we can work out the solution. The formula for the slope of a line containing two specific points is the difference in y values divided by the difference in x values. The difference in y values is $(2 - y)$, and the difference in x values is $(6 - 0)$. Plugging these values into the slope formula using the information given, we know that $\frac{1}{4}$ equals $(2 - y) \div (6 - 0)$, or $\frac{1}{4}$ equals $(2 - y) \div (6)$. Cross-multiplying and solving for y, we determine that y equals $\frac{1}{2}$, or choice (D).

2. **Since the problem does not provide a figure, you should quickly sketch the coordinate axis and indicate the point (0, 1). Instead of applying the slope formula to each of the choices, it's easier to just sketch the points—to scale—on the coordinate plane you just drew.** The point (1, 5) is "over 1, up 4" from the point (0, 1), which gives us a slope of 4. Choice (B) is the answer.

3. **Since we have algebraic answer choices, we should immediately swap a number for the variable n to make the problem more tangible.** Since n is greater than 1, let's make it 2. Point B therefore has coordinates (2, 2), which forms a slope of 1 with point A, the origin (0, 0). **As with the previous problem, sketching the points in a coordinate plane and inspecting the diagram is much better than relying on the slope formula with cumbersome calculations for each choice.** Swapping 2 for n into each of the choices gives us points of (3, 1), (1, 2), (2, 3), (2, 1), and (1, 1). The least slope for the new line segment from the origin is the point (3, 1), which has a slope of $\frac{1}{3}$; choice (A) is the answer.

    (PS: Don't let problems like this bully you. When you see algebraic answer choices, use our swapping numbers math move for variables and crank through the choices.)

4. This problem requires a little thought: it's actually asking which of the conditions ensure that the two lines are *parallel.* Since parallel lines

have the same slope (but different *y*-intercepts—otherwise the two lines would be identical), the answer is choice (C).

Solutions for Hall of Fame Problem #8

1. If the average of *p* and *q* is 6, their total is 12. If the average of *p, q,* and *r* is 8, their total is 24. Adding *r* to *p* and *q* increases their sum by 12, so *r* equals 12. The answer is choice (C). Choice (B) is a popular-looking trap.

    (PS: If you used our WIBNI move to let *p* and *q* equal 6, and then solved for r, clever you.)

2. If 12 students have an average score of 40, they have a total score of 480. If two students have an average score of 45, they have a total score of 90. Subtracting the two totals, we know that the remaining 10 students have a total score of 390, so they have an average score of 39. The answer is choice (E). Choice (A) is a popular-looking trap.

3. If the average of 4 numbers is 8, their total is 32. When one of the numbers is removed, the average of the 3 remaining numbers is 9, so their total score is 27. Subtracting the two totals, we know that 5 was removed from the set. The answer is choice (A).

4. This question is a killer rabbit: It's much trickier than it looks. **Choice (C) is a popular-looking trap, which we know should not be far off from the answer.** Since the bicyclist spends more time on the road traveling at 20 kilometers per hour than at 30 kilometers per hour, the weighted average should "tilt" towards 20. If you noticed this, you could eliminate choices (C), (D), and (E). Using our WIBNI math move, we swap an actual distance for the bicyclist to travel and then determine her average speed per hour. The number 60 is an excellent number to use for the distance since it is divisible by both 20 and 30. Traveling 60 kilometers at 20 kilometers per hour and then 30 kilometers per hour would require 3 hours and 2 hours respectively, for a total of 120 kilometers in 5 hours—or 24 kilometers per hour. Since her total traveling time given in the problem is 1 hour, the total distance she

traveled back and forth would also be 24, or choice (B).

(PS: I trust that you drew a diagram of the situation to help you think through the problem.)

Solutions for Hall of Fame Problem #7

1.   We're selecting a committee of 3 people from 5 possible candidates. **Careful, careful, careful: Try not to rely on formulas.** Since there are so few possible candidates, the safe—best—approach is to list all the possibilities. Let's say the 5 candidates are *A, B, C, D,* and *E.* Starting with *A,* we could select *ABC, ABD, ABE, ACD, ACE,* and *ADE*—or 6 combinations. That's every combination that includes *A,* so *A* drops out of the picture. Now let's list combinations with B—that don't include A, since we've already considered every combination that includes A. Okay, we could get *BCD, BCE,* and *BDE*—another 3 combinations. Now *B* drops out of the picture and we have only one possible remaining combination: *CDE.* That's a total of 10 combinations, or choice (A).

   (PS: In this question order did not matter. Notice that if we had to select not a 3-person committee, but a president, a vice-president, and a treasurer, we would get a *very* different solution. For the first selection of president, we have 5 possibilities. Once we select the president, we have 4 possibilities left for the vice-president, and then 3 possibilities left for the third selection. Multiplying these numbers, we get a total number of 60. The reason this result is so different from the original situation is that for each of the 10 original combinations, we have 6 different "versions." While the people *A, B,* and *C* can create only 1 committee—order doesn't matter—they can create 6 different president-vice-president-treasurer variations: *ABC, ACB, BAC, BCA, CAB,* and *CBA.*)

2.   With runners in a race, obviously order matters. Let's use our WIBNI math move and assume that only runner *A* can finish first. Okay, if *A* finishes first, we have 4 possible second-place finishers. Once we know who finished second, we have 3 possible third-place finishers; once we know who finished third, we have 2 possible fourth-place finishers; and once we know who finished fourth, we have only 1 person left for the last-place finisher. So if *A* finishes first, we have 4 times 3 times 2

times 1 possible combinations, or 24. Since either A or B could finish first, we can repeat the same analysis, and get an additional 24 combinations, bringing the total to 48. The answer is choice (D).

Solutions for Hall of Fame Problem #6

1. **This problem could be solved by our math move of checking the choices (start with the middle choice and check the choices until you find the answer).** Since this could have been a student response question without choices, however, let's work through the actual solution. Since AB is 10, we know that the difference in y values of A and B is 10: $k - (4 - k) = 10$. Solving this equation, we get 7, or choice (D).

   (PS: If you missed this question, you failed to check your solution, which you could have plugged back into the problem to see if it worked. Take pains.)

2. **Start by drawing out a quick coordinate plane, and then locating the points *carefully* to scale in your diagram so that you can estimate the answer.** Since we're looking for a possible center of a circle tangent to the x-axis and y-axis, the absolute value of the x- and y-coordinates must be equal. The answer is choice (B).

3. **This question absolutely requires that you draw out an xy-graph. Don't think for too long—fiddle until you find the solution.** Toss in a point for K somewhere on the x-axis. Then locate point J on your graph. Since JK equals KL, we know that J must be above the x-axis with a positive y value: eliminate choices (A), (C), and (D). K also has the same x value as J, so the answer is choice (B).

4. **If we estimate *x* and *y* values for each of the points (using the units already marked off on the coordinate axes), we can answer this question quickly.** Since we want the largest product, the x- and y-coordinates of the answer should ideally both be positive or both be negative so that as a starting point we have a positive result. Eliminate choices (A) and (C). Now we want a point as far away from the origin as possible, or choice (D).

5.   **Since a diagram is not provided, get to work drawing your own.** Let's begin by getting the *x-* and *y-*intercepts of the line by swapping 0 for *y* and *x* respectively. If *y* is 0, then *x* is 2, so the *x*-intercept is (2, 0). If *x* is 0, then *y* is −4, so the *y*-intercept is (0, − 4). The base and height of the resulting right triangle are 2 and 4, so the area is 4. The answer is choice (C).

6.   **Remember that triangles, rectangles, and circles are the basic figures we work from on the SAT Math Test. If you don't see one of these figures in a diagram, introduce a line or two to create a triangle, rectangle, or circle.** Let's drop a line from (8, 6) down to the *x*-axis, creating a right triangle with sides 6 and 8. Now extend that vertical line up a bit so that its height equals 14. Now draw a horizontal line over from (*j*, 14) to the vertical line. We just created another right triangle similar to the first. (You can verify this by tossing in a rough estimate of any angle in either triangle and cranking out the other angles; you'll see that the two triangles share the same angles.) Since the two triangles each have a long side of 8, the two triangles are in fact congruent. To get to the point (*j*, 14) from (8, 6) we have to go "up 8, and 6 to the left." If we move 6 to the left from the vertical line, we get an *x*-value of 2 for *j*. The answer is choice (B).

Solutions for Hall of Fame Problem #5

1.   **First, estimate the answer to avoid potential errors.** From the diagram it's clear that x is around 90°, maybe a bit less, so we can eliminate choice (A) at least. The interior angle next to the 30° angle is also 30° (since the two angles are vertical), and the interior angle next to the 100° angle is 80° (since the two angles are supplementary. If two of the interior angles of a triangle are 30° and 80°, the third interior angle must be 70° (since their sum is 180°). The answer is choice (C).

(PS: if you selected choice (E), you're not taking pains and checking things out. Always *verify* any assumptions you make about figures.)

2.   **First, estimate the answer to avoid potential errors.** It's clear from the diagram that *x* is greater than 80, but all the answer choices are

greater than 80. Alas the answer choices are too close in size to permit any elimination of choices—but you still should have *tried* to estimate the answer; you never know how far you can get. Anyway, from the larger triangle we know that the sum of the interior angles is 180°, so 180 = 80 + (y + z) + (y + z). Simplifying this equation as much as we can, we get y + z = 50. Turning our attention now to the inner triangle, if the sum of y and z is 50, then x must be 130. The answer is choice (B).

3. **The key to solving any angle relationship question is to work with the information the problem provides and then to crank out all the other angles until you determine the solution.** Since we have two isosceles triangles ABC and ACD, angles ADC and ACD must be equal, and angles BCA and CBA must be equal. It's clear from the information provided that triangles ABC and ACD are congruent, so if angle BCA is 65°, so is angle ACD. And if angle ACD is 65°, so is angle ADC. It's clear from the diagram that x must be less than 65, but all of the choices are less than 65 (bummer). Anyway, if angle ACD is 65, then angle BDC is 25 (because the two angles must add up to 90°), so x is 65 minus 25, or 40. The answer is choice (C).

(PS: If you selected choice (A), you didn't work things out and fell for a popular-looking trap. Take pains.)

Solutions for Hall of Fame Problem #4

1. Let's use our WIBNI math move to solve a simpler version of this question. How many numbers from 6 to 12 inclusive are divisible by 3? Three, right? Our first impulse probably is two (the difference between 12 and 6 divided by 3), so the solution rule here is to add 1 to the difference between the result of dividing the difference of 180 and 60 by 3. The answer is choice (D).

(PS: If you selected choice (C), you're not taking pains and you fell for a popular-looking trap. I warned you that this was a difficult question. The problem looked easy, so it's a killer rabbit.)

2. The pattern gives us two odd numbers for every even number, so more than half the 200 numbers in the sequence are odd. **Eliminate choices (A), (B), and (C), all of which are too small.** Now we have to take pains to decide between 133 and 134. If we divide 200 by 3, we get 66, remainder two. Of the 66 "groups" of three numbers, two-thirds are odd numbers, so we get 132 odd numbers of the first 198 numbers in the sequence. The remaining two numbers begin a new "group" of three, and so in this sequence both numbers are odd, bringing the total to 134. The answer is choice (E).

    (PS: If you selected choice (A), you misread the question.)

3. **Right off the bat, we know that 50 of the first 100 positive integers are divisible by 2, so eliminate choices (A) and (B).** Now let's use our WIBNI math move to solve a simpler version of the question: How many positive integers less than 11 are divisible by 2 or 5 or both? The answer to this simpler version is 6, and the answer to the original question is 60, or choice (C). The answer was *not* 70 because 10 of the numbers are divisible by 2 *and* 5, which we must subtract out so that we don't double count.

    (PS: If you selected choice (D), you're not taking pains and you fell for a popular-looking trap. I warned you that this was a difficult question. The problem looked easy, so it's a killer rabbit. If you selected choice (A), you misread the question.)

4. **This kind of problem in difficult territory is *always* a killer rabbit. Let's start by doing the question in the most obvious way possible— knowing that the solution we get *cannot* be correct.** If we quickly draw two vertical lines within a rectangle and cross them with two horizontal lines, we divide the rectangle into 9 nonoverlapping regions. **This solution was painless, so it cannot be correct on a question we know to be difficult.** Eliminate choices (A) and (B). If you fiddle around with this question and draw lines carefully, you'll see that the answer is 11, or choice (D) (10 is close but no cigar).

    (PS: If you selected choice (B), you're not taking pains and you fell for a popular-looking trap. I warned you that this was a difficult question. The problem looked easy, so it's a killer rabbit.)

Solutions for Hall of Fame Problem #3

1. **Swapping numbers on questions like this one is a fast and virtually foolproof method.** Swapping, say, 2 for k, we determine that the sum of the four consecutive integers beginning with 2 is 14; so s equals 14. The sum of the eight consecutive integers beginning with 2 is 44. Swapping 14 for s in the choices, we can determine that choice (D) is the answer.

    (PS: If you selected choice (B), you misread the question. If you selected choices (A), (C), or (E), I trust that you'll start swapping numbers for variables in the future!)

2. **You know the drill: Swap numbers for variables.** Let's say x is 5 and c is 100 and y is 10. I used 100 for c to convert the units immediately over to dollars. Okay, now we're dealing with a simple arithmetic question: If 5 items cost 1 dollar, how many dollars will 10 items cost? Duh, 2. **Okay, now we translate each choice into numbers—using the values we selected—until we find the equivalent answer.** The answer is choice (C).

    (PS: If you selected choice (B), you misread the question. If you selected choices (A), (D), or (E), I trust that you'll start swapping numbers for variables in the future!)

3. **You know the drill: Swap numbers for variables.** Let's say x is 40. Then angle *BCA* is 50, and y is 130. Now we translate the choices until we find an answer of 40, using 130 for y. Bingo, the answer is choice (C).

    (PS: If you selected choice (A), you're not estimating from figures, *and* you're probably relying on geometry "rules" instead of checking things out for yourself. If you got this question wrong, I trust that you'll start swapping numbers for variables in the future!)

4. **You know the drill: Swap numbers for variables.** Let's say m is 3 and x is 2. If we have 6 in the numerator, we need 6 in the denominator, so n must be 4. Now we translate the choices until we find an answer of 2, using 3 for m and 4 for n. Bingo, the answer is choice (B).

(PS: If you got this question wrong, you made an algebraic manipulation mistake of the type you could easily avoid if you used our math move. I trust that you'll start swapping numbers for variables in the future!)

5. **You know the drill: Swap numbers for variables.** Let's say x is 2 and y is 3. Now the question is a simple arithmetic problem. The numerator is $(2^2)^3$, or 64, divided by 2^2, or 4, so we get 16. Now we translate the choices until we find an answer of 16, using 2 for x and 3 for y. Bingo, the answer is choice (C).

(PS: If you got this question wrong, you are probably relying on exponent "rules" instead of checking things out for yourself. I trust that you'll start swapping numbers for variables in the future!)

Solutions for Hall of Fame Problem #2

1. **Often when you want to maximize one quantity in an algebraic thinking question, you have to *minimize* something else.** The smallest values we could make the other three integers are 1, 2, and 3, since the problem states that the numbers are positive and *different*. The greatest possible value for the fourth integer is 18, or choice (C).

   (PS: If you selected choices (A) or (E), you misread the question.)

2. **Normally we would toss in some numbers for variables, but there are so many variables here that we should try to simplify the problem first.** Okay, p has to be the largest number, because when you divide it by 3 it's still greater than or equal to all the other variables. **(That's true only because we know the variables are all positive.)** By the same line of reasoning, s has to be the smallest number. **We can now eliminate every choice that does not have p as the largest number and s as the smallest number;** choices (A), (B), (D) and (E) are out. Oh, that means choice (C) is the answer.

   (PS: If you missed this question, you either misread the question—notice that t is not on one of the two "pole" positions—or you didn't bother to take pains to check things out.)

3. **Let's toss in some numbers to see how many choices we can eliminate.** If we let x equal 3 and y equal 5, say, we can eliminate option III immediately, and with it choice (E). **Now we have to try a different set of numbers just to be sure—a different *type* of set.** Since we let y be 2 more than x before, let's let y be 4 more than x. Okay, let's say x is 5 and y is 9. Whoops, their average is now 7, so option I is out, and with it choices (B) and (D). Since x and y are both odd, their product—xy—must be odd, too, so adding 1 to the product will produce an even result. Option II is the only one that works. The answer is choice (C).

(PS: If you selected choice (D), you should have been more suspicious that such an easy solution would be correct on a question I warned you would be difficult. Take pains.)

4. We can add the two inequalities and get $x + y < 1$, which allows only choice (A). **Remember that with inequalities, we can "pretend" that the variable could be almost-almost-almost equal to the number.**

5. **Start by tossing in one set of numbers, and then check your solution with a different *type* of set.** Okay, let's start by letting x be positive. If that's the case, then y must be negative and z must be positive. We can eliminate choices (B) and (D). Now let's let x be negative. If that's the case, then y must be positive and z must be negative. Okay, we can eliminate choices (A) and (E). The answer is choice (C). **(PS: Bravo if you noticed that you could multiply the two inequalities, and get $x^2yz < 0$. Since x^2 must be positive here, yz must be negative.)**

Solutions for Hall of Fame Problem #1

1. Okay, the operation here is to subtract 1 from the product of the two numbers. Working within the parenthesis first, we get $2 \boxtimes 1 - 1$, or 1. Repeating the operation now with the number outside the parenthesis, we get $3 \boxtimes 1 - 1$, or 2. The answer is choice (E).

2.   The least integer greater than 3.1 is 4, and the greatest integer less than 1.9 is 1, so $4 - 1 = 3$. The answer is choice (A).

3.   The operation here is to divide the difference of the two numbers by their sum. Setting up the equation given in the problem, we get $\frac{(2-1)}{(2+1)} = \frac{(1-x)}{(1+x)}$. Cross multiplying and solving for x, we get $\frac{1}{2}$, or choice (C).

      (PS: If you selected choice (A), you fell for a popular-looking trap. Be suspicious of easy answers on hard questions, and take pains.)

4.   The operation here is to add 1 to the number and square the result. So translating the equation given in the problem, we get $(4 + 1)^2 + (11 + 1)^2$, which is 169. **Whoops, we're not finished yet: Now we have to translate the choices.** The answer is choice (C).

      (PS: If you selected choice (E), you fell for a popular-looking trap. Be suspicious of easy answers on hard questions, and take pains. If you selected choice (D), you forgot to translate the choice.)

5.   The operation here is to square the number and add 1. **You know the drill with algebraic answer choices: swap numbers.** Okay, let x equal 2. Squaring 2 and adding 1, we get $f(x)$ equals 5. Repeating the operation now with 5, we get 26. Translating the choices, we get choice (E).

PART VI

NUTS AND BOLTS

Taking the SAT
(Always Expect Surprises)

128 Hours and Counting: Getting Ready for the Big Day

Throughout this book we've discussed how you should get ready for the SAT beginning two to four months before the test. In this chapter we'll discuss what you should do the week before the SAT, what to expect in the exam room, and what happens *after* you've taken the test.

You want the week leading up to the test to go as smoothly as possible, so get yourself into a routine beginning on the Sunday night the week before the test (128 hours). Look at your calendar for that week and make sure you plan ahead for everything *else* in your life: homework, upcoming tests, papers due, after-school activities.

> It's easy to forget some important things you need to do this week, so have your parents read this chapter, too. They can print out a copy from the RocketReview website so you don't have to give up your book.

Go Easy on Yourself This Week

Don't overload yourself this week. In fact, do what you can to lighten up your normal schedule. If you normally participate in two or three after-school activities, consider passing up anything you don't have to do.

Your parents should know that you need to be focused this week, too. They should let you delegate some of your normal responsibilities—you can make up your chores the week *after* the SAT.

If your teachers hit you with any major assignments this week, maybe you and your classmates should ask for a minor postponement until after the SAT. Most teachers will understand if you need to slack off a bit this week—they probably remember what it was like to take the SAT and they know there's a whole lot more riding on the test these days than there was a generation ago.

Try to get into a routine in the days leading up to the test. Get to bed and wake up at reasonably consistent times. If it takes you a while to wake up in the morning, wake up an hour earlier than usual every day this week so that you'll have an extra hour on test day to clear your head; the SAT starts fairly early in the morning, and you want to be completely lucid* when the test begins.

By the way, if it's cold season, wash your hands frequently—the last thing you need going into the SAT is to get sick this week. You're not being obsessive or a hypochondriac here; most cold viruses pass from the environment to your hands, and from your hands to your face. (If you get sick the week before the test, it's not going to ruin your chances for the SAT, but do stay home from school and get well.)

*GSWLIU

Getting into the Right Frame of Mind

At the end of a season and leading up to the championship, athletes go through a "tapering phase" to make sure they perform at their peak when it counts. In a sense you've been a mental athlete, and you want to make sure that you perform at your peak when it counts: on the actual SAT.

For you, tapering consists of scaling back drastically the amount of preparation you've been doing so you can give your mind a chance to rest and rev up your motivation. During this week you should do much *less* work, but of a much higher quality. Instead of doing an entire section of an SAT, for example, spend the same amount of time focusing on three or four truly difficult questions. You'll gain far more by wrestling with a tough question for ten minutes—or more—than you will doing ten simple questions quickly.

In fact, don't do *anything* timed this week. *Rehearse* the techniques meticulously, getting everything *just* right. **Trust me on this point: the best way to improve your test-taking speed *and* your test-taking accuracy is to practice *mindfully*, being hyperconscious of every little step you do.**

This week is also an excellent time to see how far your skills have advanced since you started preparing for the test weeks ago. Get out your PSAT booklet, or your first few practice exams, and look over your work. You'll be so surprised at how you *used* to solve questions that you won't even recognize your work.

Keep up with your vocabulary work this week, but don't try to cram in more words than normal—doing so will not make much of a difference in your score and trying to do so will just heighten your anxiety level at a time when you should be taking it easy.

Don't wait until the last minute to locate your admission ticket. You can print one out from the College Board's website if you registered online.

The Day before the Test

- If you haven't already, make sure you know the location of your test center. If you don't know how to get to the center, print out directions from MapQuest.com. If you haven't taken a test before at your test center, ask around among the seniors you know to see whether there's anything you need to know about the place.

- If you weren't able to register in time and you're going to a test center as a walk-in, choose a large site that you're familiar with. (Large, well-run test centers will have extra SAT booklets on hand for walk-ins.) If you're going as a walk-in, it's also a good idea to have a contingency plan.

- Speaking of contingency plans, if someone is supposed to drive you to the test center, make sure you have a back-up plan in case the person oversleeps, gets sick, or otherwise fails to show up tomorrow morning (remember, this is the day before the test) at the appointed time.

- During the day, make sure you have a digital watch or similar timing device, ideally one with large, easily read numbers. The best timing device to use is one that counts *up* rather than down, but any digital device is better than an analog watch with hard-to-read hands.

- Also make sure you have a working alarm—or two!—in the house so you're sure to wake up in time. If you can't find one, borrow one from a friend or a neighbor.

- Although you can get some gum and maybe a bottle of water the morning of the test, it's probably a good idea if you get these things today.

- Calculators are a distraction but if you feel more comfortable having one at your side, make sure you have one handy. If you borrow a calculator from a friend, make sure you know how it operates: fumbling with it on test day is likely to be disconcerting.*

- If you didn't register in time and you're taking the test as a walk-in, make sure you have a check for the correct amount to bring with you.

*GSWLIU

- Finally, it's a good idea to have a cell phone handy on test day. If you don't have one, borrow one—and make sure it's charged.

If This Is Your First SAT—Get Excited

It's natural to feel nervous the day before the test, maybe even a bit panicked, but let's try to get some perspective on your situation. Try to think of your first SAT as an audition for college, but not the audition that really counts. Naturally you *hope* that your audition goes well tomorrow, but it's not a big deal if it doesn't go quite as well as you'd like. Half of all SAT students wind up retaking the test in the fall of their senior year. Even students who do very well often retake the SAT because they know they could have done even better.

So don't think that all your college hopes rest on how you do on tomorrow's SAT—they don't. If you get a great score, terrific, but if you don't, it's not the end of the world.

The Night before the Test

- It's fine if you want to see a movie or hang out with your friends until the early evening, but then get home. *Do* spend at least half an hour today reviewing your work, but no more than an hour. Again, you're not trying to learn anything new at this point; you're just making mental notes about things you should already know.

- Before you get too tired, lay out everything you're going to need tomorrow morning: a picture I.D., a calculator (although you don't really need one), your digital watch, your pencils, maybe a sharpener. Proctors will not allow scratch paper during the exam, so you won't need to bring that.

- Set out the clothes you'll wear for tomorrow, including any good luck items. It's a good idea to dress in layers so that if the room is too hot you can take off a sweater, or if it's too cold you can put one on.

- You might want to bring something distracting to read or listen to with you to the test site tomorrow. If so, set these out, too.

- Charge your cell phone and set your alarm!

- I've never understood why students are told to "get a good night's sleep" before the SAT; I'm not even sure what a good night's sleep is. In any event, don't stay up much later than you usually do—but don't go to bed much earlier than you normally do, either. Too much sleep tonight is just as bad as getting too little.

Waking Up on Test Morning

- When you wake up, consider taking a shower or doing some brief calisthenics or other exercise to get the blood flowing—especially to your groggy brain! If someone is taking you to the test site, make sure he or she is up, too.

- Eat a normal breakfast, but not too much or you'll be groggy. If you're used to consuming some form of caffeine—tea, coffee, cola—then doing so is probably a good idea this morning. But only if you're used to caffeine; if you're not, now is *not* the morning to start.

- Make sure you have everything with you when you leave, and allow enough time to get to the test site thirty to forty minutes before the test starts to allow for traffic delays and to get yourself into a good position for entering the exam room.

Arriving at the Test Site

There will probably be dozens of nervous students milling around at the entrance to the test site, reviewing flash cards, skimming through their notes, or muttering to themselves. If I were you I'd avoid congregating near everyone else so you can remain focused, but that's up to you and your state of mind that morning.

If you arrived super early, you can hang out in the car or find a place to sit and read your book or listen to some music. If a parent drove you to the site, have him or her hang out until the test starts just in case some emergency comes up—like you're a walk-in, the test center doesn't have enough tests for you, and you have to be driven immediately to an alternative site.

Make sure your pencil points are slightly dull. Super sharp pencil points break easily and take longer to fill in the answer sheet bubbles than do dull pencil points.

> If you're taking the test under special circumstances, or taking it as a walk-in, it's especially important that you show up to the test center early so that the proctors can accommodate you.

Entering the Exam Room

Don't just wander into your exam room casually. Try to be one of the first students into the exam room so that you can choose a good seat (assuming seating is not assigned, as it sometimes is). A good seat is one that gives you a clear view of the proctor and of the central clock in the room that the proctor will be monitoring to time the test.

When I took exams I always preferred seats in the very back of the room because I didn't like the feeling that something was going on behind my back that I couldn't see. You may be different and prefer a seat as close to the front of the room as possible. The important thing is to choose a seat that suits you, and not one that you take by default.

I recommend getting a seat either next to a window or next to a wall so that you're not sandwiched on both sides by other students. During the test you may want to take a break for a few seconds and stretch your neck; that's hard to do if you have students on either side of you. It's nice to be able to look out the window from time to time to clear your head.

As the proctor reads the instructions—*Clear your desks and put all your belongings under your seat. Print your first name and then last name, bubbling in the first few letters on page one of your answer sheet, blah, blah, blah*—don't space out. Use the time to get focused and alert so that when the test begins, you're ready to go.

Get ready to set your digital timepiece to zero—you want it to count up, not down—and await the proctor's signal.

The Scariest Moment in the Exam Room

Do you know when it is? Imagine that the proctor has finished reading the instructions and everyone in the room has his or her pencil poised to break the test booklet seal, waiting for the second hand to swing up to the twelve on the room's clock, when the test will begin.

Finally the second hand hits twelve, and the minute hand clicks once. The proctor looks out at the room full of anxious faces and announces, *Open your test booklets and begin. You have twenty-five minutes to complete the first section.*

Phwip, phwip, phwip, phwip, phwip. The silence of the room is broken by the chorus of seals being broken around the room and the flutter of test booklets being opened. Then the room is quiet, the only sound being the scribbling of pencils.

No, that's not the scariest moment in the exam, but it's about to happen.

Scribble, scribble, scribble. You're working through the problems on the first page just like you've done many times before. Everything's going along swimmingly as the proctor walks up and down the aisles occasionally.

Then, all of a sudden, everyone in the room hears a sound that draws a collective gasp: *the sound of the first page turning!*

"Oh no," everyone thinks, "I'm not moving fast enough!" All at once the head of every student in the room drops down closer to the test booklet, teeth clenched in determination, and pencils scribbling even faster. Within 30 seconds—I promise—everybody else in the room will have turned his or her first page, too, trying to catch up.

I assure you that the first person in the exam room to turn his or her page is racing recklessly through the problems—and bombing big-time. Don't be tricked into trying to keep up with that pace. Stick to our game plan. **Stay focused. No shortcuts. Take pains.** If you do so, you'll lock in at least a good score, and possibly a *very* good score. The time to accelerate is at the *end* of each section, and not before.

Ignore These Two Voices in Your Head

I want to warn you that during the test, two tiny invisible fairies will be sitting on your shoulders, whispering in your ears. You'll hear only one of the fairies, and you won't be sure which one it is until the test starts.

One of the fairies whispers gleefully, "I can't believe how *easy* this test is." The other fairy whispers ominously, "This is by far the hardest test I've *ever* taken."

There aren't really fairies whispering in your ears, of course, but I promise you that you *will* hear one of those two messages. Whichever voice you hear, ignore it—it's your mind playing games with you.

The test will *seem* much easier than your practice tests, or it will *seem* impossibly difficult, but either way it's just the way the test *seems*—it's not reality. In other words, both states of mind reflect illusions.

By the way, it's better for your eventual score that the test seem too hard than too easy. Being aware of difficulty is a sign that you are thinking about the questions and taking pains. If the test seems easy, on the other hand, it's because you're not taking pains to get the problems right. **So if the test seems easier than you expected,** *force* **yourself to slow down and take pains—** *make* **the test seem more difficult.**

Trust me on this point: you'll do better if the test seems hard. Only two types of people find the SAT easy: test-taking geniuses (1 in 10,000), or test-taking simpletons (alas, far more common than geniuses).

See also A True Story on page 638.

But Listen to This Voice

"Any question on the SAT that I *know* I can get right, I will take all necessary pains to make *sure* that I get it right. I will always take pains."

Always Maintain Your Grip during the Test—
and if You Lose It, Regain Control

One of the things you'll probably have to deal with during the SAT are distractions. Someone sniffling or coughing or tapping a pencil are one thing, but I've heard stories of distractions ranging from pile drivers at a nearby construction site to the school's band—tubas, drums, trombones, cymbals—practicing on the field outside. Some distractions are insidious,* like hearing the jingle from a commercial playing over and over in your head.

Use distractions as reminders to get back to the test in front of you. If someone in the room is distracting you, raise the hand you're not writing with to attract the proctor's attention but keep working while you wait for the proctor to get to your desk.

*GSWLIU

Keep Moving While the Clock's Ticking

Don't count on the proctor to be accurate or consistent about writing the time remaining in a section on the board. Monitor your time continually as you work through each section.

Watch out or you may enter a time warp. You start working on a difficult question that has you stumped, and before you know it, you space out. Suddenly you "come to" with a jolt and realize that you've just spent the last few *minutes* doing nothing!

To avoid time warps and spacing out in general, keep your pencil moving every few seconds, marking up your test booklet. Don't ever let your pencil lift more than a couple of inches off the page; keep it poised to mark up questions.

Speaking of keeping your pencil moving, don't spend forever bubbling in your answer sheet. It's not uncommon to see a student in the exam room artistically darkening a bubble for ten or fifteen seconds. **If you waste even two or three seconds per question bubbling in your answer, you'll waste a minute by the end of the section—or over five minutes wasted on the entire test!**

For most of the test, keep your answer sheet under your test booklet. *Always, always, always* write your answer in your test booklet *before* you transfer your answers—in groups, like once every page—over to your answer sheet.

One of Your SAT Sections Won't Count

Your SAT will have two writing sections (the essay and the proofreading questions), three reading sections, and three math sections—and another one that won't count. The section that won't count could be a math section, a reading section, or a proofreading section. (You won't have two essay sections.)

The test writers use this experimental section—"equating section" is the euphemism* the test writers use—to try out questions for future SATs. Having to take a section that isn't scored doesn't seem fair—and it isn't—but your only consolation is that everybody who's ever taken an SAT before you has had to do the same thing.

You'll know by the end of the test which *type* of section was experimental because you'll have completed an extra math, reading, or proofreading section. But how can you tell *while* you're taking a section whether it's experimental or not?

There's no absolutely certain way to spot the experimental section but here are some guidelines. First, the experimental section tends to be in the middle of the test. The SAT will begin with the essay section, and then you'll do the first multiple-choice section, which could be math, reading, or proofreading. The experimental section will probably *not* be the first multiple-choice section you take.

*GSWLIU

Second, the experimental section will probably be 25 minutes long rather than 20 minutes.

Third, if you get two math or two reading sections in a row, it's likely that one of them will be experimental (though you won't know which one).

Fourth, the experimental section tends to be harder—sometimes *much* harder—than the sections that do count. Also, if the questions lurch randomly from easy to hard to easy again, it's likely that section is experimental. (The questions in the regular sections will go from easy to medium to hard, except for the reading questions.)

If you spot the experimental section, do not blow it off or you'll have trouble regaining your focus for the rest of the test. Do the best you can on the experimental section so that you'll remain mentally limber for the remaining sections.

> Students taking the SAT under special circumstances with extra time will not face an experimental section, nor will juniors taking the PSAT.

Never, Ever Give Up on the SAT

You already know not to listen to the fairy that whispers in your ear, "This test is impossibly hard." But sometimes you truly believe that you've bombed on a section.

Don't give up. In the first place, the section in question may have been the experimental section. But even if the section you had a lot of trouble with wasn't experimental, it's possible that you didn't do nearly as badly as you fear.

But even *if* you truly did have trouble with a section, do your best on the rest of the test. Use the remaining sections to practice your test-taking techniques. Get the maximum practice value out of this test so that you'll be that much better prepared when—if—you retake the test.

> See also A True Story on page 638.

Keep Working on Each Section until the Proctor Says Stop

In baseball the umpires make the calls; their word is final. Proctors are like SAT umpires—especially about timing.

I mentioned earlier that you can't count on your proctor's being accurate or consistent about writing times on the board. **In fact you shouldn't count on your proctor's being accurate about telling everyone when to stop, either.** I've heard of proctors stopping students several minutes early, or forgetting to tell students to stop altogether!

Use absolutely every second available to work on questions, and do not stop on any section until the proctor says stop.

> After the proctor finishes reading the instructions and before the test starts, he or she will ask the class whether anyone has a question. Raise your hand and ask whether it's okay that you use a digital timer. The proctor will say of course—which you knew—but your point in asking the question is actually to put the proctor on notice that someone in the room—you—will be timing the section down to the second. In a sense, *you* become a second umpire!

Don't Overreach—a Great SAT Score Happens *Accidentally* on the Way to a *Good* Score

You may be tempted during the exam to cut corners, to stop taking pains, to rush to finish—thinking that doing so is the only way you'll get your maximum possible score.

Don't.

The way to get a great score is to take all pains necessary to lock in a *good* score—for all but the last two or three minutes of each section. Then, and only then, when you've already guaranteed yourself a good score, you can take chances and reach for the great score.

Too many students—even the strongest test takers—make the mistake of reaching for a great score from the very start. Unfortunately, reaching for a great score at the beginning of the test forces them to take too many risks too early in each section. The usual result is not pretty: not only do they not get the great score they were hoping for, but they also blow the good score they

could have gotten.

Consider Steve, who's shooting for a super-high SAT math score. He's always gotten As in math, and now, as a junior, he's acing precalculus. Steve figures that SAT math problems are way easier than the advanced algebra and trigonometry questions he's been doing in his math class, so he ought to be able to get a near perfect score on the SAT.

So he rushes in the beginning of the first math section. Steve doesn't take all the pains he should to ensure that he gets the easy and medium questions right, but then hey, he's a great math student—he doesn't *need* to take pains.

Steve's breezing through the first section just fine when all of a sudden he gets stuck on a medium question. Now, instead of tearing himself away from the question as soon as he senses trouble, he wrestles with the question. Steve figures he *has* to get that question right if he wants to get the high score he's shooting for. And before he knows it, Steve's spent several minutes on the question and he *still* hasn't solved it. He finally does but now he's in panic mode, and he races through the rest of the section. Indeed, Steve remains in high panic mode for the rest of the test—with predictable consequences for his math, reading, and writing scores.

If Steve had been merely *willing* to get a good score, he would have had no trouble jettisoning the problem that confused him and moving on. Then, if he had time left at the end of the section, he could have returned to the question and tackled it again.

Ironically, the way to achieve a great score is being willing to accept a good score. Students who *aren't* willing to accept good scores often do even worse than that.

Imagine that you're a rock climber and about to scale the tallest, steepest cliff you've ever attempted. The way to get to the top of the cliff is to *forget* about getting to the top.

Instead, focus on finding a firm hold for your right hand. Then, when you find a hold for your right hand, you test it a bit to make sure it's firm. When you know that your right hand is secure, you turn your attention to your left hand and to finding a firm hold for it. And when you do find a hold for your left hand, and you test the hold for firmness, just to be sure, you then turn your attention to your right foot, and finding a firm hold for it. And when you find a firm hold for your right foot, you're now ready to pull yourself up and find a hold for your left foot. Then you repeat the cycle again, and again, and again, until you reach the top of the cliff.

Doing well on the SAT requires the same kind of focus. If you do the little things right, the big things will take care of themselves.

Take pains.

No Matter How Well You've Prepared for the SAT, It's Always Good to Walk in Feeling a Little *Unprepared*

Taking the real SAT is always, always different from taking practice tests that you know don't count. The SAT *does* count, and you know it. It's the same difference an athlete feels between a practice game and one in the final round of a championship.

The reason it's good to feel a little—just a little—unprepared is that you won't be thrown too badly by the inevitable surprises that occur on the exam. Students who feel completely prepared are too easily thrown for a loop when things in the actual exam room don't go exactly as they'd expected.

Most of what I've said in this chapter applies equally well to the PSAT, with the big difference that not as much is riding on the PSAT as on the SAT.

Should You Cancel Your SAT Score?

Sometimes it happens: you're suffering from an awful cold the day of the test, or you panic, or whatever. If you *know* you bombed, it might be a good idea to cancel your result because *every* SAT score goes down on your permanent record. The cancellation will be noted in your permanent record, but that's much better than having a bad score recorded.

Now, sometimes you only *think* you did poorly. Emotions can run high during a big test and it may be difficult to tell how you did. Just because you realize after the test that you missed a question or two doesn't mean you did poorly (in fact, it often means exactly the opposite). And remember that one of the sections is the unscored experimental one, so if you think you did poorly on the math, say, because of one particular section, there's a good chance it was the experimental one.

Anyway, if you decide to cancel your test, you can do so either at the test site (not recommended) or by notifying the testing authorities (ETS) by the Wednesday following the test. **If you think you might want to cancel your scores, ask the test supervisor for a Request to Cancel Test Scores Form but do *not* fill the form out at the test site.** If you're not absolutely sure whether you did poorly, you should probably wait and discuss the test with your friends—you may discover that you did better than you feared—or someone else who can be objective about your options.

You can cancel your score by writing a letter with all the pertinent identification information. You don't have to explain why you want to cancel your score. Label the heading: "Attention: SAT Score Cancellation." Send it to ETS in one of the following three ways:

- Via fax (the easiest method): 1-609-771-7681

- Via U.S. Postal Service Express Mail (U.S. only): SAT Score Cancellation, P.O. Box 6228, Princeton, NJ 08541-6228

- Via other overnight mail service (U.S. or international): SAT Score Cancellation, 225 Phillips Boulevard, Ewing, NJ 08618

Remember: if you cancel your scores, nobody, not even you, will ever know how you did.

A True Story

When I first began tutoring students for the SAT, a group of them decided to take the March test. (At the time, the May test was by far the more common.) Anyway, I still remember getting the first call from one of the girls immediately after the test was over. She was in tears. She *knew* she had done "horribly, horribly."

At the time, the SAT had twenty-five antonym questions that were pure vocabulary items—pretty much either you knew the words, or you didn't (though you could use process of elimination techniques like the ones I showed you for the sentence completions). This was also the time the SAT curve was about 100 points *harder* than it is today. (Back then, only a dozen students in the entire country got a perfect score; today hundreds do.)

Anyway, as I was saying, she just *knew* she had bombed. I asked her whether she had used all the techniques she had learned. She said yes. I asked her whether she'd taken pains. She said yes. I asked her whether she recalled any specific math mistakes she'd made. She said yes, unfortunately, one or two.

After listening to her responses, I told her that she'd done much better than she feared, and in fact I thought she had done extraordinarily well. She said, "But what about my math mistakes?" I told her that the fact she remembered having made the mistakes *after* the test was in fact a *good* sign, not a bad one. Remembering specific mistakes is a sign of being hyper-aware during the test. I told her that the mistakes she recalled were probably the *only* mistakes she made. She calmed down a bit and then she hung up.

Not a minute later I got another call, this time from a boy, who was also deeply shaken by the experience. He, too, was *sure* he had bombed. "I didn't recognize half the words on the test." Again I asked him whether he'd used the techniques, and whether he'd taken pains. "Yes," he replied. So I told him not to worry.

But that afternoon I received calls from almost all the students who'd taken that test, and every single one said basically the same thing: "I'm sure I bombed." At the same time, they all reported having used the techniques without fail, and having taken pains on all the questions.

Long story short, when scores were mailed out a month later (this was pre-Internet days, so you had to wait for an actual envelope for your scores), the average improvement of the students was nearly 200 points! And the girl who'd been in tears? Her verbal score shot from a 560 to a *perfect* 800 (back then you had to answer every single question correctly to achieve an 800, versus today when you can get a couple wrong), and her score in math (not her strongest subject) went up 140 points. Her total improvement was an astounding 400 points, and remember: she was *convinced* she should cancel her scores.

True story.

While You're Waiting for Your Scores, Get Back to Real Life

For the past few weeks, if not longer, you've been preoccupied with the SAT. Maybe you've let a few things slide: homework, extracurricular activities, your friends, *fun.* Now it's time to catch up on anything that's fallen behind and to return to your normal routine.

I know you may be feeling a little anticlimactic after getting all geared up for the SAT that's now over, but don't forget other tests that may be looming on the horizon. If it's early spring now, you may have an AP test or two looming in mid-May as well as the SAT II Subject Tests, which you may also need to take in the fall. **You've worked hard preparing for the SAT and it's natural to want to relax a bit. But please, please don't blow off your AP exams or SAT IIs; in many ways these tests can be just as important to your admissions chances as the SAT.**

By the way, do not throw away all your SAT preparation materials just yet—I know you're tempted—just in case you decide to retake the SAT.

What to Do When Your Scores Arrive

Three weeks after the SAT I (or SAT II), scores are mailed out to students, but scores are actually available two weeks after the test. If you're anxious to find out before the mail arrives how you did—or if you're wondering whether you need to retake the test the next testing weekend—you can request your scores by phone for an additional $10—1-800-SAT-SCORE (1-800-728-7267), 24 hours a day—or online at the College Board website.

> **Because the new SAT has an essay that must be scored, and because I am anticipating widespread administrative "glitches" at test sites around the country in 2005, I doubt scores will be available as soon as three weeks after the test; even longer delays are possible.**

Along with your score report—which you should save—the envelope will also contain an "Additional Services Order Form." Save this form, too.

Are You Planning to Retake the Test?

I discuss the question of whether you *should* retake the SAT at length in the FAQ section (available online, see questions 7 through 10). **If you *might* retake the SAT, send away for a copy of the test and your answer sheet.** This feature is called the Question and Answer Service. It isn't available for all test dates—nor is it clear whether this service will be modified for the new SAT.

To order, complete the Additional Services Order Form mailed with your score report. **You have up to five months after the test to order your answer sheet but do so as soon as your scores arrive because it takes a month or so for your answer sheet to arrive.** The cost is $10 (though this price will probably increase a bit along with everything else associated with the new SAT).

You get a photocopy of your actual answer sheet but not your personal test booklet. Still, you'll learn a lot by reviewing your errors and any blanks you may have left. **When the booklet arrives, you'll learn an incredible amount by retaking the test—timed, using OmniProctor—and seeing whether you repeat any errors.**

Using RocketScore to Improve Your Essay Performance

Any sufficiently advanced technology is indistinguishable from magic.
—Arthur C. Clarke

The First Computerized Essay-Evaluating Software Designed for the SAT

RocketScore will not only grade your essay faster than you can say S-A-T, it will also be able—unlike a human grader—to explain *why* you received the grade you did and to offer specific suggestions on ways you can improve your grade. RocketScore's writing suggestions are even more detailed than the teacher comments you are used to seeing in the margins of your returned papers.

RocketScore also lets you revise and resubmit your essay so that you'll see *instantly* how your corrections and improvements raise your grade. For example, RocketScore might have given your essay a score of 10.2 (out of 12), but commented that your sentences were too long and that your essay could have provided more details. If you revised your essay to provide more details and shortened the length of your longest sentences, you can resubmit your essay, and RocketScore will rescore your essay with adjusted comments.

On the actual SAT, you won't be able to revise your essay. Being able to revise your essays while you practice, however, shows you the value of each aspect of your writing. It's one thing for a teacher to tell you to add another paragraph to your essay. RocketScore shows you *exactly* how much the paragraph you added improves your essay's score.

RocketScore's revision feature almost turns essay writing into an arcade game, with students revising their essays to see how high they can boost their score.

How Accurate Is RocketScore?

Amazingly accurate. RocketScore grades your essay with decimal place accuracy. (On the SAT your actual grade would be rounded to the nearest integer.) If you're interested in statistics, RocketScore predicts the grade the official SAT graders would give your essay to within 1 point (on a 12-point scale) better than 90 percent of the time. That's more accurate than an official human SAT grader could be.

Whereas a human grader is, after all, only human—and therefore subjective and inconsistent—RocketScore is completely objective. RocketScore does not have moods, RocketScore does not get tired, and RocketScore does not have personal likes, dislikes, or prejudices.

> **RocketScore's accuracy assumes that you are writing your essay with no more than the twenty-five minutes you actually have on the SAT.**

How Does RocketScore Work?

RocketScore has been trained on hundreds of student papers scored by official SAT essay graders. RocketScore was programmed to learn which features of a student's paper human graders tend to evaluate positively, and which features they tend to evaluate negatively.

In the chapter "The Essay: Basic Principles" (see page 67), I discussed some of the major features that human graders reward (such as sophisticated vocabulary) or penalize (such as informal writing). The official SAT essay graders weigh dozens of tangible and intangible features of your essay, and so does RocketScore. RocketScore uses artificial intelligence to consider not just *what* you are saying, but how well you are saying it.

> **RocketScore does not judge your writing. RocketScore merely *predicts* what an official SAT grader would have given your essay.**

How Do I Use RocketScore?

Once you are registered with your CD-ROM at the RocketReview website, www.RocketReview.com, you no longer need the CD-ROM to access RocketScore. You are free to use RocketScore on any computer with web access, 24/7, wherever you are.

RocketScore cannot read your handwriting, so first you write your essay out longhand, just as you would on the SAT. Then, when your 25 minutes are up, type in your essay exactly as you wrote it, paragraph breaks and all. You *should* fix typos, but any words you misspell should be typed in as you misspelled them.

> RocketScore is not a spell checker or a grammar checker (although it does look for certain types of grammatical errors). Think of RocketScore as a *concept* checker. It is trained to see the extent to which your essay responded to the assigned essay topic.

Everything you need to know about the actual instructions to RocketScore is fully explained at the website.

Can RocketScore Be Fooled?

Yes, but what would be the point? You can fool your writing software's spell checker and grammar checker, too. RocketScore is a tool, like a spell checker or a grammar checker—though far more sophisticated than either—that you can use to improve your writing.

RocketScore *does* include some checks on the authenticity of your essay, but otherwise it assumes that you are writing a genuine essay and not trying to see whether you can slip through a fake essay without being caught. If something walks like a duck and sounds like a duck, RocketScore will assume that it *is* a duck, and not a clever student waddling about in a duck's outfit, trying to fool it.

> To fool RocketScore, a person would first have to know how to write a good essay on the assigned topic, and then jiggle the good essay in nonsensical ways. In other words, RocketScore can be fooled by a good writer into thinking that a bad essay is better than it is—after repeated attempts—but it cannot be so fooled by a bad writer.

Can RocketScore Evaluate Non-SAT Essays?

No. The current version of RocktetScore—version 1.0—is precisely calibrated to grade essays on assigned topics only. (In addition to the SAT essay, RocketScore has sample essays for the Advanced Placement Literature and Composition Test and the Advanced Placement United States History Test.)

RocketScore is currently being programmed for other Advanced Placement Tests. RocketScore version 2.0 will be able to evaluate essays on *any* topic.

Using the Self-Updating RocketReview CD-ROM

The Latest RocketReview Tools—and SAT Updates—Brought Directly to You

The trouble with books and software programs in a fast-changing field like SAT preparation is that they can quickly get dated. That's not a problem for you and me, however, since the very latest versions of RocketReview's resources will be posted on the website as soon as they become available. Every time you run the CD-ROM from your computer, the program connects to our RocketServer and automatically updates itself.

You Can Also Access RocketReview's Web-Based Tools While Away from Your Computer

Once you've registered at www.RocketReview.com using the CD-KEY from the book, you're no longer tied down to your computer. You can log in to the RocketReview website from any computer with web access. **See the next chapter for all the tools you'll have access to at www.RocketReview.com.**

Installing the CD-ROM on a PC

To install the RocketReview CD-ROM application, make sure you are connected to the Internet, then simply insert the CD into your computer, and it will load automatically. **If the CD-ROM application doesn't start when you insert the CD, simply browse to the CD and run the "RocketReview" application.**

The first time you run the CD, you'll be asked to enter the CD-KEY for validation. You can find this key inside the CD sleeve, in the back of the book. Once you have typed in the validation code, click "Enter" to continue. A screen will ask you where you would like your program installed. If you're not sure where you should install the program, just click "next," and the program will install itself to the default folder automatically.

> **Minimum Requirements for PCs**
> *Microsoft Windows 98 or higher*
> *400 Mhz (500 Mhz or more recommended)*
> *64 Mb RAM (128 recommended)*
> *30 Mb free space*
> *An Internet connection*

Running the CD-ROM on a Mac

The CD-ROM that comes with this book is not compatible with Macs, but Mac users can simply go to www.RocketReview.com and use their CD-KEY to access all the latest CD-ROM features via the web. You'll find this key inside the CD sleeve, in the back of the book.

> **Minimum Requirements for Macs**
> *G3 266 Mhz or higher*
> *256 Mb Memory*
> *Mac OS 9 or higher*
> *Microsoft Internet Explorer*
> *Macromedia Flash Player 7*
> *An Internet connection*

Using the RocketReview Website and All the Bonus Material You'll Find There

Cool Tools at Your Disposal

The RocketReview Revolution does not end with this book. At the RocketReview website, you'll find amazing software and other resources to help you improve your SAT score. Here's just a sample of the tools you'll be able to use:

RocketScore. RocketScore artificial intelligence software can not only grade your practice SAT essays in less than a second, but it can also offer a detailed analysis of the strengths and weaknesses of your essay and suggestion on how to improve your score. (For more on this unique feature, see "Using RocketScore to Improve Your Essay Performance," beginning on page 642.)

OmniProctor. Our patent-pending OmniProctor software will time your practice tests just like a real proctor so that you get the experience of taking an actual SAT.

The Latest Practice PSAT and SAT. Because the test writers had released little information about the new SAT as this book went to the printer, I've made the latest RocketReview practice SAT and PSAT—based on the most up-to-date information about the new test—available to you for downloading in convenient PDF format so that it will look just like the real test. As new practice tests become available, they'll be posted online.

Technique Animations. If a picture is worth a thousand words, a movie is worth a whole lot more. Every major test-taking technique described in this book is also demonstrated with animations so that you can see *exactly* how and what you should be doing, whether it's solving a complicated algebra question or reading a lengthy passage.

Additional Practice Problems. You'll find dozens and dozens of practice problems of every type for each part of the SAT: math, reading, and writing. These questions can be easily downloaded in a printable format.

Additional Vocabulary Practice. In addition to the core vocabulary list included in this book (beginning on page 309), you'll find additional words, more detailed definitions, notes on etymology and pronunciation, and more.

Breaking News about the SAT. We'll post the latest updates and information about the new SAT as soon as the information is released to the public.

Use RocketReview's Tools from *Any* Computer with Internet Access

Once you register yourself with your CD-ROM serial number at the RocketReview website, you'll be able to download the latest versions of RocketReview's SAT tools and information to your computer. But these tools are also available for your use at the RocketReview website itself. That means you aren't tied down to your home computer. You can use these SAT tools not just at home, but also at school or even at a friend's house.

For more on using the CD-ROM, see the previous chapter.

A Quick, One-Time Registration Process

The first time you go to the RocketReview website as a purchaser of this book, you should register yourself immediately. You'll need the CD-KEY (serial number) included with the CD-ROM to register. It's better if you register the first time using the CD-ROM in your home computer, although this is not necessary.

The registration process will prompt you to create a screen name and password (you know the drill), and will ask you for your email address (so you can get SAT updates and other important information emailed to you). During the registration process you'll also be asked some quick background questions about your academic situation, such as what grade you're in, what subjects you like in school, when you're planning to take the SAT, and the like.

None of these background questions asks you to reveal who you are, and your responses will be used solely to provide *you* with as much specific help as possible.

Once the Website Knows More about You, You'll Get Personalized Advice

It's important that you answer the registration questions as accurately as possible. The more the website knows about you and your situation regarding the SAT, the more specific and helpful the advice it will be able to give you. As we discussed back in "How to Use This Book" (beginning on page xiii) and in the special assemblies chapter (beginning on page xix), the advice I give to you regarding the SAT might not be the same advice I'd give to someone else.

For example, the concerns of an 11th grader preparing for the PSAT are very different from the concerns of a 12th grader about to take her final SAT before applying early decision. The advice I'd give to each student concerning how to prepare for the SAT would be very different. Similarly, I'd give someone with strong reading skills and a good vocabulary—but relatively weaker math skills—different advice from the advice I'd give to someone with strong math skills but a relatively weak vocabulary.

Anyway, it will take only a minute or two to answer the questions, and then you'll be good to go.

A Crash SAT Course
with Booster Rockets:
A Summary of the Entire Book

Fasten Your Seatbelt!

You're about to zoom through every major point made in this book—in short, everything you need to know for the SAT. I'm going to throw at you so much, so fast, that you might actually get dizzy!

Don't worry. I just want to get all the important points out on the table so that you can find them in one place. You can review everything here at your leisure in the coming weeks.

A Suggestion, and a Warning

First, I recommend that you spend two or three minutes to take the quick quiz in Tutorial 3 (beginning on page 6) *before* you read this summary. Having read this summary will prejudice some of your responses to the quiz.

Warning: Many of the points below may seem obvious. But read Tutorial 9 (page 16).

RocketNotes for the SAT

As I mention in Tutorial 14 (page 26), you don't have to "memorize" the points in the book, any more than you had to memorize how to tie your shoes. With practice—when you consciously and consistently apply RocketReview techniques to solve SAT problems—you'll learn to apply everything here by reflex when it counts: on the actual exam.

From Part I: Basic Tutorials

- The SAT is way, way different from the tests you're used to taking in school. If you solve SAT math questions the way you're used to solving math questions in class, if you read SAT passages the way you're used to reading novels or even your textbooks, if you compose an SAT essay the way you're used to writing essays in English class—you'll be in for a rude surprise.

- Only perfect practice makes perfect. Merely becoming familiar with the SAT is not enough to change your score significantly. If you want to change your SAT score, you have to change the way you take the test. If you want to change your SAT score a lot, you have to change the way you take the test—a lot.

- All the advice in this book applies to *you*. Treat every rule as absolute unless I point out an exception.

- Your brain plays tricks on you as you take the SAT far more often than you are aware. Misreading questions is probably the single greatest cause of avoidable errors on the SAT Math Test as well as the SAT Reading and Writing Tests.

- The less you "do in your head" on the test, and the more you use your pencil, the higher your score. Using your pencil literally makes you smarter.

From Part II: Advanced Tutorials

- Leaving a question blank *does* cost you points. If you think blanks "don't count," what kind of SAT score do you think you'd get if you left *every* question on the test blank? As a rule of thumb, each blank you leave chops 10 points off a perfect 2400—10 points that you can *never* get back.

- Guessing does *not* hurt your score—*bad* guessing hurts your score (though only a teeny bit more than blanks hurt, anyway). Good guessing *helps* your score.

- The *only* reason to leave a question blank is to save time that you can spend on other questions. If you've already spent time on a question, *answer it*.

- For the 99 percent of students who aren't shooting for a perfect score, the speed versus accuracy tradeoff means that you'll have to leave *some* questions blank to buy yourself time. *Anybody* can finish the test in the time allowed—but only by hurting his or her score. The faster you answer questions, the sloppier you get—and the more mistakes you make. Fortunately, it's possible to sacrifice some questions—not spending a second on them—and still get a good score.

- Many of the question types on the SAT are arranged in order of difficulty: from easy to medium to difficult.

- Each question is worth the same, regardless of its difficulty, so spend your time where it's likely to do the most good: on the *medium* questions. Spend the *least* amount of time on the most difficult questions (exactly the opposite of what most students do—one reason why most students find the SAT difficult).

- Easy questions have easy, obvious, *popular* answers; hard questions have hard, unexpected, *unpopular* answers (that's *why* hard questions are hard).

From Part III: The SAT Writing Test

- The essay counts for one-third of the total points here; the multiple-choice proofreading and editing (grammar) questions count for the rest.

- For most students, the fastest SAT point gains are to be found on the Writing Test.

- You're evaluated on how well you write the *first draft* of a persuasive essay on an assigned topic.

- Follow the RocketReview formula for essays: 25 minutes to plan and write your essay is not enough time to "be creative."

- Before beginning the actual essay, spend a few minutes outlining your response.

- Write *fast*. Your essay's overall length is a *major* factor in your grade. (The graders realize that you're working under pressure, so they don't expect a polished final paper; they largely overlook minor imperfections.)

- Try to use (at least) three scholarly examples in your essay—two literary and one historical is an excellent mix. Personal examples are far less impressive.

- Give your essay a formal tone by avoiding personal statements and by putting yourself (the writer) in the background.

- Sprinkle in a few SAT words throughout your essay, especially in the first and last paragraphs.

- Use five paragraphs, and spend the initial planning time to make sure the introductory paragraph is a zinger.

- Indent all your paragraphs clearly, and remember to begin each paragraph in the body of the essay with a sentence that ties the example back to your thesis.

- Think of the multiple-choice questions as a scavenger hunt for about ten different types of grammatical errors. You don't need to know formal grammar or grammatical terms—you just need to recognize an error when you see it.

- Beware of using your "ear" to answer questions: sometimes incorrect sentences sound fine and correct sentences sound awkward.

- You don't have to memorize dozens of grammar "rules." (*Always do this. Never do that.*) There are only a handful of important grammatical concepts being tested. Five types of grammatical errors account for the great bulk of mistakes on the SAT Writing Test: pronoun errors, singular-plural errors, idiom errors, comparison errors, and parallel structure errors.

- About one-sixth of the sentences contain no error.

- In the identifying sentence-error section (short underlinings), "style" is not being tested; a sentence must contain a grammatical error to be wrong. Beware of words that *aren't* underlined since they can make something underlined wrong.

- In the improving sentences section (long underlinings), "style" is being tested; in general, the shorter the choice, the better. (In both sections, neither spelling nor punctuation is being tested.)

From Part IV: The SAT Reading Test

- Sentence completion questions (fill-in-the-blank) count for one-fourth of the total points here; reading questions count for the rest.

- Start memorizing words *today.* The sentence completion questions are largely a test of vocabulary; a significant number of the reading questions also test vocabulary, directly and indirectly. Here are the top 10 SAT words: *conventional, undermine, dismissive, aesthetic, objective, reconcile, speculative, accessible, decorum,* and *impulsive.* How many of these words can you *define* (not just "use in a sentence")?

- No matter how many words you learn, you'll almost certainly encounter some words on the SAT that you don't know—and maybe some that you've never seen before. Fortunately, you don't have to know *all* the choices on a question—just *most* of them. If the answer isn't one of the words you know, it must be one of the words you *don't* know.

- Sentence completions can be answered much faster than reading questions, so leave no sentence completions blank. If you haven't determined the answer, *guess.* When guessing, remember that easy sentence completions have easy, obvious, popular answers; hard sentence completions have hard, unexpected, *unpopular* answers.

- If you don't know what a word means, don't waste precious time trying to "figure it out." Instead, determine whether the word is "positive" or "negative" and use process of elimination to decide what could be the answer.

- Process of elimination means finding reasons to get *rid* of choices, not finding reasons to pick a choice. The answer is the choice you can't find a reason to eliminate. (Beware of eliminating words you don't know—be *especially* aware of eliminating words you *think* you know.)

- The challenge on the reading passages is not to understand the passages, but rather to understand what the choices are saying. There is no "interpretation" on the SAT: learn to read every word of a choice *literally.* Misreading even a single word of a choice can cost you a question.

- Some of the reading passages are short. Do *not* read the longer passages too closely: you'll literally overload your brain circuits. Just get a general idea of what the passage is about and then look back to verify the details when you attack the questions.

- When reading, be sure you distinguish what the author thinks from the conventional wisdom—what *other* people think. Most SAT passages *begin* with what other people think before stating what the author thinks.

- The most important sentences in most SAT passages are the last line of the first paragraph or the first line of the second passage. The final sentence of the entire passage often summarizes the author's central point.

- Unlike the sentence completion questions, the reading questions are *not* in order of difficulty—they are in *chronological* order to match the information in the passage.

- Because reading questions are so time-consuming, only the strongest readers under time pressure should attempt all the questions. Better to attempt 10 questions out of 13 in a section and get 9 right than to attempt all 13 and get only 8 right because you had to rush.

From Part V: The SAT Math Test

- Although the SAT Math Test includes a few algebra II questions, most of the topics you need to know you learned before tenth grade. What's more, the directions to each math section in the test provide most of the formulas you need.

- Try not to use your calculator. Using your calculator wastes time and takes your eyes off the page, and you shouldn't need it anyway. If you think you need it for a tough calculation, you've probably missed the point of the question.

- The SAT Math Test rewards students who *notice* things about the question, so after you read a math question, don't be so quick to rush into a mathematical solution. Try *thinking* for a moment or two first.

- The most efficient way to solve SAT math questions is often *not* the way you're used to solving them in math class. Typical classroom solutions can make many SAT problems more complicated than they really are.

- *Whenever* possible, use one or more of the master math moves to solve questions: swap numbers (on questions with algebraic answer choices), estimate the answer (on word problems as well as geometry problems), or check the choices (on word problems).

- Until you're consistently scoring above 700 on the SAT Math Test, sacrifice a few of the hardest, most time-consuming questions in a section so you have more time to spend on the remaining questions.

- Every math question you blank, however, chops 12 points off your score—18 points at the high score range. If you've spent time on a question and haven't determined the answer as time is running out, it's always better to guess.

- When you guess, avoid popular choices on medium to hard questions. Popular choices will be "nice" numbers that can be easily derived from the information in the problem. The most popular (obvious) choice on a hard question won't be right—but it won't be far off the answer.

- After you've *glanced* at a hard question, *immediately* cross off any popular-looking choices (traps) *before* you begin solving the question.

- The secret to a great SAT math score is being willing to *take pains*—to get questions right. Yes, taking pains consumes a bit more time, but you can't afford *not* to take pains. So write down all your formulas and computations; do nothing "in your head." Whenever you can, draw pictures or diagrams to help your thinking. After you've solve a problem, *check your solution.*

- "Looking over your work" for errors is almost always a waste of time. But here's one thing you must *always* do: the last step you take on any SAT math problem—after you've checked your solution but before you darken in your answer sheet with the answer—is reread the question!

- There are no such things as "stupid" mistakes on the SAT Math Test. No such thing. If you got a question wrong that you should have gotten right, then 99 percent of the time you simply didn't take pains to get it right. You either didn't write all your work down on paper, you didn't use one of the master math moves, you didn't check your solution, or you didn't reread the question.

- You've probably made a mistake on a medium to hard question if it "seemed a little easy." If the answer didn't surprise you—if you felt no *pain* while solving the question—there's a good chance you made an error! Start by rereading the question.

- The math questions within each section are arranged in order of difficulty—even if they don't always *seem* to be. A difficult question that seems easy is a *killer rabbit.*

- If you aren't sure you can solve a problem simply by glancing at it, skip the question immediately, even if it's easy. Circle the question number so you can return to the question later.

- Go through each math section in at least two passes: the first time through, scoop up the questions you know how to solve *immediately;* then on your second (or even third) pass, return to the questions you skipped earlier.

- As time runs short in a math section, choose your last few problems especially carefully. Do the remaining problems not in numerical order, but in order of each remaining problem's likely time consumption.

- Spend most of your time on the easy and especially the *medium* questions. You'll either be able to get a hard question *quickly—or not at all.*

- If you don't know what to do: do whatever you *can* do (even a simple step gets you "unstuck" and reveals the way to the solution).

- When you get to a hard question that you don't know how to solve, try using WIBNI (wouldn't it be nice if). When you "WIBNI" a math question, you solve an easier version of the hard question to reveal the method you need to solve the harder version in front of you.

- Keep your pencil moving at all times. Don't think for more than a few seconds on a question. *Fiddling* with a question is often faster than trying to solve the question using reason.

From Part VI: Nuts and Bolts

- The best time to take your SAT is when you are prepared for it. Unless you are taking it in junior high school for a special academic program, you should not take the SAT before March of your junior year.

- It's probably worth doing *some* preparation for the PSAT, but save your active efforts for the SAT.

- Start your active preparation for the SAT two to four months before you intend to take the test. (Start working on your vocabulary, however, today.)

- Get the book *The Official SAT Study Guide,* the only source of actual SAT questions for the new SAT format. Ignore the advice in the book, however; it is neither insightful nor helpful.

- Start organizing yourself and your life the week before the SAT. Settle into a routine.

- No matter how much you've prepared for the SAT, the actual test experience is *always* different from what you expected. It's best to feel a little unprepared before the test actually begins. That way you won't be flustered by the novelty of the experience.

The Best* Practice SAT Ever Created

(*Most Instructive)

Some SATs Are More Equal Than Others

I realize it's pretty outrageous to claim that the SAT in this book is the best one ever created, which is why I qualified the claim by saying that this test is the most instructive. The SATs produced by the test writers are designed to do nothing more than *test* you, to give you a score. *This* SAT is designed to test you, too—but it's also designed to *improve* your score.

I studied every actual SAT administered in the last 25 years to create an SAT *archetype**, an ideal example. I carefully selected each problem in this test to best reflect the most likely essay theme, vocabulary words, grammatical concepts, types of reading passages and questions, and math problems that you'll encounter on *your* SAT (or PSAT).

*GSWLIU

Wait! If You're a Student, Do *Not* Look at this Version 1.0 Test!

As this book went to press, the official test writers still had not released the final, detailed specifications for the new SAT or PSAT. As a result, this test is the best possible *approximation* of the new SAT.

> Fortunately, the RocketReview website—that your RocketReview CD-ROM gives you access to—includes the very latest version of the SAT that you can download to your home or school printer. I repeat: Do *not* even peek at the version in this book—you'll be tempted—if you intend to print and take the latest version (1.1 or higher) of the test from the website. If you're a junior preparing for the PSAT, you can download a PSAT version of the test, too.

If you're an adult—a parent or teacher, say—feel free to look at this version of the test. But if you're a student—and you probably are—I highly recommend that you go to the RocketReview website and download the latest version of the test. **Once you even glance at a practice SAT—without taking it—you ruin the predictive value of that test. Practice SATs must be taken under timed, proctored conditions to provide a realistic projection of your actual SAT score.** Once you download and print the RocketReview SAT Version 1.1 (or higher), be sure you use OmniProctor to administer it to yourself under realistic, test-like conditions.

STOP!

Do not turn the page. The latest version of the test in this book is available at the website for you to download and print. Do not even peek at the test in this book if you intend to take the updated version.

1 ✳ ✳ ✳  ✳ ✳ ✳ 1

Unauthorized copying or reuse of
any part of this page is illegal.

SECTION 1
Time — 25 Minutes
1 Question

You have 25 minutes to write an essay on the topic below. Your essay will be judged on how well it is written as well as how adequately you have covered the topic. DO NOT WRITE ON ANOTHER TOPIC. AN ESSAY ON ANOTHER TOPIC WILL RECEIVE NO CREDIT.

Your essay must be written on your answer sheet on the lines provided. The lined pages will be sufficient if you use all the space provided.

Directions: Consider carefully the following statement and the assignment below it. Then plan and write an essay that explains your ideas as persuasively as possible. Keep in mind that the support you provide—both reasons and examples—will help make your view convincing to the reader.

The harder the conflict, the more glorious the triumph. What we obtain too cheap, we esteem too lightly; it is dearness only that gives everything its value.

—Thomas Paine

Assignment: What is your view of the idea that people tend to value most that which they worked hardest to obtain? In an essay, support your position by discussing an example (or examples) from history, literature, the arts, science and technology, current events, or your own experience or observation.

YOU MAY MAKE NOTES ON THIS PAGE AND ON THE PRECEDING PAGE, BUT YOU WILL BE EVALUATED ONLY ON WHAT YOU HAVE WRITTEN ON THE ANSWER SHEET.

STOP
If you finish before time is up, you may check your work on this section only. Do not turn to any other section in the test.

-2-

SECTION 2
Time — 25 Minutes
22 Questions

Directions: For each question in this section, select the best answer from among the choices provided, and fill in the corresponding oval on your answer sheet.

Each sentence below has one or two blanks. Each blank indicates that something has been omitted from the sentence. Choose the word or set of words that <u>best</u> completes the meaning of the sentence as a whole.

Example:

Trends are difficult to spot until they are well established because they usually begin as minor, seemingly ------- events.

(A) momentous   (B) popular   (C) insignificant
(D) current   (E) recent

1. It was hard not to laugh at the tiny kitten's ------- gestures intended to frighten us away from its food bowl.

    (A) menacing   (B) cunning   (C) vivacious
    (D) apathetic   (E) domesticated

2. Skilled animal trainers condition their animals to associate a specific ------- with a given behavior, so that each stimulus will ------- an expected response.

    (A) discipline . . vanquish
    (B) pattern . . subvert
    (C) habitat . . elicit
    (D) temperament . . yield
    (E) cue . . trigger

3. After years of feeling that their legitimate concerns were merely ------- to mainstream interests, a growing faction of marginalized citizens have rejected ------- and become more vocal.

    (A) arbitrary . . boycotts
    (B) nefarious . . lobbying
    (C) clamorous . . narcissism
    (D) squandered . . reclamation
    (E) peripheral . . passivity

4. Far from being ------- by a succession of setbacks in his life, Native American Billy Mills was inspired by his adversity and went on to win an Olympic gold medal.

    (A) daunted   (B) validated   (C) discredited
    (D) prohibited   (E) vindicated

5. Sadly, most academic prose is perplexing if not downright -------, and certainly not a model of writing to be emulated by students.

    (A) archetypal   (B) impenetrable
    (C) nondescript   (D) creative   (E) ostensible

6. The heroic rescuer was remarkably ------- about his feat: as soon as the news crews arrived to interview him for saving so many lives, he quietly ------- the scene.

    (A) eloquent . . persevered with
    (B) meritorious . . exempted from
    (C) unassuming . . retired from
    (D) conscientious . . commenced with
    (E) accommodating . . profited from

-3-

GO ON TO THE NEXT PAGE

7. By dismissing his opponents' views as -------, the speaker hoped that the audience would fail to notice that his own position was anything but -------.

    (A) tenable . . debatable
    (B) irrefutable . . preposterous
    (C) spurious . . plausible
    (D) partisan . . dubious
    (E) moderate . . inscrutable

8. Only the aging actor's biggest fans were able to overlook that his heart was no longer in his ------- performances, and that he relied on ------- when nuanced portrayals were required.

    (A) mercenary . . paradigms
    (B) perfunctory . . histrionics
    (C) laborious . . parodies
    (D) callow . . machinations
    (E) trenchant . . kudos

9. In the modern media age in which a public figure's every expression and gesture is scrutinized, successful politicians must be skilled at -------: able to mask their true feelings and emotions to suit the occasion or the views of their audience.

    (A) relegating   (B) coercing   (C) vilifying
       (D) dissembling   (E) perpetrating

GO ON TO THE NEXT PAGE

Each passage below is followed by questions about its content. Answer the questions based on what is <u>stated</u> or <u>implied</u> in each passage and in any introductory material.

Questions 10-12 are based on the following passage.

The following excerpt is from a book on the historical origins of human consciousness.

Consciousness is a much smaller part of our mental life than we are conscious of, because we cannot be conscious of what we are not conscious
Line of. How simple that is to say; how difficult to
(5) appreciate! It is like asking a flashlight in a dark room to search around for something that does not have any light shining upon it. The flashlight, since there is light in whatever direction it turns, would have to conclude that there is light
(10) everywhere. And so consciousness can seem to pervade all mentality when actually it does not.

The timing of consciousness is also an interesting question. When we are awake, are we conscious all the time? We think so. In fact, we
(15) are sure so! I shut my eyes and even if I try not to think, consciousness still streams on, a great river of contents in a succession of different conditions which I have been taught to call thoughts, images, memories, interior dialogues, regrets, wishes,
(20) resolves, all interweaving with the constantly changing pageant of exterior sensation of which I am selectively aware. Always the continuity. Certainly this is the feeling.

And yet the seeming continuity of
(25) consciousness is probably just an illusion. The flashlight would be conscious of being on only when it is in fact on. Though huge gaps of time might have occurred, provided things were generally the same, it would seem to the flashlight
(30) itself that the light had been continuously on. We are thus conscious less of the time than we think, because we cannot be conscious of when we are not conscious.

10. It can be inferred that the dark room mentioned in the first paragraph represents which of the following?

(A) An individual's forgotten thoughts, images, memories, and interior dialogues
(B) That part of an individual's reality of which he or she is not consciously aware
(C) The state of an individual's awareness while the individual is asleep rather than awake
(D) An individual's subconscious and unconscious mind
(E) That part of reality which is inaccessible to human consciousness

11. What is the primary function of the second paragraph?

(A) To offer another metaphor of the ubiquity of consciousness
(B) To characterize the perception that we are continuously conscious
(C) To offer numerous examples of the different ways in which we are conscious
(D) To answer the question whether we are conscious all the time
(E) To show that we are not consciously aware, even though it may seem so

12. Which of the following can be inferred if things did not remain "generally the same" (lines 27-30) for the flashlight when it turned back on?

(A) The flashlight would assume that things change, as they always do.
(B) The flashlight would conclude that there might be other flashlights in the room.
(C) The flashlight would wonder how it had been turned on.
(D) The flashlight would be aware that it had not noticed everything earlier.
(E) The flashlight would realize that it had been off for a time.

-5-

GO ON TO THE NEXT PAGE

Questions 13-15 are based on the following passage.

The following passage is an excerpt from a novel written in the 1870's by a renowned female author.

     Mr. Casaubon, as might be expected, spent a great deal of time at the Grange in these weeks, and the hindrance which courtship occasioned to
Line the progress of his great work—*The Key to All*
(5) *Mythologies*—naturally made him look forward the more eagerly to the happy termination of courtship. But he had deliberately incurred the hindrance, having made up his mind that it was now time for him to adorn his life with the graces
(10) of female companionship, to irradiate the gloom which fatigue was apt to hang over the intervals of studious labor with the play of female fancy, and to secure in this, his culminating age, the solace of female tendance[1] for his declining years. Hence
(15) he determined to abandon himself to the stream of feeling, and perhaps was surprised to find what an exceedingly shallow rill[2] it was. As in droughty[3] regions baptism by immersion[4] could be performed only symbolically, so Mr. Casaubon
(20) found that sprinkling was the utmost approach to a plunge which his stream would afford him; and he concluded that the poets had much exaggerated the force of masculine passion. Nevertheless, he observed with pleasure that Miss Brooke showed
(25) an ardent submissive affection which promised to fulfill his most agreeable provision for marriage. It had once or twice crossed his mind that possibly there was some deficiency in Dorothea to account for the moderation of his abandonment; but he was
(30) unable to discern the deficiency or to figure to himself a woman who would have pleased him better; so that there was clearly no reason to fall back upon but the exaggerations of human tradition.

[1] The act of attending to or waiting on; caring for

[2] A small stream

[3] Dry and parched, as a result of abnormally low rainfall

[4] A religious ceremony in the Christian faith by which a person is immersed in water, thereby initiating the recipient into the Christian community.

13. The narrator uses the phrase "shallow rill" (line 17) as a metaphor to

(A) emphasize Mr. Casaubon's religious leanings
(B) suggest that Mr. Casaubon was afraid of his declining years
(C) remind the reader that this was Mr. Casaubon's first courtship
(D) underscore the relative depth of Mr. Casaubon's emotions
(E) point out that poets sometimes exaggerate human passions

14. The word "abandonment" (line 29) refers to Mr. Casaubon's doing which of the following?

(A) Giving up his great work to devote himself to courtship
(B) Accepting that Dorothea's deficiencies should not stand in the way of his feelings
(C) Deciding against the upcoming marriage
(D) Letting go of the search to find a woman to replace Dorothea
(E) Surrendering himself completely to his emotions

15. Mr. Casaubon is depicted as all of the following EXCEPT

(A) reflective
(B) scholarly
(C) self-centered
(D) romantic
(E) stolid

-6-

GO ON TO THE NEXT PAGE

Questions 16-22 are based on the following passage.

The following passage is an excerpt from a collection of essays on ecology written by a professor of zoology.

Every species has its niche, its place in the
grand scheme of things. Consider a wolf-spider as
it hunts through the litter of leaves on the
Line woodland floor. It must be a splendid hunter; that
(5) goes without saying for otherwise its line would
have long since died out. But it must be proficient
at other pursuits, too. Even as it hunts, it must
keep some of its eight eyes on the lookout for the
things that hunt it; and when it sees an enemy it
(10) must do the right thing to save itself. It must
know what to do when it rains. It must have a
lifestyle that enables it to survive in the winter. It
must rest safely when the time is not apt for
hunting. And there comes a season of the year
(15) when spiders, as it were, feel the sap rising in their
eight legs. The male must respond by going to
look for a female spider, and when he finds her, he
must convince her that he is not merely something
to eat—yet. And she, in the fullness of time, must
(20) carry an egg-sack as she goes about her hunting,
and later must let the babies ride on her back.
They, in turn, must learn the various forms of
fending for themselves as they go through the
different months of the spider's life until they, too,
(25) are swift-running, pouncing hunters of the
woodland floor.

Wolf-spidering is a complex job, not
something to be undertaken by an amateur. We
might say that there is a profession of wolf-
(30) spidering. It is necessary to be good at all its
manifold tasks to survive at it. What is more, the
profession is possible only in very restricted
circumstances. A woodland floor is necessary, for
instance, and the right climate with a winter
(35) roughly like that your ancestors were used to; and
enough of the right sorts of things to hunt; and the
right shelter when you need it; and the numbers of
natural enemies must be kept within reasonable
bounds. For success, individual spiders must be
(40) superlatively good at their jobs and the right
circumstance must prevail. Unless both the skills
of spidering and the opportunity are

present, there will not be any wolf-spiders; the
"niche" of wolf-spidering will not be filled.
(45) "Niche" is a word ecologists have borrowed
from church architecture. In a church a "niche"
means a recess in the wall in which a figurine is
placed; it is an address, a location, a physical
place. But the ecologist's "niche" is more than
(50) just a physical space: it is a place in the grand
scheme of things. The niche is an animal's (or a
plant's) profession. The niche of the wolf-spider is
everything it does to get its food and raise its
babies. To be able to do these things it must relate
(55) properly to the place where it lives and to the other
inhabitants of that place. Everything the species
does to survive is its niche. The physical living
place in an ecologist's jargon is called the *habitat*.
The habitat is the "address" or "location" in which
(60) individuals of the species live. The woodland
floor hunted by the wolf-spiders is the habitat, but
wolf-spidering is the niche.

16. The main purpose of this passage is to

(A) develop a metaphor
(B) offer an explanation
(C) propose a theory
(D) raise a question
(E) describe a species

17. The word "place" (line 1) most nearly means

(A) purpose
(B) location
(C) status
(D) role
(E) setting

18. In lines 7-10, the author mentions that a wolf-spider needs to keep "some of its eight eyes on the lookout for" its

(A) circumstances
(B) pursuits
(C) offspring
(D) predators
(E) prey

-7-

GO ON TO THE NEXT PAGE

668

19. The complex job of the wolf-spider referred to in the second paragraph is

    (A) finding its proper niche
    (B) finding the right circumstances
    (C) everything it must do to survive and reproduce
    (D) maintaining its place in the food chain
    (E) contributing to its environment

20. If wolf-spiders were not "superlatively good at their jobs" or if the "right circumstances" did not prevail, as discussed in the second paragraph, which of the following would be the most likely eventual consequence?

    (A) The wolf-spider's habitat would change.
    (B) The wolf-spider's line would end.
    (C) The wolf-spider's niche would change.
    (D) The wolf-spider would acquire new natural enemies.
    (E) The wolf-spider would have competitors for its niche.

21. If the author used the word "niche" in the same way as its architectural meaning (lines 45-49), a wolf-spider's niche would refer to its

    (A) environment
    (B) lifestyle
    (C) opportunity
    (D) specialty
    (E) design

22. Which of the following is probably the most serious limitation to the author's likening an animal's niche to a human profession?

    (A) An animal's niche is a much more complex job than any human profession.
    (B) The word "niche" can be used in varying contexts with different meanings.
    (C) Different animals have widely different niches.
    (D) Unlike a human being, an animal can neither choose nor change its profession.
    (E) An animal must contend with evading predators as well as with finding prey.

STOP

If you finish before time is up, you may check your work on this section only. Do not turn to any other section in the test.

-8-

SECTION 3
Time — 25 Minutes
20 Questions

Directions: You may use any available space in your booklet for scratch work, but only your answer sheet will be graded. When you have determined the answer to a question, fill in the corresponding oval on your answer sheet.

Notes:

1. You may use a calculator. All numbers used are real numbers. All figures lie in a plane unless otherwise indicated.

2. Figures that accompany problems are intended to provide information useful in solving the problems. They are drawn as accurately as possible EXCEPT when a specific problem states that the figure is not drawn to scale.

Reference Information

$A = \pi r^2$ $A = lw$ $A = \frac{1}{2}bh$ $V = lwh$ $V = \pi r^2 h$ $c^2 = a^2 + b^2$ Special Right Triangles
$C = 2\pi r$

The number of degrees of arc in a circle is 360.
The measure in degrees of a straight angle is 180.
The sum of the measures in degrees of the angles of a triangle is 180.

---

1. If $x = 4$ and $y = 20$, what does $\dfrac{2x + y}{2}$ equal?

    (A) 4
    (B) 11
    (C) 12
    (D) 14
    (E) 24

2. If j is an integer and $\dfrac{38}{j}$ lies between 7 and 8, what does j equal?

    (A) 5
    (B) 6
    (C) 7
    (D) 8
    (E) 9

3. If $n \neq 0$, then $\dfrac{100}{100} \times n =$

    (A) 1
    (B) $\dfrac{1}{n}$
    (C) n
    (D) $100n$
    (E) $10,000n$

-9-

GO ON TO THE NEXT PAGE

670

4. If p is a positive number, 25 percent of p is how much greater than 20 percent of p ?

    (A) $0.02p$

    (B) $0.05p$

    (C) $0.45p$

    (D) $\dfrac{p}{4}$

    (E) $\dfrac{p}{5}$

5. What is the probability that an integer selected at random from the first twenty positive integers will be a single-digit number?

    (A) $\dfrac{1}{20}$

    (B) $\dfrac{1}{5}$

    (C) $\dfrac{1}{4}$

    (D) $\dfrac{9}{20}$

    (E) $\dfrac{1}{2}$

6. At a certain candy store, peanuts cost $1.50 per pound and cashews cost $2.00 per pound. If a 10-pound mixture of peanuts and cashews costs $18.00, how many pounds of the mixture are peanuts?

    (A) Two
    (B) Four
    (C) Five
    (D) Six
    (E) Eight

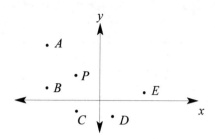

7. In the figure above, point P lies on a line (not shown) that has a positive slope. Which of the following labeled points could also lie on the line?

    (A) A
    (B) B
    (C) C
    (D) D
    (E) E

8. If $\dfrac{x}{y} = \dfrac{3}{2}$, what is the value of $\dfrac{y}{2x}$?

    (A) $\dfrac{1}{3}$

    (B) $\dfrac{2}{3}$

    (C) $\dfrac{3}{4}$

    (D) 2

    (E) 3

-10-

GO ON TO THE NEXT PAGE

9. If $xy = 2$ and $x^2y = 16$, what is the value of y?

(A) $\dfrac{1}{4}$

(B) $\dfrac{2}{3}$

(C) 2

(D) 4

(E) 8

12. The average (arithmetic mean) of 5 numbers is greater than 80 and less than 86. If three of the numbers are 94, 82, and 76, which of the following could NOT be the other two numbers?

(A) 93 and 84
(B) 88 and 95
(C) 87 and 85
(D) 84 and 80
(E) 63 and 89

10. Which of the following numbers is NOT two more than a prime number?

(A) 5
(B) 7
(C) 9
(D) 11
(E) 13

13. Let k be the greatest of 3 consecutive positive integers whose sum is t. In terms of t, what is the sum of the next 3 consecutive integers immediately following k?

(A) $t + 3$
(B) $t + 6$
(C) $t + 9$
(D) $t + 12$
(E) $t + 18$

11. If $f(x) = 8 - x^3$, then $f(-2) =$

(A) 16
(B) 4
(C) 0
(D) -4
(E) -16

14. What are all values of x for which $|x - 8| > 6$

(A) $x > 14$

(B) $-14 < x < 14$

(C) $-2 < x < 14$

(D) $x < -14$ or $x > 14$

(E) $x < 2$ or $x > 14$

GO ON TO THE NEXT PAGE

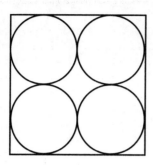

15. In the figure above, 4 circles each of radius 1 are placed inside a square. If the total area covered by the circles is c and the area of the square is s, what is the value of $\dfrac{c}{s}$?

(A) $\dfrac{\pi}{4}$

(B) $\dfrac{\pi}{2}$

(C) $\dfrac{4}{\pi}$

(D) $\dfrac{3\pi}{4}$

(E) $\dfrac{3\pi}{2}$

16. If $xy^2z^3 < 0$, then which of the following must be negative?

(A) x

(B) xy

(C) yz

(D) xz

(E) xz^2

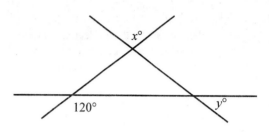

Note: Figure not drawn to scale.

17. If $x = 140$ in the figure above, what is the value of y ?

(A) 100
(B) 80
(C) 60
(D) 40
(E) 20

18. If $\dfrac{x^0}{x^{\frac{1}{2}}} = 4$, then $x =$

(A) $\dfrac{1}{16}$

(B) $\dfrac{1}{2}$

(C) 2

(D) 4

(E) 16

-12-

GO ON TO THE NEXT PAGE

673

Set $A = \{1, 2, 3, 4, 5, 6\}$

19. Two numbers from set A are selected at random without replacement and their sum recorded. How many different sums are possible?

   (A) Thirty-six
   (B) Thirty
   (C) Fifteen
   (D) Eleven
   (E) Nine

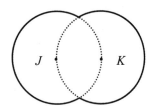

20. In the figure above, the two circles with centers J and K each have a radius of 3. What is the perimeter of the combined figure, indicated with a solid line?

   (A) 16π
   (B) 12π
   (C) 8π
   (D) 6π
   (E) 4π

STOP
If you finish before time is up, you may check your work on this section only. Do not turn to any other section in the test.

-13-

SECTION 4
Time — 25 Minutes
22 Questions

> **Directions:** For each question in this section, select the best answer from among the choices provided, and fill in the corresponding oval on your answer sheet.

Each sentence below has one or two blanks. Each blank indicates that something has been omitted from the sentence. Choose the word or set of words that best completes the meaning of the sentence as a whole.

Example:

Trends are difficult to spot until they are well established because they usually begin as minor, seemingly ------- events.

(A) momentous   (B) popular   (C) insignificant
    (D) current   (E) recent

---

1. A classic is ------- literary work that may fall out of favor with a generation of readers, and yet sooner or later will be rediscovered by another generation.

    (A) an enduring   (B) an authoritarian
      (C) a derivative   (D) an exclusively
        (E) a conservative

2. The virtues of meals by the best chefs are not ------- but rather subtle, and require the discriminating palate of the connoisseur to ------- fully.

    (A) gullible . . encompass
    (B) consuming . . savor
    (C) sagacious . . distinguish
    (D) flagrant . . appease
    (E) conspicuous . . appreciate

3. The committee's recommendation represented not simply ------- change, but rather a profound departure from the administration's previous policy.

    (A) an unexpected   (B) a redundant
      (C) an inexpedient   (D) a cosmetic
        (E) a political

4. Aspiring actors sometimes forget that fame is not guaranteed but rather -------; and even if achieved, not ------- but rather ephemeral.

    (A) intransigent . . transient
    (B) elusive . . immutable
    (C) hopeful . . permanent
    (D) mercurial . . impersonal
    (E) inevitable . . futile

5. The effects of Brian Regan's brilliant comedy routine are ------- as well as -------; they sneak up on an unsuspecting audience, slowly gathering an overwhelming comic force.

    (A) cumulative . . insidious
    (B) eccentric . . negligent
    (C) vivid . . earnest
    (D) prominent . . surreptitious
    (E) austere . . acquisitive

6. Every new scientific theory that challenges the reigning orthodoxy is viewed as ------- until it is supported by incontrovertible evidence and eventually adopted as truth.

    (A) dichotomous   (B) heretical   (C) critical
      (D) relative   (E) inconsequential

GO ON TO THE NEXT PAGE ➡

7. The effect of the introduction of improved football helmets on the game's safety was -------: because the new helmets encouraged a more dangerous style of play, the number and severity of head injuries increased.

(A) exhilarating   (B) presupposed
  (C) aggressive   (D) counterintuitive
      (E) fortifying

8. Benjamin Franklin was the ultimate -------: he was less concerned with speculating than with testing his ideas experimentally.

(A) idealist   (B) catalyst   (C) dogmatist
    (D) theoretician   (E) empiricist

9. After months of an unrelentingly ------- schedule on the campaign trail, the investigative journalist was left completely -------.

(A) dilatory . . listless
(B) soporific . . burgeoning
(C) frenetic . . enervated
(D) torpid . . moribund
(E) noisome . . obdurate

-15-

GO ON TO THE NEXT PAGE

676

The passage below is followed by questions about its content. Answer the questions based on what is <u>stated</u> or <u>implied</u> in each passage and in any introductory material.

Questions 10-22 are based on the following passage.

The following excerpt is from a book on the culmination in the eighteenth century of a race to discover a reliable method for accurately determining a boat's east-west position in the open sea, the lack of which cost countless thousands of sailors their lives over the previous centuries.

As a child, I learned the trick for remembering the difference between latitude and longitude. The latitude lines—or parallels—stay parallel to each
Line other as they girdle the globe from the Equator to
(5) the poles in a series of shrinking concentric rings. The meridians of longitude go the other way: they loop from the North Pole to the South and back again in great circles of the same size, so they all converge at the ends of the earth.
(10)   Any sailor worth his salt can gauge his latitude well enough by the length of the day, or by the height of the sun or known guide stars above the horizon. Christopher Columbus followed a straight path across the Atlantic when he "sailed
(15) the parallel" on his 1492 journey. Determining longitude in the open sea, however, is a problem that had stumped some of the wisest minds of the world for the better part of human history. To learn one's longitude, one needs to know what
(20) time it is aboard ship and also the time at another place of known longitude—at the very same moment. The two clock times enable the navigator to convert the hour difference into a geographical separation. Precise knowledge of the
(25) hour in two different places at once—so easily accessible today from any pair of cheap wristwatches—was utterly unattainable up to and including the era of pendulum clocks. On the deck of a rolling ship, such clocks would slow down, or
(30) speed up, or stop running altogether. Normal changes in temperature encountered en route from a cold country of origin to a tropical trade zone thinned or thickened a clock's lubricating oil and

made its metal parts expand or contract with
(35) equally disastrous results. A rise or fall in barometric pressure, or the subtle variations in the Earth's gravity from one latitude to another, could also cause a clock to gain or lose time.
     For lack of a practical method of determining
(40) longitude, every great captain in the Age of Exploration became lost at sea despite the best available charts and compasses. From Vasco da Gama to Ferdinand Magellan to Sir Francis Drake—they all got where they were going by
(45) forces attributed to good luck or the grace of God. As more and more sailing vessels set out to conquer or explore new territories, to wage war, or to ferry gold and commodities between foreign lands, the wealth of nations floated upon the
(50) oceans. Because no ship owned a reliable means for establishing her whereabouts, untold numbers of sailors died when their destinations suddenly loomed out of the sea and took them by surprise.
     The quest for a solution to the problem of
(55) longitude persisted over four centuries and across the whole continent of Europe. Renowned astronomers approached the longitude challenge by appealing to the clockwork universe: Galileo Galilei, Christiaan Huygens, Sir Isaac Newton, and
(60) Edmond Halley (of comet fame) all entreated the moon and stars for help. Palatial observatories were founded at Paris, London, and Berlin for the express purpose of determining longitude by the heavens. Meanwhile, lesser minds devised
(65) schemes that depended on the yelps of wounded dogs, or the cannon blasts of signal ships strategically anchored—somehow—on the open ocean.
     As time passed and no method proved
(70) successful, the search for a solution to the longitude problem assumed legendary proportions. The governments of the great maritime nations— including Spain, the Netherlands, and certain city-states of Italy—periodically offered jackpot purses
(75) for a workable method. The British Parliament, in its famed Longitude Act of 1714, set the highest

-16-

GO ON TO THE NEXT PAGE >

bounty of all: naming a prize equal to a king's
ransom (several million dollars in today's
currency) for a "Practicable and Useful" means of
(80) determining longitude.

    English clockmaker John Harrison, a
mechanical genius who pioneered the science of
portable precision timekeeping, devoted his life to
this quest. With no formal education or
(85) apprenticeship to any watchmaker, Harrison
nevertheless constructed a series of virtually
friction-free clocks that required no lubrication and
no cleaning, that were made from materials
impervious to rust, and that kept their moving
(90) parts perfectly balanced in relation to one another,
regardless of how the world pitched or tossed
about them. He did away with the pendulum, and
he combined different metals inside his works in
such a way that when one component expanded or
(95) contracted with changes in temperature, the other
counteracted the change and kept the clock's rate
constant. Harrison had accomplished what
Newton had feared was impossible: He invented a
clock that would carry the true time like an eternal
(100) flame from home port to any remote corner of the
world.

    A man of simple birth, Harrison crossed
swords with the leading lights of his day. He made
a special enemy of the Reverend Nevil Maskelyne,
(105) the fifth astronomer royal, who contested
Harrison's claim to the coveted prize money, and
whose tactics can only be described as foul play.
Harrison's every success was parried by members
of the scientific elite, who distrusted his magic
(110) box. The commissioners charged with awarding
the longitude prize—Maskelyne among them—
changed the contest rules whenever they saw fit,
so as to favor the chances of astronomers over the
likes of Harrison and his fellow "mechanics." But
(115) the utility and accuracy of Harrison's approach
triumphed in the end. An aged, exhausted
Harrison, taken under the wing of King George III,
ultimately claimed his rightful monetary award in
1773—after forty struggling years of political
(120) intrigue, international warfare, academic
backbiting, scientific revolution, and economic
upheaval.

10. The overall tone of the passage is best described as
which of the following?

(A) Lyrical
(B) Objective
(C) Mocking
(D) Argumentative
(E) Sarcastic

11. The discussion in lines 28-38 suggests that before
Harrison's invention, the chief drawback to using
clocks at sea was that timepieces of the time were
too

(A) unwieldy
(B) delicate
(C) complicated
(D) rigid
(E) expensive

12. The author mentions the great captains of the Age
of Exploration (lines 42-45) in order to

(A) illustrate that the navigation problem of the
    time was not attributable to other causes
(B) prove that even the best sailors of the time
    were lucky
(C) show that these captains were superstitious
    and did not rely enough on maps and
    compasses
(D) demonstrate that the longitude problem
    primarily affected large ships
(E) provide specific details for the historical
    narrative

13. The author uses the phrase "the wealth of nations
floated upon the oceans" (lines 49-50) in order to
emphasize

(A) the importance of navigation to fishermen
(B) that even without precise means of navigation,
    nations were able to carry on trade
(C) how much depended on successful navigation
(D) the value of minerals to be found in the
    oceans
(E) that better navigation would reduce the need
    to replace sailing vessels lost at sea

-17-

GO ON TO THE NEXT PAGE ⇒

14. The author probably mentions the famous scientists including Galileo and Newton (lines 56-61) in order to

   (A) show how long scientists had been working on the longitude problem

   (B) demonstrate that astronomers were trying to design a clock based on the movements of sun and the moon

   (C) create the impression that astronomers were the most likely to solve the challenge of longitude

   (D) argue that modern astronomy rose primarily as a result of the quest to solve the navigation problem

   (E) put the magnitude of Harrison's eventual achievement in perspective

15. As used in line 63, the word "express" most nearly means

   (A) sole
   (B) known
   (C) conspicuous
   (D) definite
   (E) rapid

16. It can be inferred that the author views the schemes discussed in lines 65-68 as primarily

   (A) impractical
   (B) visionary
   (C) tentative
   (D) ingenious
   (E) mysterious

17. It can be inferred from the discussion in lines 84-92 that Harrison was

   (A) inventive
   (B) self-taught
   (C) successful
   (D) unknown
   (E) confident

18. It can be inferred from the discussion in the sixth paragraph (lines 81-101) that which of the following aspects of timepieces did Harrison's innovations do the most to improve?

   (A) Their precision
   (B) Their popularity
   (C) Their portability
   (D) Their simplicity
   (E) Their cost

19. The phrase "how the world pitched and tossed about them" (lines 91-92) refers to

   (A) scientific disputes
   (B) nations at war
   (C) storms at sea
   (D) the movement of a clock's components
   (E) the movement of stars in the sky

20. The phrase "crossed swords with" (lines 102-103) most nearly means

   (A) inspired
   (B) condemned
   (C) joined with
   (D) competed with
   (E) attracted the attention of

21. The passage implies that the scientific elite (line 109)

   (A) had no way of adequately testing Harrison's claims

   (B) were uncertain about the contest rules

   (C) did not fully understand the workings of Harrison's clock

   (D) had submitted designs for competing versions of clocks

   (E) harbored a grudge for the favoritism Harrison enjoyed

GO ON TO THE NEXT PAGE ▷

22. The attitude with which the commissioners in charge of the longitude contest (line 110) viewed Harrison and his efforts can best be described as

(A) inquisitive
(B) acquiescent
(C) ambivalent
(D) conciliatory
(E) dismissive

STOP

If you finish before time is up, you may check your work on this section only. Do not turn to any other section in the test.

SECTION 5
Time — 35 Minutes
45 Questions

Directions: For each question in this section, select the best answer from among the choices provided, and fill in the corresponding oval on your answer sheet.

Directions: The following sentences contain errors in grammar, usage, idiom, and diction (choice of words).

      Some sentences are correct.
      No sentence contains more than one error.

In choosing answers, follow the requirements of standard written English, the kind of English found in most college textbooks.

You will find that the error, if there is one, is underlined and lettered. (Assume that elements of the sentence that are not underlined are correct and cannot be changed.) If there is an error, select the one underlined part that must be changed to make the sentence correct.

If there is no error, select choice E.

    Example:

       No matter how hard an artist <u>tries</u>, no
                     A

       individual <u>is</u> truly free <u>from</u> the influences
             B   C

       of <u>their</u> predecessors. <u>No error</u>
          D   E

Ⓐ Ⓑ Ⓒ ● Ⓔ

---

1. Now that Siena <u>won</u> first place in several regional
               A

tournaments, she <u>appears</u> somewhat <u>excited about</u>
              B   C

traveling to the capital <u>to compete</u> in the tennis
             D

finals. <u>No error</u>
     E

2. The <u>construction of</u> the company's headquarters
          A

<u>required</u> hiring additional <u>personnel</u>, increasing
    B   C

factory output, and <u>added</u> office space. <u>No error</u>
          D   E

-20-

GO ON TO THE NEXT PAGE ⟩

681

3. The remarkable leadership skills exercised by
                                         A

   General Grant in the Battle of Fort Donelson were
                  B   C

   attributable to his military experience. No error
   D   E

4. On hockey teams, players are asked to determine
                                        A

   which of their peers seems most capable to be
   B   C   D

   captain. No error
           E

5. A recently established body of minority voters

   have met with officials from the federal
   A

   government to express its distress over recent
                          B   C

   instances of electoral discrimination. No error
   D   E

6. Many of the citizens which voted in the election
   A   B

   thought the campaign's central issue so trivial
                                        C

   that they were almost indifferent to the race's
                          D

   outcome. No error
           E

7. That Frank Wildhorn composes so prolifically for
   A   B

   the Broadway stage and he knows so little about
                       C

   reading music is surprising. No error
                   D   E

8. If one is interested in becoming truly
                        A

   knowledgeable about archeology,
                 B

   you should attend digs at actual excavation sites
   C

   as well as study textbooks. No error
   D   E

9. A ranger at the state park explained to the
                             A

   students that an extremely large percentage of their
                                                  B

   wildlife relies on insects as a source of food.
           C   D

   No error
   E

10. Some advanced math concepts are difficult for
    A   B

    students to understand because they call for
                                   C   D

    students to think three-dimensionally. No error
                                          E

-21-

GO ON TO THE NEXT PAGE

682

11. Public speaking <u>often</u> causes a political candidate's
                          A

stomach to turn, <u>thereby</u> preventing <u>him or her</u>
                      B   C

<u>to speak</u> clearly. <u>No error</u>
    D   E

12. There <u>has always been</u> some degree of tension
                    A

between <u>my roommate and I</u> because we each
                    B

prefer <u>such</u> different environments <u>in which</u> to
        C   D

study. <u>No error</u>
              E

13. Each of the journalists—both <u>expecting to win</u>
                                            A

a major literary prize—<u>hope</u> to hear <u>from</u> the
                              B   C

Pulitzer Prize committee <u>soon</u>. <u>No error</u>
                              D   E

14. In his last <u>work on</u> the American Civil War,
                        A

historian Shelby Foote <u>argued that</u> the South's
                              B

economic resources were not <u>as vast as</u> <u>the North</u>.
                                    C   D

<u>No error</u>
    E

15. After Mary Lou Retton <u>won</u> a gold medal in the
                                    A

1988 Olympics, many young girls <u>who</u> wanted to
                                        B

become <u>a gymnast</u> like <u>her</u> enrolled in gymnastics
            C   D

programs across the country. <u>No error</u>
                                      E

16. The Supreme Court Justice <u>began</u> to question his
                                        A

<u>stance on</u> burning flags in public <u>when</u> he
    B   C

discussed <u>them</u> with veterans of the armed forces.
              D

<u>No error</u>
    E

17. No matter how <u>diligent</u> some students work, <u>they</u>
                            A   B

are <u>susceptible to</u> making careless spelling and
        C

punctuation errors so they should have someone

proofread <u>their</u> papers. <u>No error</u>
              D   E

-22-

GO ON TO THE NEXT PAGE

683

18. Dogs are <u>such</u> loyal creatures that it is not
      A

uncommon for <u>them</u> to travel many miles home
          B

<u>after</u> <u>separating from</u> their owners.
 C   D

<u>No error</u>
  E

19. <u>For many workers,</u> the option of working at home
     A

—an <u>increasingly</u> popular choice—seems
       B

<u>improving</u> morale <u>as well as</u> productivity. <u>No error</u>
  C   D   E

20. <u>Despite</u> scientists' best efforts to find
    A

<u>an explanation,</u> <u>certain</u> aspects of the
     B   C

<u>anomaly</u> cannot be explained fully.
   D

<u>No error</u>
  E

21. <u>When</u> deciding between the two candidates, the
    A

voters <u>apparently</u> decided <u>in favor of</u> electing the
     B   C

<u>least</u> objectionable politician. <u>No error</u>
  D   E

22. The movers <u>affirmed</u> that they would <u>arrive at</u> ten
       A   B

o'clock <u>and</u> that they <u>would try to</u> unload all the
    C   D

furniture by noon. <u>No error</u>
         E

GO ON TO THE NEXT PAGE

Directions: In each of the following sentences, some part of the sentence or the entire sentence is underlined. Below each sentence you will find the original underlined portion, followed by four alternative ways of writing the underlined part.

Choice A is always the same as the underlined part. Select choice A if you think that the original version is better than any of the suggested changes.

Otherwise, select the choice that produces the most effective sentence while still retaining the original meaning.

Pay attention to acceptable usage in grammar, sentence construction, and punctuation. These questions test correctness and effectiveness of expression, so follow the requirements of standard written English. An effective sentence will be clear and exact, without awkwardness, redundancy, or ambiguity.

Example:

Most people seem to prefer realistic art <u>than abstract art</u>.

(A) than abstract art
(B) than they do abstract art
(C) to abstract art
(D) instead of abstract art
(E) rather than art that is abstract

23. Alison worked daily to improve her dance techniques, <u>this</u> rigorous practice finally paid off when she was accepted into a highly prestigious ballet company.

(A) this
(B) therefore
(C) and this
(D) of which
(E) that

24. For many centuries, <u>using water and coal for power is more efficient</u> than using oil.

(A) using water and coal for power is more efficient
(B) using water and coal for power was more efficient
(C) being able to use the power of water and coal is more efficient
(D) there was more efficiency in using water and coal
(E) to use water and coal was more efficient

25. Henry Ford, envisioning a cheap and reliable car which would be called the Model T, <u>and this new vehicle was designed</u> with mass production in mind.

(A) and this new vehicle was designed
(B) and the design of this new vehicle was
(C) and this new vehicle having been designed
(D) and his design of this new vehicle was
(E) designed this new vehicle

26. Native Americans are often treated as a single group, but they actually comprise many distinct tribes, <u>each with its own language and culture.</u>

(A) each with its own language and culture.
(B) each having their own rules and culture.
(C) when they each have their own rules and culture.
(D) which has its own language and culture.
(E) they each have a language and culture of their own.

-24-

GO ON TO THE NEXT PAGE

27. Marie Curie used her considerable scientific skills to isolate the radioactive element radium <u>and she could research</u> the atomic properties of matter.

    (A) and she could research
    (B) as well as researching
    (C) and so to research
    (D) and the research of
    (E) and to research

28. <u>Because she was young was why Kim, a college student applying for jobs, felt that she was being denied a position.</u>

    (A) Because she was young was why Kim, a college student applying for jobs, felt that she was being denied a position
    (B) Kim, a college student applying for jobs, felt that she was being denied a position because she was young
    (C) Because she was young, Kim felt that this was why she was being denied a job as a college student
    (D) Kim, a young college student looking for a job, feeling that she was being denied a position
    (E) A college student, Kim, felt that because she was a college student applying for jobs, she was being denied a position

29. The film critic blasted the remake of *Breakfast at Tiffany's*, arguing that the leading actress had been cast not so much for her acting ability <u>but for her physically resembling Audrey Hepburn.</u>

    (A) but for her physically resembling Audrey Hepburn
    (B) the reason being her physical resemblance of Audrey Hepburn
    (C) the reason was her physically resembling Audrey Hepburn
    (D) but for her physically resembling Audrey Hepburn
    (E) as for her physical resemblance to Audrey Hepburn

30. Possibly the most colorful linguistic dialect in the United States, <u>the South is characterized by its</u> lazy drawls and slurred syllables.

    (A) the South is characterized by its
    (B) the South has such characteristics as
    (C) the South includes among its characteristics
    (D) southern accents are characterized by their
    (E) southern accents are including such characteristics as

31. Although small-scale earthquakes occur regularly on the island, <u>causing the land to shake for no more</u> than a few seconds.

    (A) causing the land to shake for no more
    (B) and yet it shakes for no more
    (C) they do not cause it to shake for more
    (D) and they do not cause it to shake for more
    (E) yet causing to shake for more

32. <u>The television series, once close to being cancelled, is</u> now one of the most popular shows on the air.

    (A) The television series, once close to being cancelled, is
    (B) The television series was once close to being cancelled, it is
    (C) The television series that once having been close to cancellation, is
    (D) The television series, because it was so close to being cancelled, is
    (E) The television series was once close to being cancelled, and it is

33. Thomas Edison was one of the twentieth century's most notable <u>inventors, this includes the creation of</u> the electric light bulb and the telegraph.

    (A) inventors, this includes the creation of
    (B) inventors, which includes the creation of
    (C) inventors, whose creations include
    (D) inventors; his creations include
    (E) inventors; this creations includes

GO ON TO THE NEXT PAGE

34. When the architect sketched his plans for the castle, <u>conventional Gothic designs were employed, but it was not strictly adhered to by him</u>.

(A) conventional Gothic designs were employed, but it was not strictly adhered to by him
(B) conventional Gothic designs were employed, but he did not adhere to it strictly
(C) conventional Gothic designs were employed by him and not strictly adhered to
(D) he employed conventional Gothic designs, but they had not been strictly adhered to
(E) he employed, but did not strictly adhere to, conventional Gothic designs

35. The historical term "McCarthyism" <u>referring to Senator Joseph McCarthy's vitriolic pursuit</u> of Communism within American borders during the 1950s.

(A) referring to Senator Joseph McCarthy's vitriolic pursuit
(B) referring to vitriolic pursuit by Senator Joseph McCarthy
(C) which refers to Senator Joseph McCarthy's vitriolic pursuit
(D) refers to Senator Joseph McCarthy's vitriolic pursuit
(E) is when vitriolic pursuit by Senator Joseph McCarthy

36. <u>Each summer hundreds of thousands of tourists travel to Florence, a city famous for its many churches and museums</u>.

(A) Each summer hundreds of thousands of tourists travel to Florence, a city famous for its many churches and museums
(B) Famous for its many churches and museums, hundreds of thousands of tourists travel to Florence each summer
(C) Hundreds of thousands of tourists travel to Florence each summer famous for its many churches and museums
(D) Hundreds of thousands of tourists had traveled to Florence each summer, which is known for its many churches and museums
(E) Each summer, famous for its many churches and museums, hundreds of thousands of people visit Florence

37. Caesar's northern armies invaded the region that was to become modern-day Belgium, ravaging the <u>land and the defeated barbarians were driven to flight</u>.

(A) land and the defeated barbarians were driven to flight
(B) land with the defeated barbarians having been driven to flight
(C) land, and the driving of the defeated barbarians to flight
(D) land and driving the defeated barbarians to flight
(E) land; driving to flight the barbarians defeated

-26-

GO ON TO THE NEXT PAGE ➔

38. <u>Overcoming severe physical limitations to become a prominent lecturer and author, historians view Helen Keller</u> as one of the twentieth century's most remarkable figures.

(A) Overcoming severe physical limitations to become a prominent lecturer and author, historians view Helen Keller

(B) Historians who view Helen Keller as overcoming severe physical limitations to become a prominent lecturer and author view her

(C) Helen Keller's overcoming severe physical limitations to become a prominent lecturer and author led to her being viewed

(D) Because Helen Keller overcame severe physical limitations to become a prominent lecturer and author, historians view her

(E) Based on her overcoming severe physical limitations to become a prominent lecturer and author, Helen Keller is viewed by historians

GO ON TO THE NEXT PAGE

Directions: The following selection is an early draft of a student's essay. Some parts of the essay need to be revised. Each sentence has been numbered for easy reference.

Read the essay and answer the questions that follow.

- Some questions are about particular sentences or parts of sentences, and ask you to improve sentence structure or diction (word choice).
- Other questions are about organization and development between sentences or paragraphs, and ask you to improve transitions or reduce wordiness.

Guide your decisions by the requirements and conventions of standard written English.

Questions 39-45 are based on the following passage.

(1) The phrase "a cappella" means "without accompaniment" in Italian. (2) In English *a cappella* usually refers to a style of singing without being accompanied by music of any kind. (3) Singing of this type can be performed individually or in a group. (4) In the United States, *a cappella* singing groups are becoming more and more common, being more popular on college campuses especially. (5) If you are in a college, there is probably a singing group there.

(6) The a *cappella* singing style, having its origins in African and Slavic folk singing, requires participants to create their own harmonies, usually in four parts. (7) Usually, *a cappella* groups will write arrangements of classic jazz and folk songs, adding and simplifying the piece for four voice parts. (8) These groups usually perform from memory, sometimes doing dance moves while singing.

(9) My own *a cappella* singing group is all-female and is called the Grace Notes. (10) We perform an arrangement of "Love Me Tender," among other pieces, and also a very funny arrangement of "In the Still of the Night." (11) We sing on our college campus and also sometimes for parties and social events. (12) I auditioned for my group and was happy to get in, since I enjoy singing. (13) It's a lot of fun, and I recommend it highly. (14) For me, *a cappella* singing means a group of friends who have a good time together and enjoy singing for other people.

39. What is the best way to combine sentences 2 and 3, reproduced below?

In English a cappella *usually refers to a style of singing without being accompanied by music of any kind. Singing of this type can be done individually or in a group.*

(A) In English *a cappella* usually refers to a style of singing without musical accompaniment, and can be performed individually or in a group.
(B) Usually referring in English to a style of singing without a piano or any other accompaniment, singing of this type can also be performed individually or in a group.
(C) Referring to a style of singing in English without a piano or any other accompaniment, singing of this type can usually be performed individually or in a group.
(D) It usually refers to a style of singing without a piano or any other accompaniment, and it can also be performed individually or in a group.
(E) Singing of this type in English usually refers to a style of singing without a piano or any other accompaniment and can be performed individually or in a group.

-28-

GO ON TO THE NEXT PAGE

40. Which of the following is the best revision of sentence 4, reproduced below?

In the United States, a cappella *singing groups are becoming more and more common, being more popular on college campuses especially.*

(A) (as it is now)
(B) Especially on college campuses, in the United States *a cappella* singing groups are becoming more and more common.
(C) *A cappella* singing groups are becoming increasingly common in the United States, especially on college campuses.
(D) On college campuses, especially in the United States, *a cappella* singing groups are becoming more and more common.
(E) Especially in the United States, *a cappella* singing groups on college campuses are becoming more and more common.

41. How should the underlined portion of sentence 6 be revised?

The a cappella *singing style, <u>having its origins in African and Slavic folk singing</u>, requires participants to create their own harmonies, usually in four parts.*

(A) (as it is now)
(B) which has its origins in African and Slavic folk singing
(C) has its origins in African and Slavic folk singing
(D) and having its origins in African and Slavic folk singing
(E) the origins of which are in African and Slavic folk singing

42. In sentence 7, reproduced below, which is the best word replacement?

Usually, a cappella *groups will be writing arrangements of classic jazz and folk songs, adding and simplifying the piece for four voice parts.*

(A) replace "Usually" with "Possibly"
(B) replace "will be writing" with "will write"
(C) replace "adding and simplifying" with "adding plus simplifying"
(D) replace "jazz and folk songs" with "jazz songs and folk songs"
(E) replace "the piece" with "pieces"

43. Which of the following is the best revision of sentence 10, reproduced below?

We perform an arrangement of "Love Me Tender," among other pieces, and also a very funny arrangement of "In the Still of the Night."

(A) (as it is now)
(B) We perform pieces, among others, of "Love Me Tender," and a very funny arrangement of "In the Still of the Night."
(C) Among other pieces, we perform an arrangement of "Love Me Tender" and a very funny arrangement of "In the Still of the Night."
(D) We perform among other pieces, an arrangement of "Love Me Tender," and "In the Still of the Night."
(E) In addition to an arrangement of "Love Me Tender," among other pieces, we perform a very funny arrangement of "In the Still of the Night."

44. Omitting which of the following sentences would best improve the unity of the final paragraph?

(A) sentence 10
(B) sentence 11
(C) sentence 12
(D) sentence 13
(E) sentence 14

GO ON TO THE NEXT PAGE

5 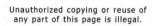  **5**

Unauthorized copying or reuse of
any part of this page is illegal.

45. The purpose of the final paragraph is to

(A) rely on earlier claims to prove the original
   premise
(B) provide a summary of the topic
(C) offer a personal anecdote
(D) explain the author's connection to the topic
(E) suggest a solution to a problem raised earlier

STOP

**If you finish before time is up, you may check your work on this
section only. Do not turn to any other section in the test.**

SECTION 6
Time — 25 Minutes
20 Questions

Directions: You may use any available space in your booklet for scratch work, but only your answer sheet will be graded. When you have determined the answer to a question, fill in the corresponding oval on your answer sheet.

Notes:

1. You may use a calculator. All numbers used are real numbers. All figures lie in a plane unless otherwise indicated.

2. Figures that accompany problems are intended to provide useful information useful in solving the problems. They are drawn as accurately as possible EXCEPT when a specific problem states that the figure is not drawn to scale.

Reference Information

$A = \pi r^2$
$C = 2\pi r$
$A = lw$
$A = \frac{1}{2}bh$
$V = lwh$
$V = \pi r^2 h$
$c^2 = a^2 + b^2$
Special Right Triangles

The number of degrees of arc in a circle is 360.
The measure in degrees of a straight angle is 180.
The sum of the measures in degrees of the angles of a triangle is 180.

1. If $2(x + 5) = 22$, then $x + 5 =$

(A) 11
(B) 15
(C) 16
(D) 20
(E) 38

2. Team M has 24 members, and Team N has 48 members, with no members in common. If $\frac{1}{3}$ of the members of Team N join Team M, how many members will Team M have then?

(A) 16
(B) 32
(C) 36
(D) 40
(E) 60

-31-

GO ON TO THE NEXT PAGE

692

3. If $x + y = 12$ and $x = 2y$, then $x =$

   (A) 3
   (B) 4
   (C) 6
   (D) 8
   (E) 24

4. What integer is between $\frac{16}{3}$ and $\frac{27}{4}$?

   (A) 4
   (B) 5
   (C) 6
   (D) 7
   (E) 8

5. The difference between two numbers is 25. If the smaller number is 5 less than half the larger number, what are the two numbers?

   (A) 35 and 60
   (B) 25 and 60
   (C) 25 and 50
   (D) 25 and 40
   (E) 15 and 40

6. The product of 2, 3, and x is equal to the sum of $2x$ and

   (A) 3
   (B) 4
   (C) 6
   (D) $3x$
   (E) $4x$

7. In the figure above, 4 congruent equilateral triangles are combined to form equilateral triangle ABC. If the perimeter of triangle ABC is 24, what is the perimeter of one of the smaller triangles?

   (A) 4
   (B) 6
   (C) 12
   (D) 18
   (E) 24

8. Four runners, J, K, L, and M, enter a race. L finishes ahead of M, and J finishes immediately after K. If there are no ties in the race, in which of the following positions could L finish?

   I. First
   II. Second
   III. Third

   (A) I only
   (B) II only
   (C) III only
   (D) I and III only
   (E) I, II, and III

-32-

GO ON TO THE NEXT PAGE

693

9. If $x^2 + y^2 = 4$, then $(4x)^2 + (4y)^2 =$

(A)   16
(B)   32
(C)   64
(D) 128
(E) 256

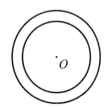

Note: Figure not drawn to scale.

10. The two circles in the figure above have
the same center O. The circumference of
the outer circle is 16π greater than the
circumference of the inner circle. The
radius of the outer circle is how much
greater than the radius of the inner circle?

(A) 2
(B) 4
(C) 8
(D) 4π
(E) 8π

11. If the origin is the midpoint of the line
segment between the points (4, 2) and
(x, y), then $(x, y) =$

(A) (8, 4)
(B) (2, 1)
(C) (2, -4)
(D) (-4, 2)
(E) (-4, -2)

12. Englewood is the largest city in
Washington County. If the population of
Englewood is 50% of the population of the
rest of Washington County, then the
population of Englewood is what percent
of the total population of Washington
County?

(A)   25%

(B) $33\frac{1}{3}$%

(C)   50%

(D) 150%

(E) 200%

13. Let $x \diamond y$ be defined by $x \diamond y = x + 2y$ for
all values of x and y. If $6 \diamond n = 36$, what
is the value of n?

(A) 12
(B) 15
(C) 21
(D) 30
(E) 42

-33-

GO ON TO THE NEXT PAGE

Questions 14 and 15 refer to the following table, which shows the results of a survey of 60 women and 40 men.

FAVORITE PETS

	Cat	Dog	Other
Women	45	12	3
Men	8	26	6

14. What percentage of women surveyed listed "dog" as their favorite pet?

    (A) 8%
    (B) 12%
    (C) 18%
    (D) 20%
    (E) 24%

15. A man and a woman are selected at random from among the persons surveyed. How many times more likely is the man to have listed "other" as his favorite pet than the woman was to have listed "other" as her favorite pet?

    (A) Two
    (B) Three
    (C) Four
    (D) Five
    (E) Six

$$pq + rs + tu$$

16. The expression above represents an odd integer. At most, how many of the integers p, q, r, s, t, and u could be even?

    (A) One
    (B) Two
    (C) Three
    (D) Four
    (E) Five

Note: Figure not drawn to scale.

17. If AD > BE in the figure above, then which of the following must be true?

    (A) $BC > CD$
    (B) $CD > BC$
    (C) $AC > CE$
    (D) $AB > DE$
    (E) $AB + DE > BD$

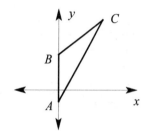

18. In the figure above, points A, B, and C have coordinates $(0, 3)$, $(0, -1)$, and $(4, 6)$ respectively. What is the area of triangle ABC?

    (A) 16
    (B) 10
    (C) 8
    (D) 5
    (E) 4

-34-

GO ON TO THE NEXT PAGE

19. A certain ice cream parlor sells 15 flavors of ice cream. The parlor's best-selling flavor ice cream—vanilla—produces 3 times the average (arithmetic mean) sales of the other flavors. Sales of vanilla ice cream account for what fraction of the parlor's total ice cream sales?

    (A) $\dfrac{1}{6}$

    (B) $\dfrac{3}{17}$

    (C) $\dfrac{1}{5}$

    (D) $\dfrac{4}{15}$

    (E) $\dfrac{3}{4}$

20. Cylinder A has volume v. If Cylinder B has twice the radius of Cylinder A and twice the height, what is the volume of Cylinder B in terms of v?

    (A) $2v$
    (B) $4v$
    (C) $6v$
    (D) $8v$
    (E) $16v$

STOP
If you finish before time is up, you may check your work on this section only. Do not turn to any other section in the test.

-35-

SECTION 7
Time — 20 Minutes
18 Questions

Directions: For each question in this section, select the best answer from among the choices provided, and fill in the corresponding oval on your answer sheet.

Each passage below is followed by questions about its content. Answer the questions based on what is <u>stated</u> or <u>implied</u> in each passage and in any introductory material.

Napoleon was asked whether he preferred courageous generals or brilliant generals. Neither, he replied; he preferred lucky generals. A society
Line that cannot accept the concept of luck is one that
(5) seeks to attach blame to every undesired outcome. Unless we can accept bad luck we are destined to be governed by a risk-blame-litigation-compensation culture that suffocates initiative.

For some, this culture can be rewarding.
(10) Tripping over an uneven paving stone, plus a note from a compliant doctor, plus the assistance of an enterprising lawyer, can yield untold riches— sometimes even without tripping. But for others, this culture is threatening. All the traditional risks
(15) encountered in our daily lives are now overhung by legal and financial risks. The whole world is now struggling to come to grips with this culture.

1. As used in line 12, "enterprising" most nearly means

(A) successful
(B) financial
(C) well-known
(D) expensive
(E) opportunistic

Who speaks Spanish in the United States? Or rather, who speaks what kind of Spanish? People who walk through the streets of Miami, Los
Line Angeles, or New York and have a sense of things
(5) Hispanic know that there is not one Spanish in North America but many—at least four: the ones used by Puerto Ricans, by Chicanos, by Cubans, and by the other subgroups.

Although Latinos share a common cultural
(10) heritage and use the same grammar and syntax, the various idioms—or, should I say, quasi dialects— they use can be distinguished only through an understanding of each group's unique national pasts. The vocabulary used by the four groups depends on
(15) historical circumstances. Argentines, for example, are less the product of an interracial mixture between the Spanish conquistadors and the native Indians, and therefore have a more Europeanized Spanish than that of say, Mexicans, who have
(20) integrated pre-Columbian terms and names such as Aztec and Mayan into their day-to-day language.

2. Which of the following is the main idea of this passage?

(A) The day-to-day language of Argentines is a truer Spanish than is the day-to-day language of Mayans.
(B) Though seemingly the same, the Spanish language in fact has more than one grammar and syntax.
(C) Different kinds of Spanish are spoken in different cities throughout the world.
(D) To appreciate the different idioms used by various Latino groups, one must explore each group's historical background.
(E) Spanish is no longer spoken on the streets of American cities.

-36-

GO ON TO THE NEXT PAGE

Questions 3-4 are based on the following passage.

Why is it we know so little about the life of
William Shakespeare—thought by many to be the
greatest writer the English language has ever
Line known—when we know comparatively so much
(5) about the lives of his accomplished but less talented
peers? Our lack of knowledge about Shakespeare
has inspired countless conspiracy theories. The
actual writing of Shakespeare's works has been
attributed to others, from his contemporary
(10) playwrights Christopher Marlowe and Ben Jonson,
to the brilliant Renaissance philosopher and
polymath Francis Bacon, to even Charles DeVere, a
nobleman of the time.
    Though Shakespeare died at just 52, he was an
(15) immensely successful dramatist who wound up
owning a one-tenth share in the actors' company
that played at the Globe Theatre (the most important
stage company of its day) as well as becoming a
prosperous property owner. Circumspect, and only
(20) too aware of political threats to playwrights—such
as the government-inspired murder of Christopher
Marlowe, the government's torture of Thomas Kyd,
and its branding of Ben Jonson—Shakespeare kept
himself nearly anonymous, despite being the
(25) reigning dramatist of London. Wary to the end,
Shakespeare led a life virtually without memorable
incident, as far as we can tell.

3. The author's primary purpose is to

   (A) propose an alternative explanation
   (B) refute a misconception
   (C) challenge an assumption
   (D) reveal a historical fallacy
   (E) provide new evidence in support of a theory

4. The author probably cites evidence of
Shakespeare's success and notoriety (lines 14-19)
in order to

   (A) show that historians know more about
       Shakespeare's life than is commonly
       supposed
   (B) emphasize the difficulty such a public figure
       would have had in maintaining a low
       profile
   (C) suggest that Shakespeare might have had
       many enemies who would have wished him
       harm
   (D) debunk the notion that Shakespeare might
       have posed a political threat
   (E) prove that Shakespeare was more successful
       than his contemporary playwrights

GO ON TO THE NEXT PAGE

Questions 5-14 are based on the following passage.

The following excerpt is from a book of literary criticism written by John Gardner, noted author and critic.

The language of art critics, and of artists of the kind who pay attention to critics, has become exceedingly odd: not talk about feelings or
Line intellectual affirmations—not talk about moving
(5) and surprising twists of plot or wonderful characters and ideas—but sentences full of large words like *hermeneutic, heuristic, structuralism, formalism,* or *opaque language,* and full of fine distinctions—for instance those between *modernist*
(10) and *post-modernist*—that would make even an intelligent cow suspicious. Though more difficult than ever before to read, criticism has become trivial.

The trivial has its place, its entertainment
(15) value. I can think of no good reason that some people should not specialize in the behavior of the left-side hairs of an elephant's trunk. Even at its best, its most deadly serious, criticism, like art, is partly a game, as all good critics know. My
(20) objection is not to the game but to the fact that contemporary critics have for the most part lost track of the point of their game, just as artists, by and large, have lost track of the point of theirs. Fiddling with the hairs on an elephant's nose is
(25) indecent when the elephant happens to be standing on the baby.

At least in America, art is not thought capable, these days, of tromping on babies. Yet it does so all the time, and what is worse, it does so with a
(30) bland smile. I've watched writers, composers, and painters knocking off their "works" with their left hands. Nice people, most of them. Artists are generally pleasant people, childlike both in love and hate, intending no harm when they turn out
(35) bad paintings, compositions, or books. Indeed, their ambition guarantees that they will do the best they know how to do or think they ought to do. The error is less in their objects than in their objectives. "Art is play, or partly play," they'll tell
(40) you with an engaging smile, serving up their non-nutritious fare with the murderous indifference of

a fat cook serving up hamburgers. What they say is true enough, as far as it goes, and nothing is more tiresome than the man who keeps hollering,
(45) "Hey, let's be *serious!*" but that is what we must holler.

In a world where nearly everything that passes for art is tinny and commercial and often, in addition, hollow and academic, I argue—by reason
(50) and by banging the table—for an old-fashioned view of what art is and does and what the fundamental business of critics therefore ought to be. Not that I want joy taken out of the arts; but even frothy entertainment is not harmed by a touch
(55) of moral responsibility, at least an evasion of too fashionable simplifications. My basic message is as old as the hills, drawn from Homer, Plato, Aristotle, Dante, and the rest, and standard in Western civilization down through the eighteenth
(60) century: one would think all critics and artists should be thoroughly familiar with it, and perhaps many are. But my experience is that in university lecture halls, or in kitchens at midnight, after parties, the traditional view of art strikes most
(65) people as strange news.

The traditional view is that true art is moral: it seeks to improve life, not debase it. It seeks to hold off, at least for a while, the twilight of the
(70) gods and us. I do not deny that art, like criticism, may legitimately celebrate the trifling. It may joke, or mock, or while away the time. But trivial art has no meaning or value except in the shadows of more serious art, the kind of art that, if you will,
(75) makes the world safe for triviality. The art which tends toward destruction, the art of cynics and nihilists, is not properly art at all. Art is essentially serious and beneficial—a game played against chaos and death, against entropy. It is a
(80) tragic game, for those who have the wit to take it seriously, because our side must lose: a comic game because only a clown with sawdust brains would take our side and eagerly join in.

Like legitimate art, legitimate criticism is a
(85) tragic-comic holding action against entropy. Art builds temporary walls against life's leveling force, against the ruin of what is splendidly unnatural in us: consciousness. Art rediscovers, generation by generation, what is necessary to humanness. Criticism restates and clarifies, reinforces the wall.

-38-

GO ON TO THE NEXT PAGE ⇒

5. The tone of the passage as a whole can best be described as which of the following?

(A) Vehement
(B) Mocking
(C) Indifferent
(D) Academic
(E) Objective

6. As used in line 8, the word "fine" most nearly means

(A) aesthetic
(B) excellent
(C) literary
(D) subtle
(E) impressive

7. The main point of the first paragraph is that

(A) artists should not concern themselves with the opinions of critics
(B) academic jargon masks how inconsequential art criticism has become
(C) art critics have lost touch with their public
(D) art critics should use simpler, more understandable language
(E) artists have become suspicious of art critics

8. The purpose of lines 14-19 is to

(A) make a concession
(B) raise a question
(C) counter a proposal
(D) create a dichotomy
(E) offer an example

9. Which of the following is implied in the author's discussion in the third paragraph (lines 27-46)?

(A) Even bad art requires more than creative talent.
(B) Too much of anything, even art, can have harmful consequences.
(C) Artists are largely indifferent to or unaware of what is at stake in the corruption of art.
(D) Art should be created for the sake of art alone.
(E) Artists create their work with the best of intentions.

10. The author uses the phrase "nearly everything that passes for art" (lines 47-48) in order to

(A) suggest that he would usually disagree with this label
(B) emphasize that he is remaining open-minded about art
(C) argue for objective standards of art
(D) point out that almost all art
(E) highlight the amount of art being produced today

11. The author probably uses the phrase "banging on the table" (line 50) in order to

(A) ask for a turn to speak at last
(B) stress the urgency of his message
(C) show that he is not above old-fashioned theatrics
(D) admit that his views on art are sometimes unreasonable
(E) distract the attention of art critics

12. The phrase "kitchens at midnight, after parties" (lines 63-64) probably refers to the

(A) author's informal discussions about art
(B) author's debates with university professors
(C) author's conception of the ridiculous state of current art criticism
(D) earlier metaphor of artists creating non-nutritious fare
(E) typical gatherings after art openings

13. According to the final sentence in the passage, which of the following should be the primary function of art criticism?

(A) To reinforce all styles of art, regardless of individual merit
(B) To describe and explain art, but neither to celebrate nor to criticize particular works or artists
(C) To remain as detached as possible from the increasingly commercial aspects of art
(D) To popularize art to a wider audience by explaining art in simple terms
(E) To illuminate the moral mission of art, and to remind artists when they stray too far from that mission

-39-

GO ON TO THE NEXT PAGE ⟩

14. Based on the passage as a whole, with which of the following statements would the author most likely agree?

(A) Art criticism is ultimately nothing more than a game.

(B) The fundamental goal of art is not entertainment.

(C) Art should not joke or be playful.

(D) Even cynical or destructive art serves a useful purpose.

(E) Trivial art is meaningless, if not a contradiction in terms.

Questions 15-16 are based on the following passage.

As long as there have been movies, there have been special effects. But in decades past, special effects served a different purpose than they do
Line now. Once upon a time—say, back in the 1970s—
(5) the visual trickery employed by filmmakers was meant to look *real*. In many of today's movies, however, the effects are meant to look *cool*.

When director John Guillermin remade *King Kong* in 1976, he and producer Dino De Laurentis
(10) went to great lengths to convince moviegoers that they were seeing an actual giant ape on the screen in front of them. With a film like 1999's *The Matrix*, however, co-directors Andy and Larry Wachowski used computer-generated imagery not
(15) intending to produce lifelike results, but to put a highly stylized accent on the visuals. In one now-famous fight scene, the female character Trinity is about to boot a bad guy when she is frozen in mid-air; the camera then sweeps around her, providing
(20) a panoramic view of the kick to come. The Wachowski brothers were not trying to convince viewers that a person could suspend herself as Trinity does. Instead, they were trying to come up with a shot that would make jaws drop.

15. The author's primary point is that

(A) computer-generated special effects are more realistic than anything dreamt of even a generation ago

(B) today's moviegoers demand more sophisticated special effects than earlier moviegoers

(C) modern directors often employ special effects for a different aim from that of their predecessors

(D) today's directors are no longer concerned with creating visual trickery that looks real

(E) the technology used to create special effects has advanced greatly

-40-

GO ON TO THE NEXT PAGE ⟩

In the Greek type of democracy, all the citizens could listen to a series of orators and vote directly on questions of legislation. Hence their
Line philosophers held that a small city was the largest
(5) possible democratic state. The English invention of representative government made a democratic nation possible, and the possibility was first realized in the United States, and later elsewhere. With the development of broadcasting in the
(10) twentieth century, it once more become possible for every citizen to listen to the political views of representative orators, and the future may perhaps see the return of the national state to the Greek form of democracy.

16. It can be inferred that broadcasting may allow societies to return to the Greek form of democracy by

   (A) allowing more orators to participate in public debates
   (B) giving citizens another way to vote directly
   (C) enabling citizens not just to listen to orators, but also to see them speak
   (D) doing away with the need for representatives
   (E) making national states obsolete

Questions 17-18 are based on the following passage.

What distinguishes the joke from the mere humorous tale is that it climaxes in a punch line—a little verbal explosion set off by a sudden switch
Line in meaning. A joke, unlike a tale, wants to be
(5) brief. As Freud observed, a joke says what it has to say not just in few words but in *too* few words. The classic joke proceeds with arrow-like swiftness, resolving its matter in the form of a two-liner ("How many psychiatrists does it take to
(10) change a lightbulb? One, but the lightbulb has to want to change."), or even a one-liner ("I was so ugly when I was born, the doctor slapped my mother"). Often a joke is signaled by a formulaic setup, which might itself, in turn, become the
(15) subject of a meta-joke ("A priest, a rabbi, and a minister walk into a bar. Bartender says, 'What is this, a joke?'").

17. It can be inferred that a "meta-joke" (line 15)

   (A) is a joke upon a joke
   (B) has no punch line
   (C) ends with a question
   (D) has a subject
   (E) involves religious themes

18. According to the passage, unlike humorous tales jokes are usually characterized by all of the following EXCEPT

   (A) a formulaic structure
   (B) brevity
   (C) abrupt changes in meaning
   (D) story-like settings
   (E) a sudden climax

STOP

If you finish before time is up, you may check your work on this section only. Do not turn to any other section in the test.

SECTION 8
Time — 20 Minutes
12 Questions

Directions: Each of the 12 questions requires you to solve the problem and enter your answer by marking the ovals in the special grid, as shown in the examples below.

Answer: 2.25

Answer: 9 / 4 or $\frac{9}{4}$

Answer: .01
Either position is correct.

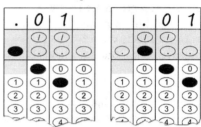

Note: You may start your answers in any column, space permitting. Columns not needed should be left blank.

Notes:

1. You may use a calculator. All numbers used are real numbers. All figures lie in a plane unless otherwise indicated.

2. Figures that accompany problems are intended to provide useful information useful in solving the problems. They are drawn as accurately as possible EXCEPT when a specific problem states that the figure is not drawn to scale.

Reference Information

$A = \pi r^2$
$C = 2\pi r$

$A = lw$

$A = \frac{1}{2}bh$

$V = lwh$

$V = \pi r^2 h$

$c^2 = a^2 + b^2$

Special Right Triangles

The number of degrees of arc in a circle is 360.
The measure in degrees of a straight angle is 180.
The sum of the measures in degrees of the angles of a triangle is 180.

1. When a number is multiplied by 4 and the product is then increased by 2, the result is 18. What is the number?

2. If a car traveling at a constant rate covers 50 miles in 2 hours, then at this rate how many miles will the car cover in the next 3 hours?

-42-

GO ON TO THE NEXT PAGE

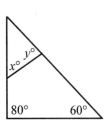

Note: Figure not drawn to scale.

3. In the figure above, $x + y =$

4. The digits 7, 8, and 9 are used to create a one-digit number and a two-digit number, with no digit repeated. What is the largest possible product of the resulting one-digit and two-digit numbers?

5. If $2^{x + 1} = 32$, then $2^x =$

6. In the figure above, $AC = 10$ and $BE = \dfrac{24}{5}$. What is the area of rectangle $ABCD$?

7. Twenty-five students are arranged in a line, and each student is assigned to one of four teams: A, B, C, or D. If no two adjacent students are assigned to the same team, and at least one student is assigned to each team, what is the maximum possible number of students assigned to A?

8. The remainder when n is divided by 8 is 5. What is the remainder if $2n$ is divided by 8?

-43-

GO ON TO THE NEXT PAGE ⟹

9. If $x + y = 6$ and $x - y = 10$, then $x^2 - y^2 =$

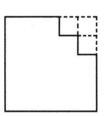

10. In the figure above, three squares of side 1 are removed from the larger square of side 5. What is the perimeter of the resulting polygon, indicated with a solid line?

11. A book collector has a collection of 1200 books, of which 900 are hardcover and 300 are paperback. If 1000 of the books are nonfiction and 50 of the paperbacks are fiction, how many of the books are hardcover and nonfiction?

12. If y varies inversely as x^2 and if $y = 100$ when $x = 1$, what is y when $x = 2$?

STOP
If you finish before time is up, you may check your work on this section only. Do not turn to any other section in the test.

Answer Key to the Practice Test

Section 2:		Section 4:		Section 5:		Section 6:		Section 8:	
1.	A	1.	A	1.	A	1.	A	1.	4
2.	B	2.	E	2.	D	2.	D	2.	75
3.	E	3.	D	3.	E	3.	D	3.	140
4.	A	4.	B	4.	D	4.	C	4.	783
5.	B	5.	A	5.	A	5.	E	5.	16
6.	C	6.	B	6.	B	6.	E	6.	48
7.	C	7.	D	7.	C	7.	C	7.	13
8.	B	8.	E	8.	C	8.	D	8	2
9.	D	9.	C	9.	B	9.	A	9.	60
10.	B	10.	B	10.	E	10.	C	10.	20
11.	B	11.	B	11.	D	11.	E	11.	750
12.	E	12.	A	12.	B	12.	B	12.	25
13.	D	13.	C	13.	B	13.	B		
14.	E	14.	E	14.	D	14.	D		
15.	D	15.	A	15.	C	15.	B		
16.	A	16.	A	16.	D	16.	D		
17.	D	17.	B	17.	A	17.	D		
18.	D	18.	C	18.	E	18.	C		
19.	C	19.	C	19.	C	19.	B		
20.	B	20.	D	20.	E	20.	D		
21.	A	21.	C	21.	D				
22.	D	22.	E	22.	A				

Section 3:

					Section 7:	
		23.	C			
		24.	B	1.	E	
1.	D	25.	E	2.	D	
2.	A	26.	A	3.	A	
3.	C	27.	E	4.	B	
4.	B	28.	B	5.	A	
5.	D	29.	E	6.	D	
6.	B	30.	D	7.	B	
7.	B	31.	C	8.	A	
8.	A	32.	A	9.	C	
9.	A	33.	D	10.	A	
10.	D	34.	E	11.	B	
11.	A	35.	D	12.	A	
12.	B	36.	A	13.	E	
13.	C	37.	D	14.	B	
14.	E	38.	D	15.	C	
15.	A	39.	A	16.	D	
16.	D	40.	C	17.	A	
17.	B	41.	B	18.	D	
18.	A	42.	B			
19.	E	43.	A			
20.	C	44.	D			
		45.	D			